PARADISE MISL

Anne Whitehead, a sixth-generation Australian, was born in Sydney but spent most of her childhood in Papua-New Guinea and England. She was educated at eleven schools and in 1972 graduated with a Master of Arts in Australian Literature from the University of Sydney.

She worked as a television producer and film director with the Australian Broadcasting Corporation and the Tasmanian Film Corporation and since 1982 has freelanced as an award-winning scriptwriter.

She has travelled extensively in Africa, the Middle East, Europe and the United States, and journeyed three times to South America to research *Paradise Mislaid*, her first book. She lives in Sydney and is currently completing a doctorate in political science.

To Tony & Peter —
with admiration and
great affection

Anne

February 1999

PARADISE MISLAID

In Search of the
Australian Tribe of Paraguay

Anne Whitehead.

Anne Whitehead

University of Queensland Press

First published 1997 by University of Queensland Press
Box 42, St Lucia, Queensland 4067 Australia

Typeset by University of Queensland Press
Printed in Australia by McPherson's Printing Group

This project has been assisted by
the Commonwealth Government through
the Australia Council, its arts funding
and advisory body.

Cataloguing in Publication Data
National Library of Australia

Whitehead, Anne.
  Paradise mislaid : in search of the Australian tribe of
  Paraguay.

  Includes index.

  1. Australians — Paraguay. 2. Collective settlements —
  Paraguay. I. Title.

335.9892

ISBN 0 7022 2651 3

To the memory of my parents
Lila and Ted Whitehead
and my sister Pamela

I came to Paraguay by a writer's instinct …

Graham Greene, *Ways of Escape*

Paraguay is not a country — it is an obsession.

Juan Carlos Herken Krauer

But now, in quest of no ambitious height,
I go where Truth and Nature lead my way,
And, ceasing here from desultory flight,
In measured strains I tell a tale of Paraguay.

Robert Southey, *A Tale of Paraguay*

Contents

Acknowledgments

No man — or woman — is an island. No book either.

I wish to thank the Literature Board of the Australia Council for a Special Purpose Grant to travel to Paraguay in 1989, and Keith Yorston and Robert Samuels at Aerolíneas Argentinas for enabling me to return to South America for the centenary of the Australian colonists' arrival in 1993.

I am most grateful for the assistance of librarians and staff at the National Library of Australia; the Mitchell Library, State Library of New South Wales, particularly Paul Brunton and Jerrylyn Brown; Kate Sexton at the University of Sydney Library and Neil Boness and the staff of its Rare Books and Special Collections Library, especially Sara Hilder who has developed a strong interest in the Australian Paraguay experiment. I would also like to acknowledge the help of Bill Richards and the staff of the Australian National Maritime Museum.

The author and publisher would like to thank the following copyright holders for permission to include material in this book: Mrs M. McCredie for the painting "The *Royal Tar* at Sea" by John Allcott McCredie; Gavin Souter for extracts from *A Peculiar People: The Australians in Paraguay* (1968, 1981); The Bodley Head and David Higham Associates for extracts from Graham Greene, *The Honorary Consul, Ways of Escape* and *Travels With My Aunt*; the estate of Pablo Neruda and Jonathan Cape for extracts from Pablo Neruda's *Selected Poems*, translated by Nathaniel Tarn and Anthony Kerrigan; Temple University Press, Philadelphia, for extracts by Mark Münzel and Eric R. Wolf from Richard Arens (ed.) *Genocide in Paraguay* (1976); Quartet Books for extracts from Eduardo Galeano, *Memory of Fire*, translated by Cedric Belfrage; and extracts from the poems "I Shall Not Sleep", "The Lover" and "Somehow We Missed Each Other" by Mary Gilmore are reproduced with permission from the Estate's publishers, ETT Imprint. Every effort has been made to contact copyright holders but some proved impossible to locate. The author and publisher would like to hear from anyone who believes they control copyright on material used here.

I also wish to acknowledge the ABC Radio Social History Unit and Jill Lennon and Jenny Palmer who produced a radio documentary series, *Paradise Lost* (1990), from my interviews recorded in Paraguay, and Brisbane Grammar School, where I spent a pleasant term as writer-in-residence.

During the long writing process I have had constant support from University of Queensland Press. I want to thank Laurie Muller and Dr Craig Munro who had faith that a book would be forthcoming when the evidence seemed against it; Judy MacDonald, Nicola Evans and Clare Forster who gave me great encouragement at the early stages of the manuscript; and finally Sue Abbey and Felicity Shea who saw the manuscript through the production process with style.

I am indebted to my brilliant agent, Dr Rosemary Creswell, and the staff of Cameron Creswell Management.

Many people contributed over the years to the research and writing of this book. Sadly many of those who offered their memories and their stories no longer survive to read them in print: original children of the colonies of New Australia and Cosme — the late Margaret Riley, the brothers Bill, Alex, Norman and Wallace Wood, Rod McLeod, George Titilah and Ricardo and Dorothy Smith. Others were Doña María Albina Cáceres de Wood and Doña Leonarda Mazacotte de Wood, Max White, and, in Australia, Eric Lane, James Mitchell and Dr Lloyd Ross.

The growing band of Australian-Paraguayans who have returned to settle in Australia were generous with their reminiscences, family photographs and friendship: Peter and Betty Wood, Carmen and Glen Touyz, Jimmy and Dolly Cadogan, Charles and Olga Wood, June and Charles Kay, and Don and Sheila Lees.

There are numerous others I wish to thank for the assistance and insights they have given me. In Australia: David Lane and Judith Armstrong, Margaret Riley's daughter Edna Watson, Mary Leeser, Steve Cooper, Brian Turner and Robyn Fookes, Nell and Ray Moody, Senator Margaret Reynolds, Penny Cook, Peter Solness, Stuart Heather, the Barcaldine Shire Council, Frank Bannan, Richard and Jane Bell, John and Marian Campbell, Harry Heumiller, Alicia Hill, Pat Ogden, and Pat and Jo Shannon of "Rodney Downs".

In Paraguay I received generous assistance from people too numerous to mention here, although many make appearances as sources in the text, especially, vitally, those descendants of the colonies of New Australia and Cosme. However, I particularly want to thank Florence Wood de White for the warm hospitality she and her husband Max extended to me, and Roger Cadogan who gave me insights into the Paraguay "the tourist doesn't see". I am also indebted to Rose Menmuir, Robin and Mette Wood, Oscar Birks, Osvaldo González Real and, in Argentina, Monica and John Blake and Luis María González.

Many friends in Australia gave me guidance, encouragement and hours of their time. I especially want to thank Mary-Jane Field and Greg Price, who translated extracts from León Cadogan's *Memorias*, and rode shotgun on my Spanish, as did Steve Gregory. Others who read the lengthy manuscript and made valuable suggestions were Rose Creswell, Janet Bell, Gil Brealey, Rod Sangwell, Alban Gillezeau, Phil Drew, Associate Professor Terry Irving, John Kerr, Christopher Koch, Roger Milliss, Frank Moorhouse, Julie Rigg, Virginia Watson and Gavin Souter.

I am also most grateful for the advice and assistance of Richard Hall, Bob Connolly, Tom Molomby, Wendy Borchers, Jane and Stuart Hawkins, Jim and Valerie Levy, Vincent Plush, Dr Tim Rowse, Dr Jenny Strauss, Eleanor Witcombe, Adrienne and John Whitehead, Jennie and Rob Woollard and Professor Michael Wilding, whose own work and publications on the Paraguayan experiment offered many insights.

Finally I must offer special thanks to Gavin Souter, without whose definitive history, *A Peculiar People: The Australians in Paraguay*, this book would not have been possible, for the encouragement I have always received from him and his wife Ngaire. And to Jill Kitson for convincing me, after a chance meeting in Patagonia, to clear the decks and concentrate exclusively on writing this book. And to John Kerr, who read and criticised the original manuscript, knocked it into shape, and was unfailingly generous with his time and expertise.

All these people added to the book; if there are mistakes, they are my own.

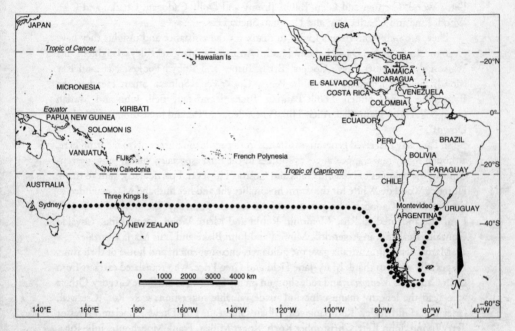

Route of the *Royal Tar*, July–September 1893, a voyage of over 14,000 kilometres

Quest

> A map of the world that does not include Utopia is not even worth
> glancing at, for it leaves out the one country at which Humanity is
> always landing. And when Humanity lands there, it looks out, and
> seeing a better country, sets sail. Progress is the realisation of
> Utopias.
>
> Oscar Wilde, "The Soul of Man under Socialism"

When the Shearers' Strike of 1891 in Queensland was put down by government forces, and hopes of a revolution, a republic, or just a better way of life in Australia faded for many people, an influential English journalist had an idea.

William Lane called on the disenchanted to uproot themselves and sail to a new place, where a society based on socialist principles and simple mateship could be founded. The site he chose for this experiment was Paraguay, a tiny land-locked country in the middle of South America. Over five hundred Australians decided to join him, and in the forest backblocks of Paraguay a small village was established, a small village with grandiose hopes and breathtaking ambitions.

But the new society soon split into two and then ultimately foundered. Most of the disillusioned colonists returned home, William Lane and his family among them. Some remained ...

*

The idea of Europeans finding themselves stranded in dense tropical jungle in an alien clime and nonetheless making do, showing their resourcefulness and what was invariably called British grit, fascinated me as a child. *Robinson Crusoe*, *The Swiss Family Robinson*, Kipling's *Kim*, Hudson's *Green Mansions* and, of course, the Tarzan books — I devoured them all.

Then my family moved to a remote house on the side of a mountain in the New Guinea highlands and I could act out my fantasies, wandering through rainforest with bow and arrows or, in a grass skirt, pre-pubescent chest bare, climbing up to my treehouse to read comics and dream of those feisty, feral and spectacularly pneumatic females, Tiger Girl, Nyoka, and Sheena, Queen of the Jungle.

Subsequent life in Australia never had quite that romance, which, it was impressed upon me, was an unsound imperialist fantasy, a tawdry metaphor of colonialism. It was time to dump the White Girl's Burden. But the old yearning to find a lost tribe from the storybooks flickered when I heard about a group of Australians who'd somehow mislaid themselves for a hundred years deep in the interior of South America.

I think I first read about them in the *Australasian Post*, the sort of strident magazine, with beach girls on its cover, that people usually admitted to seeing in the dentist's waiting room. I've since found that 1963 article in the library, with its headline: "The Australian Peasants of Paraguay — Our Forgotten Exiles". There was also a story, frantic in tone, in the *Brisbane Telegraph*: "Queenslander Tribe Found ... A tribe of South American Anglo-Indians who call themselves 'Queenslanders' ... They speak Guarani, an Indian dialect, and broken English with Australian phrases such as 'boil the billy', 'smoko' and 'fair dinkum' thrown in, in spite of the fact that there is only one Australian-born original colonist left in Paraguay — and he left Sydney when he was eight months old".

It would be some years before the idle curiosity this provoked became an obsession that would take me to Paraguay to meet that Australian-born colonist — a dignified man, bewildered by the "peasant" description — and his relatives. The next stage towards that journey came in 1969 when I was a very green film director with the Australian Broadcasting Corporation in Sydney. I was assigned to liaise with a BBC documentary crew making a series of films about aspects of Australian life for a children's television program. They had planned one, set on a sheep station at shearing time, and had arranged a location, a property near Moree in far-western New South Wales, booked transport and a light plane for aerials, when the BBC director had a nervous breakdown or perhaps a surfeit of outback Australia. The shearing couldn't wait, the station owner patiently explained, the men were already contracted. So I was plucked out to direct the film instead. Someone from the BBC in London rang me to stress that British children wanted to see nice white woolly sheep and no blood, thank you very much.

I arrived with the camera crew at one of the largest shearing sheds in New South Wales with twenty men working that season. They had to vote on allowing a woman into the shed. I had to negotiate a compensation fee so they'd slow down and avoid nicks while I was filming close up. But it didn't take long for them to sound like film buffs — "Are you going for a Wide Shot on me now or a Medium Close Up?" — or for me to sound like a greenhorn bushie as I listened to their yarns during smokoes or when we ate mutton chops served by Bluey the Cook.

There was an old shearer, his inefficiency indulged by the others because he was long past his prime and over-fond of grog, and he talked to me as if it were yesterday about the Queensland shearers' strike of 1891. His father had been involved. He said the men on strike thought they'd win, but it didn't work out that way, "because of the bloody troopers and the scabs, so a lot of them buggered off to Paraguay instead".

That fired up the compulsive interest that came to preoccupy me for many years. I read Gavin Souter's definitive history, *A Peculiar People: The Australians in Paraguay*, and, in between my film work, burrowed in libraries among old documents and letters.

I learned how the whole literally outlandish venture had baffled many people at the time it was happening and up to the present day. The 1894 edition of *Chambers' Journal of Popular Literature, Science and Art* declared:

> In the history of the world, no movement of the same kind in its principal features has been recorded. From countries with dense populations, co-operative bodies have gone forth ... But the emigrants from Australia were circumstanced as none of these were. The total population of their island continent is just over three millions; while the area of land at their disposal may be reckoned at a square mile per head. Queensland alone, which contributed the majority of the emigrants, contains 668,000 square miles — an area equal to the German Empire, France, Denmark, Switzerland, Spain, Portugal and Belgium, all together.

It was clearly viewed as absurd, outrageous, that over 500 white Australians should leave a large and under-populated country, chiefly distinguished in the 1890s for its potential, for being a place where a fresh start could be made and modest social reforms were being effected, to travel far away to a tiny, war-ravaged land, where revolutions and dictatorships were endemic, social reforms virtually unknown, the climate inhospitable, amenities of life few, transport difficult and the language incomprehensible to the newcomers. When, in addition, the overwhelming number of bachelors among them were forbidden to fraternise with the attractive local women or even console themselves with a drink, the chances for the colony's success seemed as feasible as a frog with feathers.

The whole notion was declared preposterous by the press and the Paraguayan experiment has continued to be regarded as a curious backwater to the mainstream of Australian history, though the story still demands occasional attention for its quixotic effrontery, its appeal to the national spirit of having a go.

But there seemed another way of looking at it. It could be argued that in its hopes and dreams, even if not in realisation, it was one of the most ambitious projects ever undertaken by Australians. The intention of William Lane, its ideological leader, was nothing less than to change the world but, he argued, they must first show the world that change was possible. They "must gather themselves together and go out into the desert to live their life in their own way as an example to all men".

In a remote village in Paraguay he planned to create a social laboratory, a functioning model of communalism which would be an inspiration for workers in all lands, for the industrial poor of England, France and Germany, and even perhaps for the peasants of Russia. He meant to do it not with a coterie of intellectuals or the urban disaffected, not with "soft-handed theorists" but with "hard-handed toilers", a group of knock-about Australian bushmen.

To Lane, these chosen people, the ones with "the right stuff", were already bonded by the traditions of mateship and the new trade unionism, but fortunately were not too confused by political theories. They were to be accompanied by — though this was something of an afterthought — the sort of fine upstanding women who would be the future mothers of the new society. Lane envisaged that eventually "a disciplined army of many thousands" would emerge from the Paraguayan jungle to lead an inevitable world revolution. They would write the future history of humanity on the rocks of the Andes. This was having a go in a big way.

The whole brave if foolhardy saga is described in Souter's book, and I am not here attempting to recount the detailed stages in a history already so admirably documented. He took his title from the report of a British diplomat who travelled up from Buenos Aires in 1893 to investigate ructions in the colony and found himself both impressed by the commitment of the colonists and disturbed by the unswerving righteousness of their leader. "Under good management, and on reasonable lines, the colony should prove a great success," he concluded, "but it is not improbable that William Lane's views may be found too 'straight' and his administration too strict for ordinary men. If, however, he succeeds in carrying out his ideal he will found a 'peculiar people', like Cromwell's Ironsides, and like them they may accomplish great things."

As a colony they didn't. The whole venture was a story of decline. The rocks of the Andes — rather far from swampy Paraguay to respond to any echoes — did not ring to an Australian-led socialist world revolution. No army marched out of the Paraguayan wilderness. Those who remained there came perilously close to fulfilling the dire predictions of the Sydney *Bulletin*:

> There will be a few hundred people digging and fencing in a dreary, hopeless fashion out in the great loneliness, and living on woe and unsaleable vegetables and dreams of home. And meanwhile, the founder of the settlement will be foaming at the mouth and uttering poetry beneath a tree, and wildly asking the damp ferns, "What is life?"

It *had* all been a dream, though it would be too harsh to describe it as a nightmare. Its ending didn't come in an immolation of fire, or in an excess of brutality, or corruption, or arsenic-laced Kool-Aid, but rather, almost endearingly, out of a surfeit of rectitude and inappropriateness. It simply dwindled away. But later, some of the descendants *did* accomplish great things, and in ways that William Lane could never have predicted. And most of them became proud of the idealism, however muddle-headed, that propelled their forebears across the world.

The country of Paraguay has had more than its share of dreamers — and of despots — and its turbulent, brave and bloody history came to fascinate me in its own right. Since the time of the early Jesuit missions, an attempt at communal living which lasted nearly 200 years, Paraguay's geographic and cultural isolation had attracted many utopians and visionaries, Lane and his group almost lost in the crowd of wandering pilgrims seeking some shining "city on a hill". In the name of the philosopher Friedrich Nietzsche, others attempted to breed up a German master race. Such experiments aimed to survive within a tradition of autocracy profoundly harsh even for Latin America, continent of *caudillos*.

I wondered about the "lost tribe", the descendants of the Australian socialist utopia. How were they faring, for instance, under the longest-surviving right-wing dictatorship in the world? When I made the first of three journeys to Paraguay in 1982, my welcome by those descendants was assured by a letter of introduction from Gavin Souter. I was in time to record the memories of eleven old men and women aged between seventy-six and one hundred and five years who had grown up as colony children. As I've worked on this book, all but one have died.

Many of this first generation had married into the local population, but they still went off to fight for the British Empire; and although they had no experience of Australia, some of them could recite Henry Lawson in a distinctive broad accent, sing a verse or two of "Waltzing Matilda" and bake damper for their afternoon tea.

I had a curious sense, on meeting these men and women, that I'd slipped into a time-warp, that I was talking with Australian bush-people of the 1890s, confronting the values and traditions, preserved almost intact, from my grandparents' generation. I was granted a rare picture of my own people's past, a living one, unlike the proverbial bee trapped in amber.

However, the children and grandchildren of these old people had no confusion about their identity. They are Paraguayan and proud of it.

Today the hundreds of descendants of Lane's utopian experiment encompass the political spectrum and every contradiction. Some are redheaded and freckled, in appearance classic Irish-Australian, but speak only Spanish and the Indian language, Guaraní. Others, like Rodrigo Wood, are swarthy and Hispanic looking, but he's a devoted cricketer and a fan of the Australian country singer Slim Dusty. They range from people still eking out a near-subsistence living from the land to one of the most influential businessmen in Paraguay; from cattlemen on ranches out in the Chaco to a millionaire writer of comic strips living in Denmark; from a real estate agent in Australia to an officer of the World Bank in the United States. In Paraguay Peter Kennedy was a political candidate for the ruling Colorado Party; Enrique Wood, a self-declared socialist, was arrested by the secret police three times during the Colorado regime of President Alfredo Stroessner. And there's Roger Cadogan, continuing the work of his father León Cadogan, who, though self taught, became an internationally respected anthropologist and fought for the rights of the forest Indians.

But their lives were spent in the wash of the Paraguayan experiment and what they had in common was a strong sense of that heritage. In October 1993 they came together as a group for the first time to form an association and to commemorate the arrival of their forebears one hundred years earlier.

I went to Paraguay a third time to be there for that event, making the 1,600-kilometre journey from Buenos Aires by riverboat, travelling around the country, to the two former Australian colonies, to German settlements where Nazi war criminals found harbour, and to the ruins of the old Jesuit missions. For this book I interviewed numerous descendants and asked them to talk about their childhoods and their present lives. Many had extraordinary stories to tell.

I was also interested to chart the experiences of an English adventurer, recruited in Buenos Aires, whose 400-odd letters covering his life as a colonist were donated to the Mitchell Library of New South Wales after the publication of Souter's book.

Finally, I was conscious of retracing the steps of Mary Cameron, one of the few single women to join the group, later famous in Australia as the poet and civil rights activist Dame Mary Gilmore. I wanted to discover more of her personal story, why she followed one man to the colony and married another after settling there.

I left South America by way of Patagonia — the Welsh colonies of the Chubut and some sheep *estancias* in the far south. The Gilmores and many of the early colonists who didn't stay on in Paraguay made the same exit, obtaining work as shearers and domestic help to earn their passage home.

My journey of 1993 was a final attempt to come to terms with an obsession.

PART ONE

PART ONE

1

A Feather-Headed Expedition

The Owl and the Pussy-Cat went to sea
In a beautiful pea-green boat:
They took some honey, and plenty of money
Wrapped up in a five-pound note.

Edward Lear

On the assumption that life among wild oranges and *yerba mate* scrub
has capabilities which it does not offer in Australia, one of the most
feather-headed expeditions ever conceived since Ponce de León
started out to find the Fountain of Eternal Youth, or Sir Galahad
pursued the Holy Grail, is about to set forth.

Bulletin, June 1893

S ydney Harbour: 16 July 1893. A grey blustery winter day, bullets of
rain pocking the water, didn't seem to augur well for a utopian
enterprise. There was something almost funereal about the sight of
the little barque *Royal Tar*, its square sails furled, being towed towards the
Heads, the shepherding tug on one side and a government health boat on
the other. Someone on board began singing "Homeward Bound". The
chorus was taken up among the fleet of farewelling boats and canoes,
drifting in snatches across the waves: "We're homeward bound I heard
them say, Goodbye, fare ye well …"

People watched from the wooded cliffs, they clambered onto sandstone
ledges to wave hats and handkerchiefs. They knew they were witnessing
a paradoxical event: a regally-named ship on a revolutionary mission:
Australia's own Pilgrim Fathers — and the voyagers *were* mostly men —
leaving a newly settled home to found an even newer one. A sympathetic
reporter remarked that never within living memory had the departure of
an unofficial vessel caused such a sensation on Sydney Harbour, and for
this the New Australians could thank their vociferous opponents who had,
for most people, "called into play that spirit of justice which, say what we
will, still animates ordinary humanity".

The emigrants became soaked as they crowded on the *Tar*'s deck, huddling under oilskins and canvas or in the shelter of lifeboats for their last glimpse of family and friends staying in Old Australia. Two hundred and twenty of them, eighty-seven men, forty-three women and the rest children. And above them, attempting to steady himself in one of the swinging lifeboats, the architect of their future, William Lane. The Sydney *Bulletin* called him, "the boss promoter and chief prophet of the Paraguay pilgrimage", organiser of a "harum scarum scuttle to South America".

Just thirty-two years of age, Lane seemed older with his bushy moustache, gold-rimmed spectacles and the stooped physique caused by a crippled foot. His balding head was exposed as he waved a sodden stetson hat at a group of friends in a chartered steam launch. "Three cheers for Billy!" they called to him. His American wife Anne beside him, holding an umbrella over their five-month-old baby, shared the moment of triumph.

They were on their way, despite all the opposition from the authorities and possible sabotage within their own ranks. They had complied with every niggling regulation turned up from old maritime and emigration Acts. They had been harassed and badgered, and delayed three months while they'd had a new main mast built and another cable, anchor and three more lifeboats fitted; they had been obliged to pay extra harbour dues and arrange for provisions for more than twice the expected length of the voyage. But their supporters had found the extra money somehow and at last it seemed the bureaucrats had run out of imagination.

But there was one last card up the capacious official sleeves. Just before the ship's departure, the authorities decided that the crew — mostly Association members working out their membership fees, but all with deep-sea experience — should be rejected in favour of sailors with discharges. This was an impossible demand in the middle of a maritime strike. The government had overplayed its hand and popular opinion fell in behind the pioneers. The journalist Rose de Boheme, a friend of the Lanes, jubilantly described the outcome in the *Worker*:

> An appeal was made to the Seamen's Union, with the result that over thirty men eagerly volunteered to work the vessel to her destination free of charge. The fact was published in the morning papers and the red tapeists realised that they had exceeded the limits of ordinary discretion. Very suddenly and hastily the original crew was reinspected early on Friday morning and passed as it stood. Henceforth there was nothing required but a clean bill of health,

and when Sunday morning dawned the Blue Peter was to be seen flying from the masthead and the weary waiting was at an end.

They had been checked, but they hadn't been checkmated. A banner slung between the masts proclaimed the motto of their new life: "Each for all and all for each." There were plenty of craft on the choppy harbour waters to see them off, but was that really a boatload of people in straitjackets? Annie Sibbald, one of the married women among them, later maintained that it was: "When we were all on board the *Royal Tar* the government brought out all the lunatics from the Sydney asylum and put them on a boat to sail round ours with a big banner to show they were 'lunatics come to say farewell to their brothers and sisters'."

*

William Lane professed not to care what sort of political theatre a hostile government organised against them, or how people laughed. His dream of four years was fulfilling itself at last. The people crowded on the deck below him would be the vanguard for a new communist society, hard-handed pioneer workers who would clear the land and build a city in the Paraguayan jungle. Later he hoped that thousands would join them, even as many as fifty thousand, for why not all the unemployed in Australia? The two hundred and twenty people on board were just the first batch. Thirty of them were bushmen and twenty were shearers, many of them blacklisted and unemployed since the great strike two years before. But a range of other occupations, all the skills they would need to set up their new republic, were represented. There were carpenters, stonecutters and bricklayers to build their homes; farmers and orchardists to till their fields; artisans — miners, engineers, blacksmiths, printers and a plumber — to develop their industries; and people who could make life gracious as their settlement took on the pattern of village life: storekeepers, bootmakers, tailoresses, a draper and a weaver, a baker and a nurse, even a bandmaster travelling with £400 worth of musical instruments. But at the beginning everyone would take on whatever community work was assigned them. There was full agreement about that. They were going to create a true classless society, and Lane denied the charge that they already had the makings of a new intellectual caste on board in three teachers, one of them his most devoted ally, his brother John, and a

THE OLD MAN SPEAKS:
Sixty quid's a lump, Jo,
The swag's too big to hump, Jo,
And I don't think we'll jump, Jo,
To the land of Paraguay.

From the *Bulletin*, 11 March 1893

clerk, a photographer, two music teachers and two journalists beside himself.

The important thing, he insisted, was that everyone was raring to get to work, to have a go for themselves, out from under the thumbs of the bosses. They could ignore newspapers like the *Bulletin* with its mocking, "I don't think we'll jump, Jo, To the land of Paraguay". They would rise above the prophecies of doom, the lurid warnings about the horrors ahead of them: the Paraguayan blue-bottle fly that laid eggs in human nostrils, the worm that burrowed into bare feet and the piraña fish that stripped them to the bone, the hostile natives, anacondas and alligators, not to mention the mad dictators and bloody revolutions.

One of the bushmen on board, who was a bit of a poet, was working on a reply:

> They say there's injuns whoopin' round for New Australyin blood,
> Muskeeters big as kangaroos, 'n' fevers in the mud,
> 'N' krockydiles, 'n' horrid wars — at least the papers say —
> But there's no Australyin squatters over there in Paraguay.

Paraguay ... Many of them still confused it with Patagonia, the sheep country in southern Argentina where they had first hoped to settle. If there was one thing most of these bush people knew about, it was sheep. The idea of a big self-governing sheep station, an *estancia* as they had begun to learn to call it, appealed to them. But it turned out that the Argentine government was not begging for them to settle and the Paraguayan government was. So there was nothing for it but to learn about Paraguay instead. They had all attended earnest lectures about their future home-land, they had studied the map on the wall at the headquarters of their New Australia Co-operative Settlement Association, noted the country's position, landlocked in the centre of the South American continent, and heard descriptions of the balmy climate and the land's rich potential for agriculture. "We think that an acre cleared in Paraguay will produce as much as two in most other countries," one of their prospectors had written. All that was holding things back was the lack of initiative of the native people, they were informed by an article in their journal, reprinted from *Harpers Magazine*:

> ... the men are naturally weak and indolent; and being at the same time the lords of creation, they pass their lives in meditative laziness and leave the women to do what little work is absolutely required to keep a roof over their heads ... Under the trees the oranges lie on the ground a foot deep, and the

cattle eat them and fatten well ... Nature and the Jesuits have given these Paraguayans the means of life and oblivious felicity in the shape of mandioca, oranges, *mate* and tobacco. They enjoy a climate so delightful that clothes are scarcely needed. And yet the meddlesome Europeans are surprised and irritated because they do not work for them.

It seemed the country was wasted on the Paraguayans. It was just waiting for a group of capable Australians, not afraid of hard labour. But still there were doubters, so Lane himself had written a piece for the journal, assuring them it was impossible to fail.

The world will be changed if we succeed. And we shall succeed. We cannot help succeeding. For what do we expect? Not mansions, but cottages; not idle luxury, but work-won plenty; for each a home and marriage — honest, lifelong marriage — with sturdy children growing all around to care for us when we are old. We expect that the earth will yield, and that the flocks will increase, and that the axes will fell and the hammers weld, under our own hands, as under the hands of all others who toil. We expect that the song and the dance will come back to us, and that with our human instincts satisfied, we shall joy in living. If this is a wild dream, an impossible hope, what hope is there for humanity?

But over half the men on board were bachelors, and they fretted about how they were going to find their honest, lifelong marriage and manage to produce their sturdy children. Everyone had signed a pledge to keep to themselves once they got to their new home, not to fraternise with the Paraguayans. They had agreed that made sense, just as the pledge about teetotalism did. There were only six young single women on board, ranging in age from sixteen to twenty-six. Five of them were travelling under the protection of their families.

The eldest, Clara Jones, was the sort of good-looking woman who might prove a distraction among so many lonely men. But Lane could not deny her commitment to socialism. The people who had known her in Queensland called her "Red Clara". They were fond of recounting what happened the previous year when Tom Ryan got into parliament as the first Labor member. Clara Jones, nursing at Muttaburra in Ryan's electorate, celebrated by hoisting the red flag above the hospital, scandalising the hospital committee.

No doubt it had been time for her to move on. She was nursing at Bourke when she joined the New Australia movement. Billy Wood was an organiser up there and may have recruited her, or Clara might simply have recruited herself. She turned up in Sydney when the *Tar* was being fitted out, even though Lane had stressed that single women shouldn't come until the colony was established. But she had made herself useful helping the families settle in at the ten houses they had rented at Balmain while the government delayed their departure with more petty obstacles. Her outspoken manner at the Association meetings soon nettled him though; he had put her in her place when she demanded a reading of the chairman's report without notice.

Then the health authorities announced they must have a nurse on the voyage. It seemed Clara had won. But later she claimed she'd been considering an offer of marriage from a doctor, and only agreed with reluctance to chance her future in Paraguay.

She proved her worth nursing some of the children who'd broken out in measles the week before sailing. The authorities threatened to impound the ship and the worst-affected family was obliged to pull out. As it was, some of the Kidd family children slipped through the final government medical inspection. There were rumours that Clara had helped them, giving them raspberry jam sandwiches and smearing the jam over their spotty faces. Lane feared Clara Jones was going to be a concern, a distraction for the bachelors.

He often said they were the finest people in the world, his bushmen. It brought tears to his eyes to see how they trusted him, how they handed over their hard-earned money without doubt or question. He would rather die than betray such trust. If only they didn't keep harping on the issue of the women. Tom Westwood had the effrontery to say that it was all very well for *him* because he had Annie with him, but that was sour grapes because Westwood's own wife had decided to stay behind in Adelaide. Westwood was a draper; a Queensland bushman would not have made that comment. But still it had been necessary to remind the men that once they were settled at New Australia there would be many fine single women of good moral character who would be only too anxious to join them. Especially as they would be offered a free passage.

In particular he had high hopes of Tasmania, with their surplus of women. He had been on a recruiting drive to the island, and in Launceston assured his audience that every single girl who joined them could die an old maid, if it pleased her to be so erratic, and she would be found suitable work and given full equality in voting and sharing all of her life. But, as he had told the Tasmanian women, such a spinster regime would be most unlikely "as our bachelors will be as fine a body of men as ever came together in any part of the world — strong and straight and manly with the manliness which town life destroys — and as there will be neither fear of want, or any financial difficulty to impede honest love and honourable marriage, the single girls who go will be less than human if one or other do not win their hearts and make them loving wives and happy mothers".

The sort of woman recruit Lane had in mind was exemplified by the young schoolteacher Mary Jean Cameron, who was among the group of their key supporters, the inner sanctum, on the chartered launch *Ivy*. The flotilla of small boats and dinghies was falling back, but the launch still kept pace with the *Tar*, though warned to keep its distance by an officer on the government health boat, who was still looking for ways to be difficult. Just a few days earlier she'd asked his opinion of a song, "The Men of the New Australia", she'd written to celebrate this departure:

> Oh! The men of the New Australia are ready to cross the sea,
> To form a band in a far-off land, and show what men they be;
> For the men of New Australia have turned from a hopeless strife —
> Taken the Right as a guiding light to lead to a nobler life.
> They are gath'ring in from out of the West, and in from the Central Plain,
> From where the pelican builds her nest and Drought a king doth reign.

Of course he insisted they publish it soon in the journal. Now he could make out Mary's slim figure, standing at the prow of the steam launch between Walter Head and the bulk of William Guthrie Spence. Even in

Song by Mary Cameron, published in *New Australia* journal, 18 November 1893

the grey drizzle her auburn hair was striking, also the red sash at her waist, which she said she wore as a symbol of her socialist beliefs. She was waving her straw sailor hat. He knew she would be straining to see someone on the deck just below him: David Russell Stevenson, of course.

Everything was so easy if, through no virtue of your own, you were born tall, with a strong chin and the sort of high sculpted cheekbones that women seemed mad about. But he suppressed the thought as unworthy. Stevenson was one of his best men. He had been an organiser for the Shearers' Union during the great strike and since he'd joined the New Australia movement he had become one of his most reliable lieutenants. Dave came from a landed family in Scotland; he was a cousin of the writer Robert Louis Stevenson, but he was too sturdy a socialist to boast about that. He'd worked tirelessly to raise money for the Association. When the government caused delays and all the families down from the bush were waiting around in Balmain, running out of money and food, Dave had been buccaneer enough to approach that old skinflint Sydney Burdekin, the richest man in the city. And he took it so hard when Burdekin refused. "I never felt so much like shooting a man in my life," he said. "No one could have been more likeable personally, but no appeal on behalf of the women and children, cold and sleeping hungry, had any effect, and when I was leaving it was all I could do not to turn back and kick pain into his body if I could not talk pity into his heart."

He himself had thought that reaction rather excessive, but he'd noticed how women, and Mary Cameron in particular, seemed to hang on Stevenson's every word. He didn't think Stevenson's words were so wonderful — unlike his cousin, eloquence wasn't his strength. But he had found it useful to consider Dave's other qualities when writing his novel, *The Workingman's Paradise*, to raise money for the union prisoners gaoled because of the strike. He needed a model for the romantic hero, Ned Hawkins. Even his own wife said he did not know all that much about romantic heroes, so he based him on Dave:

> ... a sunburnt shearer to whom the great trackless West was home ... Ned was a Downs native, every inch of him. He stood five feet eleven in his bare feet yet was so broad and strong that he hardly looked over the medium height. He had blue eyes and a heavy moustache just tinged with red. His hair was close-cut and dark; his forehead, nose and chin were large and strong; his lips were strangely like a woman's ... he stepped carelessly along, a dashing manliness in every motion, a breath of the great plains coming with his sunburnt face and belted waist ...

He had to concede Stevenson was a good match for a woman like Mary. He had been genuinely delighted when some months ago they'd started walking out together. He did not listen to gossip but he couldn't help overhearing the talk about how they would sit by the waterfront together after the evening meetings at Balmain, sometimes lingering so long that Dave would miss the last ferry to the city. Then, the story went, he would throw off all his clothes, fix them in a bundle on his head and swim across Darling Harbour. People laughed that he must have been keen, because everyone knew the harbour was full of sharks. They also wondered aloud, raising their eyebrows, if Mary was still with him when he stripped. It was because of that sort of frivolous chatter that he had insisted it should only be married couples at New Australia until the colony was established. Still, he had been surprised that Mary and Dave had not married so they could sail as a couple on the *Tar*. Disappointed too. She would have been a real asset at the colony; a good companion for Anne who, unfortunately, was a little aloof with some of the wives, and a wonderful example for the other women.

Mary had such dignity and had accomplished so much when you considered that she was just twenty-eight years old and had spent most of her life in the bush. She was now writing half of their journal and taking over a lot of the editing. He had told her, "You can reason like a man — indeed, I have met few men who can reason like you." But sometimes she acted on intuition too, and turned out to be uncannily prescient. A month ago, with all the costs mounting up for the repairs and refitting, he'd realised there was no money left for provisioning the voyage. He had confided to Mary that he would have to call a meeting of the executive and jettison the whole venture. It would be a sad, desperate thing to do, but there seemed no alternative. The government's obstructiveness had succeeded. The sale of the *Royal Tar* would at least finance the return of most people to their homes.

Mary had begged him to wait three days. There appeared no rational reason to do so and every day they continued on the debt became greater, but she was so insistent he had agreed. Within the three days a cheque for £600 arrived from a member in Adelaide, and Rose Scott, a supporter in Sydney, mortgaged her house for £300. They were saved. He owed Mary a great debt and he would never forget that.

He had heard some of the fellows saying that she was certainly no beauty, but it would only be a superficial man who could look into those dark brown eyes and not see her essential goodness and strength of character. People kept insisting that Mary Cameron was the heroine, Nellie Lawton, in his novel, but he was not admitting to that, not openly anyway.

> She was ... tall and slender but well-formed, every curve of her figure giving promise of more luxurious development. She was dressed in a severely plain dress of black stuff ... But it was her face that attracted one, a pale sad face that was stamped on every feature with the impress of a determined will and of an intense womanliness. From the pronounced jaw that melted its squareness of profile in the oval of the full face to the dark brown eyes that rarely veiled themselves beneath their long-lashed lids, everything told that the girl possessed the indefinable something we call character ... there was nothing drooping about Nellie and never could be. She might be torn down like one of the blue gums under which she had drawn in the fresh air of her girlhood, but she could no more bend than can the tree which must stand erect in the fiercest storm or must go down altogether.

He supposed there were elements of Mary in the description. But when Anne made sarcastic comments, he reminded her that in the novel Nellie was in love with Ned. He was planning a sequel set in South America about their experiences as a happily married couple at New Australia. He hoped it would come true for Mary and Dave. Of the success of the settlement he had no doubts, although he honestly did not know how he would find the time to write a book about it. After all, he was not really a novelist. He was a leader.

*

Mary leaned against the railing of the launch, the wind and droplets of moisture cold on her face. The *Tar* was such a fine brave sight. She wished she was on board. Of course she told people she had a responsibility as a teacher, and could not leave her pupils at Stanmore Public School halfway through the year. What else could she say?

Dave had never come out directly and asked her to marry him. He was curiously formal in some ways. He had gone to her mother instead and asked if she would agree to his proposing marriage to her daughter. And her mother had objected; apparently she had said, "Not till you've been to New Australia and found out whether it's a fit place to take Mary". She had also mentioned that his financial prospects were uncertain until the colony was a going concern. Dave was a gentleman and had not said anything further, but she knew that the understanding, though unspoken, was very real between them.

When they had embraced at the wharf today she had hoped for some declaration. She knew he cared. If only, when she had told him she would follow as soon as possible, he'd said something more definite about the future they might have together over there. Instead, he had looked awkward and answered that it would be a fine thing if she took over as the colony schoolteacher, a logical move to release a man back to the labour force, and so on and so forth. But then, she knew he was a man of few words and found it difficult to talk about feelings.

Right now she was just a confusion, a turmoil of emotions, but she could always work her way through them by writing about them. She was already wondering how she would describe their last moments together today. Someone said to her once, probably it was Henry Lawson, that it was one of the few good things about being a writer: you could turn your pain into pounds, shillings and pence. Well, payment was not an issue for the *New Australia* journal and nor should it be, but she might write about the way they parted, changing a few things, as a short short story. She would call the couple Jack and Annie. Of course people would say it was about Stevenson and herself. They would talk. But let them. The important thing was he would read it in Paraguay too …

"You are mine."

"I am?"

"Yes, you."

Annie pondered.

"You don't seem sure about it," Jack said.

"Well, no, I'm not," she candidly admitted. "I don't seem to see things the way you do, so I don't know that it would be right." To marry and join her lover in New Australia, she meant.

Jack laughed a little. During the past few moments his life had sprung away ahead of hers. But her life would catch up, and he knew it only wanted awakening; so it was that when she made answer he had only laughed. She took no notice, for she was puzzling out her thought.

"You know," she began, and stopped. "I *don't*, somehow," she added, with a lift of the head.

"Well, you'll have to."

Annie looked up at him, where he stood so strong, so straight and healthy, and an unconscious wave of passion swept up in her heart. "If he were to kiss me," she thought with a catch in her breath. The instinctive sex impulse of women against self-surrender made her turn away.

But their intense mutuality stood to them. He caught her in his arms, and she felt his heart beat.

"Well?" he queried, looking at her.

"You were right," she replied.

"The *Tar* sails almost immediately, you know," he said quietly.

She drew his hand down over her breast. "I know," she answered, and lifting her face kissed him.

There was no need of a verbal promise.

That was another good thing about being a writer, she decided. You could give your story a happy ending. You could even fool yourself some of the time …

She clenched the railing, her eyes prickling with tears. She was startled when Will Spence touched her shoulder. He said something trite about them all feeling the same, as if he could know what it felt like to see the gap widening between you and the one you loved, and know that you would not hear from him for months. He added, "Old Australia's losing a lot of her best men, but the cause is bigger. They'll have some lessons to teach us."

It sounded like a speech, she thought, but then Spence could never stop being a politician. Lane had tried to persuade him to join the first batch, but as the Australian Workers' Union president he was one of the most powerful men in the country, far too wily and ambitious to have really considered leaving it. He had almost agreed to send his son, though he'd changed his mind at the last minute. But Walter Head, editor of the Sydney *Worker*, who, as secretary of their Association, would now be running matters for the New Australia movement back here, had sent his ten-year-old son Wally. He had placed him in the care of Dave Stevenson.

She moved over beside Head who was standing quietly by himself, staring across at the *Tar*. Men were unfastening the ropes, and three boys had climbed high up on the foremast and were shouting for all they were worth. She asked if Wally was one of them. Head said he didn't think so, but the one at the top was young Voltaire Molesworth. She found it terrifying to think of a four-year-old boy up there, but knew he'd been living on the ship for months, with his father as the caretaker, and was used to climbing the rigging like a monkey.

She murmured that Wally would be safe with Dave and again tried to locate Stevenson among the crowd on the deck. Although the rain was clearing, the ship had pulled way ahead.

Walter Head grinned, pointing midships.

Now she realised why she hadn't been able to pick out Dave. She had been looking for one figure, but there were three. He was in a huddle, sharing his oilskin with the nurse Clara Jones and young Wally Head. They looked a happy family group. She felt anxiety as a sharp pain. There was no denying that Clara was a fine looking woman; some of the people who had known her in Queensland said she had real spirit too. Red Clara. Apparently she was the only single woman on board, if you didn't count a couple of lumpy adolescents travelling with their parents.

Mary Cameron resolved to travel to Paraguay as soon as single women were able. She would set her life on a course.

Abruptly the rain stopped. The *Royal Tar* was now far ahead of the launch. People on board started singing "Auld Lang Syne" and it was taken up by well-wishers in the little boats bobbing on the water.

> Should auld acquaintance be forgot,
> And nae be brought to mind,
> Should auld acquaintance be forgot
> In the days of Auld Lang Syne …

Mary felt her eyes welling with tears again — but of course she always felt emotional when she heard that old song. It was her Scottish blood. Dave was a Scotsman too. A true Highlander and from a good clan. They were so right for each other, and she knew he felt that too. It would only be a few months and she'd be able to join him. Now the ship was so far off she wasn't sure she could make him out, or the nurse either — but she could see William Lane, high up in a lifeboat, waving his peculiar American hat, like something out of the Wild West.

As the *Royal Tar* reached the swell at the Heads and the crew started to unfurl her sails, the sun came out, as if on cue to bless their venture. Double topsails and topgallants billowed, bathed in light against a blue sky. There were cries of "Lane!", "Freedom!" and "Paraguay!", followed by ringing cheers. She joined in, calling until she was hoarse, "Freedom! Paraguay!"

The government boat pulled back and the *Tar*, a stiff westerly behind her, headed through the choppy waves for the open sea, bright sunlight glancing off her sails and spars. They were off at last.

2
Something Better

The *Bulletin* wishes Lane and all those who have gone and are going the most complete success. It has not hesitated to say straight out that the scheme is unpromising to the verge of insanity ... But it will await the verdict of their ripe experience and will rejoice with them if its warnings prove to have been misplaced ...

Bulletin, July 1893

'Tis the hope of something better than the present or the past;
'Tis the wish for something better — strong within us till the last.
'Tis the longing for redemption as our ruined souls descend;
'Tis the hope of something better that will save us in the end.

Henry Lawson, *New Australia*, March 1894

On a tropical jasmine-scented night in Asunción in 1974, León Cadogan Junior took his young wife Dolly to the movies. It was almost unheard-of for an Australian film to be screened in Paraguay. It was an auspicious sign, proof of a modern nation making its presence felt.

The Cadogans' lives were in flux. They had already made the decision to emigrate to Australia, purchased their tickets and sold their house. It was the fulfilment of a dream for him, promising better opportunities. He had left his job in accountancy and she had resigned as a science teacher. León's anthropologist father, after whom he was named, had died the previous year. From now on he would go by his family nickname, Jimmy. It would suit in Australia.

They settled back to watch *Sunday Too Far Away*, relieved it was subtitled in Spanish; he had a few words of English and Dolly none at all.

It was about the lives of shearers in Queensland. That pleased Jimmy. He had been told that Jack, his grandfather, had worked there as a shearers' cook. Dolly sat beside him, rigid in shock. She stared at images of baked red plains, rough galvanised huts and rougher men who lived without comforts, singlets stained with sweat, bending their backs over sheep all day and their elbows all night over a succession of beers.

Afterwards they walked through the crowded streets of Asunción, past noisy hawkers' stalls, little restaurants and brightly-lit electronic shops. Dolly despaired. "What a hard life it's going to be," she burst out. "Australia is *so* primitive. We're going into the wilds!"

Jimmy's grandparents had come to Paraguay with much the same thoughts. He assured her the film was set in the outback, as different from Sydney as the Chaco was from Asunción.

Dolly wasn't convinced. Next day she bought another suitcase and filled it with hand lotion, soap and toilet paper to soften the harsh existence before them.

*

Sydney Harbour: 16 July 1993. The setting sun streaked the water lapping the wharf and glowed on the white, architectural modishness of the Australian National Maritime Museum. The men and women sipping white wine behind the vaulting glass windows didn't look like descendants of socialists, bushmen and shearers, but many were. Some were Paraguayan, Jimmy and Dolly Cadogan among them. Over 300 people had gathered to celebrate the sailing of the *Royal Tar*, 100 years earlier to the day.

They moved to their seats to listen to Gavin Souter, author of *A Peculiar People*. He said he believed that the story of the *Royal Tar* and its passengers and what happened to their grand vision was still compelling because it had all the makings of an Australian legend, a kind of civilian Anzac story. After all, he said, the idea of 500 Australians going to Paraguay in search of Utopia was hardly more bizarre than 50,000 Australians going to Gallipoli to fight the Turks for King and Empire. Failure against great odds was no disqualification in Australia from becoming legendary, but rather the contrary. One only had to think of Ned Kelly and Burke and Wills.

"When the New Australians sailed for Paraguay they took with them a spirit of idealism which the labour movement could no longer afford, and which has seldom manifested itself in Australian life since then. They wanted something better, and at least they had a go." That made them relevant a century later, Souter concluded, when Australia once again was distracted by unemployment, deficit and drought. But now it too was approaching a new century, indeed a new millennium, with visionary ideals, within cooee of something politically better — "not Federation this time, but constitutional reform involving a genuinely New Australia".

Perhaps thirty people in the audience were Australian-Paraguayans. Like Jimmy Cadogan, they had made the reverse journey to settle in their grandparents' homeland. Most of them had arrived without any knowledge of English, and Australian blood didn't help them avoid the usual adjustment difficulties of migrants. The first to return was Peter Wood, a stocky man in his mid-forties with calm blue eyes. He had travelled up for the celebration from Griffith in the New South Wales Riverina area, where he had become a successful real estate agent.

Peter's grandparents were William and Lillian Wood who arrived in Paraguay to join Lane in May 1895. William, always known as Billy, had been secretary of the General Labourers' Union at Bourke at the time of the shearers' strike of 1891. He had been interested in Lane's scheme from the beginning and had organised a recruiting camp in the New South Wales far-west. Henry Lawson met Wood at Bourke in 1892 and portrayed him affectionately, even if he didn't get his name quite right, in two stories, "Send Round the Hat" and "That Pretty Girl in the Army":

> Little Billy Woods, the Labourers' Union Secretary ... had a poetic temperament and more than the average Bushman's reverence for higher things — Little Billy Woods ... the best of married men, with the best of wives and children ...

Addressing the gathering in a pronounced Hispanic accent, Peter Wood said he was born in the old Queensland-style farmhouse that his grandfather built at Colonia Cosme. His mother was Paraguayan, but he grew up among a large community of relatives and family friends who found themselves in an unusual situation. They were not Paraguayan and yet not Australian either. "My father, Wallace Wood, and his brothers and sisters and those of their generation felt the great impact of their strange identity. They were brought up as Australians and it was reinforced in their speech, their behaviour, what they learned at school and so on." His uncles, Bill, Alex and Norman fought in World War I with the British, even though Paraguay did not enter the war. Australian traditions, he said, continued at Cosme even with his own generation. "Probably they're not the traditions of today, but those aspects of Australian life which held 100 years ago."

Peter described the dramatic change in his own life when Gavin Souter arrived in Paraguay in 1965 to research his book. Bill Wood, 'the clan's ambassador and spokesperson" persuaded the author to help two of his nephews migrate to Australia. The ones he had in mind were Peter, then eighteen years old, and his elder brother Francisco, aged twenty-one. (In his book, Souter remembers Bill Wood saying, "There's no point in them hanging around here. Another few years and they'll be like everyone else: walking around in torn straw hats, and sinking into the mud with big families.")

On Souter's return, he wrote an article for the *Sydney Morning Herald*, mentioning that Billy Wood had been the promptest donor in Henry Lawson's story, "Send Round the Hat", and that two of his grandsons wanted to emigrate to Australia. The point was not lost, and sponsors and financial support were found. But in the end Francisco stayed on in Paraguay to marry another Cosme colony descendant, Sylvia McLeod.

Peter made the journey alone in August 1966. He knew a great deal of family lore about the outback of the 1890s. He knew about shearing sheds, tucker boxes, smokoes and life on the track. But his knowledge of contemporary Australia was gleaned from a pictorial book about Sydney. "One picture was of a kangaroo hopping along the road with the sea in the background. When I stepped out of the plane I was expecting to see kangaroos at the airport." Worse, there were journalists and a television crew waiting for him. But friendly Wood relatives were also there, although he couldn't communicate with them except by sign language.

He went to work in the Murrumbidgee Irrigation Area and the following year was joined by two cousins. That was the beginning of a number of Paraguayans of Australian descent and otherwise coming to Australia to make a new life; people such as Jimmy Cadogan, who did well in accountancy, and Dolly, who opened a fashion boutique, "Enchanted Evenings". Paraguayans came in such numbers that Dr Fernando Cubas was appointed in 1993 as their first Consul-General to Australia. Dr Cubas was introduced to the gathering at the maritime museum. "The new Paraguay," he said, referring to the election of its first civilian president, Juan Carlos Wasmosy, "offers the image of democracy and freedom in all its ways."

I was also a speaker that evening and said that the return of these Australian-Paraguayans made me think of all the diasporas in the modern world, the mass migration of huge numbers of people from one nation to another. A new tradition had developed — of first, second and third generation migrants going back to discover their ancestral roots: Americans of Irish stock went to drink Guinness in Dublin pubs; West Indian Londoners headed off to the Caribbean; Italo-Australians with broad

Aussie accents found relatives in Italy. But with just 200 years of European settlement, Australia had only Paraguay for its own miniscule version of a diaspora. Only from Paraguay could Australia's returning chickens come home to roost.

I spoke about the journeys I had made to Paraguay in 1982 and 1989, and played tapes of my interviews with eleven old men and women, the first generation children of Utopia. I also mentioned my interest in Mary Cameron's experiences in South America. As Dame Mary Gilmore, she had become something of an Australian national icon by the time she died at the age of ninety-seven in 1962. Thirty years later she appeared, like the matriarch of the nation, on the $10 note.

*

Mary was rather grand in her old age. Whenever I visit the Art Gallery of New South Wales I stop in front of William Dobell's portrait of her. She is not just sitting, but *presiding* for the artist, ruffles of white lace at her throat, in a costume of deep green satin, arms emphatically placed and swathed in enormous folds of the fabric; the effect is of doublet sleeves on a powerful Spanish grandee. Her head in proportion is tiny and attenu-ated, wispy white hair above prune-like features. The mouth has a self-satisfied, even a smug expression; I can hear her saying, as she claimed in her old age, "The young writers I have helped, beginning with Henry Lawson, are endless". But her hooded dark eyes glint with shrewd humour. This is an old woman who seemed to be saying she had seen it all, a Dame of the British Empire who wrote a regular column for the communist newspaper, *Tribune*. For nearly thirty years, until her death in 1962, Mary lived in an apartment in Kings Cross. In those days it was the most raffish quarter of a sedate city, haunt of prostitutes and visiting seamen, but bohemian also, with artists lounging in coffee shops where their works were for sale on the walls, and Rowie Norton, the area's resident witch, glowering at her regular table. The Cross was fondly claimed to have an atmosphere like New York's Greenwich Village. It was the most densely populated precinct in Australia, with many old people like Mary, in her sensible shoes and bulky cardigan, coming out from a tiny apartment to shop in its tree-lined streets.

She received court upstairs at 99 Darlinghurst Road from politicians, journalists, oral historians and aspiring writers. Sometimes for photogra-phers she would pose with a gourd of *yerba mate*, the Paraguayan tea, taking sips of it through a *bombilla*, a silver drinking tube, as she recalled her six years in South America for yet another newspaper article.

But she had become famous for many other things besides that adventure. People thought it was because of her poetry, but her work was patchy — a few inspired pieces and much that came close to doggerel — and few people read it. She was famous simply for being a personality before the era of personalities. Ubiquitous in the newspapers, she was involved in so many issues: arbitration, votes for women, the claims of the illegitimate child and civil rights for Aboriginal people, long before their cause was taken up by the radical left. Indeed, there seemed few matters on which she did not have an opinion, whether it was a local history day for schools, pocket handkerchiefs for women in gaol, Yuri Gagarin's space flight or a memorial for working dogs.

On May Day in 1961, the year before her death, she was declared May Queen, a frail 96-year-old lady in a tiara, a red sash across her bosom. Because of poor health, she led the workers' procession in a closed car. It was, she remarked calmly, "my last glorification".

By that time she had almost completed her work on her papers. All the annotations on the huge collection of diaries, letters, manuscripts and jottings which she donated to libraries demonstrate she had no doubt that scholars would be working their way through them for many years to come. As an old woman, Mary had an unshakeable sense of her own importance, the significance of her life, and the various ways in which she'd had an impact on all the notable people she'd met.

Much of it was true — but Mary Cameron Gilmore did have a tendency to rewrite history. She could stretch the facts when it suited (and when it was a matter of saving face it usually suited), stretch them to such elongated and fanciful shapes that, coming from anyone but such a distinguished old lady, they would soon have been dismissed as bald-faced lies. Sometimes, no doubt, it was the writer in her changing the facts just to make a better story. It is extremely unlikely that as a child she was left with the Waradgery tribe, "poisoned by arsenic intended for them, I was with them on the banks of the Murrumbidgee, alone, for six weeks". But it makes a great yarn. At other times I think she just forgot, mixed up what she had read and heard, saw it so vividly in her mind that she thought she had done certain things, been at certain places.

Was she really the first woman member of the Australian Workers' Union and immediately elected to its executive? She claims she was. However, the AWU records do not in fact show it, but she had a complicated answer for that: "Being a teacher, I had to use my brother's initials (transposed) to hide the fact, or I would have been dismissed — teachers not being allowed to join unions then, or even speak of politics."

Did she actually save the *Royal Tar* expedition by begging William Lane to wait three days? "I was only a girl in experience and temperament, yet Lane looked to me for inspiration, advice and help as if I were inspired. What he told no one else he told me. But for me the *Royal Tar* never would have sailed, and the whole thing would have been abandoned." We have her account. We do not have any other.

It *is* certain that in 1890 a close friendship developed between Mary and the writer Henry Lawson, gangling, painfully shy and two years younger than herself.

> It was a strange meeting, that between the young Lawson and me. I had come down permanently to the city from Silverton; he had come from Mudgee and the mountains ... Tremulously we met, for we were both exceedingly thin and over-strung; he nervous because he thought me a scholar, I humble because I knew him a genius. Afterwards he said he fell in love with me at first sight.
>
> "But I am not pretty!" I said.
>
> "It was your eyes ..." he answered.

Mary soon assumed the dominant role in the relationship, instructing him in the use of a dictionary, commenting on his verse, "sometimes he ... asked what I thought about the words and whether other words would be better," advising on matters of social etiquette, how to hold his knife and fork and teacup, even how to give vent to his wonderful sense of humour in a way she considered genteel. His own laugh, she said, was unattractive, "being rather a sharp sound of he-he! or tee-hee!" He asked her what kind of laugh she thought acceptable and why she never laughed aloud but always silently. "I explained that the ha-ha! laugh was best, that it denoted a generous open disposition and a he-he! laugh belonged to a more suspicious and less generous nature ... From then on I never heard him laugh out aloud and in later years he was noted for his silent laughter."

They wandered the streets of Sydney together, talking passionately of poetry and the social injustice evident all around them in the lives of the poor. It is likely this was the extent of passion on Mary's side, though it seems Henry felt the stirrings of romantic love. "There was a curious immaturity about Lawson at that time," she wrote. "He was in the sappy twig stage of development. The handsome face and masculinity of later years had not then come to being. The face was weak, the chin undeveloped." This is not the memory of a woman who had been swept off her feet or out of her clothes.

Did Henry actually propose marriage, as she said, and beg her to elope with him to Western Australia? Mary claimed they would have ended up together if his mother, Louisa Lawson, had not sabotaged the relationship.

But in 1892 she met David Russell Stevenson, a bronzed and muscular shearer with a swashbuckling moustache. He was certainly a manly man. Perhaps she didn't know he was also a ladies' man. About this time, he jotted in his notebook:

> The girls are the boys for me,
> Bright faces all spanking with glee,
> Roguish and sly, some are modest and shy,
> But all are attractive to me.

It would seem that Mary reacted like the woman in her short story, "looked up at him, where he stood so strong, so straight and healthy, and an unconscious wave of passion swept up in her heart". No doubt it didn't matter whether his laughter was of the *he-he!* or *ha-ha!* variety. She fell helplessly in love.

Did Stevenson ask her mother if he could propose marriage to Mary, and were they so easily put off, as she states, by Mrs Gilmore's advice that they wait? Mary was twenty-eight years old when the *Royal Tar* sailed, surely able to make her own decisions, and at an age when the term "spinster" was often replaced by "old maid", a condition her notebooks indicate she devoutly feared.

In her account of the end of her relationship with Lawson, written after his death, Mary passed over the pain the severance must have caused him:

> Concerned in the New Australia movement, I was the more able to resist Henry. Affection I had and always would have for him; the affection of a friend who thought him wonderful, and for whom he had opened a newer and wider world. He was always urging me to write. "You can write as well as I" he used to say; but I had no confidence in myself; and besides, I had to help my family. This want of confidence made me write, when I did do anything, as others directed rather than as I wanted. This continued till I went to Paraguay.

Did Henry kneel on the wharf weeping when Mary at last sailed away? She said he did.

*

On the evening of the centenary celebration at the maritime museum, a singer, Mary-Jane Field, introduced a poem called "Rejected" by Henry Lawson. She said it was about Mary Cameron, written after Mary told Lawson he had no chance with her. She had put it to music, a haunting Latin rhythm, a combination of the Paraguayan *guarania* and the Argentine *chamamé* :

> She says she's very sorry, as she sees you to the gate;
> You calmly say "Good-bye" to her while standing off a yard,
> Then you lift your hat and leave her, walking mighty stiff and straight —
> But you're hit, old man — hit hard.
> In your brain the words are burning of the answer that she gave,
> As you turn the nearest corner and you stagger just a bit;
> But you pull yourself together, for a man's strong heart is brave
> When it's hit, old man — hard hit.

The evening concluded with a choral group from the Kings School, Parramatta, the most exclusive boys' college in New South Wales. A group of elegant students in evening dress sang:

> The free-built homes of Cosme,
> With their bare mud-plastered walls,
> And hard mud floors all carpetless
> Where damp the footstep falls —
> Are dearer far to hearts that beat
> In brotherly accord,
> Than the richest palace ever built
> For millionaire or lord.

Returning home from the evening after midnight, full of wine and goodwill, I put through a call to Asunción, Paraguay, and caught my friend Florence Wood de White, daughter of Bill Wood, the last patriarch of Cosme colony, having breakfast. I told her about the night, and all her relatives who'd gathered in Sydney to celebrate the departure of their forebears 100 years before. She said plans were already under way to do something similar over there to mark their arrival in Asunción.

She urged me to come over for it. I said money was a problem but to keep me informed.

3

The Crucible

The price of wool was falling in 1891,
The men who owned the acres saw something must be done
"We will break the shearers' union, and show we're the masters still,
And they'll take the terms we give them or we'll find the men who
    will!"

Helen Palmer, "The Ballad of 1891"

I was eight years old when the strike was on there in Barcaldine. It
was in 1891 and I can remember that because there were redcoats
sent up from Brisbane to quell the strike. They arrested the leaders
and they were sent down to Brisbane to St Helena. And my father
was out of work and this Paraguay business started, and so he decided
that we'd go to Paraguay.

Margaret Riley

The little Queensland town of Barcaldine, it could be said, was
where the whole thing began. The great Shearers' Strike of 1891
was the forcing ground for the Paraguayan experiment. Over
10,000 shearers and pastoral workers throughout central and western
Queensland held out for almost six months and the largest strike camp
and union headquarters was at Barcaldine.

June 1990, early dawn, saw me on a train coming into Barcaldine under
a mackerel sky. I stared out at a plain of yellow Mitchell grass and low
gidgee scrub across which sheep, extras without a major role but still
crucial to this drama, moved in dull flocks. It was just as I imagined,
though I hadn't bargained on the country being quite so flat. We passed
an isolated homestead or two, then clusters of them, and abruptly we were
in the town. The houses were Queensland-style: weatherboard, built up
high on stumps, tin-roofed, with stairs up dead centre at the front, broad
verandas shaded by louvres. A man came down from one of the houses
and jumped into a battered utility truck, his dog hurling itself onto the
tray as the vehicle roared off in a spume of dust. I wondered if he was a

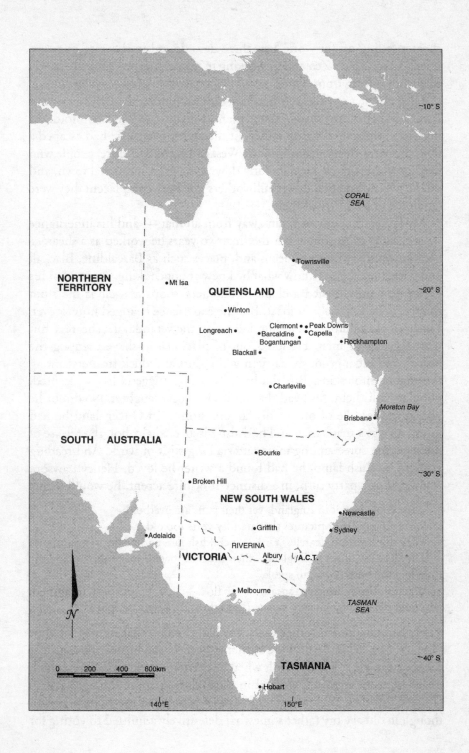

shearer setting off for work. Few these days dossed in shearers' quarters. If they weren't New Zealanders working in teams, they were mostly family men commuting from home.

I had not met any shearers until I made that film for the BBC, but since I was little I'd heard stories about them, romanticised and embroidered no doubt, from my English father. At the age of twenty he had escaped a dour property-owning family in the West Riding of Yorkshire, people who lived on a dress-circle farm looking down on a grim industrial town, and on the two-up and two-down millworkers' cottages, complacent they were landlords of over fifty of them.

My father, the only son, ran away from all that — and his inheritance — and came to Australia. For the first two years he worked as a shearers' cook in central western Queensland, places such as Barcaldine, Blackall and Clermont. I don't know what he knew about cooking, except that his Yorkshire family owned a chain of butchers' shops as well as the slum houses, so he knew about meat. But the experience changed him forever. I have an old photograph of him lolling on the veranda of a shearers' hut with a group of men. He looks out of place, clean-shaven among the beards, and incongruously natty in white shirt and duck trousers among the shabby moleskins. But the body language suggests he is accepted, popular with them, his head thrown back in easy laughter. No doubt he was in the middle of one of his famous stories. In Queensland he had found he was a man's man and he'd also discovered alcohol, the release of the drinking spree among mates after a long stint of work. And reading at night by slush lamp, he had found a writer he loved, Henry Lawson. All his life as a party turn, in a distinct Yorkshire accent, he would recite:

> They know us not in England, yet their pens are overbold;
> We're seen in fancy pictures that are fifty years too old.
> They think we are a careless race — a childish race and weak;
> They'll know us yet in England, when the bush begins to speak;
> When the bush begins to speak,
> When the bush begins to speak,
> When the west by Greed's invaded, and the bush begins to speak.

He had changed in other ways. He had decided that he was a Labor man, that he fell in behind the battler, especially the bushworker against the squatter. He still held to this when he married a landowner's daughter, qualified as an engineer, worked in New Guinea and became relatively affluent. All their lives my parents would disagree at the polling booth, though in old age my father somewhat defensively admitted to voting for an arch-conservative called Joh Bjelke-Petersen "because he's good for Queensland", though still holding firm to Labor in the Federal elections.

At the age of eighty-five my father, suffering advanced diabetes and cirrhosis of the liver, grandly ignored my mother's protests and took off on his last great adventure. From his home in the resort stretch of Queensland's Gold Coast, Australia's glitziest retirement village, he took a train over 1,300 kilometres north to Townsville. Then another train inland 900 kilometres to the mining town of Mount Isa where, no doubt in a pub, he found an old mate who wangled a permit for him to inspect the underground mine. From Cloncurry a cattle train took him on a little-used sector of the line which continued south, making a loop around the great pastoral areas of Queensland, to the far western town of Winton. It was here that Banjo Paterson (whom my father never cared for) was said to have written the lyrics of "Waltzing Matilda" at Dagworth Station. And from there another stock train brought him in late at night to Barcaldine. "They couldn't have done without me," he boasted later, "I helped with the cattle drafting."

But he had thought there'd be a buffet car on board the train and there wasn't. He had gone eight hours without food and was entering a diabetic coma when he staggered off the train at Barcaldine. The station guard helped the old man over the road to a hotel, woke up the publican, and they found a cold meat pie for him in the kitchen. He wolfed it down and went to bed. Next day he woke up, ebulliently cheerful, and walked out into the sunshine of Oak Street. He pronounced that Barcaldine hadn't changed a bit and was the best little town in Queensland. He acquired a few mates in the bar that night and was certain of it. He sent off a letter to my mother suggesting they sell up the Gold Coast house and spend the rest of their days in the pub of the best little town in Queensland. My mother wrote back that she thought it was time he came home and was he taking his insulin regularly?

My father stayed for a fortnight, then truculently returned, to give her endless reminders of her great error and the undying new friendships he had forged. "You can't beat the mates you make in the bush. Not like that jumped-up bastard next door who doesn't give you the time of day. City people! They'll take the milk out of your tea." He was a bushman again and sat quietly for many hours, ignoring the retired bank manager clipping his shrubs next door, remembering instead nights of warm and rowdy camaraderie, staring across the neighbour's swimming pool and clumps of travellers' palms, past figures in white at the bowling green across the street, to distant vistas of Mitchell grass and sheep moving in clouds of dust. Three months later he died, the great adventure over.

So I had come to Barcaldine not just because of William Lane and the shearers of 1891 but also for my father. I wished I had asked him the name of the hotel where he had stayed but expected it would be evident when I stepped out of the railway station.

"Stopping at Barky?" asked the guard. I wondered if he had been the Good Samaritan but he looked too young. The Midlander rumbled into life again and clicked away over the plain.

I walked out into dusty Oak Street. Straight ahead was the Tree of Knowledge, an elderly eucalypt under which the shearers had their meetings in 1891. Across the road were six hotels: the Union, the Railway, the Artesian, the Shakespeare, the Commercial and the Globe. I booked into the closest — so most likely candidate — the Shakespeare Hotel, and had bacon and eggs in the Hamlet dining-room. The radio was blaring "Rock'n'Roll, I gave you all the best years of my life ..." An Aboriginal woman in a tracksuit hummed along as she dusted the mahogany sideboard. The hotel's grand divided staircase recalled more genteel days when squatters' wives took tea on the top veranda. I asked the publican if he remembered an old man who'd arrived late one night, on the edge of blacking out. He blinked. "Come again?"

But there was another reason I had come to the town, an important connection with the Paraguay story, an old lady named Margaret Riley who had lived near my parents on the Gold Coast. She was one hundred years old when I met her, a bright-eyed clear-thinking woman who was probably Australia's last eyewitness of the 1891 strike at Barcaldine. Over the years she became my friend and we talked about her childhood. At one hundred and five she gave me some of her clearest memories. She died the following year, 1989, still in possession of all her mental faculties.

Margaret was the third of ten children of the carrier Denis Hoare and his wife Mary (*née* Sammon). She was born on 22 January 1883 in a little place in central Queensland called Bogantungan, a staging post along her father's carting route. He had two teams of Clydesdale horses, eight or ten horses for each wagon. Loaded with up to 20 tonnes of wool, they were faster and winning more of the work than the cumbersome bullock teams.

But a return journey from one woolshed could be over 1,000 kilometres, coaxing obstinate animals along rutted dusty tracks which became impassable quagmires after rain. Denis Hoare would be away from any town for months at a time, so he took his family with him. Margaret spent the first seven years of her life on the roads, travelling with her parents and three brothers and sisters on her father's cart and sleeping beneath it by night. "You had to be tough to survive, but it must have been hardest of all for my mother. I don't know how she coped. I can remember her sitting at the back of the cart, using a hand-machine to make clothes, and we sat up front with our father who used to give us lessons. At that time my father gave us the only schooling we got."

In 1890, when the fifth child was born, Mary Hoare persuaded Denis to buy a little house in Barcaldine, at that time a tiny settlement clustered around a railhead. Margaret, aged seven, went to school for the first time. Her father still travelled the roads, accompanied by a "spare boy", and brought the wool in from stations such as Bowen Downs, Terrick Terrick, Oondooroo, Vindex and Barcaldine Downs. Sometimes Margaret took time off school to go with him on the shorter trips and so entered a traditionally male preserve. As an old woman she laughed, remembering the scene:

> The shearing shed, it was a just a place of activity when it started. When the whistle would blow, everything was working, the machines were going, that was when they had machines. When they had the hand-shears, there'd be men bringing up the sheep, the shearers would be bent down over them, not speaking a word, they'd have their backs bent, they'd be click-click-click-clicking around the sheep and the dogs would be barking, the stockmen would be yelling. Everything would be going! The boys would be running with the tar-pot or they'd be picking up the fleece and taking it to the wool classer, he'd be classing the wool, throwing it over into the press, the press men would be working, everything would be working. Everything! It was just a hive of activity.

She met the most legendary figure in Australian shearing, who in 1892 took the world record, shearing 321 sheep in one day. Even before then, she had heard that he was special: "There was a fellow named Jack Howe. He was a very good shearer, he nearly always used to shear the most and 'ring' the shed and the others would try to beat him. I used to stand and watch them and I used to think it was a terrible place. Oh, dear! The shearers worked for their money right enough."

*

I walked along leafy streets to the rambling Shire Council offices. Galahs and white cockatoos shrieked in the branches of eucalypts and willow myrtles and shredded the red blooms of bottlebrush.

In the middle of the near-desert of the central west, Barcaldine is a
garden town. It sits on a vast underground lake; an apparently inexhaustible supply of artesian water bubbles through bores from the bowels
of the earth to supply houses and garden sprinklers. The early shire fathers,
with visions of some European arcadia, named the streets Oak, Ash, Elm
and Yew in one direction; Pine, Maple, Beech, Willow and Box in the
other.

I found the present shire fathers deep in discussion of show business.
They were planning the celebration for the following year, the centenary
of the 1891 Shearers' Strike and the origins of the Australian Labor Party.
There would be a May Day parade, the Shire president told me, and a
re-enactment at the showground of dramatic events during the strike, with
a cast of 400, local people mostly. "Some of them are getting into their
roles already. We've got to watch the blokes playing the hotheads." The
women of Barcaldine were working on the costumes and the police had
offered the use of some antique uniforms.

"We've invited Lech Walesa out from Poland for the opening," confided
Pat Ogden, a member of the committee and president of the local Labor
Party branch. "We got Bob Hawke to ask him, but whether he'll accept
or not, I don't know. But May Day is celebrated virtually all over the world
as the workers' day. He'd be a helluva attraction. They'd come from
everywhere for him. And the prime minister could use him for something
down south too."

Pat Ogden had a number of hats and was also publican of the Globe
Hotel. I had a beer with him back in the bar. He told me that his father
and all his brothers were shearers. In their day, he said, the men didn't
commute from home, but worked in teams of eight or ten men. The Globe
hotel used to be full every weekend, all the rooms taken by shearers and
twenty-three beds around the veranda. "The blokes would give their
cheque to the publican and tell him to sing out when it was finished."

But, Pat said, in the old days you didn't hear so much about the 1891
strike. People only seemed to remember it again at the time of the big
shearing dispute in 1958. "They remembered the sacrifice of those blokes.
Do you know any unionist today who'd be prepared to do bloody three
years in gaol for union principles?"

*

When the Hoare family settled in Barcaldine in 1890, the whole country
was suffering the aftermath of drought and economic depression. The

working conditions of shearers, poor before, were even worse. Men worked at the rate of £1 for 100 sheep, an apparently good income, but usually only for twenty-one weeks a year. Shearers lost money travelling from station to station, they paid for their own blades which lasted just a few days, and they surrendered a quarter of their earnings to the shearers' mess. If an overseer rejected a sheep as "cut", payment was vetoed; if rain or sickness held up work, they were paid nothing; if shearing was delayed, they lost their stand and deposit at the next shed.

The men camped in quarters without lighting or ventilation and sometimes even without floors. Their wretched conditions were described with surprising sympathy for *The Times* of London by a visiting journalist, Flora Shaw, who later became Lady Lugard. She travelled throughout Central Queensland and reported back:

> It was a hugger-mugger of food on dirty boards, just one step removed from the well filled troughs of swash and potatoes round which I have seen pigs crowd at home … They [the shearers and rouseabouts] are readers of George and Hyndman; Bellamy's *Looking Backward* is to be found in every shed …
>
> Men hardly count upon getting more than four or five months' employment in the year … the roughness of the existence in the intervals of work is probably unknown and unimagined by anyone who has not endured it … Ninety percent of the wandering population is unmarried, and they may die hungry, thirsty and homeless in the bush without greatly affecting any other human lives … You learn in this country what dying like sheep may really mean, and more men do probably so die than are entered upon any district register.

Some pastoralists still managed to live well. Margaret Riley recalled a knighted absentee landlord who came from Melbourne once a year to visit his sheep station. "He'd hire a special train — an engine, a carriage and a guard's van — and he used to bring his wife and two daughters. The train would bring him as far as Barcaldine; it was shunted off onto a line and waiting for him when he'd come back and he would hire a Cobb and Co. coach to take him out to his property. They used to stay there for a while and then they'd go back to Melbourne."

During this period two squatters dined regularly at a hotel in the neighbouring town of Blackall. After dinner and many libations, according to a family record, "they were in the habit of picking up the hotel's piano and heaving it off the first floor veranda. Then they would cheerfully reimburse the proprietor for the cost of a new piano."

*

"Grandmother Campbell used to sit in the Shakespeare Hotel and hold court like Queen Victoria. The Shakespeare Hotel was the first-class hotel — all the graziers went there."

I was talking with John and Marian Campbell, retired pastoralists. The Campbells, John proudly told me, had been in the Barcaldine district for one hundred years "and the fifth generation is on the ground now. Five generations in a straight line in the one district. They were the only large landholders who were holding land here during the 1891 strike and still are." In Scotland of course, he said, the Campbells went back into the mists, and Barcaldine Castle was their ancestral home. The district was named after it.

He showed me a fulsome obituary for his grandfather, William Henry Campbell, who died in 1919. As well as his landholdings, William Henry had been a proprietor of the conservative newspaper, the *Western Champion*. According to the obituary, the big strike in 1891 was an outstanding trouble for him: "Mr Campbell got into hot water owing to his criticisms at that time. We remember a rope was placed around the office on one occasion, and a large number of men waiting for the word to pull the whole building into the street, but wiser counsels prevailed and this was not done."

His grandson viewed me with faint suspicion and asked if I'd be writing yet another thing promoting the shearers' side? "The shearers have had far too much publicity altogether. The matter is quite straightforward; it was a law-and-order issue. The shearers were a bunch of ruffians who wanted more money than the pastoralists could afford to pay and in their pique they burned sheds down and made life hell for everybody. Something had to be done to make the place safe for decent people and that's why the troops were called up. I don't go along with this martyrdom business that my friend Pat Ogden will tell you about."

*

In the late 1880s the shearers had formed into unions to protect their interests — the Queensland Shearers' Union and, in New South Wales, the Australian Shearers' Union under the leadership of W. G. Spence. "Unionism came to the Australian bushman," Spence wrote, "as a religion. It came bringing salvation from years of tyranny. It had in it that feeling of mateship which he understood already, and which always characterised the action of one 'white man' to another." The unforgivable thing was to "scab" or "rat" on one's mates — to work non-union.

The carriers had also organised into unions, though many of them, like Denis Hoare, were owner-operators. Hoare was a member of the largest, the Central District Carriers' Union, based at Barcaldine and representing over 100 teams. He was genuinely committed to the ideas of the new unionism and his daughter remembered him as a man who read and thought a great deal about politics: "In those days he was better educated than a lot of the others. A lot of people couldn't even write, not even to sign their names. But he used to read history and books on politics and he'd get hold of any newspaper. There was one called the *Western Champion* that he read to catch up on the politics and later, of course, there was the Queensland *Worker*. He always got that."

The *Worker*, begun in March 1890, appealed directly to Hoare's interests and convictions. Its editor was a young Englishman from Bristol, William Lane, who'd come to Queensland in 1885 after a newspaper career in Canada and the United States. His thinking had been radicalised by the wave of general strikes across America in 1877, brutally crushed by police and troops and resulting in the deaths of over 100 strikers and bystanders. Lane no longer believed he was in the land of the brave and free and left for another which he thought still could be. He took with him an American wife, Anne, whom he had met in Detroit, and a bundle of books which were moulding his thinking; they included Adam Smith's *Wealth of Nations*, Henry George's *Progress and Poverty* and Laurence Gronlund's *Co-operative Commonwealth*. Australia, he believed, was a country where the creation of a fair and equal society might actually still be possible.

Within a few years of settling in Brisbane, Lane made a brilliant name for himself as a journalist. He became famous for his passionate, flamboyant articles exposing social injustice, his personal accounts of the underbelly of city life, the horrors for inmates of prisons and hospitals, in effect early experiments in gonzo journalism. He also gained a following among the wives of working men for his articles on women's issues, writing under the pseudonym of Lucinda Sharpe.

But Lane's concept of social justice was exclusively for Europeans. He admitted he "would like to sweep every Mongol, Malay, kanaka or coolie out of the country at once and for ever". He rejected the idea of "a piebald people here in Australia. We are white and progressive and we will stay white and progressive". He fulminated against the use of Pacific Islander

William Lane in 1893 (*Australian National University archives*)

and especially Chinese labour: "they debauch our children, they undersell our merchants, shopkeepers and producers, availing themselves of trade-tricks and subterfuges such as no honest community could descend to, in order to achieve the white man's ruin more happily".

Though such attitudes were common enough on the political left in the 1880s and 1890s, usually an outgrowth of job chauvinism, Lane's racism took the form of physical loathing: he would rather see his daughter dead in her coffin, he declared, than kissing a coloured man or nursing a "coffee-coloured brat".

In 1887, with a friend, Alfred Walker, as business manager, he founded his own newspaper, the *Boomerang*. In it he expressed his optimism for his adopted country: "We don't want another Rome or another England. We only want an Australia, a new nation, a glorious Republic, a free State, a country from which injustice itself shall be banished and in which every citizen shall do his duty and injure none other while protected from injury himself."

The best protection in his view for the ordinary — that is, white and progressive — worker was the new trade unionism. Lane's efforts in negotiating an affiliation of trade union organisations culminated in 1889 in the establishment of the Australian Labour Federation. The new alliance alarmed the pastoralists, who proceeded to strengthen their own organisation, the Queensland Pastoral Employers' Association. The battle lines were being drawn and Lane was one of the generals.

It was then that he convinced the ALF to finance a labour-oriented newspaper which would speak directly to unionists about the issues that concerned them. When he became the founding editor of the Queensland *Worker* his income plummeted from that of one of the highest-paid journalists in the country at a salary of £12 a week to £3, "the same as the lowliest compositor".

Through this newspaper he reached out to the men in the outback, the nomadic shearers, drovers, horse-breakers and rouseabouts, the ring-barkers, rabbit-trappers and fencers, the miners, well-sinkers, blacksmiths, bush carpenters and carriers like Denis Hoare. These bushworkers were about to play a crucial role in the life of this quintessentially urban man and he in theirs.

In the first issue of 1 March 1890 he gave them a sense of their power and the limitless possibilities available to them if they only rose to the challenge. The newspaper was only the start: "It is yours, your very own; you own it, you control it, you with your pennies thrown in a heap together … You have done it by standing together, each for all and all for each; and if you would only stand together thus for all your needs, you could snap those unjust social conditions that surround you as a seamstress snaps a tangled thread."

For the bushworkers, the shearers in particular, it was the first time a newspaper had spoken directly to and for them. They responded by contributing pieces themselves. Union subscriptions soon delivered a readership of 20,000, but many more in actual fact, as the paper became popular and was passed from hand to hand. Its circulation spread throughout Australia and New Zealand, though its power base was always Queensland.

"Billy" Lane had become the bushmen's hero and he in turn idealised these "fine manly upstanding men". He was convinced that in Australia the inevitable socialist revolution could be brought about, not by the urban proletariat that Karl Marx had envisaged leading it, but by the bushmen of Queensland.

> While the men of the South have been talking, the men of the North have been doing … The bushman has stretched out his hands to clasp in union with the tradesmen of the towns and the dweller by the sea … To all has the call gone forth to stand together and act together … And many have answered, for Australian Labor is rousing everywhere, and Queensland is leading … Together you are all-powerful, workers of Queensland, workers of Australia, workers of the world!

From the very first issue of the *Worker* he serialised Edward Bellamy's utopian novel, *Looking Backward*. First published in the United States in 1887, the book had gained an enormous following there and also in Britain. Lane said of it, "It is to industrialism what *Uncle Tom's Cabin* was to chattel slavery. It moves the world to thought because it moves the world to tears." The novel postulated a central character, Julian West, sent into a hypnotic sleep in the social misery that was Boston in 1887, only to wake in the year 2000 to find himself in a world transformed by the spirit of cooperation, equality and peace. In serialising the book, Lane suggested to his Australian readers that such a socialist future was possible for them.

For some years already, he had been mulling over the idea of establishing a "co-operative commune" either in Australia or abroad. He was interested in the Icarian Community Village scheme in the United States, and had made enquiries the previous year, 1889, about Topolobampo, a communal settlement in north-west Mexico whose founders had been influenced by the single-tax theories of Henry George. He had also been corresponding with Billy Demaine, a Queensland union leader based in Maryborough who'd spent his teenage years in Uruguay and Argentina. Lane outlined for Demaine a vision of a colony in South America of a thousand people, "men who are what the average man of hundreds of years hence will be".

But in the meantime trade unionism was the best way of consolidating a future socialist army. The immediate issues were the right for workers to form in trade unions and the employers' demand for Freedom of Contract, to engage whoever they wished, unionists or non-unionists, without restrictions on wages and conditions.

In July 1890 a financial crash in Argentina, which had become a new focus for speculation, led Barings merchant bank in London to teeter towards collapse (an event staved off, as it turned out, for another 105 years, when a young trader based in Singapore brought it down). In a salvage action, Barings made massive withdrawals of deposits from Australian financial institutions. Public works stopped, banks began to close, property owners experienced pressure on their mortgages. Pastoralists were hit by falls of up to 50 per cent in the prices for their produce and attempted to pass on their losses by reducing wage rates. Unions closed their ranks, leading to the extraordinary industrial turbulence in August 1890, affecting much of the east coast of Australia, which became known as the Great Maritime Strike.

Marine officers in Sydney demanded pay increases and walked off their ships. Seamen and waterside workers followed. Wool bales piled up at Sydney's Darling Harbour railway station but could not be shifted to the waiting ships at Circular Quay because 700 road carriers had joined the strike.

Henry Lawson was stirred by the events. He had resumed a friendship with Mary Cameron, still somewhat strained after her refusal to elope with him to Western Australia. She recalled that she was living at Newtown Road, near the university, at the time: "I lived in a fever in those days and so did Henry. There was a night meeting by torchlight. Henry first asked me to go to it. I hesitated, as I was frightfully shy about going among strangers or where strangers were, and he said, 'Perhaps better not ... It might be rough.' An hour later he was back distraught and breathless, almost dry-crying, with shock and horror. 'They have served out ball cartridge! They have served out ball cartridge! They are going to fire on the men! They are going to shoot down my countrymen!' "

As it turned out, he was mistaken, his imagination even more vivid than Mary's. "But to Henry, in his condition of anguish, the sound could have reached half round the world, and a volley sound like thunder. I got him quietened down. He had run all the way to me. Poor Henry."

Soon afterwards, there *was* violence. A convoy of horse drays loaded with "black wool" was surrounded by jeering, picketing unionists. A crowd of 10,000 gathered at the wharves. A riot broke out when hundreds of special constables and mounted police made a cavalry charge, swords raised, through the crush of union supporters. Terrified people fled in confusion.

After two months the unionists gave up, their strike funds exhausted, giving a convincing victory to the employers.

At the commencement of the 1891 shearing season, Queensland shearers were offered a new contract which insisted on the employers' right to hire non-unionists and which radically cut the rate for shed labourers. Union men refused to sign. The squatters declined to negotiate. About 200 shearers and rouseabouts left the stations and established a strike camp outside the town of Clermont. Their jobs were taken by non-union men brought up from Melbourne. Groups of armed horsemen from the strike camp rode out to intimidate the new arrivals.

*

Mr James Mitchell was waiting on the front steps of his fibro house in Barcaldine. He was ninety-four years old, tall, thin and bald with horn-rimmed spectacles and endearingly large ears. He had put on a tie for the occasion.

We sat at the kitchen table while he made me a cup of tea. Completely blind, he showed me how he had arranged everything so that he coped by knowing just where things were — the teapot, the tea caddy, the cups, and the electric jug and radio, connected to the power by a perilous jumble of adapters and cords.

As the galahs shrieked and chattered outside, he told me how, after returning from World War I and the mud of Passchendaele, he had managed a couple of properties for the New Zealand-Australian Land Company "and did a good job apparently". In 1930 the company appointed him manager of a famous property, Wellshot, near Ilfracombe. It was 309,000 hectares, 200,000 sheep to shear with 36 stands in the shearing shed. While he was manager it was listed in the *Guinness Book of Records* as the largest sheep property in the world. He had charge of it for eighteen years.

When he was young the 1891 shearers' strike was recent past history. I asked him how he felt about it.

"It depended which side you were on," he said. "Mostly what were called the working people in Australia were ex-convicts or their fathers were convicts. And the landowners were nearly all Scots or English. The owners and managers were a class on their own and they looked down on the working people. There was a sort of natural hatred between the top dogs and the ordinary men."

"You felt that too?"

"Oh, I was all on the side of the shearers!" he answered vehemently. "I was a ball and chain, convict stock too. I was born among them."

I suggested that, as a former manager of the biggest sheep property in the world, his interests were surely with the pastoralists. But he would have none of it, thumping the table for emphasis: "If you were going to be a just and proper man, you had to sympathise with those underdogs — because they were getting it in the neck and they couldn't do anything about it. They were living as low as you could live. Even their pint mugs for tea were chained to the table. The strike was the only weapon the shearers had."

*

By February 1891 twenty-one makeshift camps had been set up through-out central and western Queensland. The largest, at Barcaldine, had over a thousand men, determined to tough it out.

The *Worker* published the Barcaldine Strike Committee's response to the pastoralists: "If they want conference, we still offer it to them, but if they want fight, we offer that also ... If the worst comes to the worst we can always ride down to Brisbane and ask the Government that swamps in surplus labour to help Capitalism degrade wage-earners, what it is going to do with 10,000 able-bodied bushmen unemployed because they hung out for the fair thing."

The Queensland Colonial Secretary, Horace Tozer, alarmed at the concentration of unionists, gave instructions to police magistrates to sign up all suitable persons as "special constables". In February the Queensland government placed its military and police strength at the service of the pastoralists. It sent 107 police, 140 special constables and 150 soldiers to the Clermont camp. They brought with them a nine-pounder field piece and a Nordenfeld machine gun. All this to control 500 men, only a fraction of them armed.

The strike had become the testing ground for William Lane's social theories. He wrote directly for the men in the camps and passionately endorsed their cause. In fact he saw his role as defining it for them:

> The strike in Queensland is not just about unionism, important as that is, but about democratic rights. Only one man in ten among the shearers and pastoral workers has the right to vote. Because of their nomadic life they don't meet the property requirements of the Electoral Act ... But I have visited the men in the shearers' camps and I can speak for them all when I say that if the ballot is persistently refused us, if Parliament refuses to do us justice and scorns our demand to be made full citizens, then we shall have full justification for any action we may adopt, even if that action is revolution.

By early March over 1,000 men had gathered at the Lagoon Creek camp, a few kilometres outside Barcaldine. Tents were laid out in regular lines in a large clearing between the gidgee trees. Two flags fluttered from poles at the entrance of the camp: one was emblazoned with the word "Freedom", the other displayed the stars of the Southern Cross on a blue ground, the flag of the rebel miners of the Eureka Stockade thirty-seven years earlier.

The bushmen were drilled in weaponry on a parade ground by some old ex-soldiers. Those who did not have rifles used sticks or shovels. Men who had the means were expected to provide their own food, otherwise they received frugal rations from the Strike Committee.

The carriers were not yet officially on strike, but Denis Hoare often went to the shearers' camp with mail or a load of rations. His daughter Margaret sometimes went with him:

> I don't know that many of them had much arms out there. My father had a rifle I think, or a shotgun, but I don't think many of them had guns except the kangaroo shooters. But they intended to get arms, they intended to fight, even if it was with waddies. Another thing they had out there was what they called a "Mullengar rifle". It was a fairly big stone in the toe of a sock, and you could swing it around and hit someone on the head with it.

Life in the camps was uncomfortable. Plagued by insects, the men slept with the croaking of hundreds of frogs and an uneasy sense that police or soldiers could raid at any time. They covered their tents with leafy branches against the baking sun, and had them drenched by frequent rains. They did their own cooking, with a smoking fire in front of each tent, until a camp mess was established, which served dreary unwholesome food.

Union leaders organised cricket and diversions such as cards, draughts and chess. At Barcaldine a library was set up with 600 volumes donated by supporters. The *Worker* book exchange offered socialist literature for most of the camp libraries. Edward Bellamy's utopian novel, *Looking Backward*, was one of the most frequently borrowed. A few bushmen struggled through *Value, Price and Profit* by a little known theorist called Karl Marx.

*

Frank Bannan, the Shire Ranger, tall, dark-haired and snake-hipped, drove me out to the site of the Lagoon Creek camp. He explained that there were a number of camps around Barcaldine in 1891, and there'd been some debate about which was the main one. With the centenary looming, they needed to know for sure, so a team of archaeologists came from the University of Queensland to do a survey. They were out at Lagoon Creek for a fortnight scratching around, looking for tent eyelets, boots, fly buttons and the like. Brass things. Steel and tin did not last in the corrosive soil.

He brought the Landrover to a halt. "This is it."

A shallow gully meandered through a wide sandy area where stunted gidgee trees grew in clumps and gave off a strange acrid smell. The air felt moist and heavy. Mosquitoes hovered. A kite soared far above.

"We read so much about the Eureka Stockade," Frank said, "and that was only a few blokes and a few fellers got shot and that was the end of it. And here there were a thousand men for four and a half months, just ready to roll. If it'd flared up, if they'd started fighting, it would have been a good civil war. It got very close."

He led me to a huge compacted bed of ash, 10 metres long by about 6 metres. He kicked into it to show its depth. The archaeologists argued it was the remains of cooking fires servicing the meals of over a thousand men for a long period.

But on one of the trees was the most compelling piece of evidence, a long triangular blaze where the bark had been removed. In a photograph I had seen, taken at the time of the strike, just such a blaze bore the words:

UNITED WE STAND
DIVIDED WE FALL
ALF. THE STRIKE CAMP 1891

Like me the archaeologists looked for chiselling, but then deduced that because of the amount of writing it was far more likely to be painted on. They wrote the same words on a piece of plastic and it fitted perfectly. "Looked just like the photo."

*

Almost 2,000 men gathered at the Lagoon Creek camp on Saturday evening, 28 February 1891, for a demonstration of solidarity. They carried a banner: "EVIL BE TO HIM WHO EVIL THINKS. UNITED WE STAND, DIVIDED WE FALL". With the Oddfellows band leading they marched, five and six abreast, holding blazing torches aloft, the few kilometres into town. A top-hatted, tail-coated effigy of the premier, Sir Samuel Griffith, dangled from a pole high above the marchers.

Virtually the town's whole population, about 1,200 people, turned out to see them. Margaret Riley remembered standing with her family, craning over all the heads to glimpse the procession. The rousing drumbeat and the hundreds of flaming torches bobbing and waving seemed wonderful to the eight-year-old. "It was like the circus come to town."

The scarecrow of the premier was put on trial, convicted of conspiracy and set on fire. The crowd howled as the flames consumed it.

At the beginning of March the General Council of the ALF in Rockhampton heard fiery rhetoric from William Lane and two militant union representatives, William Bennett and George Taylor. The latter, a big, bluff, bearded man, was impatient about the chances of resolution through negotiation: "We have given moral suasion a fair trial," he declared. "If Gatling guns and militia are moral suasion they have used plenty, and the sooner we follow in their footprints the better."

That month the carriers' unions went out on strike in support of the shearers. The pastoralists had to manage with their own station wagons and animals. Denis Hoare put his horse teams at the service of the strike camps. Sometimes he took Margaret to the shearers' evening meetings under the big eucalypt in Oak Street.

> There's a big gum tree that grows near the railway station in Barcaldine and, mostly, they'd get under there at night. They'd talk about what they wanted, why they were on strike and how they were going to stay out till they got what they could. We often used to go up and sit around the railway goods shed and listen to them because my father was very interested ... You know, Australia was nearer a revolution at that time than any time in its life. Because the shearers were prepared to fight. That's why they sent up the redcoats.

The arrival on 15 March of over 100 red-coated soldiers on the afternoon train was a sight Margaret never forgot. They were greeted at the railway station by a jeering crowd of unionists and townspeople. The troops set up their tepees on the court-house reserve, handily situated to observe the union headquarters across the road. "The people didn't know just what was going to happen. The redcoats used to come into the town and parade around, I suppose, just to show themselves off. Let the people see they were there for a purpose."

The situation was explosive. By the end of March there were 10,000 shearers and station hands on strike in Queensland with an estimated 800 rifles at their disposal. Ranged against them were nearly 200 officers and constables and over 1,300 troops, mounted and infantry, and artillery-men with Gatling guns, two Nordenfeld machine guns and three field pieces.

Lane wrote in the *Worker*: "The government troops are lining up as if for the Battle of Borodino. Trainloads of blackleg labour continue to arrive and the situation is reaching the point where the men cannot be held responsible for their actions." Barcaldine had become the focus of the whole of Australia. Newspapers sent "war correspondents".

The Barcaldine Strike Committee addressed shearers and townspeople and explained that the pastoralists had rejected all the ALF attempts to resolve the stalemate. Therefore there was to be a general call-out of union members. A man rode his horse onto the platform and, rather inebriated, shouted about the power of ten thousand men with ten thousand shear-blades.

Three days later, on 25 March, "Shearblade" Martin was arrested at the railway station and charged with seditious speech. At the same time soldiers marched across the street from the courthouse reserve and sur-rounded the union office. Accompanied by a dozen police, Inspector Douglas arrested five strike committee members. They were chained and led off to the lock-up despite the protests of their supporters. A few days later a sixth member was taken at Roma. A new committee was immedi-ately elected.

Denis Hoare had been a regular at the union office since he had been on strike, collecting mail, supplies and copies of the *Worker* to deliver to the men at Lagoon Creek and other local camps. Margaret said it was fortunate he was absent when the troops raided. But she knew two of the arrested men, Hugh Blackwell and William Fothergill, her father's friends and frequent visitors to her home. "They weren't criminals, they didn't do anything very wrong. They were agitators and got the people to go on strike because they thought people should be treated better. They were political prisoners really."

Barcaldine was a town under siege. A near riot between police and strike supporters at the Shakespeare Hotel was calmed by union men.

In neighbouring towns other union leaders, including George Taylor, were arrested and charged. On 7 April a special high-security train transported these prisoners to join the others in the Barcaldine lock-up. To avoid a demonstration the authorities arranged for the train to stop at the wool scour rather than the station. But 1,000 people gathered to vent their hostility as the prisoners were led off in chains, escorted by riflemen with fixed bayonets. Over 300 soldiers and special constables held back the crowd, which included Denis Hoare and, incredibly, daughter Margaret:

> They brought Taylor down to Barcaldine to the lock-up in chains because they were a bit frightened of what was going to happen when they got off the train. There was a lot of anger. The people at Barcaldine might rush the police. My father knew Taylor and we went up to see him come down. Oh, there was a crowd there to meet him, all the shearers and everyone, and they walked with him all the way round to the lock-up and saw him go in. As he walked along you could hear the rattling. I asked my father, "What's that noise?" and he said it was the chains on his legs and arms. But anyway, nothing did happen because Taylor was smiling and he put his hands up high to quieten the people, told them not to make trouble.

According to the *Brisbane Courier*, Taylor held up his manacled hands and called, "This is Queensland freedom". A member of the crowd yelled back, "No, it's freedom of contract!" A detachment of mounted infantry attempted to clear a path through the crowd. In doing so, reported an eyewitness, they trampled over hundreds of people.

William Lane had decided he would never see his vision of a socialist society realised in Australia. He renewed his interest in a cooperative commune as an example to the world of socialism in action. In March he had held secret meetings in Brisbane and launched the New Australia Co-operative Settlement Association. The day before the demonstration for the prisoners at the Barcaldine wool scour, the Association resolved to send Alfred Walker, Lane's trusted friend and former business manager, to South America to prospect for suitable land. On 18 April the *Worker* responded to critics:

> Naturally the capitalistic opposition to the scheme is bitter and insinuating.

Some go so far as to offer money to help the bushmen go, knowing well that natural contrariness would incline him to stay if he thought they wanted him out … but the papers which publish this and such like offers don't forget to add all sorts of fancy tales about the condition of the Argentine and the price of shearing, which is set down by them at 7s 6d per 100. They do forget to add that in co-operative settlements men shear their own sheep not other people's, and dig for their own benefit not for a bank's; also that a body of settlers aren't going to be Gatling gunned in Argentine nearly so fast as wage-earners are here.

The strike leaders, acquitted of the original charges of unlawful and riotous behaviour, were arraigned for conspiracy against the British Crown under the 1825 Conspiracy Act, an archaic statute that had been repealed in England. They were committed for trial in Rockhampton.

Almost immediately Lane started work on a novel, *The Workingman's Paradise*. He did not see it as great literature and nor was it. The book had two functions: to raise money for the prisoners' families and to spread his ideas on socialism. He wrote fast, dashing off chapters as he travelled around the country, jotting on scraps of paper on his knee, hunching over a candle in outback hotels at night.

It was the story of Ned Hawkins, a rugged Queensland shearer — an amalgam of men Lane had met such as Dave Stevenson and George Taylor. Ned visits Sydney in late 1889 and meets a thoughtful young woman, Nellie Lawton, who shows him the wretchedness of life for the urban poor. Nellie convinces him that socialism can change the inequalities of this ironically-named "workingman's paradise". In the second half of the book, set in March 1891, Ned passes through Sydney again on his way back to Queensland. The ending is left ambiguous but with a suggestion that Ned is arrested for conspiracy for his part in the shearers' strike, chained and transported to Rockhampton in a locked carriage. But he smiles, confident that out of the struggle a New Order is coming, of people who will act on their vision of a better life, a "New Order which will make of this weary world a Paradise indeed".

The trial at the Supreme Court in Rockhampton began on 1 May — an ironical choice, the day when workers celebrated solidarity. Barcaldine staged a huge procession. Lane put out an especially robust issue of the *Worker*, condemning the conspiracy trial. He included a poem by "Union Girl, Clermont". Perhaps, as Gavin Souter has suggested, the fighting words were written by Clara Jones, at that time nursing at Clermont hospital:

Then forward my comrades and rush on the foe,
And deal them a death wound in every blow.
Our swords are unsheathed, we have taken our vow,
That no halfway measures will do for us now.

The fourteen strike leaders celebrated May Day in the dock in front of
Mr Justice George Harding, who did not attempt to disguise his sympathy
with the pastoralists. Lane was there every day, reporting in disgust for the
Worker. The real trial was that of Australian society, he wrote, "and one
sees how hollow the Law is and how useless it is to ever think of working
together, capitalist and labourer, for the settlement of our social troubles".

His idealised description of the bushmen in the dock offered a profile
of the kind of men he hoped would soon be recruits for his cooperative
venture in South America:

> In the prisoners' dock are the bushmen, rough-looking men, roughly dressed,
> with broad, browned hands ... If you were to see these men out West, as I
> have seen them, camping under the starry sky and gathering in on horseback
> to the great bush meetings, free handed and free hearted, open as children and
> true as steel, and simple in their habits as Arabs, you would not have said they
> were "rough-looking" then. You would have said that they fitted — but they
> don't fit here ...

The bushmen had been abused, he wrote, as if they were scoundrels.
And so they were, no doubt, through "the class-eyes of squatters, judge
and officials", the well-dressed gentry who had five courses at dinner and
knew the difference between hock and moselle. The bushmen had disturbed the established order, had attempted to "shake down the curtain
that separates the wine-press from the wine-bibbers". The article came to
a rousing conclusion, predicting that in the distant future, when people's
justice came at last, "surely then men will give a thought to the martyrs
who have made redemption possible, surely here in Australia men will
remember those who stood their trial for Labour's sake at Rockhampton
in 1891".

Justice Harding rebuked the police for having acted too leniently and
said that he himself would not have hesitated to open fire on the unionists.
He urged the jury to convict the men and, under duress, they complied.
He sentenced eleven of the strike leaders to three years' hard labour on St
Helena, a bleak prison island in Moreton Bay.

After the verdict, Lane visited Barcaldine, expressing disgust at the
swaggering behaviour of the military and special constables, who were
"rowdier than the rowdiest bushmen ... The main street of Barcaldine is

more disorderly now than ever before, and the disorder is almost wholly due to the presence of specials and military". He took the latest issue of the *Worker* with him, with a poem supporting the strike by Henry Lawson. The final verse soon became a famous battle cry for the union movement:

So we must fly a rebel flag
As others did before us,
And we must sing a rebel song,
And join in rebel chorus.
We'll make the tyrants feel the sting
O' those that they would throttle;
They needn't say the fault was ours
If blood should stain the wattle.

Lawson's inflammatory words were quoted in the Queensland Parliament to justify stronger measures to preserve order. But, despite unionists' punch-ups with blacklegs, woolshed burnings, a union deserter killed in a fight with a unionist at Barcaldine Downs, and all the firepower available to government forces, remarkably little blood flowed during the entire course of the struggle.

On his trip out west, Lane could offer faint hope to the men in the camps, most of them dependent on union rations for their survival, some suffering fever and dysentery because of the unsanitary conditions, all facing the prospect of cold outback winter nights without adequate shelter or blankets.

In June the Strike Committee advised its branches to abandon the strike. It recommended the men return to work without formally conceding freedom of contract. The camps collapsed at Blackall, Winton and Hughenden. By 18 June there were only 300 men holding out at Lagoon Creek in damp and miserable conditions, most of them hungry, many ill with Barcoo Rot, a scurvy condition caused by lack of fresh fruit and vegetables. A dismal ceremony ended it: the fife and drum band that had beaten the rhythm of camp life made its last parade to the union office, playing "Auld Lang Syne". A dejected crowd followed.

But about seventy men remained in a small camp on the banks of the Alice River. Some of them believed Utopia was possible in Australia. The Settlement, as it came to be known, lasted for a few years but was never a success.

*

In a final gesture of defiance the Barcaldine Strike Committee urged all bushworkers to register on the electoral rolls — the battle would be fought in another arena. Early in 1892 Thomas Ryan relinquished his position as an office bearer for the New Australia movement to stand as a Labor candidate for the Barcoo, the large electorate in Central Western Queensland which included Barcaldine. He was backed by most bush unions. He declared that "no rich land grabber should outvote a poor and honest man", referring to his opponent, William Henry Campbell of the *Western Champion*, who was supported by the Pastoralists' Association.

In this battle the bushmen proved victorious. Ryan won 518 votes against 322 for Campbell. The *Worker* of 19 March 1892 was predictably jubilant in announcing the result: "From Gaol to Parliament. Union Prisoner Ryan Carries the Squatter Stronghold." Nurse Clara Jones celebrated by hoisting the red flag above Muttaburra hospital. And when someone on the hospital committee pulled it down, she simply hauled it up again. But William Lane had lost faith in the parliamentary process. The problem was, he considered, that once elected delegates went to parliament, "we cannot call a meeting and dismiss them if they displease us". He was pessimistic about the continued use of Melanesian labour, which he felt "could not possibly have been forced upon the country if the people as a whole had felt in their hearts that Australia is worth keeping white, is worth having as the home of a free and contented people".

Early in 1892 he gave up editing the *Worker* to become a full-time organiser for New Australia. He travelled throughout outback Queensland and New South Wales, spending twelve-hour days on horseback, coated with dust, only his distinctive stetson hat protecting his fair skin and balding head from the fierce sun. Lane had become a bushman himself — but for a purpose.

"Come out from this hateful life," he called to the people of the west. "Come together in all unselfishness to trust each other, and to be free!"

In Bourke he met and recruited Billy Wood, Secretary of the General Labourers' Union, as an organiser. Wood's wife Lillian had her doubts about a future in South America, perhaps sensing she would never return to her "beloved home town" and to old friends and family.

Lane, Wood and other organisers, including Dave Stevenson, were spectacularly successful. Over 2,000 prospective colonists were signed up in 1892, all contributing the minimum deposit of £60. Lane himself gave £1,000 and some others also put in their life savings. The Association began looking for a ship to purchase.

"We are tired of talking Socialism," said the forceful Gilbert Casey, one of the best orators in the union movement, during a debate in Brisbane. "We are going to New Australia where we can put it into practice." His opponent, Wallace Nelson, replied: "The only thing you'll really have in common will be your poverty. Don't run away. Remain behind and fight, and make old Australia fairer and freer." But the majority of the audience laughed. Even city people were beginning to have sympathy for Lane's scheme.

To the critics who said that the New Australians were running away, deserting the labour movement, Lane asked what was one country more than another to the poor. He argued that to go far away was in fact crucial to the success of the plan: "We must go where we shall be cast inwards, where we shall be able to form new habits, uninfluenced by old social surroundings, where none but good men will go with us." He added: "Only enthusiasts will go there. Half the world lies between the new and the old. Return is difficult. Weak ones will not go; the dangers real and apparent frighten them. Our worst enemies do us the best service by abusing us and libelling the land we are going to. They help us to weed out the timid and thereby strengthen our chances of success."

Lane was by then committed to the scheme to the exclusion of everything else and his wife Anne was committed to him. His brother John had taken on William's dream long ago, to the extent that when he proposed marriage to a Brisbane girl, Jenny Cundith, it was on the condition that if William did form a cooperative commune somewhere in the world, she would take part in it. A younger Lane brother, Ernie, also planned to join the colony.

On 19 January 1893 the Association received a cablegram from Walker and the prospectors who had rejected Argentina: "Found splendid land in Paraguay."

In the Mechanics' Institutes and workers' reading rooms of western New South Wales and Queensland men and women pored over atlases and encyclopaedias to learn about a little landlocked country in the heartland of South America. They read the *New Australia* journal and discovered that the government of Paraguay had made such a magnificent offer — forty square leagues, or over 93,000 hectares — because it was anxious to encourage immigration. Those with access to city libraries could find a two-volume *History of Paraguay* by Charles A. Washburn, an American diplomat, who insisted the country "offers inducements to the emigrants from the Old World greater than any other part of South

America, if not of the world ... There is no reason why this land, so favored by nature, should not soon become the garden of the earth".

William Lane pointed out that the country had a suitably "Aryan climate". His colonists in Paraguay would preserve the Anglo-Saxon purity soon to be overwhelmed in Australia, he predicted, by Melanesians and Chinese, resulting in an inevitable "Race War". "We must be white to keep our white civilisation. Our children must be white in order that they may take the lamp of progress from us and be able to keep it burning for the generation to come."

"The Why and the Wherefore" of the venture was the subject of an article in the 28 January issue of *New Australia* by Sister Jacey, the pseudonym of Mary Cameron, the schoolteacher. Her relationship with Henry Lawson was long over; she was infatuated with Dave Stevenson and utterly committed to the movement, a regular contributor to the journal. "Going to a new country," she wrote, "with just laws and fair chances of living, there will be no need for people to fear to marry because hard times may arise and one be a clog on the other ..."

Subscriptions came in from all over the country, mostly from bachelors, though a large number of married men were putting up deposits, often having to scrape together their life savings. In the way of many nineteenth-century marriages, the men made the decisions and their wives were only cursorily consulted. If their husbands had been on strike, away in the camps, these women had already suffered a long period of privation, fending off creditors, feeding and looking after their children as best they could. Now, without the bonding conviction of unionism, they had to contemplate the total disruption of their lives, the parting from friends, family and supportive elder women, to journey to a jungle wilderness on the far side of the world where there would probably be no schools, no hospitals and where people would not speak English. They were told they had to become socialists; there would be nothing they could call their own any more.

Lizzie, the daughter of Miles and Elizabeth Butterworth, recalled later: "Mum didn't go to the meetings, so did not meet many pioneers till we got on the *Royal Tar*. Dad used to go and was eager as the rest to make the plunge from the tyranny of things as they were to the Freedom beyond the seas. Mum stopped home and had private weeps with the kids. As for us youngsters, we thought it was going to be fine fun dancing under the orange trees to the music of Pogson's Band in a land where it only rained at night."

The story was similar in the case of the large Birks family from Adelaide. Eric Birks, then a young boy, remembered: "My mother ... argued that her wedding presents were her personal effects and were not going into a 'pool' ... all of them were going with her, which explains how Paraguay first heard a piano and first saw the modern marvel — a sewing machine."

In Barcaldine, Denis Hoare the carrier made the decision that, according to his daughter, his wife Mary had been dreading for some time:

> He was out of work, and then he heard of this blooming Paraguay business ... I think it was through the *Worker* that he heard about it. He said William Lane was forming a settlement in Paraguay and he was thinking of going there. My mother didn't want to go, she wasn't keen at all. Anyway, of course, what he said was law, but she said, "I don't think it'll work." He said, "Oh, it'll work all right because there's a lot of people going and I'd like to go."
>
> Every adult was supposed to put in £60. He sold the house we had on an acre of ground, a good big piece of ground in a good position. He sold his teams, his draught horses and his saddle horses and his wagons, and he must've had a bit of money and whether he put it all in or not, I don't know. They said you had to put in whatever money you had. But I know my mother had a few sovereigns and she kept them. She said she wasn't going to put them in because she didn't know how it was going to work out and she might want them. And she did, later on.
>
> It must've been a big decision for him to make because there were seven of us and my mother had a young baby. But he said, "Oh well, you can give it a chance."

*

I was one of many making a pilgrimage to Barcaldine in May 1991. The outcome of the 1891 strike could in no way be seen as a victory for workers, but defeats are indeed often more important than victories in Australian mythology.

May is at any time the devotional season for the Labor Party and 1991 was claimed as the centenary of its birth. All the party's high priests were converging on Barcaldine: Prime Minister Bob Hawke, Queensland Premier Wayne Goss and most of his cabinet, party president and South Australian Premier John Bannon, Senator Margaret Reynolds, and a large contingent of ALP and trade union apparatchiks.

They had come to this Tolpuddle of the Bush to genuflect at the shrine of the Tree of Knowledge. On the new granite monument beside the ageing eucalypt, the eleven men convicted of conspiracy by Justice Harding had been listed as Labor martyrs.

LANE: "We'll all share alike, all be equal, and live as happy as turtle doves."

SHEARER (*whose knowledge of Human Nature is very limited*):
"But tell me, mister, who washes up?"

From the *Bulletin*, 22 July 1893

Some of the organisers were miffed that Lech Walesa had declined the invitation, with trifling matters like Poland to attend to, but nothing could dampen the enthusiasm of Pat Ogden, president of the local ALP branch. His Globe Hotel was the choice of the True Believers. Hearty choruses of old bush songs and uncertain renditions of "The Red Flag", sung by party machine men in Akubra hats, came from the bar.

To balance the Boys' Own Adventures some women speakers had been invited for a forum on May Day. I was there to talk about Clara Jones and Mary Gilmore, the Hoare family and young Margaret and the scenes she had witnessed and how it all led to her father taking the family to Paraguay.

In the evening a May Day parade was a jolly occasion and concluded, puzzlingly, with an "international theme Mardi Gras supper", stalls selling curries and satay sticks. I thought of another procession with flaming torches, grim and solemn, a century before.

Saturday morning began with another parade up Oak Street. "When you march," said Premier Goss, "you'll feel ten feet tall. And you'll have a lump in the throat." Children with fifes and drums from the Barcaldine school led the way, followed by shearers with pikes and red-coated soldiers, the beat reinforced by the Rockhampton District Band and the pipes and drums of the 42nd Battalion. Bob Hawke said there was a lesson for the Labor Party in the 1891 strike: "It is a lesson for our enemies, our adversaries, as much as for ourselves. This party, this movement, could never have survived for a century unless we had learned the hard lessons of adversity."

That night, in a grand re-enactment at the showground, the skeletal frames of woolsheds were burnt, soldiers thundered about on horseback, shearers drilled with makeshift weapons or marched with flaring torches, actors playing William Lane, George Taylor and Shearblade Martin declaimed, and Clara Jones raised her red flag. In the grandstand, pastoralists and their families, bushworkers and theirs, munched popcorn and cheered.

*

I left Barcaldine by the night train, the Midlander, rattling east in a straight line along the Tropic of Capricorn.

I fantasised. I would overshoot Rockhampton, continue unswervingly east. Skim over the Pacific Ocean with its myriad islands reflecting the vast night sky and its stars above. I would hold true to the Tropic. Vault the forbidding ramparts of the Andes. Still not a minute south or north of the latitude of Capricorn. And descend into a green and swampy land with a great river carving through it. Paraguay. The pioneers from Queensland deviated into the Southern Ocean, traversed the South Atlantic, but they too in Paraguay slept under the Southern Cross.

Before leaving Queensland, I made the journey that some of the strike leaders had been obliged to take at Her Majesty's pleasure, to the island of St Helena. The catamaran transporting the daytrippers across Moreton Bay was called *Cat o' Nine Tails*.

The flat green island was tranquil in the sparkling bay, soft meadow grass surrounding a huddle of old stone buildings. The union prisoners called it "The Rock". They did not see the beauty. The walls of their stockade loomed around them so they saw only the sky. It was the non-politicals, the ordinary thieves and footpads, who were allowed outside the beachrock walls, to work at the prison quarry and brickworks, tend cattle and grow crops.

As I walked over the bare green slopes of the island, I thought of that Atlantic St Helena and the man imprisoned there, his servants sleeping at the foot of his bed, his retinue dressing for dinner and playing old French melodies to amuse him. Bonaparte dreamed at nights of his great campaigns and of the time when he had been the most powerful man in the world.

The strike leaders on Queensland's St Helena broke rocks by day and slept by night in narrow cells. They spent their years of incarceration monitored from grim watchtowers, though the youngest unionist, Julian Stuart, wrote, "I think the sharks infesting the bay had more terrors for the would-be escapees". For misdemeanours they lost their tea, sugar and tobacco. For transgressions they were forced to run up and down the length of the prison yard heaving a cannon ball: shot drill, it was called. (I tried but failed to lift a ball off the ground.) For rebelliousness they were flogged with the cat o' nine tails, or confined in one of the dreaded dark cells. I entered one of the underground pits, ventilated only by a narrow pipe. When the lid was lowered, not a ray of light entered. Men were sent down there, encompassed by blackness and damp, buried alive for up to a month. A visitor to St Helena about the time the union prisoners were there commented: "The dark cell is a terrible punishment, as we saw. Two men who had at St Helena been sentenced to twenty-eight days in the dark cells were on the twenty-first day blueish-white in the skin of face and hands. They looked bloodless, dazed and weak."

But the union men knew that the three years' hard labour would come to an end and they dreamed of a future life. They were not allowed to read, and especially not Lane's novel *The Workingman's Paradise*, the profits of which went into a fund to aid their families. But Alec Forrester had been to Boggo Road gaol for medical treatment, and while there obtained a copy and reputedly memorised every word of it. "When he came back to St Helena," Julian Stuart wrote, "he eclipsed the exploits of Scheherazade, the lady with the record for tale-telling in the *Arabian Nights*. The hours in the wards and cells and work rooms and exercise yards, hours that were as a rule tedious and wearisome to a degree almost unspeakable, were, for the time being, brightened by Forrester's repetition of Billy's book."

Through the prisoners' grapevine they heard news of Lane and his organising out west, learned that many old friends were packing up and making for Sydney. They smuggled out a letter. A few days before the sailing of the *Royal Tar*, their message was read to a crowd of 10,000 in Sydney's Domain: "A man's life spent in such an effort is well spent."

On St Helena some of them were dreaming about South America, about a new life of freedom and goodwill in a tropical paradise. They resolved that on their release they would voyage there to join their mates. And four of them — Hugh Blackwell, Alec Forrester, Henry Smith-Barry and William Bennett — would do so.

One hundred years after them, I was also preparing to journey to Paraguay.

4
New Australia Bound

Taken as a whole, the adult members of the New Australia are probably as fine a body of men as could be got together, and the pity of it is that they are leaving the Old Australia.

Sydney Mail, July 1893

They sailed away, for a year and a day,
To the land where the bong-tree grows;
And there in a wood a Piggy-wig stood,
With a ring at the end of his nose.

Edward Lear

The immigration official peered at my passport. "Paraguay! Why on earth go there?" I was suprised at his surprise. I thought one of the perks of his job was to see the remote destinations of the world flashing past daily: Ouagadougou, Ulaanbaatar, Kanuku, Pomeroon, Essequibo. Maybe he spent his working life being astonished and never got bored; perhaps I was looking at a happy man. It was a kind of research trip, I said, historical research.

"You're interested in that lot who had some kind of socialist colony? They went there last century, didn't they?"

He knew! "They're the ones. They went in 1893."

I was unsettled by grumbling noises in the queue behind me, but he was in his stride. "Dame Mary Gilmore. She was a bit of a socialist. She went over, I think."

"She did. She was there six years."

"Well, what do you know about that!" Nothing, suggested the fretful exhalation from the woman behind me, and no desire to know more. "I've heard," said the official, "that there are still some of them left. Old blokes with Australian accents."

"Most of them have died now," I said, "I knew some of them. But their children are getting together for a party. It's a hundred years since the Australians arrived."

"I hope I hear about it some time then," he said, stamping my passport. "Bit wacky, that Paraguay business, but really kind of interesting."

*

By walking along the concourse to the gate lounge, I had already arrived in Latin America. Like so many sheep we had been corralled, tagged and sent down a chute. Sydney's multi-cultural mix had thinned out; now we were mostly Latins. The pink-faced were already the foreigners, three businessmen, a middle-aged couple walking ahead with a clutch of books, and myself. No one was taking up the invitation above a freezer in the Last Stop Shopping bay: "Take an Australian steak as a gift". To the land of beef and *machismo*? Not this little cream puff.

Ahead was a woman who seemed to have stepped off a poster for Rio, waving bangled arms below a cartwheel raffia hat ornamented with flowers and fruit. She was smiling straight at me — Mercedes Quevedo de Wood. I remembered that everyone called her Mecha. We had met over a year before at a Paraguayan get-together, just after she'd arrived in Australia with her new husband, Patricio Wood. A cousin with them from Asunción had sipped chardonnay as he looked across Sydney Harbour. He'd said, "Our grandparents left Australia looking for paradise on earth. I had always wondered what they hoped to find. And now I know. They were looking for this."

Mecha called Patricio and he joined us, a man with blue eyes and crinkly grey hair, loaded down with duty-free shopping bags. A grandson of William and Lillian Wood, he'd been one of the first of the returning Australian-Paraguayans, joining his younger brother Peter at Griffith in the 1970s. He became a successful builder but returned to Paraguay on a visit and saw Mecha, a glamorous divorcee in her fifties, the daughter of a Paraguayan colonel. Patricio was dazzled. They'd married and settled in Australia at Mooloolaba, a seaside resort north of Brisbane. When I had met her she could speak little English and I had almost forgotten what Spanish I had so we were not able to communicate much. Now she was vivacious in a noticeably Australian accent.

"Coming over for the fiesta in Asunción too? It's going to be fab."

*

Notwithstanding everything that has been said to dissuade them, every friendly admonition, every showing of just impediment, every forbidding of the banns between white upstanding Australians and a forbidding and banned community of dusky Dagoes, Lane and 210 of his followers have passed out through Sydney Heads on their way to Paraguay. The good or at least fair to middling ship *Royal Tar* is heading for the frozen Horn loaded with enthusiasts who, in the intervals of mal-de-mer, see visions of a land of golden mist and mateship under the orange grove shade, with "good grub" a certainty and just enough work to make life interesting.

The New Australians had heard many comforting things about the sturdiness of the *Royal Tar*, selected and purchased for the Association for £1,200 by one of their seafaring members, James Molesworth. They knew it had already made many voyages to America for the timber trade and they had read its specifications in the *New Australia* journal. A barque of bloodwood and blue gum, copper-bottomed and copper-fastened throughout, it had been built on the Nambucca River of New South Wales in 1876. "As a sailor she is considered one of the fastest of her size. Her registered tonnage is 598 tons and she carries between 900 and 1,000 tons when loaded; length 171 feet; breadth 31 feet; depth 17 feet."

They were aware that it had been pored over by the maritime authorities, looking for any excuse to reject it as unseaworthy, and they knew about the refitting for passenger accommodation, the cost of the new mainmast, anchor and all the other bits and pieces that had been insisted on. But intellectually appreciating all this was not the same as launching out onto the open seas and heading south to the fearsome Roaring Forties, especially for a group of people more used to vast expanses of baked red earth than water. It was an awesome realisation: they were actually doing at last what had been talked of for so long, but doing it with stomachs out of control.

"Leaving Sydney Harbour at 1 pm on Sunday, 16th July," wrote John Sibbald, a 42-year-old accountant, "we slid at once into a heavy confused sea, left by a blown-out gale, that put many, including yours truly, on the broad of their backs straightaway. Ye gods! What a time! Roll, twist, squirm, groan, how we did go it! … On the eleventh day out, however, we had the satisfaction of seeing, at 11 pm, the light on Three Kings Islands, North New Zealand, and feeling that it might yet be worthwhile to live …"

*

Our carrier was Qantas as far as Auckland, where we'd change to Aerolíneas Argentinas. The in-flight entertainment was an episode of *Mr Bean*. Rowan Atkinson's trouser-fly had become hooked with a Christmas turkey. He appeared to be having his lascivious way with the bird. I looked around the overwhelmingly Hispanic faces of passengers: they were either impassive, embarrassed or totally mystified.

At Auckland airport the Argentine soccer team surged into the VIP lounge, cameras flashing behind them. Diego Maradona and the rest of the team (though the rest of the team didn't seem important to the reporters) were on their way to Sydney for a match against Australia, a qualifier for the World Cup. With noisy conversations around me in Spanish, I sought refuge at a table with the bookish couple I had seen earlier and learned they were on their way to Montevideo where he would be giving a six-week extension course for rural field-workers. For them it was a continuing love affair with South America. Both from Melbourne, they'd met and married in Buenos Aires some thirty years before. She asked about my reasons for travelling and knew something of the story of the Australian utopians. It must have been hell going around Cape Horn in a little sailing ship, she said, especially for the women who probably had no say about being there.

*

As Captain Arden Logan steered the *Royal Tar* along the 34th parallel, the balmy weather soothed frayed nerves. The sun shone on gently rolling waves.

From the beginning of the voyage William Lane was determined to demonstrate mateship in action. He would refute the *Bulletin's* prediction that the age-old problem of "who's to do the washing-up?" would be solved "by shunting that unlovely job on someone else", leading to resentment, scheming and chaos. Lane and his wife occupied one of the smallest cabins on the ship, and he insisted on taking his turn in the galley peeling potatoes and washing dishes. Everyone was so imbued with optimism and goodwill that there weren't enough menial tasks to go around.

But in the third week out of Sydney, as the evenings continued warm and balmy, Lane's troubles began. The stuffy hold, below water level and illuminated by smoky lamps, was a difficult place to sleep. Sydney's *Daily Telegraph* had gleefully predicted this:

'Tween decks, where emigrants will live and eat and sleep and have their two months' being, are simply a mass of plain deal. Apart from the curtains to the cabins of the married women and the single girls, the place is destitute of those accessories which add to the pleasures of life. It is a wilderness of bare boards, with no entrance for the sun's rays except what may be afforded by the headlights. Indeed, a voyage in the *Royal Tar* in dirty weather round Cape Horn would be calculated to drive anyone but an enthusiast to the verge of gibbering lunacy.

John Sibbald advised that on future voyages more thought should go into providing amusement to distract members from the discomforts. In the evenings they had chess, draughts, cards and some musical entertainment, but he regretted that, although they were carrying a piano, it was packed away. He suggested that on the next voyage there should be a variety of instruments: violins, flutes, concertinas and even whistles, all of which could be used on deck to accompany the steps of the dancers. As it was, the skipping ropes they'd brought proved their worth many times over "for children, aye, and grown-ups too". A few rough shelves installed below deck held their library, and were constantly perused. "Books, of course, are invaluable, and no sort of book comes amiss — bible to shilling shocker. It is extraordinary what people will read at sea, even advertisements and parliamentary debates."

He mentioned with regret, "We did not, of course, get through our voyage without friction amongst ourselves. Such a thing is practically impossible amongst people who are new to each other, and some of whom have imperfectly absorbed the spirit of New Australia. What we did have was easily appeased, and would never have happened had work of some kind been possible for all."

James Moleworth, an experienced seamen and former stevedore, travelling with his wife and sons George, aged twelve, and four-year-old Voltaire, was laconic about the dissension: "The first revolt against Lane occurred on board ship. Lane had been given dictatorial powers until the settlement was constituted. He imposed restrictions ... We threatened to throw him overboard. The dispute was then amicably settled." But Molesworth noted the presence of "some cranks", including one who maintained he was a direct descendant of the Earl of Warwick. Pretensions to the English aristocracy were bound to provoke a mob of bush socialists. One night the Warwick descendant fell asleep at his post while on sentry duty. His boots mysteriously disappeared and later "a barefooted blue-blood swore and searched for twenty-four hours for the missing footwear".

The revolt to which Molesworth referred took place on the third week out from Sydney and began over an apparently trifling issue. The sixty bachelors, instead of cramping into the triple-tier berths in the forecastle, chose to sleep up on deck. While the weather remained warm, the women, not liking confinement below, wanted to stroll up there in the evenings too.

At first William Lane had no objection, until it came to his attention that Dave Stevenson, whom he had seen courting Mary Cameron in a way he believed presumed an "understanding", was spending most evenings in the company of the nurse, Clara Jones. In fact he seemed distinctly "spoony" about the young woman. To escape the crowd on deck Dave and Clara would climb up into one of the little lifeboats and sit there swinging as the *Tar* plunged on through the waves, talking softly together or lying back with only the starry sky as witness.

Lane was scandalised to the bottom of his puritan soul. He put up a ship's notice prohibiting all single women on deck after sundown unless in the company of their family. Clara, 26 years old and the only single female on board without relatives, recognised the prohibition was pointedly directed at her. She tore down the notice in front of Lane and stamped on it.

She was supported by a number of the pioneers who told Lane he was denying their Basis for Communal Organisation, which allowed women equal votes and "the individuality of every member". Lane replied that it wasn't intended the Basis go into effect until they reached Paraguay. The protestors thought he was changing the rules to suit himself. A number of them, no doubt including Clara and Dave, stayed on deck talking and laughing half the night to demonstrate their freedom to do so. William Lane retreated to his cabin.

In the morning he called a general meeting and offered his resignation as chairman. The dissidents were not prepared to force the issue so far, aware he held a mortgage on the ship and they were only a fraction of the Association's membership, probably constitutionally unable to elect a new chairman. The meeting refused to accept Lane's resignation and affirmed confidence in him.

I asked Mary Leeser, great-niece of David Russell Stevenson, about the episode. She said that Clara, an old lady when she had visited her on the English Channel island of Guernsey, told her she had not been expecting to go on the *Royal Tar*; the first batch was only to be bachelors and families. In fact Clara was considering marriage, and was practically engaged to a Melbourne doctor. But when the government insisted that a registered nurse accompany the pioneers, she was persuaded.

By this time too, she'd met David Stevenson and I think she thought he was very attractive. On the voyage over they did become fond of each other, but she told me Mrs Lane pulled her aside and warned that he was engaged to Mary Cameron. Whether Uncle David had anything to say about this, I don't know, but Clara was a woman inclined to shoot first and ask questions afterwards. She told me that she just said to herself, "Well, if he's been so charming to me and yet all the while he's engaged to Mary — I'll just marry the next man who asks me." That's how disgusted with him she was. She would have been a very pretty girl and she said there were miles of single men. The Lanes had the upper hand and Clara just reacted in that way, which she undoubtedly regretted for much of her life. It was one of those tragic romances.

I suggested that it could not have been a complete surprise to Clara that Dave had been courting Mary. In a letter Clara wrote to John Lane's wife, Jenny, in later years, she described an evening in Balmain before the *Tar* sailed, when they sang songs around the piano: "How well I remember that night because Dave brought Miss Cameron along and Mrs Will Lane told me she was engaged to him. She also sang 'Men Must Work and Women Must Weep' ... I never liked her voice ... As *you* always knew, Dave was the one who had my love."

She could only conclude, Mary Leeser replied, that the relationship between Mary Cameron and Stevenson, had been uncertain: "It was on, it was off, it was on, it was off. Mary might have had some encouragement — David obviously liked women and may have flirted with her a bit — but I think an engagement was her wishful thinking." She said her grandmother, Hetty Stevenson, Dave's sister-in-law and closest Australian relative, had died before she could ask about the story, but an elderly cousin had written to her about it. She read from the letter:

> I don't know much about the Paraguay business but Mary Gilmore apparently got things wrong. Unwed women were not encouraged to go out on that experiment and Mary G "was fishing maybe", according to David. She said to David, "Do you think I should go?" "By all means" said he, or words to that effect. But David, who was a sincere and truthful man, rejected the implication that he was bespoken. He went, and Mary Cameron came to visit the family.

It was an episode which had gone into family lore, said Mary Leeser. After the sailing of the *Royal Tar*, Mary Cameron arrived unannounced in Melbourne to visit her grandmother Hetty. "They were rather Establishment and no doubt the other side of politics didn't appeal to them much. But Mary Cameron turned up, saying she was engaged to Uncle David, and so was invited to stay. I've heard they felt obliged to buy a wedding present for her. So she had a present and a free holiday, but later Uncle David denied they were ever engaged. In our family she was always referred to as 'That woman!' "

Many years later Mary Gilmore recorded her own version of the failure of her relationship with Stevenson, no doubt (and understandably) putting a face-saving complexion on it: "On the voyage over Nurse Clara Jones fell in love with him. In Paraguay he told her of me. Heartbroken, she said she would marry the first man who asked her. Billy Laurence, hearing of it, proposed."

As the *Royal Tar* veered south towards Cape Horn, William Lane kept to his cabin. His nephew Eric was perhaps putting it rather too colourfully in telling me that "he had to have an armed guard across his doorway", but Lane did feel embattled. He had a special table constructed where he dined privately with his wife Anne, brother John and his wife Jenny, and a few close friends. This caused a new contretemps over disappearing cutlery. The voyage had begun with enough plates and utensils for everyone but a number of items had gone overboard and they ran short. According to a grumbling account by John Rich, Lane made this situation worse:

> When Lane moved to his new table, he took out the full complement of utensils from our tables to start it with. He was remonstrated with, and it was pointed out to him that more than one-half had been lost and that we were short now, when he said, "Oh, you can't expect us to stand the loss if you don't look after your things." We had utensils enough left for about six and had nearer thirty in the mess. The best part of it was Lane had his food oftener on deck at night, or in the cabin by day, than any of us, and I never once saw him returning the dishes, and I am certain more was lost through him than any of us.

Some of the pioneers thought Lane was behaving "like a sulky child", and he spent much of the voyage playing chess against his brother John. Meanwhile Dave Stevenson stood on the upper foredeck every morning and took a saltwater bath, a display of bushman's grit that they would eventually learn to call *machismo*, even doing so with buckets of icy water on the morning they rounded Cape Horn. And Clara continued to stroll on deck of an evening until the weather became too rough. By this stage she was permitting the attentions of Billy Laurence, a 28-year-old labourer from Western Queensland, an uncomplicated sunny personality who, no doubt, could hardly believe his luck.

In Sydney Mary Cameron knew none of this and in August was writing in the *New Australia* journal that she was certain her dream of following "our mates" on the *Royal Tar* was shared by many:

> We know also that the day will come when we, too, will go … There is not a man or woman amongst us who did not feel, as the ship sailed away, that the sorrow of staying was greater than the sorrow of parting … It is ours to remain till such a time as others can take our places, and carry on the work that must be done on this side.

In a sad little ceremony on the *Tar*, the body of a nine-months-old infant who had "succumbed to teething" was buried at sea, reminding them all of their vulnerability. John Sibbald, the accountant, still suffering seasickness, continued his record of the voyage, noting that at 4 am on 23 August they passed Cape Horn, though it was too far off to see anything. By that time, he remarked, although the temperature had dropped to less than 3 degrees centigrade on deck, all but the thinnest-blooded on board were becoming acclimatised, "so much so that when we had our photos taken next day … some out of bravado donned their summer clothes. Indeed, so mild and pleasant was the night that we actually danced on the main deck until 9 pm. How's that for the 'baldheaded devil' chewing us up to a frozen cinder that some Australian papers prophesied for us?"

The voyage was so exceptionally favourable that bitterly cold weather, flakes of snow and a full week of north winds came as a surprise, buffeting the little ship. On the morning of 31 August, one of the sharp-sighted children saw something they took to be land. Within an hour they came abreast of one of the most beautiful things Sibbald had ever seen: "An iceberg, about 200 feet high and crystal nearly a mile long; precipitous cliffs on one side and a sloping snow field on the other." They had learned that an iceberg raised only one-sixth of its bulk above water, so decided this one must be at least 360 metres in height. And the good socialists hadn't lost their commercial instincts altogether. Sibbald reported that many of them expressed a desire "to tow the mass into Sydney in summer time and see what a fortune it would bring the Association".

The little ship pushed on through drift ice under easy canvas, next day sighting more icebergs. On the evening of the third day "there rose above the horizon a monster of portentous look". They estimated it was 16 kilometres long, covering an arc of 59 degrees. The sight made Harry Taylor, a journalist from South Australia, wax poetic: "The sky was clouded, but a clear strip along the eastern horizon gave the beams of the rising sun a chance to play upon the great semi-translucent greenish-bluish mass, and we were treated for a while to a picture of rare splendor." But

Sibbald worried about such numbers of icebergs ahead and on either side that he was relieved when "we fairly turned tail and ran away westward again ..."

*

According to the cabin television screen, we were moving south at an acute angle towards Antarctica at 934 kph. I was seated next to an aeronautical engineer called Laurie. He was reading a biography, *Iacocca*. He told me gloomily that he didn't read much but, when he did, liked non-fiction. Novels were a waste of time. He didn't have much patience with his job either and couldn't wait for his retirement in two years, "when I'll do what I've always wanted to do".

"What's that?"

He smiled for the first time. "Have a garden, do oil painting, be with my wife and grandchildren. My grandson and I are building this model railway. It's a scale model of a part of Bavaria. We've got mountains, lakes, churches, it's lovely. And of course tunnels. And seven locomotives and all the rolling stock. Next time I go to the States I'm going to buy some more. I think we'll have twelve locomotives in the end."

He wanted to go on holidays with his wife, he said, camping around Lakes Entrance. But he would not be holidaying Overseas, he never wanted to see Overseas again.

*

Before the first voyage of the *Royal Tar* was halfway over, the pioneers were separating into those who believed implicitly in William Lane, and those increasingly dissatisfied with his leadership. By the time they reached New Australia two factions were clearly defined: the Royalists who supported King Billy and the Rebels who didn't. When the second batch of colonists was ready to sail, just over five months later, their brave new world was already in the process of splitting up.

The troubles in Paraguay were only cursorily mentioned in the *New Australia* journal, it clearly not being in the Association's interests to publicise them. The second group of hopeful emigrants, embarking from Adelaide five months after the *Tar*'s first sailing, had no conception of how profound they were.

Some of the most prominent figures in the Australian labour movement were on board for the second voyage, eager to realise their dream at last.

They were led by Billy Saunders, former president of the Australian
Labour Federation, a Californian with a smattering of Spanish who'd been
in the prospecting party that recommended the land in Paraguay. Also
travelling were two of the union "conspiracy" prisoners, Hugh Blackwell
and Henry Smith-Barry, recently released from St Helena gaol, and also
Gilbert Casey, the orator from Brisbane. There were also loyal supporters
who gave the labour movement its strength and weakened it by departing,
such as Denis Hoare, the Barcaldine carrier, and William Gilmore, an
unassuming but well-liked shearer from Victoria.

Of the 199 passengers on the final manifest (a handful literally missed
the boat) 132 were men. William Lane, without fully admitting to the
difficulties he was experiencing in Paraguay, had urged that it be an
all-male contingent, preferably bushmen, with the women to be delayed
six months. But the Association trustees, faced with the problem of a
number of country women and children stranded in Sydney, most unable
to return to the homes they'd sold, lodged in Balmain at considerable cost
to the Association and complaining bitterly about the separation from
their men, persuaded Lane to relent.

Nineteen wives with their children were permitted to go. It must have
been with great relief that Mary Hoare boarded a train for Adelaide with
her seven children, including Margaret and a new baby just four months
old. Nearly 2,000 kilometres from Barcaldine and their house sold, it is
hard to imagine what they would have done for six months if Lane
had not changed his mind. Margaret recalled the exercise with some
bewilderment:

> When we went down to Sydney, they weren't sure whether they could take
> the women and children so the men all went to Adelaide and we were all left
> behind. We had Christmas in Sydney. But anyway then they decided there
> *was* room for the women and children after all, and we had to go by train
> from Sydney to Adelaide. At Albury my mother saw they were taking our big
> grey box off — my father had packed everything that wasn't wanted for the
> trip into that box, her hand sewing machine, blankets, sheets and pillow slips
> — and we had to change trains. We were all roused up, some of us couldn't
> find our boots and some couldn't find their hats. Oh, such a fuss there was to
> get out of the train in time! We got onto another train and at last got to
> Adelaide and then we were shunted off down to the wharf.

Adelaide had been selected as the departure point after the obstructions
and pettifogging of the maritime authorities in Sydney, but difficulties

were encountered with a new set of bureaucrats, including an argument about the number of lifeboats.

Three days before sailing, an emissary of the Lieutenant-Governor of South Australia came on board to make an important announcement. Divulging the contents of a cable received from the Secretary of State for Colonies in London, he advised that eight of the original colonists had left New Australia and that, in the light of this, the emigrants might wish to reconsider their plans. But the secession of eight people did not seem momentous enough to dampen their fervour, indeed seemed an indicator of success, and a resolution was passed expressing "the greatest confidence in the officials and members of the Association in Paraguay".

Souter has suggested that the resolution would have been very different had the members of the second batch realised the full extent of the secession was not eight, but eighty-one people. He speculated about who was responsible for losing a digit from the cable — it was in the interests of both the Association and the Paraguayan Government not to discourage the second batch — but doubted Lane would have committed any deliberate act of deception. With cables translated from South America to London and then on to South Australia there was always the simple possibility of accident or bungling.

The *Royal Tar* made ready to depart on her second voyage on 31 December 1893. Several hundred people came to wave her off, and Gilbert Casey climbed the rigging for a speech about New Australians teaching Old Australians a lesson by which he hoped the latter would profit.

Margaret Hoare was unconcerned with adult politics. Approaching her eleventh birthday, she was on the adventure of her life. "The *Royal Tar* was out at sea and we had to load into small rowing boats to go out to the ship. Oh, it was such a scruffle! So many women and so many youngsters and they were throwing the kids up to the men on the ship and they'd just manage to catch them. It was really funny! My father was there and I can remember him catching me and putting me on the deck, and saying, 'Now you just stop there!' "

The Hoare family, with seven children, were allocated a curtained cubicle below deck. Margaret did not remember much about the first few days. As soon as the ship was under way she was violently seasick. Her mother suffered even more, and couldn't look after Dan, the four-month-old baby, who was cared for by a nurse and brought to her at feeding time. Margaret soon found her sea-legs and helped with the four younger children as the *Tar* churned through the Roaring Forties.

Oh, the ship used to roll! You'd be sitting at the dining room table — there was a ledge around it to hold the dishes — you'd be sitting there and the ship would roll and the dishes would all come your way and then they'd go back to the other side and then they'd come back again and you didn't know whether you had your dinner in your lap or what. Sometimes I couldn't eat, though I thought the food was very good. Every Sunday we'd get roast meat or corned meat and a plum pudding or rice or tapioca, but when the ship was rolling, I couldn't eat. Ooh, it was terrible sometimes.

She remembered witnessing an accident one day when Mrs Jane Kidd was on deck with her small son. His legs were in irons. "I think he'd had polio when he was younger and she always kept him near her." Suddenly a freak wave washed over the deck and the boy nearly went overboard. Mrs Kidd rushed after him, slipped, and her leg was crushed under a spar. The nurse, Margaret Grace, put it in a splint. "When we landed in Asunción, Mrs Kidd had to be taken off in a chair, they had to take her off with a windlass, right up over the ship and down onto the wharf."

On this second voyage more effort was made to provide entertainment to break the monotony. "We needed to keep amused because we were from January till March on the ship." There were card games, draughts, boxing matches and games of cricket using a ball attached to a long string. The men and the children spent much of the time fishing. When they were successful, they would take their fish to the galley and prevail on the cook. The dances on deck at night, to hornpipe, concertina and bagpipes, were popular with everybody, especially with Margaret: "I learned to dance on the ship — to bagpipe music. Oh dear, what a screech! We'd have sing-songs with a concertina and anyone who could sing or recite would do so. There was an older girl with a very good voice and she sang all those old songs — 'Annie Laurie' and 'The Blue Bells of Scotland'."

The little ship becalmed as they approached Cape Horn. Captain James Kennedy was reluctant to start the engines, wanting to sail around. "In the afternoon the wind changed and as soon as it did, the sailors raced out, you'd wonder where they came from. They rushed up the masts, looking just like monkeys. Every man knew his rope and they undid the sails and set them and we sailed around Cape Horn in great style. The ship looked lovely with all the sails filled out, and we went around and up the coast of South America to Montevideo."

As the *Tar* moved north, parallel with the Argentine coast, they encountered schools of whales and porpoises in the warm currents off Peninsula Valdés. "We saw whales, they used to come up and squirt water up in the air, dive down and then come up again and you could see the whole whale in the water. We often saw porpoises. We used to sit at the nose of the ship and watch the porpoises going by. They were all different too, we had names for all of them."

The *New Australia* journal, now largely edited by Mary Cameron, reported on the new sport:

> The second voyage of the *Tar* seems to have supplied quite a number of funny incidents to the observer, and as the passengers were mostly young bushmen to whom nothing was too hot or too heavy, it is not to be wondered at ... Sometimes could be seen about a hundred bushmen roosting along the rail as the vessel sped along under a spread of full canvas, each and every man yelling the odds on particular porpoises which sported round the ship, and the cries of "Two dividends to one on the little grey chap!", "Six to four on the spotted joker!", "Mine's in the lead!", "No, that's mine!" ... What a row they made to be sure. And how they would cheer if an albatross soared past. There were cheers for everything. A ship in sight was cheered for hours, and a whale was hailed with shouts of "another hawker!" All hands got over safely — that is the best yarn of the lot.

*

A blast of soupy music, soaring strings, woke me. On the plane's cabin screen a persimmon sun hung suspended above a glassy ocean. Rumpled passengers glanced befuddled at it and the superimposed message, *Buenos días — Good morning — Bonjour*.

Bright light gleamed under the shuttered windows. Approaching the New World from the opposite direction, the first glimmerings perceived by Columbus he took to be the coast. But they came from a species of marine glow-worm which laid its eggs between sunset and the rising of the moon. He was still only halfway across the Atlantic.

I raised the shutter to confront the jagged, ice-covered ramparts of the Andes, an immense cordillera, endlessly repeating its monstrous and heroic peaks and corrugations beneath the drifting cloud. The cabin activities seemed even more absurd, the muzak, shuffling queues for the lavatories and the captain's advice to set watches to Buenos Aires time.

The screen map showed us heading north on a steep angled course for the capital. And below was a bare tawny landscape, etched by dry watercourses. It could be outback Australia — but it was Patagonia. The name had an exciting resonance. I had read Bruce Chatwin's book, and others found in second-hand bookshops by that indomitable tribe of nineteenth-century British travellers. I hoped to get down there before I left the continent.

A hostess handed out recent copies of the *Buenos Aires Herald* with a lead story, "Maradona Fears Too Much Expected of Him in Sydney: he complained he was not the saviour of Argentine soccer".

The Falklands-Malvinas issue still simmered. British detectives had arrived in Buenos Aires to investigate alleged war crimes committed by British soldiers in 1982. They were not about to mollify the Argentine War Veterans Association, whose president had issued a statement headed, "Invasion — the Queen's Pigs Have Arrived".

But the Community News and Social Calendar proved there were still admirers of the British: St Andrews English conversation group was meeting at 6.30 pm Friday and on Saturday the Pickwick Club was having a luncheon. The Dr Smith Memorial Ladies' Work Party was going all out with a Bridge-Canasta-Gift Tea. The Reverend Couch would be speaking, followed by a video of "The Trooping of the Colour". For those disinclined to hear the Reverend Couch, there was a Bazaar and Rummage Sale at St Michaels in Martinez at 2.30 pm with stalls, games and "a very good tea".

As we descended through cloud I saw flat grey-green fields, neatly marked out in grid patterns, and, rising abruptly in the distance, absurdly enormous in all the great empty land, a shimmering metropolis.

*

I made my way through the crowds and confusion of Ezeiza airport, gave my creakingly rusty Spanish a run in order to change money, avoided the taxi touts and found an airport mini-bus.

A little blue-robed Madonna swung against the windscreen, the Virgin of Lujan, Mother of God and Patron Saint of the Argentine roads. We passed a huge billboard that unrepentantly asserted *Las Malvinas son argentinas*. The driver insisted with mournful resignation that I was British. He would tell me something, he said, about *el porteño*, the person of the port, the Buenos Aires resident. I knew what was coming ... *El porteño* was an Italian who spoke Spanish, dressed like a Frenchman and *thought* he was British. I had wondered how long it would be before someone trotted out that old saw. Twenty-eight minutes from hitting the ground.

Over a network of freeways, past a wretched squatters' settlement and rows of cement flats of breathtaking decrepitude, and we were in the city, joining the traffic in the immense avenues, cruising down Avenida 9 de

Julio, created by bulldozing rows of elegant mansions to fulfil the claim of the widest street in the world, *machismo* as urban planning. We had entered the city that *los porteños* prefer to see as its distinctive face, ignoring the Mexican squalor of its outskirts, the tirelessly promoted "Paris of Latin America", a Francophile conceit of plazas, fake Rodin statuary, rococo apartment blocks and the ornate Teatro Colón opera house, its jewel in the crown.

The city was alive and clamorous. As it was only 10 pm the early comers were stepping out to drink and dine in the restaurants, *confiterías* and little bars with bottles of vermouth and exotic liqueurs lined up in front of mirrors. The rush would come about midnight.

I was dropped off at the Phoenix hotel on the corner of Calle San Martín, just across the street from Harrods. The *boulevardier* Edward, the Prince of Wales, stayed there in 1925, and made a rakish progress through the champagne parties, hunt balls and polo matches of the Argentine elite, whom he did not seem to doubt were the loyal subjects of an obscure delightful British colony he'd just discovered, an assumption his hosts seemed anxious to confirm.

The hotel had undoubtedly declined since that heyday, but still had an eccentric shabby charm. The grey-haired accounts clerk was a man of military bearing. The receptionists were eager to practise their English. The manageress wore tight black pants and a heavy-medallioned belt. Her hair had been bleached very white and was minimalist short and assymetrical. Her earrings, bright curling feathers, brushed against her neck. There was an atrium with potted palms, the floors were marble, the elevator-cage an ornate confection of brass and wrought iron, and the plumbing was very dodgy. The Hotel Phoenix was quintessentially Buenos Aires.

5

The Big Village

A cigar store perfumed the desert like a rose.
The afternoon had established its yesterdays,
And men took on together an illusory past.
Only one thing was missing — the street had no other side.
     Jorge Luis Borges, "The Mythical Founding of Buenos Aires"

… the great sprawling muddled capital with its *fantástica arquitectura* of skyscrapers in mean streets rising haphazardly and covered for twenty floors by Pepsi-Cola advertisements.
     Graham Greene, *The Honorary Consul*

Over breakfast coffee and *medialunas*, croissants by another name, the waitress, Florencia, established I was Australian. Because of soccer this was of interest to her as it probably never would have been before, especially when I said I had been in the same airport lounge as Maradona in Auckland.

"We have to win," Florencia said, decisive.

"Why do you have to win? We're going to!"

"No, we *have* to win. It's not so important for you."

"Why isn't it?"

"Because if we don't win, we'll die."

Calle Florida, the city's celebrated shopping promenade, was just around the corner, its smartly dressed women with blank expressions and earphones tuned out from the passing parade and elegant shops and into their Walkmans. It was thought fashionable as early as 1870, when Richard Burton, the great Arabist and explorer, compared it to London's Regent Street: "Here are the best shops in the place, barbers and jewellers, mercers and modistes, hatters and bootmakers, tobacconists and lollipop vendors. The prices are double those of Europe, the quality is very inferior, but the farther up country you go, the worse you fare. Here girls walk alone by day; giving the place a gay look, and 'shopping' becomes once more possible."

Jacobo Timerman, Argentina's fearless human rights campaigner, had warned of the spurious charms of Calle Florida: "All foreigners begin that way. But that's not Buenos Aires, let alone South America."

In the lustrous fur shops faceless dummies huddled in coats, capes and stoles of nutria, mink and Magellanic fox. Businessmen hurried by, concluding deals on mobile phones. A deranged woman stared at them and muttered to herself. A shoe-shine man, definitely a man and not a boy, perched on his stool methodically polishing his boots, his own best advertisement. A clown danced with a red bubble on the end of his nose, a circle of the curious gathering. A dwarf came past, walking quickly and officiously. He was perhaps a metre in height, wearing a perfectly cut business suit and tie and weighed down by an enormous attache case.

I headed for Calle Lavalle, looking for the Tamul Shipping Company. I hoped to take a boat from Buenos Aires upriver 1,600 kilometres to Asunción and had made enquiries from Sydney and sent faxes but with confusing, ambiguous and maybe deliberately obfuscating results. My intention was to parallel as much as possible the way the original colonists had travelled. But they had arrived in Montevideo and taken the riverboat from there, for, although Buenos Aires is also situated on the Río de la Plata, over 120 kilometres wide at its mouth, it had at that time no suitable shelter or berthing facilities for ships.

A number of colonists visited the city later, and for many it represented the exit from a failed utopia. But John Lane, while not missing the opportunity for a homily on the virtues of temperance, recommended a visit as a pit stop enroute to paradise:

> On the way to Paraguay, the visitor can spend a day in Buenos Aires, the queen city of the southern hemisphere — a city as large as Sydney and Melbourne put together. Its population was twice that of the whole of Queensland. The name of the Plaza, Victoria, commemorated a victory obtained over the English in 1807. An English fleet landed a party of marines and blue jackets who took possession of the then small town; but the conquerors, overcome by the abundant wine which they discovered, became so drunk as to be easily driven out by the Argentinos. Argentine history pointed to this affair in heavy red-lettered type; English history had forgotten it.

The city's inadequacy as a port was described by an Englishman who visited Buenos Aires by yacht in the 1880s and was obliged to anchor 22 kilometres offshore, with many other vessels rolling heavily in the pea-soup swell. He thought it difficult to tell where sea began and land ended, so gradual was the incline from the vast plains of the pampas to their termination in water, with gnarled mangroves growing far out from the swampy shores. After receiving clearance, he and his crew brought the yacht to anchor in 4 metres of water, surrounded by a crowd of lighters, shallow coasting schooners and river steamers, but still a long way from shore. In a dinghy they rowed towards the end of the pier, their little craft bumping against the bottom, a large fleet of carts and bony rheumatic horses pushing through the shallows all around them. "In this extraordinary port of Buenos Ayres merchandise has to be transhipped three times … from vessel to lighter, from lighter to carts drawn by amphibious horses, and so to the railway."

The Tamul Shipping Company was a poky little office at the end of Lavalle — polished woodwork and fading pictures on the walls of paddle-steamers from their glory days, a vague whiff of Joseph Conrad about the place. Señora Hilda, the booking clerk, told me with some amusement that they'd received my faxes and there was indeed a boat leaving on 24 October. It would take five days to Asunción, landing me a day before the centenary event. My delight plummeted when she named a fare way beyond my price range. Señora Hilda seemed to be on my side and went into an inner office to plead my case. She returned, endearing in her triumph, to say that if I shared a cabin with someone I could travel for half-price.

"*Maravilloso!*" I said. "*Con otra mujer, claro?*" — That's to share with another woman, of course?

Señora Hilda grinned. "*Por qué no un hombre?*"

"*Tengo un hombre.*" — I have a man.

"*Pero — él está muy lejos!*" — But he is far away!

Two typists collapsed into giggles. Señora Hilda beamed, conscious of being the office character, as she wrote out my ticket. I asked if her name meant she had an English background. She said she could not speak a word of English but was named after her German grandmother. As I left she kissed me resoundingly on both cheeks. I decided I liked the Argentine way of doing business.

Another trip to the moneychangers to cash more travellers' cheques. The tellers all seemed to be stately hidalgo gentlemen who conferred a dignity on transactions which didn't compensate for the fact that I was going through my money at an alarming rate. I moaned about this to the Fernando Rey look-alike who was writing out my trifling exchange in triplicate. He nodded lugubriously and said it was the government's decision to put the peso on par with the US dollar. One peso for one dollar.

It had brought *la inflación* down, but they were living in a dream world. Foreign imports seemed unrealistically cheap, so local manufacturing was suffering, and they didn't have enough exports that the world wanted. "It's like a woman being laced into a very tight corset," he said. "She'll look very handsome and stylish for a while, but she'll get sick. If she doesn't bust out of the corset she'll die."

In the wide avenues and narrow cross-streets outside they were still at the stage of flaunting meretricious style. In the crowded bistros, *confiterías* and *pastelerías*, smart young people were wining and dining as if there was no tomorrow. In the Gran Cafe Tortoni, the clientele at the marble tables, refracted in the gilded mirrors, the chandeliers and lead-lit ceiling, seemed to think it was still yesterday. In Harrods, haughty salespeople presided over hectares of empty space, daring one to be impertinent enough to buy a rather ordinary blazer for $1,100, a wickerwork tray a snap at $186. The brightly lit boutiques were seductive, displaying expensive and beautiful clothes, but the elegance stopped at pavements as broken and neglected as Calcutta's. Gorgeous looking city girls clattered along in high heels and every few metres insouciantly negotiated sandpits, potholes and sudden crevasses, evidence of the yawning chasm between private enterprise and civic infrastructure.

I came across a new obstacle, a snaking queue of perhaps fifty young men and women, most of them good-looking and well dressed. They were filling in forms as they waited patiently to be admitted, one at a time, to an office. I approached a fresh-faced young girl in a leather miniskirt and asked the reason for the queue. It was for work, she said, on an estancia on *la Pampa*. There were only two jobs going. She hoped she would be one of the lucky ones.

I puzzled over this — they seemed so well turned out for a queue of unemployed — and that evening asked a *porteño* friend about it. They would be the children of the middle class, he said. They were having a difficult time of it because they had grown up with a comfortable standard of living and expectations, but for most those expectations would not be fulfilled. The future would mean a slip in the social scale.

To work on the pampas still had a certain cachet. The country's wealth had originated there in the boom years of the 1880s. Its verdant grass and deep topsoil, so the myth went, supported cattle in such numbers that a cowhand was welcome to kill a beast just to eat the tongue, providing he observed the nicety of leaving the skin for the landowner. Beef had financed the rococo splendours and architectural hubris of the city, beef brought from the pampas by rail and taken to Europe in the new refrigerated ships, to fill the stomachs of the aristocrats, the bourgeois and the new industrial rich. In the restaurants of Paris beef was presented as entrecotes, tournedos and chateaubriands swathed in subtle sauces; in the hotels and gentlemen's clubs of London as barons and ribs and galantines on silver platters. And to the kitchens of the poor the other cuts, flank and brisket, offal and sausages, sometimes made their way — when the poor were lucky. When they weren't, they thought of emigrating.

The ships taking beef to the Old World passed crowded vessels bringing the huddled masses of Europe to Argentina, peasants from the villages of southern Italy and northern Spain, to find a new life as farmworkers and cowhands, more biddable than the gauchos, on the vast flat grasslands that stretched to the horizons, and the new industrial poor of Europe who came to find jobs in the city clinging between the Atlantic and the sea of grass. They brought their skills as artisans, stonemasons, carpenters and plasterers to demolish the old Spanish colonial city and remodel it as a Francophile fantasy. They fondly called it "*la gran aldea*", the big village.

Eduardo Crawley, an Argentine expatriate writer, has said that "Buenos Aires play-acts at being a city that really belongs in the northern hemisphere, and although it somehow drifted down to the South Atlantic, it is still attached to the parental body by an imaginary umbilical cord".

The feeling is of having stepped into a diorama, a simulacrum. Like the Japanese theme park where one can do Europe in two hours, with a scale version of the Leaning Tower of Pisa conveniently near the Colosseum and the Eiffel Tower, the city grew, as if by the brush strokes of a naive artist, into a child's vision of Paris. Vistas of noble avenues and triumphal arches were flecked in, gargoyles, caryatids, spires and art nouveau iron-work, a pentimento layer in muted greys and lavenders, washed over but failing to obscure the exuberant Latin squalor underneath. *La gran aldea* presented as a rather imposing old lady, her coutourier elegance unsettled by feathers and baubles and pieces of tat from rummage sales, nameless underwear odours betraying her lack of attention to personal hygiene.

My wandering brought me to the heart of Buenos Aires, the Plaza de Mayo where, in the cathedral, a perpetual flame was burning for General José de San Martín, the Liberator and great national hero. He is found astride his horse prancing in stone or bronze in the main square of every city and town, the noble knight at the centre of a hundred grid-pattern chessboards. The embodiment of *machismo* for his courage and brilliance as a soldier, he freed his country from the Spanish, then led 3,000 men, pack-horses and mules dragging cannon, on an epic march across the high Andes to Chile and Peru to join forces with Simon Bolivar. But he is revered too as an enigma, a man who placed the welfare of South America above his personal desires, who mysteriously relinquished power at the moment of obtaining it, to retire into an obscurity denied him after his death. The flame burns for a selflessness rarely emulated afterwards.

Across the square at the Casa Rosada, the pink palace, where grenadier guards in blue and red uniforms parade every evening, government, usually volatile, often grim, harsh and dangerous, has been dispensed — or dispensed with. In the palace recesses political deals have been negotiated, parties betrayed, signatures scrawled and lives snuffed out. The square has witnessed only the outward show. Thousands gathered on 25 May 1810 to celebrate independence from the Spanish; they were there for the *caudillo* Juan Manuel de Rosas, the "Caligula of the River Plate"; and for the moveable theatre of a dozen different dictators who plotted their turn to wave from the russet stone balcony. They congregated in their hundreds of thousands to cheer and beat kettle drums for an ex-ski instructor, Juan Domingo Perón, and Evita, his Lady Bountiful; they were more subdued for Isabelita, stand-ins never having the drawing power of a leading lady, but they raised their fists in a straight-arm salute for Galtieri and his generals. They were there again in October 1983, when the military *junta* was overthrown; there for the election of Raúl Alfonsín and later for the playboy Carlos Menem.

By then many were not there. During the military regime and its "dirty war" a vast number of young people simply disappeared. There was nothing else simple about it. The Menem government accepted the figure of 9,000; sources on the left estimated as many as 30,000 *desaparecidos*. It was Thursday afternoon and in the Plaza de Mayo, for a desultory crowd and a few snap-happy tourists, the Mothers of the Disappeared were marching, keeping their grim and regular appointment. Their numbers were diminishing as old age took those who were mothers of teenagers twenty years before, and as hope of news of those whose faded photographs they clutched slowly leached away. They marched, not to learn anything more, but to force those with the Walkmans and mobile phones, the nutria furs and poodles on a leash, to remember …

One of the main streets of the city, the Avenida Rivadavia, leads off from the square, and I thought also about a young Englishman who once worked in the street in 1889. His office was situated down the other end past the Congress building, where Orthodox Jews still ran the clothing stores he'd remarked on, and new immigrants from Korea had opened electronic shops.

The Englishman was Arthur Tozer. He was in search of an adventure when he met an Australian, one of Lane's disciples, scouting for a site for paradise. "A few days ago," he reported, "I was introduced to a man who has just arrived here from Australia, via New Zealand, on a colonisation scheme."

When the first batch of pioneers on the *Royal Tar* anchored off Montevideo in September 1893, Arthur Tozer was there to meet them. His life had by then become entwined with the fortunes of the Australian colonists. Soon only William Lane would exceed this newcomer in power over their affairs.

*

Arthur Tozer came from a comfortably middle-class family who lived at Romford, then a small market town 20 kilometres north-east of London. In 1889 its population was approximately 7,000; today it has vanished from the map, absorbed into Greater London. Romford was famous for its annual horse-fair, which began on Midsummer Day, and for its local brew, Romford ale.

Young Arthur sometimes enjoyed a mug of it with his elder brother Harry, but they were both abstemious men and kept their pleasures in proportion. Arthur rather hero-worshipped Harry — Henry John Tozer — who was completing an honours degree at the new University of London while holding down a position with the Indian Civil Service. Harry stayed in lodgings in the city during the week, but when he came home at weekends they would take long walks beside the River Bourne together and discuss Harry's ideas on agnosticism, Jean Jacques Rousseau, Huxley, Darwin and human evolution, the Eight Hours question, the Irish Problem and even the rights of women. But although Harry was progressive, socialism was a subject he treated with due caution, and although concerned for the future of the peoples of the Empire, Australians were rarely mentioned. After all, he administered much more important colonials in his job in the India Office.

Arthur often felt overwhelmed by Harry and, with four other brothers and sisters making something of a crowd at home, he wanted to make his own mark on the world. He had an inchoate hunger for some kind of adventure, a yearning to find himself in the picture-book fantasies of his childhood; in a tropic clime of jagged mountains, dense green jungles and beaches with few footprints; to show his resourcefulness, like Robinson Crusoe, securing himself "against either savages, if any should appear, or wild beasts if any were in the island". He dreamed of the riotous conjunctions of nature found by the Swiss Family Robinson, of bears and monkeys, walruses and kangaroos under the cocoa-nut trees, of taking aim, to deadly effect, at a boa constrictor choking on a tiger, of "strange birds of gorgeous plumage ... wild vines and creeping plants", of "A Dangerous Night at Falcon's Nest", "An Expedition to the Savannah", of eating breadfruit and lotus leaves and drinking palm wine from a calabash cup.

When he saw an advertisement in the newspaper for a clerical position in South America, Arthur applied. It was for a British firm of sewerage engineers, Bateman, Parsons and Bateman, at 679 Avenida Rivadavia, Buenos Aires. Their sanitary services were clearly much needed, for, only twenty years earlier, Richard Burton had written of Buenos Aires: "Drainage is left to those engineers, Messrs Sun and Wind. The only washing is by rain rushing down the cross streets. There is absolutely no sewerage; a pit in the patio is dug by way of a cesspool".

Arthur Tozer arrived in the city in April 1889. With its plazas and grand railway stations, grey cupolas and copper spires, it was much more European than he had imagined, but it certainly wasn't London. It clung at the edge of a great brown river mouth with a sense of menace from the land beyond. There were stories of wild men out there who rode their horses like centaurs, and savage Indians who had escaped the extermination drives and were looking for revenge. There were also ostriches, guanacos and stampeding herds of cattle on the vast grasslands which stretched an unimaginable distance away to the Andes.

Arthur was excited and curious about everything around him and, without any knowledge of Spanish, also a little insecure. He sent dutiful letters to his "Mater" and "Pater" and, in his first despatch from Buenos Aires on 13 May, included a message for his younger sister: "Tell Grace I am sorry to hear that she is still cruel to the cat. My landlady has a cat and pigeon which play together. The cat rolls the pigeon over and over and the pigeon pecks at the cat's tail."

But he wrote to his big brother every fortnight. The letters to "My Dear Harry" unfold an extraordinary story.

He explored the city, the Plaza de Mayo and the cathedral where the flame was burning for General San Martín.

You should see the old priests here, all or nearly all are as fat as Mrs Horry, they are the fattest people in the city, nothing to do and plenty to eat. They all have shaven heads and most peculiar dresses, both white and black. A short time ago some boys put some live frogs in the holy water at the Cathedral and some ladies putting their hands in it thought it was the Devil and fainted. Some papers made great fun about it, but others took the matter in a more serious manner and the police made strict enquiries but of course without success. I sat next to a Priest in a tram car and he pulled his gown away from me as if I should defile it. I suppose he guessed I was English and therefore a Protestant.

His prospects in the new job were good provided he learned Spanish, and he was applying himself. But the office atmosphere at Bateman, Parsons and Bateman offended Tozer's sense of propriety: "Fellows in offices here smoke while they work and one has four parrots, five canaries and two other birds. The parrots go where they like, the others are caged. Plenty of freedom here, they *never* call the boss Sir and seldom Mister." He was glad to relate that things were better run at his boarding house: "Breakfast is over, it consisted of Boiled beef and vegetables, Stewed sheep's kidneys & chicken, with the usual soup, cheese, fruit & wine. It is always an hour before I can get through a meal here & it is always served in style, the napkins are placed like fans in the glasses & the knife fork & spoon arranged to stand on their handles in a pyramid."

The boarding house was recommended by a colleague, Ernesto Finck and, working together and lodging at the same place, the two men became friends. Finck was the son of a doctor who had retired from practice, having "gone wrong in the head" and his own career as a medical student had been interrupted by epileptic fits. But he impressed Tozer as "a Darwinian & an Agnostic & a clever fellow". He could converse fluently in English, Spanish, German, French and Portuguese, and he'd had a varied background; apart from his medical studies he had worked on a sugar plantation in Brazil and an ostrich farm in Argentina.

Tozer was invited to visit the ostrich farm, owned by Finck's sister and Anglo-Argentine brother-in-law, Edgar Nagel. They took a train early in the morning on the Great Southern Railway. Arthur considered the railway station very fine, and the refreshment room better than any he'd seen at a London station, offering a dinner of several courses. After the train journey and a drive to the farm through peach orchards, he was impressed by the sight of over 100 ostriches, bred from original South African stock; even more so when told of the profits to be made from them in feather dusters. In the afternoon he and Finck went riding. "My friend had a buckjumper to ride but he was not thrown as he has been used to such animals. Once the animal reared up … which of course made mine jump & which nearly threw me."

Finck was opening new horizons to Arthur Tozer. A few weeks later, another outing left an indelible impression. They took a train across the pampa, passing mud and adobe houses thatched with reeds "round which children of all colours were playing while the women were chattering". Sometimes these little mud huts were occupied by a solitary shepherd, or a gaucho with a few horses and half a dozen dogs for company. Every few miles they passed a large grazing property, an estancia, surrounded by orchards. They came to the town of Quilmes, today a suburb of Buenos Aires, the birthplace of the writer and naturalist W. H. Hudson, who described his old home in *Far Away and Long Ago*:

> The pampas are, in most places, level as a billiard-table; just where we lived, however, the country happened to be undulating, and our house stood on the summit of one of the highest elevations. Before the house stretched a great grassy plain, level to the horizon, while at the back it sloped abruptly down to a broad, deep stream, which emptied itself in the river Plata, about six miles to the east. This stream, with its three ancient willow trees growing on the banks, was a source of endless pleasure to us. Whenever we went down to play on the banks, the fresh penetrating scent of the moist earth had a strangely exhilarating effect, making us wild with joy.

But Hudson was still to achieve fame for his writings and Tozer merely remarked that a number of English people lived at Quilmes. Through the compartment window he saw "hundreds, I might say thousands, of the native ostrich, Rhea … It looks well to see 30 or 40 of these birds run at full speed as the train approaches".

As they travelled on, the country became even flatter, grasslands stretching away into the distance. They got off the train at a hamlet and sought refreshment at a country inn. Many horses, with all kinds of trappings, were tethered outside.

> Some of the horses were very fine as was also the harness. Stirrups of silver and bridles and bridle reins were of silver and the saddles made of finely dressed sheepskin trimmed with tassels and ribbon. We then went inside to see the owners. They were drinking and playing cards. Imagine a number of dark rough-looking men in highly coloured waistcoats, some made of velvet, top boots, broad brimmed felts and knives in belts or boots and with their silver spurs or short riding whips.

The men, whose playing cards depicted images of trees, coins, flowers and swords, seemed very excited, passing bundles of money to and fro while consuming quantities of alcohol. Tozer and Finck felt conspicuous outsiders. "These sort of places are frequented by all the roughs and criminal classes and it is not pleasant to be out at night in the vicinity of such a house. After having a brandy tot each and smoking a cigar we started afresh."

Their English hosts had sent horses for them. After a two-hour gallop, which tested Tozer's riding prowess to the utmost, they arrived at the estancia, surrounded by hundreds of eucalypts. Fruit trees were in blossom, blackbirds sang in the branches and flamingoes with delicate pink bodies and long yellow legs waded in a stream. "I wish I was clever enough to describe the plants, birds & animals. I could write volumes on them. I admire nature more than you perhaps think, all I want is learning to express my thoughts." He was interested to see the stock — cattle, sheep, rheas and guanacos — and particularly the horses, over 500 of them, "some worth $2,500 each".

What impressed him most were the wild horsemen he had heard about, the gauchos, famous for their distinctive dress — ponchos, baggy pants called *bombachas*, leather coin-studded belts and black Spanish hats — and for their riding skills, knife-fighting and free nomadic lifestyle. Charles Darwin had made much of them in *The Voyage of the Beagle*: "... their appearance is very striking; they are generally tall and handsome, but with a proud and dissolute expression of countenance. They frequently wear their moustaches, and long black hair curling down their backs. With their brightly-coloured garments, great spurs clanking about their heels, and knives stuck as daggers (and often so used) at their waists, they look a very different race of men."

Though the gauchos would not become the subject of English boys' annuals until after Hudson's writings, Tozer had read the epic poem by José Hernandez, which distilled a frontier myth for urban Argentines even more potently than "The Man from Snowy River" did for their Australian counterparts. "The Gaucho Martín Fierro" made these men a legend, "the lost people". But their mythic status signified that, in a new regulated society, the gauchos' old way of life was about to disappear. Tozer was lucky to see one using a lasso:

> I am speaking of the true Gaucho. I saw one here, picking out some young colts from a herd of abt 200. He rode full gallop after them & when within reach of the one he wanted, he would swing the lasso around his head & throw

it over the colt's head & gradually draw it up to the corral. These colts were to be sold in B.A. at the end of the week. I was assisting in rounding them up. It is very pleasant riding full tilt after a number of fine & spirited animals & the exercise seemed to send a thrill through me. These Gauchos are as graceful as their horses. They have such small stirrups, only large enough for the big toe. They always leave their toes free. I think I can buy an instantaneous Photo of one riding on an untamed horse & I will send it home.

Tozer had fallen in love with the outdoor life. He boasted to Harry that he could stick on any ordinary horse with ease and was about to attempt a buckjumper. But he had not necessarily fallen for the flat limitless landscape of the pampa which many Englishmen before him had found compelling. "As to scenery here, I can't say much for it … the Country in parts is flat as a table & in some places you can look to the horizon without a tree to intercept the view. It is like an ocean." He couldn't see much future for himself as a clerk, even when his Spanish improved. "I feel independent and would shift anywhere without regret."

In his next letter he asked Harry to enquire about the possibilities for ostrich farming in Africa. By late August he was thinking about going to Paraguay with some North Americans prospecting for gold, but said his friend Finck had persuaded him against it, insisting that he'd hate the insects, sandflies and heat. But he added wistfully, "I didn't expect to make anything out of it, I only wanted to see the country, which is described as enchanting. I am always on the lookout for a job anywhere. I have half a mind to work here a year or eighteen months, saving in that time about £70 or £80 or more and leave it in the Bank and to then bum the country. I mean by that, get a friend whom you can trust, buy 3 horses and go from Estancia to Estancia, working when necessary."

In November Tozer went to the pier to meet Moffatt, another English adventurer, known to his younger brother. He arranged for him to stay at the same boarding house and wrote cautiously that he thought they would get on. Moffatt soon secured a job in the drawing office of the Port Works, although Tozer thought the office was fully staffed with no real work for him. "But one more or less does not make much difference."

Finck was neglected and on a holiday feast day Tozer went to Palermo Park with Moffatt and found the sight of various groups picnicking amusing. "There was a party of niggers & negresses camping out under some willows on the river bank. They were dressed in bright colored dresses etc. A table of boards covered with a cloth was nicely laid with salads, cold meats & decanters of wine … Three whole sheep were roasting on sticks, over a wood fire, while another sheep was placed in the forked branches of a tree." The dark beauties and their lovers waltzed to the tune of four guitars, two flutes and a fiddle. He could have watched them for hours, the concentration of the musicians and "the loving looks of the couples as they glided over the grass" but Moffatt soon tired of it and was impatient to move on. "We had a look at the Zoo which has been improved recently by an addition of a number of animals & birds from Hamburg Zoo …"

*

Thinking of Tozer and Moffatt, I had coffee in an open air cafe in Palermo Park, the city's Bois de Boulogne. An old man was perched on a stool playing a violin, while soignée women in buttersoft leather jackets toyed with French pastries, Japanese tourists did their thing with Nikons, and lovers in pedal boats rippled the surface of the lake. The howl of some animal from the dank cramped cages of the nearby zoo provoked an unpleasant thought. After the military junta was overthrown, human bones were found in the monkey compound, the end for some of the *desaparecidos*.

That evening I went to La Boca, once a working-class suburb of Genovese seamen and stevedores, now raffish, flashy and trashy. This area, situated to the south of the city, became the port for Buenos Aires when a small river that runs into the bay of the Plata was dredged to admit craft. It became the headquarters of the Italian river schooners and the *barrio* was originally inhabited almost exclusively by Italians and Greeks. The English yachtsman considered it "a rather cut-throat place by reputation".

The artist Benito Quinquela Martin grew up in La Boca and did his brooding, muscular portraits of stevedores at work. The district became an artists' ghetto and later, in another inevitable transmogrification, a tourist trap. Corrugated iron and timber houses were gaily painted in a clashing cacophony of reds, blues, greens and yellows. The story goes that the seamen and stevedores who lived there brought home the cans left over from painting the river schooners, regardless of colour. It may have begun that way, but the toucan effect of the houses is now wonderfully contrived. An alleyway, El Caminito, was furnished with bold murals and sculptures of a socialist realist kind. Carlos Gardel, the great tango singer of the Depression years, was there in painted bas relief, brooding beneath his fedora; he died romantically and tragically, fulfilling all the specifications for Dead National Treasure, blown to bits in a plane crash while still young and beautiful. An artists' market was doing brisk business with watercolours of couples erotically entwined in the tango.

A new port had been dredged for shipping and the turgid oily waters at La Boca were now cluttered with rusting, half-submerged hulks. At sunset most tourists put their cameras away and left the *barrio*, and *porteños* came to the brightly lit dance halls and rowdy bars on Calle Necochea, which were all pumping out amplified rock music. In the cantina where I dined with a friend, a large mock bridal party occupied the central table. The groom in top hat and tails was an attractive young girl, becoming rapidly and uproariously drunk, the bride a pudgy boy with lopsided wig and smudged lipstick, balloons stuffed down his white wedding dress. All night he looked severe and rather conscientious, like an unwilling royal at a municipal fete.

A succession of bands thumped out Brazilian and Colombian rock, and the evening's entertainment concluded with an Elvis Presley look-alike called Roberto Sandro. Unfortunately the resemblance was to the later Elvis of the heavy jowls and corsets, but as he crooned "Love Me Tender" in Spanish, while performing fellatio on his microphone, the lights dimmed and the crowd went wild, holding flaming cigarette lighters towards him and chanting "Sandro! Sandro! Sandro!"

*

Arthur Tozer contemplated a visit to La Boca. He had been in Buenos Aires seven months and had become more adventurous. He wrote to Harry: "I am going to visit the Italian and Turkish quarters of the town as soon as I get the time. I am told it is very amusing to visit the low cafes etc to see how these people amuse themselves."

In the clubs, cafes and bordellos of La Boca immigrant workers were escaping the crowded tenements to try out the steps of a new dance. To the strains of accordion and mandolin their sliding, swaying movements seemed to fuse and meld the sinuousness of Spain's flamenco, the wild throb of the gaucho tunes of the interior, the slave's cry for a lost Africa. The tango eased the loneliness and hardships of the poor. Soon it would be exported back to Europe, titillating and scandalising, and British royalty, properly recognising disgusting foreign habits when they heard of them, officially made known they would decline attendance at parties where it was displayed.

Tozer's erstwhile friend Moffat had his sights set on higher things, wanting to join the church choir and get into society. Arthur was prevailed on to introduce him to the Reverend Ogle, but believed Moffatt's real purpose was to meet girls from the English families. He divulged nothing about his own needs or desires in this regard.

In the New Year he wrote to congratulate Harry on obtaining Honours for his thesis at London University (revised and published in 1902 as *British India and Its Trade*). But he was consumed by a growing resentment of Moffatt, his profligacy and "vulgar taste" for jewellery. "I told him a well brushed suit of clothes and a clean face would improve his looks more than imitation jewellery. He doesn't see it. His people can't be much or they would have brought him up with better and cleaner habits."

After the rift Tozer attended Spanish class more frequently and his grasp of the language improved. "I can always make people understand my wants, especially in the grub line, and I can speak without difficulty on anything connected with the office work." In February 1890 he purchased a Smith and Wesson revolver from "a fellow hard up, for half its original value". Soon he could hit a tiny piece of paper from twelve paces away. He noted that on 25 April he would have been in the country a year and had no wish to return to England.

However, he was worried by a looming financial crisis, already causing reverberations in Britain and further afield. Argentina's long delay in repaying a £1 million bond issue to Barings in London had brought that firm to the brink of bankruptcy. In attempting to salvage its position, Barings called on its loans in Australia, resulting in a depression in the pastoral industry that culminated, a year later, in the shearers' strike in Queensland. In Argentina a revolution seemed inevitable. "When I arrived," Tozer wrote, "the country was on boom and everything was going ahead but now the people are suffering from a bad and dishonest government which combined with their own extravagance has landed the country on the brink of a great financial failure which may bring on a revolution and put the progress of the country back for several years to come."

After the boom of the 1880s financial and political power had firmly consolidated among the wealthy landowners, the *estancieros*, and the major industrialists and business people of the capital. This group, possibly 200 families in all, developed links through obligation, marriage and mutual self-interest, and were collectively known as "the oligarchy". Key figures in the military were drawn into their network of influence and the justice system and bureaucracies served their interests. Presidential contenders and congressmen only emerged through their ranks and political office, with its opportunities for corruption, ensured an even greater accumulation of wealth.

The graft and paybacks under President Miguel Juárez Celman were more naked than anything Tozer had observed in England. He was genuinely shocked at the way the system worked: "The President who is the cause of this state of affairs was elected three and a half years ago. At that time he was, comparatively speaking, poor but now he is a man possessed of millions, he owns hundreds of square leagues of land which are covered with thousands of cattle, horses and sheep. He is building himself a palace surrounded for miles by land stolen from the people … All this he has obtained by fraud and robbery. His salary which is $20,000 paper per year could not purchase one thousandth of his possessions nor could he gain it by speculation."

Even Tozer's British employers, long established and respected in the city, were implicated in the corruption. "Bateman & Co are in bad odour here, it having leaked out that they paid a million dollars gold, equal to £200,000 for the concession for contracting the house drainage of this city. The above sum was paid to the President and other influential Govt people. Batemans have received no cash since November and have in consequence to reduce the number of their staff to keep down the expenses which now amount to $40,000 per month." If he was dismissed, he said he would go to Chile or Uruguay, as he saw little chance of Argentina flourishing again for some time.

Tozer had developed a natural sympathy for the Unión Cívica, a loose alliance of students, teachers and the professional middle class protesting against the control of the oligarchy. As the crisis deepened and the finance minister resigned, rumours abounded in the city that the Unión Cívica would attempt a coup.

On 15 June he thanked Harry for providing him with a "general summary of Agnosticism" which he had found instructive, and was looking forward to a promised parcel of agnostic tracts. Batemans had wound down so much that he had nothing to do at work. "I have to sit and smoke all day. I take two hours to lunch to pass the time a bit. I still expect to get the sack at any moment." One office colleague had died of smallpox, and he and Finck visited another in the squalid rat-infested general hospital. Meanwhile, the revolution moved closer, disaffected army officers were paid in lottery tickets and more and more soldiers barracked in the city. "They are nearly all red-skins, half-breeds and negroes but they march well and have two small bands which play fairly well."

On 6 August 1890 the revolution erupted. Two powerful generals, Julio A. Roca and Juan Lavalle, forced President Celman to resign in favour of Carlos Pelligrini, his vice-president. Although it would prove to be just another change of chairs at the table of the oligarchy (after all, Roca and Celman were brothers-in-law), it seemed like a victory for the Unión Cívica. A holiday was declared and Tozer joined the crowds in the Plaza de Mayo.

> The public turned out in thousands and cheered and shouted like mad people … I went to the Govt House and heard Pelligrini … speak from the balcony. He was very much cheered as he is a favorite of the people … From the 6th till 11th the rejoicing was uninterrupted. Every night bonfires were made in the streets, fireworks and bombs were cracking and booming everywhere. The processions were amusing. Some were headed by donkeys to represent the ex-president and the fellows would yell "*El burro se fue*" — "The ass is gone", keeping time by striking the poor beast with sticks. The roughs had a fine time of it. As nearly all the police are killed the force is small and bands of roughs go about the lonely streets, robbing, murdering and stabbing people. It is not safe to go out without a revolver at night …

Tozer was tremendously stirred by the events, confessing to an interest in political affairs he'd never felt in England. "There is always something exciting in politics here and there is a certain amount of danger in expressing one's opinion too freely and this all helps to make it interesting … I only wish Celman had been killed and his lands seized."

He had actually, he confided, involved himself in the revolution. "I am glad that I have seen it and was by chance detained in a house from which I had a near view of the fighting and also that I was able to empty a few cartridges on behalf of the Unión Cívica. I never expected to take part in such an affair, much less to be able to see fellows killed and wounded without feeling pity for them."

It is a chilling image: a young man with a Smith and Wesson revolver, standing on a balcony in comparative safety, picking off victims in the street below with casual sportiveness. The ruthlessness revealed is there in a different form in the account Arthur gave his brother of the letter he had received from a young Englishwoman of their acquaintance, Alice Horry (presumably the daughter of the Mrs Horry who rivalled the priests in girth): "I suppose you have heard that Alice H. had the impudence to write me a letter. She made insinuations of different kinds and wrote in a very spooney manner. In reply I sent her the following bit of 'poetry' ":

'A Fact'
A young man left England, his friends and his home,
Away o'er the wide world for fortune to roam.
His heart knew no pangs of that mystery love
For aught that's below or aught that's above.
When his birthday came round in this year of grace
A damsel possessing an unblushing face
Wrote a letter containing strange insinuations
To try on his heart to commit depredations.
But the bait wouldn't take for he well knows the sex
Though their wiles may appear to be most complex
He smiled as he read the good wishes through
And thought to himself 'This heart's not for you'.
For a lady possessing both money and land
Has just made a bid to accept of his hand,
A Spaniard by birth with many a charm,
A beautiful face and a delicate form.
So Miss Alice must wait for a far future day
For 'it's manners to wait to be asked' they say
And when next she attempts such letters to pen
Let us hope they won't be to single young men.
What a glorious home this world would make
If all young ladies would this lesson take
'To be in subjection', to exhibit less 'cheek'
To be docile, more humble, quiet and meek.

Arthur must have been proud of his vicious little poem, to have copied it out for his brother to enjoy Miss Horry's discomfort, but he added in a footnote: "The above reads rather badly but that bit about my engagement to a Spaniard will set her tongue flapping. I am hoping they (the Horries) will mention it to Mater or the girls."

On 21 December 1890 some army officers attempted unsuccessfully to bring about a counter-revolution. Despite the disruption, the Christmas mail still arrived with three books from Harry. One of them was *Looking Backward*, the novel about a future utopian society by the American Edward Bellamy, which had had an enormous impact in the United States and Britain and was serialised by William Lane in the Queensland *Worker*. Harry was no doubt later to regret having sent his brother a novel about utopia, though Arthur was already familiar with it:

"It is a book which I have read before but I am very glad you have sent it, as I had to read the other copy hurriedly and it is a book which bears reading more than once."

Arthur rejected Harry's suggestion of returning to England but still chafed for adventure in a more exotic landscape. In his mood of frustration he accused a man in the office of stealing Harry's letters. "I discovered the thief and then knocked him off his stool and when he got off the floor I sent him over again. I was reported to the boss who advised me not to take matters into my own hands but in future to report such things."

It was clearly time for a change.

In March 1891 he wrote to Harry from Río de Janeiro: "I have at last got into a country where I can satisfy my desire to see tropical vegetation in all its glory." He had taken up a posting with the London and Brazilian Bank and in his spare time he revelled in the dramatic landscape of Río, its dazzling beaches and thickly forested mountains which tumbled and plunged to a lapis lazuli bay. He made the almost vertical climb from the city, 709 metres, to the peak of Corcovado, the "Hunchback", which would not be surmounted by Landowski's great statue of Christ the Redeemer until forty years later. He crossed the bay by ferry boat and swam at a deserted beach by moonlight, "but I felt a bit afraid of sharks".

Within a week he had decided that he loathed the job, added to which yellow fever was rife, claiming twelve lives a day in Río. A bank colleague died three days after contracting it. Tozer intended "to clear out of it at the first opportunity".

Opportunity presented itself in July 1891, when he had a momentous meeting with an Australian. Alfred Walker, a former business manager on the *Boomerang* and trusted confidante of William Lane, arrived in Río to scout for suitable land for a colony. He found the young Englishman who spoke Spanish and rudimentary Portuguese a useful contact. The story he told excited Tozer's new interest in politics and longstanding wish for adventure. He wrote to Harry at length about the meeting. It was to change his life:

> I was introduced to a man who has just arrived here from Australia, via New Zealand, on a colonisation scheme. It appears that there has been trouble in Queensland between shearers etc. and property or rather run owners. They had a strike, which was of a rather serious nature. Their chief cause of complaint seems to be the bad treatment and poor pay given them by the managers of these large runs, who in the interest of their absent masters cut

things down as closely as possible. You may have seen something of this in London papers.

Arthur provided a glowing account of the utopian movement that had grown out of the strike: "The outcome of this is the formation of the 'New Australia Co-operative Settlement Association' which has now a membership of over 5,000 good men with strong socialistic views. These people propose to migrate to S. America where they hope to find land & obtain a self government somewhat on the lines of *Looking Backward*."

He had had a few chats with Walker, who was trying to obtain a land grant from the Brazilian government but, if he failed in achieving this, would try the Argentine republic. His main requirement was to find some 160 square kilometres away from other settlements, preferably on a river and fertile enough to allow a colony to be self-supporting.

Although Tozer thought that Walker was underestimating the difficulties of negotiating with Latin American governments, he believed the Australian colonisation project had more chance of success than most other such schemes: the men were used to a hot climate, hardships and opening up new country. They had also learned through experience "that united labour for their mutual benefit is the first consideration. By this post I am sending a small book containing the object & articles of the association & the benefits expected from its formation. There may be many objections to the scheme but as far as I can see the association might make a success of it. If it gets a fair start it will be interesting to people with and without socialistic views as the men are about the best class that could be obtained for such a trial. They will be of all trades and have their own machinery etc & will look to the outside world as little as possible."

Arthur concluded the effusive letter by promising to send further progress reports, and asked Harry his opinion of the plan. It soon became obvious that Harry, by then working on his master's thesis on Jean Jacques Rousseau's *Social Contract*, had strong views about the perils of compelling people to be free, equal and fraternal. He wrote that Rousseau's "insistence on the alienation of all persons and property to the State" was a perilous doctrine, which had given unfortunate impulse to the "unprecedented growth of socialistic and anarchic doctrines in this generation ... a grave menace to the peace and welfare of the State".

In August Tozer resigned from the bank in Río and took up a position with a British import firm, Jennings and Barnett, in Sao Paulo. While acknowledging Harry's doubts concerning cooperative settlement — "I have not much knowledge on the subject but can see the force of what you say" — he kept in touch with Walker, who'd reported some success. But Tozer commented dourly that the Australian's confidence was probably misplaced: "He doesn't know the Brazilian character yet. He will find great opposition if he cannot oil the palms of their hands a bit first. I am to be kept informed of the progress made & have been asked to join the affair should a start be made."

This no doubt confirmed Harry's fears. On 7 December 1891 Arthur sent news of dramatic developments. Walker had left Río and gone to Buenos Aires. He had been so successful there in his negotiations that the Argentinians had already offered a grant of 216 square leagues in the Río Negro valley at the base of the Andes. He had been given an option of twelve months to select a site; it seemed Walker had adapted to the Latin way of doing things, having expended "a fair amount of palm grease" to bring it that far.

Arthur was keen to join the prospecting expedition, particularly as he was engaged in a serious dispute with his Sao Paulo employers, Jennings and Barnett, who were in financial trouble and attempting to withhold his salary. Revealing once again his streak of cold determination, he warned Harry that "if they do that I will disfigure one or both of them for life & ruin them into the bargain. I know I can do it. I think they will settle the matter quietly — that is if they are wise — and then I shall go down to Buenos Aires".

By 28 July he was back in the Argentine capital, staying with Ernesto Finck, while he made preparations for the expedition. He would be making the journey, not with Walker who conceded he was not qualified to assess the land, but with two bushmen, agents of the Association, who had arrived in Buenos Aires. William Saunders was a Californian, a shearer, union activist and former president of the Australian Labour Federation. His companion, Charles Leck, could be depended upon in most situations. According to Souter: "Leck came from Woodstock on the western slopes of NSW. He was a short man, but very strong: one of his accomplishments was to lift a seven-pound axe horizontally in each hand and then, with arms outstretched, bring the axe-heads together in front of him. Leck had worked as a drover, bush labourer, and shearers' cook, and could turn his hand to anything."

For Tozer the longed-for adventure, the escape from "quill driving" and office drudgery was coming true at last. His excitement is almost palpable as he unfolded his plans:

My object in going with them is to see the country, improve my knowledge of Spanish, and to get some shooting. The trip will extend over a period of from two to three months. I really go as interpreter, for although Portuguese has somewhat upset my fluency in Spanish, I am still able to make myself thoroughly understood and am only wanting practice. I receive no pay — in fact I think it will take £10–15 to cover my expenses — yet I would make the trip even should a greater outlay be necessary.

They would be carrying letters of introduction from the minister of the interior to the governors of the territories of Río Negro, Chubut and Neuquen, and orders to the commanding officers to render them every assistance. He provided Harry with an exhaustive list of his purchases to outfit himself suitably, including two horses, a poncho, good clothes for visiting governors, much saddlery and harness of the South American kind, a dagger, another revolver, two rifles and more than 300 rounds of ammunition.

Saunders and Leck set off on 26 July, travelling south by train to a place called La Colina. From there, using introductions they'd collected from Walker, supporters in Australia, and from Tozer's friends Finck and the ostrich farmer Nagel, they planned to visit various estancias and obtain as much information about their proposed route as possible.

Tozer stayed on in Buenos Aires to collect plans of possible sites, then he was to join Saunders and Leck somewhere between La Colina and Bahia Blanca. The land they'd targeted for investigation was on the southern shore of Lake Nahuel Huapí near the Chilean border.

It is this district which we have to explore & here it is that the Australians hope to find land to locate themselves. The accounts which I have heard of this country — *if true* — prove it to be one of the most fertile & lovely places in Argentina. The climate is perfection, the scenery grand & the soil fit for almost anything. Its valleys are immense strawberry beds & its forests contain fine & valuable woods. Apples are fine & plentiful & cover large tracts of country. These & the strawberries are supposed to have been carried there by Jesuits some 300 years ago. There is a legend that a large and wealthy city once stood in a valley which the lake now fills and that this city was inhabited by the Incas. The priests & the city are supposed to have perished together. It is only during recent years that this district has been explored. If I reach there I believe I shall be the first Englishman ever there and in some places perhaps the first white man.

To reach the lake meant a ride of 1,000 kilometres across difficult terrain. He would be well-armed, Arthur assured Harry, because of the Chileno bandits, outlaws who'd been terrorising the country since the

Chilean revolution. "The Queenslanders are also well armed with 16 shot daisy Winchesters. I expect we shall go right along without danger or disagreeables ... I expect I shall have a good time especially when the Río Limay is reached. The scenery is said to be enchanting. Near the lake rises a mountain 15,000 feet and capped with perpetual snow. Shooting will be good, as deer, guanacos, partridges, swans, ducks, geese, otters etc are numerous. The puma and mountain cat are common and the rivers swarm with fish. I get this information from explorers' reports. I may find the reality a little different."

The last place from where he could send a letter would be Fuerte Roca, the limit of settlement, and then it would take fifteen to twenty days on horseback to the lake, "but I shall keep a diary of events and give you a full report at the end of the trip".

It must have seemed an exotic but disturbing prospect to Harry, quill-driving in the Indian Office and labouring over his Rousseau thesis in the library by night. His response was to offer financial help to his brother, who replied thanking him, "but happily I have never yet been hard up and hope I never shall be ... The fact of my having decided to undertake a journey to Patagonia is sufficient proof that I have funds, as I am to receive no pay during the three months employed in making the trip". He was already having to allow for the expense of an extra horse; the Australians were currently purchasing nine horses at about 25 shillings per head, for it had been decided that they needed three each, one to ride and the other two for pack, in rotation.

At the beginning of spring the group set off from Sauce Corto, some 800 kilometres south of the capital, authorised to select from all public lands in the provinces of Río Negro, Chubut and Neuquen.

Tozer was disappointed by the terrain after leaving Sauce Corto. "The country is all pampa, some of it as flat as a table & some rolling and fairly well wooded while a large area is covered with a thick & almost impenetrable growth of horribly thorny bushes." The fertile land gave way to sandhills, salt lakes, low bushes and sparse hard grass, then uninhabited desert cut by the serpentine channel of the Río Negro.

To the south was the Welsh colony of Chubut, first settled in 1865 which, William Saunders reported enviously, "has been in existence fully a generation and last year sold £80,000 worth of wheat". But the Welsh land, parts of which were fertile enough to carry five sheep to the acre, was already spoken for, and the group turned to the west, following the Río Negro. As they did so Tozer became more gloomy.

"This valley is much talked of in Buenos Aires; by those who don't know, it is looked on as a kind of Eden. These reports are spread by Govt. parasites who own land there and want to boom it." The fertility of the valley, he wrote, was a myth. For the last three years, not a drop of rain had fallen. Locust plagues had stripped the few trees of leaves and even of bark. But the river that flowed through this depressing land, fed by Andine snows, "is a fine one & is as wide as the Thames at London Bridge". There were two towns on its banks, one called Choele Choel and the other Fuerte Roca. "They are both nothing more than Indian settlements. The first mentioned was at one time the frontier fort along Indian territory but Fuerte Roca now takes its place."

Charles Darwin, travelling along the same route in 1832, was disheartened to meet General Rosas and learn of his plans, already well in train, for the Indians, which was: "to kill all stragglers, and having driven the remainder to a common point, to attack them in a body, in the summer, with the assistance of the Chilenos. This operation is to be repeated for three successive years". Darwin predicted that, "I think there will not, in another half-century, be a wild Indian northward of the Río Negro. The warfare is too bloody to last; the Christians killing every Indian, and the Indians doing the same by the Christians. It is melancholy to trace how the Indians have given way before the Spanish invaders."

When Tozer and the Australians arrived half a century later, the ethnic cleansing had been successful. Most of the Indians, by means of unnatural selection, had gone. The prospectors came to a garrison outpost, today known as General Roca, not far from the confluence of the Limay and Neuquen rivers. It was their intention to follow the Río Limay south-west to their destination, the huge Lake Nahuel Huapí in the shadow of the Andes. Tozer said that his companions had left Buenos Aires "with the idea that they were about to visit a land flowing with milk & honey & blessed with a mild & beautiful climate. But as we approached it we met people who had either visited the promised land or knew something about it & who gradually convinced us that the Govt. & others in Buenos Aires had deceived them".

It seemed there were no apple orchards, no valleys of strawberry beds, no Jesuit treasure to be had. The disillusioned prospectors made a stopover at Fuerte Roca and presented their letter of introduction to the commandant of the fort. "He received us well & paid us all attention, offering us soldiers & mules to continue our journey. At the same time he gave us a full description of the country & its capabilities proving to us that for our

purpose — agriculture — the land is worthless." It seemed that to proceed
to the lake would be a waste of time and money and to return was the best
course. For William Saunders it was a difficult decision. He defended it
in the *New Australia* journal:

> There is unquestionably splendid country in the Argentine. We saw choice
> parts which carried five sheep to the acre, these were taken up, but the fact
> speaks for itself ... But the scarcity of the timber, the difficulty of commu-
> nication and the nature of the seasons, which make the settler liable to frosts
> even in summer as well as to similar droughts to those so well known to us
> in Australia, appeared to us to render it very unadvisable to continue
> prospecting ...

In fact, the land the Australians were offered but never saw was some of
the finest on the continent. The site, on the southern shore of Lake Nahuel
Huapí, was spectacular: alpine meadows scattered with wildflowers, thickets of giant bamboo, forests of cypress, cedar and beech bordering the lake
and the majestic snow-covered cordillera towering above.

As the Australians did not take up the offer, the land remained unsettled
until 1902, when the town of San Carlos de Bariloche was established.
Many of the first arrivals were German and Swiss and they built fanciful
chalets, ski lodges and chocolate shops. Wealthy Argentinians flocked in
to enjoy winter sports, venison, trout and glüwein, and to be photographed with a St Bernard dog or husky in the square of their own
mini-version of Switzerland.

Today Bariloche, with its casino, discos, condominiums and boutiques
drowning in alpine kitsch, occupies some of the most expensive real estate
and is the biggest resort in Argentina. If the prospectors had pressed on,
their descendants today would no doubt be well-heeled tourist operators
— or retired to lotus-eating by the lake.

But the men were assured by the commandant at Fuerte Roca that they
had made the right decision. He exchanged their tired horses for fresh
mounts and, as a major and a captain were about to start for Buenos Aires,
arranged that they should accompany them.

It was depressing to return conceding failure, especially as Tozer still
nurtured a suspicion that "further on there would have been something
really worth seeing. It's my bad luck".

Back in Buenos Aires Alf Walker had news of a promising correspondence with the government of Paraguay. Leaving Tozer to recuperate at
the Nagels' ostrich farm, Saunders and Leck travelled north to the
land-locked country shrouded in mystery. They were overwhelmed to find

a government only too anxious to accommodate them, and were invited to inspect soft green pasture land, watered by streams and protected by great forest trees among which flittered butterflies and hummingbirds. After their ninety days in the arid wastes of the south, they had stepped into a Garden of Eden.

Douglas Stewart's poem "Terra Australis" refers to Lane's pilgrims abandoning the harsh Australian outback, but it is apt too for a deliverance from Patagonia:

> Westward there lies a desert where the crow
> Feeds upon poor men's hearts and picks their eyes;
> Eastward we flee from all that wrath and woe
> And Paraguay shall yet be Paradise.

*

In its issue of 28 January 1893, the *New Australia* journal triumphantly reported the offer of "splendid land" in Paraguay, adding: "What a rush there will be to the Encyclopaedia when this issue reaches the hands of our friends — and enemies. Possibly the Sydney *Daily Telegraph* will put a special on to 'do' Paraguay at two hours' notice. Then a sea-captain will be interviewed and a column of twaddle will appear in the King-street 'horgan' setting forth how the said sea-dog sailed his vessel right across Paraguay one wet winter, and how the lions and tigers and the grasshoppers in that benighted region howled for the blood of the crew, &c., &c."

Harry Tozer was no doubt looking up Paraguay in reference books too. But by this time his brother had an answer for any criticism: "Your remark, that seclusion for such a community would end in degeneration, is no doubt correct but only partial seclusion is intended." The colony would be, as far as possible, self-supporting and they planned to grow and manufacture from the start. "It is not expected that everything will go smoothly & happily," Arthur admitted with disarming frankness. "Discontent, selfishness, hatred & other human weaknesses will make trouble but a governing committee chosen by the people will no doubt keep these evils in check."

It was the English, Harry was informed in the next letter, who found it so difficult to adapt to new conditions. "They are too conservative & are too full of pride. They come out here with the idea that they are going to astonish the natives & start by sneering at everything not English, & are domineering & insulting whenever they can do it with safety." Arthur seemed to be repudiating his own Englishness, was on the way, with his insistence on his love of wide open spaces, to becoming an honorary Australian. "Town life will never suit me for it always brings on depression, weakness & nervousness & oh I hate it! A few weeks in the open air makes a different man of me."

It would have been no surprise to Harry when Arthur announced he was serious about Walker's invitation to join New Australia. "He has already written to Queensland proposing me as such & I have every reason to believe that I shall be elected. If it turns out as I expect, I shall soon be on my way to Paraguay to throw in my lot with the others. I believe that the socialistic theory can be carried out in practise & to believe in it & to not join in when the opportunity is presented would prove me to be very weak minded. Besides, what have I to lose?"

He was pleased to say that the area of land granted to them by the Paraguayan Government had been increased to a hundred square leagues — approximately 187,000 hectares or 460,000 acres. Its position was 32 kilometres north east of Villarrica, with the river Tebicuary passing through its boundaries. According to Walker, who had spent two weeks examining the site, there were forested areas that would yield valuable timber, but the greater part was good agricultural land which could produce a rich variety of vegetables and fruits.

The first batch of socialists had already left Australia, expected to arrive in South America in another month. Meanwhile, Arthur had received some Australian newspapers and was interested to read expressions of indignation at the prospect of the country losing so many workers. They "naturally condemn the movement, but one writer admits that the workers have some grounds for making a hit at the capitalists & wishes that they would start the colony in Australia. This is impossible, as all available *good land* has been taken up & were it not so the various colonial govts in Australia, being composed principally of big capitalists, would do their utmost to prevent concession of land for such a purpose".

Within four months Arthur expected to be in Paraguay. While he noted Harry's warnings about socialistic movements, he preferred to delay responding until he could give practical evidence. He included a cutting from the *New Australia* journal, delighted by the reference to "a young Englishman who travelled through the Argentine with Leck & Saunders voluntarily acting as their interpreter. He has since joined the Association & will meet the Pioneers at Montevideo 'as interpreter' ".

Whatever Harry thought, Arthur Tozer was about to embark on the great adventure; the die was cast:

I am admitted as a member without payment of the usual fee as the time & money I spent on the Patagonian trip has been considered more than equivalent to that sum. Walker expects to be in B. Aires early in Sept. & I am to join him there. We then go to Montevideo to receive the pioneers who are expected about the 10th or 15th prox. They are then put on board a river steamer & go direct to Asunción ...

*

There was just time for me to make a brief visit to Montevideo before I too had to board my riverboat bound for Asunción. The girls on the front desk of the Hotel Phoenix didn't think much of my plan.

"Why do you want to go to Montevideo?" asked Soledad. "It is a dirty city, not modern. It is not *beautiful* like Buenos Aires." Florencia agreed, screwing up her nose. They looked at me as if I was a traitor. I told them lamely that an Englishman who once lived in Buenos Aires and a famous Australian writer who also interested me had travelled there one hundred years before. These were definitely not viewed as sufficient reasons.

I was up very early the next morning, sheltering from the rain under an awning on a corner of fashionable Calle Florida while I waited for a *colectivo* to take me to the wharf. People hurried past the plate glass windows of Harrods, umbrellas up. A flower seller arranged buckets of blooms under a carousel that seemed incongruously bright in the grey drizzle. His colleague at the newspaper kiosk grumbled as he arranged sodden bundles of *La Nación*. Sir Richard Burton, a devotee of the seriously erotic, had complained about the "kiosk mania" imported from the banks of the Seine: "At Buenos Aires you see them even in the main square. They sell newspapers and cheap books, erotic lyrics and half-naughty photos; no-one ever knew a body who had ever entered into one of them."

Two nuns arrived to wait for the port bus, then a man with a duffle bag, and a woman in a fur coat. Further along under the same awning, an Indian woman and her son had been sleeping on the pavement. She sat up, yawned and tenderly prodded the boy, curled up under a mound of rags beside her. Another day had begun in the big village.

6

Across the Silver River

It is the perfect republic: the sense of emancipation experienced in it by the wanderer from the Old World is indescribably sweet and novel ...

W H Hudson, *The Purple Land*

It is worth coming a long way to see Monte Video.

Mary Cameron

The ferryboat, a cavernous old tub with cars on the lower deck, sat in the mud beside the wharf. It wheezed and groaned as a tug pulled it, then lurched like a cow freed from a bog. Teenagers in track suits and anoraks craned over the upper deck in the drizzling rain, full of nervy excitement, on their way to a soccer match in Montevideo. The older, seasoned travellers staked claims to tables and produced thermoses, sandwiches, *empanadas*. This boat was for people with more time than money. The income earners in their twenties to forties could travel by plane, hydrofoil or jetcat that did the crossing in a fraction of the time. The tug nosed us through a maze of channels, past an assortment of water-logged barges and old rust buckets, and through a narrow gateway. We were on our way across the choppy Río de la Plata.

The name literally means "River of Silver". Argentinians are fond of saying that its waters are silver in the morning, copper in the afternoon and gold in the evening. But the Plata is not really a river but the estuary of the great Paraná, Paraguay and Uruguay rivers and, over 120 kilometres across at its widest point, some geographers argue it is simply an intrusion of the Atlantic Ocean. Today, like most days, it was brown with silt swept down from as far away as the Mato Grosso in the heart of the continent, and rain-pocked to the misty horizon. Behind us through a squall the tall buildings of Buenos Aires dissolved in a blur.

It took three hours to chug 50 kilometres across the muddy waters to Colonia del Sacramento, the shortest crossing point. The rain cleared as a pretty wooded town came into view through drifting mist: a white lighthouse, the twin belltowers of a church among the trees, low white-washed and cream houses. Tin sheds, slipways, wharves and a rusting hulk, half-submerged, cluttered the waterfront. A smart blue-and-white cata-maran of the Buquebus company was at anchor.

I realised with a shock that my name, contained within a torrent of Spanish, was being called over the loudspeaker. I hurried to be processed by Uruguay immigration, apparently the only gringo on board, then queued for a bus for the three-hour trip east to Montevideo.

Colonia del Sacramento was established as a Portuguese settlement in 1680 and was a constant threat to the Spanish as they tried to gain control of the Río de la Plata. It developed as a flourishing centre for contraband trade, with heavy backing from the British. It was only in 1776, when the British navy had other preoccupations during the American War of Independence, that Spain succeeded in seizing control. "The Purple Land that England lost," W. H. Hudson said wistfully. But Uruguay, like neighbouring Paraguay, was still a small nation wedged between two giants, Brazil and Argentina, and that for both of them has been their fortune and their tragedy.

Giuseppe Garibaldi, that professional rebel, cut a dashing figure in Colonia in the 1840s. He commanded the tiny Uruguayan navy and an Italian legion of Redshirts in a liberation war against the Argentine forces of dictator Rosas. He returned to Italy in 1848 to take part in the Risorgimento, but continued to wear the gaucho costume of the pampas. Richard Burton conceded that Garibaldi, "then an obscure adventurer", was probably in Uruguay for the cause, not personal profit, but demanded querulously, "What business had he to fight at all?"

Burton himself wished he had a gold ounce for every throat that had been cut in Colonia. During his own visit in 1868 he shot birds from a four-in-hand wagonette, but pronounced the subsequent dinner of nettle-stalk salad and a salmi of prairie owls "well cooked and thoroughly detestable".

My bus passed through the lovely old town, giving glimpses of crumbling stone buildings with cool interior courtyards, cobbled side streets, sycamore trees shading footpaths. The way to the capital unravelled through green undulating pasture-land. Contented black-and-white cattle grazed or huddled in groups under stands of fir, pine, elms, poplars and spreading English oaks. The number of European trees astonished me; later I was told that in this part of the country they are mostly transplants, the result of a remarkable reforestation program. Small farmhouses were cosily nestled into the landscape, whitewashed adobe brick with orange pantiled roofs. Red dirt roads led off across the gentle hills, an occasional windmill reminding me sharply of Australia.

Perhaps nowhere else on earth does a city so dominate a country, like the hacienda of a vast ranch. All major roads lead to Montevideo, which has half the population, half the secondary schools and 90 per cent of all newspaper readers. It announced itself with a shanty-town and a belt of industrial development. We cruised along a waterfront and in the grey light the city across the bay seemed like 1930s Sydney in an old black-and-white photograph. Its high-rise buildings were modestly squat, grey or dun-coloured with tiny windows, some with art deco spires and fluted mouldings. They made comfortable companions with the steeples of many churches.

In the city proper, the shabbiness and neglect of the *belle epoque* buildings were testimony to a past grandeur and a troubled economic present. One gracious mansion, its ornate pediments and plaster corbels crumbling, had a sign across its portico in fluorescent tubing: "Elvis Disco Pub". It seemed as shocking as a dowager aunt in a Madonna bustier with chrome nipples.

The Old City, Ciudad Vieja, dating from 1726, was on a small peninsula near the harbour and the docks. In a narrow winding street near the cathedral I found the Hotel Palacio, seven storeys high and two rooms across, a filigree iron and brass liftwell its spinal cord. A grandfather clock chimed in the lobby, sunlight fell on floors of Portuguese blue-and-white tiles. From my brass bed I could look through shuttered windows at lace balconies, attic rooms under mansard roofs and the intrusive monolith of the Hotel Victoria Plaza, the most expensive hotel in town, where I was sure the rooms were not half so pleasant.

It was bitterly cold as I walked down to the docks and picked my way across cobblestones to the sea wall. A few derricks were loading container ships on the far side of the bay, drowsily, like sated crickets after the plague, but the old original wharf was near deserted, the doors shuttered on the *aduana*, the great red brick Customs house. At the entrance to the harbour was a conical hill, a landmark to navigators, the 132-metre Cerro de Montevideo.

I re-read an account of the scene in the 1890s, when a medley of small craft plied out to the line of sailing ships at anchor in the deeper water. The barque *Royal Tar* arrived to join them on Monday evening, 11 September 1893.

No doubt after eight weeks at sea most of the 220 pioneers were crowded on deck for their first glimpse, in the fading light, of a South American city. John Sibbald thought it looked very promising:

And so here we are, in the open roadstead that serves for a harbour, a green grass clad hill on one side 400 feet high with lighthouse on top — Monte; the old fashioned solid built flat roofed city on the other — Video. At least that's what our boys christened them immediately. One cannot express what infinite relief comes to the eye and heart at such a time after two months of immeasurable "far spooming ocean" ... Monte Video is a pleasant place to look at from the sea, or river rather, for the water here is dirty looking and only brackish, not salt. We had no time to look at it nearer for the first three days.

Alf Walker wasn't there to greet them, being detained on business in Buenos Aires, and Charles Leck was in Asunción, arranging the purchase of equipment and bullock wagons. But a wiry athletic young man they hadn't seen before came out on a launch to the *Tar*, the pioneers' first visitor in South America and their newest recruit.

For Arthur Tozer it must have been a momentous occasion to meet William Lane at last. But as is often the case, when people are caught up in events that engage their emotions and energies, they do not have time to write letters. Tozer said frustratingly little to his brother Harry about his first impressions, though it is clear from what he wrote in the weeks and months to follow that he had found someone whom he admired utterly. That first meeting must have been like the beginning of a love affair. In Lane he would have recognised someone with his own qualities taken to an extreme degree. His search for political belief was answered in Lane by passionate political commitment; his dislike of vanity and frivolity reinforced by Lane's unswerving sense of rectitude; Tozer disapproved of the graft he had witnessed in public life and here was a man who seemed totally incorruptible; and furthermore, someone whose intelligence and erudition seemed to outclass, if he dared to think it, even Harry's. Here was a worthy mentor and he attached himself and offered his loyalty. And Lane, shaken and disillusioned by the opposition he had encountered on the voyage, responded to the young man, untainted by any of those troubles, who had the shining eyes of an acolyte.

Next morning Lane resolved to go into the city and pay his respects to the appropriate authorities, with Tozer accompanying him as interpreter. He agreed that Sibbald, the expedition's treasurer, could come, and Watson, the purser, but posted a notice forbidding any of the others to go ashore until they returned. Frustration was intense and indignation loudly expressed. Lane's argument that he needed to gauge local reaction to this shipload of immigrants seemed heavy-handed, patronising and quite unacceptable to dissidents such as Fred White and Tom Westwood, the natty draper from Adelaide.

Lane called on the Paraguayan consul, Dr Alonzo Criado, who gave them "a very cordial and not over-done welcome". Sibbald was impressed to find little evidence of poverty and thought the flat-roofed houses very handsome with their tiled courtyards adorned with shrubbery and "chaste marble statuary".

On returning to the *Royal Tar* his descriptions would only have exacerbated the frustration of those left to languish on board, their resentment further increased when Lane did not return until late at night. Perhaps he and Tozer had been consolidating their new friendship with a long discussion, but it would not have been over alcohol. Lane's favourite drink was tea, copious draughts of it; as Montevideo was still very British in influence, he would have been able to obtain it.

Next morning a number of Australians, led by White, Westwood and Brittlebank, announced they were going ashore regardless. Two women joined them as they waited for the launch from the wharf. Lane warned that the Association would not pay their fares and if they were hoarding any other money they were not true to their pledges. They still climbed into the shore boat with him and were gleeful to discover he'd been bluffing: the trip was free, a service run by the port authority.

While the rebels were ashore, those loyal to Lane gazed wistfully across the water at the most impressive city the majority had ever seen. "We haven't had much time for visiting the town," wrote Harry Taylor, the journalist, "so I can't say much of it except that it looks a good big place from here, and its harbor is well filled with shipping, including several warships. There are a few revolutions happening down this way, but no one seems to take much notice of them, and everyone agrees as to the great peacefulness of Paraguay, and its immunity from pests of that description."

They were surprised when Lane and Tozer returned with Dr Alonzo Criado. "The Paraguayan Consul, a most gentlemanly Spaniard, unfortunately unable to speak English, came across to have a look at us today," reported Taylor for an Adelaide paper, the *Voice*. "He expressed himself as delighted at our coming and told us, Tozer interpreting, that the Paraguayans were looking eagerly to welcome us, and were desirous of treating us, not as foreigners, but as brothers. The earth was the gift of God to men, and what men made by their labour off it should be theirs, and he believed we would be successful, and be just the people to take the place of Paraguay's sons who had died fighting for their fatherland." The consul presented them with the Paraguayan flag and John Sibbald made a speech in response, assuring him of their intention to be loyal subjects of his country.

The occasion was considered important enough to be covered at length by *El Siglo*, a Montevideo daily. It had nothing but favourable things to say about the Australian colonisation scheme which, incidentally, it said was directed by "Señores Lane and Tozer":

> This immigration, one of the largest that has come to South America, is the offspring of English, and is composed of healthy men, strong and active, and women of singular comeliness and beauty. These form the families and members of all the sections, being for the most part agriculturalists, stockmen, masons, turners, carpenters &c. They have tents and tools to instal themselves on the first day of their arrival ... New Australia is to be established where the Jesuits had their celebrated missions in the seventeenth and eighteenth centuries, which were indeed another trial of communal civilisation with the native race, yielding great results under the fanatical religion of that period.

The article concluded by taking local government authorities to task for not having publicised the advantages of Uruguay as a place to settle and so having lost such an admirable group of colonists. Had the journalist witnessed the scene on board the *Tar* a few hours later, the reaction might have been different.

The group that had gone ashore returned that night "a bit merry", said their supporters, "roaring drunk", according to their detractors, who greeted them with the worst epithet of all, "Scabs!". A fight broke out which, after the resentments which had been brewing in cramped conditions for eight weeks, escalated with frightening rapidity. "It got to high words on both sides," John Rich wrote, "then to blows, and a few rushed for knives. The women and children were screaming and hurrying below and men were rushing on deck. One man the drink and excitement rendered quite dangerous, and he was locked up in the forepeak until the next morning. It surprised a good many of us that it ended so well as it did."

Lane called a general meeting the following evening and conceded that in the interests of future harmony he would overlook the bad behaviour. Apparently he did not feel confident of forcing the issue by expelling the worst offenders, which, while they were all still in transit, he had the power to do, and could have sent them back to Australia on the *Royal Tar*. It is understandable that he would have dreaded the mockery this would have provoked in Australia, the sneering predictions of disaster confirmed before they had even made landfall. But nonetheless such a mild reaction augured badly for his future control as chairman, particularly as the three ringleaders in the mutiny did not even bother to attend the meeting, but were living it up in Montevideo once again.

Souter has seen this as a serious error in Lane's leadership: "After acting with injudicious firmness in the matters of night strolling on deck and visits ashore, he had now shown injudicious leniency. If the temperance clause were to be retained, those who had transgressed it in Montevideo should have been disciplined in some way ... To be lenient after too much firmness was to invite the suspicion of weakness. The temperance clause remained, but drinking continued."

The next day, Friday, fifteen men went ashore, despite the fact that this needed to be a day of exhaustive hard work for everyone, transhipping all baggage and 150 tonnes of cargo from the *Tar* to a river steamer. It had originally been hoped that the barque could be towed upriver to Asunción, but its 4-metre draught was too great, water levels being low after a spell of dry weather. Tozer, already making himself indispensable to Lane, had negotiated for a paddle-steamer, the *Río Paraná*, and bought fresh provisions as they had to make their own feeding arrangements. After "a spell of work such as Montevideo has seldom seen" they were ready to leave by nightfall.

They were not likely to have been amused when the fifteen men eventually returned, their story being that they had been "treated by a few Americans". They were "a little merry" said Tom Westwood, though he admitted "Lane, especially Mrs Lane, declared them to be drunk". He added in his diary, "I can't help feeling that the movement cannot result in success if that incompetent man Lane continues to mismanage so utterly as he has done up to the present."

The *Río Paraná* steamed away at 1 o'clock in the morning with John Sibbald there to see them off, staying behind to make arrangements for the *Tar's* return voyage. Enmities seemed to have been forgotten in the jubilant farewell, which Sibbald thought must have seemed astonishing to the people on the shore: "Pogson's setting of the Marching Song given by 200 voices, 'Auld Lang Syne' and finally a perfect yell of a Cooee attended the exit of the 'mad' New Australians, and I was left behind as miserable as a bandicoot."

Back in Sydney Mary Cameron, who must have had some inkling of the real story, wrote a public relations piece for the *New Australia* journal:

> The first stage in the history of the Association was getting people together ... The first important step of the second stage was getting the Pioneers away; now the second one has been achieved; they have landed at Monte Video and are transhipping for Asuncion. A few days in a river steamer, a few hours' railway, and then — home. Home! What feelings must stir their hearts (and ours) at the thought of it.
>
> It is *home* — theirs and ours — though the land has yet to be cleared, the houses built, the fences put up ... Glad? Rather! We trust there will be a whole world glad yet, and that we will live to see it.

*

It was bitingly cold as I walked to the Plaza Independencia, the main square. I entered it through a freestanding stone archway, a relic of the wall which once encircled the Old City. The plaza was dominated by a great equestrian statue of Artigas, Uruguay's patriot hero, and his granite and marble mausoleum. He had the singular notion that no imperialist overlords were required in his country and led his people in a struggle against British, Portuguese or Spanish control. His presumption was sharply rebuked by people who felt more qualified to run things. Charles Washburn, an American diplomat, wrote: "He was a gaucho by instinct and inclination ... as ignorant as the horse he rode of all the world beyond the plains which he aspired to rule."

W. H. Hudson minced words even less, expressing the authentic, undiluted voice of imperialism:

> Is it not then bitter as wormwood and gall to think that over these domes and towers beneath my feet, no longer than half a century ago, fluttered the holy cross of St George! For never was there a holier crusade undertaken, never a nobler conquest planned, than that which had for its object the wresting of this fair country from unworthy hands ... And to think that it was won for England, not treacherously, or bought with gold, but in the old Saxon fashion with hard blows, and climbing over heaps of slain defenders; and after it was thus won, to think that it was lost — will it be believed? — not fighting, but yielded up without a stroke by craven wretches unworthy of the name of Britons!

In 1820, when Artigas was close to achieving victory, a renewed Portuguese attack forced him to take refuge in Paraguay. He spent the remaining thirty years of his life in exile there, effectively a prisoner, living on a small farm and a smaller pension. Many flowers were laid on the red granite slab.

Photographers with ancient box cameras on tripods offered to associate passers-by with greatness and drama against the Artigas backdrop. Orthodox Jews in black frockcoats and *yamulkas* huddled talking in low voices. They looked to be discussing intricacies of the Torah, but it could have been the soccer results, like the men lounging on benches nearby, sharing a communal gourd of *yerba mate*.

I turned to the account of a visiting Englishman, E. F. Knight, who called at Montevideo in his yawl, the *Falcon*, a few years before the Australians. He published a book which was on the shelves of the little library they had brought with them:

> In the evening of New Year's Day we visited the fine Plaza de Independencia, where an excellent military band was playing. Here we were enabled to study the different orders of the populace. The ladies floated by with stately Spanish walk, looking well in their black silk dresses and mantillas; but why will every South American lady so besmear her face with powder, however good her complexion be? Officers of the army strutted by in gorgeous uniforms and with the clash of sabres on the pavement; a motley crowd of the lower orders loafed about — Basques, Italians, Greeks, and the native gauchos in their barbaric but becoming costume. Here was a group of British blue-jackets slightly overcome by caña. The native soldiers were everywhere, dressed in their hideous parody of Zouave uniforms. And here were two of the Spanish bull-fighters in their picturesque off-duty dress and pigtails; smart, wiry, neat-cut fellows they were, and rather foppish in their general get up.

> On the south side of the Plaza Independencia was the handsome stone pile of Government House, and below it the vast glittering expanse of the Río de la Plata with old gun emplacements still in position along its seawall.

By the time of the arrival of the Australians, Uruguay had lapsed far behind Argentina in social and economic progress. During the 1890s two leaders of the Colorado Party took turns at the presidency, at a systematic ransacking of the state treasury and strong-arm rule that dispensed with democratic refinements. The army and navy, dedicated to keeping the regime of the moment in power, consumed up to a third of the national budget. The foreign debt, chiefly owed to England, piled up. British men-o-war patrolled the Río de la Plata, keeping surveillance over their interests.

*

The *Royal Tar* was back in Montevideo with the second batch of colonists on 20 February 1894. Under the leadership of William Saunders, they too were advised that they could not go ashore. But this may have been on the instruction of the Uruguayan health authorities, because Margaret Riley remembered that they were quarantined: "We pulled into Montevideo and the captain didn't have his papers right or something. There was no sickness on board that I remember, but we were quarantined for seven days. We had to go out in the bay and fly the yellow flag; no ship was allowed to come near us."

What she remembered most vividly were the ships flying the Union Jack. "There were these two English man-o-war boats there. When they heard about us, these Englishmen came on board and invited anyone who liked to come over to see the man-o-war boats. A lot of us went. We were rowed over and shown around, shown the cannons and everything. They had a monkey on board. There was something on in Uruguay at that time and the English man-o-war boats were there to settle it. I heard my father talking to one of the men about it. The Englishman said they were there 'to blow them to hell'. That's what he said, 'blow them to hell'! But anyway, we never found out what it was all about."

She was not aware of the explosions going on among the adults on her own ship. Alf Walker and Jim Mooney (who was returning to Australia to organise more bush workers, Lane's ideal recruits) came on board and broke the news about the disastrous happenings at their Paraguay settlement. Eighty-one of the original colonists had walked out. Walker advanced arguments in Lane's defence but added that anyone who had serious doubts and wished to return to Australia was free to do so on the *Royal Tar*. After nerve-racking deliberations, seven of the bachelors took up the offer but everyone else decided to press on.

Their quarantine clearance came through after seven days but arrangements needed to be made for a river steamer. Margaret and some of the other children were offered an outing: "We were there waiting for a river boat for quite a while and one day some of the sailors said they were going ashore and would any of us kids like to come swimming. My father let me and my sister and brother go. The sailors rowed us, nearly all of the children, across to a beach and we had a nice day there."

To the east of the city there are numerous sandy beaches. The sailors probably took the children to one of the closest, Playa Pocitos, though the beaches, sand dunes and rocky headlands continue all the way to the

Brazilian border. The bathing picnic was probably arranged to keep the children out of the way while the hard work went on of transhipping to the river boat, for they were due to leave that evening. But the sailors were late coming back to collect the children. "The tide was coming in and we couldn't get back to the ship. The tide was huge. The waves came in and washed over our little rowing boat and everybody got wet. Oh, the women were very frightened! I don't know whether the captain on the ship saw us or not but a little steamer came up and hooked on to us — they were Spanish people, they spoke Spanish — and they hooked onto us and pulled us over to our ship. The sailors all got into trouble for leaving it so late and we were dead scared, but I still thought it was fun."

*

Uruguay's most famous beach is Punta del Este, some 140 kilometres east of the capital, where wealthy Brazilians and Argentines disport themselves in March, the holiday season, baking in their gleaming thousands on personal strips of sand till the afternoon shade of the looming hotels and apartment blocks sends them in search of *aperitivos*. Argentina even maintains a summer consulate there and the daily paper, *La Nación,* opens a temporary bureau. Nearly everyone I spoke to in Montevideo asked me, beaming, if I would be going to Punta del Este. It was clearly expected of me, it was what tourists *did*. That I was an Australian and had seen beaches before was not an adequate defence.

Two hundred years ago a group of people apparently destined to become Australians sailed past that coastline and became Uruguayans instead. The convict ship *Lady Shore* left London in August 1797, transporting 75 British women and 44 men to the penal colony of New South Wales. Off the coast of Brazil, the guards — a detachment of the New South Wales Corps — mutinied, hoisted a flag "in the name of the French Republic" and sailed towards Montevideo. The Spanish seized the ship and interned everyone on board. To the convicts, a vagrant existence and a crash course in Spanish must have looked infinitely preferable to the life of felons in Australia. They adapted as best they could, the women becoming domestic servants or prostitutes, the men rediscovering old skills as pickpockets and footpads. Later many of them became respectable and all of them eventually melded without trace into the life of Montevideo.

It was also just off Punta del Este that the German pocket-battleship *Graf von Spee* met its watery end in December 1939, sunk by the British South Atlantic Squadron. But the wreck is no longer visible, most of it dismantled long ago by trophy hunters. Some of the plates from its bulkheads were used in the construction of Montevideo's city stadium, and in December 1964 its anchor was set up at the entrance to the port area to commemorate the twenty-fifth anniversary of the battle.

*

The best account of Montevideo written by any Australian colonist was Mary Cameron's. Although she published little of it, she left numerous drafts of short stories and essays about the Uruguayan capital. They reflect her excitement at her first experience of a foreign city.

> It is worth coming a long way to see Monte Video. It is like nothing Australian. One has seen it in a picture where Spanish dons figured and hidalgos dispensed hospitality — with a lordly air, and read of it in old-fashioned books where these gentry made long and wonderful speeches about nothing in particular, but till one has seen it with the eye of the body and breathed its very air, one doesn't know. I saw it for the first time … at midnight.

To jump ahead of the main narrative a little, Mary finally made the decision to go to Paraguay after the New Australia colony had broken up in disarray and Lane and 63 faithful followers acquired more land to start over again. Dave Stevenson was among that group and so was Clara, the nurse, but if Mary knew of their romantic involvement during the first voyage of the *Royal Tar*, as she almost certainly did, she would also have known that Clara had become Mrs Billy Laurence.

Mary still had hopes of Dave. No one else had had the same impact on her. She'd written in her Verse Notebook:

> This day my feet are set on the junction of three paths. It is imperative that I should choose one (or that I should drift along one). I know that if I choose I shall very likely take the wrong one, that I shall be some distance on my way before I find that out and that it will be then impossible to return. One leads to the desolate regions of old maidism; the second to the devil; the third to marriage and probable misery.

A little later she seemed to have made a decision about which path, for she wrote: "I am tired of the gilded chaff of single life and my being craves for the more substantial food of married life — even though it be rye bread."

In August 1895 Lane had written to her from the new colony of Cosme, by then established for eighteen months, asking her to join them and take charge of the school. He wrote in the same month as her thirtieth birthday, an age when the desolate regions of old maidism must have seemed to be closing in. She barely hesitated, booked her ship's passage (insisting on paying for it herself even though single women were entitled to travel at the expense of the colony), and on 31 October resigned from her teaching position.

A fortnight later she embarked on a mailboat of the New Zealand Shipping Company for Wellington, then on by a little steamer, the *Ruapehu*, to Montevideo. That in itself was an extraordinary journey for a young woman travelling by herself in the 1890s, but she still had to negotiate a paddle-steamer 1,600 kilometres upriver, the confusion of a city where few people spoke English, a steam train ride and a rough overland journey to the colony.

After leaving Wellington the *Ruapehu* took twenty-two days to reach Montevideo. At the mouth of the Río de la Plata they were driven back out to sea by a storm. It was midnight of the following day before they came in to anchorage.

> One looked out upon lines and lines of lights, straight as a bean row and judged that the city must be well lighted ... The morning brought daylight and babel, barges towed out to our boat, full of coal and cargo and chattering tongues and swarthy faces and gesticulating hands, towed out by all varieties of tenders and dancing up and down on the brown muddy water like corks ...
>
> The recent gale left the water very rough. The day before it had drowned five men in a sweep. Their boat — a man-o-war's boat — had been top heavy, had taken too much water, had overturned within hail of the shore. The waves and the sharks finished the tragedy. Nobody seemed to mind. We who landed from the *Ruapehu* were let down by crane tied in a chair, as using a gangway was impossible. No boat could stand near it without being smashed. The experience was rather peculiar. Tied, flying through the air and down, to end with a bump on a thing that jumped and danced as if it had the Tarantula, but we got down safely one after the other, being as dignified as we could be, being English in a foreign country.

I can picture Mary making her way through the crowd of sailors, dockworkers and porters, tall, red-headed and commanding respect in her long blue skirt and high-necked white blouse. She was always described as immaculate in her dress, though I wonder if she still managed it after the long cramped voyage and ungainly arrival.

She discovered there were plenty of people around the wharves who spoke English (not the case one hundred years later) so found her lack of

Spanish no great loss and decided philosophically that "a stranger is as easily cheated knowing Spanish as knowing only English". A big hotel sent a couple of English-speaking porters but Mary was determined to be independent, although "an old bare-headed scamp with a black eye had insisted on carrying my valise 'for the price of a glass of beer', one could almost fancy him saying, and seemed to think himself very hardly used when I carried it myself in spite of him. No doubt he inveighed against the wicked foreign woman, but the crowd only laughed".

The two things which struck her immediately were the extraordinary mixture of colour among the people on the wharves — "ranging from ordinary European white to the jet-black of the Brazilian Negro, who is black enough for anything" — and the amount of shipping in the bay, including English, American, Argentine, Brazilian and Uruguayan men-o'-war. "With those ships we will go to war with England," a swarthy skipper told her, pointing at one of the battleships. She laughed politely: "We all laughed, whether because of England or Uruguay, or the unlikelihood of such a thing or because we were English and the Englishman laughs at the foreigners — I don't know."

*

From the wharves I could see the splendid old building surmounted by a cupola which Mary compared to the Sydney Metropole hotel. Washing was strung out on all its balconies, refuse piled in its doorways. Many of the crumbling mansions in Montevideo's Old City have become *conventillos*, multi-family slum dwellings for refugees from rural poverty.

Poverty was evident in Mary's time too, though she thought less than Henry Lawson had shown her in Sydney's Rocks area. Montevideo she found not nearly so depressing: "There is a Relief place for those needing it which shows no more outward sign of what it is for than a small brass plate. I looked at it more than once to assure myself of the fact, for I saw through the open windows of the first ground floor room, a room full of chattering laughing women and children, poorly dressed, it is true, as the working people ordinarily are — but certainly neither abject nor careworn."

The old hotel was near the port market, the Mercado del Puerto. Richard Burton had commented on the "fine zinc dome of engineer architecture, built in Manchester", sheltering the stalls of butchers and fruiterers, and on the fountain at its centre, "which at present, curious to say, plays". The fountain was no longer playing and rubbish rotted in archaeological layers in its bowl.

I joined the couple I had met on the flight from Australia for lunch. We propped up at the counter of a *parrilla*, a grill-house in the lively marketplace, and indulged in a bender, a binge, a prodigal blow-out on beef. Helped by a large jug of *vino tinto* and spicy *chimi churri* pickle, we managed to put away most parts of the animal: ribs, chops, kidneys, blood sausage, chorizo sausage and strange bits of lung and intestine that didn't bear too much thinking about. As we worked our way through it all, an ugly sight for vegetarians, we were entertained by wandering minstrels, a group of Andean musicians with pan pipes, a flautist with two monkeys hanging around his shoulders, and black *candombe* drummers.

They were the only blacks I saw in Montevideo, though once they made up a fifth of the population and allegedly there are still 60,000, descendants of slaves. I saw no Indians for in this country, in a bout of ethnic cleansing even more efficient than in Argentina, they were exterminated. A grim monument in Prado park commemorated Uruguay's last four Charrúa Indians. They were sent as living exhibits to the Musée de l'Homme in Paris and their skeletons went on display there after their premature deaths.

On her visit late in 1895, Mary Cameron sat at the window of her *pensión* in the old city, making a detailed observation of the passing parade, of the strapping negroes, of workmen "invariably picturesque" with their striped shirts and bright neckerchiefs, of fashionable beauties who, in her opinion, wore too much rouge and powder, and children "like pictures in their colouring and texture". It was the sameness coupled with unexpected differences to familiar things which struck her most oddly. "You sit at your window and see businessmen dressed as with us, the same cut, the same material, and women in today's fashion, but, on the other hand, nine women out of ten will be gloveless, bareheaded or wearing a mantilla." She particularly liked watching "some delightful old ladies, with soft colorless skins, white hair and a deportment anyone might envy — a carriage that belongs to a people guiltless of corsets and high heels".

After lunch my friends and I walked along winding streets of once grand houses, past apartment buildings and banks, their exteriors elaborated with balconies, scrolled pediments and bas relief, and visited the cathedral, wide and imposing with two grand bell-towers. Mary admired it especially because it was lit throughout with electricity.

On the other side of the Plaza Independencia was the main shopping street, Avenida 18 de Julio, lined with turn-of-the-century buildings of decaying elegance, ornamented facades and fluted spires, the last word in architectural innovation in the 1890s, profoundly impressive to a group of bush workers from Queensland, many of whom would only have seen country towns until they set off for South America.

But the pavements were now broken and hawkers with pitifully meagre supplies of bootlaces, cigarettes or chocolates loitered at the only places doing brisk business, the cinemas showing the latest from Clint Eastwood and Sylvester Stallone. The drab dress shops were empty and tourists seemed an endangered species in the furriers' boutiques in the mirrored arcades.

"Shop fronts do not exist — not as we know them," wrote Mary Cameron, "and no goods are displayed outside a shop. Some larger places only show at the door and at a window or two … Some of the windows have the very oddest jumble of things all mixed up anyhow. Fine exquisitely painted little china cups, side by side with the very commonest glass, holy candles long enough to make a bridge to heaven, toys, prayerbooks, delft, majolica lace and probably a great heap of dates in the middle."

Today's streets were full of veteran cars, like a triumphant piece of organisation by a *film noir* art department: battered Dodges and Chevrolets, old Vauxhalls, Buicks and Packards gamely puttering along, a Hillman Minx crashing gears and blaring its horn at a pedestrian crossing. A classic bodgie's car, a black Humber Super Snipe, cruised beside the pavement, a flashback to the bad boy of the hometown of my youth. I discovered later the reason for all these ghosts. In Uruguay there is a heavy duty on all new vehicles, but those more than forty years old are exempt even from road tax.

Mary also found the transport a little behind the times: "The traffic consists chiefly of carts, things with great high wheels reminding one of the old-fashioned bicycles … There are horse or mule trams, very ugly in themselves, but redeemed by gay striped curtains."

On my last day I made my way down to the waterfront, passing a little fort belonging to the Armada Nacional. It was chill but sunny and everything felt benign. Lovers lay entwined on the embankment, a hugely overweight woman was reading a novel with her shoes off, an old couple walked gravely hand in hand. "I never saw such a fine, brown, contented-looking lot of people," wrote Mary. "Contentment seems written all over them from the muleteer astride his mule to the fat soldier on guard at the street corner, who I suppose is the policeman. If he isn't, I saw none. I saw no one looking abject and I saw no one drunk."

Kids were playing the ubiquitous soccer. They call it *fútbol* and probably do not realise it came to their country as an Englishman's game, brought by visiting seamen, clerks of the railway and the Bank of London, men like Arthur Tozer. In 1889, on this same Plata embankment in Montevideo, they celebrated Queen Victoria's birthday with a soccer match against Buenos Aires. They played under a huge portrait, suspended from the grandstand, of an old lady with a beady baleful gaze.

As Mary left Montevideo, to make her steamer trip upriver to an uncertain future, she wrote a final comment about the people she'd passed among without ever knowing, though she was already acquiring the worldly air and *sang-froid* of the seasoned traveller: "The Uruguayan, as I saw him, is strong, sturdy, fiery and quick. Full of patriotism, he despises the whole earth, the possessor of a delectable land, he wishes for no other; prompt at revolution, he craves for no change. Uruguay has more revolutions to the square mile than any country I know." (She knew one other.)

In 1903 Uruguay experienced a very different kind of revolution. Under the presidency of José Batlle y Ordóñez, it embarked on a startlingly individual course in Latin America. It was a course that surely would have met with Lane's approval. One wonders, had he despatched his prospecting expedition just ten years later, if Uruguay would have been the country he would have chosen. Batlle's social reforms and his nationalisation of public services created an audacious welfare state, otherwise unknown on the continent. It has often been compared to Switzerland, an inspiration for Batlle, and for a time was a pioneer for much of the western world. He demanded freedom of the press, tariffs to protect local industry; divorce was legalised, capital punishment abolished, education made free and compulsory, including university education for women. The population of predominantly rural workers reacted in astonishment to the rapidity of the changes, but Batlle pressed on for a free medical service, old-age and service pensions, and a workers' charter providing for a minimum wage, a set working week and holiday pay. His conviction was that "modern industry must not be allowed to destroy human beings. The State must regulate it to make more happy the life of the masses".

It could not, of course, have been allowed to last. This idealistic social progam had inevitable failings, particularly a large and notoriously unwieldy bureaucracy which became the butt of mordant humour. It was said that public servants got to work early because there were more of them than chairs.

By the 1960s civil servants made up a quarter of a workforce of one million. The telephones and electricity departments had a hierarchy of forty-five grades. The state airline boasted a thousand employees and one operational aircraft. The writer V. S. Naipaul concluded it was "a whole country living the life of a commune, work and leisure flowing together, everyone, active and inactive, a pensioner of the state".

The cost was too great. But, even more inevitably, *Batllismo* engendered bitter opponents among the landed class and the armed services. In 1973 its structures were dismantled by a military coup. A savage purge followed — of the revolutionary youth movement, the Tupamaros, but also of mildly dissident students and left-wing intellectuals. Those who could, fled. The prominent writer Mario Benedetti was one of them and estimated that, "In a country of less than three million inhabitants ... there were half a million or even 800,000 political exiles".

Now that the dictators have gone, replaced by the current ramshackle conservative regime, Benedetti and others have cautiously returned home.

*

The following morning, on a smart new catamaran built in Tasmania, we slid out of the harbour of Montevideo, past the gunboats of the Armada Nacional, and on towards the entrance in the breakwater. I turned to look back at the skyline of the solid grey city, a skyline that has changed little since the nineteenth century while its people have experienced a cataclysm. Ahead, the waters of the wide River Plate, bathed by the morning sun, shone pure gleaming silver.

7

The Good Ship *Paraná*

There is a mystery and a loneliness that pervades the scenery of the Paraná that agreeably affects the imagination; a mystery — for are not its shores unexplored forests, its sources indefinite, in an unknown region that is still a sort of fairy-land of fable and romance, even as it was when the first Spaniards came and sought the Eldorado?

E F Knight, *The Cruise of the Falcon*

You are no longer navigating the Paraguay River, nor cleaving the strait beneath the Magellanic Clouds. You are sailing behind things, unable to escape from a spaceless space.

Augusto Roa Bastos, *I the Supreme*

The *Ciudad de Paraná* was very handsome, very white, over 100 metres long, with lifeboats suspended in two rows on the top deck, their covers tautly fastened so no Clara and Dave could crawl into them. It looked a most satisfactory steamer to transport one 1,600 kilometres upriver into the heart of darkness — except that it was in fact a motor vessel and there was nothing intrepid about the voyage. I had wanted to arrive in Paraguay by cargo boat, but that kind of river traffic barely exists anymore. This was a pleasure jaunt for the 200 passengers, mostly affluent Argentines, doing the twelve-day round trip, taking in the sun and the scenery, the duty-free shopping in Asunción and a side trip to the Iguazú Falls. A banner flapped across the bow: "Magic Line. *Para vivir el río*" — To experience the river.

The pioneer Australians travelled in a paddle-steamer with a similar name, the *Río Paraná*. An article published in the Melbourne *Age* at the time of their departure from Sydney, written by a former resident of Buenos Aires, coyly describing himself as One Who Has Been There, warned them that: "Even at Buenos Ayres it is regarded as no small enterprise to make a journey into the heart of Paraguay. He who undertakes such a task is looked upon with much the same interest, I imagine,

The Río de la Plata system.

as centred around the traveller from London to Edinburgh 150 years ago. Little is known of the social life of their isolated neighbours by the Argentines, and that little is not of a flattering kind."

In the spacious lobby of the *Ciudad de Paraná* queues were forming as the harassed purser and Señora Hilda, my friend from the shipping company, processed people to their cabins. I explored the bar, casino and four decks of accommodation and wondered which of the single women I would be sharing with. When it was my turn in the queue, the purser said there was a problem with my cabin. I understood him to say there was water all over the floor. This did not seem a good start. Señora Hilda winked and muttered about "*escritora australiana*". The purser suggested I should be *tranquila* and take a drink in the bar.

We eased out of the wharf and slid along an industrial waterfront. A passenger whirred off some video footage. Soon we were out in the wide Plata but for at least an hour the skyline of Buenos Aires hovered in view like a dream city. I waited in the bar with Graham Greene's *Travels with My Aunt*, reading it for a second time, turning to the latter half so that the protagonist, Henry Pulling, and I could voyage together:

> It was eight on a July morning and the seabirds wailed like the cats in Latimer Road and the clouds were heavy with coming rain. There was one break of sunlight over La Plata which gave the dull river a single silver streak, but the brightest spot in the sombre scape of water and shore was the flames from gas pipes flapping against the black sky. There were four days ahead of me, up the Plata, the Paraná and the Paraguay ...

The passing parade distracted. An elderly gentleman with a Colonel Blimp moustache had an alarming habit of dropping his false teeth, snapping them perilously from his mouth. A lissom stewardess came past, then another more striking than the first, then a third girl so breathtakingly lovely, with long legs, heart-shaped face and tumbling curly hair, I wondered why she wasn't a star in the Argentine film industry. A courteous old man asked if he could join my table. He and his large family plomped down, his ample wife, his son, two daughters and sons-in-law. The Señor seemed impressed that I was making the trip with so little Spanish; the sheer effrontery seemed to amuse him. He insisted I have an *aperitivo*. He said he was paying for his whole family to travel, he loved them to death; that was because of his Italian blood. His son, about fifty years old, was trying to look distinguished. The old man wrenched his head down and planted a noisy kiss on his balding pate.

A black Brazilian perched on a bar stool talking to a stewardess. The sight of him would have been all too much for the American author of *Vagabonding Down the Andes*, who travelled by river steamer in 1918: "Its officers and stewards, all argentinos, were as white as you or I, though the passengers ran to all shades, and it was little short of startling to see white waiters serving and kowtowing to haughty Brazilian half-Indians and negroes."

After two hours the purser led me to a first-class cabin with twin beds. I could have it all to myself, he said. For good relations between Argentina and Australia. After he'd gone I gazed through the window at the brown Plata, herons swooping in to forage among the reeds on the shore. I was surprised at how narrow the river had become, low scrubby banks quite close on each side.

I learned we were in a channel of the Plata delta, passing the large island of Martín García. It had a turbulent history. In 1845 Garibaldi occupied it for Uruguay with the support of an Anglo-French squadron. Argentina won it back and used it as a convenient prison for state undesirables, a "pocket Botany Bay" according to Richard Burton. In 1879 the undesirables were 2,000 Patagonian Indians, shipped to the island to die after General Julio Roca's "Conquest of the Desert". Later it became a place of detention for deposed heads of state, among them Juan Domingo Perón. During the military junta's Dirty War of the 1970s, mutilated corpses washed ashore from there.

We chugged by Martín García and soon there were literally hundreds of islands, cut by a thousand channels. Every now and then, as another island slipped behind us, there were glimpses across a network of waterways, rippling away into the dusk. The lights of Buenos Aires glowed far in the distance. I had a sudden sense of how absurdly isolated the city was, clinging with its skyscrapers and European affectations to the great bare flank of the continent.

The first Spanish explorers entered and named the Río de la Plata in 1516. They were looking for an alternative route to the fabled gold and silver of the Andes. But it was difficult to find firm land in the marshy confusion of the delta and they were not a little discouraged when their leader, setting ashore, was killed and eaten by Indians. Twenty years later another expedition, under Juan de Ayolas made their way through to the Paraná and on for nearly 2,000 kilometres, past the confluence with the Paraguay River to a site with the first hills they had seen. They called it Nuestra Señora de la Asunción — Our Lady of the Assumption, and established a village. It became the capital of the Vice-Royalty of La Plata when Buenos Aires was still a swamp. This is a fact much referred to by Paraguayans and assiduously ignored by everyone else.

The evening meal was from 9 pm to midnight. The dining saloon was the focus of the cruise for many, tables set with white napery, cruets of olive oil and vinegar. The waiters were doing brisk service fulfilling orders for wine. There was a smiling woman seated opposite me with dark bruises around her eyes. She said her name was Nelly. She squeezed the hand of her husband, a sweet-faced man of perhaps eighty. It was hard to believe he would have inflicted the shiners.

A little further down Colonel Blimp was still popping his dentures. I was relieved I did not have to face him. On one side of me was a distinguished woman in her sixties from Montevideo and, on the other, an accountant from Buenos Aires who spoke good English, for which I was shamefully grateful. He talked about the desperate state of the Argentine economy which, in his view, was because of the madness of going on par with the US dollar. Tourism had fallen off, exports were at a standstill, sales taxes were prohibitive, the government was adopting frantic measures, selling off public enterprises, abolishing the old-age pension, introducing a national superannuation scheme, all of which led to more unemployment which was already fearsome. The whole system was unreal and sooner or later and probably sooner, he said, it would collapse.

It all seemed so bleak we had some more good Argentine wine to cheer ourselves up.

I thought of the pioneers on the *Río Paraná*. After the backsliding in Montevideo, the teetotal rule was strictly enforced. According to one account, admittedly written by a hostile critic of the venture, some of the parents were anxious to give their children a treat after the bland diet they had had on the voyage from Australia. They had no money, but bartered various personal belongings in order to buy a barrel of native molasses for the river trip. It was broached on the first day out of port and young and old pronounced it delicious. Then someone declared that molasses contained a certain percentage of alcohol and was therefore, according to the strict letter of New Australian law, prohibited. "Disregarding the children's tears, their mothers' protests, and the stronger language of their fathers, the newly elevated officers seized the barrel and heaved it overboard where it could harm the morals of none but the crocodiles!" If the story was true, it occurred to me that the only newly elevated officer was Arthur Tozer.

Before turning in I stood on the top deck, mesmerised by the intricate network of islands and channels, luminescent in the moonlight. The islands were flat, just above the level of the water, overgrown by shadowy vegetation. Brigands and pirates used to live on them, gauchos who'd traded their horses for canoes. Any actual mainland, I was told, was impossible to see. On the starboard side it was 50 kilometres away.

*

I woke to brilliant sunshine and what seemed to be the ocean outside the cabin window. We had entered the great Paraná River which, over 3,000 kilometres further upstream, roars through the jungled ravines of Brazil, advances in a body of water said to exceed the combined volume of all the rivers of Europe, through rainforest and rich farming land, past the cities of Posadas and Encarnación and the ruins of the old Jesuit missions, to join the Paraguay River, takes a vast horseshoe turn, the converging waters sweeping silt from the Mato Grosso and melted ice from the Andes to become this majestic waterway flowing through the Argentine pampas to the Atlantic. The Guaraní people call the Paraná the Womb of the Mother of the Sea.

With considerable justice Tom Westwood, one of the pioneers, wrote that it made the Murray, Australia's widest river, look like a creek. But, despite a hundred-year advantage in maritime technology, we seemed to have made about the same progress as those on the paddle-steamer *Río Paraná*, who awoke to see low islands but no firm riverbanks visible: "The sides of the channels through which the steamer passed were exceedingly pretty, being covered with long reeds, and in many parts bordered with willows of a most vivid green."

During breakfast we came close to the flat, reed-fringed land on the port side. Back from the river, contented cattle grazed in lush pasture to their hocks. A lone clump of pampas grass seemed an overstated announcement of our arrival at the edge of the great grasslands. A steel smelter and a huge industrial complex came into view and, beyond them, the town of San Nicholas with some high-rise buildings. Two big ships, one Argentine, the other registered in Bombay, were moored at the wharf.

A useful book in the Australian pioneers' library was *The Cruise of the Falcon*, an account by E. F. Knight, an English barrister, who spent five months in 1880 sailing the river with two other lawyers and a cabin boy as crew of his thirty-ton yawl. He wrote about the considerable shipping on the Paraná at that time, vessels from North America and Europe loading hides, bones and alfalfa at the quays of Rosario. But beyond that point, where the shifting shoals and channels were treacherous, the navigation was almost exclusively in the hands of Italian seamen, the people who made the capital's port *barrio* of La Boca their home. A voyage far into the continent's interior, a round trip of almost 8,000 kilometres, could take them a year:

> Their vessels are handsome schooners, of little draught but great beam, with enormous spread of canvas, and great square top-sails high aloft to catch the wind above the trees. The running-gear is generally of plaited hide, a very excellent substitute for rope. They go up against the stream, laden with wines and European produce, even as far as the centre of the Brazilian province of Matagrosso ... They return to Buenos Ayres and Montevideo with cargoes of cedar and valuable hard woods from the virgin forests of the Chaco, of oranges from Paraguay and other produce of those rich but little cultivated countries.

We passed a small settlement — two-storey villas in a parkland setting, sweeping lawns broken by stands of cypresses and pencil pines. Couples played tennis on courts in the background; a young girl was riding a pony along the sandy beach. Yachts bobbed at a marina, seemingly one for every villa. A high security fence surrounded the whole complex. It was a country club estate, I was told; they had become popular with the affluent class wanting to escape the crowding and crime of the city. Many of them had a school, pony club and golf course within the grounds. The husband (for the assumption was that he'd be the only one working) would commute to Buenos Aires or Rosario to pay for it all.

Far away to our starboard side was Entre Ríos province, also called Mesopotamia, for it is a green and fertile triangle in the fork of two rivers, the Paraná and the Uruguay. A scent of hay arrived on the breeze; the rich pasture has made Entre Ríos famous for breeding stock.

In September 1893, as the paddles of the *Río Paraná* churned upstream, boatmen on passing craft waved their hats and called out "Australianos!", for the expedition had attracted much bemused interest and been written up in the Buenos Aires and Montevideo newspapers.

By mid-morning in October 1993 the poop deck of the *Ciudad de Paraná* was crowded with the middle class at play, bodies good and not so good oiled and exposed to the sun, chatting groups on the plastic chairs. I received indulgent smiles for the word had gone around that I was an *escritora australiana* and I had a place in the scheme of things. Señora Nelly joined me. Her English was as bad as my Spanish, but she was determined to explain how she had received her black eyes, miming as in a game of charades.

"In Buenos Aires, you have seen" — she marched a few steps, pointing at the deck. "You have seen how they are *rotas?*" She brought her hand down in a swift karate chop. Indeed, I had seen the state of the pavements. She was walking with her son. She did not look where she was going for a moment ... I grabbed her as she re-enacted her fall. "Now you look at me." She grinned wryly. "People think my poor husband do it."

He was her second husband and he was eighty years old. Before he retired he had been Chief Inspector of Taxes for Argentina. Her first husband had been in the army and her son took after him and was a colonel in the Patricio Regiment. He was very strict, he liked things in perfect order. I was beginning to dislike the son. Four years ago she rang him and said, "Just imagine, your mother has received a proposal of marriage."

"I'll have to think about that. I'll just have to think about that."

"No, you won't," she told him. "I've already done the thinking and it's settled."

She loved her new husband. He had insisted on paying more so they could have a cabin with a *cama de matrimonio*, a double bed. She winked.

The activities coordinator, José Mazzetti, made an announcement which drew rumbling complaints. On the itinerary we had been due to stop at Rosario, but would not be doing so because we were behind schedule. We were 320 kilometres upriver as we passed the city, built on a bluff, its high-rise buildings sprouting abruptly from the pampas, ocean-going vessels at anchor at the wharf.

There had been similar complaints in 1893 when the *Río Paraná* stopped for an hour in Rosario to take on fresh provisions and William Lane was the only one of the Australians to go ashore, probably in the company of Arthur Tozer. He sent a cable to Walter Head, the Association leader in Sydney: "It is imperative that migration be confined to unquestionably earnest members." Head responded by sending a circular to all delegates instructing them not to enrol anyone who was "not really ready to 'go mates' in the fullest sense of the word".

Rosario is often called the Chicago of Argentina, an industrial centre servicing a large agricultural hinterland. I remembered, four years earlier, passing through its back streets by bus at night, through the shanty settlement on the city's fringe, past houses of unfinished brick, rough-mortared mechanics' workshops and sheds, high-rise apartment blocks with washing strung out on balconies and tumbledown shops advertising batteries, diesoline and galvanised iron. That was the tradesmen's entrance. From the river the city put out the welcome mat. Its main claim to fame, the colossal Monument to the Flag, dominated a park near the waterfront. The architect Angel Guido, in some fever of patriotic hubris, had perpetrated the 78-metre obelisk; the base or pouch to this phallus served as the crypt for General Manuel Belgrano, the designer of the Argentine flag.

Richard Burton, after observing wrestling bears and a bullfight in Rosario, decided:

> Ugly church, ugly steeple,
> Ugly square and ugly people.

The English barrister on the *Falcon,* voyaging a few years later, was also unimpressed:

> There is but little to say about these modern Spanish South American cities. They are very uninteresting. In describing one you describe all. The same straight streets drawn at right angles to each other, with the dismal, one-storied, flat-roofed houses. Tramways everywhere. A square or two. A cleanly prosperous look about the whole, inhabitants included … At the end of each street is the desert … It is indeed a marvellous contrast; a wilderness untilled, inhabited by wild half-breeds clad in a barbaric costume, coming up to the very streets of cities where every article of European civilization is to be found …

About 20 kilometres further upriver there was another outlet for patriotism. As we passed smokestacks and a coal-loader, the tireless activities coordinator, Señor Mazzetti, announced that this was San Lorenzo, where General San Martín had made a heroic stand against the Spanish. The passengers, mostly descendants of Spaniards, gave three rousing cheers and launched into a song, the gist of which was, "Ar-gen-tin-a! We shall win!"

The low reed-covered banks had been replaced by cliffs or *barrancas,* the vast flat pampas stretching away behind them. An American scientist on an expedition to Argentina in 1912 wrote, "I have crossed the prairies of Minnesota and the Dakotas, of Kansas and Nebraska, of Manitoba and Alberta; I have travelled over the steppes of Russia; but in none of them have I seen such absolutely level lands as those which lie between Rosario and Irigoyen. The horizon is that of the ocean; an upturned clod attracts attention; a hut looks like a house; a tree looms up like a hill."

From one to three in the afternoon the big event was the four-course lunch. Everyone had their own bottle of wine, corked from the previous meal with their cabin and table numbers marked.

After a siesta I took a turn around the deck to watch the sunset. The river was silvery-rose, dappled with shadows, our passage causing gentle hump-backed waves which slapped against the submerged bases of trees on the port side. Bare petrified branches were thrown into silhouette by the crimson glare of the setting sun. To the starboard, the moon was riding up into a violet sky above the distant dark shore. I ran for my old Pentax. When I came out the sun was suspended just above the trees, a great ripe persimmon, spilling colour like luscious juice across the sky. A woman passenger did a long slow pan with her video, exclaiming at the sumptuousness, "*Hermoso! Muy lindo!*"

A girl of about eleven was calmly roller-blading along the deck. She made me think of Margaret Riley who, with characteristic enthusiasm, revelled in the two-week trip upriver, especially the time after sunset. "The nights were lovely, the scrub was all lit up with fireflies and fire-beetles. I used to sit on the deck and stare out at the land and see the fireflies sparking in the darkness." She would usually wait up for a special treat. "My mother was feeding the baby and she liked to take a cup of cocoa before going to bed, and so did I. She used to put a few teaspoons of cocoa into a billy-can and give it me to get boiling water. I would take it down to the galley and ask for *agua caliente* — so the cook used to call me that. Whenever he'd see me, he'd say 'Hello, *Agua Caliente*.' "

Another New Australian child, Eric Birks, voyaging a year later, did not make himself so popular with the crew:

> From the very bowels of this boat rose and fell, mysteriously, a shining great beam of steel. One perched, precariously, on the top guard rails, around an opening in the top deck, and with precision aimed banana skins at the bald pate of the Scotch engineer below. Once a miss proved no better than a mile, for he pounced upon me from behind a ventilator.
>
> "Ye little devil, a-messing up my gratings! And a-clabbing up of my head with your bits of skins — take that! and that —"
>
> So I took my first licking from a marine engineer, on the *Parana*, steaming along in the type of boat made famous by Mark Twain.

Every evening the lounge became a casino for bingo. The calls, despite the glamorous croupier in a glittering dress, sounded as leadenly dull as they do in English. "*Sesenta y dos … Seis … Dos … Sesenta y dos … Quince! Uno … Cinco … Quin-ce!*" I wondered about the dramatic intensity in the atmosphere, the intermittent uproar, jubilation and dashed faces, till I learned that the stakes were at least US$3,000 a time.

And after dinner, for those who could last the distance, a musical combo provided dancing until the small hours, the lounge transformed into a dark and moody nightclub where lovers danced cheek to cheek and elderly *porteño* couples did the tango, gliding together with practised melancholy.

*

The next morning Señor Mazzetti was whipping up enthusiasm for shipboard fun and games, dividing passengers into teams and timing them running around the deck. I beat a hasty retreat to the poop deck with my notebook. The pampas rolled by. A little wooden cart was being pulled by a bony horse along a red road that cut straight across the illimitable flatness. A flowering ceibo tree at the water's edge was an excitement, a man fishing from a canoe a major event.

Over lunch Señora Nelly told me she had a daughter married to a Brazilian and living in Sao Paulo. Her grandson was growing up learning only Portuguese and she had difficulty communicating. So she was going to buy a parrot, teach it to speak Spanish and send it to him.

As we were served dessert, a musician moved to the dais with a Yamaha synthesiser. Señor Mazzetti made announcements about our visit to Corrientes the following day. Our arrival time would be uncertain because the captain had to navigate cautiously through the shallow waters. He continued with other announcements. The musician launched into a tango and I heard mention of "*la australiana*". Applause as Señor Mazzetti swooped towards me. He wouldn't dare, I thought with a sinking feeling. He would. In front of a room full of people who'd been dancing the tango inside their mother's wombs, I trampled on his toes.

As the sun set across the pampas that evening, skyscrapers appeared on the skyline, rolling pink clouds behind them. The town of Santa Fé as a surrealistic painting, a vision of Magritte or Jeffrey Smart. Riding towards the town was a horseman with a fleece under his high-pommelled Spanish saddle. In a cloud of dust, he was overtaken by a Landcruiser.

When the old way of life of the horsemen of the pampas had all but gone, the Argentines romanticised them as *la gente perdida*, the lost people. Metropolitan poets manufactured ballads about them and city people decorated their barbeque areas with their daggers, belts and *mate* gourds.

William Lane had a similarly coloured view of the "tall, straight and manly" Australian bushmen but did not comment on the gauchos. It was after his time that W. H. Hudson embroidered the legend for British readers, while conceding that the old days had gone "when the gaucho had more liberty and was a more lawless being than he is now or can ever be again".

Still, I had been sufficiently influenced by what Bruce Chatwin called "all the cant about the gaucho" to have been thrilled, four years before, to have spotted a relic. Travelling by bus, I had passed through Santa Fé and, sometime after midnight, we had stopped at a little cow town set out in the usual grid pattern with the usual statue to General San Martín in the square. And there he was, loitering with a group of local lads outside a roadhouse, splendidly surly, wearing a saucer-shaped black hat, a string under his chin, black blousy trousers and knee-high leather boots. And he didn't give a fart for his tourist appeal.

"Don't talk to me about the gauchos," remarked an Anglo-Argentine passenger. "They may have slept on their saddles, but that's because they were too stupid to get a decent pillow together."

We had negotiated a channel which brought us closer to the right bank of the river and to the pretty town of La Paz, white buildings with red roofs among acacias and sentinel cypresses, set high on a *barranca*. E. F. Knight stocked the *Falcon* with provisions here: "The river being flooded, the butcher's shop on the beach was under water, so we were able to row right inside it to buy our beef, which was highly convenient."

The river had broadened into a noble stream, maybe 2 kilometres across, but apparently with many shallows and shoals. Our draught was a constant problem and this cruise would be the last until the following winter. A heron made a grave evening constitutional along a sandbar; rafts of *camelote*, floating water hyacinths, drifted past, some with birds hitching a ride. It is said that jaguars and other wild beasts used to travel downstream this way — perhaps a fluvial myth.

As night fell, the stars were brilliant in the enormity of vaulting dark. I located the Southern Cross and was comforted to have come so far and still have the company of an old friend.

A man leaned against the deck railing and started singing in a pure voice, the words not Spanish. People gathered to listen; someone whispered that he was singing in Guaraní. The notes of his song rippled out over the water and no one moved until he was finished.

I discovered he was Paraguayan and a doctor. His name was Luis Alberto Aliende. He told me he loved travelling by river, it was in his blood. His father had been in Paraguay's Prefectura Naval, the Maritime Police, and often used to speak about the last two paddle-steamers still working from the early days — the *Pingo* and the *Olimpo*. Owned by a Paraguayan shipping company called Camihort, they did the run from Buenos Aires to Asunción right up until 1930.

Mary Cameron wrote in 1895: "When I went aboard the *Olimpo* I was obliged to take a boat to go out to her. It was a rough day and I had to get a four-oared boat. She danced so that everything loose had to be stowed and I had to watch that I did not lose my balance and take an unexpected dip."

*

On Thursday morning I woke to discover that the river was now almost 3 kilometres wide. It seemed hard to credit that this was possible 1,300 kilometres inland. It was because we were approaching the junction of the Paraná and the Paraguay, the confluence of two mighty streams. But although the expanse of water appeared so vast and deep, the previous night while passengers were sleeping our ship had run aground; we had been stranded for an hour before the tide had refloated us. Margaret Riley's paddle-steamer was "stuck on a sand bank till nearly midday the next day. They thought everybody would have to disembark to get the ship off but anyway the tide lifted us".

Ahead of us an elegant concrete arc, the Puente Belgrano, made a soaring span across the Paraná, a prodigious feat of engineering to connect the towns of Corrientes and the capital of the Chaco province, Resistencia. The *Ciudad de Paraná* eased into the port of Corrientes, occupying the full length of the cobbled wharf. The town was a haze of colour, jacarandas, poincianas and rose-pink *lapachos* in bloom along the waterfront, its air of tranquil indolence belying a troubled past.

Indian resistance discouraged Spanish settlement until 1588 when Jesuit priests moved down from Asunción. Almost three centuries later, the Paraguayan dictator, Francisco Solano López, back from Europe and with Napoleonic dreams of empire, cast his acquisitive gaze on the port on the Paraná. In April 1865 five of his warships appeared offshore, seized two Argentine gunboats and occupied the city. This piece of insolence initiated the signing of a treaty between Argentina, Brazil and Uruguay, designed to teach López a lesson and, not incidentally, to divide up the spoils. Argentina's president, Bartolomé Mitre, announced his nation's goal as, "To the barracks in twenty-four hours; on campaign in three weeks; in Asunción in three months!" But he underestimated the ferocity and passionate nationalism of the Paraguayan soldier. Though it almost destroyed the country they defended, the War of the Triple Alliance lasted five bloody years.

Our ship's passengers, with dire instructions from Señor Mazzetti about time limits, fanned out into the town in sensible sunhats, new Reeboks collecting dust, unmistakable as tourists. In a shambling group we moved up Calle Mendoza, past old colonial buildings of crumbling stucco and some eyesore blocks of flats. Cameras went into action in front of the sixteenth-century church, the Convento de San Francisco, spare and lovely in its whitewashed simplicity. A group of men lounging on the opposite street corner hardly gave us a glance. A few were wearing woven ponchos and I was abruptly conscious of being in Indian territory. The local people were darker skinned than in the capital, many with high cheekbones and aquiline features.

In 1880 E. F. Knight felt threatened by the Indian presence, especially by the nomadic people who came across river from the Chaco, a vast sparsely settled scrubland extending all the way to the Andes:

> On landing in our canoe on the tosca beach, we found … an encampment of men, women and children, whose barbaric costume and hideous faces betokened them to be Indians of the Chaco. They were Guacurús, a ferocious tribe, and spoke a harsh, guttural language, sounding very unpleasant after the tongue of the civilized Guaranís. These Guacurús had come over the river in a huge canoe which they had drawn up on the beach; they had brought firewood and skins of wild beasts to exchange for salt and other necessaries. They were of a very dark colour, with long coarse black hair hanging down their backs; some had tiger-skins, but most had merely filthy blankets wrapped round them. The women were, if possible, uglier than the men. Corrientes is really more Indian than a Spanish city, for not only do the savages from the Chaco often throng its streets … but, as far as I could judge, quite three-quarters of the inhabitants are Guaranís, and speak that tongue.

The pioneer Australians, arriving on the *Río Paraná* some years later, did not disembark, but their paddle-steamer lay in close to shore while supplies of meat and vegetables were brought aboard. They pressed against the railings to stare out at the town, the dusty pot-holed streets lined with orange trees, the horse-drawn trams and bullock carts, Indian washerwomen and young senoritas with mantillas over their long hair, Argentine soldiers and dark-skinned men in ponchos. They would have seen the campaniles of several Jesuit churches and heard the story of one, containing a sixteenth-century cross, which had defied all the attempts of Indians, hostile to the new Christianity, to burn it. For the first time since they had left home, they were witnessing a way of life that had little to do with Europe.

Tom Westwood studied the scene through field-glasses and, in the garden of a large house near the water's edge, he discovered a young woman swinging at her ease in a hammock while a small antelope or gazelle grazed on the grass beside her. "I don't know which is the prettier," he wrote, "the dear in the hammock or the deer on the lawn."

William Lane had decided that the journalist Harry Taylor should disembark at Corrientes and return to Montevideo to join the *Royal Tar* on its voyage back to Australia. The reason he gave to the pioneers, called together for a general meeting in the saloon of the *Río Paraná*, was that they needed a representative on the ship which was, after all, the property of their Association. This argument was treated with scepticism by some of the disaffected members. Souter has suggested that later events make another interpretation credible: Lane may have already been anticipating a schism at New Australia and given Taylor instructions to raise funds for an alternative tract of land as an insurance policy. He may have already been actively planning for failure.

While Taylor waited for a steamer to take him downriver, Corrientes was recovering from a revolution which had erupted a few days before. Some shots had been fired between a government ironclad moored just off port and dissidents in two smaller boats. Eleven men had been killed and sixteen wounded, but Taylor downplayed the drama for the *Voice* in Adelaide: "It seems to have been a very tame affair, and the alarming accounts which, from time to time, appear in the papers are evidently drawn largely from imagination, so as to give picturesqueness and vividness to what is, in reality, exceedingly dull and commonplace."

In the Plaza 25 de Mayo, I inspected the inevitable statue of General José de San Martín, arrested in mid-prance on his horse, then the ship's hooter sounded from the river, summoning us back.

*

As the *Ciudad de Paraná* chugged away from Corrientes and under the arch of the Puente Belgrano, it was as though we had passed through a gateway. Just 40 kilometres to the north we came to the confluence of two of the world's great waterways and took the fork to the west. We had entered the Paraguay River, still over a kilometre wide, and the treeless pampa was far behind. On either bank the trees closed in and on the starboard side was the secretive land the Australian pioneers had been seeking: Paraguay. John Lane gazed across the river as a flock of flamingoes took off from the eastern shore in a cloud of pink. Usually such a sturdy pragmatist, he felt he had literally entered a paradise. "In Paraguay, the river's borders had a beauty and softness unknown in Argentina. The very air blew as from a garden … Fishes scaled in gold and silver splashed glitteringly in the sunshine."

As dusk was falling our ship juddered to a halt on a hidden shoal. Among the towering trees on the eastern shore were some ruins, the gaunt red wall of a church and a shattered tower. The Paraguayan, Dr Aliende, was tremendously moved by the sight and by the fact that it was here that we should become stranded. It was Humaitá, he said, a sacred place for his country-people, where a legendary siege took place during the War of the Triple Alliance. In 1865 at this southern river gate to his country, López had tried to hold back the invading armies of Brazil, Argentina and Uruguay. He succeeded for three years.

Commanding a position at a horseshoe bend in the river, Humaitá was Paraguay's Sebastopol. It had a fort on either bank, an impressive row of gun batteries, and chains across the river connecting a deadly network of submerged torpedoes. López had been advised in his strategy by a brilliant English ballistics engineer, William Whitehead, whom he had engaged to build his formidable arsenal at Asunción. Incredibly, within the Humaitá fortress itself, Whitehead had established an iron foundry which produced other armaments including two 12-tonne guns cast from church bells, firing 70-kilogram projectiles.

For three years fierce battles were waged there, the Allied gunboats aiming their cannon and heavy artillery at the Paraguayan forts. Over 80,000 men and every advance of modern warfare were at their disposal, including spy flights over the Paraguayan entrenchments by mercenaries, the American Allen brothers, in a hot-air balloon. In February 1868, taking advantage of an exceptional rise in the river, the Brazilian squadron at last forced through the blockade, bombarding the chain mountings.

At dawn next day some thirty canoes, disguised by clumps of water hyacinths, eased up to two Brazilian ironclads. Naked men climbed to the upper decks. They found the hatches closed. "The Paraguayans," wrote Burton, "attempted to throw hand-grenades into the port-holes and ran about seeking ingress, like a cat attacking a trapped mouse." Abruptly two other ironclads steamed alongside and opened fire. A few Paraguayans dived overboard; the rest were slaughtered.

López retreated with his retinue but ordered the resistance to continue. The Paraguayans fought. Their country was threatened, they loved it passionately and they would die for it. They died in thousands. The starving garrison of Humaitá surrendered finally in August 1868.

"I will never forget that I saw Humaitá," wrote Mary Gilmore, "where to prevent the oncoming boats of Argentina with their cannons and their legions, the Paraguayans stayed them with ropes made of lianas … The war left its myths, its ghosts and its haunts. But above everything one great fact stands out and that is the pride of race, the courage and the endurance of the coloured man in Paraguay as a defender of his country."

The war dragged on for another nineteen months, López determined to keep at it while any men, however wounded or crippled, or any boys, however young and untried, were left. Accompanied by his Irish mistress Madame Eliza Lynch, he moved his line of defence further north, torturing or flogging those of his officers unwilling to fight on.

But just after the sacking of Humaitá, the most illustrious of all British tourists came cruising along the river: Captain Richard Burton — soldier, explorer, scholar, poet, diplomat, botanist, linguist, translator and lover of *volupté*. He dropped by in September 1868, and again in April 1869.

Burton was already famous for his expedition in Africa in search of the source of the Nile, and for his romantic foray to the sacred Islamic cities of Mecca and Medina in black-face disguise. Not yet a knight, he was already a nineteenth-century superstar. But for three and a half years he had been languishing as the British consul in Santos, Brazil, while petitioning the Foreign Office to return him to Arabia, "the land of my heart's predilection". So he had taken time off to go by riverboat to Paraguay during the bloodiest conflict in Latin American history. He had made a study of the Guaraní language to equip himself for the trip. With the best connections and introductions, insatiably curious about everything he saw, his *Letters from the Battlefields of Paraguay* was essentially a travel book, a nineteenth-century precursor to *Holidays in Hell*.

His river steamer, the *Yí*, he described as "a brand new 'floating hotel', with her plated silver dazzling, her napkins stiff-starched, and her gilt mouldings upon the untarnished white panels clean as a new sovereign". He thought a common English passenger steamer would have been far plainer but proportionally more comfortable. The splendid saloon all along the second deck would soon, he predicted, wax dingy, and there was no possibility of walking in the open air. Furthermore, "the three stewards are expected to do the work of one man; they are exceedingly civil, and they do nothing". The cook had bolted, in fear of enlistment, and another steward had also fled, first locking up the pantry, so "the party of pleasure began, as usual, painfully".

The ship could average 10 to 12 knots an hour and had cost £30,000, making it a marvel in South America, though Burton, who was a man who'd seen a thing or two, commented that for the United States it was "some ten years behind the age".

As on my ship 125 years later, "by far the favourite amusement ... is hearty, thorough, whole-souled gambling, which makes the fore-saloon a standing hell. One passenger is said to have lost during the excursion $8,000. The Brazilians are the hottest players, pushing on far into the small hours".

The *Yi* carried a full complement of VIPs, travelling in dress-circle seats to view the progress of the war and the death of a nation: Segundo Flores, third son of the recently assassinated Brazilian president, was making the trip to obtain a clothing contract for Brazilian troops, and the elegant Hector Varela, later to become Madame Lynch's biographer, was writing a column for the Buenos Aires *Tribuna*. Also among the "tripsters", as Burton called them, were the wife and daughter of General Juan Gelly y Obes, the Commander in Chief of the Argentine forces.

Just before they reached Humaitá they were joined by General Gelly himself, dashing in magenta-coloured kepi with gold braiding, blue frock and long riding-boots. Burton found himself impressed with this man, rumoured to be of Paraguayan descent, who had begun his working life as an auctioneer: "He has been the life and soul of his motley force, ever in the saddle, and ever *au grand galop*. But this active and energetic soldier has not been fortunate, and his enemies have soundly abused him for failing to do some great deed."

As they approached the famous fortress, Burton stared in disbelief. Where was "the great stronghold" which had been looked on as the keystone of Paraguay? How could the pathetic camp he saw have resisted such a bloody and protracted siege?

Accompanied by General Gelly, he went ashore, inspected the iron foundry where Whitehead had cast guns, and explored the presidential "palace", a brick shed bespattered and pierced by shot. They found quantities of Parisian furniture, still unpacked from its crates. This was the only "civilized loot", which otherwise consisted of rusty guns, cases of bottled palm oil and some sacks of *yerba mate*. But underneath Madame Lynch's gilded bed, General Gelly had earlier discovered a pair of black satin shoes. He had sent them to his wife in Buenos Aires, and she had written back with frank admiration: "I received the booty of Madame Lynch. After three years blockade, Madame Lynch leaves her elegant latest fashion shoes lying about ... It's a pity that woman is not López's wife.

Her heroism would be worthy of every eulogy, for following the destiny of her husband."

Humaitá was a stronghold that had fallen, and the occupying troops had no reason to love it. Water lay in filthy pools. The soldiers camped in mat huts or tents. Just as American grunts in 1970s Vietnam called their sandbagged foxholes "Beverley Hills Ramada" and "Hollywood Hilton", so the occupiers of Humaitá gave their hovels "the ambitious names of Hotel Francais, de Bordeaux, and de Garibaldi". Burton encountered a jumble of nationalities and idlers, ruffians, musicians, cut-throats and prostitutes — all the types he had known from Arabia and the East.

But, in all that devastation, it was the Paraguayan guns which most moved him. Just ninety guns in seven batteries had held off the invaders for years, yet the evidence before him showed that some dated back to manufacture in Seville, Spain, in the 1670s, antiques honeycombed with rust, quaint museum pieces in the 1860s. Even the modern weaponry — Whitworth muzzle-loaders, Krupps cannons, self-rifling shells, hand gre-nades and rotating rockets — were a motley collection, absurdly eclectic, hopelessly inefficient. Cannons were wadded with circles of twisted palm. Shot was packed in leather, not metal. Grape shot was made from available materials — screws, broken rifles, old locks, chopped-up pieces of iron — and bound with strips of hide and liana. They indicated a people fighting almost literally with everything they could lay their hands on. "To be killed by such barbaric appliances would be another sting to that of death."

As he viewed the remains of the Paraguayan arsenal, Burton wrote that, "I felt something of the hysterical passion at the thought of so much wasted heroism. And this personal inspection of the site where the last struggle had so lately ended impressed me highly with Paraguayan strength of purpose, and with the probability of such men fighting to the last."

The Paraguayan arsenal had reached its most formidable strength at the beginning of the war in 1865. This was universally attributed to the policy of its brilliant English director, William Whitehead. It deteriorated that year after his suicide from an injection of concentrated nicotine. It was acknowledged as a major strategic disaster for Paraguay. A former López employee, George Masterman, who escaped to the Brazilian side, wrote: "Mr Whytehead, the chief engineer, died, to the deep regret of his friends, and the serious loss of the Paraguayans. He was a man of remarkable skill, and had raised the arsenal to a state of great efficiency."

My researches later uncovered a fact that made me almost as emotional as the Paraguayan, Dr Aliende, about Humaitá. It seemed that William was of the same industrial north England family from which my engineer father was descended. William Whitehead, who abetted López, was one of my own ancestors. Perhaps some tribal memory was at the basis of my obsession with the country.

Four hours later the tide lifted us and we chugged on in the darkness, leaving the ruins of Humaitá behind. We had cleared the blockade and entered Paraguay at last, land of dreamers and despots.

*

Morning found us in the tropics. The vegetation had changed; forest had become jungle. Palm trees and stands of feathery bamboo jostled luxuriantly against broad-leaved forest giants, tangles of creepers and flowering vines restrained half-drowned logs at the water's edge. Señor Mazzetti advised passengers to look among the trees and they might be lucky enough to see monkeys or other wild animals. Retired bank managers, company directors and the former Chief Inspector of Taxes rushed to the railings.

The pioneers *did* see monkeys, parrots in flocks and alligators basking in the sun along the river banks or sliding into the water as the waves from the paddles alarmed them. Tozer was delighted by the screaming and gaudy plumage of birds, the hum of insects, having missed them since his Brazilian sojourn a year before.

From a book they listed as having in their shipboard library — *Paraguay: The Land and the People* by Dr E. de Bourgade La Dardye — the Australians learned that there were an alarming number of creatures other than alligators swimming in the waters beneath them: the *manguruyú*, growing to 6 metres in length and weighing up to 200 kilograms; the *dorado*, loved by game fishermen for its fighting form, and the *surubí*, a huge spotted catfish, the last two both good eating. But there were a number of strong-jawed little fish good *at* eating — unwary swimmers, for instance — and feared most of all were the pirañas. Mouths crammed with razor teeth, they worked in schools and "leave anything with an exposed wound fleshless within minutes; nothing else can produce a skeleton from living flesh so quickly. Alligators' armour does not exempt them. The men, when swimming cattle across piraña-infested water, will sometimes kill one animal or an alligator, throw the carcase downstream. While the pirañas flay it, the troop crosses elsewhere". There were other unpleasant creatures: a ray with a long spike which inflicted a wound difficult to heal, and the water-serpent or anaconda, much more to be feared than the boa constrictor. La Dardye wrote that it was "known in the country as the *mboy-yagua* (serpent-dog). They will upset canoes, and drag bathers down into the water. The Indians have an intense horror of them. During my exploration of the Ygatimi, I saw one cross the river a little way ahead of our boat, and I am confident it was not much under ten yards [10 metres] in length".

Mary Cameron, travelling two years after the first batch during December, the height of summer, found the heat intolerable: "The atmosphere almost reaches the point of saturation. It is impossible to be cool anywhere and one sips iced lemonade and fans oneself in sheer desperation while the perspiration runs off in streams. As for baths — they are not easy to get, as the South American prefers powder to a bath." Mary arranged with the chief engineer, an Englishman called Dysart, to have the use of his bath every morning. "The whole ship's crew, cooks, stewards and all not on actual duty, used to gape with astonishment."

But afterwards, until the sun forced her inside, she leaned against the steamer's railing, enthralled by the luxuriance of the river scenery — and claiming perhaps more than her reasonable quota of exotic sightings:

> ... the forest lies on each side of the river, dense and impenetrable. The monkey swings from tree to tree, the jaguar, the puma, the ocelot crouch in their lairs, thousands of gay coloured birds nest in the branches, the tree cactus stands on sentry among the forest giants, the tecoma climbs everywhere seeking the sun, in the pools and *riachuelos* (little lagoons from the river) cranes stand dreaming, while the flamingo, startled by the snort of the engine, rise in flights to wing their way to greater distances and denser safeties ... In the mud along the river bank the cayman lies lazily in the sun or drifts like a log in the moody waters waiting his prey, fish swim and flash as they leap for flies, a thousand varieties of insects live and have their lives, by night a chorus of sounds, frogs, crickets, all manner of things.

She had been reading Charles Kingsley's *Westward Ho!*, partly set in Paraguay. Not realising the author had never visited the country, she agreed with his verdict that it "should have been called Paradise because of the beauty of its forests, its verdure, its rivers and its birds".

Mary had a theory that "England wanted Paraguay" and so had intrigued to prolong the War of the Triple Alliance. Even more startling, she declared this imperial vision was part of a secret agenda for the New Australia movement: "One of the dim dreams of William Lane ... that we should spread and expand and by a peaceful penetration of the land would become British and a British colony would lead the world in world collectivism." In fact, she wrote, the dim dream had firmed into a specific and grandiose plan: "In choosing Paraguay for New Australia, William Lane (who believed the British the world's chosen race) intended raising the British flag there, and so in the end adding all South America to the British Empire."

It was a vision, she admitted, which at the time she shared. Later she was embarrassed by its presumption: "By that time I had lived long enough in South America to have ceased to think the British any more wonderful or civilized than at least the South Americans ... When I think of our ignorance when we went to Paraguay! We talked of 'these foreigners' — we ourselves the foreigners, charitably housed in their country after being refused even a foot of ground for our settlement in every colony of Australia."

Some of the British had already recognised Paraguay's attractions. The barrister on the *Falcon* was immensely cheered, on entering the mouth of the Paraguay River to see on the right-hand shore, "several white-clad damsels standing, who waved their hands to us and laughed musically as we sailed by, as if to welcome us to the Land of Women". That was almost literally what Paraguay had become after the War of the Triple Alliance. Two generations of women, famous for their beauty, had resigned themselves to celibacy or polygamy. It was indeed a boys' paradise, a fact not lost on visiting Englishmen. Knight and his friends went ashore at Pilar, the first Paraguayan town, and found their first impressions most agreeably confirmed:

Numerous women passed us, each clad in the snowy white robe of the country, bare-footed, and bearing something on her head, a jar of water, a pumpkin, a bundle of cigars ... They stalk through the streets with a soft, supple, panther-like tread, that is most beautiful, for they do not indulge in high-heeled boots and stays, but step out as Eve herself might have done, quite unimpeded by their simple dress, which is merely a short tunic tied round at the waist, and adorned with the pretty native lace. These tunics have short sleeves and very low necks, and reveal the statuesque shoulders and breasts rather more than would be considered delicate in Europe. Nearly all the Paraguayan women have large dark and fine eyes, and I think they know this ... These Paraguayan women seem to be always happy and laughing, and their kindness and good-nature towards each other is very discernible.

The Australian bachelors must have noticed the charms of the women when the *Río Paraná* put in at the wharf at Pilar for another transhipment.

Paraguayan country women in the 1890s. They were celebrated for their beauty, but for two generations were resigned to celibacy or polygamy. (One of the "magic lantern" slides used to attract Australian recruits to Paraguay) (*University of Sydney Library*)

From that point the river was too shallow for the paddle-steamer and the pioneers had to travel on to the capital in a small ferryboat, the *Pollux*.

*

The *Ciudad de Paraná* also paused at Pilar, a collection of stucco buildings and tin sheds, thatched huts at its straggling fringes. A tender came out from the jetty to collect a disembarking passenger. I thought of an anecdote from Richard Burton, of the looting by Brazilians and Argentines after the fall of Humaitá. At Pilar he saw three soldiers staggering down to the waterfront, two of them supporting a drunken comrade. The "drunk" turned out to be a life-size statue of Christ stolen from a church and kitted out in trousers and blue jacket.

Señor Mazzetti announced that because of the delay being stranded, we would be six hours late arriving in Asunción. I was exasperated and anxious, for the celebration for the centenary of the arrival of the Australian pioneers was to begin the following morning.

It was after midnight when, against an indigo sky, the dark silhouette of a perfectly-shaped conical hill came into view, the Cerro Lambaré. For Asunceños it announces their return home the way the harbour bridge does for Sydneysiders. The doctor looked emotional as he told me it was named for a famous Guaraní chieftan who resisted the Spanish. It was the first respectable hill that the *conquistadores* led by Juan de Ayolas had seen on their voyage from the coast and they decided to establish a settlement. After a three-day siege the Indians surrendered and sent six young women as peace offerings. The Spaniards had not found gold, but they had found tractable Guaraní people for servants and wives, and they settled down to the serious business of living in lotus-land.

The *Ciudad de Paraná* rounded a point and came into the Bay of Asunción, the lights of the city dancing in the water. The Presidential Palace glowed on the cliff above, a fanciful structure built by child slaves. The first dictator to occupy it tortured the architect in its cellars. The last, so recently removed from office, signed many death warrants there. Its towers, turrets and pinnacles were lit up with fairy lights like a picture-book castle.

8

Landfall

… they all would sail "without a woman aboard" to Paraguay…

"They have the highest ratio of women to men in the world, due to Lopez, who almost extinguished their manhood in his wars; it's impossible for women to tyrannize over men; none of the men do any work; they sit around all day long watching the women do the work. They're appreciated."

Christina Stead, *Letty Fox: Her Luck*

I came to Paraguay by a writer's instinct … I knew nothing of the city, but I believed I would find in Asunción some mingling of the exotic, the dangerous and the Victorian which would appeal … How right I proved to be.

Graham Greene, *Ways of Escape*

It was the small hours of the morning of Saturday, 30 October, and the quay was dark and almost deserted. There was no cargo to be unloaded and few passengers disembarking, most staying on the *Ciudad de Paraná* for the round trip and the duty-free shopping. We were six hours late into port and my hosts had given up waiting and gone home to rest before the big day. I walked through the empty streets, past shuttered tourist shops. Asunción is a relatively safe city for strangers; the violence for which it became notorious was inflicted behind doors, in the cellars of the secret police, on its own people. At last I found a battered yellow cab with the driver hunched asleep behind the wheel.

The rambling port authority building hadn't changed much since the colonists arrived on the *Pollux* on the morning of 22 September 1893. They were met by an important reception committee, including the President of Paraguay, Dr Juan González, the Foreign Minister, Dr Venancio López, who was also the Minister for Colonisation, and the elderly British consul, Dr William Stewart. These dignitaries came on board and formed a receiving line in the saloon while the colonists filed past to be introduced and sign their names. Arthur Tozer, as he pointed

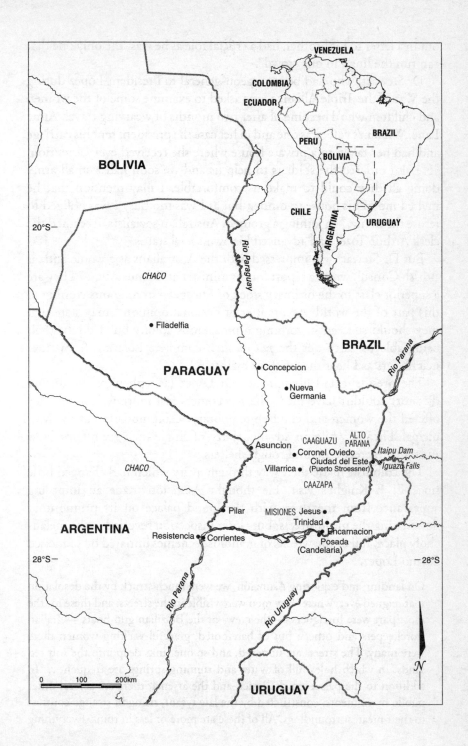

VENEZUELA

COLOMBIA

ECUADOR

PERU

BRAZIL

BOLIVIA

CHILE

ARGENTINA

URUGUAY

BOLIVIA

20°S—

Rio Paraguay

CHACO

• Filadelfia

PARAGUAY

BRAZIL

• Concepcion

Rio Parana

• Nueva
Germania

CAAGUAZU   ALTO
              PARANA
Asuncion   Itaipu Dam
       • Coronel Oviedo
          Ciudad del Este
Villarrica • (Puerto Stroessner)   Iguazu Falls

CHACO

CAAZAPA

MISIONES Jesus •
• Pilar   Trinidad •

ARGENTINA   Encarnacion
       Resistencia • Corrientes   Posada
                                  (Candelaria)

28°S—   —28°S

Rio Parana

Rio Uruguay

N

0   100   200km

URUGUAY

out in a letter to his brother, had a crucial role as he was "the only one that can run the lingo in our crowd".

Dr Stewart, who had been surgeon-general to President López during the War of the Triple Alliance, was asked to examine some of the women and children who'd become ill after two months of wearying travel. Anne Lane, William's wife, was one and in her case the president sent his carriage and had her taken to a private house where she received every attention. "He also ordered the soldiers to help us and we soon had a small army doing all they could to make us comfortable. I may mention that he invited me to his house to dinner, but as I was too busy I was obliged to refuse the invite." In joining a group of Australian socialists, it seemed the clerk Arthur Tozer had advanced his own social status.

But Dr Stewart was impressed with the Australians as a whole and, as British Consul, wrote a report for his minister at Buenos Aires: "They are a superior class to the ordinary stock of European immigrants coming to this part of the world. As a matter of personal opinion I may state that they should succeed in forming a prosperous colony but I doubt their being able to carry out the *fad* of such complete isolation from their neighbours as I hear they wish to maintain."

The president and his minister Dr López (a nephew of the former dictator) couldn't have made the newcomers feel more welcome. They offered the women and children temporary accommodation at the Municipal Theatre while an advance party of single men set off for New Australia to erect tents and rough shelters.

The colonists made their way through a city which had changed little since E. F. Knight's visit. He thought Asunción made an imposing appearance from the river, with the grand palace on its promontory dominating the mean streets; but closer inspection revealed it as a melancholy place, full of the wrecks of grandiose schemes initiated by Francisco Solano López.

> On landing and exploring Asunción, we were much struck by the desolation that reigned everywhere. Few men were visible in the streets, and these for the most part were foreigners — the crews of the Brazilian gun-boats — Italian storekeepers and others; but of barefooted, graceful-walking women there were many. The streets are unpaved, and so one sinks deep into the soft red sands, in which holes full of water and running springs are frequent … In addition to the palace on the beach and the arsenal, there are several other public monuments, constructed by the late tyrant, rising in strange contrast to their mean surroundings. All of these are more or less in ruins. Everything

that López planned was on the most ambitious scale, but was never completed, for the war burst out in the midst of these great works. There is a noble theatre, and a Pantheon destined to be the last resting-place of a long line of emperors. But no actors ever find their way to this impoverished capital, and the house of López fell even before its founder was enabled to wear that imperial crown which he had commissioned a Parisian jeweller to construct for him.

The country the Australians had chosen for their utopian experiment had a sombre and bloody history. When Paraguay won its independence from Spain in 1811, the most eloquent spokesman at a congress in Asunción, Dr José Gaspar Rodríguez de Francia, declared that his people had been "humiliated, oppressed, degraded and made the object of contempt by the pride and despotism of our rulers … These unfortunate times of oppression and tyranny have ended at last." They had just begun anew. The nation was now free to have its own oppressors. Of the three dictators who followed, the first, Dr Francia, was the most sombre, the last, Francisco Solano López, the bloodiest.

Francia, an austere remote man, trained in theology and the law and with a passion for astronomy, soon exercised absolute control over the Congress and in 1816 was appointed dictator for life. He had gained many of his political ideas from reading Rousseau's *Social Contract*; he believed that people, by compact, gave up their natural liberty for the sake of social security. As *El Supremo* he removed the Paraguayans' freedom and offered security as he decreed it. He maintained a deadly hold, governing by terror, control of the army and a network of spies. Political prisoners were shackled without light or ventilation in underground cells until they rotted. Suspected conspirators were bayoneted under the dictator's window while he watched.

He severed relations with the Vatican, challenging the Pope to come to Paraguay so he could "make him an altar boy". He closed off the country's borders, forbidding all trade with the outside world, or even for anyone to enter or leave without permission. Born in Paraguay of Spanish and Portuguese descent, Francia hated foreigners, especially pure-blood expatriate Spaniards, the property-owning establishment. Many were gaoled, murdered or exiled. In 1814 he introduced an edict, in force for 26 years, banning Spaniards from marrying among themselves, but only with *mestizos* (people of mixed Indian and Spanish blood), Indians or blacks. The ruling crippled the establishment and prevented them extending their control genetically. It was popular with the bulk of the population, assuring a genuine mingling of races.

But with isolation and absolute power, Francia's edicts became more grotesque: he ordered all dogs in the country to be killed; no subject was allowed to look at him as he passed in the street. He went in disguise among his people, listening for treachery. When he died in 1840, Paraguayans greeted strangers, just in case, with "*Viva el difunto!*" — Long live the deceased one!

From behind the curtain around their country they emerged, a relatively prosperous people with a fierce sense of their distinctiveness, though accustomed to a tradition of absolute autocracy. They were becoming a predominantly *mestizo* race, more homogeneous and darker-skinned than in the other southern countries of the continent. The Indians had effectively absorbed the Spanish and almost everyone could speak Guaraní.

Asunción in the 1890s. This image of a prosperous, substantial city was used to attract recruits from Australia. (*University of Sydney Library*)

Today Paraguay is an officially bilingual nation and Dr Francia is revered as a great patriotic hero. Even his severest critics, in assessing him, concede that he was a man of total honesty and frugality, utterly incorruptible, and that he sincerely loved the nation he oppressed. He had qualities which found a minor echo in another austere fanatic who became *supremo* of a tiny commonwealth within the nation's borders, William Lane.

From the chaos that followed Francia's death a new leader emerged, Carlos Antonio López, a landowner and, like most of his people, a *mestizo*. He initiated and won approval for a republican constitution and was nominated as the first president. Unlike his predecessor, López amassed a vast fortune during his period in power, the visual metaphor for which was his prodigious girth. Richard Burton described him as "hideous, burly and thick-set ... With chops flying over his cravat, his face wears, like the late George IV, a porcine appearance". He silenced critics, but without the savagery of Francia, and is remembered as a relatively enlightened despot. He revived relations with the Vatican, opened up the country to trade, established a school system, built roads, churches and a cathedral. And in 1843 his government was the first in the Americas to liberate slaves, passing a law that all slaves were automatically to become free on attaining their adulthood — in that way allowing a gradual transition to a new basis for the economy's labour force.

Foreigners with skills the nation needed — surgeons, engineers and mechanics — were invited to settle in Paraguay and the most useful proved to come from Britain.

Dr William Stewart, who had been among the reception committee for the Australians, was one who arrived. A veteran of the Crimean War, he'd gone to the Argentine province of Corrientes in charge of a boatload of British colonists. When the colony failed he visited Paraguay, impressed the president and his eldest son, and was given military rank and authority to organise a hospital service.

George Thompson, a railway engineer, was another and in 1858 his firm, Burrel, Valpy and Thompson, commenced work on Paraguay's Central Railroad. One of South America's first rail lines, it was serviced by British-made equipment, much of it Crimean War surplus.

William Whitehead, with whom I had discovered a family connection, was a key recruit. López commissioned him to construct an arsenal in Asunción which employed thirty English technicians and 300 local workers. An iron foundry and steam saw-mill were also set up and within three years the arsenal turned out seven steamers, which were first used as mail-boats from Asunción to Montevideo, and later armed for war. Sixty-eight pounders and other heavy artillery were cast for the batteries of Humaitá.

Paraguay had come out of its seclusion, but Goliath neighbours resented a young David brandishing a slingshot. To the south, Argentina still refused to recognise the country's independence. Brazil, a huge threatening presence to the north and east, had a continuing quarrel about access through the Río Paraguay to its territory of Mato Grosso, and disputed the definition of the border. Meanwhile, to the south-east, a chronic state of political turbulence existed in Uruguay. The possibility of war on any of three fronts could not be discounted; that it could happen on all fronts at once was too absurd to contemplate.

Carlos Antonio López made his eldest son a brigadier-general and commander-in-chief of the army. Francisco Solano López was just nineteen years old with a volatile temperament. (Mary Gilmore unearthed the obscure information that, after his birth, "he bit the nipple of the breast till it bled".) Francisco pushed for funds, gained with his father's reluctant approval, to build up the army. Soon it would become one of the largest, though still inadequately equipped, in South America, providing an intolerable irritant to neighbouring countries.

In 1853 Francisco went on a mission to Europe to buy armaments. An assertive young man of short stature, he had long found consolation by comparing himself to Napoleon Bonaparte. He studied his great battles, concentrating on the victories, without learning the lessons about tactical withdrawal contained in the defeats, and he luxuriated in dreams of empire. Now he had uniforms made like those the Corsican had worn, and donned a tricorne hat. He was going to Paris, the fountainhead for his obsession, to astonish the Europeans with a vision of Bonaparte reborn. As he sailed down the river away from his country, its almost total destruction lurched closer.

*

My taxi puttered along Asunción's main thoroughfare — Avenida Mariscal Francisco Solano López — past decaying stone mansions with pillared porticoes — neo-Gothic, neo-Palladian and, a millionaire's replica of Tara, neo-*Gone with the Wind*. It was 2 o'clock in the morning and they were all in darkness, except for the floodlit bunker of the American embassy, located with apple-pie cutesiness at 1776. We turned in to Calle Leandro

Prieto and, opposite the little chapel of Santa Rosa de Lima, pulled up at a place I knew well, the home of Florence and Max White. A whitewashed villa with a pantiled roof, it was as I remembered it four years before, bougainvillea rambling over the wrought-iron grille work, a riot of palms, jasmine and flowering plants in the garden, a blue kidney-shaped swimming pool, half-empty then, half-empty still.

Florence answered the door in her nightdress. A redhead with warm brown eyes and an excitable, effervescent manner, fiercely Paraguayan, her grandfather was William Wood, secretary of the General Labourers' Union at Bourke. She was exhausted by her organising for the celebration at the Municipal Theatre which would begin in a few hours time. The date, October 30, though a month after the colonists actually arrived a century earlier, was the only time that the Australian ambassador based in Buenos Aires could attend. She fretted about whether he would turn up with the plaque as he'd promised, and if the Mayor of Asunción would be there.

Her husband Max emerged sleepily in a blue velour dressing-gown and poured a Smirnoff vodka at the carved mock-Spanish bar. A large shambling man with a mid-West drawl from St Louis, Missouri, he was a former cartographer with the United States Airforce and NASA and did the tracking orbit for Skylab. On my earlier visit he had told me, "I did my computer projection and a colleague did his and when we put them over one another there was hardly any difference. All the same we drew a hairline between them and presented that as the orbit, so that if the thing crashed, well hell, no single one of us could be blamed!" He had laughed wheezily. Max was still enjoying the way his pension stretched by retiring to Asunción: "We can get this house and a pool and a maid for the same money that'd get us a closet back in the States. Johnny Walker whisky's four dollars a bottle, American cigarettes are thirty-five cents a pack, because they're all contraband, everything runs on contraband here. And shoot! I like the damn weather!"

I had stayed with them on a visit to Asunción in 1989 and they had been wonderfully kind to me. As the daughter of Bill Wood, the last patriarch of Cosme, Florence assumed something of the role of ambassador for the Australian descendants in Paraguay. With her cousin Rodrigo she was an organiser of this centenary event. "Now that our grandparents and parents have gone," she said, "it would be so easy to let it all slip away. We want to keep in touch with each other and for the next generation to understand their heritage."

*

In the sunny garden a tiny green hummingbird hovered, flittering and whirring, over a hibiscus shrub beside the swimming pool. As I finished the cup of breakfast coffee, wanting more, lots more, to feel human again, Florence clattered out in high heels, elegant in a beige crepe suit. "The taxi's here. We have to be at the theatre by 10."

Max had decided to pass. "Florence has some wonderful relatives and she loves them very much," he drawled, grinning. "But all of them together, yabbering on in Spanish and remembering their goddamn socialist origins or whatever the hell it was all about, no thank you."

The Municipal Theatre was a small, no-frills version of a Viennese opera house, built in 1863. With a domed roof and tiered galleries, it was on the corner of Presidente Franco and Alberdi streets, not far from the river. Over 100 people had gathered under its awning, embracing in the Paraguayan way, a kiss on each cheek, volubly exchanging news and gossip. Blondes, redheads and coppery *mestizos*, they were just a few of the possibly 2,000 people whose presence in South America could be sheeted back to the dream of one man, William Lane.

One of them, Sylvia McLeod de Wood, with a milk-coffee complexion, clear blue eyes and a halting command of English, had a pedigree like a *Mayflower* or First Fleet descendant. Her grandfather, Rod McLeod, a thirty-year-old labourer from Bourke in New South Wales, had arrived with Lane and the first batch on the *Royal Tar*.

Oscar Birks, one of the most successful businessmen in Paraguay, was there because his great-grandfather Alfred embarked on the *Tar's* second voyage from Adelaide, along with a brother and a cousin.

Santiago Butterworth, an accountant who did some cattle ranching on the side, was also descended from second batchers, Miles and Elizabeth Butterworth from Sydney.

Members of the big Wood clan were greeting each other, as turbulent and contradictory a family as any described by Gabriel García Márquez, all descended from William and Lillian Wood of Bourke.

Three children of León Cadogan made an appearance; their grand-mother, Rose Summerfield, had been a notable figure in the Australian union and women's suffrage movements.

A young doctor, Carlos Alberto McLeod, was from a different branch of the McLeod clan. His grandfather Allan, also from Bourke, had been a carpenter and at Cosme was in charge of building, sawing and wheelwrighting; he was remembered for playing the fiddle beautifully at the evening socials.

Two grandchildren were there to represent Edward Jacks, an Australian who'd married Minnie Richards, one of the single women recruited by Lane in England. The granddaughter, Lilita, ran a fashionable furnishings shop, Casa Inglesa.

There were other descendants of English recruits: the Apthorpes, grandchildren of Leonard who'd come to Cosme in 1900. "We love each other so much, we colonists," said the ebullient Lily Apthorpe, hugging everyone in reach, "we had a glorious childhood!"

The Kennedys were descendants of James Craig Kennedy from London, who settled at Nueva Australia in 1899 and ended up with a cattle empire.

There were the grandchildren and great-grandchildren of Alfred and Mary Davey, who came to Cosme in 1897. Originally from Liverpool, Alf had worked as a Queensland farmer and a miner in New Guinea, and married a Sydney girl, Mary Ann Rayner. Their daughter Elsie was, at eighty-one, the eldest colony descendant present. With a wicked grin, she looked around the mixed group of people, some of them very swarthy, and exclaimed, "See how we've married into the niggers!"

I puzzled about two young men, Carlos and Alfredo Stephens, as I couldn't trace their forebears in anything I'd read about New Australia or Cosme. Carlos laughed. "We're nothing to do with Australia. Our people were English and Italians and settled at another colony, Nueva Italia. But someone said that we should come. It's all the same, isn't it, Nueva Australia or Nueva Italia? We're all Paraguayan now."

Rodrigo Wood, a burly dark-skinned man wearing a large straw hat, looked like a cattle man; in fact, although he does have a ranch in the Chaco, he is a successful financier. He seemed very flustered; he just couldn't decide where to mount the bronze plaque. The theatre people had insisted it couldn't be attached to the wood-panelling of the foyer as they hoped one day to restore a beautiful old mural underneath. His cousin Patricio followed him about, arguing. They decided to fix it to the tiled wall under the awning outside, near a bus stop. Rod extracted a virtue from this: it would be good to draw the attention of commuters to the history of the Australians in Paraguay. I noticed that the arrival date was incorrect but, as it was cast in bronze, it seemed too late to mention it.

The Australian and Paraguayan flags were draped across the plaque as the Australian Ambassador, Hugh Wyndham, discussed the order of procedure with Rod. A reporter from the Australian Broadcasting Corporation set up lights to videotape the event. I took time out to peer inside the theatre, at the three tiers of fretwork balconies, the red plush chairs and velvet curtains. Florence's father Bill Wood had brought me there eleven years before and explained how he'd done a repair job on the domed wooden ceiling. The place smelled musty. Primary schoolchildren in bright red and yellow costumes were rehearsing for a school concert, chanting while skipping in a disorderly attempt at unison across the stage.

*

When the young Francisco Solano López brought *la concubina irlandesa*, his Irish mistress Madame Lynch, to the theatre in his home town, she provided much the best show, to the fury of the president and the López ladies. Hector Varela, a shrewd eyewitness and one of Richard Burton's companions on the river steamer *Yí*, left an account:

> The high society of Asunción attended. In the box of honour, the broad-faced and corpulent dictator sat with his equally corpulent wife and two obese daughters decked out like Bavarian Eggs. In the next box sat General Francisco López and Baron Von Wisner; but seated in the centre box, gorgeously dressed and displaying many jewels, was Madame Eliza Lynch ... more resplendent and enticing than I have ever seen her. The gentlemen in the audience all watched her with definitely respectful admiration. The ladies gave her hostile looks, the meaning of which was perfectly clear.

Thirty years later, in September 1893, the Australian women and children were camping in the theatre, bedding down on the plush seats. The government had assigned a company of soldiers to cook and look after them. One of the young women wrote back to a friend in Balmain: "The Spaniards used to bring us eggs, oranges, meat, vegetables and water and would not hear of payment ... Some of the boys used to hand us in oranges and cigarettes through the gates and the soldiers would peel them for us with their swords. They would tell us we were very pretty..."

The men camped outside. "We slept in the open in the Paraguayan capital," wrote James Molesworth, "an object of surprise to the white-robed women, hatless and bootless, but all smoking huge cigars. Naked youngsters played among the Gwaranee gutters in the refuse. The Paraguayan male smoked and drank — while his woman worked."

But the colonists were surprised, given the tales of heroism and horror they'd heard about the War of the Triple Alliance, never to see a cripple.

Mary Gilmore later wrote that Dr William Stewart, surgeon-general to "that would-be Napoleon of the New World, Lopez II", had exercised a policy during the war of allowing medical aid only to the very slightly wounded. "The others — what was the use? Even if they survived operations there was nothing to keep them alive on. That is why one never sees either the one-armed or the one-legged in Paraguay."

Around every corner the city presented scenes both fascinating and alarming in their difference to anything the Australians had known, though the rutted and poorly paved roads were familiar enough. "They are in a disgraceful state," reported John Rich, "and want attending to, as we used to say in Tasmania." Horse-drawn trams and bullock wagons threw up dust which filtered in a haze around the orange trees on the pavements, the street vendors in their loose chemises, the señoritas half-veiled by lace mantillas, the barefooted soldiers carrying swords and muskets and the fashionable young men lounging in the shade and showing off their lacquered boots. "An old woman, seated on the skull of a bullock, sucked an orange ... A toucan, a species of huge parrot, fought a dog for possession of a bone, and a group of Chaco Indian women, who had been marketing in the town, were preparing to return to their forests."

Today Asunción retains an atmosphere of nineteenth-century indolent charm, despite its clump of glass and steel skyscrapers, many unoccupied and rumoured to belong to the Stroessner family. Women with baskets of bread or fruit on their heads climb the hilly streets, some still paved with cobblestones, which slope up from the two fanciful palaces, presidential and legislative, the cathedral, the docks and the wide curve of the Paraguay River. Bright yellow Belgian tramcars rattle along beside lumbering buses. Though sickening now with the petrol fumes, orange trees still line some sidewalks. In a leafy square, under jacarandas and poincianas, Indians selling feathered arrows, and elderly photographers with hooded box cameras on tripods, wait for the rare tourist.

A curious Saturday shopping crowd, passing the Municipal Theatre, glanced at the group of over 100 people gathered under the awning. If it was known they were Australian descendants this would have been of no great interest, for Paraguay is a country of immigrants — Germans, Russians, Mennonites from Canada and, in recent years, Koreans, Taiwanese and Japanese. But a number of soldiers going by — the army is still the biggest employer in Paraguay — scrutinised the girls, particularly the blondes and redheads, colouring unusual enough to be worth another look.

Juan Carlos Wasmosy, the first democratically elected civilian president in the country's history, had been invited but declined. The Mayor of Asunción didn't show. But Woods and McLeods, Cadogans and Butterworths, Daveys, Birks, Kennedys and the Italian Stephens brothers, listened attentively as Ambassador Wyndham addressed them in Spanish. He said that the celebration fortified links between Australia and Paraguay; that 100 years before, Paraguay hadn't been what it was today, that the country had changed, but what hadn't changed was the search for ideals and justice. (This seemed a masterly piece of diplomatic understatement. The brutal dictatorship of President Stroessner had ended just four years before.)

Descendants applauded as the ambassador and the director of the theatre, José Luis Ardissone, pulled back draped flags to reveal the plaque with its Spanish inscription:

23 August 1883 — 23 August 1993
To commemorate the centenary of the arrival of a large contingent of Australians to settle in this country, their descendants wish to honour and record their arrival at this theatre which served as their first refuge. In a quest for a more just society they crossed oceans and confronted many difficulties.
Signed by the Municipal Mayor of Asunción, Dr Carlos Filizzola
and the Ambassador to Paraguay, Mr Hugh Wyndham.

As the colonists actually arrived on 22 September 1893, the plaque, cast by a firm in Melbourne, was out by one day, one month and a whole decade. But errors set in bronze have a way of becoming history.

The party then repaired to the ballroom of the Gran Hotel del Paraguay for lunch and more speeches. This rambling building, set in a lush tropical garden on the suburban outskirts of the city, was formerly the mansion of Madame Lynch, the mistress of the dictator Solano López. In many ways it was a suitable venue. The welcome the Australians received in 1893 was so generous because the legacy of López had been so disastrous. The country was a graveyard.

*

In 1853, when the young López arrived in Paris expecting recognition as a man of destiny, he proved instead to be a minor object of derision, worth a titter over champagne, coming from a country remote and obscure enough to sound like a fanciful invention. With his retinue of forty, his lavish purchase of favours and, most of all, his absurd uniforms, a travesty of Bonaparte's but embellished with lace and feathers and enormous silver spurs, he was mocked as "the man from Paraguay" and "this half-civilized monkey in the mountebank attire".

But he had a fat purse and ships to buy, so at last a private interview with Emperor Louis Napoleon III was actually arranged. But López was not impressed with this bored and exhausted nephew of his hero and was astute enough to know when he was being patronised. He bought his ships in England instead, although Queen Victoria said she was "quite too busy to see the little savage". He brooded privately about the day when he would prove to the world what a great military commander he was. Meanwhile he took from Paris a beautiful young Irish courtesan, Eliza Alicia Lynch.

Eliza was just eighteen years old at the time and every report, even by her many enemies, describes her as exquisitely lovely with fine skin, blue eyes and abundant golden hair. Since she was fifteen she had survived on the fringes of the upper class by that beauty and her considerable intelligence, and had acquired fluent French, Spanish, social polish and accomplishments. But times had become difficult. She had a Russian protector who had become untenable with France involved in the Crimean War and she needed a new one. The "man from Paraguay" was unstinting in his indulgence, crudely sexual in a way that intrigued her after the effete courtiers she'd known, and he whispered in her ear that she might be an empress one day.

When Francisco and Eliza arrived in Asunción by riverboat she was pregnant, and was promptly ostracised by the old president and his family, the diplomatic corps and what passed for high society in the capital. She had more innate refinement than most, but was dismissed as a whore from the Paris slums. The French ambassador insisted on the Irish slums and pronounced he would "as soon break bread with a nigger as accept a morsel from that devious Irish slut".

Her lover, the heir apparent, has been almost universally described as squat, ugly and uncouth. The British adventurer, R. B. Cunninghame Graham, compiled a list of his qualities: "Sadism, an inverted patriotism, colossal ignorance of the outside world, a megalomania pushed almost to insanity, a total disregard of human life or human dignity ... an abject cowardice that in any other country in the world but Paraguay would have rendered him ridiculous."

However, the English engineer Thompson, who knew him personally, was prepared to concede: "He is, when he likes, very smooth and gentlemanly, and capable of imposing even on diplomats, and making them believe anything he wishes." As events unfolded Thompson was to describe him as "a monster without parallel".

Eliza was installed in a mansion in town and also given a country house, now the Gran Hotel del Paraguay. With the national coffers footing the bill, she established such elegance of style that she became a favourite of the Buenos Aires newspapers, which reported, "Many of Madame Lynch's brasses and porcelains are museum pieces and the French tapestries and Oriental rugs are distributed with excellent taste and in a manner to delight the eye".

Meanwhile Solano López assumed more control of government as his father became increasingly corpulent and fatigued, and he embarked on an ambitious program of public building, extended the arsenal and dramatically increased Paraguay's defence forces.

As word spread of the lively discussions at Madame Lynch's *salon* evenings, the fine entertainment at her *musicales* with chamber groups imported from Europe, plus her position as "The Favourite" of the heir-apparent and the mother of his children, the calling cards arrived in sheaves. But not from the First Families of Asunción. Eliza was desperate to win them over and thought dispensing culture might do the trick. She invited Monsieur de Cluny from Paris to open a French Academy, which proved so under-attended that he soon departed. Two ageing French ladies, the Mesdames Dupart and Balet, came to run a finishing school for young ladies. The First Families replied, in effect, that they weren't entrusting their daughters to a couple of Paris tarts and the Mesdames fled.

At last an occasion arose which Eliza hoped would establish her position in society. A group of French agriculturalists were forming a colony not far from Asunción. All the high-ranking Paraguayans and the diplomatic corps were invited to the opening ceremony, and Eliza persuaded López to make her the official hostess. The men were to travel to the settlement by horseback and coach, their wives to follow by river steamer. As the society ladies, led by the French ambassador's wife, Madame Laurent-Cochelet, came up the gangplank, Eliza waited, smiling graciously, to receive them. Every one of them walked right past her without acknowledgement, and joined in animated groups on the deck as the boat sailed out into the river. They continued to ignore her as platoons of liveried servants laid out a magnificent banquet lunch. The ladies crowded around the hams, roast turkeys and suckling pigs, apparently so oblivious of the existence of their hostess that they prevented her from even getting near the table. Eliza smiled, then quietly, but in a way that didn't brook argument, ordered the waiters to throw everything overboard. The ladies gasped and stared as all the food and wine and even the Limoges china went into the river.

According to a number of sources, both hostile and in favour of her, Eliza then instructed the captain to anchor midstream until further orders and returned to her isolated chair. She calmly stared at and through her hungry, perspiring and near-apoplectic guests. "By ignoring Madame Lynch from the moment they boarded the ship," a biographer observed, "the Ladies had made their point. By the time the captain received permission to weigh anchor and return to Asunción — *ten hours later* — Madame Lynch had made hers."

Everything changed in 1862 when, on the death of his father, Francisco Solano López succeeded as head of state. Eliza threw a masked ball to celebrate his election to the presidency. Even the furious First Families knew it was wise to attend and, what was worse, were instructed what to wear. The American envoy in Asunción, Charles Washburn, left an account: "At this fancy ball she prescribed the dress for all — assigning the garb of a Swiss shepherdess for one, an Italian fruit seller for another, and prescribing for each some peculiar style of costume." With wicked glee, Eliza asked the lumpish López sisters to come as "Guaraní Indian maidens", and Madame Laurent-Cochelet, the leader of the opposition against her, to be Queen Victoria, not a role that gave much scope for glamour. Eliza herself, in billowing skirts and fluted collar, a crown on her golden hair, was arrayed "in the gorgeous style of Queen Elizabeth". Francisco Solano López came, naturally, as Napoleon Bonaparte "on the day of his coronation as Emperor of the French".

In Buenos Aires, Richard Burton claimed to have actually seen a plaster model of Napoleon's crown, commissioned by López and sent out by a Parisian house. It had been embargoed by the Argentine Government, together with furniture ordered by the Marshal-President. "The furniture, destined for one room and worth about £400, consisted of fine solid curtain hangings, showy chairs, white, red and gold, and tinsel chandeliers with common cut glass and white paint showing under the gilding. It bore the arms of the Republic, but it was evidently copied from the Tuileries. A hard fate caused it to be sold by auction at Buenos Aires."

All too soon any humour was to disappear from the story of Solano López and Eliza Lynch. The numerous histories, biographies and popular accounts of their relationship and the course of the War of the Triple

President José Gaspar Rodríguez de Francia, 1814–40

President Carlos Antonio López, 1844–62

President Francisco Solano López, 1862–70

Madame Eliza Alicia Lynch in middle age

Alliance tend to polarise dramatically. One school, predominantly Western historians, relying heavily on the memoirs of disaffected Britons and Americans resident in Paraguay during the war, present a view of López as a cruel and vicious megalomaniac whose mammoth ego and increasing insanity led his people to almost total annihilation, and of Lynch as his conniving, ruthless doxy who made off with what was left of the nation's treasures. But Burton warned: "Interested motives had spread evil report against Marshal-President López, and with few exceptions the press of Europe was so well packed that even Our Own Correspondent, the Consul of Rosario, was not permitted to print a line in favour of Paraguay."

The opposing school of thought, increasingly resurgent in the country today, sees Solano López as a great national hero and military strategist who defended Paraguay against impossible odds and engendered in his people such devotion to the Fatherland and himself as its leader that they fought almost to the last man. A leading Paraguayan writer feverishly declared that "a whole Race was incarnate in him, a youthful, artistic and courageous Race, who knew how to snatch from the claws of death the secret of Immortality". Madame Lynch, according to this view, was a consort who matched him in bravery and passion for her adopted country, who fought by his side when she could have fled back to Europe, who after his death was left penniless, duped out of any rightful inheritance, and was buried in Paris in a pauper's grave until reclaimed by the country she loved.

An unsavoury supporter for the latter view was Generalissimo Alfredo Stroessner who, until his ousting in 1989, no doubt had a particular interest in rehabilitating perceptions of bloody dictators. But a number of moderate historians in Paraguay today continue to see the West's view of López as yet another example of racism and scholarly imperialism. The safest route perhaps, like Max White and his colleague's tracking orbit for Skylab, is a hairline course between the two.

Though the origins and course of the War of the Triple Alliance were complex, its outcome was devastatingly stark.

Solano López saw himself as a statesman among the powers of South America, perhaps destined to assume an imperial role. He perceived his greatest rival as the only emperor on the continent, Dom Pedro II of Brazil, the grandson of John VI of Portugal who had fled from Europe during the Napoleonic Wars. Dom Pedro controlled the second largest empire in the world with a population of 10 million and an impressive fleet of

President Francisco Solano López and his increasingly irrelevant Cabinet

warships. The men enrolled in his National Guard outnumbered the entire population of Paraguay.

In 1864 Paraguay had just over half a million people and only nine fighting ships, some of them adapted ferryboats with only one gun, but in that year it was a mouse that roared. What Marshall López, to use his self-bestowed title, did have, after years of building it up, was an unevenly developed military infrastructure and a standing army of 64,000; by pulling in reserves of boys and old men it increased to 100,000, though with an inadequate and untrained officer corps. Paraguay's fighting strength was still remarkable in relation to its population (in the same year, Argentina had an army of only 6,000 and, after the war began, President Mitre had difficulty raising another 20,000 men). López could possibly have triumphed against one adversary; that he resisted so long against three was astonishing.

When Brazil made an armed intervention into Uruguay, he responded, claiming he was defending a sovereign neighbour, and seized a Brazilian ship making its way up the Río Paraguay to its territory of Mato Grosso. He then, disastrously, alienated Brazil's traditional rival, Argentina, by encroaching on its borders. On 1 May 1865 Argentina, Brazil and the by then puppet state of Uruguay formed a Triple Alliance. The Allies' combined troops convincingly outnumbered Paraguay's in men and fire-power. They were going to share the mouse between them for dinner.

The war was confidently predicted to be over in a few months but lasted

five horrific years, the bloodiest war in the history of Latin America, until
the mouse was squashed flat. The Paraguayans fought with almost unbe-
lievable bravery to defend their homeland. They had a strong sense of who
they were, a proud and homogeneous people who had long been isolated
from the world, while the majority of Brazilian soldiers were black slaves
pressed into the war. The Allies were divided, factionalised and generally
handicapped in having to transport their armies and supplies long distances upriver. They also made the initial mistake of viewing Paraguay's
fighting force with contempt.

Captain Richard Burton did not make that mistake: "It is a fatal war
waged by hundreds against thousands; a battle of Brown Bess and poor
old flint muskets against Spencer and Enfield rifles; of honeycombed
carronades, long and short, against Whitworths and Lahittes; of punts and
canoes against ironclads. It brings before us an anthropological type
which, like the English of a past generation, holds every Paraguayan
boy-man equal, single-handed, to at least any half-dozen of his enemies."

For three years the Allies were held off at Paraguay's gateway, the
riverside fortress of Humaitá. For most of that heroic stand Eliza Lynch
was there with López, under constant bombardment, separated from her
children, wearing the uniform of a colonel, organising the women behind
the lines and overseeing the hospitalisation of the wounded. But in the
end the odds against the Paraguayans were overwhelming, including being
led by a president who seemed, by any definition, increasingly deranged.

He made stupendous blunders. At the battle of Tuyutí almost three
quarters of the Paraguayan force of 20,000 were casualties. An Englishman
on Lopez's staff wrote: "That battle ... may be said to have annihilated
the Spanish race in Paraguay. In the front ranks were the males of all the
best families in the country, and they were killed almost to a man;
hundreds of families, in the capital especially, had not a husband, father,
son or brother left." The Allies heaped the corpses, painfully thin from
the years of deprivation, in piles of hundreds to burn them. "They
complained that the Paraguayans were so lean that they would not burn."
The corpses that were left were picked over by the wild dogs, the *perros
cimarrones*.

However, on rare occasions, López showed military strategy worthy of
a Bonaparte. According to Burton, at one devastating battle at Curupaiti,
the Allies lost 5,000 troops and the Paraguayans only 54. But this victory
only prolonged the war. López had insufficient forces to press on and rout

the enemy but was too inflated with Napoleonic grandiosity to consider the offered peace negotiations.

As the course of the war turned against him, he blamed his officers with a desperado's ruthlessness. The motto for his troops was *Vencer o morir* — Conquer or die. López was said to have supervised the executions of any commanders who emerged from defeat, as well as hundreds of his countrymen suspected of passing information to the enemy, including two of his own brothers. But, writing while the war was still proceeding, Richard Burton suggested that as regards the "atrocities of López", his reported ordering of tortures, floggings, shootings and bayonetings, "the reader will, I venture to assert, do well to exercise a certain reservation of judgment, like myself ... The fact is that nothing about Paraguay is known outside the country, and of its government very little is known even inside its limits. The foreign employees themselves must generally speak from hearsay, and some of them have not failed to supplement their facts by fancies, theories and fictions."

As López's soldiers fell in their thousands, old men and young boys joined the battle, children fighting beside their grandfathers. A Boys' Regiment, aged from eleven to fourteen, struggled in a hopeless rearguard action at the battle of Acostá-Nú. All were massacred.

Fear was not the only motivation for the Paraguayans, but some fanatical almost mystical love of their country and their leader. In attempting to explain the phenomenon, a new Minister of the United States to Paraguay, General Martin T. McMahon reported to the US House Foreign Affairs Committee: "There certainly exists among the people — and I think among quite a majority of them — a most devoted attachment to López. It is a devotion that surpasses anything that I have ever witnessed before."

Then the women of Paraguay took to arms as a fighting force. Although the story is almost certainly ludicrous of Eliza Lynch, in breeches and cape, leading a cavalry charge of women against the enemy, one of her harshest critics, writing a virulently biased account of the war, still wondered why she remained at her lover's side. "López's determination was, according to all laws of reason, inexplicable; Madame Lynch's decision to be part and parcel of her Friend's lunacy is incomprehensible. Why did she not surrender with her sons to the oncoming Brazilians, instead of fleeing with the remnants of López's government every time a capital was about to be overrun? Was it, as some of her defenders maintain, a sense of loyalty towards López that precluded her abandoning him? Was it López's refusal

A Paraguayan soldier during the War of the Triple Alliance, 1865–1870 (*University of Sydney Library*)

to let her go? ... Is it even possible that her pride would not permit her to admit defeat?"

At last, on 5 January 1869, Asunción fell and the Allies declared victory. López and Madame Lynch pushed north, 500 kilometres through the jungle. Hundreds of Paraguayans, weakened and starving, the wounded "hobbling ... their bandages caked in mud", followed to continue the fight, although there was now nothing to compel them to do so and everything to dissuade them. Richard Burton was again in Paraguay, reporting on the war, when it moved into this third and final phase: "Marshal-President López, safely sheltered by the mountains, determines upon a guerrilla warfare, and collects for that purpose the last of the doomed Paraguayan race."

On 1 March 1870, beside the Aquidaban River near Cerro Corá, still refusing to surrender, Francisco Solano López was lanced to death by a Brazilian cavalryman. It is eyewitness record from the Brazilian side, rather than the folk legend it would seem, that Madame Lynch dug a grave for her lover, and their son who had fallen beside him, with her bare hands.

"*Muero con mi patria!*" — I die with my country! — López was reputed to have cried as he fell, which turned out to be true enough. The figures are almost too extraordinary to comprehend, no doubt the most devastating slaughter of a people in modern history. Paraguay had a population of 525,000 before the war. In a census taken by the victors in 1871 it had been reduced to 221,079 of whom 106,254 were women, 86,079 children and just 28,746 were men. In other words, Paraguay had lost approximately 90 per cent of its manhood and those who were left were mostly the old, the disabled and young boys. Burton felt that "seldom has aught more impressive been presented to the gaze of the world than this tragedy; this unflinching struggle maintained for so long a period against overwhelming odds, and to the very verge of racial annihilation".

It was "a time of misery such as few nations have ever witnessed", wrote Mary Gilmore, who became obsessed by stories of the war, "when women and children flocked in thousands to Asunción, begging for food, and fell by the way till the roadsides were lined with the bodies of the dead and the dying, and Asunción itself had become a plague spot more awful than any battle field". For at least two generations, the women of Paraguay resigned themselves to be the labourers and share the few men in a polygamous society, while the Church looked the other way.

"The peace that came to Paraguay," the historian Hubert Herring has said, "was the peace of a windswept graveyard: the women were widows;

the children were orphans; the men were old and mutilated. Promiscuity was general; the Brazilian soldiers who occupied the land until 1876 fathered a new generation of Paraguayans. The country was broken and defenseless..." Argentina and Brazil levied huge war indemnities which the crippled nation was quite unable to pay and annexed 142,500 square kilometres of its territory. Few educated Paraguayans survived the war and few technicians. A tradition of textile-making was lost and deranged people wandered half-naked. With the able-bodied men gone, starving women and children struggled to cultivate the land or lived off roots, berries and the one abundant resource, wild oranges. The jaguars, having acquired a taste for human flesh from the corpses of the slain, came out of the forests looking for more.

The tragedy was expressed in a famous poem, "Nenia". It is the lament of a native girl who grieves, like the near-extinct *urutaú* bird calling plaintively in the forests. She has lost parents, brothers and sisters in the terrible war:

Llora, llora, urutaú,
en las ramas del yatay;
ya no existe el Paraguay,
donde nací como tú.
Llora, llora, urutaú.
Weep, weep *urutaú* bird,
in the branches of the *yatay* tree;
no more is there a Paraguay,
where I was born, like you.
Weep, weep, *urutaú.*

*

It was just over twenty years after that crushing defeat that William Lane's prospecting party arrived, asking the Paraguay government if there would be any interest in a large group of settlers, experienced in working the land, who, at the beginning at least, would mostly be single men!

Such immigrations had been forecast by George Masterman, an English apothecary formerly employed by López, who escaped to the Brazilian side at the end of the war:

The Paraguayans exist no longer — there is a gap in the family of nations; but the story of their sufferings and of their heroism should not perish with them. For myself, I think of them with regret and sorrow ... Their gaiety, their politeness, their unaffected kindness and charity to each other, when no shadow of the Government was upon them, their obedience to superiors, shown so strangely in the cruelties they suffered and inflicted, their love of home and country, their courage and endurance, made them most estimable to me. The sturdy German and the Anglo-Saxon will soon fill the void this war of extermination has made; permanent prosperity will banish all trace of its devastations. It is well that it should be so...

When the first group of Australian colonists arrived in 1893 it was only eight years since Madame Eliza Lynch's last hopeless visit to South America, her final attempt to gain restitution for what she insisted·was her rightful legacy under López's will. She claimed that 220,000 gold pesos, his provision for her and her sons, had been taken out of the country by López's trusted physician, Dr William Stewart. The American envoy, General McMahon, made a deposition that he had witnessed the will.

However, the whole issue is murky. Some sources claim that Eliza Lynch, in the time-honoured tradition of dictators' wives and mistresses, had long before smuggled out of the country as much wealth as she could lay her hands on, and still managed to carry a casket of jewellery with her as she fled. There were also imputations, but unaccompanied by any evidence, that General McMahon may have deducted a handsome commission for his support.

Whatever the truth of it, Eliza was either outraged and needy enough or, alternatively, greedy enough, to have taken the trouble to sue Dr Stewart through the Scottish courts for over a year. Under oath the doctor denied any knowledge or obligation but when Madame Lynch, astonishingly, considering how rapidly she'd been bundled out of Paraguay, was able to produce a receipt, he was forced to admit that it was in his handwriting. ("The defender undertook to transmit the said specie to this country, to lodge the proceeds thereof in the Royal Bank of Scotland in his own name, and to hold the same for behoof, and on account of the pursuer, until the amount should be restored to her.") The verdict in Edinburgh went against Dr Stewart, but he declared himself unable to pay and filed for bankruptcy.

In 1875 Madame Lynch returned to Asunción to re-open her claim, but was allowed to stay only three hours before being deported under armed guard. In 1885 she made another attempt but received word in Buenos Aires that she was forbidden to enter Paraguay. Her enemies were in power. Dr Venancio López, the Foreign Minister, was no friend to the memory of his uncle, who had ordered his own father's execution.

Dr Stewart had returned to settle in Paraguay as the honorary British consul and had curiously recovered from his insolvency enough to be one of the most fabulously wealthy men in the country. He was the same Dr Stewart who was with the reception committee to welcome the Australians when they arrived on the *Pollux*.

The Australian settlers, most of them single men, had received such a handsome welcome from the government of Paraguay because they were expected to provide fresh bloodstock.

The Government was unaware that one of the pledges all intending colonists had been obliged to sign was observance of The Colour Line. Membership was forbidden to "any person of colour, including any married to persons of colour". There was to be no racial fraternising. Paraguay was nearly 80 per cent women, of a beauty and seductiveness attested to by many observers, and the Australian colony was 80 per cent red-blooded bachelors. For a certain breed of adventurer, well-heeled young men like Knight, a visit to The Land of Women was a chance to combine their wanderlust with the other kind, the nineteenth-century equivalent of a sex tour. The Australian men were soon to find this was all testing the faith rather too sternly. But they were unable to drown their frustrations in grog; they had also signed the pledge to teetotalism.

*

In October 1993 in the old ballroom of the Gran Hotel del Paraguay where Madame Lynch and Solano López had once demonstrated the waltz, the minuet and the polka, accompanied by an orchestra imported from Paris, a painted scroll among the flowers and fruit entwined on the frescoed ceiling warned *In Vino Veritas*. The colony descendants, a handsome group of people, most of mixed Paraguayan blood, were enjoying culinary delicacies washed down with good Argentine wine.

As they took turns to address the gathering it was clear that, unlike their parents and grandparents, they had little confusion about their identity. They were Paraguayan and proud of it — but most spoke of wanting to consolidate an Australian heritage before it disappeared.

Rodrigo Wood said he felt strongly the spirits of their ancestors around them, and he thought they had come together to repay a debt of honour.

"I think that company of people," said Carlos Jacks, "like most socialists, had more good intentions, poetry and dreams than they had clear plans or understanding of human reality. But anyway, here we are after a hundred years."

Dr Carlos Alberto McLeod confessed he was too overcome with emotion to speak.

President of the largest travel company in Paraguay, Oscar Birks, marvelled at the tremendous journey his Australian forebears had made in search of an ideal, but added that he was glad that communism was now failing world-wide. Peter Kennedy, a millionaire cattle rancher, agreed. But Enrique Wood, a veterinarian and dealer in livestock, said he greatly admired the solidarity and support the Australians had given each other. He was proud to come from that socialist tradition and he still considered himself a socialist.

Florence Wood de White encouraged all those present to join the new Australian-Paraguayan association. Lilita Jacks reminded them that many English recruits came to the Australian colonies too, and she hoped they would not be forgotten. "I absorb much from the influence of the English, who love animals, their homes and the chimney in winter."

Julie Cadogan de Cáceres and Roger Cadogan spoke about the work of their father, the late León Cadogan. Born at New Australia, he became an internationally recognised authority on Indian groups in Paraguay and did pioneering studies on their languages and culture. In defending the rights of the Indians, Cadogan clashed many times with the repressive Stroessner government. "He was concerned," said Julie, "with what we should all be concerned with here today: the liberty of the human being."

In a country long oppressed by dictatorships, the descendants believed they had entered a new era of democracy and prosperity. Few of them had any thought of emigrating to the land of their forebears. But one couple in the ballroom, Patricio and Mercedes Wood, had travelled from Australia to take part in the event. Patricio, born at Cosme, was a successful builder on Queensland's Sunshine Coast but expressed a yearning to come back for his retirement years. He said, "Australia has become a home and there are so many facilities to make life easy. But Cosme, the land where I was born, that's my roots, my real home. The spiritual things are here in Paraguay. So now us true blue Aussies are coming back to live." His Paraguayan wife Mercedes seemed unconvinced.

After lunch many people in the group, including most of the Wood family, drove in convoy to a large house in a leafy suburb to continue the party. Rodrigo Wood, with a crowd squashed into his Mitsubishi Landcruiser, changed the cassette on the tape deck to Slim Dusty. He bellowed along with it as we roared through the streets:

It's lonesome away from your kindred and all,
By the campfire at night, where the wild dingoes call;
But there's nothing so lonesome, morbid or drear,
Than to sit in the bar of a pub with no beer ...

On Avenida Aviadores del Chaco we passed a sprawling mansion set back among the trees and it was pointed out to me as the former home of Nata Legal, the mistress of President Alfredo Stroessner. He was arrested there, on one of his regular assignations, on 2 February 1989. A short distance further along the avenue, Slim Dusty still blaring at startled pedestrians, we accelerated past the huge white statue of a warrior woman, something of a hybrid between Boadicea and Joan of Arc. With one hand she protected a small child but with the other brandished a flag, straining onwards and upwards towards some obscure but clearly heroic destiny: Madame Eliza Alicia Lynch.

9
Into the Wilds

The World was all before them, where to choose
Their place of rest, and Providence their guide
They hand in hand with wand'ring steps and slow
Through Eden took their solitary way.
                    John Milton, *Paradise Lost*

At daybreak we got up, and set about our preparations for removing
as quickly as possible to the Promised Land ... where we intended
to take up our abode.
                    Johann David Wyss, *Swiss Family Robinson*

Florence Wood de White and I walked across the Plaza de los Héroes where soldiers from an elite cavalry corps were guarding the Pantheon, a miniature of Les Invalides in Paris where Napoleon's remains are interred. Francisco Solano López decreed it as a tomb for himself and, as an afterthought, for his father and a few other Paraguayan heroes to make it look respectable. A small urn may or may not contain what was left of the gaunt and gloomy Dr Francia. It is said that his bones were dug up and hurled into the river by an angry mob.

Madame Eliza Lynch is not there among the exalted dead but, in 1961, another who appointed himself one of the nation's *supremos* found a place for her. President Alfredo Stroessner had her remains exhumed and brought back from Paris, according to one story accompanied by "four kilos of pure Lebanese hashish".

On the morning of 25 July 1961, declared a Day of National Homage, the crowds gathered at the Asunción docks. An urn containing what was left of Madame Lynch, "our national heroine, our national martyr", was carried off a gunboat. President Stroessner, in all his medals and peaked aviator's cap, was chief pallbearer in the procession to the Pantheon. To please the crowds she was ceremonially placed beside the matching urn of her lover — but, as their union had not been sanctified by the Church, was forbidden to remain there, ending up instead in a hastily organised and threadbare Madame Lynch Museum.

Nine years later, on 24 July 1970, Paraguayans had another day of national celebration, this time for the centenary of their crushing defeat and near-extermination in the war, rewritten by patriot historians, as "a heroic epoch in our glorious history". A special mausoleum had been built for Madame Lynch at La Recoleta cemetery. A huge statue on the slab represented her clutching a cross, having just buried her consort.

President Stroessner, about to embark on his own regime's most fearsome stage of torture and repression, was reported to choke with emotion as he read out the tribute to "Elisa Alicia Lynch, who with Abnegation Accompanied the Greatest Hero of the Nation, Marshall Francisco Solano López, until his Immolation at Cerro Corá".

*

At school Florence Wood de White, like all young Paraguayans, had studied the War of the Triple Alliance. In a national history that featured few women except for the Blue Virgin of the Miracles of Caacupé, she'd particularly admired Madame Lynch and her independence of spirit. She herself had grown up too strong minded for most Paraguayan men. "I think that was the Australian side of me. I was very direct and men don't like that here. They want to be the ones who are in command and a woman has to be very gentle and docile and go along with what they say. I'm, on the contrary, very opinionated and strong-willed, and that's why I could never find a Paraguayan husband. I found boyfriends, but when they had to clash with my mind, it was a 'Goodbye' and that was it."

But once she had married Max, her American husband, she took the traditional form for her name — Florence Wood de White — though she knew that many feminists in Paraguay now objected to the "de" which seemed to assign them as a man's property. "I guess I'm a bit traditional as well."

We walked down towards the river, past the busy official money-changers and the furtive black-market touts, the shops where Koreans and Taiwanese sold electronic goods, the street vendors with racks of pirate cassettes, the perfume hawkers, shoe-shine boys and old women selling bundles of herbs for *mate tereré*. The Makká Indians were forlornly seeking out tourists, without much conviction holding out strings of beads, woven headbands and arrows trimmed with bright pink feathers. At the old picture palace, Cine Victoria, across the square from the Hotel Guaraní, the movies were *Solo Para Adultos* and allegedly steamy. "*Caliente!*" screamed the posters, "*Sexo Explícito!*"

Margaret Riley, arriving with her family a few months after the pioneers, thought the capital needed a good scrubbing:

> We didn't see much of Asunción at that time because we got in at night and they unloaded the ship and we got on the train in the morning. But I thought it was a very dirty city and the people didn't seem to be clean either; nothing seemed to be clean and my mother was very particular, so she didn't like that a bit. She said, "The sooner I get out of here the better".
>
> About 12 o'clock everything was shut down; the shops were shut and everybody would sit down and have their siesta. You'd see them propped up against door posts or against anything at all, their hats over their eyes, fast asleep. About 2 o'clock everything would come to life again. Oh, I thought they were lazy lot of people! They did nothing with the country! The men in particular were very lazy, they'd just saunter about all day and do nothing.

In the Plaza Uruguaya flamboyant trees and rose-pink *lapacho* were in bloom and men were sauntering about, or sitting in groups sipping *yerba mate,* refilling the communal gourds from thermoses. Only later in the day would the plaza become the beat of prostitutes. Ahead of us was the colonnaded railway station, with an intrusive sign sponsored by Esso advising us of this fact, in case the railway tracks emerging from the building and crossing a city street didn't make it obvious.

Across a narrow lane from the station was the Plaza Hotel. Apart from a new sign on its crumbling facade, it was as modest as the hotel in the 1890s where colonists were advised to stay: "If not met by a colony agent in Asunción they should go to the Hotel de Paris, near the railway station, where it has been arranged for Cosme folk to get reduced rates ... They should have nothing to do in Asunción with boatmen, carters or touts of any kind, who only swindle them."

I had wanted to travel by train to Villarrica, the way the early colonists did, but Florence displayed the town-dweller's contempt for the railway that I had noticed before in Buenos Aires. "Go by bus," she said, "*everyone* does. And the train to Villarrica leaves at night and gets in at 2 in the morning, so you wouldn't see anything." But she had agreed to come with me on the regular service to Areguá, which would take us some distance along the same route.

The railway station was completed in 1861, under the administration of Francisco's father, President Carlos Antonio López. Inside, pigeons fluttered in the shadowy gothic-arched cloisters and the vaulted roof was supported by ornate iron columns of British engineering. E. F. Knight thought it looked like a Grecian temple, and as old, judging from its wrecked appearance. It still had the feeling of a ghostly ruin. Few people turn up for the departure of the weekly Internacional bound for Buenos Aires and there seemed little information about when it departed and less about when it arrived.

By 1864, at the outbreak of the Triple Alliance War, the railroad constructed by Burrel, Valpy and Thompson had reached to the town of Paraguarí. During the war it was used by Marshall President López for an armoured train carrying a field gun. After the war it was sold to British interests and the line extended to the Argentine border. It was bought back by the Paraguay government in 1961 but some of the wood-burning locomotives still date from the earliest era and are an attraction for steam buffs from all over the world.

A number of tourists were clustered at one end of the platform, photographing the wood-burning engine of the train for Areguá. The driver standing on the plate, and his assistant shovelling logs from the skip behind the coal box, smiled perfunctorily. The enthusiasm of these *gringos* did not help their pay but maybe kept them in jobs. The fare for the 50 kilometres to Areguá was less than US$1. The locomotive was hooked up to just two carriages: first class, with torn upholstered seats, full of tourists, mainly German and Swiss, and second class, where for the same fare one could spread out with just four Paraguayans making the trip.

The advance party of Australian pioneers, the men going ahead to make a camp, arrived at the railway station on Friday evening, 22 September, the day they had landed in the capital. They were impressed with the station building, which one of them reported was "a handsomer one than Adelaide's, though not so large", but probably not with the hour of departure which was the same as Florence had warned me about. They arrived at Villarrica at 2 o'clock in the morning.

The whistle for our departure sounded at 12.15 pm and we were off, the driver working the hooter with buccaneer enthusiasm as we clattered across city streets on unguarded rails, holding up traffic. With nonchalant cool, some youths made a running leap aboard as we passed through the backyards of a shantytown. Little shacks of scrap-iron vibrated, laundry flapped on strings a metre from the train, but there was barely a flicker of interest from the woman scraping mandioca into a bowl, the toddlers playing in an open drain, the ducks, chickens and a skinny piglet foraging among the rank grass beside the tracks.

We left the town behind and came into more open country, villas with
large gardens and small farmlets. At a level crossing Florence pointed out
that the airport was half a kilometre away. Her sister Nelly had been a
stewardess with Braniff Airlines and Florence and her father used to come
out on the train to see her between flights. The guard would be worded
up in advance and at the level crossing the train would slow down so that
Bill Wood, sixty years old at the time and looking dashing in his panama
hat, could jump off, then catch young Florence.

The main party of Australians came this way in three groups on the
Saturday, Sunday and Monday after their arrival. Their trip was bumpy,
for the track was rough, almost unballasted, and the sleepers were often
removed by country people for firewood. The line was unfenced and
bullocks often strayed onto it and were run down. If the engine driver saw
a beast in time he would stop, blow his whistle loudly and the passengers
would get out and pelt stones to encourage it on its way.

Arthur Tozer reported to his brother that their train, going at express
speed, took nine hours to reach Villarrica. "This is quick for Paraguay
where everything is slow & in keeping with the easy going habits of the
people. The journey was pleasant & as wc wished to see all we could of
the country we did not find its slowness at all tedious. The country is really
beautiful …"

The pioneers gazed through the windows at the typical landscape of
eastern Paraguay: low rolling hills and the wide flat grasslands known as
campo, studded with small palm trees and watered by streams. Some of
the hills were covered with dense primeval forest which they soon learned
to call *monte*, the effect being of wooded islands in a sea of grass. They
would also have felt at home seeing some stands of eucalypts, for these
trees were not introduced to the country by the Australians, but were
planted during the regime of Carlos Antonio López. Little mud and lathe
houses with thatched roofs nestled among groves of oranges, banana,
mango and papaya, each surrounded by a garden of maize and mandioca
(a bland starchy tuber, also known as cassava or manioc, the staple food
of Paraguay).

One hundred years later, the scene was not so different. The patches of
forest were thinning out, with evidence of bulldozers at work, as more and
more entrepreneurs entered the timber business. The grasslands were still
given over to cattle pasture, though here and there broken up by giant
advertising billboards, a brickworks or small strip of industrial development. The little houses were now mostly constructed of thin orange bricks,

roofed with curved terracotta tiles, though the mud and thatch huts increased in number as we travelled further from the city. Orange trees were everywhere, piles of golden fruit lying rotting under most of them. The Jesuit fathers carried the seedlings from Spain in the seventeenth century. They adapted in such profusion that citrus groves can be found deep in the forests.

As we stopped at the stations of small towns and villages, women with baskets of oranges or bread on their heads crowded around the train windows, calling "*Naranjas!*" and "*Chipá!*" just as the colonists described. These days there wasn't the preponderance of women as in those desperate years after the War of the Triple Alliance. The Scottish parliamentarian Robert Bontine Cunninghame Graham, whom Lane had praised as one of the ablest leaders of the British labour movement, left an account of his experience as a train passenger in Paraguay just after the war had ended:

> Women in long white sleeveless smocks (their only garment) went about selling "chipa" — the Paraguayan bread of mandioca flour, flavoured with cheese, as indigestible as an old-fashioned Pitcaithly bannock — and pieces of sugar-cane, oranges and bananas ... The sun poured down upon the platform, crowded with women, for men were very scarce in Paraguay in those days. They kept up a perpetual shrill chattering in Guaraní ...
>
> Differences of classes may have existed, but only theoretically, like the rights of man, equality, liberty, or any of the other mendacious bywords that mankind love to write large and disregard. No matter what the passenger unused to Paraguay paid for his ticket, the carriage was at once invaded by the other travellers, smoking and talking volubly and spitting so profusely that it was evident that no matter what diseases Paraguay was subject to, consumption had no place amongst them.
>
> The jolting was terrific, the heat infernal, and the whole train crowded with people, who sat in open trucks, upon the tops of carriages, on footboards, or on anything that would contain them, smoking and chattering, and in their white clothes as the train slowly jolted onwards, looking like a swarm of butterflies.

Margaret Riley and her family made the train trip in March 1894, six months after the pioneers, and she remembered its snail's pace with some amusement: "The train was overloaded with all our gear and all the passengers and it just crept out of the station, you could get out and walk alongside it. And we'd see orange trees at the side of the track or a little distance from it. We'd jump out and run across and grab some oranges and run back and catch the train. When the driver saw us coming, he'd put on a bit of a spurt and send the train along so that we'd have to race after it."

We stopped briefly at the station of a little town called Luque, once the capital of Marshal-President López in retreat, after the Allies had taken Asunción. Florence, looking nostalgic, confided that her first serious boyfriend used to live at Luque. A great spreading lapacho tree drooped its dusky lavender flowers over a fence. As we puffed away, gathering speed again, a man sprinted and hurled himself into our carriage, grinning in triumph. "Silly galoot!" Florence whispered. She was surprised when I said it was Australian slang. It was just a word her father used for someone a bit mad.

The gradient became steeper, and the engine made heavy work of it as we passed between two ranges of wooded hills. It was even slower going in Margaret Riley's time. "They'd shunt back, then they'd go forward a bit, then back and crawl forward some more. We used to think we'd never get to the next station!"

After two hours we had come 50 kilometres. We rounded a bend and the blue waters of Lake Ypacaraí shimmered below us and beyond were the dark cordilleras, mountains twisted into fantastic Rider Haggard shapes and covered by virgin forests. A few Mbyá Indians still lived there — hunting naked with bows and arrows — those who had eluded the rounding up and transportation to stern government reservations. On the further lake shore German settlers had once established a colony, Nueva Bavaria, which became the centre of the German Nazi Party in Paraguay during the Third Reich. Today it is the resort town of San Bernardino, a popular watering-place for the affluent.

Our train pulled in to the station of Areguá, a leafy town beside the lake with a large white church on top of the hill and gracious old houses in established gardens. We had lunch at the Mozart Restaurant, dark-panelled, beer steins hanging on pegs along the bar, pictures of youths in *lederhosen* and a thoughtful Wolfgang Amadeus.

In 1880 Knight and his lawyer friends came to Areguá by train and attended a dance where they were delighted with the ratio of 500 women to 100 men. He thought it "a happy childish assembly" which reminded him of clean children at a school-treat in an English village. As he watched the women dancing the Palomita he admired their beauty once again, though it "was curious to see a girl and her partner puffing away at their long cigars across each other's shoulders while waltzing vigorously".

He was less eager to meet a fat Guaraní priest who, at his house, "has many mistresses and a nursery full of children", as well as a parrot on the veranda that could mumble the litany of the Latin service, several indecencies and a few blasphemies. Even more disappointingly, he and his friends were unable to mingle with the women during the supper break:

> We aristocrats were forced to dine in the stifling room ... Our meal was a luxurious one; chipa, roast parrots, and stewed iguana or lizard being but a few of the many delicacies that were spread before us. The padre did not dine with us, as he had drunk himself into a state of imbecility, as is his wont on every such occasion. The women of the place had tucked his fat carcase into a hammock and were engaged in fanning his apoplectic-looking visage.

The Australian pioneers continued on the train, through the town of Paraguarí, overlooked by a high saddle-shaped hill, across the Tebicuary River and at last came in to Villarrica in the small hours of the morning. A British resident of the town allowed them to doss down in one of his sheds.

Villarrica, 175 kilometres from the capital and halfway to the Brazilian border, announces itself today with a giant statue of a conquistador. It has always been an important commercial centre for the surrounding countryside and was the big smoke for the colonists. But even today its population is only 50,000 — about the size of Asunción in their time — a town of comfortingly low-rise colonial buildings, a small university and a graceful white cathedral. Horse-drawn taxis called *kaxapés* clatter along the streets. Outside the railway station, mingled with battered old vehicles and Ford pick-up trucks, the bullock *carretas*, the great high-wheeled wagons suited to negotiating the rutted country roads, are still lined up

Soon after the Australians' arrival they learned that up to 1,000 Guaraní Indians were still squatting on the site of their land grant. The Government had made a vague attempt to order them off, without taking it any further. Apparently if the new landlords wanted the Indians to go, it was up to them to evict them.

Lane had already seen some of the bachelors admiring the bare-footed Paraguayan women in their revealing white chemises. He was reluctant to establish his new settlement where there would be a constant temptation for the men to break their pledge and cross The Colour Line. In fact he wanted little fraternisation of any kind with the local people, in order not to sully the purity of his experiment. "We must go where we shall be cast inwards," he had always argued, "where we shall be able to form new habits, uninfluenced by old social surroundings, where none but good men will go with us." He was therefore determined to find some resolution to the situation before his main party of settlers arrived on the land, but in a way that did not characterise them as a new generation of ruthless conquistadors. He immediately hired horses and rode out to the land grant with an interpreter who spoke Guaraní.

Lane was starting the way he intended to continue, impressing his authority on the local people. But he lacked the imperious manner of a British missionary who'd arrived just seven years earlier: the Reverend William Barbrooke Grubb came to Paraguay in 1886 and later published his precepts for dealing with the native Indians:

> Assume at all times and under all circumstances superiority and authority … Perhaps a few general instances given here will best illustrate the way in which I carried out this policy. On arriving at a village, I insisted, as far as possible, upon all the people ministering to my personal comfort. I ordered one to prepare my resting place, another to make a fire, a third to bring me water, and another to pull off my knee boots. When the heat was great or the flies troublesome, I made two sit by me with a fan. When on foot and having to cross a swampy patch, I made one of them carry me across — in fact, I avoided doing anything myself that I could persuade them to do for me …

By comparison with the lordly progress of Barbrooke Grubb, Lane was conciliatory to the point of self-abnegation. He assured the Indian squatters that they would not be made homeless but, if they were in the way of the planned settlement, they'd be given land elsewhere on the extensive site.

The squatters submitted and Lane seemed to have brought off a diplomatic coup, although *El Centinela*, an Asunción newpaper, reported the incident with resentment verging on apoplexy: "Let the Australian Gringos come! Let the whole world come to cultivate our soil and to sell sweet potatoes! But do not let them come asking for justice when they have need of it, for consideration when they deserve it, or for public freedom, because these things are not produced by the soil. They are permitted only to ask for sweet potatoes, because that is the only thing that is produced here in the soil."

Meanwhile Charles Leck, one of the prospectors with Tozer in Patagonia, had been busy in Villarrica arranging the hire of twenty *carretas* with their drivers. On Monday afternoon the convoy of Australians set off, each cart or *carreta* with its huge wooden wheels drawn by six or eight bullocks yoked in pairs, the drivers urging the teams by the use of a goad — a long pole with a steel point suspended over the animals' backs. Women and children perched on mounds of luggage, the men walked alongside, and in this way they made the trek to their promised land.

In the darkness they negotiated a crossing of the Tebicuary River, the bullocks floundering in water up to the axles of the wagons, and collapsed at a camp prepared by the advance party on the further shore. Mosquitoes swarmed around them but they were too exhausted to care. "We pegged out in the open," wrote John Rich, "under the broad canopy of heaven, among some long grass, and soon fell asleep."

But they were still a long way from their goal. Next day they set off again through dense forest — the *monte* — the children thrilled to see monkeys swinging in the trees, macaws and brilliantly plumaged parrots screaming overhead and butterflies flittering out of reach. The parents were agitated in a different way, as evening closed in, when they heard from the drivers that the forest was inhabited by wolves and jaguars.

Margaret Riley, arriving with the second batch, remembered wild beasts howling at night as they huddled by the wagons around a campfire. She said "Oh, anything could happen in those *montes*, anything at all could happen, they were thick with undergrowth and the vines that used to come down from the trees. I thought we must really be going into the wilds. And I was right — we were."

And Eric Birks, the boy who'd been in strife with the riverboat engineer, lost some of his cockiness: "At nights, beyond the fires, I could see eyes gleaming. Foxes. I said my prayers, for I was very frightened. At last I slept beneath the *carreta* — with the men. Even today it is a pleasure to wipe my feet on a fox-skin rug. It seems the proper place for a fox."

On Wednesday the pioneers reached the site that had been chosen by Leck and Alf Walker and where a rough camp had been established. But Lane and some of the advance party had already decided that the site was too damp and low-lying and probably too close to the Guaraní squatters. Scouts had been sent out who returned with reports of more suitable land 12 kilometres further on.

The following morning, 28 September, the settlers claimed their New Australia, an expansive area of grassland encircled by *monte*. It seemed auspicious to the sheepworkers among them that the place was known locally as Puesto de Las Ovejas — The Sheep Station. Now that their long and wearisome journey was over at last, William Lane hoped that the tensions, petty squabbling and divisions into factions would come to an end, that all differences could be healed as they worked one for all and all for one. In this green and pleasant land with its towering forests, orange

One of the Regulations of the
Paraguayan Colonists
All persons
Over 18 Shall be at liberty to leave the
Settlement at any time."

Bulletin, 13 May 1893. The journal's mockery in this instance was wrong: natural predators were the least of the colonists' problems.

groves and lush pasture watered by streams — so different to the parched outback Australian landscape familiar to most of them — he felt it should be possible.

But James Molesworth remembered their arrival as chaos, and a few hours later the almost daily tropical downfall drenched them. "It was an inauspicious beginning."

And later on that first night, according to a critic of New Australia, the camp was woken by a blood-curdling cry. People cowered in their tents, convinced a jaguar was lusting for their blood. "For the rest of that night armed men patrolled the camp, and fires were kept burning brightly to scare away savage beasts. In the morning the animal whose awful note had so alarmed the sleepers was found to be a donkey."

10
The Promised Land

The land, judging from the accounts which have reached us, is flowing with milk and honey; you have merely to scratch the earth and it laughs back fruit and flowers.

Sydney Mail, 22 July 1893

The sailor relates that in Utopia neither money nor private property exists. There, scorn for gold and for superfluous consumption is encouraged, and no one dresses ostentatiously. Everybody gives the fruits of his work to the public stores and freely collects what he needs. The economy is planned. There is no hoarding, which is the son of fear, nor is hunger known. The people choose their prince and the people can depose him ...

Eduardo Galeano, on Thomas More's *Utopia*

Another billboard flashed past. *Tome Coca Cola!* exhorted a copper-skinned señorita. On the green savannah plain behind her, Zebu and long-horned cattle grazed between low caranday palms. I was travelling along the straight well-sealed Ruta 2, the nation's showpiece of roadmaking, along which cars are smuggled from Brazil to Asunción and tourists make forays to the famous Iguazú falls and the duty-free shopping of Ciudad del Este, a vast border-town supermarket run by Koreans and Taiwanese.

Between the two destinations the road slices 330 kilometres across some of the loveliest countryside imaginable, the undulating subtropical heartland of eastern Paraguay, described by so many visitors as arcadian. Except for the billboards: like the fading tattered image of the Pope — Juan Pablo — waving to his Paraguayan flock, a leftover from his visit in 1988. A thatched farmhouse, a grove of orange trees, a German restaurant with steep gabled roof and geraniums under the shuttered windows, a lavender burst of jacarandas and the Marlboro Man loomed up, square-jawed and unrepentantly blonde under his cowboy hat.

I was on my way to the site of New Australia.

On my first journey to Paraguay in 1982 I hadn't managed to see it. We had sped past the turn-off in a big American car and Rodrigo Wood had casually pointed to the sign: Distrito Hugo Stroessner.

"You wouldn't want to go there," said Rod's 83-year-old father, Norman. "There's nothing of interest there, and no one who speaks English." I'd protested weakly but Don Norman wanted to get on to Cosme. He had a passion about the place where he was born. And a lingering grudge against the old rival colony.

Seven years later I was back in Paraguay, making my way there by bus. By chance I'd met up with an Australian, Steve Cooper, a retired trade union research officer calling in on his way to Brazil. Through the bus window we watched the driver of a huge-wheeled *carreta* goading his hump-backed bullocks past a roadside shrine where a woman was kneeling to place some flowers.

I said it seemed that New Australia and Cosme had become Stations of the Cross for the Australian radical left on its final march. Steve agreed that he felt a bit of a pilgrim, in search of what survived of a legend. But his interest, he said, had been inspired by a meeting with Dame Mary Gilmore when he was a very young man. He'd been working for a small journal in the 1950s and published an article about the 1804 convict uprising at Castle Hill in New South Wales. Dame Mary had written, commending him on the piece, and invited him to call at her flat in Kings Cross.

"Dame Mary didn't exactly hold court," he said, "but I know she encouraged a lot of young writers. She certainly seemed impressive sitting there, although she was well into her eighties at the time. I found her a fascinating woman. She told me that her grandmother had heard the screaming of the convicts being lashed after that uprising. And she talked a little bit about her days in Paraguay. From that time I'd always wanted to come here."

*

Sing the song o' pizen snaix,
Across in Paraguay;
The Indians whooping for our blood,
The skeeter and the fly;
An' all the other bitey things
The papers said we'd meet

When we chucked Australia up
With its tramp o' weary feet …

So Mary wrote in the *New Australia* journal of 18 December 1893, returning a serve to the *Bulletin*.

An' sing the song o' sixpence,
The pocket full o' rye,
The disappointed editor
Awipin' of his eye;
For the children aint astarvin'
The women aint undone,
The boys aint ventilated
By the Paraguayan gun.
But everybody's hearty
In a wholesome sort of way
In the land of full and plenty
Which we once called Paraguay.

It was *once* called "Paraguay", Mary explained in a footnote, because the correct pronunciation was "Par-a-whi". She was still teaching in Sydney, but work on the journal consumed her outside school hours. She yearned to leave for the colony, having received so many letters imbued with goodwill and optimism.

Arthur Tozer wrote in a similar vein to Harry, declaring they had obtained the finest tract of land in Paraguay, the scenery as beautiful as the land was fertile. "All the rising ground is forest — not too dense — & the level land is grass or what is known as savannah country. This gives a park-like appearance to the whole & makes it look as if the grassland was at one time under water, & the wooded country the islands & shores of an immense lake."

Although they'd only been at the site for three weeks, he boasted, they'd already put up rough housing sufficient to accommodate everyone comfortably. A terrace of twenty-four rooms for the single men, using a wattle and daub construction, was partially completed; William Lane was fond of comparing it to the barracks for the Indian acolytes at the Jesuit missions three centuries earlier. Many acres of ground had already been ploughed and planted with beans, potatoes, melons and mandioca, grass had been cut for thatching, and the timber felling continued apace. Suitable clay had been found close by, brickmaking was proceeding and the site for a town was already laid out. It was to be of noble proportions, looking ahead to its future as a great communist city. The streets were to be 45 metres

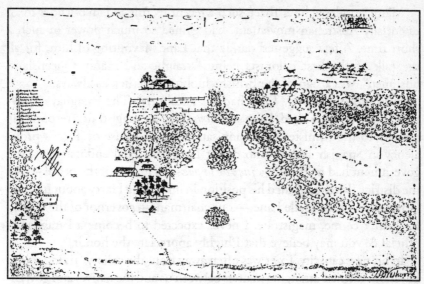

Plan of New Australia by Tom Westwood (*University of Sydney Library*)

wide, bordered by orange and other fruit trees, leading to a town square and hall for public meetings and entertainments. The quarter-acre allotments would all have a 22-metre frontage and a depth of 55 metres. It was agreed that the present rude dwellings would serve later as stables and outbuildings.

The colonists had been working ten-hour days to establish their new home, and in a few weeks they expected over 200 more people from Australia and "then we hope to make things hum & have plenty to shew for our work". It was even raining just when they needed it for their crops.

It seemed nothing could dampen Tozer's enthusiasm, not even their isolation. "We are quite out of the world here & since I left Montevideo I have heard nothing of how it wags. Still, I am happy & hope all will go well. The life is rough, but very healthy & free from all worries & cares which are unavoidable in towns & cities when a man has to depend on a boss for his existence."

There were already some at the settlement who thought Tozer, with his Smith and Wesson stuck in his belt, was assuming the manner of a boss himself. James Molesworth wrote that, "A picturesque revolver-girded Scot, named Tozer, was appointed Lane's aide-de-camp. He purchased 2,000 head of cattle for us. One was killed daily. The tongue was supposed to be distributed in turn ... But many of us never saw the tongue — nor tasted it."

Many wondered how Tozer, such a recent recruit and an outsider to an essentially Australian movement, had gained so much power in such a short time. A few suggested darkly that Lane's favouring of him, for all the talk of the best colonists being "straight and manly Queensland bushmen", was a sign of the British clubbing together, as always.

Even more irritating, Tozer had legal authority. The Paraguayan government had appointed Lane as *intendente* or magistrate, responsible directly to the Minister for Colonisation. But because of Tozer's proficiency in Spanish and also no doubt Lane's personal endorsement, the government had made him a *juez de la paz* — a justice of the peace — for the district. Tozer upgraded his position in informing Harry about it: "The Government have made Lane — our chairman — governor of the colony & district & me, magistrate. I never expected to become a Paraguayan official & you may believe that I highly appreciate the honor."

In his new capacity Tozer was often away from the colony "riding round in various districts arranging matters between us and the natives and government officials". When not doing that he, like all the colonists, worked in the department — farming, dairy, stock, building, smithy, forestry or gardening — to which he'd been assigned. Tozer spent time wielding an axe and extracting tree stumps from the burnt-off land so presumably was in the forestry department. In the evening he conducted a Spanish class, while William Lane discussed English literature, and someone else, general science. Dan Pogson, the bandmaster, whom Tozer described as "a professor of music", offered lessons in playing a musical instrument.

But there were rumblings about the way their labour was distributed: why some people had been placed in one department rather than another where they believed their talents were more suited or where the work was easier or more attractive. The man tilling the vegetable patch envied the stockman herding cattle; the stockman thought the schoolteacher had a soft job, and the teacher wondered why Pogson and his band members gained work credits for having fun.

But a united front was presented for the colony's official opening ceremony on 11 October 1893. A tarpaulin was thrown across the end of the partially-thatched hall, cloths were spread over a long table knocked together from boxes, a ten-metre bamboo pole was erected to receive the tricoloured flag of Paraguay.

The sounding of a horn announced the arrival of the official party. The colonists assembled to greet a cavalcade of horsemen guided in by Alf Walker: the minister, Dr López, wearing a poncho; the German secretary to the president, who spoke English; the administrator for the local Department of Ajos and a few other notables, flanked by an officer and four soldiers of the presidential bodyguard.

The party was led into the hall for refreshments, then the horn sounded again for the official ceremony. Dr López, an amiable man, who "with a round, red face might have been taken for an English squire", unfolded the Paraguayan flag. He and Lane linked arms, advanced to the flagstaff and hauled it up together as the soldiers fired their Winchesters.

The minister made a short speech, translated by the secretary, which assured the colonists that the flag would always wave over and protect them. William Lane responded, expressing their gratitude. The drama of the occasion made an impression on James Molesworth's four-year-old son Voltaire. Many years later he recalled the red, white and blue flag fluttering in the tropical sunshine and the speech of the minister proclaiming "the establishment of the New Australia Colony in the land which his uncle had ruled as dictator — and had ruined. The 200-odd pioneers from Australia cheered the flag to which they now gave allegiance, and again cheered the motto inscribed on it of 'Peace and Justice'."

*

The New Australians failed to preserve the appearance of harmony and unity of purpose for long after the formal opening. Slanders were spread, grudges nurtured, bitterness erupted in angry words and fist-fights. Within two months irreconcilable differences meant a split was inevitable.

The factionalism which hurtled the colony to collapse has been documented by Souter. In broad terms those harbouring the resentments formed an alliance, the Rebels, opposing "King Billy Lane" and his Royalist supporters. In the nightly meetings, Voltaire Molesworth described how the two groups aligned themselves explicitly as a parliament: "Two large logs were drawn up close to the perpetual fire, the opposition selected one log and the government the other. Tomorrow's job was thrashed out. The shortage of milk supplies, and a hundred and one things formed the theme of the bush parliamentarians."

But the Rebels viewed it as a parliament without true democratic representation, presided over by a not always benevolent despot. Lane had absolute power as director because he had the majority of proxy votes of members still in Australia or about to depart for Paraguay. Some of the Rebels were on the opposition logs because of disappointment at the discomfort of living conditions, the paucity and monotony of the food, the colony's difficult access to road and river transport and Lane's general dictatorial approach. But many of them still believed in the ideals that had brought them to Paraguay and hoped that matters would come to rights as more settlers arrived, material conditions improved and the Basis for Communal Organisation was fully implemented.

Arthur Tozer assured Harry that he continued to have confidence in the colonists as a group: "I find the people — the Australians — a very agreeable set to live with & although some are rough in manner, there is something so true & straight about them that you cannot help liking them. They are mostly bushmen & of a type similar to the descriptions I have read of the north American backwoodsmen. They would not hesitate to send a man who played them false to the other world & would divide their last crust with a chum or one of their party."

But four of the Rebels were unrelenting and strident in their criticism of Lane and of two basic principles of the Association, Teetotalism and The Colour Line. They were Louis Simon, a miner from Clermont in Queensland, and the three ringleaders of the drinking spree in Montevideo: Fred White, the Adelaide draper Tom Westwood, and the engineer and photographer from Albury, Arthur Brittlebank.

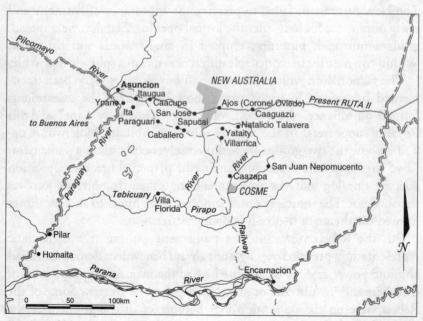

Area around New Australia and Cosme

The dominant figure, Fred White, had an ambiguous past. A gloomy, taciturn man in his thirties, he had worked in western Queensland and may have been a special constable during the shearers' strike. Certainly that was rumoured. John Sibbald, the former accountant, thought White enlisted in Adelaide with the avowed intention of disrupting the Association. Historian Gavin Souter was unable to confirm or deny this view but agreed he was clever, unscrupulous and bent on causing mischief. In his documentary novel, *The Paraguayan Experiment*, Michael Wilding suggested that White, the nephew of a police magistrate, deliberately infiltrated the colony as an agent provocateur.

While Queensland pastoralists were no doubt delighted to see their enemies, Lane and militant union leaders, abandon Australia, they lost many skilled rural workers with them and would not have welcomed an extension of the drift, particularly as Lane had spoken in terms of a colony of 50,000. It is not an outrageous speculation that they might have been prepared, perhaps in concert with the Queensland government, to pay what would have been for them a comparatively negligible retainer to a saboteur to see the whole venture collapse.

Whatever the truth of the matter, the record of Fred White's actions shows him as consistent and adroit in manipulating every circumstance to work against Lane and the success of the colony. It was almost certainly White, with his probable background as a special constable, whom Arthur Tozer described to Harry as the exception to the true and straight bushmen: "There is one black sheep amongst us & we are only awaiting some proofs against him from Australia before action is taken against him. At present he is afraid & refuses to leave the camp. He knows only too well that if he did he would never return."

A short time later White did so dare. On 29 October Tom Westwood's diary mentioned a visit to a Paraguayan friend in the village of Ajos, whose wife "made cigars and rolled the leaf on her naked thigh". On 18 November he noted that he went to Ajos with White and Simon and the following day, "Attended Mass at 6 o'clock. At 11 o'clock had a good meal at the priest's house. He produced a bottle of wine of his own making and good wine too".

There were also reports of commune tools being exchanged for liquor. *Sub-intendente* Tozer was severe in policing any attempts at barter with Guaraní neighbours, on the argument that all property and labour belonged to the community as a whole and therefore trading with either was theft. Arthur Brittlebank did some repairs for a Guaraní family and accepted milk laced with *caña*, the Paraguayan white rum, as payment. Tozer was so incensed that, although he had a broken arm at the time, he knocked Brittlebank down with two blows from his good arm.

He informed his brother that difficulties on the colony had begun with "three fellows breaking the regulation respecting drink. I as J. P. put a stop to it as far as possible but it was still continued secretly. One of them threatened to punch my nose so I went to him & invited him to start right away. He didn't seem inclined to carry out his threat so I started on him & in a few minutes finished him. He then left the colony. Soon after, the news got into the Asunción papers which stated that the J. P. of New Australia carried out punishments himself ... and disdained to use the soldiers placed at his disposal."

Tozer's fierce zealotry extended to his role as storekeeper. Voltaire Molesworth recalled that a system of supplying food at the communal store in exchange for coupons was instituted and for a while worked satisfactorily. A few industrious housewives, "whose cooperative principles had not fully developed kept back a certain number of coupons each week and eventually decided to have a good old shopping day", But when they presented their accumulated coupons they were dismayed to learn they were only legal tender for the week of issue. "Thus was capitalism crushed in its early stages."

A major cause for dissatisfaction was Lane's insistence on The Colour Line, the preservation of the racial purity of his Anglo-Saxon enclave while it worked towards its great destiny. "We have isolation from a society," he wrote, "whose seductions would draw our thoughts when they are needed to organise and build". The seductiveness of the local Guaraní women continued to draw the thoughts of the bachelors.

Edward Channing marvelled for the *New Australia* journal: "Fancy, in the town of Ajos, about nine miles from here, there are between 300 and 400 women and only 14 men. Every native seems to have one wife, but he has also three or four women about." Not only were the women comely, Channing continued, but they seemed so easy to please. "Some two or three months ago one of the natives saw me on the bicycle and could not understand how it was. They, being very superstitious, told the priest, and he and about 100 of the people, mostly women, came out to see what they called the iron horse. They fetched the town band with them — about six brass instruments — and I had to give a performance like a circus. It would have done the heart of a circus man good to have seen the audience laugh. The simplest things seem to amuse them most."

*

Our bus pulled in at Coronel Oviedo, the midway point on the route to the Brazilian border, a charmless strip development of roadhouses, *hamburguerías* and gas stations for the long-distance transports and *rápido* buses. Once it was called Ajos and was a sleepy dusty hamlet, though still capable of offering temptations for wayward colonial bachelors.

An old man at a roadside stall knew about the *gringos australianos*. We should take a *colectivo*, a local bus, he said, to Distrito Hugo Stroessner. We should ask for Señor Ricardo Smith. He'd been one of them, but he was old now and blind.

Not wanting to arrive empty-handed, I purchased the only gifts available, the local *chipá* bread rolls, some tomatoes and a bunch of bananas.

*

"At a feast day in Ajos," wrote Lane's ally Alf Walker to secretary Walter Head in Sydney, "the rules relating to drink were again flagrantly broken, and one man openly announced his intention of bringing a native woman into the colony to live with him." He'd also heard that the sexual favours of an Australian woman had been promised to a local man in exchange for those of a Guaraní beauty.

Arthur Tozer condemned such fraternisation, but wasn't immune to the frustration and loneliness. He wrote to his brother: "Have you anyone in view yet? At present I am not thinking of getting spliced but if any nice girls come out from Australia I may get caught & then it would be all up with me. Anyhow I shall want a very nice girl & a very nice girl is likely to want someone nicer than I am."

The bitterness and ill-feeling in the community festered and found poisonous release after Lane and Walker returned from a visit to Asunción. They'd been negotiating with the authorities, attempting to preserve the principles of New Australia, while complying with the requirement to register it according to the labyrinthine complexities of Paraguayan company law. With no provision for a cooperative association, they had been obliged to register the Sociedad Co-operativa Colonizadora Nueva Australia as a limited liability company. One of its articles stipulated that "the president of the company during his term of office shall act as the agent of all the shareholders in Australia".

Souter has argued that there seemed no evidence of personal corruption in the decisions taken by Lane and Walker — the Sociedad did not replace the Association and Lane was still answerable to a two-thirds vote of the trustees — but there were definite signs of political naivety and indifference to public opinion. They made no attempt to explain their mission and the Rebels chanced on the articles of the Sociedad listed in the newspaper *La Democracia*. Lane and Walker returned to uproar. The Rebels' poor Spanish led them to believe that no dividends would be paid for twenty years and a "gigantic land swindle" had been perpetrated.

Lane made a half-hearted attempt to defend his actions at a tumultuous community meeting. "If Lane felt as he looked, he must have felt queer, for I never remember him looking so bad," wrote John Rich. "He was accused, in plain old English, of double-dealing and deceit, and was told that the majority had lost confidence in him. He offered to resign when the next batch arrived, then expected in about two months."

If the situation failed to improve in six months, Lane had a secret plan to leave with his supporters. He increasingly blamed himself and turned to the religion he had formerly rejected. He revealed his agonised state of mind to Walter Head in Sydney:

> The malcontents are so buried under mountains of selfishness that they will not help us to do right. Our loyal bushmen and those who we know joined us because of the religion of the movement are doing most of the work and least of the grumbling. Of course it is my fault, as there are some among us who would never have joined us had they known that under the movement was a real, albeit a flickering, belief in God. I organised too much on material lines, and as a result am reaping the reward of materialism. But I brought these people here and must use every endeavour to get them to go for the right.

On 5 December a petition to the Paraguayan government was drafted by White, Westwood and Simon and signed by twenty-four colonists. It announced an intention to sever connections with New Australia because of "serious differences and complications" and their rejection of the policy of "isolation and exclusiveness". As practical agriculturalists they desired to establish individual holdings and asked the government for a new grant of land close to rail or river communication.

A few days later White went to Asunción with the intention of seeing the Minister for Colonisation. Lane left for the capital at the same time in order to get in first. Before departing he prepared notices expelling White, Westwood and Simon for infringements of the temperance rule. He defended his action in a letter to Walter Head: "There is nothing for it but for me to stand on my full rights as chairman — subject to suspension by two-thirds of trustees — and do what I think is right. The crooked ones will have to go."

The expulsion notices, dated 15 December 1893, advised the miscreants that a wagon would take them to Villarrica at 7 o'clock the following morning. If they remained on the colony after that time, they would be forcibly removed by the police.

Tozer had under his command a cavalry captain, a sergeant, four soldiers and also, when needed, the national guard of the district, described by one colonist as "a nondescript body of payless cut-throats". When the expelled men refused to leave voluntarily, Tozer executed the order, obviously with some relish: "I rode into Ajos, a village near here … and brought out the captain & six soldiers. We then ordered three of the worst to leave the camp or they would be forcibly ejected. At first they said that they would have to be carried before they would go but when the soldiers went to do it they soon gave in & went like lambs."

"It was the most brutal exhibition of power I have ever witnessed," Charles Manning reported to the Sydney *Bulletin*. He claimed that Tom Westwood had been laid up for a fortnight with dysentery, but "was forced from his bed and given half an hour to pack up his effects".

Westwood's nine-year-old blind son, Foley, went with his father and the other expelled men. The image of them being hustled away by armed guards devastated many colonists, particularly the Queenslanders, reminding them of scenes they had fled to avoid experiencing again. There were mordant reflections on how passionately William Lane had railed against the use of force in former days.

"Many of the women called upon us to resist the troopers," wrote Manning. "But I feel sure we adopted the wiser plan, as nothing would have pleased some of Lane's satellites better than the sight of the police firing upon us."

Manning and six other "Rebels" walked out the following day. He noted bitterly that Lane issued an order that their luggage be searched in case they were removing Association property. Tozer was given the task. "No less a personage than the deputy chairman was cut out for this dirty job. And he did it well. Women were compelled to open up their boxes and exhibit their baby linen and underclothing to his vulgar gaze."

Nineteen men signed a petition stating they had been unjustly treated and their individual liberties unduly restricted. "Hard words have been said and deeds have been done which, in our opinion, render reconciliation upon our existing basis absolutely impossible. There remains but one remedy — separation." But partition of the land was refused. For those determined to go, meagre payouts were offered from the depleted general funds.

The colony was in chaos, but Tozer wrote to Harry that he was anxious to be free "from all our bad fellows and we shall then go on smoothly". He was comfortable that another shipload of colonists would be leaving Australia in a few days. "There will be plenty of work for them here & we are looking forward to their arrival. W. Lane, Chairman, tells me that they will be a far better lot than are already here. Anyhow I don't think they can be better & if so they will have to be very good indeed. Our men, especially the single ones, are as fine a lot as you would find anywhere. They seldom grumble, are cheerful & very hard workers, & put up with any inconvenience."

By the end of December, when the *Royal Tar* was leaving Adelaide on its second voyage, New Australia had lost more than one-third of its population; Souter's count is eighty-one people, thirty men, seventeen women and the rest children. William Lane offered them free transport, either to Villarrica or to Colonia González, a government-backed private enterprise colony over 70 kilometres to the south. But one group, departing, could not make themselves understood by their Paraguayan wagon driver. They passed Charles Leck, a Lane supporter, on the road, and the driver asked where he should take them. Leck shouted in Spanish, "Take them to hell!"

*

"Distrito Hugo Stroessner," said the *colectivo* driver, letting us off at the edge of a leafy village green.

Its citrus groves were deserted but for a white horse and a few pigs snuffling at fallen oranges. It was dominated by a memorial, an ugly bravura structure that would have done Mussolini proud: two concrete tusks supported an idealised bust that looked like a Roman senator. It was of Hugo Stroessner, a Bavarian brewer not famous for anything much except producing a son, Alfredo.

The little village had been renamed in the 1970s. Oscar Birks, a descendant of New Australia based in Asunción, explained to me how it happened: "A Colorado Party senator, not knowing what else to do to please President Alfredo Stroessner, rose in the Senate one day and said, 'I don't see any reason to have this name Colonia Nueva Australia. What does it mean to us? It merely pays homage to kangaroos! We should change the name to Hugo Stroessner — the man who gave us this great citizen who is conducting our country so brilliantly!' Everyone applauded — what else could they do? — and there was a law immediately, renaming the place for the father of the dictator."

But at the time of my visit there in 1989, it was about to be changed again. All over Paraguay, after the coup of 2 February, the name Stroessner was being excised. Portraits of the son had been removed from official walls, busts and statues were tumbling down. They hadn't got to this village yet. I hoped it would revert to its original name. Oscar Birks, an influential businessman, was confident of it. "I'm going to get in touch with the other Australian descendants," he told me, "and we will present a letter to the Senate requesting that the name be returned to Nueva Australia. That would only be fair."

*

Mansfeldt de Cardonnel Findlay was a shrewd and elegant career diplomat, at thirty-one years of age Second Secretary at the British Legation in Buenos Aires. He travelled up to Asunción in response to an urgent telegram from Dr Stewart, the elderly British honorary consul, who'd been besieged by a number of disaffected Australians.

On 23 December Findlay had a discussion with the seceders, led by Westwood and G. W. W. Pope. He listened to their complaints and requests for assistance as the loyal British subjects they claimed to be. He was aware of the diplomatic delicacy of the situation — how the remaining colonists could resent any British intervention and the wider implications. "As the movement had caused considerable excitement in Australia among the Labour and Socialist parties," he wrote in his report to the British Foreign Office, "it appeared to me most desirable to avoid anything which might possibly embitter the feelings of the Australians towards the Home Government."

He advised the seceders to attempt a reconciliation. They responded that Lane had made their lives unendurable, they were terrorised, their wives insulted by foul language, and it was all because of asking inconvenient questions. Having left Australia with hopes of a happier life, they said, all they wanted to do was return there. Findlay suggested that they had acted rashly in leaving the colony and abandoning their shares, and their best course was to approach the Paraguayan government for aid. He himself would visit the colony in the near future and attempt to bring about a reconciliation if it seemed possible.

Later the same day Findlay and Dr Stewart had a meeting with President González, during which it was agreed that it was generally undesirable "both for Paraguay and for the good name of Australians" if the group of people departed the country as paupers. His Excellency the President was left in no doubt that Her Britannic Majesty's Government would be obliged if the seceders could stay on and earn at least a subsistence living. As a result, land was offered to them at the government-supported González colony.

On 24 December Dr Stewart sent a telegram to Mr Pakenham, the British Minister Plenipotentiary in Buenos Aires, informing him of the differences at New Australia which had caused "eighty-five souls" to leave. The seceders had requested this news be conveyed to their friends in Adelaide before the imminent departure of the *Royal Tar*. It was cabled on to the Foreign Office in London, but the message that reached Adelaide referred to the secession of "8 Australian settlers". The emigrants decided so few was no cause for alarm and the *Tar* left on its second voyage.

Findlay arranged to visit New Australia, encouraged by Dr López, the Minister for Colonisation who, the diplomat noted, seemed "prejudiced against the seceders, having, like myself, heard only one side of the story". He arrived by train at Villarrica on 30 December and met with a number of the rebels, whom he found "very respectable people, but on enquiring as to their trades, I found that they were mostly artisans and townspeople — only a small minority being agriculturalists. This appeared to me partly to account for their having failed to get on in the colony". They repeated all their complaints and accusations against Lane but Findlay was keeping an open mind. When they asked for British Government assistance with passages back to Australia he reminded them "that they had come to Paraguay on their own responsibility, and that the only government assistance they could possibly expect was such moral support as I was endeavouring to give them". He advised them to consider the offer of land at the González colony, which they all seemed loath to do, and at last he agreed that he would use whatever influence he could with Lane to provide them with passages on the return voyage of the *Tar*.

While in Villarrica, Findlay had a meeting with the urbane, well-educated Englishman, Doctor Bottrell, who had treated the Australian colonists and knew most of them well. "I was not surprised to find that he considered the quarrel to have originated in the intrigues and ill-conduct of two or three bad characters, especially of White, one of those expelled; that the feud, thus begun, had been carefully kept alive by these men, and had been embittered by the quarrels of the ladies."

Next morning Alf Walker, representing the Lane faction, brought him a mount for the ride to New Australia. They swam their horses across the Tebicuary River and, after nine hours in the saddle, arrived at the settlement. Although they had passed through fertile green country, Findlay thought "the Australians had been given the very cream of it".

After lunch he had a long conversation with Lane, telling him frankly what action he had taken in the matter and asking for equal frankness in return. He got it. Lane's first remark was that he could not see why the British Legation had any right to interfere, to which Findlay responded that it had a duty to listen to the formal complaints of British subjects. He went on to give Lane a list of those complaints and carefully considered his responses.

Findlay could see the difficulty in registering the Association as a limited liability company and agreed that, according to the Articles, no financial statement was due until March. But as to the breaches of the teetotal pledge, he argued that surely the "occasional lapse from the strict path of righteousness" could be encompassed as, among so large a number of men, "many admittedly accustomed to a rough life, some such lapses were sure to occur". Expulsion, after a man had forfeited his life savings, seemed to him an extreme penalty. But Lane remained intransigent and replied that to *him*, a pledge was absolutely binding. "In fact," Findlay observed, "on every point I found him unwilling to admit extenuating circumstances, and throughout our conversation his tone was most unconciliatory."

But in the end, although he found it difficult to concede that the settlers had received full information about the site before leaving Australia, Findlay decided that most of the accusations against Lane were without foundation or were based on a faulty understanding of the Articles of Association. "The men of both parties have strong views and are extremely independent. Misunderstandings which had arisen had evidently been used by White and others to stir up faction, and Mr Lane is not the man to smooth away difficulties."

The main problem, he could see, was Mr Lane's personality, particularly his inflexibility. This was demonstrated once again when Findlay repeated the request of the seceders to return on the *Royal Tar*. Lane answered that, having left the Association, they had no right to make such a request and Findlay dropped the matter to avoid a direct refusal. As he took his leave he suggested that, although they differed on many subjects, their private relations could still be friendly. Lane responded that, as they differed on such grave subjects as the binding nature of a pledge, little sympathy could exist between them.

The records of long-dead bureaucrats have always been an invaluable source for historians. Only very occasionally does a human being shine through the copperplate. The summing-up for the British Foreign Office reveals Mansfeldt de Cardonnel Findlay as a remarkable man — acute, fearless, perspicacious and fair:

> Mr Lane has very strong, and very narrow ideas, an unsympathetic manner and a dogmatic way of laying down the law and refusing to depart from the letter thereof which is calculated to arouse opposition. It has evidently done so, and unless I am mistaken, will do so again. On the other hand I am perfectly convinced that he is honest, and that the accusation that the colony is a swindle is completely false. On the contrary, if it were worked on reasonable lines, it could hardly fail to succeed.

He concluded with great generosity and prescience that, "it is not improbable that William Lane's views may be found too 'straight' and his administration too strict for ordinary men. If, however, he succeeds in carrying out his ideal he will found a 'peculiar people', like Cromwell's Ironsides, and like them they may accomplish great things".

*

Arthur Tozer informed his brother that they had had a visit from the Secretary of the British Legation in Buenos Aires. "He was surprised at the progress made and on his return to B.A he wired the Paraguayan Government thanking it for the way in which it has assisted us and expressing satisfaction with the manner in which the colony is governed. Very kind and condescending on the part of the British Legation. The kind of condescension we don't require."

They had had other visitors at the colony, a German and two Austrians touring South America looking for speculative opportunities. One of them was a nephew of the banker Baron von Rothschild. "They also were surprised at our progress and were not so condescending in manner as the Legation man. Therefore they received better treatment. Lane almost converted Rothschild's nephew to socialism but had he done so I am afraid he would have soon drifted back into his former way of thinking." But

Rothschild had offered the colony an interest-free loan, if they ever cared to apply.

On New Year's Day, William Lane, as *intendente*, performed a joint marriage service for three couples. He had a personal interest in the wedding of his American sister-in-law, Eleanor McQuire, to Jack Delugar, a young bushman from Queensland; and of Clara Jones, aged twenty-six, to Billy Laurence, an amiable young man whose "golden tenor" enriched the evening sing-songs.

What Dave Stevenson thought about the union is not recorded, but Mary Cameron in Sydney published an account in the *New Australia* journal, no doubt with great personal interest herself: "The triple wedding was engineered by Will Lane in the single men's quarters at 5 pm, and judging from the manner these couples have stuck to their own respective domiciles during the past week a very good job has been made ... There are not many more marriageable girls. If there were we should soon have no single men, now that the ice is broken."

Tozer thought the colony had never been better with the malcontents gone. Although they had lost eighty persons, only thirty were men and of them only eleven good workers — in fact, they had been carrying a lot of drones. Now they were looking forward to the arrival of the *Royal Tar* at the end of February, with a complement of single bushmen, "free from most of the vices with which townsfolk are inoculated".

William Lane was not in such an ebullient frame of mind. He had despatched his wife Anne to Montevideo to join the *Tar* on its return voyage. Her mission was to recruit single women in Australia. Some colonists believed Lane had sent her as an act of self-abnegation, to prove to the bachelors that he could live without a wife and not be tempted by the local women — and so could they.

The expulsions and departures had depressed him deeply and he blamed himself for having repudiated his religious faith. He expressed his confusion and torment in a letter to Walter Head: "For God has given a task to me who am unworthy, and has not deserted me altogether, though for years I have tried to do His work without declaring Him openly, relying on my own intellect rather than on the Supreme will, and shrinking from the scoffs and jeers of men. It is reaping of my own sowing that the Settlement we have tried to build has been uncemented by the sense of God, without which there can be no firm trust among men."

This was not a train of thought likely to inspire confidence in intending colonists, but Head published the letter in *New Australia*, giving the

Bulletin the opportunity to mock Lane's "awful vein of snuffle, self-glorification and pious frenzy".

The colonists' greatest source of encouragement was the continuing support of the Paraguayan government, but even that seemed shaky. There were rumours of a revolution, although Tozer believed the existing government would survive.

*

A bell rang at the whitewashed Colegio Nacional Hugo Stroessner and the students, in neat pressed blue and white uniforms, came streaming across the village green. Some stopped to play netball with fallen oranges. They watched amused as I photographed an insignificant plaque at the base of the memorial to the dictator's father.

It read, "*A Los Colonos Precursores del Distrito Hugo Stroessner. La Comunidad Agradecida. 1893 — 17 de Mayo de 1894*". Those colonial precursors of 1893, I told them, were Australian, although it did not say so. I was interested because that was where I came from too.

"*Sí, sí! Australianos también!*" they choroused, and pushed forward two of their number, a girl with freckles and carrot-red hair and a boy with the Paraguayan milk-coffee complexion but clear blue eyes. Peter David Kennedy was fifteen and Sady Karyna Smith-Coherne two years younger. Neither spoke any English, but they seemed pleased, if a bit bemused, to be descended from the Australian colony. They had heard that their great-grandfathers were socialists — or something like that.

Sady directed us to her grandparents' home, a large brick bungalow across the road from the plaza. A sleek silver-grey Mercedes 3000 was parked in the drive, long-horned bullock skulls decorated the veranda. A servant ushered us into a gracious living room: a high cathedral ceiling and an expanse of tiled floor with scatter rugs, a Regency sideboard, a Welsh dresser with fine porcelain on its racks, antimacassars on the chairs and a grandfather clock tocking in the corner.

I hid the bread rolls and bananas behind my back.

*

The second batch of colonists arrived by riverboat in Asunción in March 1894 and were met by a few of the seceders. Only one man, William Kempson, a shearer from Barcaldine, was sufficiently unnerved by the horror stories to head straight back to Australia. The others, including the

Hoare family and young Margaret, pausing only to look around and decide Asunción needed a good clean-up, made the train and *carreta* journey out to the colony.

At the age of 105 Margaret recalled her first impressions:

> We arrived at the main settlement of New Australia some time in March, I think. They had built a few houses there with thatched walls and thatched roofs, but there wasn't a house big enough to accommodate a man and wife and seven children, so we lived in a tent for a few months. It seemed to be a very wild country. The settlement was on a plain, just outside a big *monte*. There were orchids up on the trees and I used to climb up to have a look at them, because my mother wouldn't let us pick them. The wildflowers were beautiful too, verbenas and poppies up above the tall green grass.

A new settlement, Loma Rugua — Hill End, was established 20 kilometres to the south. Fifty single men and ten families of the second batch, including the Hoares, moved there. "They built us a house," Margaret said, "two rooms and a big open breeze-way for a dining-living room with mud walls and a thatched roof. The kitchen, with an open fire, was outside, because they had to be very careful with the thatched roofs in case they caught alight. Our outhouse did burn down one day and my father had to build a new one."

Another terrace was erected for the single men and they came to the communal dining room for their meals. "You could get roast beef, corned beef, steak and kidney or what they called a sea-pie, stewing steak with suet pastry."

Margaret did seem to have had a generous memory of the food, for other colonists recalled a diet of beans, maize and mandioca as the staples, with beef a rare treat when one of the cattle was slaughtered. But soon her mother, Mary Hoare, decided she wasn't satisfied with the fare at the communal dining room and wanted to do her own cooking. That was the pattern that developed: the men worked on communal projects and the wives, particularly as friction continued in the camp, tended to retreat to their own houses and remain individualists.

William Lane had taken up temporary residence at Loma Rugua and Margaret remembered him as also retreating to his house, some distance away from the rest of the camp. "He wouldn't join in with the common people. He had a two-bedroomed house with thatched sides and a thatched roof. He'd come into the settlement and say what he wanted to say and do what he wanted to do, and then he'd go back to his cottage. My father said he wouldn't mix in with the rest of them."

Despite the political troubles, Denis Hoare wrote to a friend in Barcaldine that he liked the life in Paraguay: "I never felt so easy in my mind as I do since I came here. Nothing seems to trouble me. I just go out to my work in the morning and return at night and sleep quite happy. I am working at the timber and building houses. The only thing is that I would like to see some of my old mates here as there are very few amongst the men here that I knew before but they are a fine lot of men and very sociable."

*

"Hoare?" the 92-year-old man shouted, leaning forward in his rocking chair and staring in my direction with blind, rheumy eyes. "Old Denis Hoare? Of course I knew him. Knew him well! I could tell you about all those old families here at the colony, before I lost my memory. But now, I'm afraid, I can't remember sometimes whatever happened yesterday. But I can remember what happened ninety years ago. I have a perfect memory for that. And I still have days when I can remember everything well. And put it into words too. But I'm fast losing my English."

Ricardo Smith could not have known Denis Hoare. He arrived at Nueva Australia in 1909, twelve years after the Hoare family left. His wife Dorothy, born in 1904, couldn't have known them either. But she had been a colony child and her parents, the McCreens, knew all the original people. She had heard the names from them and Ricardo had perhaps absorbed them from her, taking on part of the tribal knowledge. Or else he was simply trying to please a visitor from Australia who had arrived at his door, eager for memories. There had been a constant stream of them, ever since he'd been mentioned by name as a "sight", a living relic, in a tourist handbook. He tried to oblige. And it was true that not much had changed at the old village of New Australia in the eighty years he'd been there. Except the name.

A Paraguayan manservant motioned us to seats beside the rocking chair. Old Ricardo chuckled: "Feliciano and I have been together forty-four years. All his life. I'll tell you what that means. I know all his bad points and he *knows* that I know them!"

*

The Hoare family and others of the second batch had come halfway around the world, inspired by William Lane's notions of a life of harmony, equality and mateship. They arrived to find a colony seething with discord and enmity. Many of them felt betrayed; some were shocked by Lane's dictatorial manner, others by the inaccessibility to markets; the single men resented the lack of women; a number of the wives were appalled by the primitive conditions — even fresh water had to be carried some distance to the camp. Within the first week at Loma Rugua, according to Souter's count, three men walked off without a word and twelve more in the second.

But William Lane and the trustees genuinely attempted to make the newcomers feel welcome. A cricket match was arranged, the first ever held in Paraguay. The New Australians travelled to Villarrica to play a scratch team, the Englishmen of Paraguay, organised by Dr Bottrell. In the first innings the score was England 63 to Australia's 56. An eleven-course dinner followed at Villarrica's best hotel, after which, wrote Frank Birks, "we had songs and boxes of cigars, which are very cheap, and as we New Australians couldn't get drunk on wine, we tried on ginger ale and iced lemonade, leaving the wine to the Englishmen, who were not slow in putting it away". Their abstemiousness paid off in the second innings when the Australians scored 71 to the Englishmen's 63, just carrying the match.

On their way home in the dark, the Australians lost their way and hired a guide in Ajos to lead their horses along a bridle trail through the *monte*. "Tree ferns of a dozen different kinds met over the path," wrote Frank Birks, "and sprinkled dew over us as we passed under them or pushed them aside, and the moonbeams which managed to come through the thick roof of trees and creepers here and there were no small addition to the lovely scene, it was fairyland pure and simple."

The children were unconcerned with the vagaries of the adults, pleased the interminable discussions left them on the loose. "For a child it was a lovely life," said Margaret, "a real good life, because it was free and easy. Half the time there was no school." She and her brothers and sisters would take off into the *monte* with the eight children of Edwin Jones, a farmer from Bundaberg: "Those Jones kids were the biggest characters out! They'd make out we were going somewhere for oranges. They'd call us up and we'd start off at daylight. If we couldn't find a bag we'd take the slips off our pillows and get into a row when we came home. Away we'd go for miles through the *monte*, looking for the sweetest oranges. It'd be dark when we'd come home and we'd get into trouble for being late."

But although the children thought they had landed in paradise, among the adults the complaints and simmering resentments continued. The group from the second batch at Loma Rugua met with some of the disgruntled settlers at Las Ovejas and decided affairs could be run better by an elected board of management. The leader behind the move was Gilbert Casey, a nuggety, forceful man with wide experience as a trade union organiser. He'd been one of Lane's strongest supporters in Brisbane, declaring in a public debate, "We are tired of talking Socialism. We are going to New Australia where we can put it into practice!" Many who had hesitated had surged forward to sign up.

Now Casey was talking about an elected board of management and exerting his considerable will to achieve it. He claimed to have consulted and won endorsement for the scheme from some leading Lane supporters. On 30 March, the morning after the cricket match, he walked from Las Ovejas to Loma Rugua and invited William Lane to step out into the *monte* for a chat. According to his account they sprawled in a forest glade and talked for eight hours. Casey proposed that Lane should remain as chairman but accept the advice of a managing board. "At one time during our conversation," he wrote, "I had Lane almost convinced I was right. In fact he was withdrawing from the position he had taken up, and he started to make a statement that he would reconsider the matter, when just at that time a thought entered his mind of supposed loyalty he had to the fellows who had backed him up. He stopped, and refrained from saying what he had intended." At the end of the discussion Lane was intransigent. He would not act as chairman without power, and if the majority objected, he would resign.

Next morning Casey addressed people at Loma Rugua and proposed that all settlers should gather in a plenary session. The following day, 1 April, at a meeting held midway between the two camps, Lane witnessed the resolution for a board of management overwhelmingly carried by 106 votes to 4. His own supporters abstained.

Margaret Riley remembered the meeting and heated arguments among the adults about Lane: "He was very much better educated than a lot of them, because he was a journalist, but I think he *thought* he was better, and of course, they didn't think so. They had common sense and knew what they wanted. But Bill Lane wanted everything to go his way and said they should do a thing whether they liked it or not. They thought they'd rather have the board of management and let it settle what was right and wrong. Give them all a chance to have their say."

Lane was effectively deposed from the chairmanship, but with a sufficient number of supporters to have remained, if he had wished, a key member of the new management body. However, that was not his style. He responded by proposing that the Basis of Communal Organisation be immediately established instead of waiting, as originally agreed, until 500 members were settled in Paraguay. He then announced his intention of withdrawing from the Association once the change was instituted. He would gather his sixty or so disciples around him and start again in a new colony.

With his characteristic talent for perceiving a victory in disaster, he wrote to Walter Head: "As a matter of fact, the best thing has happened which could happen ... When men refuse your help, refuse your brains, refuse to even carry out a contract, there is only one course open — to close the contract ... Saunders, Leck, Tozer, Mabbott, Stevenson are among those who are with me. Send money if you can. We are starting *anyway* ... a *quiet, safe* start on bedrock."

At the end of the month Tozer posted Harry a long letter from Asunción, warning him not to write back until he had been given a new address. He had been both disinclined and too busy to write until then, he said, but would outline the recent difficulties. After clearing out the dangerous element among the pioneers, things had gone smoothly until the arrival of the second batch in March. Initially they had seemed a decent group of people and he had been favourably impressed. Soon they were well housed in rain-proof tents, "but then began murmurings & growls about various things". A party of them, together with some of the malcontents of the first batch, started to condemn Lane, his organisation and the lack of luxurious food, even questioning his honesty and "accused all those who had done most for the formation of the colony, of anything bad they could invent". Finally "the discontented push" succeeded in getting their wish for an elected board of management by, he misinformed Harry, "a few votes".

> The result is that they have elected a new chairman etc & Lane hands over the chairmanship on 1st May & also resigns membership. There are fifty men, nine of them married, & twelve children leaving to form a new colony & to carry out the ideal which is upheld by Lane & them. They leave without any compensation whatever & are ready to struggle & work against difficulties visible & invisible. They have no money but hope to raise a little by selling watches, chains, rings, brooches etc. We take the cream of the colony with us. Lane takes only those he knows to be true, others have wanted to come but have been refused.

He himself was currently in Asunción, he said, with Saunders, one of his Patagonian companions, negotiating with the government for more land. They had had two interviews with Dr López, the minister, and had been offered any unsettled tract in the republic. He hoped they might locate themselves on a navigable river, and was shortly off to prospect a site once occupied by the old Jesuit missions on the Upper Paraná. But it was painful, he said, to leave the land they had laboured over for six months and to abandon the crops and cattle. In fact there had been talk of Lane and their seceding group taking over a portion of the colony of seven square leagues, subject to the approval of the members. It had been put to the vote but lost by a two-thirds majority. When he had told López about this incident, "he was greatly disgusted & said that for our services alone they should at least have given us ten leagues and a few hundred head of cattle". But he insisted that Lane and other stalwarts were confident of success and, though it was hard to leave, "better that than to live amongst a crowd of growling & selfish men & women whose highest object in life is to quarrel & to fill their accommodating bellies at the expense of another". The women had been the worst:

> Until I came to New Australia I had a good opinion of women in general but there I had my eyes opened. With a few exceptions they are all extremely selfish, scandalmongers, liars & growlers. Not content with that they would influence their husbands in every way possible & always for the bad, always doing their utmost to cause trouble by lying about their neighbours & interfering in matters which have nothing to do with them. Those we take with us are young & have received a sort of training from their husbands who have advanced ideas & train up a wife in the way she should go, but we wouldn't have one of the old hags we leave behind us even if her husband was perfection itself. One of these snarling, lying, backbiting, inquisitive, selfish, ugly old scarecrows can do more harm than a dozen badly minded men.

But a badly minded man, according to Tozer, was one of the most influential at New Australia: Gilbert Casey, "a man who upholds marrying Paraguayan women & canceling the law respecting alcoholic drink. Nothing could be more fatal to a colony than to allow these two things & their introduction will be rapidly followed by a general breaking up of the colony". However, the faithful would ensure the ideal was not lost: "Lane, who leaves the colony a penniless man, is determined to shew the World that his theory can be put into practice."

Casey declined the presidency of the colony's new management committee, confident the position was his when he wanted it. In the meantime he planned to return to Australia and win control of the Association's assets. The new president, effectively in a caretaker role, was Frederick Kidd, the bootmaker from Albury whose wife still hobbled on a stick since her accident on the *Royal Tar*. The members of the management committee included only two of the pioneers, Edgar Neill, a former labourer, and Dan Barrett Pogson, the bandmaster. The others were all from the second batch: Henry Smith-Barry and Hugh Blackwell, both conspiracy prisoners who had done time on St Helena, Thomas McLure, Allen Whitehorne, and Margaret's father, Denis Hoare.

Everyone on the colony seemed to be sending off letters to Australia with their version of events. Hoare was moved to do the same, informing two carrier friends in Barcaldine: "We had a split and Lane has cleared out and we are not sorry because him and us could not get on. He wanted to be Jesus Christ and us to be a lot of fools but we wouldn't stand him so he is gone and a lot of his disciples ... There were a few growls but they are gone with Lane."

Having dealt with the politics, Denis Hoare got down to matters of serious interest "concerning the Natives and their teams". He went on for some pages, a professional talking to colleagues who would appreciate the niceties of the Paraguayan teams, the *carretas* with great wooden wheels over two metres in height, and the six yoked bullocks drawing a tonne. He conceded that the drivers had their animals well trained and "never travel in the heat of the day but early and late and they are as happy as a sandboy".

As a bunch, Hoare found the Paraguayans very likeable:

> They do not care whether they work or not and they never are in a hurry. They are very friendly to us. If any of us goes to their places they will give the best they have got. My wife with two other women and the children went to a place near here the other day and they made a lot of them, especially the baby ... If they happen to see you outside if they have seen you before they shake hands and try to make you understand their lingo and give you some cigars and will feel offended if you do not take whatever they offer you.

He and his wife were well satisfied, Hoare concluded, and his only regret was "that I did not come here long ago and not to be slaving in Queensland as long as I was. There is no doubt it is a splendid Country. I cannot speak too high of it ... The Children are all well and looking well and like the place well. They are nearly living on oranges and are as fat as fools ... Remember me to everyone and let me know when you intend to come here. Let me know how Tom Cooney is getting on with my Teams, allso how the carriers getting on, allso let me know how the union followed up. I haven't heard anything about it ... Tell Harry that I will never go back to Australia untill I am a Millionaire".

He added in a cheeky postscript: "The next time you want to spell the bullocks and there are a drought on just bring them over here. Plenty of grass and water. No droughts here."

*

"So you want to talk about the colony?" Old Ricardo Smith smiled. "I like that. We had someone here the other day wanting to talk about it too. But most people are not interested now."

His full name, he said, was Ricardo Lille Smith. He was given the middle name because his great-grandfather was imprisoned in the French fortress of Lille during the Napoleonic Wars, but escaped, commandeered a French ship, the *Vanessa*, and took it back to England. His great-grandfather was awarded the ship as a trophy of war. "He became a sort of privateer."

His own father, Henry Alfred Smith, had been a British naval captain who resigned because of bad health. His doctor had recommended a warmer climate, so he came to Paraguay in 1909. He had known about the Australian socialist colony and had been one of the subscribers to the cause. "But he was not a socialist although he always said 'Give them a chance!' Well, they had a good chance!" Ricardo Smith made a wry face and dropped into a ruminative silence. After a long pause he added flatly: "I imagine that socialism will never work. It goes against human nature, I think."

His wife Dorothy came in, a tall dignified woman of eighty-four. "My father *was* a socialist and that's what *he* came for," she said, deadpan. Her father, Syd McCreen, was an Australian seaman who, by his own admission, used to bore holes in the hulls of blackleg ships during the great "maritime strike" in Australia. The McCreens came to Paraguay to join the colony in the late 1890s — but not on the *Royal Tar* as Mrs Smith seemed to believe. She was born and grew up at New Australia, married Ricardo and had remained there ever since. Her sister married another colonist, Arthur King. Both died some years before.

The dining table was being set by a maid. "I expect you're hungry," Mrs Smith said. "Have some lunch before you talk more." Steve Cooper and I protested that we weren't expected. She smiled drily at the bread and bananas I was hiding and said she could see I'd brought a picnic but they could do better than that. We sat down to a spicy beef stew and finished with brownie cake. Ricardo said, "We have it all the time. The colonists had the recipe. Brownie is quite passable when it's made with milk and eggs. In the old days they were made with corn meal and water and we called them 'tombstones'."

He liked remembering the old days, he said, and was happy to have a chance to speak English again. He was twelve when he came with his parents and brother to New Australia, and there were quite a few of the old families still settled there. They had an English school and an Anglican church, maintained by the Bishop of the Falkland Islands. (Paraguay seemed a bit of a hike from the Falklands, I thought, then recalled the small stone churches outside Sydney, once part of the diocese of Calcutta.) The clergyman, doubling as the schoolteacher, was the Reverend Charles Newbould; he enjoyed his time at New Australia and his regular game of chess with the postmaster. But eventually the funds were not sufficient to keep paying his stipend "so it all fell through and there was nothing left".

Mrs Smith was five years old at the time and her elder brother Bert became Ricardo's friend. "We were very good in school," she said. "We never played up and made a noise like they do these days. We had one big room with all the classes in there. We were easy to teach because nobody made a noise. But I only went until I was in second grade. We had to pay and my people were poor. It was a hard life. We all worked, the women, the girls and the boys, just the same."

When Ricardo and his family arrived, the little houses were still of mud and lathe construction, with either thatched roofs or shingles. "The Australians split the shingles, a lot of work. They made them when the colony was still a communistic affair."

Mrs Smith snorted in disgust. "They always went rotten, those shingles. Those places are all gone now. Awful old places!"

Her father, Syd McCreen, was an atheist. When one of his children died of a blood infection in 1900, he insisted on burying the child without ceremony or coffin outside the front door of his house. As time passed, Mrs McCreen became morbidly obsessed by the thought of every visitor to the house trampling over her dead child's grave. Her husband was too pragmatic to be troubled by such niceties. The neighbours took pity on her and persuaded Syd to take his family to Villarrica for a holiday. Then they burnt the house down and, by the time its owners returned, a new dwelling had been constructed some distance away.

*

William Lane and his sixty-three loyalists walked out of New Australia on 12 May 1894 and made a temporary camp beside the Tebicuary River some 50 kilometres to the south-east. According to Souter, the Association provided them with transport, tents, tools, food supplies to last them three weeks, and withdrawal payments of 14 shillings each, amounting to only £40 between them. In addition they were given £55 worth of cattle, in lieu of money paid by supporters in Australia. It was a paltry sum with which to buy land and livestock, perilously little for sixty-four people to start a new life. Women contributed their brooches and wedding rings but the situation seemed desperate. One wonders what happened to the offer of Baron von Rothschild's nephew, now that it was needed.

Though they had no material prospects, they had, wrote Harry Taylor, "an abundant faith in our leader and full trust among ourselves, and a certain deep-seated feeling that the giving up of all for the Truth's sake would surely be rewarded in the long run".

The reward came soon: Dave Stevenson unexpectedly received £150 from his affluent family in Scotland and donated it all to the common fund. They had been saved, even if by a narrow margin, and the jewellery was returned to its owners.

The seceders were optimistic and, with the possible exception of Clara Laurence, who had other reasons for being with them, utterly committed to Lane. "Of his fitness for generalship we had no doubt," Taylor recorded, "but mainly we were prepared to follow him whithersoever he would because we had been near enough the man to feel the warmth of his intense devotion to the Cause, and to be touched by the sweet winsomeness of his personality."

It must have pained Lane to have left two of his old friends behind at New Australia. Alf Walker, who had been his business manager in the early days of the *Boomerang*, remained, according to Tozer, out of a sense of duty to assist the New Australians in their dealings with the government. Another former loyal supporter, John Sibbald, now saw Lane as "one of the most inaccessible of men. His temper leads him into a kind of hysteria ... One of the results of his one-sided mutual trust conception is his failure to see that a mixed body of men should not be driven, but drawn".

But Lane still had his devoted lieutenant. Arthur Tozer's admiration was boundless. He warned his brother that he would see biased accounts in the newspapers about New Australia, but the fact was that Lane had been slandered and unfairly blamed for everything. "He has done his best & leaves a poor man. Now we shall see what they can do without him and also what he can do without them."

The biased accounts (or were they?) were not long in coming. In Sydney the *Bulletin* fairly crowed, its predictions of disaster confirmed in just a few short months:

The great scheme went to pieces chiefly upon the dismally vulgar question — who was to wash up? ... It has proved itself just like every other expedition, and the result is only what might reasonably have been expected. Man will drink and gamble and prowl round to the back-doors of the dusky daughters of the land till the end of time, and every scheme that fails to take these facts into consideration is certain to come to grief. The constitution of NA was based on the assumption that it is possible to create a community where every person is sober, moral, religious and full of holy yearning for self-sacrifice, and the collapse came about because there is no such community outside heaven, and never will be. If Lane was aware of this at the beginning, he perpetrated on his followers about the meanest "have" of the century; if he was not aware of it his ignorance of human nature was so vast as to be past reasoning about.

11
The Workingman's Paradise

Ah love, could thou and I with Fate conspire
To grasp this sorry Scheme of Things entire,
Would we not shatter it to bits — and then
Remould it, nearer to the Heart's Desire!
   Edward Fitzgerald, *The Rubáiyát of Omar Khayyám*

There is no happy valley to which the profane do not penetrate
sooner or later.
                                    Sydney *Truth*, June 1893

Afrer Lane and his supporters had left, the colonists at New Australia
celebrated with another triple wedding in the orange grove. The
occasion made a deep impression on young Margaret Hoare: "The
new president, Mr Kidd, married them. I thought it was a beautiful setting
for a wedding. The trees were white with blossom and the ground too and
petals were falling on the brides and grooms during the service. They had
orange blossoms for posies, mosquito net for veils and the dresses were
made of calico. I thought it was very romantic. There was a big spread
after at the dining hall."

But many of the bachelors were painfully aware that the colony could
not offer brides for them and the negative publicity in Australia would
deter single women recruits. And despite the departure of Lane, a majority
of trustees on the Board of Management still upheld his views on The
Colour Line.

One by one the men began to slip away. Margaret remembered: "People
were always leaving Las Ovejas — it was just falling apart. There was
nothing much there for the single men. They were told they could not
mix with the natives of the country, although they were nice friendly
people. I think that's why the men got so dissatisfied."

Tozer, with Lane's group at a temporary camp beside the Tebicuary
River at a ford called Paso Cosme, was delighted to report on fractures
and defections at the colony they had abandoned:

Kidd the new chairman is a dense pigheaded, smallminded, mule-like animal elected to that position because his brother mules see that he is one capable of falling in with their views & becoming their willing tool. I don't describe him thus because I have any dislike above what I should always have for such a man but because he is really as I describe him. In fact I may say that amongst those left behind there are not ten who are in any way fit to govern the colony & the few decent ones there have not been elected to any office. The schools for both young & old have been stopped as amongst the members there are none fit to carry on the work.

In fact, he informed his brother, everyone who knew anything about the movement realised that without Lane the thing was dead — but only as far as the old colony was concerned. Among the faithful the idea was as much alive as ever.

He omitted to mention the defections among the Lane loyalists. One night five men disappeared from the camp, stealing the dinghy from the *Royal Tar*, which had been left on the river bank, and in it made their way downstream to the Paraná. A few days later three more men withdrew. After these departures the rest of the group closed ranks solidly behind Lane.

Tozer posted his letter to Harry on 27 May from Asunción, where he was negotiating a concession of land found by the advance prospectors. It gave him the opportunity to further his acquaintance with the Minister of Colonisation and the Exterior. "I have frequently to visit Minister López at his private house. He is a stout man about 32–35 years old, recently married to a good looking young lady of about eighteen. His house is comfortably furnished but everything is very plain. There is no attempt at show — as a comparison I may say that our house is richly furnished compared with his. He is very chatty & pleasant & apparently wishes to do his best for us. He was speaking about the coming elections the other day when he said that either Eguzguiza or Decoud would be elected president & that he would probably retain his office as Minister of Exterior for two years."

The Minister's confidence was misplaced. In a bloodless revolution on 9 June 1894, President González and all his ministry were overthrown by a faction of their own Colorado Party. Lane had an appointment with Minister López at 2 o'clock that very day, but the minister was arrested by the rebels at 11 in the morning, while engaged in discussions about land with Alf Walker.

Tozer described events: "López and Walker walked up to the troops

surrounding the Chamber of Deputies; they, the soldiers, allowed them
to pass within the ranks & then arrested López. Walker was not touched.
The president & all the ministers were arrested & shipped off to Argentina
next day."

After the subsequent election, in another factional putsch General Juan
Eguzguiza was confirmed in power. Tozer complained that the revolution
had interfered with their negotiations. They had ended up buying five
leagues of land in the fork formed b the Pirapó and Capiibary Rivers,
and were working on the new government for a grant of an adjoining five
leagues. Meanwhile, he was buying bullocks and horses in readiness for
transportation to the site.

The property, purchased for £360, was 72 kilometres south-east of New
Australia, on the other side of the large town of Villarrica and some 20
kilometres from the nearest village of Caazapá. It was in two parcels,
forming 9,380 hectares altogether, a mixture of *campo*, or grassland, and
monte, dense forest. The fact that it was situated in the fork of two rivers
with a tendency to flood did not seem to alarm the colonists unduly.

On 27 June an advance party of twelve men went ahead to clear trees
and establish some huts. An early decision was taken to name their new
home after the river crossing where they had camped: Colonia Cosme.

Tozer reported that the main body of colonists hoped to be settled at
Cosme within a fortnight. Meanwhile, they had had encouraging news
from Australia: all the officials of the cooperative movement still remaining there had resigned in order to side with Lane. New Australia was
"practically bust", he said, and in desperation Gilbert Casey had gone to
London to try to recruit new members. He didn't think much of his
chances but in London, "Casey will no doubt get hold of some of the
Labor leaders & probably you may get to hear his lecture or get a report
of it. Try to find out something of what he says & let me know. He is a
good speaker but talks with a sneering twang. I don't think he will run
Lane down but will rather speak of him as a man who has the ideal at
heart but not the knowledge to put it into practice".

The last of the seceders settled at Colonia Cosme in July, and in their
publicity discouraged all but the most earnest from joining them: "To save
needless enquiries, everybody should understand that Cosme is for English-speaking Whites, who accept the Life Marriage, The Colour Line,
and Teetotalism among their principles, and who realize in their hearts
that COMMUNISM IS RIGHT."

*

"I get mad as a hornet when I think about William Lane," said Ricardo Smith. "I like talking about the old colony, but not about him, the big despot!"

I was surprised Lane's name meant so much to him, as the Smiths had not come to New Australia until long after the colony had reverted to individual titles. But he remembered "that autocrat" was mentioned all the time by the old crowd, though no one had anything good to say. "They reckoned if you took up a position against him, he was an enemy for life. He could not stand opposition. He wanted to be the big mogul and what he said had to go. That's why they made a division and made the two colonies — Cosme and New Australia."

I asked the Smiths if they remembered much contact between the New Australians and the people at Cosme. "In the beginning yes, two or three cricket matches," Don Ricardo replied, "but afterwards, through bad communications they didn't visit each other. There were hardly any visits from one colony to the other. There was still bad feeling."

"Does it still linger on today? Certain bitter memories?"

"The rivalry? Yes! But it doesn't go on anymore because all of them have all died off."

*

In 1894 a trickle of recruits still came to New Australia. George Napier Birks, a 56-year-old homoeopathic chemist from Adelaide and his wife Helen arrived in June to join their adult sons. George, a distinguished man with a bushy white beard, wrote to his brother back home that he mustn't be alarmed by the fearful conditions described in the Australian papers. Most of it was untrue, although he had to admit their total house accommodation was less than their old sitting room in Adelaide, and they were "absolutely destitute of household furnishings except the few pots and pans we had to buy in Asunción to carry us on". On the other hand, he found their condition peaceful and orderly, "work is going on uninterruptedly — we have never been near starvation, there is very little bad language heard in public, there is no quarrelling, the decencies of life are observed, and we are hopeful of something better in course of time".

Naturally Lane's defection had made a great difference to them, he admitted, and they had to look forward to a period of enforced economy after the withdrawal of so much of their labour force. He'd heard that two more men had left the settlement of Loma Rugua because they, like some others, "find living under rules irksome both as regards drink and native women, and the share and share alike part of the business has no charms for them; however, they have had their fun, and now they have their reward for they will have to go out without anything, the Assocn not being in a position to pay out withdrawing members".

But he and his family were content. They enjoyed the view over the plain to the *monte* all around them, broken in the distance by openings giving glimpses of plains and further *monte* beyond.

About the same time, Tozer reported from Cosme that he had not heard much of New Australia since they had left three months before, except some smug statements from the new management that everything was flourishing and all the members were satisfied. "Through other channels we hear that all rules are ignored & that members do pretty well as they like. Some drink, native women sleep in the camps & the colony's goods & tools are fast disappearing, it being known that members are bartering them for native produce, especially rum. Under these conditions & knowing the class of men there I am not surprised to hear that they are satisfied."

A third settlement had been formed at New Australia in optimistic expectation of new British arrivals. It was both unpromising in its name — Tuju Rugua or Mud Pocket — and in its genesis, for some Paraguayan families living there were asked to leave. The Hoare family moved to Tuju Rugua, but Margaret remembered the eviction of the locals with regret:

> I don't think it was right to put the natives out of their homes. They were settled there and quite content to live their own lives. But a lot of them had to go. There was a chap there, Don Eduardo, he was a Spaniard, married to a Guarani; he had to leave his place and he was quite annoyed about it. I think they took some of his cattle too. When we went there to live he turned up one day. My father couldn't speak the Spanish so well — he learned it from books and gave it his own pronunciation and you couldn't understand him — but we'd learned it from the natives, so he had to get one of us to speak for him. Don Eduardo wanted to know if he could get his cattle. My father told him to go out on the run and take what cattle he wanted. He said, "There's nothing to stop you," so that's what he did.

Don Eduardo moved some distance away, but visited often. He had a small sugar mill and used to sell treacle to people in the neighbourhood. Margaret's mother, Mary Hoare, earned a little income by sewing for other colonists such as the Stanleys, a family from England, and some of the single men. She made shirts and calico trousers and with the proceeds bought treats for her family such as *galletas*, *chipá* bread and treacle. One day Don Eduardo ordered some clothes. "She outfitted him in a plain loose coat and trousers, not tied in around the ankles, and he thought he was just made. Because he could dress like the Australians. Anywhere you went, the Australians were thought a lot of. They didn't think so much of the English people, but the Australians were somebodies."

Margaret was shocked to see the Paraguayan men sauntering about while the women did all the work. "The men seemed to be very lazy. It was good land and could grow anything, but they didn't want to bother. But, do you know, out in the country, I never once saw an old man. There had been a war there and most of the men had been killed off. There were quite a few young men who used to come around after Bill Lane and the others had left. But if you went to a fiesta, you'd never see an old man, though there were plenty of old women, and young ones too."

The colonists celebrated the anniversary of the establishment of New Australia in September. Denis Hoare reported on the event for his Barcaldine carrier friend, William Price Junior:

> You may think that our life here is a drudgery but there you mistake. On the 16th of Sept was the anniversary of Nueva Australia being proclaimed a Colony by the Paraguayan Government. We had a public holiday. We invited several people from Villa Rica thirty miles from us, allso some from a village called Ajos seven miles from us. We had some athletic sports in which some of the Visitors took part. At night we had a concert and the singing class came out in their true colours and astonished the Visitors. I must now tell you about our amusements. In the first place we have one of the best music masters that was in Australia. D.B. Pogson ... has got a brass band here of over twenty members, he is allso teaching all the girls over thirteen to play on the Violin and the boys the fife. He allso teaches anyone that wishes singing. He has a very large class.

There were still departures at New Australia, including a trustee, Henry Smith-Barry, one of the former conspiracy prisoners. But some prodigals returned, people who'd walked out at the time of the big revolt against Lane. Most of them had found it a frightening experience being adrift without Spanish or any funds to return home.

About sixty of the Australians who had taken up the offer to settle at the government-backed Colonia González found themselves in desperate straits after the revolution. The new government showed no particular commitment towards them, and twenty-five of them made their way to

Buenos Aires to throw themselves on the mercy of the British legation. Another nineteen followed them and the last Australian left Colonia González in October 1894.

The British Minister in Buenos Aires, the Honourable F. J. Pakenham, described them as in "a perfectly destitute condition", but could receive no undertaking from the New South Wales or Queensland governments to repatriate them — although the latter eventually assisted with passages for three families. Some of the former shearers made their way to Patagonia to find work on British-run sheep estancias; the Salvation Army in the Argentine capital helped some of the others, but Souter concludes that, "It is not possible to account for everyone who left New Australia: some stayed in South America, some went to England, some returned to Australia".

Writing many years later of the subsequent lives of some Australian colonists, Mary Gilmore offered a lurid tale of the trouble-makers and suspected saboteurs: "There was Louis Simon who, with T. Westwood and another man named White, arranged to capture a Spanish gunboat (that for safety had crept up the Plate River to Asunción during the Spanish-American war) and go privateering." In another version she wrote that the captured gunboat had crept upriver, far north near the Brazilian border, and the Australians only failed in their scheme because the American envoy notified the Paraguay Government "that this boat being allowed to remain in Paraguayan waters was an unfriendly act towards the United States and she had to be ordered out. Paraguay didn't like it, all her sympathy being with Spain, but there was nothing for her to do but obey, which she did, while three disappointed ex-Australians cursed international law and reckoned, 'what a chance they had missed'. I daresay that, by now, that gunboat has grown to a man-o'-war in their imaginations, and their sense of loss great in proportion".

According to Mary, Louis Simon was later "suspected of engineering a rising in one of the provinces of Brazil". Souter notes that Tom Westwood and his son returned to Australia, "where Foley, despite his blindness, became a successful violin teacher". But of the later career of the mysterious Fred White, the suspected ringleader and former special constable, there seems no further trace.

Meanwhile, those remaining at New Australia enjoyed another celebration, diplomatically accepting an invitation to come to the nearby town of San José on 23 November to commemorate the inauguration of the Paraguayan republic. Denis Hoare described the festivities for his Barcaldine friend:

When our people were approaching the town, our band struck up the Nationale of Paraguay. It caused a great commotion amongst the people here who are very true Patriots. Some of the old people who remembered the War in Lopez time were seen to shed tears and the younger people were jumping with joy and shouting Bueno Nueva Australia (good New Australia) and anything they had was not too good for our people ... The Government of Paraguay stood the whole expense, they even sent carts to take our people and brought them home again after two days and nights of singing, playing and dancing.

*

Gilbert Casey had arrived in Sydney in September, with the intention of taking over the New Australia Co-operative Settlement Association, but was opposed by the secretary, Walter Head, a staunch Lane ally.

The members in Australia were understandably restive about the £60 deposits they had invested. According to the Articles of the Association, if they decided to withdraw they forfeited £10, but everything over that sum would be returned to them from the Savings Trust Account where it was to have been lodged. After the disturbing news from Paraguay of a split, the majority of members demanded refunds — only to discover that the Savings Trust Account did not exist. The money had been expended for the refitting of the *Royal Tar*. Though the ship was still an asset for the Association, the other assets were land, livestock and equipment in Paraguay, and so quite useless to members planning to withdraw in Australia. When they confronted Walter Head, he referred them to the trustees at New Australia.

Some of them sued, and in a ruling of the Sydney District Court, Head, although he had resigned from the Association at the time of Lane's secession, was deemed legally responsible. Bombarded with writs and lawyers' letters, he wrote to Lane that he feared going to gaol: "Nice blanky position ain't it?"

Mrs Anne Lane, staying in Sydney with Mary Cameron at her lodgings in Newtown, was instructed by her husband not to recruit women for Cosme until the situation clarified.

But Gilbert Casey was keen to attract women to New Australia and aroused the interest of Rose Summerfield, a poet, campaigner for women's suffrage and a capable organiser for the new Australian Workers' Union. She was not to make the journey herself for a few more years, at the time being married to an elderly tailor.

Meanwhile, Walter Head — overwhelmed by troubles, having lost a child in the Gippsland bush the previous year, and with his eldest child Wally in the care of Dave Stevenson in Paraguay — tried to sort out his obligations to the Association. In November 1894, while threatened with criminal prosecutions on all sides, he discharged Lane's mortgage on the *Royal Tar* to a firm of Sydney merchants, with a second mortgage in the name of William Saunders. He arranged an audit of the Association's books, with power of attorney given to another Lane sympathiser, Tom Hicks-Hall. Then Head left for Melbourne and quite simply disappeared.

Those who were close to him, such as Mary Cameron who'd worked beside him at the Association office, always maintained that Head was scrupulously honest but, in a situation not of his causing, he was legally vulnerable and liable for up to fifteen years' gaol. Casey and the New Australia supporters saw his disappearance as incriminating. Objectively it is hard to view his actions, if not for personal gain, as anything other than heavily partisan for Cosme. Anne Lane wrote to her husband in Paraguay that he must always feel kindly to Walter Head, "for he has always been true to us, no matter what reports say — and there have been terrible ones". Saunders, in a letter to Lane of 6 December, admitted that he had seen Head, who had taken on a new identity: "The worse of it is Walter must keep scarce and cannot come and fight it out. Anyway I am satisfied. I waited and saw him and when you feel sure a thing is right it does not matter what outsiders say."

Souter documented Head's trail to New Zealand, then to Tasmania, where he assumed the name of Walter Alan Woods, edited a Labour periodical and entered politics. He helped found the Tasmanian Labor Party, was a member of the Tasmanian parliament for seventeen years, and served two terms as speaker.

On 6 March 1895 the *Royal Tar* was sold, on the authority, according to Mary Cameron, of a letter which forged Head's handwriting, for a sum variously given as £1,100 or £1,750. Lane issued a circular to all the original New Australia creditors, accepting responsibility for liabilities. Souter says that it seems that many claims from Australia were, in fact, paid "and until the end of his life William Lane is said to have sent money whenever he could afford it to any in whose debt he still stood".

Anne Lane departed for Paraguay on 15 March. She was followed one week later by Tom Hicks-Hall and a former conspiracy prisoner, Alec Forrester, who sailed from Newcastle for Valparaiso in Chile, planning to make their way to Cosme across the Andes. It seems likely that this circuitous route was to give people in Australia the slip, particularly as Forrester at this stage changed his name to Alec Lewis. But there would have been no great detective work in presuming their destination; at about the same time, their wives and children left Sydney with a party of seventeen bound for Cosme. Also on board were William Wood, the former secretary of the General Labourers' Union at Bourke, his wife Lillian and infant son William.

Gilbert Casey had been given the keys to the New Australia office, only to find that the cupboard was bare. He stayed on in Sydney for two more months, then he too sailed for Paraguay with fifty-one adults and children, recruits for New Australia.

*

Denis Hoare wrote from Paraguay on 9 December 1894 to William Price Junior at Barcaldine:

> Dear Will, you have heard many conflicting reports concerning us which are utterly false, but as Gilbert Casey is in Australia with full instructions from us to let the people of Australia know, it is not necessary for me to go into details. The only thing that we want is to let the people know the truth and then they can come if they like. We do not want to lure anyone here under false pretence. Enough for me to say that we are here and a big majority of us would not change for anything we ever had before. Speaking personally the more I see of the Country the better I like it and even if the association were to bust up as the papers says it has allready done, nothing would persuade me to return to the old life in Australia again. The only thing that I regret is that I did not know as much about Paraguay ten years ago. I would not have wasted so much of my life trying to live in Australia.

Although the split with Lane had done them harm, Hoare continued, they were now beginning to reap the benefit. Some people who had walked out were returning and they had had numerous enquiries from interested parties in England and North America. There were good opportunities for a man with about £200 to make a comfortable living. The soil was good and the climate mild: "If you do happen to get a day a little hot, you are sure to have rain the next. There are no sham rains here, if it looks like rain you can be sure of getting it." He would very much like to see some of his old friends come over, he wrote, "but no matter how much I would like it I have made up my mind not to advise no one. Let everyone please themselfs". He could see hard work for at least two more years, but after that a bright future. He hoped to look back with pride to the time when they were struggling and be able to relate to his children and friends the difficulties they had surmounted at the start of their great movement.

"There was no starvation whatever on the settlement," his daughter Margaret told me. "There were fish in the rivers and we had plenty of fowls — domestic fowl and wildfowl — and plenty of eggs. The women used to make flour from grated mandioca and bread from cornmeal. We had a big cultivation of maize, sugar cane, peanuts and other vegetables, so we were not short of anything in that line. We could not get tea but we drank *yerba mate* and we could not get white sugar but we had molasses. There was plenty of fruit — orange groves just everywhere — and mandarins, limes and guavas."

But Lizzie Butterworth, one of three children in her family, remembered that there was not enough food to go around and then "the romance faded out of the picture". Her father would come home depressed from New Australia meetings, because the single men complained about supporting the colony children. "Dad used to tell them that the kids would keep them when they got old, but the single ones wouldn't see it that way. And week by week all that could got away home again and the family people had to stick it."

George Napier Birks' grandson, Eric, wrote that after the split the colony sold off most of its cattle for cash, and soon beef became a fond memory. After about nine months with pumpkin and oranges as the staple items in their diet, most members of the family were looking speculatively at Dear Old Pals, his little sister's pet rooster:

> Plainly we were sick and tired of pumpkin. Secretly, into the pot went "Dear Old Pals". Much boiling filled the hut with an appetising smell which was but a memory of good days, meat days. Boiling made him palatable even for his playmate. Suddenly a long leg bone was identified as the very leg of the pet rooster, and a wail went up from the heart, "Oh, Dear Old Pals!" As far as I know, Mrs Jones got the bird. I do know we went back on to pumpkin.

The Birks family — with professional backgrounds and establishment connections in Adelaide — were often described by the other colonists as "silvertails".

But Eliza Jones, the bushwoman from Bundaberg with eight children, had developed a firm friendship with Eric's mother, Grace Birks. It probably stemmed from the morning when Grace, feeling ill, was trying to do the family laundry in makeshift conditions, drawing water from a well and scrubbing clothes under a shelter of smelly green hides. "Get out of this," Mrs Jones told her, taking over, "and if ever I see you fooling round in here spoiling your good clothes, and making such a silly mess of things, I'll break your bloomin' neck!"

Grace responded by helping Eliza when she had her occasional bouts of epilepsy. "She would stagger in to me when she felt the seizures coming on," Grace wrote, "and say, 'I'm on strike for today,' and then lie on my bed while I looked after her baby, and kept the other children out of mischief."

The children — Jones, Hoares, Molesworths, Birks, Pogsons and Butterworths — were expert at mischief. In the dense *monte* which enclosed their settlement they found creatures to inspire fear, wonder, alarm and, more often than not, hilarity. Three species of monkeys were to be seen around New Australia: the little brown capuchins, the large dark howlers, which kept the colonists awake at night with their wails, and the tiny spider monkeys. "They wouldn't come down near us," Margaret said with a laugh, "but we used to see them up in the trees and we'd throw oranges at them and they'd catch an orange and throw it back down at us." She paused, remembering the stories about the Cosme settlers eating monkeys in the early days of privation. "I don't know how they could have eaten monkey meat. Oh, you couldn't, you couldn't! They're too human! You know, the little monkeys put their hands over their eyes and cry, just like a baby."

In the forest there were possums, red deer, the strange armour-plated armadillo which would roll itself into a ball when disturbed — "we never ate them but some of the people did" — gaudily plumaged macaws, the toucan with its droll, top-heavy beak and clouds of butterflies. But the favourite for Margaret was the hummingbird that nested in the orange grove behind her house. "We'd stand back and look at it but my mother would never let us go near it to touch it or frighten it away. And it used to come and hum and hum and hum over the nest. It was lovely to see. It was such a tiny thing, you could hardly see it, for the flittering of its wings."

There were creatures to dread — the fox, wolf, puma and, feared most of all, the jaguar, nearly alway called a "tiger" in Paraguay. "We caught a jaguar once," Margaret said. "We always had to lock the fowls up at night-time and set a trap, because the foxes used to prowl around after them. I'll never forget one morning there was a jaguar in the trap. The men shot him and brought him into the camp and we all had a good look. It was a dumpy sort of an animal, not as big as a leopard or a lion, but spotted all over and with big teeth. I wouldn't like to meet him anywhere."

The Australian bush children, the Queenslanders especially, had left a

land with some of the most venomous snakes in the world, but ironically
were more in awe of the snakes of South America — the boa constrictors
and rattlesnakes — which featured more dramatically in adventure books
such as *Chums*.

Eric Birks wrote that, "One little tree snake there is, I forget his name,
but he guarantees death, which follows his bite, most times in a matter of
minutes. One day my sister was playing in the shade of the hut, and my
mother and I saw one of these snakes. It moved towards my sister. We
stood stick still; the little fair-haired child sang on to her dollie. The snake
ran between my sister's bare legs and away. My mother fainted. I have
never liked snakes since then; the only good snake is a dead one." He
recommended a Paraguayan treatment for snake-bite: splitting a chicken
down the breast with a machete and then clapping the bird over the
puncture. "If the patient dies, then the chicken was not killed quickly
enough. This method did not appeal to us much after Dear Old Pals had
gone the way of all flesh."

The New Australian women learned to tolerate non-venomous snakes
camping in their grass-thatched roofs, but they "threatened to strike when
an army of black monster ants invaded the huts". As the ants attacked
only food and insects, they finally came to see these visits as those of a
garbage collector.

The most unpleasant insect, according to Eric, was the *chigre*, or
"jigger" as it was called. "This flea-like pest evidently produces a preponderance of females. It lurks near ground and attacks the toes and feet where
it quickly burrows into the flesh, there to lay eggs. If not meticulously
removed each night with a lance, festering sores and ulcers form." The
children had to line up every night for jigger parade, but Eric's mother
was often too busy to check her own limbs and "paid the price for the rest
of her life".

The children's usual play route was across the *campo*, where wild
poppies were in bloom, and into the dark *monte*. In pools of sunlight they
saw brilliantly coloured orchids, tree ferns stippling the shadows, and,
imitating the monkeys, they swung from the vines. One day Margaret and
some others emerged from the forest at a ford across the river. Just beyond
was a waterfall with a deep pool beneath.

> We peeled off everything, left our clothes up on the bushes and got into the
> river and had a good swim. Suddenly a mob of cattle stampeded down; some
> of our men had brought them and they had been travelling and were thirsty.
> We rushed out of the water and climbed up into a tree — but there was an

ants' nest up there and we had no clothes on and they nearly ate us!

But for us children it was a paradise. It was the best life ever because it was free and easy. You could go anywhere you wanted and the natives used to marvel at us, the way the Australian kids used to go walkabout. We hardly ever had to bother about school. Sometimes somebody would take it into their head to collect the youngsters and start a school and teach us something. Well, that'd fall through. Then we kids would run wild again.

One of the colonists who took on the thankless task of schoolteacher was Kyffin Birks. His nephew Eric remembered skittishly: "Near by the barn was the school; with its black-board, stools, desks and its window made with frame and glass from a picture donated by my grandparents; it was a tribute to ingenuity, and no doubt a credit to early enthusiasm. On Saturday, October 19th, 1895, that school was burnt to the ground. I deny having anything to do with the fire. I did not even help to put it out. The fact that one of my name was the head, and only master, gave me no pangs."

"Our last teacher," Margaret said, "was Hughie Blackwell. I knew him well from Barcaldine where he had been a friend of my father's." Blackwell had been one of the conspiracy prisoners on St Helena. With his oiled hair parted almost comically dead-centre, he looked like a mild-mannered clerk. But during the shearers' strike in Queensland he had been viewed by the authorities as a dangerous firebrand. At the trial in Rockhampton his letters were tabled as evidence of a conspiracy to overthrow the government: "Things are quiet in Clermont," he had written. "First shot fired there may be the cause of the Australian Revolution. The men are very determined here, and anxious to be at work. What work I leave you to imagine."

"When Blackwell left," Margaret said, "as the men dwindled away, we didn't have a schoolteacher. No more formal schooling but my father used to teach us. He'd set the lessons and correct them at night time."

Denis Hoare also set lessons for himself, studying Spanish after a hard day's physical work. "He learned it from books — but that's different altogether to the way that people speak. When he'd talk they could not understand him because he'd give it his Australian accent. So he often got my brothers to speak for him — they had learned their Spanish from the children we played with. The natives were very good to us. They'd give us a feed and bags full of oranges."

Life wasn't so good for George Napier Birks. One of his lungs had been haemorrhaging for thirty years and was not getting any better in Paraguay's humid climate. At fifty-six he had not adapted well to the rigours of communal living; he had lost weight and suffered from boils. He was in fact on a rapid slide to his early death. With his background as a pharmacist, he still acted as a doctor in emergencies, as he did when Denis Hoare almost amputated one of his toes with an axe, and a little girl's fingers were caught in the sugarcane crusher. But Birks was in desperate need of medical attention — and counselling — himself.

He wrote to his brother that he recognised that one's previous mode of living and one's age made all the difference, but he was finding life insufferably monotonous. The difficulties of pioneering with such an ill-assorted group of people were vastly greater than he had anticipated. They had been so short-handed it had taxed all their labour power to cope with prosaic crops such as mandioca, sweet potato, maize and sugarcane. The planting of ornamental and fruit trees had been postponed, "and no one has cared to do anything on his allotment here, feeling that *he* would not reap the fruits of his labour — this with some few notable exceptions, to whom be honour. Such is the Socialism that we have brought with us: we will do as little as possible for the public good, and nothing at all if he thinks another individual will reap the benefit".

Some of the women — "who came because they had to come" — were the worst offenders, he observed, but there were still good men and women on the colony who would do their best to make the thing a success, "but they have a heavy task, not only to endure their own troubles, but to listen to others, to have their every action misconstrued, and to be generally distrusted".

The former accountant, John Sibbald, agreed that the trouble with Utopia was that you had to know everybody. "In Adelaide one can choose his friends. You may 'know' your next-door neighbour or not as you please. But in New Australia you must know him and his 199 neighbours and neighbouresses. He has a brother's right to intrude into your most sacred precincts."

They were all getting fed up with each other.

"The fact is," wrote Henry Connelly, a bushman from Queensland, "we ran up against ourselves, and at the same time made the acquaintance of others at close quarters, and in doing so found that however workable communism may be for angels, we were not suited for it. Communism is an exceeding high religion. In practice it is only a chosen few who are fit to live that high life."

In February 1895 Dan Barrett Pogson, the bandmaster, his wife

Rebecca, pregnant again, and their seven children left. His music had helped make New Australia a happier place, but life on the colony was not giving him joy anymore and his rheumatism had worsened. He was entitled to take his band instruments as his tools of trade and sold them to finance their fares.

With her dreams of dancing under the orange trees over, Lizzie Butterworth complained she "had to turn out early to help milk the Colony cows, then help Dad with the pigs, then help teach school. Then I had to help three other girls clean up the single men's rooms, make beds and do mending for them; and then they said they were keeping us".

One by one, old customs from Australia were replaced by a Paraguayan way of doing things. Eric Birks recalled "the stock of tea was exhausted, but that, quaintly enough, was no hardship because the native *yerba mate*, which is sipped through a *bombilla* from a gourd, is a quickly-acquired habit".

His grandfather, George Napier Birks, was by then desperately ill, possibly from cancer of the bowel, and died on 14 September 1895. During his last pain-racked days, when he spoke disjointedly of happy times and tea and hot buttered toast in Adelaide, Eric and some of the other children kept him company. "Lying on his death-bed, in a mud hut, he made pictures for us on scraps of paper with invisible ink. These I carried to the fire where the heat brought the pictures to life and great pleasure to us both."

George's widow, Helen, and most of her large family made arrangements to return to Australia. Eric's mother tried to make the last Christmas in Paraguay a memorable one for the children, with fireflies tied to the tree instead of candles, making it "as brilliant as any tree in an English manor or castle ... dolls made of sawdust and old rags; home-made toys of many kinds, for boys who had no toys other than the ones they made for themselves". Meanwhile, Eric "lorded it a little over my white companions, and a lot over the natives, both boys and girls and men, with an old clock the hands of which spun madly, for a spring was twisted".

During the festive season some colonists celebrated with *caña*, Paraguay's potent white rum. According to Margaret Riley, they had found a handy local which offered other attractions as well:

> There was no grog actually on the settlement. But there was a place between the settlements where a chap used to make *caña*. He used to fly the white flag when the rum was on and the men used to go there and get their drink. We often used to visit because it was a very nice place and he'd always give us a

meal, bacon and mandioca and corn on a great big dish for us children to help ourselves. We used to call the man Father-in-Law because he had two very nice looking young daughters. We used to reckon the men came there to see the girls. But I never saw a drunken man all the time that I was there.

Maybe, but Arthur Tozer exulted about further evidence of New Australia "going to the dogs.": "Some of the colonists have intercourse with the native women & natives of both sexes attend their balls & socials. The rules are ignored and drinking common. At a recent cricket match with the English residents many got drunk & even boys were carried off the field in a state of intoxication. A number of the members have received money from friends but none of them pay it into the general fund. They either bank it or buy horses etc with it for their own use."

Margaret's memories of the dance nights were of lively, innocent social events:

I think mostly all the children learned to dance bare-footed and on an earth floor. We'd kick up the dust a bit! Sometimes we'd have our brass band or bagpipes, but mostly it was concertina music. The natives used to have a violin and they were very fond of dancing. They'd come to our dances and we'd go to theirs. It was all very friendly. They'd try to give us a supper at their dances, even if it was only *chipá* bread and boiled eggs.

They used to dance our dances — the quadrille, the Lancers and the waltz, the Schottische and the barn dance. But their native dances were really different, with more rhythm. There were two men and a woman up one end, and two women and a man down at the other, and they'd meet one another and jiggle around. Hah! Really some of their dances were something after the shuffle they have today. You know, you were just shuffling around bare-footed on an earth floor. I didn't call it dancing but it was fun.

The Paraguayan women, and later the colony women too, used to dance with fire beetles or fireflies in their hair. The fire beetle is bigger. It used to flick its head and when it did the lights would come on. We kids were always chasing after the fire beetles to catch them.

*

In her modern bungalow at the site of New Australia, Mrs Dorothy Smith took a scrap of mosquito netting. She bunched it up and pinned it in her short grey hair.

"We'd trap the little fireflies inside these bits of net and pin them all over our heads. That was a trick we learned from the Paraguayans. It was romantic, I suppose."

Her husband Ricardo looked ahead with sightless eyes as she gazed into a mirror, smiling softly.

I said that the young women at New Australia must have looked beautiful to him, dancing with the fireflies glowing and flickering around their faces.

He paused, considering. "Well, there was none of them that you'd call beauties, but they were all passable. Quite passable, I suppose."

*

The Anglican clergyman sent by the Bishop of the Falkland Islands found the dances at New Australia, "delightfully friendly and refreshing, although weird and primitive". The Reverend Charles Newbould commented on the mud floor, the few wooden chairs around the walls and the orchestra of guitar, accordion, fiddle and mandolin, playing by lamplight. "The everyday dress of the guests has been brushed up a little, but lethal weapons still ornament leather belts, and spurs are only removed from top boots if manifestly in the way."

But Arthur Tozer was determined to see a den of moral turpitude and came to investigate for himself. He visited New Australia at a time when the trustees were considering a Village Settlement Scheme, a loose association of self-governing communities. The plan was to reduce friction between colonists and demonstrate to the Paraguay government that, despite dwindling numbers, the large land grant wasn't going to waste. But it would shift the colony further away from communal towards private ownership. "All this is rather sad," lamented *Cosme Evening Notes*, "when we think of what we all hoped New Australia would be." Although the trustees could not reach agreement on the details, it was determined that two new settlements would be established: *La Novia* (The Sweetheart) and *Los Amigos* (The Friends).

As William Lane's emissary, Tozer came bearing a letter to the trustees enquiring whether Gilbert Casey intended to discharge the liabilities of the Association in Australia. He did not receive a definitive reply, but returned with some splendid gossip. "One of the historic sights," reported *Cosme Evening Notes*, "was Tozer being pumped last night. Every man took his turn at the handle and in just two hours Tozer was dry. Anyway the pump was sucked. The only good thing he was heard to say was in approval of the two-storied barn."

New Australia had already sold off half its original herd of cattle and now sold off all the remainder, except for 500 breeding cows, but for a price well below their market value. In another desperate measure they gave an English contractor the right to take 50,000 trees from the *monte*, but again the profit was disappointing. Despite Casey's return and election to the chair of the Board of Management, the departures continued. Ultimate dismemberment of the colony was inevitable.

"There was no money coming in," said Margaret Riley. "They had sold a lot of the cattle, but it was all handled by the Board of Management. No one was paid for the work they did. People got very dissatisfied, because they were getting short of things and the men liked to have their smokes and do what they wanted to do with a bit of money."

Eric Birks remembered the sense of failure. Despite all their labour, clearing, ploughing and building, things had gone from bad to worse. Tools and equipment were left outside to rust or rot because "it was the other fellow's job to bring them in". His parents acknowledged it was time to go, though two uncles, Kyf and Alf, remained.

> Mother sold her wedding presents. All was excitement. My last sight of the sewing machine was the proud native owner seated in the centre of a large ring of relatives and neighbours paddling like one possessed of a devil more than of a machine. I did a trade with the old alarm clock. I swopped it for a model canoe which I placed beside a case in a *carreta*. My own affairs thus wound up, I was ready to go. Alas, before we came to the first river the little boat was crushed to pulp.

The departures produced another sanctimonious bulletin from Arthur Tozer. The depth of New Australia's decline, in his view, was demonstrated by Gilbert Casey cohabiting with a Paraguayan woman. Casey later married her — María Antonia Sosa — adopted her daughter Valvina, and they produced two sons together, Lorenzo and Gilberto. But these domestic arrangements aroused jealousy among some of the New Australian bachelors and disapproval from the more conservative settlers. "As far as I know," Margaret Riley told me, "Gilbert Casey was the first of the men to mix with the native women. They said he was living with this native woman. I never saw her but my father used to meet them. Later a number of the men did take Guaraní wives. Well, whether they all married them or not I can't exactly say, but they were quite happy and satisfied with them."

Denis and Mary Hoare found it disquieting that their daughters were receiving attention from Paraguayan men. Margaret remembered Juan, a suitor who regularly tethered his horse outside their house. "My mother was teaching me to crochet and to sew on the hand-machine, and he'd come and sit beside me and talk while I was doing it." What irritated her mother most was that she could not understand what he was saying to Margaret in Spanish. "She thought he was paying me too much attention, and one day she said, 'I don't want that fellow sitting near you anymore. Tell him not to come!' I didn't care whether he came or not, because I didn't bother about men. Too young, I suppose."

Margaret's interest was more engaged some time later, when she went to a New Australia dance at the home of Mrs Prior, a lively woman with a fondness for parties.

> Mrs Prior often used to give a dance and invite a few of the natives around. There was a chap who asked me for a dance — he looked to me to be more Spanish than Guaraní — and we ended up having two or three dances, shuffling and parading around the room. When I went back to the seat, Mrs Prior came over and said to me, "What a good looking fellow that is!" I said, "Yes, he is nice looking." She said, "If he comes back and asks you for a dance, you should tell him that *I* want to dance with him." So anyway, he did come back and I told him. "Oh!" he said, and went and got her up and that was the end of him. I said to my sister, "I've lost my good-looking chap." She said, "Serves you right for introducing him around!"

*

By October 1896 the New Australian residents were welcoming departures so that the ultimate division would mean larger shares for those who stayed. Souter records that in January 1897 the colony assets were valued and divided equally between the seventy-eight remaining adult members. Those planning to leave could sell their lots.

After his long and devoted service to the colony, Alf Walker claimed his share and left, planning to find newspaper work in London. He died soon after his arrival.

Gilbert Casey stayed on at New Australia with his new wife, as did the Edwin Jones family from Bundaberg, the Syd McCreens and their daughter Dorothy who would later marry Ricardo Smith, the Miles Butterworths, Thomas Kings, the Stanleys, O'Donnells, Jacobsons, Henry Connelly and Kyf Birks.

The Paraguayan government, generous to the end, granted each remaining colonist 45 hectares of land and almost 11,450 hectares for communal use and division among descendants and new settlers.

*

Ricardo Smith, arriving in 1909, was one of the beneficiaries. He became animated remembering how, as a young man, he had practically lived in the saddle, wearing a sombrero, a leather fringed apron over his trousers, a revolver in his belt. "Of course we all used to carry a gun, because in the olden times we had wild cattle and we often had to take out our revolver — to shoot a bull if he got too obstreperous, to save the life of a cow or even one of the people travelling with us. We had to defend them."

Unlike Cosme, the farming land of New Australia was well placed near a main transport route. Many of those who stayed after the reversion to private title did well, and about half the land in the district is still held by colony descendants. But Ricardo said that most of them survive on very small lots and see themselves as Paraguayan; they don't have much interest in their family's singular history.

He believed the colonists in the old days had not understood about cattle, and the few beasts they had were puny and inbred. When he went into the cattle business he started in a small way and gradually worked up. Now his sons all had their own properties and he himself still had three estancias, some 13,000 hectares which, he pointed out, was a considerable holding for Paraguay, on rich land supporting some 30,000 cattle. "And all well developed. Electric light and running water. It was all very primitive in the old times, but now our estancias are very up-to-date. Our cattle are practically pure bred. All white! It's nice to see them coming up to the corral. A stream of animals, seven or eight hundred beasts all walking in line, all of them white."

It had been a good life and peaceful, he said, despite a recent disturbance: "Some months ago we had an upheaval here. They threw the government out and put all new people in. But life went on just the same. I never personally had anything against old President Stroessner. In fact he was a friend of mine and he did me two or three good services. Someone tried to take a piece of land off us and he soon put a stop to that! I can't say he was an intimate friend, but I knew him and I'd always defend old Stroessner. He was never as bad as they're making him out to be. He certainly was a dictator but he did a lot of good here."

I wondered if he thought the district's name would revert to New Australia. He answered, "It'll come back now that the government has been changed."

*

As private landowners the former colonists became increasingly Paraguayan, spoke Spanish if not much Guaraní, took to the local cigars and *yerba mate* and the loose clothing of the horsemen. And some began to take Paraguayan wives.

The notion that some of the Australian girls might actually consider Paraguayan husbands was treated with more alarm. In 1897 Margaret Riley was an attractive blue-eyed fourteen-year-old and quite a few of the local men had romantic ideas about her. She recalled with amusement: "Some of them were very handsome and some had more than one wife. If I'd stayed there I might have been one of the wives. The women used to ride on the back of the horse behind the man if they were going any distance. I often used to get on the back of the horse behind this Spanish-type chap — *he* was very interested — and go off to a dance somewhere. The dances always used to go on till daylight. My mother used to go mad about it, but I still went."

Her mother was desperate to return to Australia. She had always hated Paraguay, and at last, with so many other colonists leaving, Denis Hoare capitulated. "There was nothing there for him. No work and no money coming in. And they didn't like the idea of us mixing in and marrying into the natives. I don't know why my mother felt so strongly about that because they were quite decent people. I felt a bit sorry about it. It was a free and easy life for us, and it wouldn't have been such a bad thing. I suppose we would have lived on the country the same as they did. It all depends on who you'd marry."

Margaret related the story of her family's journey home with her usual cheerful stoicism:

We came down to the Argentine and my father was going to get a bridge-building job on the Río Negro but then that fell through. Anyway we all got the measles and had to go into hospital in Buenos Aires, and my youngest brother died there in hospital. After that my father came and got us out of our sick beds because he had heard that a British cargo vessel had come into port and he had decided we'd go to England on that. Well, we were only out at sea a week or so when my eldest brother contracted smallpox. So the captain called in to the port of Santos in Brazil and decided to take him off the ship. He said otherwise the ship would have to be quarantined and he didn't want that. My father announced that we'd all get off. But there was very bad yellow fever in Brazil at that time and the captain said it wouldn't be wise. In the end my brother was left in the hospital in Santos, in the care of the British consul. We waited six months in England for him, but he didn't turn up until long after we were back in Australia.

*

Although New Australia had lost many people, new hopefuls still came. "In spite of the epitaph mongers," Gilbert Casey wrote in June 1897, "we are very much alive and prosperous." He was president of the recently formed New Australia Industrial Co-Partnership, a loose association with emphasis on individualism and personal profit.

In 1899 the former Rose Summerfield arrived in Paraguay with Harry, her son from her first marriage, and her new husband, Jack Cadogan, a qualified schoolteacher who had chosen to work as a shearers' cook and a journalist on the *Democrat*, a magazine endorsing the Single Tax theories of Henry George. Rose herself had become quite famous in Sydney as a poet and lecturer on socialism and women's rights. She was pregnant when they landed in Asunción and soon after gave birth to a son, Léon. He grew up at New Australia and the first language he learned to speak fluently was Guaraní.

Arthur Tozer wrote that, "New Australia colony is coming to the fore again. It now has a population of over 100 persons and a much greater proportion of adults and workers than on Cosme". The government had made it a separate municipality with autonomy on local matters. It no doubt vexed Tozer to observe that the majority of the colonists seemed in good circumstances and had small herds of cattle, some up to 200 head. "New colonists from time to time arrive & few if any leave. One man just arrived bringing £2000 capital."

The capital-bringer was James Craig Kennedy who, with his wife Sarah, came from England in the same year as the Cadogans. In 1900 Kennedy succeeded Casey as president of the Co-Partnership.

*

I wanted to visit Nigel Kennedy, the only other original colonist left in the district. A phone call was made to him out on his estancia and, despite the siesta, an awkward time to call in Paraguay, he agreed to see Steve Cooper and myself. Ricardo Smith insisted that his servant Feliciano would take us in the Mercedes.

As we swung out of the village, I recognised two huge trees, erupting at their crowns in rust-coloured sprays: silky oaks, the Australian native *grevillea robusta*. We drove along a rutted red dirt road through soft green country and I thought how fortunate the New Australian colonists had been compared with their compatriots at Cosme.

We were still on the original New Australia grant as we passed through the gates of Ña Sarah, a 9,000 hectare estancia, and across undulating pasture. At the crest of a rise was a *hacienda* with a Spanish-tiled roof and roses in bloom behind a neat fence. Nigel Kennedy was waiting on the veranda, a lean handsome man, aged seventy-four, a knife and a Colt 45 in a holster on his belt.

His attractive Paraguayan wife, Señora Valentina Otazú de Kennedy, took Steve off for a tour of the rose garden. The living room with its bare floorboards was sparsely furnished, drawing the eye to a collection of family photographs, weddings and christenings and framed sepia portraits of earlier Kennedys. One wall was dominated by coloured pennants and brass plaques for the prize-winning *Ña Sarah* cattle.

Don Nigel spoke haltingly: "I've lost my English a little. I'm losing practice in English. I don't speak it very much these days. Here we speak Guaraní, more than Spanish almost. We spoke English when we were young, with mother and father."

His father James Craig Kennedy had three sons by his first wife. When she died he married a girl from Keswick, Sarah Jane Swindale, after whom the estancia was named. He was active in labour politics in London but in 1899 made the decision to come to New Australia, apparently unaware of the disintegration of the original ideals of the colony.

An elder son, Juan, wrote that the main reason his father came was because of the strong recommendation of a close personal friend, the Scottish parliamentarian, writer and adventurer, Robert Bontine Cunninghame Graham. A legendary figure, the aristocratic Cunninghame Graham had represented the mining constituency of North-West Lanark from 1886 to 1892 as a Gladstonian Liberal, and fought to improve the working conditions of miners and factory workers. In 1888 he spent six weeks in prison for his part in demonstrations for Irish patriots in Trafalgar Square. He had spoken out so passionately against the inequalities of class and wealth that he earned the approbation of the editor of a workers' newspaper in faraway Queensland, William Lane.

But Cunninghame Graham had long yearned to return to Argentina and Paraguay where he had spent eight years in his swashbuckling youth, working with horses and gauchos. In his writings he recalled his adventures and would have inspired James Craig Kennedy with his vivid descriptions of Paraguay:

The towns buried in vegetation, the sandy streets, all of them watercourses after a night's rain, the listless life, the donkeys straying to and fro, the white-robed women, with their hair hanging down their backs, and cut square on the forehead after the style so usual amongst Iceland ponies, the great unfinished palaces, the squares with grass five or six inches high, and over all the reddish haze blending the palm-trees, houses, sandy streets, the river and the distant Chaco into a copper-coloured whole at sunset, rise to my memory like the reflection of a dream. A dream seen in a convex mirror, opening away from me as years have passed …

Kennedy was forty-five years old when he came to Paraguay and Sarah only eighteen. At Nueva Australia they had six sons and one daughter, who all grew up helping on the family property. The eldest, Jaime, later ran two estancias in the Chaco; Juan established a successful trucking business; Alexander was shot dead, an accident with a gun at fourteen; Douglas was killed in the 1932 Chaco War while a prisoner of the Bolivians; Kenneth had died at the age of seventy-two. At the time of my visit only two of the sons survived: Nigel, the youngest, and Allan, who had an estancia some distance away. Their only sister, Hilda, had married the brother of Ricardo Smith.

His father could have had a brilliant career in politics in England, Don Nigel said. He often wondered what he had been running away from, why he had chosen to come out to such a desert.

Looking through the window at the rose garden and beyond to the *campo*, where long-horned cattle cropped the lush pasture, I protested that it was hardly a desert. "A wild place," said Nigel Kennedy. "There were tigers here yet. And monkeys. But not many people. Unpopulated. When I was a boy it was still wild. There were *bandidos* about. Now the tigers have disappeared and the people have come."

He had never been to school in his life, he said. Before his time there had been a religious school that the Australian and English children attended. But by the time he was old enough to go, it had closed. "There were only Paraguayan schools here which were very low class. So I never went to school." But his father had brought a large library from England and told his children, "You only need reading and writing. They are the pick and shovel to dig out the treasure I have here".

When they were growing up, Don Nigel said, they never heard much about politics, about the reasons why the socialist colony was founded or why it all failed. "I know Mr Casey had trouble with William Lane and then it all fell apart." I was curious to know his memories of Gilbert Casey. His answer was guarded. "He was a smart old chap. He had some queer habits …" After a pause he continued: "He left his wife and took up with an old Paraguayan woman here. An old black woman. They had two sons, Lorenzo and Gilberto." Still with the note of disparagement, Don Nigel said that Gilberto died young, shot by a *bandido*. "He had some argument with him and was shot in the arm. And from that wound he died."

The Australian identity of the settlement was further diffused when new migrants came from Britain, Europe and the United States, people attracted by the idea of being part of a community of Europeans while pursuing opportunities for commercial success on a new frontier. A few of these people still came because of an attachment to the colony's original socialist objectives, even as late as 1909 when Henry Alfred Smith, Ricardo's father, arrived.

The Kennedy family lived on their allotment and grazed the communal land. "We all worked, sometimes from about five years old. Anything we could do. As soon as we could ride we went out on the camp with our brothers." When they grew up, "three of my brothers went to the Chaco and took work there as *mayor domos* with an English firm. I bought land in the Chaco too."

From 1932 to 1935 the Chaco became a bloody battlefield as Paraguay fought against Bolivia. Nigel and his brother Douglas volunteered. "I had papers to say that I was English if I'd wanted to use them. But I'm Paraguayan and I thought I should go and fight. My other brothers wanted to get us out of it, but I said 'No, I want to go and have a bad time'."

The war took Douglas Kennedy's life. He was buried at Cochabamba, high on the Andean altiplano, in 1935.

James Craig Kennedy never recovered from the shock, and died the following year. All his children were entitled to a share from his land grant. Nigel took over his father's original holding in 1941. It was hard in the beginning. He earned a small income from harvesting wild oranges for their oil or *petit-grain*, used in the perfume industry. "I really had to work for anything I've got now. Nothing was handed on a plate." He was proud to say he had extended his father's 45 hectares to 9,000 today, shared with his wife, four sons and a daughter. "I buy land and put it in my sons' names."

He took us walking across the rolling green pasture of the estancia where contented cattle were grazing. Don Nigel explained that his three main breeds were Zebu, Nelor and Brahmin. He also had Santa Gertrudis, and the Paraguayan native cattle, the silvery white *tava-puá* and the long-horned reddish *vacas criollas*. He was currently conducting breeding experiments, crossing some of these animals with Limousin, Hereford and Indo-Brazil.

We reached an outcrop of *monte*, an island of dense forest on a rise. Pushing through the trees and overhanging vines, Don Nigel revealed a little cemetery where a number of the early colonists were buried. Two substantial and well-maintained tombstones were for James Craig Kennedy and his wife Sarah. Undergrowth and cowpats obscured most of the graves and the names Murray, Prior, King, Gorman and Butterworth were hard to decipher. Some of the headstones were broken and scattered. I wondered if this was where George Napier Birks had been laid to rest. Certainly somewhere there, in unmarked graves, Rose Cadogan — the former writer and activist Rose Summerfield — was lying beside her son Hugh. The 1915 *Australian Worker* had published a nostalgic poem she had written, yearning for the country to which she would never return, concluding:

> I am longing for my own land,
> My dear land, my home land;
> I'm sighing for its peaceful shore,
> 'Neath its blue gums again to stand,
> And scent the wattle blooms once more.

Don Nigel pointed out Mr Shepperson's cross, half-missing, and the smashed marble of Thomas King's tombstone, the date 1905 on a shard of its own. He shook his head. "We tried to stick the pieces back together but it didn't work." Stray inscriptions — "In Memory of ...", "A better life ...", "In Sorrow ..." made a poignant jigsaw puzzle.

We left the little cemetery, walking through the old *lapacho* fence posts. The gate was lying in the long grass. Nigel Kennedy said: "A fellow stole the hinges. I knew who he was and I said at the time, 'He won't last long. He's stealing dead men's things'. I was right. Six months later the man died."

*

Returning to the flat sheep plains of Barcaldine was a difficult readjustment for Denis Hoare. "It wasn't easy to come back to the place he had left," Margaret said. "He found it hard to get work — because he was an older man, of course, and he wasn't trained to do anything much. He was a handy man but he had to take any job he could get."

In 1907 public baths were opened in Barcaldine, fed by the abundant artesian water supply. The first caretaker, who kept the position until his retirement, was Hoare. His job was to collect the admission fees, empty and scrub the pool every weekend, and come down hard on boisterous behaviour. The *Western Champion*, owned by that old opponent of socialists, William Henry Campbell, praised the appointment, stating that "a big strong determined man like Denis Hoare is needed to put down larrikinism and filthiness".

Margaret said they all just had to settle back into life again: "We went to school for a while and then we got jobs. We weren't trained for anything and we got domestic work. We had to do the best we could." She married a policeman, Edwin Riley, a World War I veteran who had returned wounded from France. "But I didn't marry until I was in my thirties. I was the third child in my family and there were that many babies I was sick of babies — so I left it until later in life so that I wouldn't have too many."

The couple had three children — Bill, Edna and Edwin Martin, always known as Mick. During World War II, Mick was one of the crew of HMAS *Sydney*. He went down with the battleship when it was sunk by a German raider with the loss of all hands. Margaret Riley looked away and said quietly, "That was a terrible time."

Just after her 105th birthday, I showed her some of my recent photographs from Paraguay — the grandiloquent memorial to Hugo Stroessner at the site of New Australia, the schoolchildren of mixed Paraguayan-Australian blood who spoke only Spanish and Guaraní, the river steamers, oxen *carretas*, crumbling stucco buildings and Jesuit churches, the headstones in the Las Ovejas graveyard and the sweeps of grassy *campo* and dwindling stands of *monte* where monkeys no longer chattered in the trees.

She lingered over them. It was the best time in her life, she said, and in her father's life too, although her mother was never persuaded to like it.

Her father did not involve himself in politics after their return. "But he was still a Labor man and still believed in the Labor Party and better conditions for the worker. He'd still fight for that if he got the chance. Well, he thought the working class was the backbone of the country. If he was alive today, he'd still be Labor. And I'm still Labor too." She laughed with a rebel glint in her eyes and a continuing delight in life.

She had become something of a celebrity where she lived with her daughter and grandson on the Queensland Gold Coast, interviewed regularly by the press and asked to give her recipe for long life (an occasional glass of champagne). As one of the last originals of the great shearers' strike and the Paraguayan experiment, she could be relied on to

Bulletin, 31 March 1894

THE PRODIGAL.

Old Australia (to New ditto): "Well, young 'un, you have had enough of 'true mateship', and have come back to the old camp. Come in, you'll find some cold veal in the pantry, and when you've pulled yourself together a bit you had better take a pick and shovel and dish and make up for lost time."

produce a sprightly anecdote for television when needed. On 5 March 1989, aged 106, Margaret Riley died peacefully at home.

*

As we headed back to where Feliciano was waiting patiently with the Mercedes, fireflies were sparking in the shadow of the trees. It was a Paraguayan village now, said Don Nigel. There were colony descendants but almost none who spoke English. "My children don't speak it either. They understand some, but they don't speak it."

I asked if he thought the name of the district would be changed from Hugo Stroessner. He smiled and said that since the new government came to power, he had been talked into becoming head of the *seccional* or local branch of the Colorado Party. And one thing he had been pushing for very strongly was to have the name changed. The decision had now definitely been taken, and they were only waiting for the decree from the government. "So it will be Nueva Australia again?" I asked, pleased. Señor Kennedy, the son of an Englishman, smiled portentously and shook his head.

We left Distrito Hugo Stroessner at dusk in a lumbering local bus and passed another making its way towards the village. Chalked on the headboard was its destination, the officially approved new name: *Nueva Londres* — New London.

12

New London

We live not in Plato his Commonwealth, but in times wherein abuses
have got the upper hand.

Francis Bacon

A handful of earth
That did I seek from you,
That do I have from you.
Herib Campos Cervera

About 20 kilometres before Coronel Oviedo, the former village of
Ajos, the bus driver braked to let me off. The *gringos australianos*
lived up there, he said, pointing where a red dirt road branched
at a right angle. I should wait for a *colectivo*. He started up again with a
crash of gears.

The roadside hamlet was once Los Amigos, one of the five settlements
established on the New Australia land grant. It was late 1993 and I was
back, curious to see what had changed and what survived.

Opposite the turn-off was the only building in sight, a little flat-fronted
cantina, a mournful song in Guaraní crackling from a tinny radio. The
sun beat down. Long-horned cattle cropped soft grass. The red dirt road
led away across a rise, enclosed at its crest by tall trees. A peaceful bucolic
scene, except for the trucks grinding past on Ruta 2.

I walked over to the cantina, past pecking fowls. An old man in overalls
was leaning back at a precarious angle on a chair beside the door. He had
a swarthy complexion and lank grey hair under a red baseball cap
advertising "Old Spice". He looked up and studied me, assessing a business
opportunity. His eyes were a startling blue.

There had been an arrangement that Nigel Kennedy would be sending
a car for me. I asked the man if anyone had been waiting. He shrugged.
"*Quién sabe?*"

He hadn't seen a vehicle waiting at all? *Nada* — nothing, he said. He
volunteered that Nueva Londres was eight kilometres up the road and the

Kennedy estancia further still. But there'd be a bus, I persisted, a *colectivo*? I'd been to Nueva Londres before; there'd been a bus.

"*Nada.*"

I ordered a coffee. He returned with it and sat beside me. He was seventy years old, he told me, and his name was Stanley-Hijo. Slightly baffled, I wrote it down. He meant *hijo*, the word for "son"? He nodded at the slow learner. His grandfather's name was Stanley, he said. He'd been an Englishman. His father spoke English too, and could read and write it. But he himself was Stanley-Hijo. I realised I was seeing the evolution of a surname, the way names like Robertson and MacDonald had developed.

His grandfather Stanley came out from England to live at Colonia Nueva Australia, he told me. I remembered that Mary Hoare had done sewing for an Englishman, Lionel Stanley, had made him calico trousers with tapes at the ankles. But his grandfather was never a socialist, Stanley-Hijo insisted, oh no! Only one man had been — Gilbert Casey. As an afterthought he added that there *was* another man, but he couldn't remember his name.

"William Lane?"

He said yes, William Lane had begun the *cooperativo*, but that was a long time before. Some time after the War of the Triple Alliance. Then he'd left and started again on the other side of Villarrica, a place called Colonia Cosme. William Lane was *very* socialist. But all the Australians had gone now from Nueva Londres. The last one was Señora Dorothy Smith. She died about a year ago, and her husband Ricardo some years before that.

Saddened to hear it, I told him I had met the Smiths four years earlier. Stanley-Hijo nodded, unsurprised. Now many Australians came here, he said, *muchos profesores y escritores*. He had seen them all. He muttered something about a *canguro*. I didn't get his drift. He gestured for me to wait, and disappeared into the kitchen. He returned in a few moments with a plastic bundle and spread out the contents on the wooden table. Proudly he displayed a felt patch which looked to have been detached from a tracksuit, the Australian coat of arms, a kangaroo and emu supporting a shield.

There was also an assortment of business cards and scrawled addresses from various Australian pilgrims. It was being impressed on me that Stanley-Hijo was something of a media personality. He shuffled the cards, pointing to the degrees and diplomas. He then emptied some small change from a purse — Australian, New Zealand and British coins. These were *regalos*, presents to him from the people who came. He waited expectantly for my reaction. I fished around in the bottom of my handbag and gave him an Australian $2 coin. He briskly added it to his collection, then asked if I wanted to take his photograph. I took up the offer and he posed with seasoned professionalism, saying that all the Australian visitors took his photograph, all the writers and journalists and teachers. They liked his blue eyes. His sister did the cooking, but they didn't want her, she didn't have the blue eyes. His father didn't have them either, but his grandfather Stanley, the Englishman, he'd had the blue eyes too.

I felt the sister was being discriminated against, and said I would like to take her photograph. She was too busy cooking, said Stanley-Hijo. She always had too much work. *Mucho trabajo*.

A cowhand tethered his horse just outside the door and came in, heavy iron spurs on his boots clanking. He slumped on a chair with brooding authority. The media personality scurried away and returned almost immediately with a plate of *milanesa*, cold crumbed beef with mandioca on the side.

I asked if there was a telephone anywhere so I could ring Señor Kennedy. Stanley-Hijo shook his head and told the *vaquero* that I was an Australian writer. All the Australian writers came to take his photograph. The *vaquero* grunted and ate noisily.

Stanley-Hijo disappeared into the back room and I heard him talking to his sister. I glanced at the newspaper on the table: a graphic photograph on the front page of the corpse of a murder victim, a detailed description of the rape of a nine-year-old girl by her uncle at Ciudad del Este, and an account of the arrest of smugglers by customs agents in the Alto Paraná region. I studied the goods for sale in the glass case under the counter. Cartons of eggs, bottles of wine and Olde Monk whisky, bags of *galletas*, tins of Beefeater corned meat, a small rack of lipsticks and one aerosol can of Faberge Brut deodorant. A skinny dog stirred under my feet and gnashed at its fleas.

As the *vaquero* clumped out he asked if I was going to Nueva Londres. I nodded hopefully. He muttered that there'd be a *colectivo* along in a few minutes and the fare was 2,000 *guaraníes* (about $2 Australian).

I paid for the coffee, adding a hefty tip, as a covered utility truck pulled up at the turn-off, passengers sitting on benches at the back. I walked towards it. Stanley-Hijo scuttled ahead, saying he would speak to the driver and arrange a fare of 7,000 *guaraníes*. I said I'd come all the way from Asunción for half that and I could talk to the driver myself. I paid the standard fare and joined the cheerful group of villagers crammed on the benches. As we roared off I waved to Stanley-Hijo, who did not return the compliment.

"One makes friends quickly in Spanish countries," observed the author Peter Matthiessen in *The Cloud Forest*, "and loses them just as fast."

We rumbled along the red dirt road through undulating pasture land, stopping to let people off at little *ranchos* half hidden among fruit trees. At the top of the hill we came to the village square. The remaining passengers climbed down into the shade of tall Australian silky oaks. The monument to Hugo Stroessner was still there in the orange grove, the small plaque to the obscure colonial precursors weathered and tarnished.

The driver took me on to Estancia Ña-Sarah. A sprinkler was playing in the rose garden, yellow alamanders entwined an arch at the front gate. The long low house with its red tiled roof seemed deserted, all the shutters closed along the veranda.

An Indian girl with a cleft palate met me at the front door. I understood her to say that Señor Kennedy and his wife had been expecting me, but now they were having their siesta. I asked her not to wake them. She gestured hospitably for me to sit on the veranda and sat beside me, beaming. She said her name was Sacumina Ovelan Underra. I guessed she was about eighteen. We were joined by a girl about four years younger, Norma Aguillera, small, barefoot and shy. We sat companionably, watching the Zebu and long-horned cattle grazing on the *campo*.

Don Nigel Kennedy emerged, a little more frail at seventy-eight years of age. He embraced me in the Paraguayan way, then strapped a pistol holster onto his belt.

"Didn't Stanley-Hijo give you a message that we had a driver there to bring you? He's a bit mad, that Stanley-Hijo."

We sat down to afternoon tea with Doña Valentina and spread wild orange marmalade on freshly baked scones. "Old Mr Stanley was a good man," Don Nigel fretted, "but that little Stanley-Hijo, he's silly. His sister Hilda is a good woman. She works hard at that place they have on the *ruta*. But Stanley-Hijo has never really worked. He might cut firewood or something, that's all. I said to him years ago, 'I can't do anything to convince you. Go your own way and fall in the mud!' He won't listen."

*

Don Nigel said he wasn't so good at walking any more. We drove across the *campo* to the little cemetery hidden among the trees.

Black and white plovers shrieked. A huge many-branched cactus, like a synagogue candelabra, provided something of an ecumenical atmosphere. But there was now little to see except for the two large Kennedy family tombs inside the neat enclosure with its new spring-loaded gate. Outside the fence, two weathered headstones, the names indecipherable, and a rusting iron cross, were all that remained to indicate the resting place of other colonists.

"Nearly everything has gone now," said Don Nigel. "People took the stones. When I was a boy, there used to be a very old lady called Mrs Prior. She used to tell me where everyone was buried."

I remembered Mrs Prior, resented by young Margaret Hoare for dancing away with her good-looking bloke, grasping her pleasures where she could and now long buried herself.

Don Nigel paced about under the trees. "Mrs Prior used to say: 'This is where the Kings are. Mr Adams is under here. And Mr Murray over there …' I used to know it all once. But now I forget. People come here from Australia and I'm sorry they have to see it like this. I can't maintain it."

He looked troubled and anxious and I felt guilty being another of the visiting pilgrims, adding to his sense of responsibility as custodian of a history that was only marginal to him.

"The new Paraguayan cemetery is a better run place," he said, brightening. "Would you like to see it? It's a short walk through the *monte*." His legs weren't up to it, he said, but the maids would accompany me.

Sacumina and Norma led me across the *campo*, negotiating around cowpats and thistles, to the brooding line of forest along the rise. We followed a well-worn cattle path in among the trees to a magic, shadowy world where leaf litter subsided gently underfoot. Rotting logs bristled with bright green moss and huge orange toadstools sprouted in the pungent earth. The branches of a small tree were studded with shiny black fruit like olives. Sacumina picked off a handful of them. "*Es bueno*," she said. She showed me how to slide off the dark skin, revealing a fruit like a lychee. It was succulent, slightly bitter and refreshing. We walked on, sucking the fruit and spitting out the pips.

We emerged abruptly from the *monte* to find the official Nueva Londres cemetery just ahead. It was treeless, like a new housing estate, the little vaults in serried rows, all sharp bright angles, new concrete and fresh paint. Two grave-diggers, leaning on their shovels, shouted something ribald to the girls as we passed.

The most ostentatious structure was a cream brick vault about the size of a garage. I peered inside at the lace-draped altar, vases of plastic flowers in front of two framed photographs. They were of Ricardo Lille Smith, 1897–1990, and Dorothy McCreen Smith, 1904–1991.

They would have approved of their final home, I thought, so shiny and neat with its terazzo patio and amber glass door. It was satisfactorily distant from "those awful old places" with rotten shingles, built when the colony was still "a communistic affair".

*

I recorded Don Nigel as he spoke calmly about his horrendous experience of the Chaco War. Then it was time for me to depart to connect with a bus back to Asunción. He provided a driver to take me to the crossroads at Coronel Oviedo. Unlike Colonia Cosme, the site of New Australia is convenient for day trippers. I feared that soon far too many Australians would be coming to visit this gracious old man, disrupting his life, with less and less for them to see.

As I said goodbye, I asked him if he kept in touch at all with the descendants of Cosme. "Very, very little," he answered. "I've always said that I would go to see what Colonia Cosme is like, but I haven't." He looked at me, suddenly very curious. "You *have* been there?"

I told him that I had, but it was very remote, still unconnected to electricity, and it wasn't nearly as prosperous as this district.

"*Sí!*" he exclaimed with unmistakable satisfaction. "Perhaps I'll go there one day."

13
Virgin Ground

I descended a little on the side of that delicious vale, surveying it with
a secret kind of pleasure (though mixed with my other afflicting
thoughts), to think that this was all my own; that I was king and lord
of all this country indefeasibly ... I saw here abundance of cocoa
trees, orange and lemon, and citron trees, but all wild ...

Daniel Defoe, *Robinson Crusoe*

I was fortunate to be in Asunción ... like my character Henry Pulling
when the National Day was celebrated by the ruling party, the
Colorado. In a country where Communism is a crime and even the
Jesuits have their telephones tapped and where no criticism of the
United States was allowed in the Press it surprised me to find when
I woke that the whole of Asunción had gone Red — red banners,
red skirts, red scarves, red flowers, red ties, red handkerchiefs ...

Graham Greene, *Ways of Escape*

I first went to Cosme in 1982. At that time, also my first visit to
Paraguay, Asunción had fewer skyscrapers, fewer tourists, more orange
trees in fruit on the sidewalks and more overt charm. There was also
more censorship, more soldiers in the streets, guards goose-stepping
outside the presidential palace, a greater sense of menace. A dictator was
at the height of his power and he and his henchmen were accumulating
vast wealth from the massive Itaipú hydro-electric project developed with
Brazil. His portrait hung everywhere. In the main square a message flashed
constantly: "Stroessner — Peace — Work — Well-Being".

That was the kind of newsflash President Alfredo Stroessner approved,
but the headlines were being dominated by another catastrophe, a struggle
for a few miserably cold and windy islands in the South Atlantic. It was
May 1982 and, after weeks of rattling diplomatic ultimatums, naval fleets
out of mothballs, Harriers and Vulcan bombers over Port Stanley, the
Falklands-Malvinas war had erupted. Britain announced a 200-mile air
and sea blockade around the Falkland Islands. "We still have a certain kind

of majesty," said Mrs Thatcher, "and we're not bad when it comes to might either."

I was travelling with a friend and colleague, Julie Rigg, a broadcaster with the ABC in Sydney, on holiday leave. As we flew in to Santiago, Chile, on 5 May, we were appalled to learn that the British had just torpedoed the Argentine battle-cruiser, *General Belgrano*, outside the exclusion zone, with the loss of 668 lives. I reluctantly revised my plan which had been, before going on to Paraguay, to visit Río Gallegos in Patagonia where Mary Gilmore had lived for a year. That windswept southern town had now become the main barracks and transfer point for Argentine troops heading to the war zone. Two British journalists had just been arrested there. Julie argued, with undeniable logic that, as I was carrying a professional tape recorder and camera, my protestations to the Argentine authorities that my real interest was an Australian woman poet who had lived there some eighty years before might seem somewhat thin. We proceeded directly to Asunción instead.

We booked into a pensión and went to the news kiosk of the main tourist hotel, the Guaraní, to get an update on the progress of the war. Tourists were mainly conspicuous by their absence, but the Buenos Aires newspapers were selling out fast to Paraguayans who milled around, talking in huddles. The ancient grudge against Argentina was being subsumed into a larger cause, Latin Americans closing ranks against the *gringo* imperialists. We received some hostile glances. An Argentine businessman in the hotel coffee shop asked if we were British.

"Australianas!" we insisted loudly, beaming.

"You people are helping the British," he answered coldly. "You lent them a frigate."

Before coming to Paraguay, I'd written to Señor Guillermo Wood, the unofficial spokesperson for the Australian Cosme descendants. He had replied warmly, suggesting that as he was not on the phone himself, I should ring his youngest daughter Daisy when we arrived in Asunción. I rang the number. Daisy spoke English with a pronounced Hispanic accent. Her father was looking forward to our visit, she said, and expected us for afternoon tea. We would be able to meet quite a few of the family. It was lucky that we had arrived on the day of a special annual celebration: it was 12 May, Cosme Foundation Day.

*

The sixty-three colonists who seceded with William Lane felt optimistic about the new home where they planned to spend the remainder of their lives. The last of them walked out of the original colony of New Australia on 12 May 1894, a date that became enshrined as their foundation day, although a permanent settlement had not been established.

Then a prospecting party — Lane, Saunders and Leck — found what seemed a suitable site: just over 9,300 hectares in the fork between two rivers. The land was fertile, a mixture of pasture and dense forest and, 72 kilometres south-east of New Australia, far enough from their rivals. A purchase agreement was reached, thanks to Stevenson's handsome contribution of £150 received from his family in Scotland. Negotiations with the Paraguayan government were interrupted by the small hiccough of a revolution, then the new administration approved the land transfer.

They named their new home *Colonia Cosme*. The main body of settlers moved onto the land "on a bleak day in July, 1894," John Lane recalled, "when the hired native *carretas* left us and our belongings in the long, wet grass at the edge of that Paraguayan *monte*, which we were to call home. But though it soaked our garments, the rain could not damp our spirits, for dissensions were left behind, and we were on our own land. Before nightfall, all were under shelter of some sort; tents, with grass-thatched flys, huts of saplings, with grass roof and sides".

A red clay anthill was hollowed out for a baker's oven and by that first night, wrote Harry Taylor, "was flaming the great communal fire that for nearly three years was never once to be allowed to die down into ashes". For the next few months, the swing of axe and crash of falling timber echoed through the *monte* as clearing went on with feverish haste. Although the season was already late, their survival depended on producing a crop.

By August Arthur Tozer was able to inform his brother: "We are getting along far better than I expected. We have water-tight grass *ranchos* up, on a temporary site, for all hands. There are about 20 acres of grass land ploughed & partly harrowed & nearly the same amount of virgin forest felled. Of this one acre has been cleaned, stumped & planted & another acre is cleaned & partly stumped. In this planted acre we have up & doing well, turnips, carrots, parsley, tomatoes, water & rockmelons, marrows, beet, cabbages, radishes, lettuce, sweet potatoes & tobacco, also peas. We shall soon be planting out mandioca, sugar cane & as soon as possible we shall sow maize etc. There is considerable labour in clearing the forest but it pays in the end." In fact, he added, they soon hoped to reduce the working week from six days to five, and then those who worked Saturdays could stockpile holiday credits.

The Paraguayan government would allow them a degree of autonomy, he said, "and we are going to appoint Lane and myself as *Intendente* and *Sub-Intendente* respectively". They had formed new rules for running the colony, "as bitter experience has taught us the need for them. We form this colony on certain lines for a certain end. We shall allow *free* entry on the understanding that the new member abides by *our* rules. He has then to undergo a long probation before he is accepted as a *full* member".

But Tozer overstated their ability to sustain themselves from their efforts. While they waited for their crops to mature and saw many fail, a supply of beans and maize had to be purchased locally. James Molesworth later recalled Tozer's stoicism: "He would eat the beans at Cosme and then go outside and vomit. He refused the sick allowance and got more and more hollow-eyed, but kept at his work."

As they could rarely sacrifice a working bullock, they relied on the skills of the hunting department for occasional fresh meat. Eels were sought out in the swamps, the cooks learned how to make stews of little birds or agouti — the local guinea pig — to remove the plates of armadillo and prepare its flesh, to overcome uncomfortable moral qualms about carving up a monkey. *Cosme Evening Notes*, read around the campfire every night, recorded in October: "Monkey, whether it be the low class lemur or the most intelligent of the apes, is indeed a dish fit for a Cannib — I mean a king. Never shall a Cosme colonist be able to say that he owes nothing to his ancestors but the bare fact of his being."

Good humour got them by. "We were never reduced to rags," wrote Harry Taylor, "though we used sometimes to look speculatively at the large forest leaves, and long before funds would allow of the purchase of rough trousering and shirting material our garments used to look like pieces of fantastic patch-work quilting."

In the *Notes* of 10 November, William Lane acknowledged the probability of no money coming from Australia until Christmas and the need to tough it out. "It must not be forgotten that if we bear hardship, hardship also bears on us. Two months ago there was hardly a man in camp but showed signs of being under-nourished, the women the same. It is no use blinking the fact. It was so. And from this we have gradually worked out, most of us. Shall we risk dropping back?"

They were upheld by their *esprit de corps*, with concerts and dances in the dining hall, games of draughts and dominoes, lectures on the poetry of Adam Lindsay Gordon and Robert Burns, and debates on many issues. The bushman, Arthur Tozer wrote, "is generally a big reader, not of novels, but of books of the better sort, & when a number of them get round a camp fire an argument gets started & each gives his idea of the question. Here in Cosme there is generally a debate on about some reform, such as Single Tax or Land or the merits of some writers compared to others etc etc, all of which are very interesting & instructive. Lane is always one of the debaters & sometimes the arguments continue until after midnight & cover quite a wide range of subjects. In fact I think I should be right in saying that the average bushman is more intelligent than the average townsman".

They came to the end of 1894 in good spirits, celebrating with a four-day holiday. Lane gave an address on the origins of Christmas in a dining hall decorated with ferns and flowers, followed by a veritable feast: roast pork and chicken, plum pudding, blancmange and a dozen different tarts. Entertainments were held each evening — carol singing, dancing, a farce and black minstrel show — and the summer days were spent swimming at the Capiibary River and with a cricket match against the Englishmen of Paraguay, made more enjoyable by an Australian victory. Tozer didn't fail to mention his contribution: "I happened to score the greatest number of runs, making 34 in the two innings."

*

Don Guillermo Wood was white-haired with very blue eyes. He had the frailty of eighty-eight years, but held himself very upright, with a natural dignity. His long, low bungalow, painted bright blue, was in a suburb of Asunción near the cemetery. "Welcome to Paraguay," he said, kissing Julie and me on both cheeks. He led us past lemon trees in the garden to the front door, where we were introduced to an amply-proportioned woman with heavy Indian features — Eulalia, his cook.

The front room was sparsely furnished with three vinyl armchairs and a bookcase. This was the parlour, Don Guillermo said. I saw a volume of *Collected Poems of Henry Lawson* and a much-thumbed copy of Gavin Souter's *A Peculiar People*. A calendar on the wall advertised a pharmacy in Ballarat with an idealised Australian bush scene: sheep streaming in golden light down a slope towards a river. Don Guillermo said an Australian cousin had sent it.

We went down the hall to the kitchen where a tall man with a weathered olive complexion was waiting: Don Norman Wood, a younger brother, who had been summoned down from the northern river town of Concepción especially to meet us. He had a rangy athletic physique which belied his eighty-three years; even without his false teeth, Julie and I later agreed, he was the sexiest old man we'd ever met. "Gidday," he said with a mischievous smile. "So you're going to have some tucker with us?" I realised with a jolt that both men spoke with an Australian accent — not the fast and rather slurred one of the present day, but a slow, broad and stately accent, the way I remembered Dr Evatt speaking on the radio when I was a child. But the elder brother had been a baby when he left Australia and the younger had never been there.

"It's all settled," said Don Guillermo. "I'd like you girls to stay here, as long as it's not too rough for you. I'd enjoy the company and a bit of a gossip. Especially talking English again. You know, I've never really liked talking Spanish, never all my life. And if, as you said, you want to do some recording with me, we can take our time. I wish I could come to Cosme with you."

"It's a bit much for him now he's nearly ninety," said Don Norman, skittishly confident himself, "so I'm going with you. We might have to ride horses for the last bit if the Pirapó river is in flood. We might have to swim the horses across, and that's a bit much for Bill these days."

Don Guillermo saw Julie and me exchange a nervous glance and laughed that we needn't worry about Norman. He had spent most of his life on horseback, working on cattle estancias in the Gran Chaco. "We'll go in two days' time if that's suitable," said Don Norman. "My son Rodrigo can drive us out there."

The third brother arrived, Don Alexander Wood, aged eighty-five, a distinguished old man with courtly manners. "Never mind this Don business," he said. "Call me Uncle Ack. Everybody does."

"Then I'm Bill," said Don Guillermo. "Uncle Bill." He said we would meet their other brother, Wallace, the youngest at eighty-one, at Cosme. Their only surviving sister, Rose, lived in South Africa.

The kitchen table was set for afternoon tea. Eulalia came in with a big teapot and a freshly made brownie cake which would have won prizes at a church fete in Australia. Bill Wood poured cups of real Indian tea from the pot. We understood this was a special treat in a country where the local herbal brew, *yerba mate*, was a way of life.

Every year on Cosme, he said, they celebrated 12 May by having a general holiday. "They knocked off work and had some celebration up at the social hall. On Cosme it was not the accustomed thing to have alcohol. But there was always plenty of lemonade and *yerba mate*."

I asked if it was usual for the Wood family to still celebrate Foundation Day. "Always!" said Don Alex. "We have a cup of tea. If two or three are gathered, we have a cup of tea."

Eulalia placed a bottle of wine on the table. "And nowadays maybe just a small tot," said Bill Wood.

*

William Wood Senior was from a Scottish family who had emigrated to the colony of Victoria. As a young man he had taken up the nomadic seasonal life of a shearer. "Melbourne could never hold me in my youth," he wrote. "When the call of the sheep-shearing time came, I simply had to go. Train to Echuca then up with my swag and off for the Murrumbidgee or Lachlan and never mind the sore feet or tired shoulders, for what joy there was when the tramp was over, lazing around waiting for the start, swapping yarns with the crowd."

By the time of the shearers' strike of 1891 he had become a union organiser, Secretary of the General Labourers' Union at Bourke in far western New South Wales. There he met and married a girl of Irish stock, Lillian McClaskey. An early photograph shows her wasp-waisted, wearing a winsome expression and a perky hat.

Henry Lawson got to know them in 1892 on a trip to Bourke, funded by J. F. Archibald of the *Bulletin* in the hope of getting the writer off the grog and back in touch with the bush people that he wrote about. Wood and another shearer, Tom Hicks-Hall, were organising a recruiting camp for William Lane's South American adventure. Lawson put "Billy Woods" in a couple of his stories, mentioning that he had "a poetic temperament and more than the average Bushman's reverence for higher things ... the best of married men, with the best of wives and children ..."

After Lawson's death William Wood wrote a memoir, recalling that on a hot Christmas Day in 1892 the writer had been with them in Bourke. "After the meal, Henry, Donald and myself came back to my house, and, as my wife was away visiting her people, we got off everything that we had on, except our underpants, and sat under a spray on the veranda most of that afternoon drinking beer. It must have been 115 [46°C] in the shade that day. The spray of river water was a great idea and kept us beautifully cool." Later they'd all gone boating upstream, camped at a bend in the river, "boiled the billy, and had something to eat as well, afterwards

smoking and yarning until late evening, when we drifted gently downstream. Those were very pleasant days, and we enjoyed them to the full".

William and Lillian lost their first child, a baby girl. Afterwards they
moved to Sydney, planning to sail for Paraguay, but their departure was
delayed by the discovery that Lillian was pregnant again. They had
lodgings in Surry Hills, a suburb fiercely Irish working-class in character,
of narrow winding streets, grimy tenements and small factories near the
Central Railway station. William took odd jobs while he worked for the
New Australia movement and Lillian was employed as a waitress at
Mathesons Hotel until her confinement. On 5 September 1894, William
Wood Jr was born.

The baby was six months old when William and Lillian sailed, making
up a special contingent with fourteen other Lane loyalists. They arrived
at Colonia Cosme on 12 May 1895, the first anniversary of Foundation
Day, just in time to take part in the festivities recorded in *Cosme Monthly
Notes*:

> Foundation Day annual meeting. Holidays and general rejoicing. A minstrel
> show, cricket match and much dancing. We killed a fat pig and had a great
> public dinner ... William Lane spoke on "Cosme and Communism" and the
> need for patience and forbearance ... New arrivals were William Wood, wife
> and baby ...

William and Lillian were never to leave Paraguay. In that country they
had seven more children. In all they had six sons and two daughters, a
tribe of grandchildren and great-grandchildren, founding an Australian
dynasty that is well known in Paraguay today.

The Wood brothers were fond of the story of their parents' first night
at Cosme. Norman described his mother's reaction to the special spread
that had been put on for Foundation Day.

> The old hands asked my mother, "Would you like a little feed of sweet
> potatoes?"
> She said, "No thank you."
> "Would you like some *yerba mate*?" they asked.
> "No thank you," she said.
> "Some yams?"
> "No, thank you."
> And then she thought, "My God! I suppose they have nothing else!" So she
> said, "Yes, I will have some of that." It was mostly beans.

What happened after the festivities also became family lore. Exhausted by their long trip, the Woods retired with baby Bill to the tent they had been given beside an "island" of *monte*. Lillian carefully placed her precious belongings, things she had guarded all the way from Australia, beside the central pole of the tent. "When they were asleep during the night, a bullock poked his head in and knocked her belongings flying. So she lost most of her prized crockery that first night."

Don Guillermo said that their father never talked about the Queensland shearers' strike or the political reasons that brought them to Paraguay, but he often became nostalgic about the old way of life. "He had a great friend, Billy Laurence, who used to come down quite frequently in the evening and they'd sit in the front room by the chimney fireplace and we kids would gather around listening to them talking about the shearing sheds and the people. What struck me as marvellous was their memory for names and places. Billy Laurence for example, would say, 'Do you remember Ted Morrison, the ringer in such and such a shed?' I suppose if Dad didn't remember him he'd agree that he did, and they'd talk about him and what happened and things like that. But they never discussed, that I can remember, any of the troubles with the government. I don't remember the first thing about their reasons for leaving Australia. All we heard from Dad was that he had worked as a union member."

But William Wood sometimes mentioned Henry Lawson, with whom he had kept vaguely in touch after the visit to Bourke. After Lawson's death in 1922, Wood said in his memoir that he had asked the writer to come to Paraguay:

> Before I left Sydney … to come here, I had a couple of nights with Henry, and we farewelled each other. After I had been over here about four years, I wrote, inviting him to try and make the trip and spend a few months with us, but, unfortunately, it didn't come about; most likely the getting together of the necessary cash was the obstacle. Had Lawson got here, he would have been able to get together plenty of data for some capital yarns.

In about 1914, Don Guillermo said, Lawson had sent his father autographed copies of two of his books. "We used to have them on the colony but I won't guarantee that they're still there."

"Lawson was deaf," said Don Norman. "Dad always said he was deaf as a post. Apparently he drank a bit too."

Don Guillermo poured us all a "tot" of wine and proposed a toast to Cosme Foundation Day. Julie and I followed with a toast to the Wood family.

"*Salud!*" said Don Norman. "But it's not much to crow about, is it?"

"Why not?"

"Well, our father arrived at Cosme and that was that. He might have been a member of parliament in Australia. That's what they used to say about him."

Don Guillermo wanted to make a speech and spoke solemnly for the tape recorder: "You can tell Australia that we're proud to be able to call ourselves Australian. After all these years without much contact, we still are quite proud of being Australian."

"*Salud!*"

*

Just over a week after the Woods' arrival, the Lanes' eight-year-old son Charlie was sent to the Cosme barber for a haircut. He stopped on the way to join in a game of cricket on the oval. Young Wally Head, Dave Stevenson's ward, bowled a ball which hit Charlie on the chest. He fell and died within minutes. Tozer wrote there was "no bruise to indicate that the ball struck him with any great force & the boy bowling is hardly old enough to do any damage". It was freakish bad luck and a hard blow for Anne and William Lane. Some colonists later claimed it as the first dark omen for Cosme.

Tozer became fiercely protective of Lane. He sent Harry a number of his articles, asking him to submit them to various journals, supposing "you don't object to the trouble these enclosures may give you" and "relying on your good nature".

Harry's refusal came as a shock. Tozer's letters lost their tone of brotherly warmth:

> I regret that I troubled you with those things for publication. I ought to have been more thoughtful. I ought not to have expected you to assist me in circulating matter supporting a cause in which you have no belief, with which you have no sympathy & against which you are lecturing. I note what you say about Lane, but it is useless for me to argue the matter, all I can say is that I feel sure that if you knew him as well as I do, you would alter your opinion. It is likely that Lane will visit England early next year & then you may meet him (this is private) ... I am grateful to you for your offer of money for personal use but I can do without it. Money for the colony's use I do not expect you to send & even were you willing to contribute, I don't think I should be right in accepting it for that purpose, seeing that you do not sympathise with us.

Nevertheless, he asked for a copy of Harry's recently published translation of Rousseau's *Du Contrat Social*, although he wondered rather waspishly, "What is there in your translation of that work which makes you think it worth your while when there are other translations to compete with yours in the book market?"

In early July Tozer, using up his holiday credits, took off on a three-week boating trip with Dave Stevenson and Bob Miller. They had planned it some weeks before and, in their spare time "cross-cutting and hewing" with axe and adze at a big timbo tree, they had made a solid canoe 5 metres long and a metre across the beam. They dubbed it the *Pioneer*.

It was the sort of Boys' Own Adventure Tozer had always dreamed about, a 130-kilometre trip down the Capiibary and Tebicuary rivers to the town of Villa Florida, where they would sell the canoe and return on foot. They even had attractive female company for the first few days: Rebecca Sims, the thirty-year-old wife of Joseph Sims, and her young daughter. ("They were model passengers, taking the rough with the smooth uncomplainingly, sitting still when we were trying for a shot at game and flying round at cooking and washing up times.") In Stevenson's gung-ho account, published as a supplement to *Cosme Monthly Notes*, "Three Men in a Boat … A true tale of the adventures encountered and privations endured", Miller was described as the captain, Stevenson as the mate (or general rouseabout) and Tozer as the agent (or providor and pathfinder). Tozer sent it to Harry, obviously proud to feature as a key player in such a rollicking adventure:

> The agent and mate had now become more expert with the paddles and sent the old *Pioneer* along 6 knots an hour. A big kingfisher was sighted, sitting in a meditative attitude on a tree overhanging the stream, and the agent was instructed to fire on him from a distance of about 100 yards to try his skill. The bird went the same evening the way of all flesh — killed or cadged, good, bad or indifferent — down the mate's throat at suppertime. Shortly after the murder of the bird the senora uttered a faint gasp of horror and pointed towards the bank, where a grisly monster of an alligator 8 or 10 feet long was lying motionless asleep. Our sharpshooter, the agent, sent two bullets into his brain. The mate begged the skipper to put back and get his tail for tucker but the current had swept the *Pioneer* onwards and the remainder of those on board expressed no yearning for alligator fritters, so the 1st officer took to his paddle again in a bad temper.

After escorting Rebecca Sims and her child to the railway, the men drifted on in the canoe, looking for a camping site. "The last two hours we pulled," Stevenson wrote, "were by moonlight, and very romantic and weird the river looked by the light of the silvery goddess. We felt the beauty of the scene each in his own way. Even the agent, practical man though he is, began to tell us about the ideal woman of his heart."

The subject seemed a preoccupation not just for Tozer, the agent, but consuming for the mate as well. Observing two flamingoes on a sandbar, Stevenson compared their plumage to the "delicate roseate pink ... which tinges the cheek of sweet seventeen at the first words of spoken love". Further downstream, after meeting some Paraguayan *carpincho* hunters who invited them ashore to share some *yerba mate*, he was much taken with one of their women, "with fine eyes, a resolute mouth and the rich red blood flowing under a clear dark skin which is so suggestive of health and vigor".

They stopped at an estancia to buy milk. A solidly-built young Guaraní woman studied Tozer with undisguised interest, "flicking a very substantial leg with a riding whip, the while assuming a thousand airs and graces". Tozer asked whether he would be entitled to her flock of sheep if he married her. "She put her lower lip out about three inches in a pretty pout and wriggled herself, evidently somewhat pleased," Stevenson reported. "After we had left some distance, she pursued us with the thin excuse that she thought by our packs we had something to sell, but really to have another look at Tozer. That youth considered her an *animal*, but she was not. She was merely a young woman who thought herself more fascinating than nature intended her to be. A common enough failing in her sex, Tozer says."

Towards the end of their journey, the three men made camp in an orange grove, inviting two women from a neighbouring house to prepare a meal for them. The mother and daughter agreed, "evidently deeming us men worthy to be waited on by woman — the which we will not deny". Stevenson thought it a noble sight, as the sun sank in the west and the old woman prepared a fire "and made things hum generally". But he was absorbed in contemplation of Favriana, the daughter:

> ... a girl about 18 or 19 years of age and more than interesting to look at. Her small head with its oval clear brown face was crowned by rippling waves of hair. The forehead was broad and low, the nose small and delicately formed, short upper lip, rounded chin and smooth full throat. But it was the extraordinary swiftness and grace of her movements that chiefly struck us. Doubtless much climbing of the hill, on whose side she dwelt, to the neighbouring village, balancing her market produce on her shapely head had lent to her limbs and figure its additional share of litheness and strength ... Now when

a European woman, cased in a combination of steel hoops and whalebone and with long skirts starts to run, the general effect is not encouraging. But this young savage had on a garment which left her lower limbs unimpeded, she required no corsets for obvious reasons and when she ran she lost none of her grace.

After serving their supper, the beautiful Favriana wound a mantilla about her head and returned to her home.

The three men laid back on their swags, puffed cigars, and agreed "that it would be a fine thing to escort the first batch of single girls which comes to Cosme, and some perhaps of our married women round the country to learn by the force of example a woman's duty and respect towards the nobler sex".

As they bade farewell in the morning, accepting a bumper of warm milk, Stevenson concluded:

Sweet Favriana, you will, we suppose, grow old like other women; your step will slow and falter and your temper at times prove uncertain. Your husband — when you get one — will probably now and then, after the manner of husbands, be sorry that he was born, but to us you will ever remain the embodiment of youthful Paraguayan strength and beauty. Kind of heart and fair of form, may the sun and stars in conjunction ever shine on your doorstep!

All this effusiveness clearly left little room for thoughts of Mary Cameron, encased in her discouraging whalebone corsets and long skirts, still teaching in Sydney. But the evidence would suggest that Stevenson was rarely far from her mind. No one else had replaced him in her affections, although she had made many friends in the socialist and trade union movements.

One was a wild, one-armed anarchist called Larry Petrie; for a time she hid some dynamite for him, placing it in a bottom drawer at her lodgings in Newtown. Later she professed to be unaware of his plans for it: "It was not till I went to South America that he told me that while I had it the police were scouring Sydney for it."

Henry Lawson still visited Mary, sometimes rather inebriated. Anne Lane, who was her guest at the lodgings until she returned to Paraguay in March, was withering about him. "Mrs Lane used to ask me why I troubled with him as he was 'only a weakling' and 'a waster'. She had no patience with 'wasters'." Anne no doubt compared Lawson with a manly fellow like Stevenson and encouraged Mary's hopes, reminding her that Clara was now Mrs Billy Laurence.

Before the split at New Australia, Mary had written for the *Journal*: "A woman has lived vainly, and without the crowning joy of living, unless from among manly men she has chosen in free will a husband upon whom, in all purity and virtue, she can pour out the passionate affection that is in all true women's hearts."

On 16 August 1895, just two weeks after the boating party returned to Cosme, Mary Cameron turned thirty. At the same time Cosme opened its first school, with John Lane the schoolmaster of eleven pupils. But he was an experienced horticulturalist who had received training at London's Kew Gardens and his skills were desperately needed elsewhere on the colony. In the same month William Lane wrote to Mary, entreating her to come and take charge of the children's education. She made an abrupt decision and began preparing a stock of teaching materials, including (as the piano had remained the property of New Australia) a keyboard of wood and cardboard for music lessons.

In a letter written to Mary nearly thirty years later, Walter Head (who had moved to Tasmania and changed his name to Walter Alan Woods) described his memory of her before her departure for Paraguay.

> You were a tall, straight, lissome, alert-eyed and jolly-voiced maiden, in a white blouse and (I think) a scarlet belt ... Weren't you sort of engaged to Dave Stevenson? What happened to that and why? ... As to your influence. Of course it was great, but not so very surprising when I come to think of it seeing you's you ... one whose value as a good mate to the men, personally and collectively, was by no means lessened by the amazing but incontrovertible fact that your mateship with the men-folk fanned no tiniest spark of jealousy among the women-folk. They trusted you, too! They knew you absolutely unselfish and clean and straight with that unconscious and unparaded straightness which delights all good women and disarms all the not-so-good.

The wives may not have felt so very threatened. Mary's biographer, W. H. Wilde, describes her at the time as "a formidable woman": "She had grown to well above average height [five feet nine inches — 175 cm] and was, as an experienced schoolteacher, of commanding, even imperious presence. Her contemporaries, male and female, saw her as a somewhat daunting person — a radical blue-stocking, competent, assured and forthright. Few men would have entertained romantic notions about such a woman and those who did would have had to have been made of stern stuff to believe themselves worthy of being considered her mate and her equal. Dave Stevenson probably was such a man — Mary always spoke of him with admiration."

The colony to which she intended to make her way had a population of eighty-four (seventeen women, forty-five men and twenty-two children) and a leader who was increasingly introspective and inclined to depression. William Lane had not come to terms with Charlie's death. But on 6 September Cosme celebrated his thirty-fourth birthday with "a grand social and ball, both men and women turning out in their very very best clothes".

Arthur Tozer mentioned to Harry: "I think it likely that Lane will be going to England in a few months time. I want to know if Pater, Mater and you would like him to call? I couldn't tell him to visit you unless I thought he would be thoroughly welcome. I would also like to know if he might expect to put up at our house for a few days without being thought a bother. I would like you all to know him because I feel sure you would change your opinion of him pretty quickly after a few hours conversation. No special arrangement would have to be made for him as he has 'toughed it' both here and in the Australian bush & would consider your style of living luxurious."

Mary Cameron resigned from the New South Wales Department of Public Instruction on 31 October 1895. Writing years later about leaving Stanmore Public School for the last time, she said that the children wept in the streets. Among the items Mary packed in a saratoga trunk for the journey was a length of white hailstone muslin, suitable for a wedding dress.

In Paraguay, William Lane had been afflicted with a serious abdominal illness and his life hung in the balance. Dr Bottrell, the English physician based in Villarrica, was holidaying in England so Lane was under the ministrations of an unqualified man from Caazapá. His condition worsened. The settlers, recognising a real emergency, cabled an eminent Asunción physician, asking him to hire a special train and come immediately. Dr Ossorio arrived at great expense, declined to use opium to stop the violent diarrhoea, watched his patient decline for seven days, then gave up the case. "The camp very gloomy," John Dias recorded, "reckoned he was past recovery, but still hoped. On that night he lost all power of the muscular system ... It was decided to go against Dr Ossorio's orders and stop the diarrhoea at all hazards, as he was going to die anyhow from weakness." Astonishingly, Lane began to improve. He was taken to a house in Caazapá to convalesce, tended by his wife Anne, eldest child Nellie, and Arthur Tozer.

Souter observes that during this period Lane's writing "took on the same intensely religious tone as it had during the darkest days at New Australia".

Lane thanked God for his deliverance, while still expressing gratitude to all those at Cosme who had stood by him. "I couldn't have been nursed better, anywhere or anyhow, and everyone of our push felt kindly to me and did all they could. How different to New Australia? Our poor chaps! ' have cost them over 50 head of cattle and not one grudges it, except me, I know."

There were stories — probably overstated — of Lane becoming over-fond of brandy at this time, and other stories — probably true — of his difficulty as a charge. Billy Mabbott wrote to Will Saunders that he "tried the patience of our nurses and his wife, wanted all his own way, took to brandy and wine like a babe does to the breast, but insisted on calling it Tonic. Arthur Tozer says he was a pig of a patient and suggests we get up a farce with that title and take him off when he comes back, also to ask him to give us a lecture on intemperance". If this was a genuine recounting of Tozer's attitude, no matter how short-lived and provoked by stress it was, these would seem his first harsh words against a man he habitually idolised.

On 28 November Tozer wrote to Harry, expressing relief that Lane was out of danger, and admiration for him as a person whose habit of self-denial had brought him so low he had sickened. "It would have been a very bad thing for the colony if he had died but I think our fellows are too united to give in under such a blow after surmounting so many difficulties. We are all very thankful that he is well again & intend to see that he takes better care of himself in the future than he has done in the past."

At the time, Mary Cameron was preparing to leave Sydney. Years later she described how Henry Lawson became more gloomy and depressed as her departure drew near. "The night before I sailed he broke right down. He knelt to me and begged me not to go. 'If you go I am ruined,' he said. 'My life will never be worth anything again'."

The next day, 15 November, Henry was at the wharf to see her off with his mates Jack Jones and John Le Gay Brereton. According to a later account written by Jones, they "nearly stowed away on the boat that left for Paraguay". But like Henry's earlier talk of elopement, the plan came to nothing and he was left to make a final farewell to the woman it seems he had loved. "I sent my own people away," Mary wrote, "then Brereton, then Jones, and Henry's sad face was the last face I saw, his voice the last I heard. He looked like one lost and hopeless."

*

Julie and I were up before dawn on the morning of 14 May, huddling around the fuel stove with the elderly brothers, Bill and Norman Wood, drinking *yerba mate*, an acrid brew which seemed at first like an infusion of old cigarette butts, but which I'd begun to enjoy. At 5 am Rodrigo Wood, Norman's second eldest son, arrived with a gust of energy and the streetsmart style he had retained from his final year of high school in California. In his late thirties, his dark *mestizo* good looks acquiring the weight of good living, he had become the manager in Asunción of a private bank called Progreso.

Don Guillermo followed us out to farewell us as we piled into Rod's large American car.

Don Norman said, "This will probably be my last trip to Cosme."

"You always say that," said his brother.

"Yes, I keep going back," said Don Norman. "I'd like to be buried there, but my old missus won't let me."

Rodrigo donned a jaunty red baseball cap as we drove through the empty streets of Asunción in the pale morning light. Workmen were draping scarlet bunting — the colour of the ruling Colorado Party — around the statue of Madame Eliza Lynch. We were making our journey on Paraguay's official Independence Day and all over the country people were wearing a touch of red. They were celebrating their freedom from the Spanish yoke by thanking their dictator for imposing another yoke on them. Graham Greene's retired bank clerk Henry Pulling encountered a similar scene:

> Most men in the street wore red scarves round their necks, and many scarves were printed with a picture of the General ... There were red flags everywhere: you would have thought the town had been taken over by the Communists, but red here was the colour of conservatism. I was held up continually at street crossings by processions of women in red scarves carrying portraits of the General and slogans about the great Colorado party.

We passed a huge billboard which shouted the lie of the nation's advance under the dictator: "ARRIBA LA PATRIA CON STROESSNER!"

"Old Alfie will always be there," said Don Norman, "so we may as well go with the strength. The Liberals would probably be just as bad if they got into power." He grinned and added that his father used to have a saying, "The Colonel's lady and Biddy O'Grady are sisters under the skin." As women, so rulers apparently.

Beyond the straggling fringes of the capital we came to the little town of Itauguá, the traditional centre for Paraguay's famous *ñandutí* or spider-web lace. The weavers had spread their webs at their doors to catch tourists flying past, bedspreads, tablecloths and doilies of work too absurdly fine for the ordinary world. "Imagine how the hearts of white women are ravished at the sight of a handkerchief of lace so light that it can be blown across the room with a breath," Eric Birks had written. In the square the children were assembling for the Independence Day celebrations, girls in white dresses, boys in navy trousers and crisp shirts.

The road ran straight across the *campo*, rust-coloured earth on either side, stands of eucalypts as windbreaks, in the gardens of small farmhouses papaya, banana and huge dark mango trees, morning glory clambering exuberantly over tree trunks and adobe outbuildings, tiny butter-box shrines marking sites where people had been killed on the road.

In Caacupé, 54 kilometres from the capital, the fiesta had begun with a procession, a brass band and much beating of drums. This town is Paraguay's most important religious centre, its Lourdes. Rodrigo explained that there'd been a great flood in the 1600s which threatened to devastate the countryside until a Franciscan priest, Father Luis Bolanos, blessed the waters. As the flood receded a casket floated to the shore. It was found to contain a wooden statue of the Virgin Mary, carved by an Indian. Since that time, every year on 8 December, the Feast of the Immaculate Conception, people came from all over the country, from Brazil and Argentina as well, to pay homage to the statue of the *Virgen Azul de los Milagros*, the Blue Virgin of the Miracles. The president usually dropped in by helicopter, but most pilgrims walked, penitents whipping themselves with leather thongs. They celebrated with fireworks, candle-lit processions and displays of bottle-dancing, pyramids of bottles balanced on the dancers' heads. But despite all this devotion, the Virgin had recently seemed unhappy with the simple church where Her statue resided, showing Her displeasure by not healing the sick anymore.

But we saw a grand new basilica was nearing completion, the cobbled plaza had been enlarged to accommodate a crowd of 300,000, the streets were lined with tourist shops selling all manner of religious kitsch and lurid bleeding hearts, business was booming and, apparently, the Virgin was mollified and back at work again.

In the little town of San José, where some of the New Australian backsliders used to come to drink *caña*, the local people were spruced up in their best and waving red pennants on the grassy plaza. A statue of a soldier on a plinth, commemorating Paraguay's involvement in the Chaco War, looked uncannily like his digger counterpart in stone or bronze in any Australian country town.

A short distance further on, a dirt road led off to the left and a sign announced: Distrito Hugo Stroessner.

"It was once New Australia," said Rodrigo. Julie and I looked longingly up the road.

"You wouldn't want to go there," said Don Norman. "There's nothing of interest there and no one who speaks English. Let's get on to Cosme."

We turned south at Coronel Oviedo, once the village of Ajos. Now we were getting into the real countryside, *monte* on the higher land in the distance and sweeps of *campo* studded with cabbage-tree-like coca palms, called *mbocaya* in Guaraní. Rod said their fruit was a hard shiny brown nut liked only by monkeys, and there weren't many monkeys left to enjoy them these days. The farmhouses now, instead of being brick and tile, were mostly thatched-roofed, with walls of cracked brown *pug*. We passed high wheeled *carretas* pulled by oxen, some with a rough yoke of two branches to prevent them getting through fences. Occasionally and spectacularly, a horseman came riding by wearing baggy *bombachas* and a straw sombrero, nonchalantly astride a high-pommelled Spanish saddle with a sheepskin underneath.

Rod sang a little song in Guaraní. He said it was a very sweet and lyrical tongue, preferred by most Paraguayans for love-making. The president, he said, was devoted to the Guaraní language.

In the pleasant leafy town of Villarrica, the teenage girls of the Young Paraguayan Movement were marching. In their tight red jackets and short white skirts, they stepped out to a rousing rhythm from drums and cymbals. The drum majorette twirled her swagger stick, they kicked their legs high in their white leather boots. President Alfredo Stroessner, a paunchy 69-year-old, was said to enjoy the salute from the Young Para-guayans, one of his less onerous duties of state. The girls were a little old for his taste — fourteen years of age was about the cut-off for him; after that he usually passed girls on to his generals — but he could appreciate maturity when he saw it.

We detoured round the crowds gathering for the celebrations and, on a corner just off the plaza, found the graceful whitewashed villa of the English physician, Dr Bottrell, its wide verandas festooned with grape-vines. Tozer had described the doctor as "a good looking active man with the appearance of a country squire much given to sport and hunting", who had come to South America because of a heart condition, believing he could live longer in Paraguay's climate than elsewhere.

A man with a poncho over his shoulders was sitting on the sidewalk outside the house. He looked up and smiled shyly. He was pure-blood Indian, his face seamed and hawk-like.

At a *copetín* we stocked up on provisions for the weekend and, as we did, Uncle Norman beckoned a woman in the street carrying a cloth-wrapped basket. He passed around warm crusty rolls of *chipá* bread, made with corn flour, mandioca, eggs, cheese, aniseed and pig fat — and perfectly delicious.

Out along a dirt road through green rolling countryside with jagged blue mountains in the distance and we sped past a turn-off for San Juan Nepomuceno. According to an anthropological work I'd been reading, banned in Paraguay, there had been a slave market held there as recently as 1949. Some Guayakí forest Indians, the survivors of a manhunt and massacre, "were taken naked and in chains to the nearest town of San Juan Nepomuceno and there exposed for public sale".

More oxen *carretas*, more horsemen in *bombachas*, and we rolled into Caazapá. It was well known to me from reading *Cosme Monthly Notes*, the nearest marketing centre for the colony. The Australians had sometimes come in to watch bullfights, especially when toreadors from Spain performed. A little town of wide dusty streets, crumbling stucco houses with pantiled roofs, horses tethered at sliprails, John Wayne or Clint Eastwood could have come around a corner packing a six-gun, no problem. I bought film in a *farmacia* with high wooden shelves stacked with ancient medicaments and coloured glass jars. But there was one new house going up, brick, with ostentatious concrete balustrading. "At least *somebody* believes in Caazapá," grinned Don Norman.

He said that one of his first jobs had been as a mail-boy for the colony. "I used to ride into Caazapá and ask for the mail and get away as quickly as possible back to Cosme."

"Why?"

"The Paraguayan boys in the town didn't like us gringos. We didn't sit very tight in the saddle and they'd see our bums going up and down and they'd laugh about it. So one day I had to fight the ringleader — and he got the worst of it. It was under that tree over there."

Don Norman beamed and pointed to the scene of his triumph over seventy years before.

In Caazapá as elsewhere, a fiesta was in progress. Horsemen and onlookers gathered on the grassy plaza in front of a simple white church with colonnades on each side. "My brother Bill fixed the windows on that church," said Don Norman.

Birds flittered in the coolness inside. A massive and intricate altarpiece reached to the height of the nave. Five gilded alcoves contained sculptures of saints and apostles in high Baroque style. The sixth, in the centre, held the Virgin and Child, and only the detail surrounding them, flowers and fruit entwined, a carved white bird over the Virgin's head, were at odds with the pomp and ceremony of Europe and came, joyously, from the forest world of the Indian craftsmen.

Outside the church was a statue of its founder, Fray Luis Bolanos, a Franciscan priest who arrived from Spain in 1575, only eighty-three years after Columbus. Even before the establishment of the famous Jesuit missions, Father Bolanos was encouraging Indians to congregate in village settlements and adopt Christianity. He mastered the Guaraní language and translated a prayer book for his followers. He pushed eastwards to Guairá province, spreading word of his God, and within five years had established eighteen such villages, including Caazapá.

A local legend was relayed to me by Alcides Wood, a lawyer and another Cosme descendant. He said Father Bolanos, who had blessed the flood-waters at Caacupé, was resisted by the Indians around Caazapá. They demanded proof of the power of his god. The priest climbed the nearest mountain and, at the summit, rapped his stick against a rock. "Water came gushing out," said Alcides. "The spring is still there today. It never dries up."

The Indians converted to Christianity, but were endlessly vulnerable to raids by the Spanish landowners looking for labour for their farms and to capture by the *bandeirantes*, slave hunters from Brazil. They lacked the military defences later set up on the Jesuit missions, and they succumbed to diseases brought by the Spaniards. Father Nicolás del Techo, writing a history of this early period, recorded that 300,000 Indians lived in Guairá when the Spaniards first came and, even before 1600, "scarce the fifth part of that number remains".

A wooden cross was erected at Caazapá on the grave of Fray Luis Bolanos. Alcides' wife told me there was a popular belief that if you took a splinter from the cross, you got married soon afterwards. Girls came from all over Paraguay to get a splinter. I laughed. "It works," she said abruptly. "I got my husband that way."

*

Mary Cameron probably did not know about Father Bolanos's splinter, or I think she would have tried it. She had made an intrepid journey for a woman travelling alone in the 1890s, with no language other than English and, at last, her goal was close. She had an undoubted commitment to the ideals of Cosme colony, but it also seems undeniable that she hoped to marry Dave Stevenson.

After her 22-day voyage in the little mailboat *S S Ruapehu* and unceremonious arrival in Montevideo, slung down in a chair to a launch which "jumped and danced as if it had the Tarantula", she had explored that city with delight, writing up her observations. Then came her river trip in the paddle-steamer *Olimpo*, suffering dreadfully as they moved into the tropics, sipping iced lemonade, fanning herself in sheer desperation while the perspiration ran off in streams, and braving the banter of the crew to avail herself of the chief engineer's bath in the mornings.

She arrived in Asunción on either New Year's Eve or New Year's Day 1896. Either way the city would have been full of carousing crowds, the train schedules even more lax than usual, and the midsummer heat oppressive. She may have stayed overnight at the Hotel de Paris near the railway station, where Cosme people enjoyed reduced rates.

> Once in Asunción,
> Long, long ago in Paraguay,
> I woke to hear the sentries' call,
> The hours of night go by.

She visited the nearby cathedral, and wrote, "one is struck by the sight of the choristers & incense bearers going about in vestment trimmed with almost priceless lace yet with bare feet". She described a Nativity tableau at the cathedral: "The sun was blazing down on the sand outside the church, the perspiration ran down one's face in streams while the flies were a source of torture. But the snow remained intact all round the holy group, children's sixpenny lambs followed the shepherds, and the air was full of angels, cupids and lovely ladys cut out of cigar and hair restorer ads."

Having sent a telegram to the colony, Mary took the train from Asunción to a siding called Sosa, just over 30 kilometres west of the settlement. She must have expected and hoped that Stevenson would be there to meet her — but no one was. She then went on to González, the government colony, and was not at all impressed with the people there. "The colonists were Paraguayan with an odd German, English and

Frenchman. Here one learned what a 'poor white' is. He is the most miserable and squalid of beings, living on his wife if he has one, or his mistress if he has not, and when he has neither, living anyhow." Mary was considering her options, for one of the mistresses ran what passed for an accommodation house, when John Lane arrived, leading a horse for her.

According to John's son Eric Lane, a lively, garrulous septuagenarian when I interviewed him in Brisbane in 1988, his father also led a packhorse for Mary's luggage. "The train had come in a day earlier than expected. She was waiting in a wayside shanty. They set out on the return trip but darkness fell and they had to go back and stop the night."

Mary's disappointment must have been crushing, and her emotions in turmoil on that first night of the new year and her new life. But on the arduous ride next day, "hearing the oranges go squish, squash under our horses' feet", she caught up on recent events at Cosme.

> John Lane told me of the illness his brother had had, and of the colony anguish in the dread of his death. The strong man in whom all faith, all hope centred, he who was governor, guide, and father had lain for weeks where the shadows are thickest, and no man knew whether he would ever again see the sun. Somehow he rallied. Perhaps the necessity for him pulled him through.

Cosme Monthly Notes recorded Mary's arrival on 2 January 1896 and that she was "warmly welcomed". There is no mention of warmth from David Russell Stevenson who, according to John Lane's daughter Hilda, "was a bit of a Casanova … I don't think he considered himself engaged to Mary, for when she arrived he refused to go and meet her and poor Papa had to ride twenty miles through the pampas".

Eric Lane said his father remembered a Welcome Dance for Mary: "But most men thought her a very unattractive female. They drew straws — the unlucky ones with the long straws had to dance with her. Peter Pindar drew a long straw; when he saw her he tried to get rid of it. After the last dance Mary hooked into Pindar's arms. He disengaged himself and said 'Follow my moleskin trousers and we'll get you home'."

"She was a joke in Cosme — arrived after the battling had been done," Hilda Lane wrote of Mary. "She was a very poor teacher and couldn't keep order … No love was lost between her and my father tho he would never allow us to joke about her — but he'd talk to his men friends about her funny ways." Another colonist described Mary as "the hysterical man-woman", and I had heard similar gibes from the Wood brothers. It is tempting to dismiss all these comments as mere scuttlebutt, but they are revealing, coming from children of original colonists relaying the views of their parents. There is an element of hostility that goes beyond Mary failing to come up to scratch as a great beauty (after all, another of the few single women, Nurse Margaret Grace, was no sylph at 76 kilos, but was always mentioned in friendly terms). It has to do, surely, with Mary being a threatening figure, especially to a group of bushmen, in her height, education, confidence and articulateness. As well as all this, there is the simple possibility that Mary was irritating. Some of the grandiosity in her memoirs is irritating to me. But the comments of descendants certainly reflect the gossip-ridden place Cosme was, one of the reasons for the ultimate breakdown of the colony.

In January 1896 most colonists seemed to be aware of how Mary's expectations of Stevenson had been rebuffed and they busily relayed the news back to friends in Australia. "She is *not* married, no prospect," Tom Hall wrote. "The old affair is off. But she is well liked by all of us. My wife who is looking over my shoulder whispers — 'Not me', but then she isn't trustworthy in this matter."

William Wood, who had come to know Mary in Sydney, obviously found her impressive but difficult: "She is a great girl and I would like to see her get married to one of our best fellows. No sign that way as yet tho! Of course, it's not every man would suit a girl of her description, is it?"

Many years later, in a letter to the poet Hugh McCrae, Mary gave her version of the failure of her romance. As her biographer, W. H. Wilde says, it was "an unlikely but totally understandable account (since nobody likes to be jilted)":

> David, cousin to Robert Louis Stevenson, and to whom I was engaged in the early New Australia days, and perhaps would have married but that another woman so broke her heart over it she married the first man who asked her and suffered and suffered. When I went to Cosme and passed her house (she was then married) I used to hear her crying when she thought no one could hear.

Mary coped with the public humiliation and settled in to her new life. The food was a shock. "At the time of my arrival in the settlement things had not long passed the stage of utter and continued hardship, the time when food consisted solely of beans relieved by an occasional monkey." Fearing scarcity still existed, she maintained that in the first week she was afraid to eat in case someone else should go short. But in all her time at the colony she found the food unappetising, indigestible and had to force it down.

During the first few weeks she stayed with John and Jenny Lane. Then a little house was completed for her, next to the colony dining hall.

My first house was of grass — grass walls, grass windows, grass roof. It had no fireplace. It had no door. The floor was of clay. If you sat too long in the sitting room, the legs of the stools (we had no chairs at this time) sank inches deep in the floor ... The humidity of the atmosphere was such that my dressing gowns mildewed, hanging on the line I had put up as a wardrobe. Things in my saratoga and steel trunks kept well enough, but anything in open and unlined wood became quite damp — kid gloves and boots suffering most ... I put a packing case across the doorway to keep out any too inquisitive bullock, mosquito-driven horse, or soap-devouring cow.

It was unpleasant to wake up and find ants all over the bed, flowing like a river across the floor, speeding up the walls and through the roof. But the scatteration of frogs, toads, crickets, lizards, tarantulas, spiders, and probable snakes, made up for all unpleasantness, and when morning came and one swept up fragments of legs and claws, mandibles and wing-scales, it was with a feeling that there is a law of compensation, after all, and that, in spite of everything, one's day will come at last.

*

On a deeply rutted road, 20 kilometres from Caazapá, we came to the Pirapó. It seemed a disappointingly narrow muddy stream but was notorious for flooding its banks with astonishing rapidity, marooning Cosme from the world.

"So we don't have to swim the horses across today," said Don Norman. "That makes a nice change." We rattled over the old timber bridge which Allan McLeod and other colonists had helped to build, and sloughed another 5 kilometres along a furrowed track, the *monte* closing in on both sides.

Quite suddenly we emerged into open space and bright sunlight. "Guantanamera" was booming from a loudspeaker. We were on a village green fronted by a dozen houses, one of red brick, a couple of cracked mud, but most of them neatly whitewashed and thatched.

"Colonia Cosme," said Don Norman softly, looking around with immense satisfaction. "I was not sure I'd ever be back."

A kind of rodeo was in progress for Independence Day. Young men wearing straw sombreros, fleeces under their saddles, were coaxing their horses through a series of jumps, applauded by the *campesinos*, the local swarthy-skinned country people, and numerous excited children.

A wiry athletic man of perhaps forty with fine-boned good looks and a bushy moustache came forward and embraced Norman and Rodrigo, then kissed us on both cheeks, greeting us in Spanish. This was Francisco

Wood who, as a young man, had almost gone with his brother Peter to Australia, but had stayed instead to marry Sylvia McLeod, another colony descendant. We were introduced to Sylvia, whose high cheek bones and aquiline features seemed uncannily both Scottish and Spanish. She was one of the three teachers at Cosme's school and claimed to have only *un poco inglés* because she had found no use for English in recent years.

An old man, white-haired and achingly thin, made his way through the crowd. He was convulsed with glee, exposing toothless gums, as he hugged Don Norman, his childhood friend. This was 81-year-old Rod McLeod, not related to Sylvia but the son of Allan McLeod, a carpenter from Bourke in New South Wales. "We used to wag school together," laughed Don Norman, "and go hunting in the *monte*. Remember that, Rod?"

"Eh?"

"Remember, we used to wag school."

"Course we did! School was a waste of time!"

The music blaring from the loudspeakers changed to Harry Belafonte's "Banana Boat Song". The young men of the village steadied their champing horses at the edge of the field. Don Norman explained that this event, the *sortija*, was much beloved in Paraguay. Rod McLeod giggled. "All the fellers show off to their girls!"

A large cross, entwined with leaves and flowers, had been erected in the centre of the ground. Two tiny rings, the size of large wedding rings, dangled at each end of the cross beam. In twos the young men on horseback charged, thrusting their lances like medieval jousters. The idea was to successfully spear a ring at full gallop and race one's rival to the finishing line.

Norman Wood and Rod McLeod, arm in arm, led us across the field, skirting the horsemen as they thundered by, past pits of glowing charcoal where hunks of meat were skewered on green saplings. Ahead, screened by a row of Chinese cedar trees, was the slab timber farmhouse built by William Wood Senior. It looked for all the world like something out of nineteenth-century Australia — which essentially it was.

On the rickety veranda an old white-haired man was waiting, Wallace Wood, aged eighty-one. He was the only one of the brothers to have stayed on at Cosme, and had eked out a living, subsistence farming. He stumbled as he rose to greet us, obviously very ill. Apparently he had collapsed the previous night, a recurring angina condition, and I'm sure had only struggled out of bed because of us.

His wife, Doña Maria, a gnarled and bent country woman with slightly

Indian features, a headscarf tied low on her forehead, greeted us. She was shy and embarrassingly deferential, and disappeared back inside to cook over an open fireplace, preparing the mandioca to go with the joints of *asado* beef that Rod had purchased from the fiesta.

To allow her more time, Sylvia McLeod de Wood led us away to see the schoolhouse, accompanied by her three young daughters — Mabel, Diana and Shirley — and Francisco, a *macho* fourteen-year-old version of his father. A group of curious, giggling children also followed.

Sylvia was their teacher, and at her request the children took their places at desks in the spartan, brick schoolroom. In Guaraní they dutifully chanted a patriotic poem about Paraguay. A carrot-haired, freckled boy, a larrikin Ginger Meggs, ducked below the desk, overcome with mirth that these visitors had so little to do with their time.

*

"Soon after my arrival," Mary wrote, "I was given charge of the school. A many windowed, wooden building with a bungalow roof, it was furnished with the ordinary fittings of Australian schools. The curriculum was our own, as we kept in every way non-Paraguayan. The Queensland Readers in use, however, were supplemented by Spanish Readers."

Mary had definite ideas on "The Training of Children". She expounded these for the adults at an evening meeting in February. Her twelve pupils, aged between five and fifteen years, who had had a sporadic schooling thus far, found themselves plunged into a rigorous schedule:

> The subjects taught include Reading (which takes in spelling and words, meanings and derivations), Writing (including transcription, dictation and printing), Arithmetic, English History, General and Physical Geography, English (which takes in grammatical construction, parsing, composition and style), Spanish, Singing, Sewing, Plaiting, Weaving, Drill, Object Lessons and Natural Science. Under the last two headings have been given lessons on ants, coral insects, teeth, cardinal points, finding the north, elephants, organs of the body, names and kinds of joints, outline of lessons on the heart, elementary botany (taking in sex in plants), metals and minerals, slate, papermaking, wood, clocks and watches, observation of birds, lines and perspective and how the eye measures distance, movements of the earth, ideas relative to God, Mohammedanism, general causes affecting temperature and climate, wind and current, solids and liquids and gases, blood, grasses, process of amputating limbs, burns and scalds, stoppage of bleeding from cuts and wounds, stages of development of peoples, modes of seed distribution, development of the

writing pen, mammals, insects, moths, butterflies, with lessons on ethical
subjects whenever it is appropriate to give them, also on Cosme and what it
means in the same way …

Phew! I imagine the Cosme kids had the same reaction.

There were woodpeckers' nests in termite mounds near the schoolhouse
and, as part of the "observation of birds", Miss Cameron wrote, "I had the
egg daily removed from one of these. The bird laid no less than eighteen!
When fresh they were of a beautiful lavender or lilac colour, but in a few
days this faded to white."

At the time of Mary's arrival in January, Cosme was officially proclaimed a colony by the government, which offered to cover the cost of
the five leagues of land they currently occupied and grant them an
additional league, on condition that seventy-two families were settled
within two years. William Lane was confirmed as *intendente* or magistrate,
and Tozer as *sub-intendente*.

But Lane had not fully recovered from his illness, as Mary Cameron
soon observed: "It was not all over, even at the time I got there. The leader
was still a white shadow of a man, easily exhausted by effort, physical or
mental. Indeed he was never really and truly himself till after he left
Paraguay for good, though he would probably not admit the fact." Tozer
took on most of the colony's official business and told his brother that he
was obliged to visit Asunción at least once a month, had attended meetings
with the minister of colonisation, and had looked up his old friend,
ex-minister López, once again living in Paraguay, "who was very cordial".

In March William Lane had a relapse. He was placed under the care of
Dr Bottrell, back from vacation, who was able to diagnose the real problem
as a rupture of the abdominal membrane and constriction of the bowel.
Tozer, returning from Villarrica where he had arranged accommodation
for Lane and his family, wrote to Harry that, "he will aways be in
considerable danger until it has properly healed … but he never takes
enough care of himself & hates the extra expense to the colony".

Lane was still planning a recruiting trip to England and had asked Tozer
to come as his aide. "My part of the work will most likely be the usual
office drudgery with occasional trips from London to the provinces.
London would be headquarters. Lane intends to start organising & assist
it by running a Communistic journal. He would want me to remain with
him about a year & then I should return to Paraguay." Tozer thought the
government would pay Lane's fare, but canvassed the possibility that
Harry and the family might come up with a third-class fare for himself,

adding somewhat ungraciously: "I confess that I don't much like the idea of living in England for even a year but I certainly should like to see you all again & that would more than compensate for the unpleasant part of the trip." He concluded by affirming his faith in a future, even if not a spectacular one, for Cosme: "We may never influence the World much one way or the other but there is some satisfaction in knowing that you are living straight & that your children will have a chance of doing the same. We are more likely to do good than harm in the World and that alone is something."

He couldn't say the same for New Australia, although he admitted, "my besetting sin is, I believe, bitterness. I can't quite forgive the New Australians their treatment of us in the past". Their offer of a friendly cricket match against Cosme was sharply rebuffed. Glorying in his contacts, Tozer confided that the Minister of Colonisation viewed "NA as very disorganised" and he knew for a fact that the British Minister in Buenos Aires was preparing a dossier on the two colonies, because Dr Bottrell had been asked to give his opinion. He hoped Harry could get hold of the consular report. "Any information given by Bottrell is reliable. He knows what is going on in both colonies & does not believe in either Socialism or Communism. He is about the best known man in Paraguay & very influential with the govt. Also he is well read & intelligent generally & quite capable of judging the colonies. I take him to be very honorable & don't think he would write what he didn't believe to be absolutely correct."

Harry, generous in the past with offers of money to his younger brother, remained reticent on the matter of the fare, although Arthur renewed his request, stressing that Lane would need him in England and Dr Bottrell considered his company essential.

After four months, Mary Cameron had settled into colony life with real enthusiasm, judging by a letter she wrote to W. G. Spence, though loyalty to Lane may have coloured her words:

> The plainest thing written on the face of this Colony is success. It has succeeded far beyond my expectations ... Everyone in the place seems as a matter of course to be homely and friendly and alright and you feel it at once. In all my life I have never had such a "home" feeling as here, and I have never worked so freely and with such a feeling of individual independence — a feeling that if I were asked to do what I thought unfair I could straightway object, and that if my objection were legitimate it would be alright, and that if it were not I should be shown it were not ... I am satisfied of the justice and the possibility of communism. I am satisfied with my own lot, I am contented

and I feel I have learned more since I came here than I had ever hoped to learn in Australia ...

A reason for her sudden contentment could have been the intimate association with Dave Stevenson almost every evening. They were rehearsing a play, *Engaged*, by W. S. Gilbert (without the music of his partner Sullivan), to be staged in the new wooden barn as the main event for the third Foundation Day. Mary and Dave, both of Scottish extraction, were playing two lovers, Maggie Macfarlane and Angus Macalister. Stage directions called for frequent kissing and embracing. Although there were roles for four other women, Clara Laurence did not take part.

Mary also made her presence felt at the evening social gatherings, one Sunday night reading two of her original short stories. Perhaps one was an early draft of "Santa Rosa — A Tale of the Pampa". In that story an Englishman was parted from his beloved, living a hard life on the pampas, although, "he had kissed her in England". He failed to write, because he was "a man who writes with difficulty and to whom writing is a pain ... But she was on her way to him, on her way to the Argentine". Unaware of this, the Englishman decided, " 'Better be dead, dead and forgotten and no more remembered', and he looked down at his hands in bitterness of soul." On a fateful day a *carreta* came to his door, the sun dazzled his eyes and he struggled with a thousand memories:

> Then he saw it was she. As she came to him, he moved back. She stood, as also did he. She looked into his eyes, with the eyes of England and the eyes of love. He looked back at her ... then slowly held out the hands of a leper.
> "Look" he said, as they lay before her.
> "I know" she said.

The message would have been clear, not just to new devotees of Sigmund Freud, but also to the veterans of intrigue at Cosme: the lover who turned his back on love would be blighted — but he could accept the healing devotion of a good woman.

Mary was sometimes seen of an evening walking with Stevenson in the *monte*. The forest was a revelation to her in its richness and profusion of palms, ferns, cedars and creepers, "like some vast Botanical Garden let loose". She described it as she knew it on her evening walks:

> The sun was growing perceptibly lower every minute. Soon it would be dark and already there were signs of night in the chattering of the monkeys, the scurrying to cover of the coons, and the clutter and fluster of the flocks of

macaws which so far we had not seen but had only heard screeching far overhead in their flight Brazilwards from the cold farther South.

*

As we finished Doña María's *asado* beef and mandioca a storm broke, with violent crashes of thunder, tree branches rasping against the iron roof. The little slab timber house was in darkness but for sudden flares of lightning, a flickering oil lamp and the smouldering fire in the kitchen. Once Billy Laurence had sat in front of that fire, *mate* gourd in hand, talking about the old shearing days with William Wood. Now, sitting with a glass of whisky, Wallace Wood was enjoying himself, despite his illness. He astonished his brother Norman by wanting to talk about Mary Gilmore.

"I'm only going by the gossip we heard around here," said Don Wallace, "but I suppose the people who gossiped knew what they were talking about. They said what attracted Mary to Cosme more than anything else was Dave Stevenson. He was a wonderful attraction for a number of the women. There were two or three only too happy to walk in the *monte* with him."

Rod McLeod chuckled. He said his father always had a very humorous look when he talked about Mary walking with Dave, "with the moon going down over the banana patch".

"They used to say she followed him with the hope of eventually getting him to propose to her," said Wallace, "but he never did. He didn't propose to any woman until he could marry Clara."

Don Norman looked sceptical. "Where'd you get all this, Wallace? You were hardly born."

"Mum used to talk about it all the time," said Don Wallace, defiant. "And I can see Dave's point. Have you seen a photograph of Mary Gilmore?"

"I saw one somewhere," said Don Norman, a ladies' man himself. "I wouldn't fall violently in love with her."

"She had a rather *decided* look, as if she meant to get what she wanted."

"Well, she didn't get our Dave!" Rod McLeod exploded in a fit of giggles. They all laughed — heirs, I thought to myself helplessly, of the male chauvinism of the bush mateship tradition of 1890s Australia, crossed with Latin *machismo*.

"Stevenson was a real character, a wonderful dancer and a great conversationalist," continued Don Wallace. "He was a bit of a hero for us."

Don Norman nodded agreement. "He looked like a soldier, a man of military bearing." He said his brother Bill always remembered how Stevenson was "so perfectly clean. A real spartan. In winter time he'd put a kerosene tin full of water out to get cold, to get a little shroud of frost on it. He liked to break the ice to have his bath as soon as he got up in the morning."

"Remember the picnics?" said Don Wallace. "He used to take us kids down to the blue gums."

"He would get a remittance from Scotland once a year," explained Don Norman, "and he didn't want the money, so he'd put on a picnic for the kids. The women would make the goodies — I remember Mrs Laurence's patty cakes and lemon cheese tarts — but Stevenson paid for the lot. Apparently his people had money."

"Well, of course, he was a relation of Robert Louis Stevenson, the writer," said Wallace.

"Where'd you get all this stuff?" asked Don Norman. "I never heard these tales."

"Dad used to say so," said Don Wallace. "And anyway, I read it in Gavin Souter's book. Until someone stole it."

I found the copy I'd brought of *A Peculiar People* and gave it to him, amused that Cosme talk had been a source for the book; now the book was a source for Cosme talk.

"I always say, 'A Queer People'," said Don Norman.

Julie played a cassette she had brought, the folk group Redgum singing about a group of Australians who sailed away to start a new life in South America.

> … And the Paraguay skies and nights are cold,
> You can forsake your country and lose your soul …

On the small recorder, the plangent rock chords dominated the words.

> … We won't drop anchor till we reach Altamira Sound,
> Heave away, we're New Australia Bound,
> Virgin Ground.

"What's it saying?" Don Norman asked, leaning towards the speaker, a trifle irritated. "What's the damn thing saying? I can't make it out."

"It's what I like," said Rodrigo, clicking his fingers, "Elvis!"

*

The trip to England hung in the balance. It depended on whether Arthur

Tozer could make it, and that hinged on his brother financing a fare. And Harry was not forthcoming. His last letter had irked and mystified Arthur, suggesting that Lane's presence might cause "a bit of bother at home". Arthur failed to see what the bother could be and insisted that Lane was not an invalid. His sickness had been caused by a rupture of the intestinal membrane, he had been careless about his food and too fond of riding, the cause of his setbacks, but now he understood that greater care was required.

On the other questions Harry had raised, he went fiercely into battle. It was Lane, not his brother, who was his mentor now:

> It appears to me that you are afraid that Lane is going to make a miserable failure of his visit to England, that he may get a relapse, & that then the both of us would come on the family for support. If that is your idea you needn't worry about it. The organisation may not be a success & he may get one or more relapses but he won't want to make Romford his hospital nor a convenient refuge if he gets down on his luck. Lane has friends in England, more than I have, so that if he requires charity, as you call it, he won't go to Romford for it.

Harry's remarks "re the tyranny of Lane & the committee in the matter of holidays" were also ill-advised and uninformed. It was absurd to talk of tyranny at Cosme. Although Tozer conceded the potential was there, it could never creep in to any great extent as there were too many checks against it. The holiday credit system had been put to the vote in the usual manner and passed by a majority. With the recruiting trip still uncertain, he planned to use his credits in July to join another boating expedition with his old companions, Miller and Stevenson. But he would prefer a draft from Harry to pay his passage to England instead.

Tozer's indignation left scant room for news, but he did reveal, with almost endearing casualness, that he was considering moving into a little house. For the previous two and a half years he had been living in a tent, but it was now rotten, falling to pieces and would not repel water any longer. "It is a very healthy but rather inconvenient sort of residence. I never catch cold when living in a tent but as soon as I sleep in a house I am sure to get one."

On 12 May 1896 the colonists enjoyed their anticipated celebration for Cosme's third Foundation Day. At a public tea, toasts were pledged — in *yerba mate* — to "The Race We Spring From", "The Land We Live In", "Cosme and Communism" and "Sweethearts and Wives". William Lane, apparently recovered from his long illness, spoke encouragingly of the progress made during the year despite various disappointments (a poignant comment; one was the death of his son Charlie): "But we may safely say that we are beyond the reach of starvation, that we have broken the back of actual pioneering and that the coming year will see progress made in the essential of actual permanent settlement. And there is still among us that goodwill and friendliness which is of all communal treasures the most precious, because without it all communism is in vain."

Lane then inaugurated the new barn on the hill, a handsome wooden building some 30 metres long by 20 metres wide. Everyone gathered inside, people sitting on corn sacks, children sleeping at their parents' feet, two-year-old Bill Wood on his mother's lap, for the long-anticipated event, a full-length production of Gilbert's *Engaged*. "The comedy itself was played in a way which spoke volumes for the dramatic capacity and careful study of the players."

William Wood appeared in the leading role as Cheviot Hill, a young Englishman of property. But as oil lamps dimmed in brackets along the walls, the scene opened on a garden in Gretna Green, with Mary Cameron as Maggie Macfarlane, "a pretty country girl … spinning at a wheel and singing as she spins".

Dave Stevenson, as Angus Macalister, "a good-looking peasant lad", crept softly towards her, placing his hands over her eyes. He declared he was not the man "to deal in squeaming compliments … I love thee dearly, as thou well knowest".

To which Maggie replied that if such a "gude, brave, honest man, will be troubled wi' sic a puir little, humble mousie as Maggie Macfarlane, why, she'll just be the proudest and happiest lassie in a' Dumfries!"

"My ain darling!" Angus cried, and they embraced.

But although the love of Maggie and Angus was soon fraught with difficulties and complications created by others, a final consummation came for them at last. The play concluded to thunderous applause as all the couples paired off and the actors embraced: Mary and Dave, William Wood and Miss Margaret Grace, Charlie Boys and Mrs Cantrill, Allan McLeod and Mrs Kushel.

Some of Mary's early poems have a passion and sexual intensity which could date them to this period:

> I shall not sleep,
> I cannot sleep —
> He kissed me twice today;

He took me in his arms,
I could not say him nay.
He took me in his arms —
O God! the flash of light!
I cannot sleep, I will not sleep
I shall not sleep to-night!

In June the social evenings were not so well attended. In the Paraguayan winter, according to *Cosme Monthly Notes*, people enjoyed "the greater attraction of the home fires". Even Arthur Tozer now had a fireplace in his own house. "The furniture consists of two carpenter made beds, a table & two three-legged stools. My valuables & property in general is hung round the walls or kept in a trunk ... The floor is made of hard beaten clay & the walls are plastered with a paste made of clay & cow dung. It is a very comfortable little place & is quite a palace when compared to the tent."

Tozer set off in late July on the boating trip, down the rivers Capiibary, Pirapó and Yibicuarí-guayu to the Paraguay and the port of Corrientes. This time they had a sawn-timber boat, with a dug-out full of provisions, and four passengers — according to *Cosme Monthly Notes*, two women, a man and a boy — travelling, as Rebecca Sims had done, as far as the railway connection near Punto Fierro. The passengers were not named, but the "School" report for the *Notes* of July mentioned that the children rejoiced in four days' holiday while the schoolteacher went boating, and were given additional holidays for Settlement Day, and another day for "teacher's business".

So Mary Cameron had a full week off school in Stevenson's company, passing through tranquil and beautiful scenery and camping on the banks at night. Presumably, during the production of *Engaged* some relationship had been renewed between them. But the whole venture seemed eccentric, especially in the middle of winter. Mary's presence on the boat must have been at Stevenson's invitation and, in Cosme's hothouse society, would have produced a fever of speculation. It is frustrating, therefore, to be unable to locate any written evidence. Everyone is oddly silent on the matter. Mary did not write about the trip. There was no gung-ho account from Stevenson. Tozer was too cross with Harry to bother sending him a letter.

Was Mary, like Rebecca Sims in Stevenson's opinion, a model passenger, "taking the rough with the smooth uncomplainingly, sitting still when we were trying for a shot at game and flying round at cooking and washing up times"? Was she offered examples of the Paraguayan "woman's duty and respect towards the nobler sex"? And how did she get on with the hot-tempered and assertive Tozer? They must have had some sense of competition as Lane's two leading acolytes, but they are consistently and curiously unforthcoming on the subject of each other. And, above all, how did Mary get on with Stevenson? We can only speculate from her poetry:

He took me in his arms yesternight, yesternight —
The grass was hung with fairy dew,
The moon looked down upon us two,
He kissed me, did my lover true,
Yesternight, yesternight.
His hand lay near my heart, yesternight, yesternight —
The wind went by us into space,
My hair flew backwards out of place,
I felt his breath upon my face,
Yesternight, yesternight.

But whatever happened on the boating trip, it culminated with her hopes of Stevenson at a bitter end. Mary returned to Cosme at the beginning of August, but the school was closed for a further week according to the *Notes*, "on account of sickness of teacher".

Some clue to her ailment — perhaps rejection — is given in the postcard she wrote on 5 August to her old sweetheart, the man she had also rejected, Henry Lawson. She knew he had recently published a new volume of verse, *In the Days When the World Was Wide*. But she didn't know that on 15 April, a few months after her departure, he had married an attractive young woman, Bertha Bredt. Perhaps she had thought he would always be there in the background, ready to comfort her when she needed love. Suddenly, the idea of Henry coming to Cosme seemed very attractive to Mary.

Dear Harry,
I've got such a lot to say to you that I write on a postcard in order to say something. I am glad about your book but I haven't seen anything approaching a criticism of it, no one having sent me any papers. As for you, I believe you forgot me — but I know you didn't — only you might have sent me a copy of the book. Send me one anyway. How is it going? Tell Brereton to write to me and write yourself. I'd give a lot to see you here. The place teems with copy, the life makes it. I wish to Heaven I could write it up. I could cry when I see how it goes to waste. We are all originals, every one of us but as life becomes easier it will grow more commonplace and none but a see-er can write of us

as we are now.

Communism as we have it is alright, Harry, and we are getting on — slowly of course, but in a year or two what now is, will have gone, drowned by prosperity. And the country! — It is a constant wonder to me, so beautiful, so rich in bird, insect and plant. And the history! — and the stories of the war! If you were only here, Henry. Don't let someone else snap your chances. Come while the field is new — as a visitor I mean, though I'd like you to come for good, only I don't think you would. I am satisfied with life anyway — and I wish everyone found life as good as I do. Come if you can, dear old friend. You know I wouldn't ask you if I didn't think it worth it — even from your standpoint.

M.J. Cameron

p.s. I didn't get married.

14

Falling from Eden

It is stated and indeed proved that the Garden of Eden was in this place, in the centre of the New World, the heart of the Indian continent, a real, physical, actual place, and that here man was created. Any of these trees might have been the Tree of Life ...

Augusto Roa Bastos, *Son of Man*

The colony is a garden of Eden to look at, full of fruits and flowers. But, the orange and banana excepted, the fruits are generally grubby. But the rent day never comes round, nor the grocer's assistant to collect his little account. There is no paying into a club for medical attendance, nor worry over the doctor's bill, no watching for advertisements for situations for the girls and boys ...

Mary Gilmore, "Colonia Cosme"

Cocks crowed, a piglet snuffled outside the bedroom window under the Chinese cedars. In morning sunlight after the storm, Colonia Cosme was beautiful. The villagers were moving around the little whitewashed houses, ducks, geese and guinea fowl foraged in the meadow grass, and pale hump-backed cattle wandered the track deeply carved by *carreta* wheels. A *campesino* went by on horseback, a rifle slung over his shoulder, and waved to Norman Wood and Rod McLeod. They wished him good hunting as he headed towards the *monte*.

Julie and I walked on with the old men to take a look at The Flat where the colonists first made their settlement. The present site was all *monte* when they first came, Don Norman said. "They made a hard job of clearing it. Instead of doing like the natives did, just cutting down the trees and burning off, they wanted to use their ploughs so they had to take out all the stumps."

The narrow track was bordered by clumps of bamboo and huge mango trees with feathery flowers. Green and yellow parrots flittered between them, shrieking and chattering.

"This was the Two Chain Road," said Don Norman. "We still call it that. On the old Cosme plans it was marked two chains wide."

It was designed as a grand thoroughfare, nearly 50 metres across, to connect all the self-governing industrial villages and terminate in a noble plaza where citizens of the communist city could gather for uplifting speeches. "The plaza and the streets will all be lawned with buffalo grass," wrote Harry Taylor, "all to be lined with orange and other fruit trees, many of which are already planted in position." He predicted that in a few years it would be "a place of green-lawned loveliness, with wealth of fruit and flowers, a place of happy people and romping, laughing children".

"Hard to get a *carreta* along here now," laughed Rod McLeod, who found nearly everything a source of amusement. "Place is a hole. But we like it."

He didn't always, commented Don Norman drily, adding that Rod had a dark past. It seemed an unlikely load for the frail old man with the infectious laugh to carry.

"It was years ago," said Don Norman. "He had an argument with a policeman and threatened to shoot him. And the policeman went for his gun and said he'd get him first. So for a long time Rod stayed away for his health, isn't that right, Rod?"

Rod McLeod chuckled, but wasn't saying.

Don Norman stopped and pointed. "The social hall was there. We had many a dance there."

No trace of a building remained, just a citrus grove, the trees heavy in fruit.

"I don't remember the first hall here, it got burnt down," said Don Norman. "But they built another one in the same place. It was open on both sides with a shingle roof. Our floor was a marvellous floor, well planed and waxed, slippery as glass."

"They used to rub candles into it," said Rod McLeod. "We were always falling tom-tit."

"So you used to come courting here?" I asked.

"We courted anywhere!" laughed Rod.

*

The boat party — Arthur Tozer, Dave Stevenson and Bob Miller — returned at the end of August 1896 in time for a special evening at the social hall.

It was to welcome a colourful new addition to the Cosme community,

Laurence De Petrie. An anarchist of Scottish and French ancestry, Larry had an impressive black moustache, but only one arm, the other having been lost as the result of a scuffle between unionists and "scabs". In eastern Australia he had been famous for attracting an audience by singing the "Marseillaise", waving his stump in the air at the chorus, "*aux armes, citoyens!*" He would inspire the crowd with his vision of a future of liberty, equality and fraternity, achieved through mateship. "Hurrah for the Social Revolution," he'd declaim, "the abolition of white slavery, Kanaka slaughter, misery, prostitution, the unemployed, landlords and sundowners."

He arrived at Cosme after stowing away to Honolulu and "jumping the rattler" in the United States. He had suffered months of privations, appalled to find "the struggle for existence so keen that the poor hate one another". Eventually he managed to work his passage as a deckhand from New Orleans to Montevideo. Petrie never did anything quietly. William Lane's younger brother Ernest (who didn't come to Paraguay himself until 1903) counted him as a friend and remembered, "I have known many rebels, but Petrie was in the super-class."

Mary Cameron met him in Sydney in 1893 and hid some dynamite for him in her bottom drawer, later rather implausibly maintaining a belief that he planned some quarrying. Petrie became notorious in July that year, accused of planting a bomb on the steamer *Aramac* which was transporting blackleg labourers to Brisbane. Ernie Lane said that Petrie "vowed he would travel on one of the scab boats and blow it and the scabs up". Someone else reckoned they had heard him say that he'd "make an example of some plutocrats and double-breasted parasites". When the explosion actually occurred, the forecabin filled with flame and two people were slightly injured. Petrie was discovered on board and promptly arrested.

"I had seen the paragraphs in the papers relating to it," Mary wrote, and knew the police were scouring Sydney looking for a cache of explosives, "but never dreamt that what they were looking for was what Larry had asked me to keep for him."

Petrie's union mates raised money for his defence, and the Queensland *Worker* thundered in his support and published Mary's poem, "The Crows Kep' Flyin' Up", her identity hidden by a *nom-de-plume*:

We hear that worse than crows is agettin' at him now —
Worse than them goanners that dined upon the Chow.
We ain't worth much to look at, but Rome and me will wait,
An' do whatever we can do for Larry, man an' mate.

But the police had a sound case against Petrie, enough to have him hanged according to Ernie Lane, but lacked evidence of where he had obtained the dynamite. They overplayed their hand in getting a dealer to perjure himself. Petrie's defence collected proofs of the frame-up. "Not daring to face the public exposure of these police methods," wrote Ernie Lane, "the Attorney General filed a No True Bill and Petrie was discharged. I never saw him again, having left Sydney when he returned. He managed to get across to Paraguay and joined Cosme Colony."

Though Petrie had been two years on the journey, "with his face set for Cosme all the time", Harry Taylor was sure "the unrestrained joy and heart-felt warmth of welcome that greeted him at the termination of his journey must have gone far to repay him for the bitter weariness and semi-starvation of those two years".

William Lane joined in the welcome, no doubt in excellent humour. The British Embassy in Buenos Aires had provided the Foreign Office with a report which rated Cosme as "without a doubt one of the most, if not the most, orderly and best conducted colony in Paraguay". For over two years, it said, the Australians, "teetotalers without exception ... have laboured with praiseworthy energy and extraordinary perseverance, and their efforts, so far, have been crowned with success".

Larry Petrie was inclined to agree. He wrote to W. G. Spence that "Communism is all right" and was "slowly but surely rubbing out the barbaric elements born and bred of Modern Civilization ... I do not mean to say that we are perfect but I do say that I have not felt mad with anyone except myself since my arrival".

But Lane had no intention of resting on any laurels and urged the community to adopt a new Plan of Village Organisation. He envisaged a future when there would be a federation of self-governing industrial villages, each with at least a hundred families. He could offer British recruits the chance to become part of an army of upstanding, teetotal, Anglo-Saxon communists who would set an example to the world and could, ultimately, emerge from the *monte* to lead it.

Lane, departing for England with Tozer within a fortnight, was further gratified that the Paraguayan government had finally decided to pay both their fares, so formally acknowledging Cosme as a suitable destination for British immigrants. The immediate program was to attract enough re-cruits to fulfil their undertaking to the government of seventy-two families settled by June 1898. As there were only sixteen families so far, their task was formidable.

They were particularly anxious to find single women for the colony's thirty-three bachelors. There were presently only three spinsters and one of them was about to leave: Nurse Margaret Grace was returning to South Australia to care for her invalid mother. That left Nellie Bilby, a teenager who already had a suitor in the colony librarian, Dick Rae, and the one genuinely unattached female, Miss Mary Cameron.

Mary's problematical on again, off again relationship with Stevenson was definitely over, but few men had the nerve to approach such an impressive woman. She was now editing *Cosme Evening Notes*, and not only demonstrated supreme confidence in reading aloud stories and poems at the evening meetings, but quite often had written them too. "Mary Gilmore wasn't very popular," wrote John Lane's daughter Hilda. "She had a wonderful speaking voice and they loved to hear her read — but she *would* sing."

People could not have been more astonished when Mary was seen more than once in the company of one of the shyest and most unassuming of the colony men, William Gilmore. A 31-year-old shearer from Victoria, he was undoubtedly handsome, described by the journalist Harry Taylor as having "the sort of head that young girls rave about, clean cut features, nose somewhat aquiline and forehead crowned by a big bunch of bushy black curls". He was well-liked, practical and capable, but he wasn't one of the colony's intellectuals, never known, like Stevenson, to give a dissertation on Tennyson, Shakespeare's *Richard III*, or even, despite his Scots blood, on Robbie Burns. He had shown little interest in such matters and, as his formal schooling had stopped at the age of ten, he read and wrote with difficulty.

So when Gilmore was laid up in the colony hospital and Mary visited to read to him, even the inveterate gossips made little of it. He had a lacerated back and sprained ankle, the result of an accident typical of his good nature: he had seen a post collapsing on the children's swings and taken its weight, so saving the children from mishap and injuring himself. Hilda Lane observed that Mary read to him every day "and by the time he was up and about they were engaged. (That's how she 'got' him.) They all said 'Poor Billy' as he was the idol of the Cosme people, especially women and children".

When he had recovered, Gilmore accompanied Mary on evening strolls into the *monte*. Mary was obviously aware of the humiliating gossip about herself and was at this time emotionally fragile, if her illness after the boating trip and her rather desperate note to Lawson are any indication. It seems Henry could not face replying to her, but some time in September she received a letter from his old friend, John Le Gay Brereton, with the news that the writer had married a "little nurse" who seemed "much in love with him and looks after him as though she were his mother — or a young stepmother".

Mary wanted a husband. The obsession with Stevenson had cost years of her youth. She had just turned thirty-one; time was running out. Gilmore was a good, kind man and what's more, "a manly man", handsome enough to make her pulses race. If it was he who proposed marriage to her, and after such a brief courtship, he showed an uncharacteristic assertiveness. It is more likely Mary made the proposal herself, or at least drew him towards it.

She later dated their decision to marry to 6 September, the evening of the celebrations for William Lane's birthday. But the public announcement was not made until 15 September, the night before Lane and Tozer departed for England. According to a rather spiteful account from Tom Hall, once again revealing the hostility to Mary, it was not quite the surprise it might otherwise have been: "An accidental *rencontre* with an agouti shooter in the *monte* a few nights previous had prepared us for the announcement. Neither of the two look any the better for it. He is quieter than ever and the lady looks as if she has had a fit."

*

We followed the track, thickly overhung by trees, down a steep hill and emerged on The Flat — a bowl of sallow grassland, the size of three football fields, bordered by heavily wooded rising land. The *monte* stretched away to a range of low mountains in the distance. There was no evidence of human habitation, no visible ruins from the time of the Australian settlers. Their little houses, built from the substance of the earth, had sunk back into it. But at the edge of the forest, reflected in a pond, some blue gums they had planted were flourishing.

It was easy to see why the pioneers first settled there on the *campo*. They didn't have to clear trees and it seemed deceptively good farming land. The Queenslanders compared it to the Darling Downs and the sweeping grassland did appear uncannily Australian, especially with the eucalypts.

But walking, one's feet squelched; pools glistened between the grass tussocks. The soil was too sour and soggy for farming and at night mosquitoes descended in clouds. Eventually they copied the Paraguayans and cleared the *monte* on the higher ground, discovering soil fertilised by aeons of forest humus. As they cleared they moved to the new village up on the hill, but for a long time the community straggled between the two settlements.

Reddish termite hills, some of them nearly two metres high, dotted the plain. Marshal López used to stretch his prisoners to die over such mounds.

"There used to be a lot of owls settling on them, looking for ants," said Rod McLeod.

I recalled Mary Cameron's early fears of the blood-curdling cries in the dark, perhaps a wolf prowling:

> But at last the nerve shaking thing of the night was discovered to be just our little friend Mr Owl of the ant hill … One may see a hundred of these termite hills, and a little brown owl on the top of every one. In the twilight or among the white light and black shadows of a moonlit night the effect is most unearthly. One feels as if one were set down among a maze of heathen altars, upon every one of which stood the image of a god.

"The owls seem to have all gone now," said Rod McLeod. "And the armadillos too. There used to be hundreds of armadillos down here. Good eating."

We had walked across the plain to the dark brackish waterhole in which the blue gums were reflected. Don Norman said it was the old brick pit. His brother Bill used to swim there as a boy. A few baked bricks were scattered in the long grass, but neither of the old men could identify any of the sites of the original houses. They were born up the hill, they explained, with a certain chauvinistic pride. Bill might have been able to say, if he had been with us.

"But about here," Don Norman waved his arm expansively, "was the old cricket oval. I guess they had it in better condition in those days."

The oval had been fenced, levelled, sown with English grasses and fine turf for the pitch, and a neat pavilion offered shade for the spectators. Now the knee-high yellow grassland stretched away.

"Watch where you step," said Don Norman. "You'll be treading on a rattlesnake or something."

*

The day after Lane and Tozer's departure, The Englishmen of Paraguay arrived for a few days of cricket and entertainment. The visit "boomed social affairs considerably". The team was captained by Thomas Blackmore, brother of the author of *Lorna Doone*, and included Dr Bottrell and W. J. Holmes, the new British Consul in Paraguay. The scores were Cosme

41 and 92, The Englishmen 14 and 29, with Cosme winning by ninety runs, its victory "chiefly owing to the bowlers".

The visitors were entertained with a minstrel performance on the Saturday night, readings of poetry and short stories on Sunday and, on Monday night, Gilbert's *Engaged* was staged again. "The company was the same as before, but improvement was marked."

Years later, Mary Gilmore remembered how they had improvised: "Being poor we had what props we could. When we needed white stockings and had none, we raw-starched or pipeclayed our legs; when we needed a castle we did as Shakespeare did: we put up a placard with 'Here is a castle'." Looking back, she thought that their production of *Engaged* was unintentionally modern, in that it "anticipated the open ended stage, the unfinished colony barn being the theatre. The end wall still being out, our back stage was the fierce Paraguayan forest, the sky, the stars & the moon when it rose. I had to make a reference to the moon, she was there, a beautiful moon, but only half the audience thought to look skywards to see it. The kerosene footlights were between them & the heavenly light."

After the play, refreshments were served, then dancing until dawn, Mary Cameron and Will Gilmore much together as the colony's newest couple. According to *Cosme Monthly Notes*, "The guests were impressed with the Englishness of everything and when they left it was clearly understood that their visit was to be an annual institution."

But in fact it was to be one of the last truly carefree occasions at Cosme for a very long time. Souter has suggested that William Lane's absence in England served as the beginning of the end for Cosme, and, with hindsight, "an extraordinary sequence of tragedies, difficulties and withdrawals from the colony endowed his departure with unfortunate symbolic importance".

A baby, John Kushel, fell into a well and was drowned. A 34-year-old man, Robert Pindar, was caught in the machinery of the sugarcane grinder and crushed to death. And news came from England that one of their socialist mentors, William Morris, had died.

But spirits lightened with various activities for the festive season, an all-night ball, a communal dinner on Christmas Day and a maypole dance performed by the colony girls. The Christmas tree, which glimmered with fireflies, "was loaded with presents for the children, the elders being by no means forgotten. The sight of the happy faces must have well repaid Miss Cameron who was responsible for this seasonal treat. Toy shops are unknown to Cosme and the making of the carts, horses, barrows, whips, dolls and sundries had been carried on very secretly for several weeks. After the tree came the dance".

Mary and Gilmore planned to delay their wedding until Lane returned from England so that he could officiate. But recognised now as an inseparable couple, they enjoyed themselves again at the dance on New Year's Eve when they and other Cosme Scots, including Stevenson, took to the floor with bagpipes accompanying.

Most of the colonists were moving from the soggy Flat to a permanent location up the hill which they called "Homestead" (though the name never really took), the present site of Cosme village today. Will Gilmore started building a little house up there, with Mary assisting in the furnishing. Evidently they had decided not to wait much longer, for on 6 February 1897 she was replaced at the school by John Lane, her service dutifully noted: "Miss Cameron's resignation of the teachership, the natural accompaniment of her approaching marriage, has been held back owing to the delay in the permanent site building. As this is now to be pushed on, the happy event will now be able to take place in a short time, as soon, we understand, as the house on the hill will be ready. Much as the need for a change in the school management is to be regretted yet the

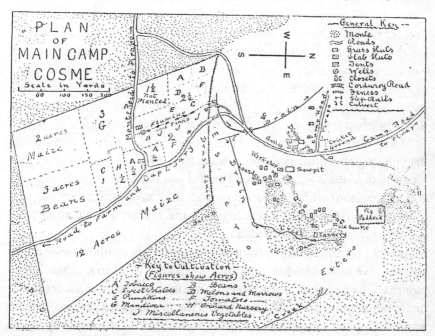

Cosme plan c.1897, drawn by John Lane

special circumstances which makes the change necessary calls forth the heartiest good wishes and congratulations from all of us."

On 25 February Anne Lane gave birth to a fifth child, William Robert, and cabled the news to her husband in England. Lane had a punishing schedule in February and March, a series of public lectures in London and from Portsmouth in the south through Liverpool and the industrial towns of the Midlands and Yorkshire to Glasgow and Edinburgh.

Meanwhile, Arthur Tozer remained in London interviewing interested applicants. As there were disappointingly few of these, he was not hard pressed. There was now no need for him to write to Harry, so his usual fulsome account of his activities is sorely missed in trying to piece together a record. He spent time with his family at Romford and recruited a local, one of the most promising contenders for Cosme, eighteen-year-old Edward Thompson. In 1965 Mr Thompson was still living at Romford and told Gavin Souter that he and Tozer discussed his recruitment on a long cross-country walk. It was agreed he would take over as the Cosme schoolteacher. But Thompson had another offer a few days later, an elder brother persuading him to join the rush to the Yukon to seek their fortunes on the Klondike field. Gold outweighed Utopia.

Nearly six months after Lane and Tozer's departure, the first of a number of small groups of British recruits set sail for Paraguay. They were for the most part urban tradespeople and, of the first ten to arrive at Cosme, only two stuck it out longer than a year. Like many subsequent newcomers from Britain, they found life at the colony too rough and resented the clannishness of the Australians, who were fond of assuring them they had it easy compared to what *they'd* been through.

Mary Gilmore said later that the introduction of strangers, who lacked the bonding of mutual experience, was a fatal step. "In the first place the pioneers of Cosme were the little handful out of the great gathering — and people don't drift together into close relationships for nothing — further they had suffered much together and more than that there was real friendly love amongst them all."

Another reason the new people didn't stay, in her opinion, was Lane's absence. He had intended returning to Cosme in March, after seven months. Given the lack of British enthusiasm to participate in a communist vanguard for the world, this seemed the most prudent course. There was little apparent justification for his lingering on, as the response in no way justified the financial burden to the colony. But Lane did linger. He was away from Cosme, his wife, family and new child, for a full seventeen months. This suggests there may have been another attraction for him.

Tozer definitely had another attraction. He had met a young woman called Amy Cadwallader.

*

Mary married William Gilmore on 29 May 1897, a fortnight after Cosme's fourth Foundation Day. Her wedding dress was made up from the length of white hailstone muslin she had brought in anticipation of another groom at her side. The night before, Mary had "kept everyone awake singing all her old songs over for the last time single". Gilmore, having no wedding ring, fashioned one by cutting the centre out of a shilling piece. The ceremony was conducted by William Saunders as acting Homestead chairman and government registrar. He read from the Cosme Marriage Service, written by Lane, almost certainly with Mary's collaboration:

> It is moreover a sinful thing for any Cosme man or woman to enter into marriage save for love only, since we are not as brute beasts, but are men and women with human feeling which we must keep pure and undefiled lest we debase and degrade ourselves. In Cosme there can be no fear of want nor greed of gain nor any unnatural pressure to excuse the weakest for so sinning.

At the wedding social the bridal couple danced to the colony's newly acquired musical instruments — two violins, a banjo and a harmonium. But it was not a widely applauded match. Hilda Lane commented that her father said that Billy Gilmore "never smiled again". Unlike the glowing account of the wedding of Nellie Bilby and Dick Rae just a month earlier, *Cosme Monthly Notes* was understated: "At Homestead on May 29th, William Gilmore and Mary J. Cameron were married." For a more effusive response they had to wait some months, when Gilmore received a letter from Lane:

> All the usual friendly messages seem so stupidly insufficient to express how much I wish you all joys and every happiness. Marriage isn't a picnic. Or perhaps, even if it is, you will have found as I very speedily did — at least I suppose you will — that it is a picnic on ground where there are some ants and an occasional mosquito. But if you and your wife are as happy as I would wish you, you will think 98 degrees in the shade not enough to make the world an aching void; and if you are as happy as I have been these fourteen years and more you will be far happier than any man can claim of his own deserts. Only, William, always remember that a woman is like china which must be handled

with care or else it is apt to break. But you're not the sort to forget. All joking apart, Will, there is no true life excepting the marriage life and the men and women who let their married life be spoiled don't know what they miss.

Lane's recruiting efforts resulted in another four men, one woman and a child coming from England in June, and *Cosme Monthly Notes* anticipated the arrival of fifty more recruits, including ten single women.

A new bridge was completed across the Pirapó river in July and, although most people kept to their home firesides with the onset of cold weather, the hunting department had a very good month. The men caught a large carpincho or "river pig" which proved good eating, though the same could not be said for a crocodile almost two metres long found close to Cosme camp. "The record deer was shot in July; it weighed 100 lbs [45 kg]. The few dogs are now made use of in hunting. Armadillos and agoutis are frequently shot by those who take the trouble to hunt them."

Cooking pots and utensils were turned out at a new village forge, where the children gathered to see the great bellows pumping and sparks flying from the anvil as William Wood, the blacksmith, went about his work.

On 17 July 1897, a second son was born to Wood and his wife Lillian. Alexander Francis was soon known to everyone by his pet name, Ack.

In August Dave Stevenson gave an evening lecture on the verse of Banjo Paterson and the children were delighted by magic lantern slides brought by one of the newcomers from Scotland. Mrs Mary Gilmore resumed public life by taking a dancing class for beginners.

The following month another family came from Scotland: William Titilah, a bootmaker, with his wife and five children, including seven-year-old George, who was to remain at Cosme all of his long life.

*

"George was never any good as a carpenter," said Don Norman, pushing past a rough sapling gate.

A little pug and thatch house was ahead of us, compressed mud on a lathe framework, the construction method of the early colonists and still of poor villagers today. Two rooms were connected by an open thatched breezeway with a beaten earth floor.

George Titilah, ninety-two years old, hobbled out bare-footed, leaned on a gnarled stick and watched us approach. He had a shock of white hair and a straggling beard. Don Norman called to him in Guaraní.

"He's a bit deaf," said Rod McLeod. "We're all a bit deaf."

George studied Julie and me with startled blue eyes. "*Buenos días*," we said. He continued to look anxious and stared at our tape recorders.

"They're from Australia," said Don Norman. "They want to know how you're getting on."

"How I am doing?" Speaking English came back to him slowly, then with force he remembered the word he wanted. "Rotten! I feel rotten!" He pointed at the recorders. "What's those things there?"

We explained. He was incredulous. "You want to put all that I say in a box?"

We put the intrusive machines away and sat with the old men on benches in the breezeway. A great-granddaughter with coppery skin, about six years old, came round the side of the house, a sheep trotting behind her. She studied us solemnly with huge black eyes.

"When did you last have a shave, George?" asked Don Norman. "You look shocking."

"Can't do it anymore," said George. "Shake too much."

"You want to straighten up a bit. Are you about finished?"

The question was matter of fact and so was the answer. "I'm done for," said George. "We're all getting to the end of our lives."

Don Norman was undeterred. "Where's your razor? The girls will do it."

He gave the child an instruction in Guaraní and she came back from the cookhouse with razor and soap. George leaned back, delighted with all the attention, making jokes in Guaraní, while Julie shaved him and I snipped his long wispy hair.

"Trim his eyebrows too," said Don Norman. "Make a new man of him."

The result was none too professional. "Have you finished?" George shouted. "Thank God for that!" But he held up a little mirror and grinned at himself from different angles.

We said goodbye to Cosme's oldest colony survivor, aware with some guilt that he was still bewildered, though not displeased, by our visit.

*

The fourth party of British recruits arrived at Cosme in October and, at last, there were single women among them. The sisters Georgina and Annie Noon from Hawick were met at the railway station by two bachelors, Charles Leck and Harry Buckley, who had drawn straws and won the privilege. They didn't waste time. The girls were effectively betrothed before they reached the colony. Georgina and Charles were married the following month and Annie and Harry five months later.

Meanwhile, in England William Lane was arranging his winter season of lectures, to be illustrated by a number of magic lantern views of the colony. But he had lost his lieutenant.

Arthur Tozer had married his new love, Amy Cadwallader, and in October sailed for South America with a fifth batch of new recruits, mainly from Scotland. He wrote to Harry from on board the *Southern Cross* and posted the letter from Las Palmas in the Canary Islands:

> Amy has been very unwell & only made her first appearance at table this morning. The main cause was probably seasickness but I think she is alright now ... We have about 28 passengers on board ... Captain & officers are a very decent lot & most of the passengers are alright. The missionaries have been very sick but constant prayer has enabled them to get well later than anyone else ... The unmarried one is very energetic & has already, between his attacks of seasickness, tried to convert the ship's company & passengers but so far without any result. He asked me if I was a Christian & I told him that I was happy to say that I was not. He is quite kind & much interested in my future & in every one else's; of his own he has no doubt ... Amy also sends love. Any letters for Lane may be forwarded to Paraguayan Consulate 18 Eldon Street, London EC.

Dave Stevenson and other Cosme men had been working on a surprise for Tozer and his bride, "a very acceptable wedding present ready for them on their home-coming in the shape of a snug two-roomed house with veranda and small kitchen".

But Stevenson did not wait for their arrival. On 25 November he took a year's leave of absence to visit Scotland. As the mating season seemed to be preoccupying many of his old friends, the Cosme gossips must have speculated that he would put paid to his enforced celibacy and return with a bride himself. But this was not to be the case.

The end of celibacy certainly seemed to have suited Mary Gilmore, whose writings suggest she had fallen deeply in love with her husband. She burst into print in the *Evening Notes* about the joys of a housewife.

> It's singin' in an' out,
> An' round about the place,
> Here an' there, an' up an' down
> An' feeling full of grace.
> It's rollin' up your sleeves,
> An' whitenin' up the hearth,

An' scrubbin' out the floors,
An' sweepin' down the path ...

The poem concluded that all these domestic chores were a pleasure because of one main joy: "Her man is comin' home."

Tozer wrote to his brother from Asunción on 19 November, saying that Saunders, his old friend from the Patagonia expedition, had met them at the port and conveyed the disappointing news that "the people from England & Scotland are not, generally speaking, giving satisfaction to the old members who want people of a better type". Lane had been advised to return at once, and he enclosed a private letter for him, asking Harry to pass it on.

He wrote again just before Christmas, when they had been settled at Cosme for a month. Amy had been unwell and needed medications prescribed by Dr Bottrell, but "she takes to the colony life better than I thought she would & she doesn't find the food at all unpleasant. Of course she misses many of the things to which she has been accustomed but she is getting over that. Neither of us have seen much of the colony or its inhabitants yet, as we have both been obliged to rest & take care of ourselves".

This resting and taking care of himself was a new theme for Tozer, who had ridden over a thousand kilometres in Patagonia without complaint and for two and a half years lived in a tent until it fell to pieces. Dr Bottrell suspected consumption (tuberculosis, a major killer in the nineteenth century), and advised complete rest.

Though he seemed pleased with their new house and impressed with the work done at the colony during his absence, Tozer regretted that "in social matters things have gone back rather than forward".

The year had been a disheartening one for the colony. An extraordinary amount of sickness, including malaria, was brought on by heavy rains filling the swamps to overflowing. These troubles were added to, in Tozer's opinion, by the new recruits:

Of all who have arrived from England, including those who came with me, only six are good men and one of those has just left. Of the seven single women (whose passages were paid) two are good, two indifferent, two were turned out of the colony for bad conduct on the voyage out & one, whose conduct was also bad, I left in Buenos Aires. This single women business has been a great disappointment & the whole organisation in England is here regarded as a failure. And so it really has been. With all our selection we have only been able to get a few who are able & willing to adopt our mode of life as explained to them by Lane & in the *Monthly* & other printed matter. These unwelcome newcomers, together with two or three of the old members who are "agin the government", have formed themselves into a little party which is sufficiently dangerous to the well-being of the colony as to make it needful to break it up. They — the members of it — want more individualism & the sooner we give it them the better. They can get all they want outside the colony.

The hope was, he said, that Lane could put things to rights when he got back. If he acted firmly, he believed this was possible, but half measures would result in a repetition of what happened at New Australia. Tozer still professed himself a great admirer of Lane, convinced that "without Lane the colony becomes weak & I feel that if death deprived us of him the colony, in its present condition, would have a short life".

Christmas passed off pleasantly, with the usual communal dinner, presents for the children, and another cricket match in which the Englishmen beat the Cosme-ites, 83 runs to 64. After the New Year's Eve dance heralding in 1898, parties were made up to picnic on the banks of the Pirapó river, "camping out in some instances for several days, and passing the time bathing, fishing, hunting or idling".

Mary Gilmore warbled in the *Monthly Notes* about the happiness of being "Wedded":

> It's us two when it's morning,
> And us two when it's night;
> And us two when it's troubled,
> And us two when it's bright;
> And us two don't want nothing
> To make life good and true,
> And lovin'-sweet, and happy,
> While us two's got us two.

But mid-January brought a dramatic change. William Saunders and Arthur Tozer, two of Lane's most devoted allies, abruptly resigned from their acting positions as village chairman and secretary. Their places were taken instead by John Lane and Charles Leck. "This matter has been thoroughly thought out by me," Saunders stated, "and ... is not the outcome of a moment of pique or anger." He did not publicly disclose the reason for his resignation, but at a subsequent committee meeting in March presented a letter. John Lane left the chair while it was discussed. The committee, which included Gilmore, returned the letter to Saunders and resolved unanimously that it could not reach a decision "on a conversation that took place between two persons without corroborative evidence".

Souter, considering this turn of events, concluded: "It is not clear from the surviving records, or from the recollections of survivors, just what the trouble was at this time."

But Tozer's letter to Harry of 23 January gives an explanation. It is bitter and emotionally overwrought. He declared he wanted to leave Paraguay as soon as possible, was anxious about his health, felt weak and enervated, and Dr Bottrell still suspected consumption. He was also worried about money, but there were other reasons for resigning. Colony people were tending towards individualism and boasting of getting "nearer Nature" in a way he found deplorable:

> This getting "nearer Nature" is simply resulting in slovenliness, filth & carelessness as to decency & anything which goes to make social life agreeable. The children here now number about forty-five — the colony started with eleven — who are, for the most part, perfect little gutter-snipes ... Seeing how Cosme is & the direction it is taking & looking at the rising generation as an indication of what its future will be if it lasts any length of time, I think the best thing to do is to get out of it & confess that it is useless to try these social colonies & expect them to succeed in any useful sense. People must be educated up to a higher life gradually & not have it pushed down their throats before they are ready to digest it.

He said Saunders, who had brought his new wife to the colony two years before, had resigned, "disgusted with the whole business". He then got to the nub of it, warning Harry "I have something still less pleasant to tell you", something which had happened in England:

> I have always thought Lane worthy of any trust although I didn't always approve of what he did, but what I am about to tell you entirely upset all my ideas of him. About a fortnight ago I rec'd the following information. In June last Lane was staying at the house of a man & his wife who were interested in Cosme. The husband was away at his work all day & left Lane at home with his wife. One day Lane, by suggestion, attempted to make the wife unfaithful to her husband but without success. Suggestion having failed he tried force but again without success, but he left his finger marks on her throat. Then by threats & entreaty he at last prevailed on her not to tell her husband about it but she worried so that at last she informed a friend. This friend then told the husband. The wife, still in fear of Lane, made her husband promise to do nothing in the matter & I suppose he didn't want a useless scandal anyhow. He ought however to have reported the matter either to me or to the colony. I am not in a position to do anything because all the details I have are second

hand and from one to whom the wife simply told them & one cannot accuse on that sort of evidence but I am certain that all I have heard is reliable & some of it is confirmed by some of Lane's actions which at that period I could not understand & by some of the expressions he is said to have made use of & which are too like Lane's to be mere inventions. It is because of this information that I resigned the secretaryship so soon after accepting it. I don't care to do that sort of work & have Lane at the head of affairs after a revelation of this nature. Had I known of this while in England I should not have returned to the colony.

The letter to which Tozer referred was obviously the one tabled in a closed session of the village committee. The personal content regarding William Lane would explain why his brother John felt obliged to absent himself while it was being discussed.

The conclusion reached by the committee, that no decision could be made or a man condemned on hearsay evidence, is surely also the only one for a reader one hundred years on. Nothing can be known now about the aggrieved woman or the real nature of her acquaintance with Lane, or about her husband, who conveyed the story, or the relationship between them.

But it seems clear that Tozer and Saunders genuinely believed the allegation, sufficiently to abandon a man they had always supported, a communal ideal to which they had been committed, and a village where both had settled in with their wives. Tozer, in his actions and his writings, had often revealed himself as vengeful and prejudiced, but Lane almost always remained the object of his admiration; only the previous month he had expressed a wish that Lane should return as soon as possible, being the only person capable of holding the ailing colony together.

If the allegation had been given much credence by members of the village committee it surely would have leaked out in other correspondence — if not then at least the following year during more wranglings and high emotions — but it seems not to have done so. Mary Gilmore, who must have heard of it from her husband, a committee member, always wrote of Lane with respect and affection.

The village committee, at its meeting of 11 March, heard a statement from Saunders and accepted his resignation. According to Tozer, Alfred Davey, a former Queensland farmer who had also worked as a miner in New Guinea, "and understands tropical agriculture and stock, the most practical and intelligent worker we have had", decided to join the Saunders couple in a storekeeping and farming venture at the small settlement of Yataity, near Villarrica.

Tozer told Harry that Dr Bottrell considered him too ill, with the aftermath of "galloping consumption", to consider moving yet, but as soon as possible he would join them in the enterprise. "We shall work together on purely individualistic lines & make no more attempts at socialism or any other ism. I now feel more individualistic than I have ever been before & am convinced that if communism is ever to be attained it will only be done by a gradual evolution of race or races as a whole ... We are expecting Lane here in about a week. The condition of affairs will give him a bit of a shock."

Three days after Saunders' resignation William Lane arrived. The *Monthly Notes* recorded this with a brevity — "On March 14th William Lane reached Cosme from England, coming alone" — which suggested voluble discussions behind the scenes. But the unsuspecting general readership was offered a cheerful poem about monkey stew:

Those whose appetites capricious
Yearn for oysters, shrimps and snails
But reject a dish delicious
'Cause their fathers once had tails
Can keep right-on a-sneering
While we keep scoffing too
We can beat 'em pioneering
And at scoffing monkey stew.

In Tozer's account, he did not see Lane for a few days, but then they had a long talk. Lane was vehement in denying the alleged incident in England. He maintained that the colony was as good or better than it had ever been, except for the harmful influence of a few, notably Tozer and Saunders, saying that they "had done more to disturb the peace than all the others combined":

He could not explain to me how & no matter what I spoke about he wriggled away from the point and avoided facts. I could not get him to admit that anything I brought forward was wrong so the interview ended without giving on either side. However I don't think that he himself really believes that things are alright. He will probably content himself ... with having a colony of any sort so long as it is a colony and if high ideals are not in reach I suppose he will adopt low ones ... It looks as if Lane will soon have to depend on a faithful few, who regard him as infallible & who are always ready to do his bidding & on those whose large families or lack of grit bars their leaving. Thus he may always have a colony but it will be of no moral use to its members or the world in general.

One of the faithful few was Mary Gilmore, who was involved in the Dramatic Club's presentation on 19 March of a farce, *The New Boy* , to celebrate Lane's return. Mary was four months pregnant, but took a leading role as Martha Hav'em, then danced until daybreak.

It is unlikely that Mr and Mrs Tozer attended. "We are having very little to do with the colonists now & we don't visit. A few of the fellows spend the evenings with us & that is about all the social life we wish for here. Lane keeps away from us & I have only had that one talk with him since his return."

Tozer seemed to spend most of the time brooding on his health, still convinced he had tuberculosis, a diagnosis never convincingly confirmed, though supported by news from Romford that his sister Annie had contracted the disease. He wrote that he often became despondent but, although his wife Amy had not been well either, she was a comfort to him. "She has plenty of go & grit & I don't in any sense regret becoming a husband, except that I wish I was sound in the lungs ... I don't do any work that will hurt & no work at all for the colony."

His lack of effort for the commune, while consuming its food, caused resentment. Tozer reacted in righteous indignation: "Some of the worst of the people here are talking about my 'idleness' and they don't like my getting better food than they, although they know perfectly well my condition. At first I didn't like it but now I have hardened myself to that sort of thing & can stand any amount of it. I am just going to suit my own convenience in every way & shall simply follow Dr Bottrell's instructions no matter what is said."

He had become very friendly with the doctor, who refused to accept any payment. "I understand that he never charges Englishmen & only sends in his bill to the well-to-do of other nationalities, whereas Dr Stewart — the army doctor in López the tyrant's time — gets all he can from everyone." Bottrell's advice was to wait until winter was over and then to consider going to a country with a hot, dry climate such as Australia.

In any case, Tozer continued, Lane had suspended payment of withdrawal shares until the annual general meeting on 12 May 1898, Cosme Foundation Day. Many colonists were talking of leaving, "but I think all or nearly all will want to see what the Annual Meeting brings forth. It is likely that after the middle of May resignations will become frequent".

But the flashpoint came earlier. In defiance of commune rules, Joseph

Sims and John Pindar had been fattening two weaner pigs which they then slaughtered, sharing the meat with a few friends. Tozer said that the piglets were from the litter of a sow that had died. The men were asked to hand them over to the communal piggery, but they refused, arguing they would have died anyway if they had not taken the trouble to rear them.

On 9 May the village committee resolved unanimously to expel Sims and Pindar. At the annual general meeting three days later, the twenty-seven voting members endorsed the decision, nineteen votes to six. However, none of the newcomers were yet enfranchised and the wives of colonists did not have the vote. The six dissenters promptly decided to leave the colony also, beginning a mass exodus which resulted in forty people departing within two months.

Tozer actually agreed that the two men deserved expulsion, but argued that the manner in which it was done was not fair: "They were charged with trumpery breaches of the rules which most of the members have been guilty of & which have until recently not been considered wrong. The real reason for their expulsion was their getting hold of newcomers & sowing seeds of discontent among them but as the colony could not well prove offences of that kind they decided to charge them with something they could prove ... The meeting was a farce. Lane's object in expelling these men just before the annual general meeting was to have no opposition & questions re his actions in England."

He said departing members were being offered withdrawal shares of less than £3: "This low sum has been obtained by a deliberate under-valu-ation of the assets ... The colony is now about bust up. It will probably linger on for years but its future is hopeless." He added that some really good men had resigned and were leaving the colony with the bad ones whose departure Lane obviously welcomed.

One of them was Larry Petrie, whose freewheeling anarchism could never have made him comfortable under Lane's strictures for long. He declared: "Whips of dogma, stacks of selfishness, yards of words and absolutely no liberty. Therefore as my ideas and the ways of Cosme did not harmonise I *got*." In a letter to W. G. Spence, Petrie blamed the furore on what he saw as Lane's fanaticism: "He is a madman, a knave seized with the madness of ambition, overpowered with a sense of the divinity of himself and his mission, and for that he will barter truth, justice and the whole world plus the handful of bigots he terms the faithful. I believe everybody can perceive how shamefully he betrays his friends, cheerfully leaving them to bear a burden of reproach which he at least should share."

Tozer, now a grim Savonarola, told his brother: "I am looking forward to the next *Cosme Monthly* which is likely to be fuller of cant than usual. Lane will try to make capital out of this expulsion business but I doubt if it will work."

He was wrong. The June issue, while certainly defensive, could not have been more bleak and understated: "*Maintenance of Principles*. On May 9 by unanimous decision of the chairman and committee, two members were expelled from membership for antagonism to and violation of the communist principles of Cosme. On May 11 at a special general meeting the action of the committee was approved by nineteen votes to six. Most of those voting in the negative subsequently resigned and with others left the colony. Withdrawal shares paid ... School taken charge of by Mrs Gilmore — to enable working strength to be increased."

The whole episode obviously had a devastating effect on Will Gilmore, for he vacated his position on the village committee, though still maintaining his loyalty to Lane. Mary returned to teaching but, as she was seven months pregnant, this could only be a stop-gap measure.

Cosme's population was now just ninety-six: thirty-six adult men, twenty-three women and the rest children. This was a smaller community than before Lane and Tozer's trip to England. The recruiting drive, undertaken at great expense, had been a disaster: only four of the British men and five of the women still remained. Lane's grandiose notion of a communist army and a federation of self-governing villages was stillborn. Even the more modest ambition of seventy-two families settled on the land would obviously now never be achieved. However, the Paraguay Government, which had completed registration of land titles in the colony's favour, at no time made any recrimination.

Lane must have been in a very fragile state of mind at this time; the series of articles he began writing on "Belief and Communism" are rambling, disjointed and larded with pious zealotry. The vexing question of Arthur Tozer would not have helped his mental stability. Tozer had done no work for the commune since his return from England and demanded a special diet as an invalid, though he was not laid up in bed. He could be seen, a constant irritant to those who spent a hard day labouring, pottering about his house. The village committee decided he was fit enough to report for work, and Lane sent him a note to that effect.

Tozer raged in a letter to his brother that, but for eggs, all his food "extras" had been terminated.

So I went to Lane and had a regular row with him. I also told him about his

conduct in England but he denied the whole business, even when I showed
him a letter confirming what I told him, from the husband of the woman he
is said to have attempted to wrong. He admitted that they had been trying to
boycott me out of the colony & said that such action was justifiable when I
showed that I was withholding my sympathy for his party. Anyhow I am done
with "brotherly love" now & I don't think I shall ever regret it. I was an ass to
ever believe in it.

He no longer considered the store at Yataity a proposition, for Saunders
and Davey had already dissolved their partnership. ("Their wives could
not agree and life became unbearable.") Davey and his wife had returned
to Cosme and Saunders was continuing on with the store alone. Tozer felt
he didn't want to take Amy "to an out of the way place like that with only
one English-speaking woman for a companion".

Instead, he had been to Asunción and spoken with the British general
manager of the railways. He had been offered a clerical position at a modest
salary, had already accepted it and resigned membership from the colony.
"I don't like the idea of office work, but anything is better than remaining
here."

By mid-July he wrote to Harry from the headquarters of the Paraguay
Central Railway in Asunción, saying that he could tolerate the job and
had been given a very good house, with large rooms, floors of ornamental
tiles, and orange and guava trees in the garden.

Towards the end of the same month, the Cosme school was closed for
Mary Gilmore's confinement. Although Will wanted to accompany her
to Villarrica, he could not be spared from the colony's working strength.
Years later, Mary remembered her journey alone as harrowing:

> A month before my child was born I went into Villa Rica. Imagine me, a
> delicate woman, who had been a weakly baby and a frail child … starting from
> home with my husband at 4 am in a spring cart and two horses, and an hour
> later having to get out and wade through water often over my knees, wading
> thus, with an occasional "lift" in the cart where the water and mud were not
> too deep … till about 11 am when we came out on a plain where the keen
> June wind cut like a knife. I didn't dare ride then for fear of a chill, and I had
> to walk on to keep up the circulation till we reached the Railway Station just
> as the 1 o'clock train was heard to whistle in the distance. We had just time
> to change a note and get my ticket. I got into the train wet, cold and alone,
> for we did not feel justified in spending money on a ticket (1s 8d) for my
> husband. And there I travelled in a filthy third class carriage full of natives, of
> whose language I was quite ignorant — all smoking, men and women alike,
> with baskets of meat here and there on the floor — game-cocks perched on

the backs of the seats, and young pigs in bags among our feet. I got into Villa
Rica about 6 o'clock. God knows how I escaped fatal harm; yet somehow I
got through alright. Vitality I suppose.

In the town she rented a room with Mrs John Kushel, a former member
of the colony, who assisted as midwife. Mary was later censorious of her
heavy drinking, but did not mention that the woman had lost her own
baby, drowned in a well at Cosme, less than two years before.

On 21 August 1898 Mary gave birth to a son whom she called William
Dysart Cameron Gilmore — the second name bestowed in honour of the
friendly engineer on the riverboat *Olimpo*. Mary said afterwards that she
longed to send a wire to Will at Cosme but resisted because of the expense.
"But I never think of that telegram without a feeling of sadness."

After two weeks she returned to the colony. For Gilmore his new son
was a wonder and a joy and he set about making a cot for him:

> Will split the timber — lapacho, a hardwood and heavy — with maul and
> wedges, then he trimmed down the splintered sides with an adze, after which
> he split the pieces with an old saw. He was weeks over the work — the wood
> was so hard — then with a plane and a spoke shave he smoothed all the
> surfaces. It was a bit out of plumb in some of its legs, but it would take a
> beautiful polish ... I never put the boy to bed in it except by day. It seemed
> so cold-hearted to put him away in the night — and we thought he might
> feel lonely — "besides," his father said, "he is such a little fellow".

For the August *Monthly Notes*, William Lane wrote a stern lecture on
"The Fate of Communities", warning that failure was the usual result.
They only succeeded, he said, when people accepted a belief in communism as part and parcel of their being; without it, "as the sowing so is the
reaping" and "surely we turn back to the whips and fleshpots and false
gods of Egypt".

A falling off in social activity was mentioned in the September *Notes*,
lamely accounted for by the straggling nature of the village, the distance
between the houses on the Flat and the new settlement on the hill. But
the real distance was between the original ideals of the community and
the present reality. The dismemberment of the utopian dream was provided with nightmarish symbolism by a massacre at the fowl-yard. A
marauding beast killed over 100 fowls and some rabbits. "The slaughtered
were quickly divided around and supplied the baked meats for their own
funerals." The culprit was an ocelot, a ferocious but beautiful leopard-like
cat, which Will Gilmore later killed with a single shot. The skin was
advertised for sale. The colony, to attract extra income, was now in the

curio trade and through its newsletter offered jaguar and alligator skins, black howling monkey pelts and armadillo shells.

Tozer, in Asunción, had only occasional news of Cosme, although he subscribed to the *Monthly*. From England he heard that his sister Annie had died of consumption. Now that he had left Cosme, Tozer's own ailments and his wife's improved remarkably. "Freedom from petty worries has done us both good ... After the colony, life here for her is a Paradise and for me too."

At the end of November Dave Stevenson arrived back in Paraguay, after a year's leave of absence. He visited the Tozers, delivering a parcel from Arthur's family in England, and no doubt heard a highly-coloured account of recent Cosme politics.

The colony to which he returned for a lack-lustre Christmas was a defeated little community which had just had the dubious benefit of Part Four of William Lane's continuing lecture on "Belief and Communism". It had virtually fulfilled the prophecy of the Sydney *Bulletin* five years before: "There will be a few hundred people digging and fencing in a dreary, hopeless fashion out in the great loneliness, and living on woe and unsaleable vegetables and dreams of home. And meanwhile the founder of the settlement will be foaming at the mouth and uttering poetry beneath a tree, and wildly asking the damp ferns, 'What is life?'." But the *Bulletin* had in fact been generous. The colony had less than a hundred people, and the majority were children.

During the Christmas celebrations, Tozer reported, William Lane, who "is supposed to be at times a bit strange in his head ... sat alone and no one could cheer him up or rouse him from his moroseness".

The informant was Clara Laurence, who stayed with the Tozers during January. She and her husband Billy were still mourning the sudden death of their infant son. Clara was never to have another child. Tozer received her as a welcome guest, "one of the two women that Amy liked on the colony".

> She is clean and, unlike most Cosme women, bright, energetic and intelligent. She gives anything but a glowing account of the place and says that the effect of the split has been the reverse of satisfactory. The social life is now very dull owing to the reduced membership and the leaving of nearly all who had any talent for getting up entertainments. New differences are springing up amongst the men and some are getting hopeless. Also the continued unsatisfactory diet combined with excessive work in such a climate is telling on the men & some seem to be broken in health & no longer fit for the life. The

women are getting more & more dissatisfied & all are longing to leave, not excepting Mrs W. Lane. The scandal mongering and bitterness among the women is on the increase & there is hardly one who is not at enmity with one or more of her sisters. They are divided into cliques, each daggers drawn with the opposing group.

As the drift and departures continued and those who remained bickered among themselves, Mary too was desperate to leave. She was anxious about her health and, especially, that of her baby son. And she had developed an obsessive fear of snakes, the result of unpleasant encounters:

Once, just as I stepped into the bath, suddenly a great green snake uncoiled on the wall plate ... There was not only a sense of the intrusive eye, but there was the perception of (apparent) unlimited area of vulnerability. You never know what size you are, or how much skin you possess till a snake can strike you anywhere he likes!

There had been an alarm when she was teaching at the schoolhouse: "A girl heard a rattle in the grass beside her. She rushed in to me, white faced, shaking, panting. As some authorities denied the existence of rattlesnakes in South America, doubt was thrown on her story. However a year or more later the doubt was removed, a snake with nine rattles being shot in a thicket near some of the colony houses."

Crisis point was reached in March when there were three snake incidents in a row. A rattlesnake — a Paraguayan *cascabel* — was shot close to the colony pigsties. It was just under 2 metres long, "as thick as one's wrist and the possessor of eight rattles". Then Clara Laurence was bitten by a snake, fortunately a non-venomous one, when she disturbed it near the wood-pile. And Mary's horror fantasy came true: as she was feeding baby Billy a snake dropped from the ceiling and landed on her neck. Its mate was found in the rafters and killed. *Cosme Monthly Notes* commented cheerfully: "These little episodes make up to some extent for the absence of bus, tram and train accidents. But our Australians can still proudly claim that reptiles are nothing here to what they are in the land of the kangaroo."

It was all too much for Mary. The serpents had entered her Eden and she wanted to leave.

Some of the Australian men who had left the colony had gone shearing in Argentina and were making reasonable money. Gilmore decided to do the same in order to earn their fares. However, he was once again on the village committee and reluctant to leave while Lane needed him.

But Lane was now embittered with even his most faithful friends. He blamed the failure of his dream on the inadequacy of the human material with which he had tried to implement it. "The devil of the Labour movement," he wrote to W. G. Spence, "is having to work with dirty tools."

His supporters were saddened. Harry Taylor, living back in South Australia but kept informed of events at Cosme, concluded of Lane: "He is still incorruptible, disinterested in motive, and unswerving in pursuit of what he conceives to be the truth; but the mental outlook has narrowed, something of bitterness has entered into his soul, and with the drawing-in of his human sympathies there has departed from him, in great measure, the old winsomeness of manner, the sweet loveableness of spirit, the indescribable something which of old knit men's souls to his for life or death."

It was not surprising that no one wanted to be reminded and no fuss was made of Cosme's sixth Foundation Day on 12 May 1899. There was no point in celebrating the foundations of a structure when the walls were collapsing and the roof caving in. "To me this Labour movement endeavouring to build walls of sand against the incoming tide of destruction is a hopeless thing," Lane said. Instead, his gesture for the anniversary was to decline any office on the committee. The following month he announced his intention of leaving Paraguay. He applied for honorary membership of the colony and arranged that power of attorney for the land titles, held in his name, be transferred to his brother John, the new chairman.

Tozer heard of it in early July from Stevenson, who was his house-guest for a few days.

> Of course he gave us a lot of Cosme news but he is very discreet & kept the dark side of life there more or less to himself. He surprised us by saying that Lane and family are leaving *for good*. Lane has given no explanation (except perhaps to a chosen few) of his reasons for leaving other than that he wants to pay off the New Australian debt (£200), that his health is bad and that he feels that his duty is in propaganda work. By propaganda work he evidently does not mean organising for Cosme but spreading the Gospel of Communism wherever he may go. He is going to New Zealand. He went through to Asunción yesterday and I saw him but we didn't salute. Mrs Lane and four children are waiting in V. Rica until time to catch the boat down the river. So they have already left the colony.

But it seems that the Lane family did briefly return to Cosme, for the *Monthly Notes* recorded their final departure from there on 2 August 1899. It was without the benefit of a farewell social. It must have been a muted, bleak scene as their cart trundled out of the village, Anne pregnant again, Lane looking back for the last time at the little collection of thatched huts in the forest clearing, the mere outhouses for the great communist city he would never build. He was just a few weeks short of his thirty-eighth birthday.

John Lane, sturdy and loyal to the end, defended his brother's departure in the Queensland *Worker*, even contriving good news from it: "Those who are personally acquainted with the first editor of the *Worker* will of course know that as captain of the Cosme ship, he would have stood by her to the last had she been in a sinking condition, and that therefore the fact of his leaving the colony shows that in his opinion the prospects of Cosme are assured."

Tozer wrote that he had heard from Stevenson that work was going more smoothly at Cosme under the new chairmanship. Paraguayan labour was being employed for timber felling. Of this development he remarked, "it strikes me that it is the thin edge of the wedge which will bust up the 'brotherhood' ". But if the colony held together a little longer he felt it would be because John Lane was more practical and broader minded than his brother and understood that it was neither wise to try nor possible to make all men think and act as one. "Stevenson, since his return, has been the leader of the opposition on Cosme and he looks forward to all round better conditions in the near future ... He also says that it is absurd to credit themselves with practising either Communism or Socialism; that at best they are co-operative with a little of the others thrown in."

"We were not communists, we were Laneites, with a degree of capability for communism," Mary Gilmore wrote later. Without William Lane, she saw it as inevitable that the commune would collapse. She insisted — rather defensively, in the face of the evidence — that many colonists besides herself would always remember him with respect and love; they still knew him to be straight and true, even when he left, "bowed in spirit and broken in health" and that was "a tribute few men have had and greater than that of words".

Ten days after the Lanes' departure, the Gilmores resigned from the colony. Will headed south to Patagonia looking for shearing work. Mary stayed on at Cosme with baby Billy for nine months, a disillusioned and unhappy woman, expressing her anxieties almost daily in letters to her husband, even when she could not post them for lack of an address:

> I often dread your feeling sorry you left the Colony. Don't for my sake, darling. We can't be much poorer than we were here, you surely won't have to work

harder … Surely it will never be as bad as that again. We can hardly go to a more trying climate than this, and hardly worse moral surroundings, bad children for the boy to grow up with, a constant straining to individualism, the native girl outside, and the *caña* almost for the asking. When we get settled again we will bring the boy up with the idea of community life even if there are only ourselves … Perhaps he will be our only child and you must take care of yourself for his sake as well as for mine and your own. It is cold tonight and I think I will hurry off to bed. Goodnight, dearest, and keep your heart up.

But in the middle of all the defeatism, William and Lillian Wood had something to celebrate: the birth of their third son, Norman James, on 11 July 1899.

*

Don Norman had made it into the world in time to overlap his presence at Cosme with William Lane's by just three weeks.

The old man sat by the fireside of the Wood homestead with his brother Wallace. "It's a wonder to me how people could believe in a man like Lane," he mused. "He must've been a bit mad."

"Mum said it was after his son was killed by the cricket ball," said Don Wallace. "He was never the same again. She said that when it happened Mrs Lane cried, 'Oh, Cosme, Cosme, I'll never love you anymore.' And they didn't, neither of them."

"It's a pity so many people followed them," said Don Norman. "But Dad had promised and he wanted to keep his promise. He promised rashly. He would've been better off in Australia."

"No, he always said, 'I would have been dead by now if I'd stayed in Australia'."

"I know. Funny how he always said that."

15

A Wild Colonial Childhood

During this time, I made my rounds in the woods for game every day, when the rain permitted me, and made frequent discoveries in these walks, of something or other to my advantage.

Daniel Defoe, *Robinson Crusoe*

Here all we little children have just come along,
You'll listen for a minute till we sing a little song,
When we all lie abed at the tooting of the horn,
That we may all be fed, you go to hoe the corn.
We clap our little hands, shake our little feet,
Oh! My! But Cosme corn is sweet;
Oh! folks they must be saucy when they call it nigger meat.
Oh! My! But corn is good to eat.

Tom Adamson, "Children's Corn Song"

According to the *Manchester Guardian*, Cosme was an arcadian retreat similar to the court of the exiled duke in Shakespeare's *As You Like It*. Probably it was John Lane who wrote the response in the March 1900 *Monthly Notes*. Cosme was grateful for the compliments, but "we really are not the only durable communist village in the world" and "our Amiens and Jacques do more axe work and hoeing than singing and moralising".

But if the colony was their stage, and the original men and women merely players, the few I'd cast in leading roles in this personal view of the Cosme drama had made their exits — William and Anne Lane to New Zealand, Arthur Tozer to the offices of the Central Railway in Asunción, and Will Gilmore to Patagonia. Mary still lingered at the colony until May 1900, but in the sense of any real participation she had already departed. Dave Stevenson and Clara Laurence had committed long-term, though apparently forever separated from each other by her fidelity to her husband.

A new cast were about to make their entrances, the children, according

to Jacques in *As You Like It*, "creeping like snail, unwillingly to school".
The Cosme children crept very unwillingly, for the *monte* was far more
exciting. Born to parents from Australia and Britain, they handled Spanish
better than the adults and soon most of them were speaking Guaraní. They
were growing up Paraguayan.

Arthur Tozer did not think much of the upbringing:

> They are dirty, ill mannered little savages & those of them, boys & girls, old
> enough to learn anything at all, know enough about sexual matters to act on
> that knowledge at every opportunity. Most of the parents practically make no
> effort to check them in anything & the result is that one would have to look
> to the slums of some big city to find children to equal them in depravity &
> other disagreeable things. The children are not to be blamed. When they do
> wrong they are considered smart & their parents & others joke about it …

We peered over a fence at Cosme at the corn patch adjacent to the
whitewashed house of a Paraguayan villager. "John Lane's school was
here," said Don Norman. Though he remembered John Lane — "he
found me up a loquat tree once and made me come down and he spanked
me" — his daughters had made a more vivid impression: "Two of them,
Ettie and Alice, were big girls, young ladies. I remember being in the girls'
room when they were dressing and I was such a little fellow they didn't
take any notice of me. But I noticed."

Don Norman said he was too young to have been taught by John Lane
— "I was about five years old when he left" — but his elder brothers were.

"My memories of school started with John Lane," Bill Wood told me,
"and the first school was the one they built down on the Flat. But I only
went there for a few months and then they built a little wooden school
up on the hill and John Lane continued as schoolmaster there. I'm afraid
he found it very difficult to teach us all because there were teenagers —
Dave and Allie McLeod, Wendy and Bessie Titilah — and we seven and
eight-year-olds had to take pot luck because he couldn't be teaching
everybody at the same time. He would teach a bit for one and bit for the
other."

Alex Wood remembered him as a stern disciplinarian. "With John Lane
you couldn't sit around shooting marbles or anything like that. And if I
didn't show up he'd find our mother and say 'Where's Ack? He didn't turn
up at school.' And then I'd be for it! He always had a cane and any boy
that didn't jump to obey got a good hard smack on the behind. He taught
very well, but I always thought that his heart was in Australia."

"I think I can safely say," said his brother Bill, "that he took a disliking to me for something. I may have been worse than the others, but he certainly used to keep me in after class. He'd smack me on the hands and give me something to write over and over as my penance. I could hardly hold the pen after being belted with that switch of his. He was rather hard on all the children, even on his eldest daughter Ettie, who was still at school. But I suppose that we learned quite a lot."

Bill Wood said that he was five and a half when Mary Gilmore left the colony and he didn't think he had ever been taught by her. But he had a vague memory of her as one of the people who worked on the *Cosme Monthly*. "She was one of the high class people and was much appreciated. The only source of information I had was Allan McLeod talking about her. Apparently she didn't get on well with all the women, she had her likes and dislikes. I think that she fell out with Mrs John Lane. I think they were the main antagonists. They were both what they called blue-stockings or highly educated women."

*

"There is a lot of anger just now over Mrs J. Lane," Mary wrote to her husband, incensed that Jenny Lane had accepted presents from Mrs John Pindar, one of the people who had been expelled. The presents seemed paltry enough, washing soap and blue. "She offered some to Mrs Delugar I hear. Mrs Delugar refused it, saying, 'No Jinny, I don't care to accept things from people I helped to put out of the colony.' "

Mary was now desperately lonely, a bitter, unhappy woman. Her mood was not lifted by joining the large group which took the traditional holiday fishing, bathing and camping out at the Capiibary River, the colony's southern border. What seemed to infuriate her most was the sight of Jenny Lane frolicking in the water with Dave Stevenson. "She bathed among the men. D. S. taught her to swim, one man's costume consisted of a belt and a pouch — just about. 'She' doesn't believe in mock modesty, and stripped in the presence of both women and children — but enough of disgusting things."

Cosme as a community no longer commanded Mary's loyalty. That was now focused on her son Billy and on her husband in Patagonia. She had few letters from him and fretted about how he was faring in the cold climate. On 12 December she wrote that Dave Stevenson had called to see her the previous evening and assured her he had heard the area was "thoroughly suited to English people, so I am hoping the cold will not be as real as I had feared".

Stevenson no longer seemed to have any power over her; it was her love for Will Gilmore that was her lifeline to sanity. "You don't understand how I am — and have always been — haunted by the dread of losing you ... I don't suppose if anything happened to you I would die or go mad — though I could easily enough go mad if I chose to allow myself. I would probably make an idol of the boy but life would be a living death and the spring would never bloom again for me."

For Will, she felt, she was prepared to give up everything, even her vocation as a writer, a rash offer she later found impossible to keep:

I often wonder if the thought of me gives you such joy as the thought of you gives me, yet I think it can't because I am not as good and as gentle — as great dispositioned as you, and then I think perhaps it does because you love me, dear. I often think of the words "Blessed art thou among women". If all women were as blessed as I am how happy all life would be — but then there is only one Will in the world.

People here say I mean to be a writer, and that is why we resigned. They know nothing about it. I wouldn't be a writer in case I should let the love of it grow into my life and perhaps owe to it what I only want to owe to you — or that it might set up another aim or tie in which you would not be the centre.

In her general mood of disillusion she repudiated any belief in communism, another position she was later cautiously to revise, but for the present she felt that it was "not attainable, real Communism that is, and enforced Communism is worse than none. I think after all co-operation with equal sharing is the truest and most possible — gives most good with fewest ill results".

She wrote that the colony offered nothing "to balance its snakes, its fever, its jaundice, and its generally infernal climate" and longed to leave. But bubonic plague had broken out in Asunción and she was unable to do so because of quarantine restrictions. She stayed on until May 1900, aware that she was a financial burden to the colony, isolated and critical of almost everyone except Clara Laurence, Mrs Alf Davey and Mrs Dick, whose kindness she noted; of John Lane she wrote, "He is worth all the rest of the crowd put together". Billy's health was a constant anxiety and in April he had fever once again, "but not as badly as Norman Wood".

*

Norman Wood remembered being told he nearly died of *chuchu* fever as a child, but he was growing up a sturdy little boy. One of his earliest memories was of waking up to hear music thumping in the distance and he looked through the window "at a great big moon up in the sky, as big as a melon". So he got out of bed and toddled through the long grass to the hall where the Full Moon Social was being held, oil lamps in brackets along the walls and the women dancing with fire beetles pinned in their hair.

"I remember Allan McLeod playing his fiddle — 'The Cock of the North' or something like that — and I was dancing around under people's feet. I got into trouble and had to go and lie in a cot in the little room where the ladies used to leave their babies."

Unlikely though it seems, Bill Wood insisted Mcleod's violin was a Stradivarius. It needed adjustment and another colonist, going into Asunción, undertook to deliver it to the music repair shop. But the colonist had a few drinks on the way "and he started swatting the horse with the violin and that was the end of the Stradivarius".

After that, the main music for the monthly Full Moon Socials was from piano and accordion. "Jack Black, I remember, was a splendid accordionist," said Bill, "and my dad used to be able to grind out the dance music also. They had all those ancient old dances, Scottish reels and mazurkas, the Schottische, Lancers and Caledonians, and square dances like the First Set and the Alberts. People such as Billy Laurence and Dave Stevenson seemed to be almost professional dancers, lively as crickets, picking up everybody in turn. The social hall floor was made of sawn timber, all carefully planed with no ridges to catch the feet, and they used to scrape wax candles over it so it was slippery as glass. It was very easy to slip and fall on that floor but it made dancing very light and pleasant."

Despite the imbalance of the sexes, Bill Wood was vehement that he never saw a man dance with another man; in fact he seemed scandalised by the thought. "No, no, I never once saw such a thing!" The men who did not have partners or who were not interested in dancing, he said, sat up on the little dais used as a stage and played chess or draughts.

"Anyway not everybody wanted to be in the square dances because they were intricate businesses. The music kept changing from polka to waltz time and you had to memorise what part came next and where you were supposed to be, circling round and clasping hands."

Standing on the site of the old social hall at Cosme, Norman Wood agreed. "Those square dances were very complicated things." He and Rod McLeod circled each other in the grass, chanting a routine from over seventy years before: "First couple retire and bow. Second couple retire and bow, next couple the same, then all swing," and the old men linked arms and swung around, avoiding cowpats, shaky on their legs. "Now promenade. That means you canter around the square." They passed on the cantering.

They remembered that between dance brackets people would often recite or sing. "Mrs Bethune or Mrs Lane or Mum would get up on the stage," said Don Norman, "and Jimmy Sime had songs about ancient Scottish history, something about Prince Charlie or somebody in the North Sea. Then my father always used to do the sword dance."

"Our dad was a bit of a specialist," said Bill Wood. "He had a show of his own, the sword dance, which everybody would vociferously demand. They'd make a cross on the floor with machetes and he would jump around among them while old Allan McLeod played 'Long May the Keel Row'."

On other nights there were readings from Shakespeare, minstrel shows, the "highbrow people" would read their own poems, or there'd be *kinderspiel* for the children. "Our colony people, right from the beginning, wanted to make life bearable for the kids. We had 'Little Boy Blue' with someone blowing the big bullock horn used at Cosme to announce meal-times, and 'Jack and the Beanstalk'. As Jack, I had to sing some doleful dirge about 'My mother and I have of late felt poverty's pinch once or twice'."

About 9 o'clock in the evening a bonfire was lit behind the hall, and drums of water boiled to make *mate cocido*, their preferred way of brewing the Paraguayan tea. "And every housewife would contribute sandwiches or cake, boiled eggs and on special occasions pork pies. Everybody thrived on the 'interval' as we used to call it. We kids grew up thinking that 'interval' meant something to eat."

Courting couples were notorious for slipping away into the shadows of the trees during the interval. Mary Gilmore was appalled to observe eighteen-year-old Bella Lewis with Ned Dyer, a member of the colony committee and twenty-five years Bella's senior.

An engagement was quietly announced in April. Mary wondered how Bella's parents, Alec and Mary Ann Forrester-Lewis, could possibly approve the match. Alec had been one of the heroes of the 1891 shearers' strike, a conspiracy prisoner, who'd changed his surname to Lewis on coming to Paraguay. When a wedding followed the engagement with indecent haste, conducted by John Lane, with only Bella's brothers in attendance, Mary vented her outrage in a letter to Will:

> You will understand what that means. I have only a contemptuous pity for the girl. She is so young and so ill-developed mentally, morally as well as

physically. If I meet her I shall speak to her. For the man I feel the utmost scorn — I shall have no recognition for him … It would serve that man right if every man in the place rope's ended him and then threw him into a ditch … When the chairman asked Alec if he was aware of certain matters and hiding them, I believe he almost fainted … The shock sent the mother delirious … The father forbade Ned the house, refused to speak to him and forbade the children going to see their sister.

Nonetheless, the couple settled down to married life and five months later Bella gave birth to a daughter. But Bella's mother was not there to see her grandchild.

All the colonists had been through devastating strains in the year preceding, witnessing the departure of Lane and so many other colonists, and the dismantling of so many dreams. For Mary Ann Lewis, to experience on top of all that the scandal concerning her daughter and perhaps to be aware of the censoriousness of so impressive a woman as Mary Gilmore, it was too much to bear. On 25 July she walked into the *monte* surrounding Cosme and from one of the tall forest trees she hanged herself.

*

The episode demonstrated Cosme's complete moral collapse, wrote Arthur Tozer, although he expressed sympathy for Mary Ann: "The poor woman had had a hard life and it is alleged that her husband treated her brutally and it is more than probable that this, added to her daughter's conduct, unhinged her mind." Naturally, he said, the Cosme people were trying to keep the story dark, with no mention of it in their journal. "The *Cosme Monthly* is an utter fraud … but as it may charm and entrap some poor beggar who hankers after brotherly love it serves the colony's end."

Mary Gilmore heard news of the suicide in Villarrica. Unable to tolerate the colony any longer, she had moved there on 13 May 1900, just after the seventh Cosme Foundation Day.

It had been arranged that she and young Billy would share a *carreta* into town with John Parish, a Yorkshireman recruited by Lane from Bradford. Although a relatively recent arrival, the June *Cosme Monthly Notes* made much of his departure: "A very successful farewell social was given on May 5th in honour of John Parish. John is already much missed. He is now in Buenos Aires working at his trade of wood carver."

There is no indication of the farewell social including Mary, leaving at the same time, who had been a key figure in the movement for eight years and at Cosme for almost five. No doubt the snub was intended, for the same issue of the *Notes* stated baldly: "Mrs Gilmore has gone to live in Villarrica pending joining her husband in Patagonia."

There was a party the night before they left, with the old empty brick-shed down on the Flat turned into a banquet hall, but this was for Foundation Day. "Cigars, speeches and songs followed the supper after which an adjournment was made to the dancing floor." If there was a speech for Mary's departure it was not mentioned. Unlike her husband, she had never been popular.

She was still only thirty-five years old. Of the sad, beautiful little village that had absorbed so much of her life she wrote, "I left the place without the faintest pang of regret. I looked at everything as I passed and wondered why I could not feel sorry ..." No doubt she made an affectionate farewell to the few women she liked, including Clara Laurence, once her rival in love, and to John Lane, whom she had always respected. Almost five years before, it had been John who collected her at the railway siding, when it was Stevenson she had been hoping for.

Her parting from Dave Stevenson, who had consumed so much of her emotional life, must have been difficult. She was never to see him again. But some years after returning to Australia, when she and Will were living in a country town in Victoria, she published her first volume of verse. There is one poem in it that is surely about her abortive, wasted love affair with Stevenson:

> Somehow we missed each other,
> Passed each other by unknowing;
> I who sought you, you who sought me,
> With hearts that throbbed for hopes and fears,
> Passed each other in the early going,
> Missed each other in the early years.
> Somehow we missed each other,
> We two poor bankrupt souls, sowing
> A harvest that we recked not of;
> Now, others' sorrows claim our tears,
> Others call us in our later going,
> Others hold us in our later years.

In Villarrica Mary was able to rent the same house where she had had her baby, thanks to the negotiations of her old friend, Larry Petrie, by then working as a watchman at the town's railway station. "I feel more homely in this little hut than I ever did on Cosme," she wrote to Gilmore, "and there are no prying eyes looking for scandal and gossip, and tongues to retail it and make harm out of everything."

Relieved to have left the tensions behind, Mary enjoyed sitting on the veranda until nearly dusk. "After a week of this my landlord and his six daughters came one evening to see me and remonstrate. 'It wasn't safe' they gave me to understand; 'there were *bandidos* about.'" The landlord insisted she double-lock the door before sundown and demonstrated how she should jam a sapling against it. "Some weeks afterwards, finding the door rattle in a high wind, I examined the hinges. There were no screws in them, only nails, old rusty nails, about two to each hinge. I smiled. The thing was so like Paraguay."

After his seventeen hours of duty at the railway station, Petrie often came to visit her. " 'Larry, Larry, you foolish fellow' I used to say — 'Why don't you go to bed instead of coming up here?' 'Bed!' he would reply, 'How can I sleep? The carpenters work beside me and the lampmen are in and out all the time, and so it's a case of get drunk, or come and talk to you', and he would stay and talk till his nerves quietened and then tramp wearily back to his little lamp-room for an hour's sleep."

Sometimes he recalled his old roaring days in Australia, the time he bombed the blackleg ship, the *Aramac*. "The funny thing was," he told her, that the moment the bomb went off, "the first thing that came to my mind was to save people. I did everything I could to help." He confided that he was saving to buy some land, and Mary predicted he would eventually marry a local woman, "as he hasn't much chance of marrying anyone else and his sympathies are considerably Paraguayan".

She got in touch with Arthur Tozer once again, for her husband was planning to return for her during the harsh Patagonian winter and was anxious to pick up some casual work. Tozer had been appointed manager of the railway's central workshops at Sapucai. For people to get employment there, Mary wrote to Will, "I think Tozer has to recommend them".

Tozer had his own anxieties. Amy had recently given birth to a daughter, but had not recovered from a difficult labour and remained in Villarrica under Dr Bottrell's supervision. He only saw her at weekends and the baby, also recently very ill, stayed with him in the care of a wet-nurse. Tozer had become emotionally involved with the progress of the Boer War, and registered his daughter, Dorothy Ethel, as a British subject, "because I don't want her to be Paraguayan in anything, much less in nationality. I am getting so blessed patriotic now that I feel like adorning our empty flag staff with a Union Jack and I would if I had one to run up".

He offered work to Gilmore, but accommodation in the single men's quarters. Mary was briefly reunited with her husband in August, then he took up the job in Sapucai, a company town where all the workers were Paraguayan, the clerical staff English and Tozer reigned supreme.

After three months the Gilmores left for Buenos Aires, and in November 1900 headed for Patagonia for the summer shearing season. Later, on my own journey home from Paraguay, I followed their path down there.

Meanwhile, I tried to pursue the trail of Mary's idiosyncratic friend. Larry Petrie had a hot head that had often brought about his temporary downfall, but it was his warm heart that caused his end. The year after Mary left Villarrica, in March 1901, he was working at the railway station when the station-master's little daughter strayed onto the line just as a train was coming into the platform. Petrie jumped down and pushed her to safety, but was hit by the train, his ribs forced through his lungs, killed by the impact. Rose Cadogan from New Australia, who as Rose Summerfield had worked with him at the AWU in Sydney, claimed his body and arranged a funeral.

Larry Petrie had become a favourite of mine. In 1993 I searched for his grave in the cemetery at Villarrica, passing by the vaults and marble angels, the condominiums of the affluent dead, looking for some untended and more humble plot, befitting an obscure one-armed Australian anarchist. But I could not find his name. Perhaps Petrie lies somewhere in the unmarked earth at the little New Australian cemetery at Ña Sarah, a further cause for anxiety for Señor Nigel Kennedy, fearing more Australian researchers whose questions he cannot satisfy.

*

An odd assortment of teachers shared the responsibility — or the blame — for the patchy schooling of Cosme's children. At eighty-eight years of age Bill Wood said he regretted most his lack of a proper education. "In Australia, I'm sure, the schooling would've been much more strict. On Cosme there were long periods when there was no real teacher so we children just went to the house called the school and sat there amusing ourselves instead of learning something."

Often it was the teachers also who crept "like snail, unwillingly to school", appointed willy-nilly when the village committee decreed that was how they could best do their share. After John Lane came Jim Sime, a former weaver from western Queensland. He had shown some interest in literature, having given an evening lecture on the poetry of Robert

Burns, but he wasn't remembered as a good teacher. "I don't think that we children paid much attention to Jimmy," said Norman Wood, "because he had a pretty pronounced Scottish accent and it was hard to make out what he was saying."

"He was too easy-going altogether," said Bill, "he didn't keep our noses to the grindstone."

Next was Billy Bennett, a former conspiracy prisoner and hero of the shearers' strike, but no hero at school. As chairman of the Barcaldine Strike Committee he had written that "staring down soldiers' rifles ... is an education in itself". His conception seemed not to have advanced beyond that. "It was an impossible task for him," said Bill Wood. "Apparently he wasn't a schoolteacher at all. He used to get us all seated and busy on something or other, and he would sit and read books the whole school time. He only lasted until John Lane went away to organise new members for the colony."

John Lane's natural skill, as Souter has noted, was managerial, not, like his elder brother, inspirational. His moderation, common sense and conciliatory manner helped hold Cosme together after the bitter events accompanying William Lane's departure. But the colony's failure still seemed inevitable without an injection of new lifeblood.

The community was just eighty-four in number, the majority children. The recruitment drive in Britain had never produced more than a trickle of immigrants and that had all but stopped. In 1900 only one family arrived: Leonard Apthorpe, his wife Laura and their young daughter Mabel. Although Apthorpe became a long-term member, people were soon muttering about his laziness, his reluctance to pull his weight.

The annual meeting of the village committee in May 1901 resolved that experience showed that bush people were better than Britons as colonists; the time had come to mount a new campaign in Australia.

The recruiting organiser was chosen by ballot among the voting members of the community; in two rounds the votes were fairly evenly shared between Dave Stevenson and John Lane. In the third round Stevenson stood down. Lane was elected for a job much to be envied despite its undoubted challenges: after eight years away, a chance to see Australia again, its cities and the bush, to meet up with relatives and old mates, to catch up with politics in a new federated nation.

The Paraguayan Government, still supportive of the colony, paid the return steamship fare via England. John Lane departed in July and Billy Bennett took over as chairman of the village committee.

No doubt it was with relief that Bennett stepped down from his post at the school. "Then we had a whole series of people filling in for a week or two," Bill Wood remembered. "I don't think any of them were really great teachers. Allan McLeod taught us for a while, but he was such an important man as the colony's chief carpenter, they couldn't spare him for wasting his time with children."

Don Norman said he liked Allan McLeod's classes because he taught "all sorts of queer things and he would accompany his lessons with the fiddle to drum things into us". They learned about the states of Australia and the outback and the shearing sheds and the ringers in the sheds who could shear 300 sheep a day. "We could hardly understand how they could do that."

There was a new addition to the kindergarten group, little Mabel Apthorpe. Seven-year-old Bill Wood grandly ignored her existence; in later years he would notice her a great deal and pursue her to become his wife. In the meantime real life, as far as the Cosme boys were concerned, was to be found in the *monte*. "We were out all day practically," said Norman Wood, "absolutely free. Except when we were getting home at night. Then we worried about the belting we'd get."

*

The *monte* was their secret world, their enchanted retreat, their Green Mansions. There were flamingoes, Norman Wood remembered, down on the Flat, shy deer in the forest glades, and macaws and parrots screeching overhead. High up in the canopy the monkeys held a chattering parliament. The children swung through the trees, years before Edgar Rice Burroughs dreamed of Tarzan and his special mode of transport. "There were vines hanging everywhere," said Don Norman, "so we'd swing from them, usually over a gully. We'd tie on a piece of wood to make a seat and somebody would push and you could swoop a long way. One day I just stopped in time or I'd have swung right down on top of a wild pig."

But you had to know how to walk in the *monte*, he said with a certain pride. "You had to take a knife to cut the vines that got in your way and wrapped round your legs. When you got pretty good you could even run in the *monte*, but you had to know how."

Every day the boys set out, armed with shanghais, axes and machetes, accompanied by their dogs, usually returning with something for the pot. "We small kids weren't allowed guns," said Bill Wood, "but Dave McLeod, a bigger boy, had an old muzzle-loading shot-gun. Before we were in the colony workforce we used to go out to the surrounding *montes* and catch small animals, which were much appreciated at home."

Their dogs would get the scent of a raccoon or an agouti, a creature like a large guinea pig, and chase it into one of the abundant hollow logs. "Then we'd come along with an axe and cut the agouti out. But the only way to get a deer or armadillo was to shoot it because they could outdistance the dogs. Once armadillos got down into their burrows, there was no hope of digging them out. So you had to shoot them on the run. When we got one, we'd come home singing, 'Armadilla, armadilla, armadilla for tea'."

Dining on armadillo was considered a real treat; its flesh was white and odourless, often compared to chicken. The women dried the armour-plated shell and used it as a little basket, handy for knitting wool.

Remembering Margaret Riley's stories of roaming far into the *monte* at New Australia, I suggested to the Wood brothers that surely some Cosme girls accompanied them on their expeditions, their sisters Rose and Kathleen, for instance. Bill Wood looked astonished. "Not *hunting*," he said. "That wouldn't have been suitable for young womenfolk. And they had their work to do around the house, sewing and embroidery and so forth."

I felt depressed for the girls, sitting in a little thatched shack, having to pretend it was some genteel parlour of their mother's memory in a land they had never seen. I would have wanted to heave the embroidery out the window, strap a knife to my leg, take off into the *monte* and swing from the vines.

Don Guillermo seemed to pick up on my thoughts. "Besides, my sister Rose didn't like the *monte*," he said. "The only person on Cosme who was bitten by a venomous snake was Rose. She trod on a *yarará*, the most poisonous snake in Paraguay, but she managed to survive somehow."

I wondered if the girls got to read *Chums*. Many newspapers and magazines were sent to Cosme from friends overseas and were shared around until tattered. From Australia came the *Worker*, the Sydney *Bulletin* and *The Lone Hand*. Supporters in England sent *The Weekly Welcome* and *Home Chat*. But the paper the Cosme boys waited for most anxiously was *Chums*.

It was full of gung-ho adventure stories set in exotic parts of the world, aimed at prep school boys in Cheltenham and Reading who had "elevenses" at recess and climbed the stairs with teddy-bears to say their prayers. For the Cosme boys, many of the stories simply seemed to be about themselves, even if a bit dodgy on the detail. "We used to thrive on *Chums*," said Bill Wood, remembering one story in particular which impressed him so much that Jimmy Sime coached him to read it out at the Saturday evening social:

> It was a blood curdling tale about a boy travelling out onto the grasslands on his own with a tree here and there. He was suddenly attacked by a furious mob of wild pigs, but he managed to scramble up a tree. He was, of course, scared out of his wits but, remarkable to relate, unlike most boys unless they were secret smokers, he happened to have a box of matches in his pocket. This horde of pigs, circling round the butt of his tree, apparently hadn't destroyed the dead grass there. The boy began striking matches and throwing them down while the pigs tusked away at his tree. Luckily, the very last match set fire to the chaff underneath and the pigs all thundered off, scared to death. Then the boy just climbed down and went home.

Bill Wood said as an eight-year-old he didn't want to analyse or criticise the story. "I just swallowed the yarn whole." A short time later he and his brother Ack and another boy were fishing down at the river late in the afternoon. It came on to rain and they started for home. "We were hurrying along in the rain when suddenly, beside the track, there was this big mob of wild pigs, smashing their tusks like castanets. Ack stopped with his mouth open, the other boy stared, forgetting he had a gun in his hand, and I started climbing a tree. I got up about a metre and bumped back onto the ground again. I don't think a box of matches would have been much use to me. But luckily the pigs cleared off into the *monte*."

Sometimes they would hear a crashing sound in the bushes and it would be an *mborebi*, a tapir, that strange pig-like creature of the rhinoceros family, lumbering away from them. "A harmless thing," said Bill Wood.

Nor had any of them been alarmed by encounters with the wolf of the *monte*. "It's smaller than the European wolf," said Don Bill. "In Guaraní it's called *aguará guasú*, large fox, and that's more what it's like. It's very timid. You might see it from a long way off but if it sees you it goes for its life. They feed on small animals and birds but they're never known to attack a human."

Perhaps Mary Gilmore did not know this, for in her book, *More Recollections*, she made high drama of her meeting with one:

> One evening as I sat reading, just at dusk I saw a big dog walk in under my veranda. This being the first I had seen about the colony I was greatly interested and delightedly called out to him.
> "Hello, old man, whose dog are you?" I said in a friendly way.

As I spoke I went up to pat him, putting my hand on his great head. When I touched him I thought what a harsh, hard lot of hair he had. I went on stroking him and he bore with me for a while, then he edged away, sniffing round for any scraps of food that might be in my rubbish box. I spoke and patted again, and still he made no response. So I concluded that he only knew Guaraní or Spanish, and had not yet learned English.

For three nights, she wrote, the animal visited and she woke to find him sniffing and padding around her bed. But she had no fear of dogs so drowsily greeted him and went back to sleep again. She inquired about him and, being told that the colony had no such dog, assumed it was a stray. A few days later, at dusk, William Lane called with Charlie Leck, who was carrying a gun:

> "Don't make a light," said Mr Leck as he entered, and added, "I want you to go into the bedroom and not to make a sound, as I have come to get that *lobo* of yours."
> "*Lobo*! What is a *lobo*?" I asked in astonishment.
> "A wolf!" he replied.
> And even then I did not feel fear, the thing had seemed so tame. Yet all the mothers in the place had been in a panic for fear their children would be devoured. I think I was the only person who did not know it.
> He was a timber wolf, and if you took your very largest Alsatian and gave him a collie's tail, you would have his double, only the double would be a little smaller in the neck and head, and a little shorter in the teeth.
> Later we caught him in a wolf-trap made on the colony ... The wolf in the cage filled me with terror. Yet I had patted him as a dog without fear and without harm! But I confess that, in spite of the fear, I grieved to think that he had to be killed for he seemed so like a dog.

The animal with *gravitas*, with serious sex appeal as far as the Cosme boys were concerned, was the jaguar. Most of the old men were eager to tell a story of a personal experience with a "tiger".

As a boy, Wallace Wood had come across one when out riding, and his horse Prince had bolted. His brother Alex had seen one jump on a bullock, kill it by breaking its neck and slowly devour it.

Rod McLeod said they were very rare these days, but occasionally one still came out of the *monte* at Cosme and took someone's dog or chickens. He laughed. "It's a wonder they never gobbled us up. We used to go down to the river, a league through the *monte*, and see tigers' footmarks all over the place." But he gave one a good scare once. He was about to climb a tree to collect orange leaves — "they made scent from them and you could make some money" — when high in a fork he saw a tiger. "I yelled and beat the butt with a good sharp machete and the thing sprang down and rushed off, breaking vines and bashing into trees. It might be still going for all I know."

Bill Wood, aged ten, was out riding one day with a Paraguayan woman. They had harvested corn cobs and mandioca from a garden patch and, with the bags slung on the saddles in front of them, were riding back to Cosme through the forest. He was riding "old Jean, the black mare who generally resented me trying to stop her if she wanted to get home". They came around a bend and there was a jaguar standing in the middle of the track, "about as big as a donkey, patchy coloured, spotted red and black, with huge wonderful paws. He was staring straight at us. So I hastily pulled old Jean to a stop and the Paraguayan woman did the same, of course. I stared at the jaguar for quite a while and I felt my hair go up on end. Then he suddenly turned around, swung his head forward and bounced into the *monte*".

Later Dave and Allie McLeod, aged sixteen and fifteen, went after the jaguar with a Paraguayan professional hunter and his dogs. "Their dogs savaged the jaguar but it ran off and sprang up into a fork of a tree. It lay on a branch looking down at the dogs and the hunter increased the load in his old muzzle-loader and shot it in the chest. It fell down amongst the dogs and they all dashed in to bite it. But it was quite alive enough to dispose of them, and killed three dogs with its paws, then limped off for a couple of hundred yards before finally dropping down."

I was saddened for the jaguar, but did not want to say so and confirm the notion that the suitable thing for the womenfolk was embroidery and tatting.

Don Norman remembered the carcass of a jaguar being carried into the camp by Paraguayan hunters who were handsomely recompensed by two Frenchman. One of them, Dr Housin, was a naturalist, and he and his younger brother stayed at Cosme for six months. "They skinned the tiger very carefully," said Don Norman, "because they were going to have it stuffed. The natives used to bring them birds too and we watched them stuff them. They had a whole collection — hummingbirds, sparrows, thrushes, macaws and *monte* hens."

Don Guillermo remembered the two men vividly. "Apparently they were very high-class Frenchmen. Dr Housin considered my mother a beauty and painted her portrait. The younger brother, who spoke no English, was a great hunter and nearly every day he would go into the *monte* and shoot a couple of monkeys. He would hand some of them around, so that's when I got my first taste of monkey meat. It had a very powerful smell of the wild but we enjoyed it. But my mother didn't like to dispose of the hands, so like human hands with soft black skin on the palms."

*

The old men led the way along a track which became a tunnel as it entered the *monte*. Julie and I followed. Rod McLeod looked up into the trees from which ganglions of vines descended. It was a long time, he said, since he had seen a monkey around Cosme. "The Paraguayan people go out hunting them and the Indians eat them too. I suppose they'll finish them all off in the end."

There were chack-chacking monkey sounds behind us, then a splutter of giggles.

"One of the Titilahs," laughed Rod McLeod, and called out in Guaraní. The carrot head and freckled face of the Ginger Meggs boy we had seen at the schoolhouse bobbed up from behind a bush, then down again. Young Diana and Shirley Wood crouched beside him, understandably amused by the mad *gringas* going about with microphones reverently recording everything. Earlier in the day they had caught us taping the quacking of ducks. More monkey sounds and giggles.

Don Norman said his mother used to hate the sound of the howling monkeys in the night. They would come down to steal the corn. He remembered George Titilah going out to his corn patch and leaving a dish of treacle with some white rum in it. "The monkeys came and they all got drunk and then George was able to take his time, knocking them off with a machete."

We said it was a horrible story. Rod McLeod bent over, choking with glee.

The children stayed behind as we followed the track further into the gloom. The *monte* was silently avaricious, sticky creepers attaching as we passed, elkhorns clinging to tree-trunks, moss and brilliant fungi to logs, tangles of lianas, like carelessly hung nets, holding sagging loads of rotting leaves and fallen branches, tree ferns straining for the light.

Abruptly the forest opened into a clearing stippled with sunlight. The grass had been cropped to parkland by wandering cattle. A spring gurgled into three brackish pools with suds at the edges. Don Norman said the colony women used to wash their clothes there and today's villagers still did.

At the edge of the glade were a few old orange trees, fruit weighing down the branches and rotting beneath them. Julie and I marvelled at the abundance.

"People don't like these ones," said Don Norman. "They're *apepús*, wild oranges. Only very poor *campesinos* bother with them."

The *New Australia* journal in 1893 had informed intending pioneers:

> Paraguay is the land of orange trees … There are several varieties, notably the *apepú*, a very acid orange, which, from its Guaraní name, some believe to be a native variety while the sweet orange, the bigarade (Citrus bigaradia), the mandarin and various kinds of lemons and limes, were undoubtedly introduced by the Jesuits. The great orange season is from May to August when … may be seen the picturesque processions of laughing and screaming girls and women, who carry basket after basket of fruit on their heads from the shore to the ship, like a swarm of busy ants. Up to the present no industrial use has been made of the orange. Some sixty millions are exported annually, the same quantity is consumed by the natives, and perhaps treble that quantity is devoured by monkeys and birds, or left to rot on the ground.

We sat down in the grass, Don Norman carefully lowering his tall frame. He deftly skinned some *apepús* and passed them to us. They were bitter but not unpleasant, in the heat very refreshing. In this place, we remarked, comparisons with Arcadia did not seem so very fanciful.

The old men were conversing in Guaraní, making gentle plosive and clucking sounds. We asked what they were saying.

Rod McLeod chuckled. "We were hoping that the little white boy won't come and get you."

Don Norman laughed at our bafflement. It was a story they learned long ago from the Indian children, he said. A legend about a little white boy who lived in the *monte*. It had nothing to do with the Australian gringos who came to Cosme. The Guaraní people had known the story for generations. The little white boy with fair hair and blue eyes was the *yasy-yateré*. He could be heard and sometimes seen among the trees, especially at dusk. If you were a child he lured you into the *monte* with wild honey, making beautiful noises like a bird. But if you listened to the *yasy-yateré* you lost your wits and were never seen again.

"Rod knows all those old ghost stories," said Don Norman. "Guaraní is his main language. He's lived with Paraguayans and Indians all his life." There was also, he remembered, the *luison*, which was like a big dog. When a family had only boys, the seventh would be a *luison*. During the night it would go to the cemetery and eat dead bodies. Don Norman grinned. "We were lucky we had a couple of sisters in our family."

"There's the *pombero*," said Rod, "covered all over with brown fur like a monkey. He comes around the house at night, whistling under your window. If you don't want trouble, you've got to leave cigars out for him."

We laughed.

Rod McLeod nodded emphatically. "It's true. I believe it."

*

At the beginning of November 1900 the Gilmores left Buenos Aires on a rusting tramp steamer, the *Santa Cruz*. The 2,600-kilometre voyage south, expected to take six or seven days, lasted a month. Mary suffered acute diarrhoea and young Billy was so ill with measles and inflammation of the lungs that the ship's doctor prayed over him, certain he'd die.

But as the steamer headed towards the treacherous port of Río Gallegos, on the same latitude as the Falkland Islands, Mary, despite her troubles, was stirred by the drama of their destination. They were a short distance from the Straits of Magellan. She'd been reading about the great navigator, how he sailed and charted the narrow waterway, "named the land on one side of it Tierra del Fuego, the Land of Fire, from the camp fires of the Indians along the shore (not from volcanoes as we were school taught) and named the land on the other side for the Patagones, the tribe of Indians living there (the Tehuelches) who he said had big feet; probably they were skin-covered because of the cold".

Patagonia inspired her. From the moment of her arrival she was alert, intensely curious about everything around her. The bitter, complaining woman of Cosme disappeared. She was, like Marcella, a well-read young woman in one of her draft stories, wryly amused and prepared for whatever the strange new world might deliver:

> She was new to Gallegos and its ways and hoped much from what the hitherto unknown held for her. So she stood on the rotten timbers of the pier, with her handbag in her hand, and watched the launch go puffing back to the far off ship, watched it bobbing up and down in the rough like a cork … Where the wind never ceases, people grow used to legs … when she held her skirts her hat blew over her nose, when she held her hat, her skirts inclined to do the same.

From the driver of a mule cart she learned of another constant, bad

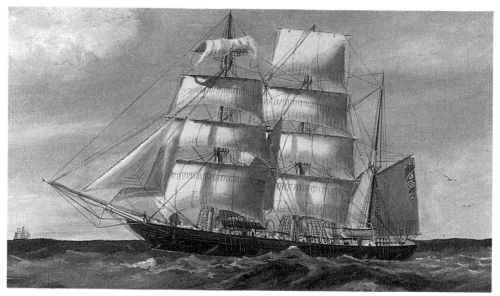

"*Royal Tar* at Sea", painting by John Allcott McCredie

Jimmy and Dolly Cadogan at Asunción airport in February 1974, about to depart for Australia with their sons John and Henry

Henry Lawson in 1890, the year he met Mary Cameron.
"There was a curious immaturity about Lawson at that time ...
the face was weak, the chin undeveloped."
(Mitchell Library, State Library of New South Wales)

Mary Cameron, aged 30 in 1895, the year she went to Paraguay *(Mitchell Library)*

Wedding photo: Denis and Mary Hoare, late 1870s

William Lane in the year he led his followers to Paraguay *(From original in the Rare Books and Special Collections of the Library of University of Sydney)*

Strike leaders sentenced in May 1891 to three years' hard labour on St Helena Island in Moreton Bay. *From left, rear:* Henry Smith-Barry, William Fothergill, Alec Forrester, Julian Stuart. *Centre*: George Taylor, P. Griffin, E. Murphy, Hugh Blackwell. *Front*: A. Brown, R. Prince, William Bennett, D. Murphy. *Reclining*: William Hamilton. On their release, Blackwell, Forrester, Fothergill and Smith-Barry went to Paraguay. *(John Oxley Library)*

On board *Royal Tar*, Sydney Harbour, 16 July 1893 *(Mitchell Library)*

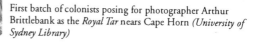

First batch of colonists posing for photographer Arthur Brittlebank as the *Royal Tar* nears Cape Horn *(University of Sydney Library)*

The promised land in sight *(University of Sydney Library)*

Asunción docks, presidential palace in background

Downtown Asunción in 1993, orange trees and petrol fumes

Cathedral, Asunción

Florence Wood de White contemplates the bust of Francisco Solano López at Asunción's central post office

October 1993: descendants of Australian colonists outside Asunción's municipal theatre for the centenary of the arrival of their forebears.

Wood family descendants with Australian
ambassador Hugh Wyndham at Asunción's
municipal theatre

Patricio Wood and his wife
Mercedes Quevedo de Wood

Statue of Madame Eliza Alicia Lynch in Asunción

Monument to Hugo Stroessner, the dictator's father, at former site of New Australia

Ricardo Smith in 1989

The author and Nigel Kennedy at his ranch on the original site of New Australia

Margaret Hoare (later Margaret Riley), aged fourteen in 1897, had many Paraguayan male admirers

Margaret Riley at 105 years of age

Stanley-Hijo, descendant of New Australia, at his roadside cantina in 1993

Top: Village of Nueva Londres, originally Nueva Australia, in 1993. Trees on right are *Grevillea robusta*, the Australian native silky oak.

Above left: Don Guillermo (Bill) Wood, aged 91, at his home in Asunción in 1985 *(Peter Solness)*

Above right: Lillian Wood, *left*, with her sister at Bourke before departing for Paraguay

Left: William Wood at Bourke in about 1892, the time of Henry Lawson's visit

Colonists at Cosme in late 1896. *Left group, from left*: Ettie Lane, Jenny Lane, Margaret Grace, unknown woman, Mary Cameron (white apron), Clara Laurence (white dress). *Right group, from left*: Dave Stevenson and ward Wally Head, a McLeod child, Jim Sime, Peter Pindar, probably John Kushel, Jack Black, Cosma Lane and another child, W. Moffatt, Charlie Rae (with horse), Harry Taylor and Dick Rae. *(Mitchell Library)*

Wood family house at Cosme, built by William Wood about 1906 *(Gavin Souter)*

Anne Whitehead with Norman and
William Wood in Asunción in 1982

Independence Day 1982. Drum majorettes of the
Young Paraguayan Movement — favourites of former
President Stroessner

Once the Villarrica home of Dr Bottrell,
physician and friend to the Australian colonists

Caazapá, the nearest settlement to Cosme. Colonists came to shop, watch the occasional bullfight and a few to drink in its cantinas.

Rod McLeod, a Cosme original aged 81, greets Rodrigo Wood in 1982

Youths at Cosme competing in a rodeo on Independence Day 1982

Cosme workshops and the barn which served as the theatre for an 1896 production of W.S. Gilbert's *Engaged (University of Sydney Library)*

Pirapó River bridge constructed by Cosme colonists under the direction of Allan McLeod *(University of Sydney Library)*

Colonists reading *Cosme Evening Notes*. Billy Bennett *second from left*. Arthur Tozer sprawled *at centre. Extreme right:* William Wood reading, then Alf Davey and Billy Laurence. *(University of Sydney Library)*

Cosme kindergarten group with artwork, about 1898.
Cosma Lane, first child born at Cosme, is wearing bonnet
and white apron. Her elder sisters are the teachers:
Ettie *at left*, Alice, *right*. *(University of Sydney Library)*

Cosme children with *carreta* outside colony store and
printery. *At left:* Ettie Lane. *(University of Sydney Library)*

Group of Cosme colonists, c. 1900. *Back row from left:* Mrs John Lane, Mrs Apthorpe, Billy Bennett (waistcoat), Jack Delugar,
William Titilah, Jim Sime, Tom Adamson, Mrs Adamson (hat), Dick Rae holding daughter Haidee, Nellie Rae holding
daughter Nora. *2nd row from left:* Jack Parish, Leonard Apthorpe (cap) holding daughter Mabel, unknown man, William
Wood, four unknown men, then Allan McLeod. *Front row from left:* Wally Head (straw hat), Dave Stevenson (reclining),
Harry Baker, Ned Dyer (beard and cap), Billy Laurence (open shirt and waistcoat), Mrs Fanny Bennett, Mrs Margaret
McLeod and Jack Wilson. *(University of Sydney Library)*

Billy Laurence, *left*, and William Titilah in the *monte* at Cosme about 1900 *(University of Sydney Library)*

Allan McLeod after the death of his wife Margaret in 1903 with his nine children (young Rod on his left knee). Cosme colonists, notably the John Lane and William Wood families, took on the upbringing of a number of the children. *(University of Sydney Library)*

John Lane family at Cosme in 1904. *From left, rear:* Alice, John Lane holding Hilda, Ettie holding Charlie McLeod. *Front:* Mrs Jenny Lane, Cosma, Daisy McLeod. *(University of Sydney Library)*

Raphael, Ruben and Lorenzo Titilah at their Cosme home in 1985 *(Peter Solness)*

Former children of Cosme colony in 1982. Rod McLeod, aged 81, George Titilah, 92, Norman Wood, 83.

Herbert Stanley Felton, who employed the Gilmores on his Patagonian *estancia*, with his wife Emma, son-in-law Henstock, baby son Carlos and daughter Millie — "the most awful girl that ever lived".

William and Mary Gilmore and young Billy, c.1910
(University of Sydney Library)

William Wood family at Cosme c.1907. *From left:* William Wood Sr, Alex, Wallace, Lillian holding baby Kathleen, Norman, Rose, William Jr. *(University of Sydney Library)*

Cosme work party at the lagoon in the Capiibary River below the "Stony Crossing" *(University of Sydney Library)*

Rose Menmuir at the Asunción home of her niece
Florence Wood de White in 1989

Sylvia McLeod de Wood and Francisco Wood in 1985
with their two elder children, Francisco Jr (known as
Kiko) and Mabel, both in the uniform of the Young
Paraguayan Movement *(Peter Solness)*

VENCER O MORIR

Mabel Wood honouring the memory of Francisco Solano López and the War of the Triple Alliance *(Peter Solness)*

Alex, *left*, and Bill Wood in Jerusalem, 1919 *(University of Sydney Library)*

Dave Stevenson during World War I. He rejected the opportunity to take up a commission — "probably he had some political idea about it all". *(University of Sydney Library)*

Donald Lane, William Lane's eldest son, killed in action at Gallipoli in 1915 *(University of Sydney Library)*

Norman Wood, aged 19, in British Army uniform

William and Lillian Wood and their family outside their house at Cosme, c.1922–23. *From left, rear:* William Wood Sr (hat), daughter Kathleen, sons Alex, Wallace, William Jr (tie), Donald and Norman. *From left, front:* Neighbour Minnie Black, unknown child, Lillian, aged 50, holding grand-daughter Margaret Rose (Peggy), unknown girl, youngest son Frank (at front), Peggy McLeod de Wood holding her son Sandy, unknown child. *(National Library of Australia)*

Donald Wood, back from fighting in the 1932–35 Chaco War, in Asunción's Plaza Uruguaya

Wallace Wood, in *gaucho* trousers, in Corrientes, Argentina, in 1933

Concepción from the river, art-directed
for a Graham Greene film

Pony carts at Concepción's wharf
waiting for the weekly riverboat

Concepción, Don Norman's patch of Paraguay
(Stuart Heather)

Norman Wood, his wife Doña Leonarda
and two grand-daughters

Centre: Don Norman Wood and his dog Fury,
at home in Concepción in 1989

Bottom: The author with Norman Wood's son Enrique,
a veterinary surgeon and the only self-declared socialist
among the Paraguayan colony descendants

Rose Cadogan c.1899. She was well-known in Australia as the poet and activist Rose Summerfield.

León Cadogan, aged 22, working as a translator in Buenos Aires

León Cadogan in 1962 with his daughter Connie and the son of Chief Pablo Vera of the Mbyá-Guaraní

León Cadogan and his grand-daughter Maria Mercedes in 1962. He told her the Guaraní legend of the Blue Bird.

León Cadogan with two
Aché-Guayaki Indians

Roger Cadogan (*on right*) and his half-brother Benito with
Chief Vicente Gauto on land purchased by the Léon
Cadogan Foundation for the Mbyá-Guaraní in the 1970s

Lillian Wood in the 1940s at Cosme,
"beached on a foreign shore by William
Lane's dream"

Rose Wood, shortly after her marriage to Alan Menmuir, a Scottish engineer

Doña María Albina Cáceres de Wood with her son Francisco

Rose Menmuir, in South Africa about 1949, with Virginia and Alan

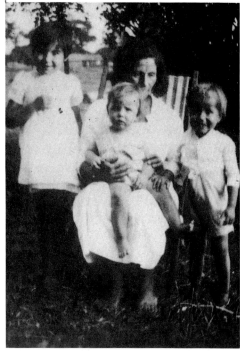

María Albina Cáceres de Wood at Cosme about 1949, holding youngest son Peter, flanked by son Francisco and daughter Dora

Bill and Mabel Wood in early 1940s with four of their nine children. *From left:* William III, Florence, Charlie and John.

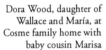

Dora Wood, daughter of Wallace and María, at Cosme family home with baby cousin Marisa

Francisco Wood and friend swimming their horses across the flooded Pirapó in 1965
(Gavin Souter)

Donald Wood, his wife Deolidia (*née* Fernandez) and their children in early 1970s. *From left*: Alcides, Carmen, Lucy, George, Gladys, Annie and William.

Florence Wood in 1968, operating radio for Inter-American Geodetic Survey in Asunción

Peter Wood at Sydney airport in 1966, greeted by Australian relatives with whom he communicated in sign language. Mrs Torry Hyatt (*née* Johnston, *on his right*) used to correspond with his grandfather. (*Gavin Souter*)

Two children of Norman Wood in 1989: Rodrigo, a banker, and his sister Marisa

Alan Wood, reunited with his biological family at Cosme in 1982. *From left:* Francisco, Wallace Wood, Dora, Alan, his mother María Albina Cáceres de Wood, youngest brother Peter.

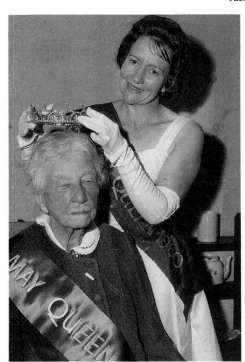

Dame Mary Gilmore crowned May Queen in 1961, the year before her death. It was, she said, "my last glorification". *(John Fairfax Limited)*

Clara Stevenson in retirement on the island of Guernsey. She died in 1964 aged 96, surviving Mary Gilmore, her old rival in love, by two years. *(University of Sydney Library)*

Peter, George and Alcides Wood in the NSW Riverina district in 1967
(University of Sydney Library)

Florence and Max White at their home in Asunción in 1989

Robin Wood in his early 30s on a visit back to Paraguay, with
his young cousin Carmen at Encarnación

Peggy Wood — career blonde

Big Wood with Makká Indians

Robin Wood today

Robin Wood, aged 14, overseer of timber workers on the lawless frontier of the Alto Paraná

Cosme village in 1993

Sylvia McLeod de Wood at the old family homestead at Cosme, 1993

Francisco Wood, with the last of the morticed fence posts made by the Australian colonists at Cosme

Descendants of two rival socialist colonies, Florence Wood de White of Cosme and Jimmy Cadogan of New Australia, reunited in a new democratic Paraguay in 1995

Gerald Wood, son of Sandy Wood, at a monument in Asunción to the dictator Francisco Solano López
(Peter Solness)

Iguazú Falls, on the borders of Paraguay, Brazil and Argentina, "a miracle undiminished"

language: "*Carajo!* If you don't gallop I'll cut your entrails out and feed them to your mother!" Mary resolved to learn Spanish as soon as possible and to get shorter skirts with hems weighted with shot, to acquire some top boots, and to wear these "all the time she remained in this infernal country". As she gazed at an "endless vista of sand, shingle, *barranca*, and the monotony of a treeless landscape with a galvanized iron house fastened down to it here and there," she came to the conclusion "that the ways of civilisation did not suit this place, and that being used to civilisation did not fit one for Patagonia ..."

Will had hoped to have longer to settle Mary and Billy in suitable accommodation, but the extended voyage had put paid to that. On 5 December he was contracted to start work at Killik Aike, the estancia — or ranch — owned by Herbert Felton who'd employed him earlier that year.

Mary stayed at a boarding house in the town, struggling to make herself understood with her few words of Spanish. When she learned that the English governess employed by the Felton family had left, she sent a letter proposing herself for the position. Six weeks later, to her delight, she was on her way. "Everybody whom I have seen," she wrote to Will, "seems to think that for us to go to Feltons' is like going to Heaven. They talk about them having 'everything' in almost a tone of awe ..."

*

The Gilmores were given a little cottage outside the garden of the main homestead. On my own later visit to Estancia Killik Aike I found it: a neat two-storey gingerbread house, with walls clad in painted corrugated iron, two bay windows and a red roof shaded by a giant pine tree. It smelled musty. On the mantelpiece were a few cloth-bound editions of Charles Dickens. Once there had been a complete set. Argentine soldiers, billeted in the cottage during the 1982 Falklands-Malvinas war, burned the others for fuel.

The narrow bathroom, though a luxury for mere employees, was cold and dismal. The wind whistled through a wide crack in the door. I tried to picture Mary Gilmore lying naked in the claw-footed bath, but doubted there'd ever been much languishing. Bathing would have been a hasty, unpleasant business, especially in winter. Mary described how she kept a barrel of water outside the cottage door. In winter it burst, leaving a block of ice.

Beyond was the Big House, built by Herbert Felton in 1893. Many

sitting areas, glass-protected, with chintz-covered chairs, looked out to a
garden of lilac hedges and herbaceous borders, sheltered by windbreaks.
Felton memorabilia still cluttered the cellars: an Edwardian cane lounge
with a folding leather hood, a Wimbledon croquet set, butterfly nets,
fishing rods, saddles and sheepskins and a matched set of cabin trunks
suitable for the Grand Tour. I studied a fading sepia portrait of the Felton
family, the original owners of Killik Aike. In evening dress Herbert Stanley
Felton, the *estanciero*, looked more like a Yorkshire mill-owner, portly and
bewhiskered, peering down his long nose with the complacency of a
self-made man. His wife Emma, in ruched brocade, her dark hair gathered
in a curly top-knot, was elegant, fine-featured, even beautiful. But the
lumpish blonde daughter Emily — usually known as Millie — took after
her father, a bovine sullenness undisguised by elaborate frills. (Perhaps I
had become party to Mary's prejudice concerning her pupil.) Another
man, Millie's husband, had a calculating look and an etiolated waxed
moustache. A child, little Carlos Felton, with his golden curls and
winsome smile, basked in the certainty of being forever adored, forever
indulged.

A worn green volume, the *Killik Aike Wages Book 1896–1902* included
the accounts for W. Gilmore in spidery copperplate. His debits from the
estancia store were modest — matches, tobacco and candles — until
Mary's arrival produced a flurry of purchases: potatoes, onions and beans,
tins of butter, jam and milk, bags of sugar, salt and flour, a packet of tea
and a bottle of Currie. But his wages record indicated a sturdy worker who
put in long hours.

*

The Australian shearers scorned the Spanish tied system, where the sheep's
legs were first trussed by rouseabouts. Tom Hicks-Hall, one of the first
Cosme men to shear in Patagonia, wrote: "There was quite a gape of
wonder and astonishment when I calmly untied my first sheep as a
preliminary to shearing it, and I was conscious of many inquisitive eyes."
According to Mary, never given to understatement, her husband was soon
"said to be the best shearer in Patagonia".

Mary began teaching her pupil, Millie Felton, whom she described as
"the most awful girl that ever lived".

> She was 16; looked 18, and called herself 14. She knew everything ever known,
> and what I told her one day, told me back in a day or two as entirely her own.
> Among the items of her own peculiar knowledge was that "she knew the

woman who made all the lace for Queen Victoria's wedding". Her mother was a nice woman, her father a big man with a thin nose, a high voice, and a character and reputation to match …

But though Mary didn't care for her pupil or her employer, she was content. Her husband and son were with her, and she'd begun to make friends.

There was Stephens, the cook at the men's quarters, who drank hard but baked good bread and kept his kitchen clean. He lent Mary books, "in a land where there were but few … In return I gave him a copy of the *Decameron* that had been given me by a friend who had not wished it to fall into the hands of certain lads he knew, yet being a book lover dared not burn".

Another of the English employees who'd known finer things was Harry Marsdon. He was alarmed by Mary's interest in collecting Spanish oaths. "Look here, little girl," he told her, "you leave this question of swearing alone. You're too fond of investigating and studying and looking for experience. You're an experience for us just as you are and we like it. We don't want you to do the things that we do or to know the things we know … These swine down here don't understand you, they don't know your kind." She had to understand that women were the slaves of circumstances.

"In my country," I said, "they are the slaves of men."

"Yes?" His tone was of polite interest. Harry was always polite. He took that from his English bringing-up.

"Yes," I said stoutly, "but they're working to get the vote and then they will be *free!* "

"Yes, but will that make any difference?"

I laughed. "*Olé,* as for that I don't know. I doubt it myself."

There was "that old sinner" Bristol Tom, an ancient British ruin who cadged his way around the various estancias and wore rags that only his dirt held together. "Thirty seven years I bin tryin' to get away from this b——y country but they won't let me go!" he'd tell her. On his visits she'd open the door to clear the air. "Bristol wasn't partial to any kind of water except that known as 'strong'."

One friend was a young *peón,* a lowly odd-job boy called Jesús María. The Gilmores' protestant notions found "Jesús" objectionable; they called him José instead. By day he chopped wood, broke up coal and carted it indoors, sifted cinders, filled lamps, cleaned knives and polished boots. By night he slept in the cookhouse.

José had come from Buenos Aires in search of work and had never experienced a Patagonian winter. In May snow began to fall and the ground was icy. Even in the heated schoolroom, Mary's breath formed frost flowers on the window. She suffered despite her lambskin petticoat and wool-lined clogs laced high up the leg. "Even then I felt the frozen earth under my feet." While other station hands donned snow boots, fox-skin gloves and storm-collared ponchos, José shivered in dungarees.

Mary noticed the boy's hands were "like mutton hams from chaps and chillblains". She asked why he hadn't brought warm clothes, purchased some from the estancia store, or had them advanced against his wages.

"I had no money, Señora," he replied, "and the *patrón*, the master, would not let me have any."

"The brute!" I said under my breath. "You wait and I will get Don Guillermo, my husband, to see about it." I added to the boy, "In the meantime, let me do something for your hands."

She bathed them and prepared an unguent of honey, fat, white of egg and eucalyptus. She gave him a pot of the mixture to apply every night. Some days later she saw José again, beaming, proud of the warm clothing Will had obtained for him. His hands were healing, but he'd finished the ointment. Mary made more and offered it to him next time he walked by her cottage.

They were observed by Herbert Felton. "*El patrón* came past, eyeing us out of the corner of his eye and whistling as he went ... He went round to the store, waited half a minute then sent the book keeper to tell José he was wanted. José went at once."

An hour later Will came home, shaking with rage. "José's got the sack." Wesley, the foreman, had ordered him off the property.

Will believed that Felton had insisted on it from spite, resenting a mere *peón* talking to a white woman. José had done his work well so there could be no complaint on that score. He was well liked and the men had made up a subscription of £3 but "that won't last him long".

In the morning the boy's departing tracks were erased by a fresh fall of snow. Mary watched the flakes come down with a deepening sense of gloom and hatred for the place, despairing that Will could not break his contract.

At 11 o'clock Will returned for breakfast, but admitted his mind was plagued too: "I can't do anything for thinking of him." He drank his coffee hastily, deciding, "I will go after him."

> My heart stopped. Yet what could I do? I put my arms round him and kissed him, of all men the most *lovable* and the most to be revered. He would do his duty though we were all, husband, wife and child, turned out for it.
>
> I brought him his snow boots and a storm coat. He took an iron shod stick and started out ...
>
> As for me I could do nothing but look out the window and dream of despair, and even Billy's chatter could not rouse me. The fire burned out, the room grew colder and colder, ice thickened on the window panes, the sun passed behind the hills ... but my heart seemed darker and colder than anything inside or outside the room ...

It seemed a very long time before Will returned. She rubbed his hands and removed his boots before letting him speak. She knew the great fact, and other things could wait.

> At last I said "You found him —"
> "Yes," replied Will softly, "I found him." Then he added, "His troubles are over."
> "I thought so," I responded in the same tone.
> I think I cried all night. Will slept from sheer exhaustion.

The following morning Wesley, the foreman, complained that since the Australian had been on the property he'd had nothing but insolence and insubordination. Then he went up to the Feltons' house and got drunk. Later, he seemed subdued, even abject, when he met Gilmore. Mary believed "he feared what the authorities might say if they got to know of things, and he knew we would not be afraid to speak".

Hasty arrangements were made for José's burial. Stephens the cook was ordered "to take two men and dig a grave beyond the woolshed and say nothing about the occurrence".

*

Mary's unpublished story, "We Called Him José", was, I believe, essentially true. She made no attempt to fictionalise the names of the key characters — they're all in the wages book — and in references to Herbert Felton in her correspondence, her contempt never wavered.

I can find nothing but the events surrounding the boy's death to explain her next move. The Gilmore family had a comfortable cottage at Killik

Aike, Will was contracted until the next spring and Mary had her governessing work, albeit with a disagreeable pupil.

But on 12 August 1901, still deep in the Patagonian winter, she and young Billy moved to Río Gallegos. The wages book indicates Will resumed board that day at the single men's quarters. Did Mary walk or was she pushed? Did she have words with Felton about José's death? Probably she would not have jeopardised Will's job, the income they needed for their passages. But her dislike of the owner must have been palpable, matched by his uneasiness in her presence. Perhaps he informed her, with all the usual expressions of perfunctory regret, that the cottage was no longer available, making her continued stay on the estancia untenable.

Whatever the cause, it wasn't marital discord. As soon as she arrived in town she began her loving, lonely, almost daily letters to her husband. She had no job prospects but lodged at the Hotel Inglés. The wife of the English manager agreed she could stay in exchange for work at the hotel, sewing and minding her children.

Mary visited the deputy governor, who advised her to give English lessons to adults, despite her protests that she could not speak Spanish. "Oh, but you are such a good English scholar," he told her, "you should do well at it." Her first pupil was Don Vicente Cane, local manager of the Bank of Argentina. He brought others and the deputy governor sent more. "The first month of teaching was dreadful. I felt such a fraud, for I hadn't the use of twenty words of the language, though with dictionary I could read fairly well. As the lesson hour came round my knees used to shake with apprehension lest Don Vicente wouldn't come, and my stomach grow sick in dread of the lesson should he come. Whichever way it was awful."

Her Spanish soon improved and she had as many pupils as she could manage. Best of all, "the teaching I am doing now does not take nearly as much out of me as teaching Miss Felton".

By early September she was able to rent a two-roomed house of her own, near an English couple, the Lanes. Soon these kindly people were reading *The Workingman's Paradise* by their namesake. "If you were to come in now," Mary wrote to Will, "you would come to the most comfortable home we have ever had. If it were not for the money aspect I should feel in Heaven."

But she was alert for any chance for him to leave Felton's employment. When she heard of one, she wrote immediately: "Can you shear with a machine? And can you instruct others?" The local doctor had told her Estancia Condor, 80 kilometres to the south, was "putting up big works for machine shearing and will want a Capataz … I should say that even if you had not worked a machine you know all about it and could say you were out of practice to get a day or two to get your hand in."

Will got the job — on the basis of living at the single men's quarters. He finished up at Killik Aike on 16 October 1901, collecting his wages of £9 13s 0$^1/_2$.

Mary wrote to Will that she'd been told "of the awful roughness of living down at Condor. So I am sending a couple of old forks which will be no loss if lost … I am very pleased to hear that you have started the machines and made a satisfactory trial of them".

She felt she'd been tense during his visit between estancias and wanted to make it up to him: "Indeed, I have often thought that my irritability was enough to make you care less and less for me, and I have loved you for your patience and gentleness and felt over and over again how much I wanted to tell you so, only we can write so much more easily than we can speak …"

There was reason for her stress. On the day Will left Killik Aike a long-smouldering dispute between Argentina and Chile erupted again, this time over the border along the Straits of Magellan. Soldiers drilled daily at the back and front of her house, beginning at 2 am. Carrier pigeons were put into training. Chilenos were arrested in the streets. Rumours abounded.

In November she wrote to Will that an Argentine man o' war was anchored in the river and the military doctor feared war. "It will be a serious matter for all the English, as there is no British Consul here and consequently no safety. No woman will be safe and all the men whom they can lay hands on will be forced to bear arms. I earnestly hope it will come to nothing." She was hardly consoled by the assurances of the English bank officials, who promised to defend British women with everything they had. They had been issued with two bullets: one to save a lady from a fate worse than death, the other to use on themselves.

Mary slept with an axe, two or three carving knives and a whistle under her pillow, recalling later how her pupils impressed upon her never to open her door at night.

She was desperately lonely. "It is terrible to be always alone — and sick," she wrote to Will in mid-December. "Not a friend to turn to to say 'Send someone to stay with me' or 'Let me stay with you'. No one but a child to speak to all day and all night — except as regards lessons. It is no wonder I grow low spirited and depressed. And I am not strong enough to keep from writing letters that I know will make you miserable."

Mary had suffered chronic diarrhoea with rarely a break since she'd left Paraguay sixteen months before. At last a military doctor diagnosed amoebic dysentery.

Another constant enemy was the brutal wind, which put her in a mood "either to swear or cry". It was worse for women, whose skirts almost sent them into flight.

> Half the lessons I gave at my own house, the rest at the houses of pupils, and many and many a day the wind blew my little boy off his feet as we hurried along to a lesson, or dashed me against a telegraph post or a fence. The wind is incessant. Except in the dead of winter when all is frozen it never ceases. I have been half an hour going 100 yards, and holding on to fences all the way, and I have seen men — who wear no skirts — have to put their hands to the ground to maintain their balance.

Although the threat of war receded with the arrival of an arbitration commission, she wanted to leave on the first available boat. "I wish we were away."

Just before Christmas, Mary narrowly avoided Herbert Stanley Felton in town. "I was so glad to have missed him." She wouldn't have been one of Felton's favourite people. Some months before, the authorities had harassed Wesley, his foreman, with enquiries about the death of an obscure *peón*. "They say 'a bird in the air will carry a thing'," Mary wrote enigmatically, "and one could almost believe a bird had done it, only that no bird's voice broke the frozen stillness of the pampa. Yet the fact of José's death leaked out and got to town somehow." An official demanded to know why the death on the estancia had not been notified, why a burial had been performed without authority.

Mary must have been considered a prime suspect as the informant.

The outcome was an inconvenience for the *estanciero*. The foreman raged. Two men had to take picks and crowbars and, at the back of Killik Aike's woolshed, exhume a small frozen body for the coroner. Bullocks were yoked up, and the dead body wrapped and put on a *carreta*. Also some wine as a handy bribe. The team had to make the long journey, travelling far up where the river narrowed to cross on the ice. Two bullocks slipped and broke legs. The driver got drunk. It took a week to get into town. Mary concluded:

And when they got in the coronial enquiry was only a matter of form to enable the official to draw his fee. His interest in the cause of José's death was nothing, and his liking for Wesley's wine much. Besides, what did a *peón* more or less matter, there were plenty more. So the little stiff body of the lad was taken out and by the aid of more picks and crowbars deposited under a foot of earth, where he made things decidedly unpleasant in the summer, poor little wayfarer from a warmer clime …

And such was the passing of José — and such also is life in Patagonia when the man in possession rules.

The Mary Gilmore who emerged from Patagonia was strong and feisty, observant and humane. She was ready to gather together her powers as a writer. It was time to go home.

Mary and Will took a boat from Río Gallegos in early January 1902. Their voyage to England, travelling third class, was horrendous because of an outbreak of influenza and whooping cough. The family all went down, Billy's case worsening to pneumonia. Mary, ill herself, tried to nurse her husband and son, and was near collapse as their ship berthed at Liverpool in drizzling rain. A message arrived from Henry Lawson and his wife Bertha, inviting them to stay in London. "Bed's made and cot's ready for the little fellow," Henry wrote. "Come at once, am simply mad for the sight of an Australian face."

*

John Lane had reached London a few months earlier, in August 1901. "The village to us is better than the city," he wrote for the *British Socialist News*, "the cottage than the mansion … We would rather our children play with orange blossoms than lead soldiers." During a month in England he signed up seven new recruits for Cosme, including a future son-in-law, Harold Wallis, a studious Quaker from Yorkshire who later married his daughter Ettie.

Lane travelled on to the new Commonwealth of Australia which now had sixteen Labor members in its Federal Parliament. He had arrived at the wrong time, the end of a devastating drought, purveying unfashionable wares. He offered the prospect of formidable challenges in a difficult place, when people only wanted to improve their present lives. As Souter has said, "the tide of practical politics had overwhelmed almost all support for Utopianism".

Doughty, resilient, never one to be easily deterred, John Lane bought a bicycle for £7 in Adelaide, and on this he set off into the outback. He had a special water-tank made, fitted to the front part of the bike, and he wore a woollen pullover on the proposition that, drenched with his sweat, it would keep him cool. At the height of summer he pedalled over 1,000 kilometres through the desert to Broken Hill, White Cliffs and Bourke, then another 650 kilometres to Glen Innes in northern New South Wales.

His son Eric told me: "Dad had a lovely set of letters about the trip which Mother destroyed. But he told some fantastic stories. The emus cottoned onto the shine from his handlebars. He would start riding at half past four in the morning and the emus, hundreds of them, would follow him right through until the afternoon. When bindi-eyes ripped the tube of a tyre, he stuffed it with grass. Sometimes he'd come across bicycle tracks in the desert and realise they were his own and he had gone full circle. The drought was terrible. There were carcasses everywhere. When he stopped at a waterhole he would have to skim away the bodies of hundreds of dead rabbits before he could get some water to boil."

Lane somehow juggled along with him a collection of Paraguayan butterflies, a magic lantern and slides of Cosme. He invited the people of the outback to join a socialist village in a green and tropical land. The men and women who listened to him in the little bush halls and Mechanics Institutes had already read in the Australian press that the socialism was a failure, the village a dump and the land mostly swamp.

Eric Lane said that his father called at one little hut, way out on a flat plain, where a woman battled on alone with a number of children while her husband was away working. "He said she was just like Henry Lawson's 'Drover's Wife'. She had been out there in the drought in this tiny vacant place month after month without her husband. So he gave the collection of South American butterflies to the little kids. He always had a soft heart."

The task was a near-hopeless one, but Lane pressed on. His epic bicycle journey is described in *A Peculiar People*, and receives honourable mention in a history of the bicycle in the Australian bush.

Between April and September 1902 he rode through the flat sheep plains of central and western Queensland, the womb of the great shearers' strike and the Utopian dream. But there was no chance of another conception. In the little towns of Clermont, Barcaldine, Longreach and Winton, the bush workers and their families listened to him, heard him out in Hughenden, Richmond and Charleville, but few signed up.

He concluded that the old unionism of the bush had gone, replaced by a new imperialism and a desire to shelter under the British flag. "The Socialistic idea has become much less prevalent. In fact it is only occasionally in these parts you drop across a socialist ... I now realize how very different things are here to what they were in the early nineties."

He had pedalled thousands of kilometres. But at the end of it all, just eighteen men, women and children made the trip to Paraguay and all of them left within two years.

John Lane arrived back at Cosme on 2 December 1902.

He found a colony in rapid decline, with a departure almost every month. And it was having its own flirtation with imperialism. The new British recruits were skewing the old radical allegiances. Events in the Boer War had been followed with avidity, and sympathies were not always, like John Lane's, with the Boer peasant farmers. There had been cheers at the Boer surrender and pride in an empire reasserting its dominance. Arthur Tozer saw this as a healthy development, whereas before, "Cosmeism tended to kill national sentiment which I now feel is not good for Britishers, especially if the white races are to be on top".

In June 1902 Cosme had thrown a party to celebrate the Coronation of Edward VII. The Union Jack was raised and Cosme children sang "Rule Britannia".

*

The Anglican Bishop of the Falkland Islands had decided his scattered diocese included Paraguay. Just before John Lane's return, Bishop E. F. Every had "turned an episcopal eye on Cosme" and determined there were British souls in need of saving. In November he visited and baptised three children, though later in the *South America Missionary Magazine* he deplored the way they "grow up practically heathen".

John Lane replied to the bishop in *Cosme Monthly Notes*:

> In Cosme there is no social evil, no drink evil, no extremes of wealth and poverty, no idle rich, no outcast poor. The children's ideas and lives are moulded by their surroundings which assist them in keeping their bodies in temperance, soberness and chastity; in not coveting nor desiring other men's goods, and in learning and labouring truly to get their own living. Moreover in this simple community the children wonder why in Christian England so many die of hunger while there is plenty of food in the country; why so many are poor and overworked while others are rich and idle ... In their simple heathen way our children regard as evil-doers those who live in luxury while their fellow creatures are starving. They would even look upon a Bishop as

wicked who rode in a carriage while tired women tramped the side walk.

If these unorthodox views are carried out in practice as the Cosme children grow up, then the little heathens are perhaps not so far from the Kingdom of Heaven as Bishop Every fears.

Nine colony children were suddenly left motherless when Mrs Margaret McLeod died at the beginning of 1903. The father, Allan, by then blind in one eye and no longer with a violin to play, kept the elder children. The five young ones were cared for among the colony people. Young Rod McLeod spent most of his time with the Wood family, accepted as another brother by Norman and Wallace.

As Tozer expected, colonists continued to depart: "Many of those in the colony are there only because they have large families and fear starting afresh in the outside world ... As time goes on Cosme will find it more and more difficult to keep new members because the old hands are getting narrower and narrower in their ideas and newcomers won't stand it."

To earn their passages to Buenos Aires, many of the refugees were employed by Tozer at the Sapucai workshops. He considered them human wrecks: "The women are old before their time and their complexions are yellow and wrinkled. The men one by one get sick and some who a few years ago were fine strapping fellows are now fever racked, weak and low spirited." One of them called Sapucai "a sort of convalescent home for those who are recovering from the fever of Cosmeism". But Tozer was dismissive with people who were not friends from the old days. Jack Taylor approached him about a job, deferentially taking off his hat. "Tozer looked up at me and said in a very cold way, 'It is not usual for a visitor to this office to remove his headgear.' "

Tozer was fretful, uncertain whether to emigrate to Australia or Africa, and he had a new dependant. In February Amy, still in poor health, had given birth to a son, promptly named Harry. "So far have had no reason to regret his birth," he wrote to the baby's namesake. "He is not being pampered nor stupidly trained and he practically lives in the open air. He is certainly a blessing to Amy and adds to her happiness in a way I cannot explain nor yet understand." He added with some relish: "Cosme is still in existence although, if people who have recently left there are to be believed, it cannot last much longer."

In despair John Lane watched the colony disintegrate. The loss of experienced people, including pioneers such as Charles Leck, could in no way be balanced by the few new arrivals, even though one was a Lane. This was John's younger brother Ernest who, according to Souter, had visited William and Anne Lane in New Zealand on his way to Cosme and been told, "See you back soon."

New recruits rarely stayed long, but Ernest Kell, a young man with an accountancy background who came from England in May 1903, was to end his life in Paraguay. Ernie Lane described Kell, a gentle vegetarian, as "most unselfish but not a fighter".

Fighting was needed apparently, for in Ernie Lane's opinion Cosme had divided into two camps, and the "opposing party — cooperators, non-Communistic" was led by David Russell Stevenson, "a brainy, unscrupulous individual, with a couple of avowed adherents". (It would not have made the Lane men any fonder of Stevenson to have heard that, during John's absence in Australia, he had been out riding with Jenny Lane and had "got fresh", to the extent, she told a friend, that she "had to use the whip on him".)

At the annual general meeting in 1904 Ernie Lane wrote that Stevenson "had the audacity to state that Cosme wasn't and never had been Communistic ... In the past years, S. would never dare to have said such things, but now he feels his majority and shows the cloven hoof. If John and all of us were to have fought we could have squashed him — but to what purpose? If members here want the S. type of Communism, let them have it. There isn't room for the two parties here."

The heart had gone out of Cosme as a socialist colony and John Lane had lost the will to hold it together and any optimism about its future. "I myself considered that Cosme's only chance of keeping white was to grow," he wrote later. "If it failed to grow it must ultimately become Paraguayan. I could not take that risk for my children, so I decided to return to Australia."

In May 1904 — the same month that the community hall and its piano were destroyed by fire — he resigned as chairman and in November he and Ernie, with their families, departed. John worked his way back to Australia on a cattle boat and obtained work as a teacher in Brisbane to raise the fares for his family waiting in Buenos Aires.

For the first time since the inception of the movement twelve years before, there was not a Lane connected with it. The movement barely existed, and the most powerful personality on the colony was Dave Stevenson.

*

Ernest Kell was not a powerful personality. One hundred years later he would have been described as a Sensitive New Age Guy. He lived in a little hut at the edge of the *monte* and demonstrated a talent for gardening.

Julie and I surveyed a patch of brambles at Cosme while Norman Wood and Rod McLeod recalled how it had once been set out in neat beds, the beans properly strung up, the corn flourishing, under Kell's tender care.

"He had two kerosene tins on a yoke over his shoulders, and he would go down to the bottom of the hill to get water from a well. You'd see him struggling up, then watering the rows, backwards and forwards."

But this was only part-time work for Kell, who had been appointed the schoolteacher. The children did not make it easy for him. "I don't think we respected him very much," said Don Norman. "We thought he was queer because he was a vegetarian and he did not like people to shoot birds with a shanghai. He wouldn't wear leather boots because they came from cow-hide."

"He said we should brush the mosquitoes instead of hitting them," laughed Rod McLeod.

With sardonic amusement Don Norman recalled the time that Mr Kell, crossing his legs, accidentally trapped a grasshopper.

" 'You brute! You've gone and killed it,' I said.

Mr Kell looked as if the end of the world had come. Then he shouted, 'No I haven't! See, I haven't!' Tenderly, beaming with relief, he dusted off the grasshopper and sent it on its way."

They remembered that for his teaching Kell relied on a little book called *Beecham's Help for Scholars*. "You could find almost anything in that. Avoirdupois, troy weight and all that sort of thing."

Bishop Every of the Falkland Islands made another visit to check on the errant children of Cosme.

"He didn't like the way we spoke," said Don Norman. "He said it was not proper English, more the London cockney way of speaking. And he didn't like our Australian sayings like 'tucker' and 'knock-off'."

"He didn't like 'I ain't'," chuckled Rod McLeod.

"No, he didn't like 'I ain't'."

Bishop Every took action and sent up an English schoolteacher from Buenos Aires named Arthur Groves. According to Bill Wood he was a Cambridge-educated man. "The bishop had seen the necessity of getting a real teacher for the colony kids. But Groves had a defect by not having a palate so it was difficult to understand what he was saying."

Another defect in his opinion was that Groves insisted on following the same syllabus he had taught in England. "We got to know all the names of the shires or counties in England, their capitals and what rivers they were on."

"He gave me a map of England," said Don Norman, "with a slide-rule to measure how far each town was from London. We had to uphold the Empire in those days, we were very proud of seeing those maps all painted red where the Empire was. I knew the capitals of each English county by heart, and the rivers on which they were built. I can still tell you ... Winchester on the Itchen, that's Hampshire I think, and Bodmin on the Camel, that's Cornwall."

A little testy, Bill Wood said it was not much to extract from all those years. "Groves might have been a good teacher, but it was not exactly what we needed to learn. All this rubbish about English counties was a waste of time for us. I found my main benefit from his teaching was learning how to spell. He put in a lot of time on spelling."

Don Norman thought Groves improved their Spanish too — "we learned about irregular verbs" — and he taught them a little Paraguayan history:

The War of the Triple Alliance and so on, but it was not popular with him. He wanted to teach us about English history. We studied from the beginning, about the Roman conquest of England, 55 BC and then about the Danes and the Saxons and the reign of King Alfred and then came William the Conqueror in 1066. There was William Rufus in 1087 and some other one? Well, there were about four or five of them, I think, from the Norman line and it ended with Stephen. That was the history of England. Then there was the discovery of America. But we didn't learn about the American War of Independence — it was not properly English.

But it was always difficult, he said, understanding what Groves was saying because of his cleft palate, though they got used to him in the end. "But I think he was a knowledgeable man. He used to write stories and essays himself, and he used to collect stamps."

Bill Wood said Groves was his last teacher "because I had to start working for my living".

A man whose great natural intelligence was obvious, he looked away, fighting emotions, then burst out: "I suppose by learning how to read and write and spell and a bit about world geography we were about the same category of education as the boys around the district. If one wanted a secondary education, you had to be sent down to Asunción and that was impossible for us. So, if I start lamenting a college education, that would be a waste of time. We were lucky to be able to get enough to eat and live the primitive life that the natives were living."

"Our kids have done well," said Don Norman comfortably, proud of his son Rodrigo, manager of a private bank.

"Some of the younger generation have big jobs these days," Bill Wood agreed, "but one of them said to me, 'It seems strange that we have forged ahead so wonderfully and you oldsters have remained glued down to the same standard you were on Cosme'. I told him he was totally wrong. 'Nearly all of you finished secondary education because we oldsters realised that with education you could get a better start in life. We oldsters, you must remember, paid for that education for you.' "

*

The two octegenarians climbed through a fence and gallantly held the wires apart for us.

"Cosme cemetery," said Don Norman softly.

The graves were overgrown, hummocks of soil marked by nondescript wooden crosses. The red earth mound of William and Lillian Wood was wide and comfortable, like a big double bed.

"When Mum was buried beside Dad," said Don Norman, "Wallace had a prayer book and read the service and Rod here was alongside him, the only other one who understood English."

"We did it properly," said Rod McLeod. "The only thing Wallace said was that we needed the thing in Spanish because all the people who come around now don't understand English."

"These days they're burying the native people here too," said Don Norman. We left him standing quietly by his parents' grave and followed Rod McLeod through the brambles.

Rod explained that his own mother was buried down on the Flat, but there were a lot of McLeods here. He pointed to the last resting place of his father Allan — "I had a large stone on his grave but someone stole it to sharpen knives" — and to the unmarked graves of his brother Eddie, and the other Cosme McLeods who were unrelated, Colin, the father of the schoolteacher Sylvia, his brother Monty, and Rod, the grandfather, who came on the *Royal Tar*.

"Here," he continued uncertainly, "is Mrs Bethune, then there's Mrs Minnie Jacks. She went strange in the head and died in the *monte*. They found her because of the vultures circling."

"Over there is Mr Collins," said Don Norman. "Remember, he was killed by the *bandido*." It was Gaspar Flore, a famous bandit, who killed him, Rod McLeod told us. "He had been killing people round about. He did it just for sport. Now, over there's Bessie Titilah and some other Titilahs."

"And before too long," said Don Norman, "old George will be here. And you too, Rod, and Wallace."

"You might turn up here if you get your way."

"I might. But I doubt it. My missus won't let me."

*

We heard high-pitched squealing from near the Wood homestead as we returned to the village. Francisco was killing a young pig in honour of our last night at Cosme. The children, pushing dogs away underfoot, carried a bowl of blood to Sylvia for making black pudding. As the butchering proceeded they took other tributes: offal, intestines, trotters.

Don Wallace had been ordered back to bed by a Paraguayan doctor who was still there, sipping *mate tereré* on the front veranda, blood spatters on his shirt from a previous house call delivering a baby. He told Don Norman that Wallace's condition was serious, a bad heart condition and fluid on the lungs. It was agreed that back in Asunción a phone call would be made to Peter, Francisco's brother in Griffith, Australia, who returned nearly every year to see his parents. On his last visit he had installed a septic toilet and a shower in the old farmhouse.

Julie and I, embarrassed to be there at such a difficult time, went to the kitchen to help with preparations for the *asado*.

Wallace's wife, Doña María Albina Cáceres de Wood, a tiny woman with a deeply seamed face and the high cheekbones of the Guaraní people, aged seventy-three, was peeling mandioca with intense concentration. We begged her to let us help Sylvia with the cooking while she joined her husband. She answered, still shy with us, that he was sleeping quietly and the best thing for her was to keep occupied.

As we worked I asked Doña María if she would tell us something about her childhood. She laughed and said that it wouldn't be of interest. With a little more persuasion she began hesitantly, then with some eagerness, Sylvia translating from the Guaraní language in which María was most comfortable.

She was born in Santa Caterina, a village near Cosme. When she was twelve she became a boarder at a school in Asunción, where she learned about cooking, spinning, weaving and needlework.

"The sort of skills a woman should have," said Don Norman approvingly, coming into the kitchen and taking a straight-backed chair by the fireplace.

When María was fourteen there was a revolution in the country — the revolution of 1921–3, a bitter struggle, two factions of the Liberal Party fighting for supremacy. Soldiers burst into the school. The girls were locked in the storeroom and told to keep silent. They could hear angry voices, furniture thrown about, the school ransacked. They were very frightened — they'd heard terrible stories about what soldiers did to young girls — but fortunately they were not discovered. After that she returned home and taught needlework for a while, then she met Wallace Wood. And that, apparently, was that.

Through the doorway we could see Francisco, Rodrigo and a darker-skinned Paraguayan raking the coals in the *asado* pit, arranging saplings for the meat. I asked who the other man was.

"That's Chilito," said Don Norman, "María's son ... Not by Wallace though." He paused. "Why don't you ask her about him? She may be prepared to tell you."

This was more difficult. Doña María laughed, looked embarrassed, spoke rapidly to Don Norman in Guaraní. He said at last that she did not mind if *he* told the story.

When Doña María returned from school in Asunción, he said, she had married a Paraguayan who turned out to be a brutish fellow and an alcoholic. She had Chilito by him, then the husband went off to fight in the Chaco War. While he was away she found employment as a domestic servant.

Then she met Wallace Wood and began a relationship with him which resulted in the birth of a baby girl, Dora. The cuckolded husband returned from the war to discover this situation and did not like it one little bit. He hired a man to murder Wallace. When the assassin arrived to do the job, Wallace managed to talk him out of it and the man slunk away.

The whole thing was brought to a satisfactory conclusion, in Don Norman's opinion, when the brutish husband, who had obviously made a bad fist of things altogether, staggered home drunk one night, fell into the Pirapó river and drowned.

Doña María ladled chunks of mandioca from the big pot on the fuel stove and was not going to comment.

Don Norman said it was time for a tot of whisky and headed out to join the men.

*

There are moments that you consciously engrave on your memory, take a mental snapshot of to hold for the rest of your life. Sitting around the glowing charcoal pit beside the old Wood farmhouse at Cosme was one of them for me. The place seemed imbued with the spirit of those who had been there a hundred years before, who planted the blue gums, and sat as we were, around the fire of an evening.

Birds swooped in to nest in the branches of the white cedars, fireflies sparked in the shadows, a silvery bullock cropped just beyond the fence, its neck-bell clunking. A horseman rode past, disappearing among the trees.

"He's not afraid of the little white boy, going into the *monte* at this time," said Don Norman.

He refilled our glasses of whisky, a dispensation, we realised, not normally accorded the womenfolk. Julie and I made a final attempt on our huge plates of barbecued pork, grateful for the generosity but starting to dream a little of parsley, of salads. We whispered a quiet toast to the memory of Ernie Kell, the Cosme vegetarian.

Word of the *asado* had spread. As well as the Wood family, Rod McLeod and old George Titilah were there, and Chilito and his wife and children, and all of us were now replete.

Don Norman was in a gentle, abstracted mood, conscious of his brother fighting for his life inside the house, aware that we were leaving in the morning and he might never see him or Cosme again. But his old colony friends were around him and our persistent questioning had reopened the storehouse of childhood memories. The talk turned with nostalgia to an Australia they had never known.

"What I don't understand, what has always puzzled me," said Sylvia, grand-daughter of a *Royal Tar* pioneer, "is why so many people left such a rich country to come to a place like this."

"It was to do with the shearers," said Don Norman. "There was a sort of revolution in Australia. The blackmiths were making pikes for the men to use as bayonets, so it seems there was a lot of trouble at one time in Australia. They were dissatisfied with the system there altogether and the government was using soldiers to put them down and so on. So they decided to have a try with William Lane in some other place." He chuckled darkly. "But if they were afraid of revolutions, they made a mistake in coming here!"

Rod McLeod doubled up, wheezing laughter turning to coughing.

"I could sing an Australian song if you like," Don Norman offered, and began:

There was a wild colonial boy,
Jack Dowling was his name,
Of poor but honest parents
He was born ...
Where *was* he born?
I don't remember ...

He said that instead he would sing another one that he knew well. He had heard it first in the Argentine, at the estancia of an old friend, Finch, who was an Australian. "He had the record and he played it, and it was very nice. I liked all the *simpático* Australian words, the billabong, the jumbuck and the swagman ..."

He was pulled up by Sylvia and asked to explain.

The jumbuck, Don Norman said authoritatively, was a wether, "what we call a *capón*. And the swagman was the man who went outback shearing sheep. He would hoist up his swag by the strap and say 'Come on Matilda', because it was the only woman he had."

He began singing:

Once a jolly swagman camped by a billabong,
Under the shade of a coolibah tree,
And he sang as he sat and waited till his billy boiled,
"You'll go a waltzing Matilda with me ..."

And Don Norman continued to the very end, at each chorus joined in harmony by his son Rodrigo, who gave the old song an up-tempo Latin rhythm.

*

Back in Asunción, a Paraguayan journalist interviewed me about the nineteenth-century Australian socialists and their descendants, who "speak English with an archaic accent". He described my visit to the country as "a voyage across history and time". His article, published in the newspaper *ABC Color*, observed:

The political history of Australia has always been characterised by its prefer-ence for evolution rather than revolution. The nearest the Australians ever got to social disorder was a clash between 10,000 unarmed shearers and 3000 heavily armed agents of law and order. This resulted in some bloodshed, but not enough to flow to the river. Rather it crossed the ocean.

The epoch was the 1890s decade. The world was suffering from an economic depression — one of the periods of adjustment which are followed by renewed growth and expansion. But the shearers had lost their faith in capitalism and placed their hope in utopian socialism.

Led by an articulate English journalist, William Lane, they decided to leave Australia. They went to another country where their beliefs could be implemented without government interference. They chose Paraguay ...

When the article was published on 30 May 1982, Bill Wood, pleased with the attention, sat down and laboriously wrote me a translation from the Spanish.

The journalist, Ricardo Caballero, said the paper had received numerous calls from readers wanting to know if the Australian settlement in Paraguay had actually happened, "or whether we were just inventing it as a sort of Capotesque non-fiction reportage".

What Paraguayan readers found most bizarre was the choice of their country for its lack of "government interference".

ABC Color was the only newspaper which regularly dared to criticise the Stroessner regime. In March 1984 fifty soldiers with machine-guns enforced the order to close it down and its editor was thrown into gaol.

PART TWO

PART TWO

16
Coming of Age

We thought to find the Happy Land,
A blissful land all fair and free,
On that far-off delightful strand
Where blooms the golden-fruited tree.
But late we found, alack! alack!
The Golden Age comes no more back.
    Harry Taylor, "To a Disappointed Communist"

But now that we have made the land
A garden full of promise,
Old Greed must crook 'is dirty hand
An' come and take it from us.
    Henry Lawson, "Freedom on the Wallaby"

November 1989. It was the Day of the Dead in Asunción, *El Día de los Difuntos*. Hymn singing, full-throated and fervent, reverberated into the night from the little chapel over the road, the Capilla Santa Rosa de Lima. Florence Wood de White opened the shutters to let it flow into the house, into her thoughts. The maid was over there, she said, singing her heart out. On this day, loved ones who had gone crowded one's thoughts all day.

Now over at the chapel the priest was calling out names, followed by spirited applause from the congregation, a joyous affirmation of a life that had passed, a summoning to memory of everyone in the neighbourhood, everyone close to someone in the chapel, who had died.

The calling, remembering and clapping went on long into the night. It was mesmeric, insistent, demanding attention for the dead.

I recalled the Cosme people I'd met who had now gone: George Titilah, whom we'd given a shave and haircut, was the first. His death in 1983 was not unexpected. A few months before it, Wallace Wood had written to me from Cosme: "Yesterday Rod McLeod and I went up to see George who had fallen into the fire as he was trying to light a cigar ... It was not serious. We didn't stay long for one now needs a slate and pencil to converse with George."

The death of Alex Wood in the same year, at the age of eighty-six, was a shock, although he had been suffering for some time from suppurating ulcers on his legs. His brother Wallace, with a chronic heart condition, had been expected to go first, and succumbed in May 1985, aged eighty-four.

By a strange coincidence a friend of mine, the photographer Peter Solness, was in Paraguay and Don Norman had decided to accompany him to Cosme. They arrived just five hours after Wallace's death, in time to attend the funeral in the little Cosme cemetery. Peter sent me a postcard: "It was bizarre timing for Norman to arrive, he seemed to contain his loss rather well ... It was a still sunny afternoon and as a sweating Paraguayan rammed the damp red earth that covered Wallace, the passing of an epoch was starkly obvious. Rod McLeod is still well, he arrived at the funeral in a dapper pinstripe suit ... Cosme is beautiful but at the moment a little sad."

Don Guillermo — Bill Wood — was shaken by the deaths of his brothers, but kept to his regular routine. In his bungalow in Asunción he sat down every Sunday to write to his many family members and friends, and sometimes included me. "I have no doubt that in the photos you took of us we still look the same old 'sorry remnants', so don't go sending us dozens of them." Eulalia, the maid, was caring for him: "She no doubt considers me a necessary evil ... I go to have a look at my bees as soon as Eulalia comes to take over the kitchen in the morning. My main group of orchids growing in the front garden have just finished flaunting their beautiful flowers and another simple variety on the old orange tree are bursting from their sheaths."

Another time he wrote, "I note that your Dad proposes writing to me. As you remarked ... we differ on religion. I believe there must be some intelligence directing everything, but the thousands of cults and creeds have caused more bloodshed than anything else."

On the Queensland Gold Coast, my father kept bees, much to the irritation of his neighbours. He wrote to Don Guillermo recommending Maeterlinck's *Life of the Bee*, "in case you haven't read it", and said he knew the sheep districts where William Wood Sr had worked and was going to visit them again.

"I received a letter from your dad and found it very interesting," Don Guillermo reported. A letter from Norman had also just arrived, "but it was a poor effort". Norman had been back to the old colony: "He is a devoted Cosme-ite and declares he is going to ask in his will that his ashes be buried at Cosme."

Later, a more wavering hand informed, "Rod McLeod, whom you met on Cosme, has been with me for the last couple of weeks. He is trying to get a document entitling him to a pension and benefits. I enjoy having him here as we yarn together, mostly of old time Cosme memories, and have a couple of games of cribbage before midday and evening meals. I wouldn't mind if he stopped here permanently, but I suppose Cosme will pull him back."

In 1984 he wrote that he had celebrated his ninetieth birthday on 5 September with a pleasant party and "just enough people rolled up".

His letters stopped and then I received one which began: "My name is Florence White, and I am writing for my Dad, Bill Wood. I am No. 6 in the 'Wood tree' and have just arrived from Saint Louis, Missouri, USA, with Max, my husband, to live in Asunción ... Dad has been awfully sick and we thought he would leave us many times."

Florence had come home to Paraguay to nurse her father. After being bedridden for five months, Don Guillermo Wood died on 18 July 1985. Don Norman wrote to me: "Asunción is different with Bill away. He was not happy in the end. Couldn't hear. Wouldn't look at you and try to guess what you were saying." He added a quotation, "One by one crept silently to rest."

In 1989, three months before I travelled back to Paraguay, 88-year-old Rod McLeod, the last of the originals still living at the colony, died. "He was one of the Chaco War heroes and a childhood good friend of mine," wrote Don Norman. "He was our last sad link with Cosme." He was acutely aware that of the colony children, only he and his sister Rose, who lived in South Africa, were left.

I returned because I couldn't stay away. In February 1989 there had been a coup, the dictator Stroessner had been overthrown, and Paraguay was making its first tentative steps towards democracy. And Don Norman had written from the northern town of Concepción that he was turning ninety and I should visit, "because I'm not going to last forever. When you come it will be no trouble to give you a room and tucker ... My sister Rose who lives in Johannesburg will be coming for my birthday. No doubt she would be delighted to tell you about the sins of my youth ... I asked her to come and live with us but she prefers to stay over there. Plenty of trouble for those Africans in the future, I suppose. Too many black people being oppressed with no democracy and no rights. No vote."

I couldn't make the journey in time to be at Don Norman's birthday fiesta in July, but two months later was indeed offered a room and tucker in Asunción by Florence and Max White.

Vividly attractive in her early fifties, with the red hair and freckles of the Scots on her paternal grandfather's side, the emotionalism of the Irish on her grandmother's, and with a directness of manner which she identified as Australian, Florence was, above all, intensely Paraguayan. After her father's death, she had persuaded Max, who was ready to retire, to stay and make their home in Asunción.

Earlier in the day, like almost everyone else in the country on *El Día de los Difuntos*, we had gone to the cemetery. La Recoleta necropolis was crowded, a Roman carnival atmosphere, people with great armfuls of blooms moving between the stone sarcophagi, marble statuary and crucifixes, the pine trees and cypresses bordering the paths. In the English section we laid sheaves of flowers on the tombs of the Wood family and other Australian descendants. León Cadogan's slab had a simple inscription: *Tupá Kuchuvi Vevé*, dragonfly in Guaraní, the name the Indian people he worked with had given him.

Florence knelt by the graves of her sister Diana, her uncle Alexander, and wept for her nephew Donald, Rodrigo's son, killed just a few months before at the age of fourteen, an accident with a gun. She lingered, saying a prayer beside her parents, Mabel Wood *née* Apthorpe and William Wood. "Cosme's Loved Patriarch" was chiselled on the marble headstone.

We walked back along Avenida Mariscal López, past the bullet-pocked walls of the Presidential Escort Battalion's barracks where Alfredo Stroessner was suspected of hiding during the coup, and turned into a street where a lavish villa was under construction, commissioned by Chile's General Pinochet for his retirement.

When we reached the pretty whitewashed house at Calle Leandro Prieto, Florence's aunt, Rose Menmuir, had already arrived for lunch. An elegant woman with sculpted cheekbones and a floss of wavy white hair, clearly a beauty in her day, her eyes were clouded by cataracts. But at the age of eighty-five she had scraped the money together and travelled from South Africa to be at her brother Norman's ninetieth fiesta. "We had a roasted steer," he had written to me, "and plenty of wine and whisky and beer. I never had such a blow out."

She had stayed on with him in Concepción, but the following day was flying to Buenos Aires, then home to South Africa.

Max White was presiding behind the bar; they had already started on their second whiskies. Max had been looking forward to Rose's visit and had told Florence: "If I'd been a few years older and your auntie had been a few years younger when we met, well hell, we would have jumped into bed together and we wouldn't have climbed out for a week!"

Florence had laughed. "I know."

Over lunch of *asado* beef, salad and a good Argentine *vino rosado*, Aunt Rose explained that she lived in an old people's home in Johannesburg. She was almost blind and it hadn't been easy to make the trip. "I saved and did without in order to come. And I'm glad I did."

She said she would be happy to talk about the old days at Cosme, especially to divulge some of Norman's sins, so after lunch we retired to the living room.

*

Rose Menmuir kicked off her shoe to show me the angry purple blotch on her ankle. "See, that's where the snake bit me at the age of nine."

She had been in the McLeod cane patch with the other children, pretending to be a pig, when she trod on the snake. Later they found it, a *yarará*, also known as a *fer-de-lance*, one of the most poisonous and aggressive snakes in South America. Rose walked home, feeling sick, and announced, "Mummy, a snake bit me".

Lillian Wood sent for the nurse, Clara Laurence, who swore she could save Rose with a snake-bite cure from Queensland. She had the shoots of a banana tree cut up and put through a mincer. "Ooh! but that juice was a terrible taste. I cried every time I had to take it."

Rose lost consciousness, bleeding from her mouth, nose and ears. She woke nauseated by a disgusting smell. "They kept changing the cloths, as the dirty stinking blood came out of my veins and saved my life. But I was left with a twisted face for a long time." Later she asked why she hadn't died and was told that it was because the snake had only got one fang into her.

Rose Menmuir massaged her foot. "That was seventy-six years ago and it still feels as if worms are crawling there."

After that she and her younger sister Kathleen didn't play in the *monte* very often. "The boys finished school at lunchtime, but we girls had to return in the afternoon for lessons in sewing, embroidery, crochet and knitting. The colony ladies taught us. I enjoyed it and won prizes for my embroidery. But what I really wanted was a pair of football boots."

Her brother Norman's famous sin was aiming mudballs at Groves, the teacher, with his shanghai. "Mr Groves was a Cambridge man, not used to that sort of thing. He'd swing around from the blackboard, but Norman would be innocently writing at his desk." She had reminded Norman when staying with him recently. "He denied it, with a smirk."

The happiest times she remembered from her childhood were when she gathered with her brothers and sisters while their father told them stories. In the summer he let them sleep outside, under the trellis-work. "He used to make a cow-dung fire that kept the mosquitoes away and he would tell us all about the stars and the moon and its eclipse until we slept." In the winter they'd huddle around the fireplace, sitting on sheepskins while he read from Charles Dickens, Robert Louis Stevenson, Sir Walter Scott and R. D. Blackmore — she loved *The Heart of Midlothian* and *Lorna Doone*. "All winter long in the evenings Dad would read to us by the big log fire."

*

Then there was "the divide". In 1909, when Rose was five years old, the failure of Cosme as a socialist community was formally acknowledged by carving up the remaining assets and establishing private titles.

At a meeting three years before, in December 1906, the original constitution had been effectively annulled after a motion put by Dave Stevenson and the colony was redefined as a partnership. It was agreed wages would be paid for community work, the cash flow to come from leasing grazing land and allowing timber rights to a group of American sawing contractors.

But still Cosme failed to prosper. Its main crop was sugarcane, but despite the employment of Paraguayan labourers in the cutting season and the installation of an expensive steam engine to power the crushing works, transport costs made it difficult to compete.

"As a descendant," Don Guillermo told me, "reading about those dozens of leagues of good land at New Australia, I marvel why Lane insisted on getting away to Cosme which was actually an impossible place for progress, in the fork of two rivers often in flood. I think the early colony people did wonders to get steam engines there for example. They must have had tremendous teams of bullocks. But any heavy carting, even logs from the *monte*, had to be done when it was perfectly dry and I remember whole years when there was not a day you could reach the surrounding towns without going through a certain amount of water."

"The Cosme people didn't know how to go about making money," said his brother Alex. "They were always getting further into debt. I used to ride on the old mare ploughing sugar-cane and being cut on my bare legs. But for all the blood and sweat and tears, they couldn't make it pay."

"Cosme isn't the sort of land where you can make a big plantation," Norman Wood agreed. "There are pockets that fill with water at flood time, only good for the frogs yelling their heads off. There was a lot of work and very little money in it, that's what disheartened most of them."

Foundation members, such as Alec Forrester-Lewis, with his sons Charlie and Rod, weakened the community by their departure. "The Lewis boys," said Bill Wood, "had ideas that they'd like to get away to some civilised place where they could get a girl to talk to and fall in love with." Wally Head, who had grown up in the charge of Dave Stevenson, went to try his luck elsewhere and ended up marrying and going into business in San Francisco. Ned and Bella Dyer, the couple who had scandalised Mary Gilmore, went to New Zealand. Harold Wallis pursued John Lane's daughter Ettie, married her and settled in Sydney.

Bill Wood was thirteen years old when large groups of people left, dissatisfied with the prospects for their children's education and the unreliable food supply:

It was getting so that the families were producing what they wanted for themselves and there was never enough. There was always jealousy — about getting different parts of an animal that was killed, different quantities of milk and eggs. A couple like the Laurences, who had no children, had abundant supplies for two, but a family like the Titilahs with eight or nine kids were always struggling. Some of those who left went down to the Argentine looking for work to pay their passages, but that was impossible for a family like the Titilahs. In the end the father broke away and went to Sapucai and got a job.

The departure of colonists left an inadequate labour force to break in new land or prepare produce for market. The problem was exacerbated because there were some hard workers and others who complained and did not pull their weight. The drones — "like Len Apthorpe, the Englishman who later became my father-in-law" — were always being criticised.

Another cause for dissension was the employment of Paraguayan labour, begun in 1899, which Tozer had predicted would "bust up the 'brotherhood' ". With colony numbers reduced it became essential to hire local help for timber felling, sawmilling, cane-cutting and sugar extracting. Tozer

wrote that by "exploiting the native" the colony hoped to work its way
out of financial trouble, "but as a rule the native prefers working for
himself and won't allow a 'communistic-socialistic' colony to sweat him".

Bill Wood said he was very young when the *peones* first came in, "to
help with the sugarcane which is very filthy and hard work. And the colony
boys readily learned to speak to them in Guaraní, long before we learned
correct Spanish". As they worked together, friendships developed. "The
colony boys would go riding around the district and Paraguayans are
hospitable people. They don't feed expensively but they seem to be good
at making very tasty dishes. If they asked us boys in once or twice, we'd
be happy to return, so we gradually got used to mixing with the Paraguayans."

The *peones* brought their wives and children to visit Cosme. Lillian
Wood's skills as a midwife became known. "There were cases where the
local midwife couldn't get results, so they'd hastily send for Mum to attend
to them." Young Bill sometimes went with her. He remembered one case
in mid-winter, when they went on horseback to a house some 5 kilometres
away. "The woman, who was having a pretty tough time, seemed to get
new hope when Mum arrived. After about an hour the baby was delivered
but the woman was shivering, so Mum stripped off her woollen pants and
put them on her. That always stuck in my memory. She was too good
altogether. The people never offered to pay her, they'd just accept her as
something that came from heaven."

With the increased social mixing with what Bill Wood called "the
Paraguayan element", some of the Cosme parents were uncomfortable
about the possibility of their children marrying into the local community.
"When all was said and done, a lot of them decided that it was not being
run on the William Lane idea — what they'd all come over for."

When it became obvious that a divide was inevitable, Bill Wood said
the old hands "decided to chase out anyone they did not think entitled to
profit from the remains of Cosme". Newcomers were discouraged so
there'd be fewer to share the spoils. By the end of 1908 there were nine
male members — wives not being eligible under the guidelines. Five were
married — William Wood, Leonard Apthorpe, Alf Davey, Rod McLeod
and William Laurence — and four were single — Jim Sime, Dave
Stevenson, Ernest Kell and the widower Allan McLeod, father of nine of
the colony's remaining twenty-one children.

The land was surveyed and divided, but the Monte Viscaino, the most
valuable timber stand on Cosme, had to be sold to pay the surveying bills

and the lawyers. Wood, Apthorpe, Kell and Allan McLeod hired a Paraguayan lawyer but the other five, disagreeing with his approach, employed Gilbert Casey, their old rival from New Australia, by then freelancing as a bilingual agent.

The Paraguayan lawyer, Don Antonio Vasconcelos, stayed with the Wood family during the negotiations. This warm-hearted man was a big hit with young Rose Wood and her sister Kathleen. "We loved him so much. Kath and I used to vie with each other as to who could get up the earliest to sit on his knee while he and my dad sucked *mate-bombilla* from 5 to 6 o'clock in the morning in front of the sitting-room fire. Don Antonio used to go into the boys' room and wake my brothers, shouting, '*Arriba, muchachos, arriba!*' "

The divide was legally ratified at Caazapá on 12 August 1909. Souter has unravelled the complexities of the final allocation: "Each of the nine members received a house lot of fifteen hectares (thirty-seven acres) at the township site and a parcel of at least 200 hectares (494 acres) of *campo* and *monte*, the larger areas varying according to their proportion of valuable *monte*. The plaza site, the social hall and the barn remained public property and a large area of land was retained as communal *campo*. Cattle, horses and all tools and equipment other than household goods were divided into lots, which were drawn for by the householders. In the case of families with several children, cash payments and/or an additional draw were allowed."

Their lives had changed irrevocably. "So here is the question," Mary Gilmore had written in an Australian newspaper in 1902. "Will the colony keep to its ideal, and remain poor, or will it relax, and become well-to-do? I do not for one moment suppose that it will ever become individualistic. I think it is more likely to break up altogether than do that; and I do not think it will break up." The unthinkable had happened. They were no longer communists or colonists, but individualists, small independent farmers, having to scratch a living like most of the ordinary citizens of Paraguay.

Norman Wood remembered the divide because Jimmy Sime went among the colony children handing out pesos to correspond with their ages. "I was ten years old and he gave me a ten peso bill. I'd never had such luck. I went to a feast in Caazapá and bought a tin whistle and when I got tired of that, some other boy traded it for fifty cents. I went to the market and bought five *pasteles* and had a good feed."

But the windfall had gone to Sime's head and he kept spending. Four years later, William Wood wrote to a friend: "Here you have the puzzle of the crowd ... Sime until the divide never touched liquor. Immediately after he set to, and has been going hard ever since. I reckon he has got through some 30,000 Paraguayan dollars since the divide ... He has already sold one of his pieces of land to Rod McLeod. It is a moot question as to whether his property will suffice to bury him. My word he did make things hum."

On the other hand, Leonard Apthorpe lost his money without having fun. He put it in a bank in Asunción, the bank failed and he lost everything. Rose Menmuir said her father fortunately had his money in a different bank, "and he lived on the proceeds until about 1916. After that, he had eaten the whole lot away. Then he started selling things around that belonged to him. There was nothing left for us children. Nothing at all."

At times William Wood spoke of returning to Australia. Don Norman remembered: "He had high hopes. They were always talking about a gentleman who was coming to buy the land and in that way they'd have the money for the passage back. 'When we go home,' they were always saying. I used to think, 'Why should we be planting this corn? We're going to Australia. I wonder what I'll do with all my marbles? I'll give them to somebody else, we're going to Australia'."

Don Guillermo thought that Donald Macdonell, an old associate from Bourke, had attempted through the union movement to raise funds for the family's return. "But I don't think Dad was really keen on the idea. Mum's main ambition was to get back again but Dad seemed to fit in on Cosme, he enjoyed the life. There was nothing very wonderful about it, but we had enough to eat, our clothing was simple, so he did not really have to work".

After the divide, he said, his father derived an income from the timber on his 400 hectares of land. As the best Spanish-speaker of the community he also dealt with the timber merchants for the other ex-colonists and quite frequently went to Asunción. Any Paraguayan government officials visiting Cosme came to him, so his Spanish continued to improve. "He was never shy about speaking to anybody. He would chat to the president or a cane *peón*, just the same."

But Bill's sister Rose had a more acerbic memory of their father at this time: "He just loafed around. When all his money went, he lived off his sons. Mum slaved and Dad lay on his back."

Lillian Wood wrote to her sisters in Bourke and dreamed of returning home but saw the likelihood drifting away, especially as she was pregnant again. In the meantime the old Cosme connections had not been severed by the signing of a legal document. The Wood home was where the former colony women — Ada McLeod, Mary Davey, Laura Apthorpe and Clara Laurence, all still meticulously addressing each other as "Mrs" — got together for their morning "smoko". "Not that any of them smoked," said Bill Wood, "but that was the name of their half-hour's rest at 9 o'clock in the morning. They'd have a gossip and a cup of *mate* or tea if someone had sent them a packet."

There was no longer a dining room for the single men and they had to make their own arrangements. Ernest Kell lived off his vegetable patch and tried to earn money making marmalade from *apepús*, the bitter wild oranges. "Dad and I made a big copper pot for him, but it was not a good idea. Poor Ernie, nobody wanted his marmalade."

Dave Stevenson entered an interesting *menage*, paying to have all his meals at the Laurence household. "He almost lived there. Billy and Clara both enjoyed his conversation. Dave was a connoisseur of food and Mrs Laurence was a wonderful cook, no doubt the best on Cosme."

Sometimes the former colonists would get together for a communal feast. Alex Wood remembered enjoying pork for Sunday lunch at the home of Alf Davey. He was so impressed that he bought a suckling pig himself.

> I took it home and I used to feed it and it grew up. This was after the divide, but when the pig was killed, everyone came around for a share of it.
> "But that's my pig," I said to my father. He told me, "No, we've got to share it. That's our way of life. That is communism."
> "Then I'm not a communist," I said. "I won't be a communist!"

At the time of the divide, Bill Wood was fifteen years old and his father's holding was too small to support him. He had to find a job. He said he had no training or technical skills, apart from having sometimes helped his father in the colony's blacksmith's shop. "So I could only get low-type work and started as a counter-jumper."

He was employed as an assistant at a store in Yegros, some 30 kilometres from Cosme. This settlement was the former Colonia González, which had never been more than a private enterprise cooperative. The new name signified that even that degree of social organisation had been abandoned. It was an eclectic community of German, French and Italian settlers, intermarried with Paraguayans, and a handful of Australians who had left New Australia years before. "We knew two families there, the Williams and the Henrys. But the Yegros people were different from Cosme's because they had perfect communications; they had the railway line running through their properties so they had no problems in getting rid of any of their produce. They'd planted yerba trees and grape-vines."

Bill Wood's employer was a German-American, Otto Meyer. "He had a domineering wife who was not satisfied with him as a husband and had taken to herself one of the shop assistants. Meyer found out all about it and sacked him, so they had to get somebody else."

He could place the year he started work there, Bill Wood said, because he was very homesick and remembered lying at night in his little room behind the shop, gazing through the window at the starry sky and the trail of a great comet streaking across it: Halley's Comet on its 1910 visitation.

He was not happy in the job because the wife was always finding fault with him. "I was not nearly as satisfactory as the man who had been sacked. I was apparently too simple minded for anything she thought worthwhile, too young for those gallantries." Each Monday morning as he started work, he yearned for the coming weekend when he would rejoin his brothers and sisters at Cosme.

Alex, aged thirteen, was helping his father with the sugarcane crop, but Norman, eleven, Wallace, nine, Rose, six and Kathleen, four were still at school, at Arthur Groves' behest still placing a slide rule on the map between London and various towns. There was a new toddler in the Wood family, two-year-old Donald, and Lillian Wood had just given birth to her eighth child, Frank.

Dave Stevenson had become irascible in the presence of small children: "If he heard a baby crying he would yell 'Smother it! Kill it!' The poor mothers did not like him shouting those things." But on some weekends Stevenson would take the young people at Cosme in hand to teach them etiquette. Bill Wood recalled: "He would invite a group of us to his house and Clara Laurence would provide some sweet biscuits and a bucket of lemonade. He would teach us how to sit straight, and walk with an upright military bearing like him. And he'd show us how to prepare a table and where to put the knives and forks, how to eat with our mouths shut and our elbows off the table, that sort of thing."

Stevenson was forty-eight years old and his legendary attractiveness was becoming distinctly resistible; some women viewed him as a pest. Rod Mcleod remembered his sister Peggy, who had grown into a very pretty adolescent, complaining that Stevenson was always trying to chase after her. "She was afraid of him."

Norman Wood agreed. He had heard a story of Stevenson pursuing Mrs Davey around a table until she was out of breath protecting her virtue. I thought it a wonder there had not been more such stories. Stevenson was obviously a man of strong sexuality, but for seventeen years he had been a bachelor in Paraguay. Surely he had had a covert relationship, a local woman like the beautiful Favriana he had admired on the boating trip?

Rod McLeod, who'd had a Paraguayan wife himself, was shocked by the suggestion. "He wouldn't touch them. Definitely not. He didn't want to send his blood around about here amongst the Indians."

Don Norman said with his usual directness: "He used to work it off with work and walking around having afternoon tea with the ladies. When it was still a colony some of the married women were quite liberal. They may have thought, 'This poor man's alone here. He needs it and why shouldn't we share it out with him?' "

They mentioned the names of two colony women who seemed to enjoy many cups of tea with Dave, usually when their husbands were working in the *monte*. Rod McLeod thought that one of them produced a son who had the Stevenson nose and chin.

"You're too evil-minded for words," laughed Don Norman.

But both of them were emphatic that Clara Laurence was not one of those women. "She was too dignified and careful of her reputation. Nobody ever made a snide remark about Clara Laurence."

The weekends that people enjoyed most were those spent bathing and fishing at the Capiibary River. The favourite swimming place was "the stony crossing", a pool above a natural rocky dam broken by narrow channels forming rapids. The crossing was sometimes used by the men moving stock across the river. Below it was a deep lagoon, some 300 metres long by 100 metres wide, once a port for rafting cedar logs from the *monte*. The men used to fish in the lagoon, while the children swam in the shallower pool above. At one time Cosme-ites had a thick rope strung from one bank to the other at the head of the rapids, so children could cling to it if they were swept away by the current.

Rose Menmuir said she loved going to the stony crossing. "We used to spend every weekend down there with Daisy McLeod and all my elder brothers. We used to cut up reeds, put a blanket over them and sleep there, get up on Sunday and swim and fish and have a lovely time."

The men went swimming in their undershorts, Bill Wood said, and the women and girls "in petticoat and brassiere, I suppose. I did not investigate too closely. Our Paraguayan neighbours used to go in naked, I believe. They weren't so worried about sex, apparently".

The lagoon below the crossing was swarming with fish with ferocious teeth, "the English people called them 'sharks' ". Although the fish had an immense network of bones, their flesh was delicious. The Cosme boys flattened them and dried them in the sun. There were alligators in the lagoon too, but "they were *yacarés*, timid things," said Rose Menmuir. "Nobody that I knew was bitten by one. They'd come sliding down into the water between us, part of the family. They're not like the crocodiles that eat people; they're only interested in fish."

On Sunday evening they would walk home, following a path that wound 5 kilometres through the *monte*. "I'd be worn out and Daddy would say, 'Get up on my shoulders Rosie', but I'd tell him that I could make it by myself."

There were still occasional evening theatricals at the social hall. At the Cosme Foundation Day get-together in Asunción, the three Wood brothers recalled a "nigger minstrel" evening after the divide.

It began with Eddie McLeod wandering about the stage wailing, "Where, oh where, has my little dog gone?"

All the dogs about the place had been collected up and Billy Laurence, playing the black-faced murderer, threw them one by one into a machine and turned the handle. It was a sham: the dogs actually went through a trap-door into a pit under the stage, but it seemed they were being turned into mince-meat. "The dogs were barking and yelping and all the little kids were howling with fright because strings of sausages were coming out of the other end of the machine." Eddie continued moaning:

Oh where, oh where has my little dog gone,
Oh where, oh where can he be?
With his hair cut short and his tail hung long,
Oh where, oh where has he gone?

Then Billy Laurence grabbed Eddie and tossed him into the machine, more sausages came out, while the audience chanted, "Turn away, murderer!"

"That became one of our sayings," said Don Guillermo. "'Turn away, murderer!' "

It was their favourite show. They choked with laughter, remembering how Norman had collected all the sausages in a basket and dumped them in front of the resident vegetarian. "Ten pounds of sausages for Mr Kell!"

Soon afterwards, Ernest Kell was taken ill and admitted to hospital in

Asunción. He refused the meat dishes offered, wasted away and died, apparently of malnutrition. "He suffered in silence," said Don Norman, "a martyr for his vegetarianism. He was a good man, a sort of protector of animals and little birds. I always thought he was something like Jesus."

Occasionally the former colonists held a dance at the social hall and soon Cosme boys were inviting Paraguayan girls as their partners. But the girls would arrive with their families and friends and Bill Wood said that the spreads put on at interval had to be abandoned. "After the divide we tried to keep to the tradition of feeding halfway through the dance. Someone amongst the colony people would take a tray of food and walk around the group seated around the edges of the hall. But the natives would take it by the handful; they wouldn't just take a sandwich and be content, they'd take a dozen and wrap them in their handkerchiefs to take home to the kids. So after the Paraguayans came to our dances the idea of feeding was given up. If they wanted something to eat they could bring it for themselves."

It was about this time too that alcohol first appeared at Cosme. *Caña*, the local white rum made from sugarcane, became a favourite tipple at the end of the day. In fact, according to Norman Wood, some Cosme men began making *caña* for sale.

> They had the molasses and the machinery for crushing sugarcane, and the pans to boil the juice and they built a still to make the white rum. They all started taking a drink and Jimmy Sime was more or less permanently drunk. My mother was very much against Dad having *caña* in the house. She said, "I'll throw it all out, if you bring any here". And he would just laugh. Billy Laurence would steal a drink whenever he could get away with it without his missus seeing him. When they went together in the bullock cart to town, he had a little bottle tied under the axle of the cart. He had an offsider, a little Paraguayan boy called Valentine, and the boy would ride alongside the cart and look at the wheel. Billy would say, "What's wrong with it?" and Valentine was trained to answer, "I don't know, it looks something to be wrong". Billy would get off the cart, get under it, and have a swig.
>
> "Shall I get down, Billy?" Mrs Laurence would call, concerned, and he'd say, "No dear, you stay where you are. I'll have this right in a minute."

It was a long way from the scrupulous teetotalism that saw molasses thrown overboard on the Paraná River in 1893.

Don Guillermo remembered Laurence, Stevenson and an Englishman called Dale, playing bridge all through the night with a bottle of *caña* on the table constantly replenished.

This would all have come as no surprise to William Lane, who had long gained bitter satisfaction from predicting the worst for Cosme. He had become a leader-writer, soon to be editor, of the right-wing *New Zealand Herald* and, under the pen-name Tohunga, the Maori word for prophet, his fiery rhetoric supported the forces of conservatism and imperialism. It seemed only two tenets of faith remained constant from the old days — his distrust of non-whites and his detestation of alcohol.

But the introduction of drink at Cosme would have been a great disappointment to Mary Gilmore, who had gone on record that, if she had her way, she would "go as far as the women of Finland and allow alcohol to be sold only by the Government, and then for medical, industrial or scientific purposes alone".

Mary was living with her husband and son in the town of Casterton in the Western District of Victoria. In 1910 she had published her first volume of poetry, *Marri'd and Other Verses*, and for three years had been editor of the Women's Page of the New South Wales *Worker*. It gave her a platform for her views. In the issue of 7 January 1909 she devoted a major article to "Alcohol and Life":

> It is to women, the waiting mother, the trembling fear-stricken wife … the broken woman sitting by the feeble-lifed, the idiot-minded, the criminally tainted, that the evil of drink is so apparent. Man takes his drink and comes home. If the home is cheerless, he jingles his coins in his pocket, goes out and drinks again. What matter to him the mental, moral and physical enfeeble-ment of the child his wife bears to him …

In June 1911 Will Gilmore went farming in north-west Queensland and Mary moved to Sydney to write full-time for the *Worker*. They announced it as a temporary separation, necessitated by circumstances, but it lasted for the remainder of their lives. In Sydney Mary immersed herself in her journalism, essays and poetry and soon became prominent in the city's literary milieu. The love of writing, which she had fought, expressing her fear and conflict in a letter to Will in Patagonia, could no longer be denied. It was now her centre.

Meanwhile, Bill Wood had abandoned the unhappy situation in the store at Yegros, dabbled at being a carpenter, and trailed through a number of different jobs. Through the dispensation of Arthur Tozer, who had become powerful as the Superintendent of the Paraguay Central Railway, he obtained work at Sapucai as a railway assistant and an engineers' cook. He left to train with a firm of electrical engineers and then landed a job he really liked, with the Asunción Tramways Light and Power Company.

He worked in the sub-station on the rotary converters which aligned the alternating current of the carbon candle street-lighting to the same voltage that drove the city's trams. A revolution during 1911–12, another struggle between Liberals and Colorados, was irritating: a number of the street-lights were shot out.

The Liberals won power but were incapable of maintaining political stability. For the next forty years, revolutions were a commonplace of Paraguay life, provoked not by major political issues but by the usual turbulent egos and factional rivalries.

*

In August 1914 a war broke out in Europe that had no impact on the average Paraguayan. But it was different for the young men who had grown up at New Australia and Cosme. They had a sense of belonging to the British empire. All those red patches on the map had to be defended.

The first Cosme-ite to go was Rod's elder brother, Dave McLeod. He had been employed by the Paraguay Central Railway, but had no heart for the work and decided to enlist with the British Army in Buenos Aires.

"It sort of fired my imagination and I wanted to go immediately," said Bill Wood. "I was then twenty years old." But his boss told him he couldn't leave his job until he had trained three replacements, so he was obliged to stay on until January 1915.

At Cosme a number of the men volunteered. It was no surprise when the schoolteacher Arthur Groves, a stalwart of the imperial spirit, headed for the recruiting office in Buenos Aires. Young Allie McLeod, who had always accompanied his brother on hunting expeditions in the *monte*, decided to join Dave on the battlefield. Jim Titilah followed. Then two of Cosme's older men, both of central importance in Clara Laurence's life, enlisted: her husband Billy, aged forty-nine, and Dave Stevenson, aged fifty-two. Clara promptly offered her services as a nurse but, presumably because she was 47-years-old, was not accepted.

The colony postmistress, Minnie Jacks, wrote to Mary Gilmore in Sydney, describing the men's departure from Cosme, how the Union Jack fluttered on the green and they all cheered as they rode off, but "as horse and rider disappear into the *monte* we don't look at each other and we don't say much either".

At the end of January Bill Wood took leave of his family and young Mabel Apthorpe, in whom he had started to take an interest. Alex had decided to follow him as soon as possible. Norman, still too young, was chafing to go and volunteered as soon as he came of age.

In the end sixteen men from the two former socialist colonies answered the call, ten from Cosme and six from New Australia, including three Kennedys, soldiers defending an Empire they had learned about at school.

By March 1915, Bill Wood was in Buenos Aires, his first visit to the city he found impressive but bewildering. He was one of almost 5,000 expatriate British and Anglo-Argentines offering their services to King and Country. The newspaper oriented to their interests, the English-language *Buenos Aires Herald* reported: "Ties of blood and kindred and devotion to the Motherland brushed all other considerations on one side." Bill presented himself at the British Consulate-General, as an Australian-Paraguayan providing another bizarre variation in the motley crowd the *Herald* described: "There one rubbed shoulders with reservists, old soldiers, old volunteers, many of whom had seen active service in the South African war, and others anxious to give the most practical evidence of their patriotism."

But he learned shocking news of a Cosme friend who had been like an uncle to him all his life. Billy Laurence had been rejected as unfit for service, but elected to have an operation at the British Hospital in Buenos Aires in the hope of curing his condition. "What Billy had was a stone in the kidney, but he had left it too long before seeing a doctor and by the time they operated he was too far gone and they couldn't keep him alive. He died on the operating table."

At Cosme Clara waited anxiously, and asked Norman Wood to ride in to the telegraph office at Yegros. He told me: "When Clara learned that he had died, you could hear her crying from a long way off, all through the night, 'My poor Billy, poor Billy, that doctor was a butcher!' Whatever people say, I'm sure she was very fond of Billy."

Dave Stevenson arranged for Laurence to be buried in the Chacarita cemetery in Buenos Aires, then proceeded on alone. "D.R. Stevenson is in Egypt," wrote Minnie Jacks to Mary Gilmore. "He says he will return to Cosme for the rest of his life."

Arriving at the Buenos Aires recruiting centre, Bill Wood met up with a young Englishman from Manchester, Horace Moulds. He had met him first in Asunción and had helped Moulds get casual work with the Asunción Tramways Light and Power Company. They sailed together — "my first time on an ocean ship; the British Government provided free passages," he said, still jubilant about that — and arrived at Liverpool on 1 April 1915.

Moulds invited him to his home in Manchester "and gave me a wonderful insight into the life of an English family. His father was an engineering assistant in a cotton-spinning factory. They were very hospitable people and looked after me like a long lost son".

Because of his electrical experience, Wood joined the Royal Engineers, 10th Irish Division, and was given training as a signaller. "I was sent to Chatham and different parts of England and Wales and learned how to lay electrical cables for telegraphing."

In August 1915 he was sent to Gallipoli.

He was part of Kitchener's Army, in one of three British divisions that landed at Suvla Bay, the bleak salt-pan country to the north of Anzac Cove. The plan of the British commanding general, Sir Ian Hamilton, was that the landing should surprise the Turks, whose attention would be diverted by a feint, a three-pronged attack by the Anzacs, taking the Turkish position at Lone Pine and pushing on to the heights of Chunuk Bair. According to the strategy, the 25,000 men of Kitchener's Army would then press forward to gain control of the peninsula.

They were to be landed late on the moonless night of 6 August. At 5.30 pm the Australians began their almost impossible assault on the strongly fortified Turkish trenches at Lone Pine. It was a massacre — the Turks mowing them down as they rushed the bare slopes.

But the Australians prised the log coverings from the trenches, they crawled over their own fallen in the maze of tunnels. By 6 pm, against all the odds, Lone Pine was taken. But hundreds of Australian dead lay on ground too exposed for corpses to be identified or given burial, sacrificed to draw Turkish attention from the British landing.

About 11 pm the three British destroyers came close to shore at Suvla Bay, according to a midshipman, "making the devil of a noise as only one of them muffled her cable". Motor-lighters proceeded ahead of them, bobbing on the swell. But for the sucking of the undertow and waves slapping against a low cliff to their starboard, everything was quiet and still. "Suddenly, I distinctly heard a sharp click ashore," wrote the midshipman, "which must have been the cocking of rifles, for only a few seconds later there was one shot followed by hundreds ... I got inside our wheelhouse while the boat's crew lay down as best they could on the lee side of the firing ... I might add that the soldiers were naturally not too keen to get ashore and especially at the end, it took quite a lot of persuasion from the sergeants to clear the lighter."

Bill Wood was among the men wading ashore, the water above their waists, while shells rained on them. In the darkness they staggered around, frightened and confused, waiting for orders. "The Turks were occupying the east hills, so under cannon fire we ran to the hillocks on the western side, but we did not know what we were supposed to be doing."

The British divisions failed to press forward to outflank the Turks while the opportunity presented itself. Another soldier at the landing wrote: "All the while the Tommy troops were being landed and sent inland. Time and time again men doubled back and asked us where the front line was. They had no idea where to go. They'd head off into the scrub, thick bush it was. Officers and men alike asked us 'which way to the lines?' They were all green, inexperienced … We couldn't see anything of what was happening to the Australians. We heard terrible reports."

This inaction has subsequently been attributed "largely to the lack of energy of the commander, Sir Frederick Stopford, who preferred to remain on board his ship during this critical period. By the time they were ready to move inland it was too late — Turkish reserves had already been brought up".

While the British floundered, the Australians were asked to make another diversionary action to draw enemy troops from Suvla Bay. At dawn on 7 August, Light Horsemen on foot stormed Turkish trenches on The Nek, a precipitous and narrow ridge. The enemy was to be distracted by a British bombardment from the sea, but this cut out seven minutes earlier than planned, just as the Australians were making their bayonet charge across exposed ground. They had been ordered to leave their rifles unloaded for close combat. The slaughter of the Australians was ferocious, machine-gun bullets ripping hundreds of them to pieces. A second wave of men fell on the bodies of their comrades, a third line and then a fourth, charging to certain destruction for no strategic gain. C. E. W. Bean, in his official account of Australians in World War I, wrote: "In the history of war there is no more signal example of reckless obedience than that given by the dismounted Light Horsemen at The Nek …"

But Kitchener's Army was ashore at Suvla Bay. Bill Wood was attached to the 29th Brigade. On his second night, he was required to establish a communications link between his brigade and two others. His job as a signaller made him a prime target. With a group of young soldiers he pulled a cable drum mounted on a trolley across rough terrain in the darkness, unreeling 3 kilometres of wire, constantly exposed to enemy fire.

During that trek he discovered what war was. "We managed to get to the 30th Brigade with the cable, but the bullets were zapping around us. I got down into a trench to get out of the way and stepped on a wounded soldier; then I saw the trenches were full of wounded." As they continued their nightmarish journey to the 31st Brigade headquarters, a maimed soldier feebly lifted his arm to attract their attention. "Our sergeant refused to stop. I asked one of my pals if I'd be left like that if I got hit. He said, 'No, we look after our own', which consoled me a bit. I was not very keen on being just left on the roadside."

The shellfire had burnt all the grass from the edge of rising country right down to the shore. "I was at the front of the wagon and we couldn't see more than a few metres ahead. Suddenly I was confronted with a corpse swollen to about a metre high; apparently it'd been lying in the sun for days. I skirted around it and stepped right on another dead soldier."

The front-line trenches of the 31st Brigade were under heavy fire. They found the brigade headquarters and the slit-trench housing the telegraph equipment. Wood felt an exhaustion beyond anything in his experience. "I collapsed on the lip of the trench. One of the telegraphists looked up and said, 'You'd better get down out of that, one of our pals was just killed there.'"

After a few days some English regiments, including Wood's, were sent to reinforce the Australian Infantry Force. "Our battalion was transferred to Australian command," he said "and I was sent over to Anzac."

I expected this to have immediate emotional impact for him, to be with large numbers of Australians, his compatriots, for the first time in his life. But of course the overwhelming impact was the constant fire from the Turkish guns and he did not have time to savour the irony of the situation, even when he saw a man who eerily resembled himself, like a double, his *doppelganger*.

We crossed over from Suvla Beach in a little red-wing auxiliary craft. When we arrived at Anzac Cove, my pal Moulds pointed out a man and said, "My God! That Australian there looks just like you. He must be some relation of yours."

With shame I say that I looked at this Australian and he had been sunburnt very badly in Egypt and he had a bright red face and he did not look very handsome, so I didn't bother going and introducing myself. I've always been very sorry I was stupid enough not to have found out who he was. He may have been one of my relations. But I suppose I was not very interested in knowing anybody special then, but only in getting out of the road of the shells bursting overhead and the bullets that seemed to be whizzing past and hitting everything except me.

He was chosen to relay the daily instructions from Anzac headquarters. "I don't know why, but I was selected to represent my company in the Australian commander's evening gathering, when he ordered what each section under his command had to do the following day." What struck him most was the easy camaraderie between the Australian officers and the ranks. "I couldn't tell who were the officers. It was all first names — Harry, Dick, Bill — and everyone was telling jokes all the time."

His role was to maintain and repair the lines of communication between headquarters and the trenches. "It did not matter if there was an attack in progress and people were getting their heads blown off, if the line got cut, you had to follow it along till you found the break and repaired it."

Despite his liaison job collecting the daily orders, he got to know few Australians. "Although I travelled round amongst them, I never had any real contact with them. They did not mix with me."

As far as the men of the AIF were concerned, he was a Tommy. Charles Bean reflected in his diary the spirit of egalitarianism which caused many diggers to lack respect for the British soldier:

> The truth is that after 100 years of breeding in slums, the British race is not the same, and can't be expected to be the same, as in the days of Waterloo. It is breeding one fine class at the expense of all the rest. The only hope is that those puny narrow-chested little men may, if they come out to Australia or NZ or Canada, within two generations breed men again. England herself, unless she does something heroic, cannot hope to … To my mind this war, as far as I have seen it, is just Britain's tomahawks coming home to roost … They have neither the nerve, the physique, nor the spirit and self-control to fit them for soldiers.

Bill Wood had no opportunity and no inclination to explain that he was an Australian who, because of an experiment in egalitarianism and socialism in a wild circuit to South America, had ended up on that Turkish peninsula in a British uniform. He said that soon after his arrival the main body of Australians moved on. "I think they went further south towards Cape Helles, the southern tip of Gallipoli. I didn't see them round about where we were after that."

He remembered Gallipoli as a blur of horror. "I was under fire every day that we were there. There were bullets smacking around everywhere we were. There was no getting away from them because the Turks were on the top of the hills and we were a couple of hundred yards lower down in full sight, so they could blaze away at us day and night." Only in the saps, the trenches over two metres deep, was it possible to escape.

He considered it a miracle that he did not get wounded. The immensity of the slaughter came home to him when he saw a stack of rifles, "there must've been a couple of thousand, nearly two metres high and about seven metres long". They had belonged to soldiers killed in action.

His twenty-first birthday came around on 5 September 1915, "but it was no celebration in that hell-of-a-hole, with swarms of flies settling in the latrines and on corpses, killing off hundreds from dysentery".

He was not aware that elsewhere on the Gallipoli peninsula another Cosme boy was also defending the Empire. Corporal Donald Lane, the 22-year-old son of William and Anne, was with the New Zealand 16th Waikato Company.

Shortly after landing, Lane led a machine-gun section to Zulach Point, where the Turks had their fire-power concentrated on the allies' boats. The Waikato men were ordered to advance across a gully and join the Australians on the next ridge. Going down into the gully, Don Lane was shot in the right forearm. According to a comrade, who considered him "one of the bravest men on the field", an officer urged him to go back but he declined, insisting the wound was nothing.

> He still kept his section together as well as he could under the enemy's heavy shrapnel and machine-gun fire until the platoon reached the Australians' position. When this contact was made they lay down and formed a joint firing line. Just at that stage Don Lane was again hit, a bullet striking him in the muscle of the thigh. Even then he would not go back, but insisted on staying in the line, and went on giving orders and controlling the fire of his section. Two ambulance men came along with a stretcher and wanted Don to let them carry him to the rear, but he would not, saying that he had only received another flesh wound. Then it was decided to charge. Don Lane rose to his knees and was giving the necessary order to his men to advance, when a bullet from a machine-gun struck him on the forehead, and the brave fellow fell back dead.

For William Lane it was a savage blow to lose yet another son. One year later, on the anniversary of the first landing in the Dardanelles, he wrote in the *New Zealand Herald*: "The message from Anzac is graven on hearts that throb with mingled pride and grief as the earth turns and swings in its path to the re-dawning of that holy day."

*

Norman Wood sat quietly at the scrubbed wooden table in the little house in Asunción while his brother recalled the horror of Gallipoli. A silence settled, broken only by the amplified throbbing from next door of a love song in Guaraní.

Don Norman asked if I knew the poem Henry Lawson wrote about the Dardanelles. I said I'd read it once, and reached for the battered copy of Lawson's *Collected Verse* I'd seen on the bookshelves.

"No need, I remember it," said Don Norman. He closed his eyes and, while his brother twisted and folded a handkerchief to disguise his emotion, he recited five verses, word perfect, and concluded:

> The sea was hell and the shore was hell,
> With mine, entanglement, shrapnel and shell,
> But they stormed the heights as Australians should,
> And they fought and they died as we knew they would.
> Knew they would —
> Knew they would;
> They fought and they died as we knew they would.

*

Bill's brother Alex had been serving with the 2nd Battalion of the Black Watch regiment in Mesopotamia. They learned with grief of the death of Dave McLeod, the leader on their childhood hunting expeditions. He had been with the Argyll and Sutherland Highlanders in France and was killed by a German shell behind the lines. "He was a born horseman," remembered Bill, "like the man from Snowy River."

Allie McLeod was wounded by shrapnel and repatriated to Paraguay.

Dave Stevenson was also fighting on the grim battlefield of the Western Front, as a sergeant. According to his great-niece, Mary Leeser, he had rejected the opportunity to take up a commission. "Apparently some English general had particularly wanted him to do the officers' course. But he did not approve of authority. I'm sure it wasn't because he couldn't accept the responsibility, but probably he had some political idea about it all. He wanted to be amongst the men."

In late June 1916 the Commander in Chief of the British Forces, Sir

Douglas Haig, launched a major British-French offensive against the Germans at the Somme River. Over a million men attacked along a 72-kilometre front, after an artillery bombardment of unprecedented intensity on the German positions. But the offensive was unsuccessful in causing any major breakthrough of the enemy lines and German forces inflicted appalling casualties on the British and French infantry.

Of the First Battle of the Somme, Charles Bean concluded: "Almost the whole of the 500,000 British troops who — according to calculations made before the battle — were available for expenditure in casualties, were duly expended; and the question arises, how far that sacrifice was justified by the results." He believed that General Haig's contention of success was "unlikely to be upheld by posterity".

Dave Stevenson was one of the casualties, hit in the chest in the cross-fire at the village of Beaumont Hamel, near Pozières, in a hideous wasteland of shell holes, broken wire and churned mud in which bodies lay in every state of decay and mutilation.

Doctors operated but decided that the bullet was too close to his heart to be removed. Stevenson was sent to a service hospital in England to convalesce.

His great-niece, Mary Leeser, then told me a story that surprised me. Her understanding was that when he was hospitalised, the widowed Clara Laurence came from Paraguay to nurse him. "I have a definite memory of Aunt Clara telling me that she went as a 'camp following' nurse to the war. She may not have been properly registered in the army nursing service, but she came to care for Uncle David."

She said her memory was confirmed by her own father, Allan Flores Stevenson, who was an officer in the Australian Flying Corps, at that time stationed in England with the Australian Fourth Squadron. "He spoke of meeting Uncle David with Aunt Clara during the war. He remembered that Uncle David disliked being saluted by an officer. He felt saluting was the wrong thing to be doing."

Mary Leeser thought it inevitable that Dave and Clara had finally got together. "From their obvious devotion to each other in later years, I think the spark had always been there between them."

*

Dave Stevenson was discharged from the British Army late in 1916 and he and Clara returned to Paraguay. At Cosme they were able to marry at last and set up house together.

Bill Wood took a pragmatic view of their union: "Clara, as Billy Laurence's widow, had one of the Cosme lots and Dave had another, so they decided to pool their resources and get married. But for Dave it was not a marriage like it usually is for young people, to produce a family and so forth. It was just pure convenience. Clara, who all her life had tried to get Dave, eventually got him because of her good cooking and wonderful house-keeping."

His brother Norman stoutly disagreed. "I think they really enjoyed living together. In *every* way."

As an old woman, Clara wrote to Jenny Lane that for her the marriage was the consummation of a thwarted love that had survived for twenty-three years: "As *you* always knew, Dave was the one who had my love. Had I not heard Dave was engaged to Mary Cameron he would have been my husband instead of poor Billy who deserved a better wife than one without love. Still I did my duty and I think I made him happy."

At Cosme the girls were knitting socks for soldiers at the front. Norman Wood took lessons in military drill from Stevenson. He was anxious to follow his brothers to the war and had been applying from the day he turned sixteen.

William Wood wrote to Mary Gilmore that George Titilah had enlisted, making "my boy Norman the senior boy ... To the credit of all who have gone, each went self-urged. No law was required to force them. That is only what might have been expected of boys reared in Cosme ... Anyway, the war has shown me that all British should be under one flag."

In August 1918 Norman Wood received the call. In Buenos Aires he encountered Allie McLeod, returning wounded from France. "His brother Dave had been killed and he told me, 'You're a fool. Why are you going?' I said it did not matter what he thought. I wanted to uphold the Empire. 'All right,' he said, 'they'll make a man of you.' "

Norman boarded a boat in La Plata with other volunteers from Argentina and Chile, but he was the only one from Paraguay. They sailed across to Sierra Leone and joined a convoy of a dozen ships going to England. "We had a man-o-war accompanying us in case a submarine decided to chase us."

He was talking to a group of people on board when dinner was announced. "I said, 'Tucker's ready,' and a man jumped up and cried, 'You're an Australian?' 'No,' I said. 'But that word "tucker" is Australian.' I said, 'I suppose it is. My father and mother are Australian, so I have a lot of Australian blood in me'. Another man came from Cornwall and I told him, 'Your capital is Bodmin on the Camel'. He was astonished by that; he knew the Camel estuary but he did not know the capital of his own county. But I couldn't get into the way of talking of these English people. They had all sorts of accents and ways of saying things. I always felt myself a stranger amongst them. I did not get on with them."

Arriving at Liverpool, Norman, a tall and robust nineteen-year-old, had no trouble with the standard medical inspection apart from bemusement: "I had to wander around naked with just an overcoat between a dozen doctors."

He was inducted into the British Army and sent to camps at Swanage and Bovington. "I did not feel like an Englishman but I knew more about England than some of those people in the army. They seemed an ignorant lot of boys. But I think they loved their king more than I did." The sergeants gave him meaningless jobs, "cleaning drain pipes and so on". It soon became apparent he was not going to be posted anywhere. He had arrived too late to see any action. He chuckled as he told me an old joke, newly minted to him: "The Germans saw me coming and they said, 'What's the use?' and they threw in the sponge!"

He was sent to the demobilisation centre at Winchester. "Whenever you asked for leave there, they'd give it to you. They wanted to get rid of you, I suppose. If you were going to travel anywhere, they'd give you a half-fare voucher."

He began a flurry of visiting and sight-seeing. "I went to see a relative of my father up in Wales but I did not get on very well with them. They didn't like me, I think the women thought I was too rough. I couldn't behave socially." He had better luck with people with a Paraguay connection. He visited Billy Laurence's sister in London and went to Dunbar in Scotland to see the widow of Dave McLeod who had been killed in France. "She was the daughter of the vicar in Dunbar and they were very nice to me." Kindest of all were the Moulds family in Manchester: "Their boy Horace had stayed at our place in Paraguay for a time and they treated me very well." But he did not visit Arthur Tozer, who had returned to live in England in 1918.

Norman went to concerts in London put on by a society formed to help South American volunteers. "They asked me what I needed and gave me money to buy a suitcase and some clothes, because I'd thrown the stuff away that I'd brought with me."

One day in London he passed Australia House. "I was curious and went in. I saw a copy of the big nugget that somebody had found on the

Australian goldfields. I thought it must be a rich country. But they didn't have much time for me because I did not have this hat the Australians had, so I was not welcomed. I wanted to leave my kit-bag there while I went away sightseeing. I told them I was Australian but they said, 'You're in the English Army, you've got their uniform, we have our own men to look after. Go to your own people.' They didn't like me so I went."

Like all the men from Paraguay who had gone to the war, Norman was offered alternative repatriation, to Australia or to remain and settle in Britain. The alternatives appalled him. He couldn't wait to be home.

He returned by steamer to Buenos Aires and upriver to Asunción with some of the volunteers who had gone from New Australia. He took a train to Yegros, "and there I found an old friend who gave me a horse to ride home to Cosme".

*

After Gallipoli, Bill Wood was based in Macedonia. In late 1917 he was posted to Egypt, then to the railway workshops at Lod in Palestine, halfway between Jerusalem and the coast. He was responsible for maintaining signal communications on the line. "I spent over a year there, till the end of the war."

In an Arab village near the railway camp he had an initiation that still put a glint in his eyes when he told me about it at the age of eighty-eight. "I made love to a little Arab girl who seemed to be quite amused with my approaches. She had a brother who was a dishwasher at our camp and he taught me some Arabic and told me what to say to the girl. She said to me, 'My brother said that you want to kiss me.' I said, 'Yes, have you any objections?' She said, 'Well, all the men I know generally don't ask. They just help themselves.' It was quite an experience. She was young but she was apparently well up in her wisdom of men."

In memory it seemed to have had as much impact on him as those first nights at Gallipoli.

As an old man, Bill Wood had qualities now undervalued in the country from which his parents came: honour, decency, gentleness and even innocence. I think those qualities would have been much in evidence when he was twenty-three.

In 1919 in Jerusalem he was reunited with his brother Alex. "He had been in Mesopotamia as an infantryman with the Black Watch regiment. When we met up, Ack was wearing a kilt and had a thick Scottish brogue.

I suppose he had learned their way of talking. He complained about my Australian accent and seemed rather embarrassed by it."

Alex Wood had been to Damascus and Baghdad and later said that by doing so he had satisfied an ambition he had harboured ever since reading *The Thousand Nights and a Night.*

Bill and Alex Wood remained together in Palestine for some months. They did not realise that yet another old childhood friend, the youngest of William Lane's sons, was stationed somewhere in Palestine with the New Zealand Army: 22-year-old William Robert, born at Cosme while his father was away in England on the recruiting trip. Had they met up, he would have been able to tell them of his father's death but, as they barely remembered the architect of their early lives, the news would have made little impact.

The Wood brothers were sent back to England but were separated in the demobilisation process at Winchester. They were offered a choice of repatriation, but there was no hesitation about their answer: Paraguay.

They did not meet up again until they were back at Cosme, greeted by the little community as returning heroes.

Their experience, and that of the other Empire soldiers of Paraguay, had already inspired a poem in the *Australian Worker*:

> Since I left my home far far to roam,
> Over the trackless sea,
> I have seen fair lands, and I've crossed the sands,
> The desert wastes to see.
> I have met dear friends at the world's wide ends,
> Who were very kind and true;
> Still my thoughts stray back to Paraguay,
> To my dear old home and you.
> I have fought the fight, both by day and night,
> That few but the brave men wage;
> I have led the life and faced the strife,
> And the hard world's savage rage.
> Still I surely know that where'ere I go,
> I'll go back again some day
> To the green, green fields and flowing streams
> Of far-off Paraguay.

17

The *Guabirá* Tree

"Look round!" said he, waving a lazy hand, "and see the works of
God, and the place of Paradise, whither poor weary souls go home
and rest, after their masters in the wicked world have used them up,
with labour and sorrow, and made them wade knee-deep in blood
… Leave us here in peace, alone with God and God's woods, and the
good wives that God has given us …"

Charles Kingsley, *Westward Ho!*

Ah! if we only could
Blot out the bitter thought
Make life the thing we would
And shape it as we ought.

Mary Gilmore, *Worker*, 1902

"I thought of going to Australia," Bill Wood said about his decision
at the end of the war, "but I came back to Paraguay. It was my family
and where I grew up. It's like cattle will walk a hundred miles to get
home. It's a terrible thing, homesickness."

"We advise them all not to come back if they come through," Minnie
Jacks had written to Mary Gilmore, "but to go to Australia." But she knew
there was no question of it: "To read their letters one would think there
was only one country in the world, and that was Paraguay … There is a
'claw' in this country all right, which drags people back!"

The claw had a lacerating effect on Lillian Wood, who had seen the
war as her big chance for escape. Her daughter, Rose Menmuir, told me:
"Mum begged Bill: 'After the war, go to Australia, see your relations, work
there, save money and help us all to get back.' But not Bill, he came home,
and Ack and Norman too. Apparently the outside world didn't appeal to
them. They were just mad about Paraguay. There's an old story we were
told as kids by the local people, that if you ate the fruit of a certain tree in
the *monte*, you'd never be able to leave."

"Among the great trees of Paraguay," writes historian H. G. Warren, "is the *guabirá* whose oval leaves end in a small spike. He who eats fruit of this tree becomes enamored of Paraguay and is content to spend the rest of his life there."

In the mythology of the Guaraní, a young Indian girl called Guabirá, endowed with supernatural powers, was in training to become a sorceress. She fasted and took a vow of chastity, "almost impossible feats among the Guaranís," according to Warren, and passed many tests without faltering. A final ordeal, which many a postulant had failed, was to drink *jugo de muerte*, the "death juice" seeping from decomposing bodies on funeral platforms in the trees. Guabirá won through to be a powerful sorceress. She could charm snakes to come to her, give meaning to the present and see into the future.

Perhaps she even saw but could not change her own tragic fate. She became deeply enamoured of a Spaniard and ran away with him to the forest where they enjoyed a passionate idyll. But the Spaniard became fretful for his homeland and the company of white women and soon abandoned her. Guabirá was inconsolable, and outcast from her people for having broken her vows. Then the great god Tupá felt compassion for her plight and gave her eternal life, transforming her into a beautiful forest tree with yellow fruit. "Once a man eats of this fruit, he no longer yearns for the land of his birth, and the maid who loves him need have no fear that her lover will go away."

"My brothers must have had some of it," said Rose Menmuir.

*

Because of the disruption of the war, news which two years earlier had produced mixed obituaries in Australia and New Zealand had been slow in filtering to Paraguay. William Lane had died on 26 August 1917, aged fifty-six; a bronchial condition had weakened his heart.

"His death didn't cause much comment at Cosme that I remember," said Rose. "I know my mother felt very sorry for his wife Anne. She'd had such a hard life, having to bear all the anger at the colony directed against him, losing two sons and then her husband."

Lane's death had come just weeks before the Bolsheviks seized power in the October revolution in Russia, an event which, as an ultra-conservative, he would have thunderously condemned.

The *New Zealand Herald* declared, "This journal has lost a great editor and the country a great Imperialist." His old paper, the Brisbane *Worker*, said that it was the memory of his earlier days that would live in Queensland, "and it will live as long as the Labour movement lasts".

John Lane's son Eric told me how the news reached the family in Queensland: "I remember the day that the telegram came. It was a Saturday morning and I was sleeping out on the veranda. Mum was in bed — she always had a headache — and my father came in and said that he'd just got a telegram that William had died. My mother said, 'Poor Will.' My father's answer shocked me a bit. He said, 'Poor Will died twenty years ago.' "

A few weeks afterwards, John Lane received a letter from William's widow, Anne:

> I have to face life without Will so must make the best of it, altho' until just lately I felt it was an impossibility. I was so fond of him. We never became indifferent to one another and the fact that he was first and foremost with me made it all the more difficult to face. I used often to wish that I was more his equal intellectually, but I comfort myself now with the thought that the great love I bore him counted for more, perhaps, in his life.

Robert Ross, a former friend, long estranged from Lane as their political views polarised, gave his verdict in his paper, *Ross's Monthly*:

> "Billy" Lane is dead — dear old "Billy" Lane. And he died in the camp of the enemy! There's the infinite tragedy of it. Nevertheless, peace be to his ashes! … He was so much to so many of us … years ago. Never phrase-maker so magical, nor personality so picturesque, nor preacher so magnetic, nor propagandist so mighty — to us of the 90s … Those who came under his influence were stirred to the depths, mentally and spiritually. He made all things New. He gripped — and across all those years he grips. He was prophet, priest and king … We shall not look upon his like again. And he died in the camp of the enemy!

*

It was good to be back at Cosme and the Wood brothers resolved to stay if they could manage a living. The old homestead, which their father described in a letter to a niece in Australia, had never been far from their thoughts while they'd been at the war:

> Just picture a wooden house with a shingle roof, with a fairly big flower garden in front — roses, violets, geraniums, phlox, stocks, dahlias, mignonette, carnations and sweet peas in it. On the right of the main house and close up is the boys' room of boards with thatched roof. On the left another long room

of wooden slabs, upright, with corrugated iron roof. On the left of that is the vegetable garden, cabbage, onions, leeks, carrots, beetroot, parsley, tomatoes, lettuce, cauliflowers and potatoes … Back of the buildings is a banana grove with some forty clumps in it; six peach trees, seven mandarins and a loquat. Outside scattered about are dozens of orange trees in full fruit. Then picture the cattle, horses, fowls and dogs and a forest close at hand, and you have a rough picture of us on Cosme.

William Wood confessed he was "developing a keen interest in growing roses and may yet become a crank in that respect". But his sons discovered that he had become overly fond of *caña* and much less inclined to hard manual work. Bill and Norman took on the timber business together, exploiting the cedar on the family allotment.

Lillian, their mother, looked after the flourishing vegetable garden and kept the little bungalow spotless, constantly sweeping the dust which filtered from the thatched roof. She had been a beauty but her looks were going, ravaged by hard work and disappointment. "My mother said she thought it was a lark when she came to Cosme," said Rose Menmuir. "She never dreamed she wouldn't be going back to Australia."

Lillian hated the isolation of their life in Paraguay, the heat, hardship and shortages, the Spanish language which she never troubled to learn, and the *bichos*, a handy word she did adopt for all the annoying creatures, from insects to snakes, that invaded her house.

One day Norman came into the parlour to find her dealing with a particularly nasty *bicho*. "A very poisonous big yellow snake had come up through the floor and was trying to swallow a frog. When the snake saw Mum it dropped the frog and tried to go back down his hole. But she caught it by the tail, drew it out and hit it with her slipper until she killed it. Then she put the frog in front of the dead snake and said, 'Now you just look at that!' "

But in their absence, to the young men's surprise, Lillian had made one adjustment to Paraguay. She had taken up smoking the small brown cigars popular with the local country people. Her "smoko" get-togethers with the other women were now aptly named.

Their sisters, Rose and Kathleen, had been children when the war started. Now they were attractive young women, though overtures from local admirers were frowned upon. The girls were graduates of the modest finishing school conducted by Dave Stevenson after he had returned from France with a bullet lodged near his heart.

"When Mr Stevenson came back to Cosme," said Rose, "he taught us how to dance and how to behave at table. For instance, he took Morty Apthorpe and me to his house and cooked the dinner, then asked me, 'Now, what flavours are in the salad?' I could pick out tomato and lettuce, but he would insist, 'Can you not notice any other flavours?' He told me I had to be taught how to appreciate life. The next day he would have another couple of young people and another dinner for them and so he went through all us kids, taking two at a time. He'd say, 'Now, on your right you have your glass and on your left you have your plate, this is the way you do it. These are the knives and forks you must have'. We learned how we should behave. I think he did a lot for us."

The girls had had their "coming out" during the war years at a fancy dress ball. Rose went as Mary, Mary, Quite Contrary. "I was a little fat thing holding a basket of flowers, but my sister Kathy was thin and dainty and went as a fairy with wings on her shoulders. Mum was Queen of the Night, dressed all in black with fire-beetles under a net on her hair. Mrs Black was a toreador with a cape over her shoulder, and Teddy Jacks was Little Boy Blue. Old Jimmy Sime went as Robinson Crusoe with a sheepskin at his front and back and a straw thatched umbrella."

With the family reunited again, the young men helped their father to kill and butcher a pig, scalding and scraping the skin. William's speciality was making bacon, hanging it up in the chimney to smoke. And sometimes in the evenings they would gather around while Lillian played the piano and William, standing at her shoulder, would sing all the old songs from Australia.

At other times, in a rush of nostalgia, he would read stories and poems by his old friend Henry Lawson, and remind them how he had nearly persuaded the writer to come to Cosme. A new Lawson poem, "Song of the Dardanelles", was painful for Bill, his own memories of Gallipoli too raw, but Norman learned every word of it.

In late 1922 they were saddened to receive a letter from Mary Gilmore with news that Henry Lawson had died in September, alcoholic and poverty-stricken. He had been given a State funeral in Sydney, she told them. The cathedral was so full of politicians and dignitaries that his old mates could barely find standing room at the back.

*

Revolutions were yet another aspect of Paraguayan life that Lillian Wood disliked, and she was given plenty of scope to dwell on this. The country was in a constant state of political turbulence during the years 1919 to 1924, with five presidents turned out of office.

Norman and Bill, cutting down trees in the *monte*, rafting the timber to Yegros and returning with a boatload of *yerba mate*, were not too concerned. "We could hear the cannons booming," said Don Norman, "but we were quite happy and calm and no revolutionary soldiers molested us."

In fact, he remembered the revolutionary period as rather a jolly time, with various people coming to Cosme for sanctuary. "One of the visitors was a nephew of the President. Musicians and people from town would come out and we had dances in the social hall. Ack began flirting with Peggy McLeod and I flirted with her sister Dora."

But, at New Australia, houses were ransacked and a number of settlers decided it was time to leave Paraguay. At the village of Santa Barbara, near Villarrica, Rose Cadogan's son Hugh was captured and threatened with a firing squad.

"The bloodthirsty Paraguayans have been at their old game of Revolution," William Wood Sr complained to his niece Torry Johnston in Australia. "Well, they say it is over now and I'm sure I hope that we have no more for although we here were not molested, yet the whole trade and work of the country is paralysed and that means we all suffer in pocket anyway." But it was not over. His daughter Rose was stranded in Buenos Aires for Christmas and New Year while the fighting continued.

Rose had begun nursing training at the British Hospital there and kept in touch with Mabel Apthorpe and her sister who had taken up governess positions in the city. They were soon joined in the Argentine capital by Bill Wood and young Kathleen.

The mating season seemed to be the reason for the move in each case. For young people of marriageable age, the pool of potential partners at Cosme was small. In 1922 Kathleen Wood had written to her Australian cousin: "So Nellie is sweet 21 is she, and never been kissed? Hasn't she got a best boy yet? Rose was sweet 18 the 9th of March, and she hasn't got one yet!! I was sweet 16 on the 8 of May and I don't want one yet!!! Any way it's no use looking for one here, because there isn't any! When I'm 18 I'll make a dash for good old Aussie."

There *were* suitors in the district among the Paraguayan community. Kathleen had an approach from Antonio Codas, son of a wealthy neighbouring land-owner and nephew of a former government minister. Rose Wood recalled: "My sister Kathy was beautiful; she was semi-blonde, more towards titian, and she could dance like a fairy. But she had a temper, though everyone loved her, especially the men. Antonio Codas fell in love with Kathy, but she didn't return his love; she had various irons in the fire and she was a real flirt. He went to my father and said 'Don Guillermo, *por favor* … If you can persuade her to marry me, I will give you my best bull.' My father was highly amused to think that Kath was worth a first-class bull. But she hit the roof !"

"Kathy, I think, would easily become an accomplished flirt," William Wood observed to his niece, "if given plenty of opportunity. Rose is a great girl and awfully good-natured and would make a good wife for the right sort of man." The right sort, in his opinion, was a man of British stock. He was outraged by the assertion in the *Windsor and Richmond Gazette* that "nearly all the second generation has gone native in Paraguay". He sent off a sharp reply: "The greater number have not done so, and have married into their own nationality. So far as Colonia Cosme is concerned, there is not one instance!"

Even more infuriating to him was a description in W. A. Hirst's book, *Argentina*, claiming that the Australian colony "remnants" had attracted the serious attention of the South American Mission, "whose ordinary field of work lies among the Indian aborigines of the Chaco. In the tropic forest a man's moral and mental horizon appears to shrink in direct proportion to the range of his physical vision".

To this, Wood responded caustically, "But we can still see the sun, moon and stars".

Kathleen made a dash for Buenos Aires, accompanied by her eldest brother. The attraction for Bill was Mabel Apthorpe, whom he had visited on his way back from the war. A tacit understanding had been reached, and he took a job in a shipping office so that he could lay siege to Mabel.

Clara and Dave Stevenson settled into married life, but during the revolutionary period had a financial disaster. Clara sold off the old Laurence allotment and Dave advised her to bank the proceeds with Lloyds. But Clara found a better interest rate with one of the South American banks so made her own decision, depositing with them. Presumably she didn't have Leonard Apthorpe's experience as a warning; his money may have been with the same institution. When the bank crashed "someone came rushing up the street with a telegram, screaming 'Mrs Stevenson, Mrs Stevenson! You've lost all your money!' Clara said, 'Oh, is that what all the fuss is about? Come in and have a cup of tea.' "

My informant was Dave's great-niece, Mary Leeser, who had stayed with Clara on the English Channel island of Guernsey. "She had quite a stiff upper lip and Dave was obviously fairly stoical too. She told me that he never rebuked her for not taking his advice."

Another story indicated a deep affection between the couple. During the revolutionary period, supplies to the colony were interrupted. Clara appreciated fine china on her table, but despaired that most of hers was broken or chipped. "So Uncle David went into one of the local towns and found a porcelain cup and saucer for her. The river was up when he returned, and he had to swim the horse across, holding the porcelain cup aloft. That cup remained her most treasured possession. When I knew her in the 1950s she had it still, and asked that it be buried with her."

After five years of revolution, William Wood Sr thought once again of returning to Australia, encouraged by George Reeve, a genealogist in Sydney, who unsuccessfully petitioned the Australian Government to finance the repatriation of former colonists. "Cannot some efforts be made on our side to bring these unfortunate people to their homeland?" Reeve demanded.

He supported the case by publishing a letter from Wood: "I am sure we would joyfully pack up and go back to our native land, Australia, if we had the opportunity. We are still here and we hope the time will come when that happy occasion will eventuate. Although I may never again see my native land, I have hopes that my children will do so."

But William Wood's sons had eaten from the *guabirá* tree. Paraguay was their mother earth and they were firmly extending their roots.

Alex had married pretty Peggy McLeod, who had once had such trouble eluding Dave Stevenson. They presented William and Lillian with a grandson, christened Alexander but soon known to everyone as Sandy. William Wood professed alarm at his arrival: "Consequently I'm Grandad now. To tell you the truth, I don't gloat much about that title but his grandmother and his uncles and aunts take good care it is fastened on to me. So I think I shall now have to let my beard grow and do my bit. For you know the only use for Grandfathers is to have beards for grandchildren to pull."

The following year Sandy had a little blonde sister, Margaret Rose, to help with the beard pulling. Everyone called her Peggy and agreed she was angelic. Later many revised that opinion.

Bill Wood's courtship of Mabel Apthorpe continued at a snail's pace according to his father, who considered "they are both getting on in years, she being about the same age". Bill returned from Buenos Aires with the understanding that Mabel would follow. "I decided I was going to remain at home for a considerable time," he told me, "so I fitted myself into a work program to be able to keep myself there. I got a small steam engine and installed a circular saw." Soon he was attracting business from Yegros and Caazapá and was in a position to offer marriage.

Clara had sold her allotment to Paraguayans, the Fernandez family. The first *mestizo* family settling right in Cosme village signalled a new era. The newcomers rapidly consolidated their holding and influence in the community, also buying the lot of Jimmy Sime who was still drinking his money away.

But most significant was that Señor José María Fernandez had five attractive daughters. Before long, by a not too mysterious process, his home was the meeting place for the young Cosme men. Bill Wood said that every evening the colony boys would go down to their house, "and sit in the gloaming talking to the family and the girls. It was quite a centre of social activities".

Mabel Apthorpe returned and joined the evening gatherings at the Fernandez place. With her marriage to Bill in 1926, Cosme celebrated yet another linking of second-generation colonists.

Other nuptial announcements followed. "The arrival of the Fernandez family," said Bill Wood, "marked the beginning of Cosme people intermarrying with the Paraguayans. Eventually, one of my brothers, Donald, married Deolidia, one of those girls, Roddy Jacks married another, and my brother-in-law, Mort Apthorpe, married a third. Old man Fernandez, I suppose, was quite happy to get his family into this class of people, these gringos, who seemed to be superior to the local talent."

It would have been unthinkable in the old days, when the colony pledge was quite specific: "We hold not merely life-marriage, but the colour line — that is to say, we refuse to mix with coloured races; we want our children to be as white as we are, capable of upholding our principles and understanding our ideals."

But Bill Wood did not remember any unfavourable reaction among the former colonists, "not that it would have mattered one way or the other. By then they were all just individualists, with no need to consult with their neighbours about this thing or that".

The issue mattered to Mary Gilmore who, in 1902, had written a series of articles about Cosme for the Sydney *Daily Telegraph*:

> The merging with the Paraguayan is the thing to be dreaded. There are people in the colony who had, as far as we knew, absolutely no intention of ever

leaving it, yet who expressed themselves confident, from what they saw and knew of other people, that there were those then resident whose children would marry natives. This speaks for itself … The universal rule is that a man who marries a native becomes a native, living the easy-going animal existence that has no complexities and no ideals — a human vegetable by sheer inertia of the brain. This, then, is what the colony has to dread …

*

"It's not the same," said Bill Wood to his brother Norman, across the dining table of his house in Asunción. "You've got to admit it's not the same."

"The same as what?"

"As having an Australian or English wife. You've got to admit that the Paraguayan woman is second class as a wife. She might be all right for the cooking and so on, but she's not a real companion. It's not the same."

Don Norman, usually distinguished by his laconic, humorous style, looked at his brother with something approaching fury. "As you know, my old missus is Paraguayan," he said quietly, "and she's a good enough companion for me."

*

In 1927 Dave and Clara Stevenson sold up their interests in Cosme and went to Britain. Dave had inherited a substantial amount of money. "The rest of the Stevenson clan had died," said his great-niece, "including his sister Jean. It all went to Uncle David and the Australian side didn't get a penny." The Stevensons purchased an annuity, enabling them to settle on the Channel island of Guernsey and live the rest of their days in modest gentility. "They stayed in boarding houses; not the poshest places, but very comfortable, with entertainment turned on in the high season. The retired gentry lived there on the coast and the seasons came and went."

Arthur Tozer and his wife returned to South America to live in Buenos Aires. Their son Harry joined them with his new bride, Dr Bottrell's daughter, Beattie.

At Cosme, Bill Wood had his carpentry and his brothers Wallace and Frank tilled the land, but most of the young people had to leave in search of work, especially if they had a family to maintain. Alex and Peggy took up farming near Asunción, Norman Wood and Mort Apthorpe were both offered jobs on cattle estancias in north-eastern Paraguay and Donald Wood left with his new wife Deolidia to work in the forestry industry.

In 1931 Kathleen Wood was working as a governess in Córdoba, Argentina and had met her future husband, a Scottish businessman, Oswald Lees.

Her sister Rose enjoyed her nursing career in Buenos Aires and had established a wide network of friends. But in that year a bout of illness brought her back to Paraguay for a holiday. One day Rose and her mother joined friends from the Bank of London for an alfresco lunch at the golf club in Asunción. And there she met a Scottish engineer, Alan Menmuir, visiting from South Africa. He had been brought to Paraguay by the Liebig's company to inspect their meat extraction plant.

"It was a whirlwind romance. We were married three months later," said Rose.

After some time at Cosme, where Menmuir set up a fully operational sawmill which he sold to his brothers-in-law, he returned with Rose to South Africa. They lived on cattle properties there, and in South-West Africa, the comfortable life of the white establishment.

"When we have made some money we hope to tour the world," Rose wrote to her Australian cousin, "so in the next ten years I may run across you. We have no kids as yet. I went to Buenos Aires for an operation to have my womb put straight so as to have a few — but I can always sling them on my back and continue my wanderings like the black Jins."

Rose continued childless. Then she arranged with her brother Wallace at Cosme to adopt three of his children, two daughters and a son. She brought them from Paraguay to raise as the offspring of herself and Alan Menmuir.

I expressed surprise that María, the children's mother, had agreed to the arrangement. "It was to help Wallace," Rose answered briskly. "He found it difficult to provide for all his family."

The Menmuirs moved to Kenya. There Alan contracted a mosquito-borne virus which caused his death in the 1970s after eight years of long and painful illness.

*

"It was such a wonderful childhood at Cosme," Rose Menmuir said, returning to a happier subject. "In all my eighty-five years, those days were the best ..."

She gathered her things together as Rodrigo's wife arrived for her. She had to be early at the airport in the morning; there was a good flight connection in Buenos Aires and she would be back in Johannesburg by midnight.

I asked if anyone would be meeting her and she laughed at the very idea. She would simply get a bus into town and then a taxi from the bus station to the old people's home.

But she was so glad she had made it back for Norman's ninetieth birthday, she said, and "for this last visit to Paraguay. I would have liked to go back to Cosme and see the old house, the cemetery and the stony crossing one last time. Well, not *see* them, because I'm blind as a bat, but stand there where we used to picnic, take in the smells and the feeling. But you can't do everything."

As she left, in the chapel over the road the hymn singing had already begun for *El Día de los Difuntos*, the Day of the Dead.

18
Heart of Darkness

... a will and desire awakens to go off, anywhere, at any cost ... that superfluity which grants to the free spirit the dangerous privilege of living experimentally and of being allowed to offer itself to adventure: the master privilege of the free spirit.

Friedrich Nietzsche, *Human All Too Human*

It had become a place of darkness. But there was in it one river, especially a mighty big river, that you could see on the map, resembling an immense snake uncoiled, with its head in the sea, its body at rest curving afar over a vast country, and its tail lost in the depths of the land ... The snake had charmed me.

Joseph Conrad, *Heart of Darkness*

The Legislative Palace loomed like a medieval fortress on the cliff above the tin sheds and shacks of the Chacarita, the squatter settlement at the edge of the river. The squatters enjoyed a view across the wide glaze of water of the Yacht and Golf Club Paraguayo, at US$500 a day the country's most exclusive hotel resort. "You can get anything you want over there," Max White told me with a rumbling laugh, "and I mean *anything*."

In the pearly morning light Asunción glowed, its modest row of skyscrapers softened and air-brushed, offering a golden reflective wall for the turrets and pinnacles of palaces, the domes and spires of churches.

Rust streaked the white hull of the *Carlos Antonio López*. It was a sturdy working vessel of Paraguay's state merchant fleet, Flota Mercantil del Estado, delivering passengers and cargo to ports all the way up the great river to the border with Brazil.

A Paraguayan naval band on the dock, the musicians smartly turned out in white uniforms and gold braid, lent our departure a ceremonial importance. It was intended for three gunboats of the Brazilian navy moving out midstream and downriver. Officers and crew lined up and saluted on the decks.

Our hooter sounded, engines throbbed, and with a churning of muddy waters we swirled away in the opposite direction. Florence waved from the wharf. I was on my way to Concepción, 310 kilometres north, to visit her Uncle Norman.

On the deck, third-class passengers made camp, fixing string hammocks to stanchions and funnels and setting out bundles to mark territory — bags of bananas, baskets of cackling fowls and a kid goat with its legs trussed.

Leaning against the railing, watching the gunboats and city recede, were five fair-skinned people. The three men, Brothers Grimm, were dressed in brown trousers, high-buttoned shirts, dark blue cardigans. They had blunt pudding-bowl haircuts and bushy grandfather beards. The women wore long blue dresses and white bonnets. They were Mennonites, like the Amish a branch of the sixteenth-century Anabaptists. I knew there was a vast colony of them in the Chaco, a more successful colony than William Lane's.

We left Asunción's river shanties behind; although we were 1,600 kilometres from the sea, the river was still more than a kilometre wide. We passed under a concrete span, another triumph of engineering, connecting Asunción by road to the Chaco and Argentina. Soon, the low scrub on each bank was interrupted only by the occasional brick-and-tile *rancho* or a Spanish colonial waterfront mansion.

Drizzling rain began. The Mennonites fled, the squatters dismantled bedding and bundles, fowls squawking, goat bleating, and scattered to claim new places in the corridors below. I stowed my things in my cabin on the top deck, next to the captain's, two bunks to myself, sharing a bathroom with a cabin on the other side.

I hurried through the growing squall to the first-class restaurant. It had the sort of shabby old-world comfort that the English on the Grand Tour once expected as the minimum — dark wood panelling, flock wallpaper, tables with linen napery — though they would have dispensed with the portrait above the bar of that avuncular old dictator, Carlos Antonio López. A sallow, bearded Brazilian man read a newspaper, three German backpackers played Tiddliwinks, some young tourists with Yorkshire accents argued over a game of dice.

The grey-brown river was choppy; rafts of *camelote*, water hyacinth, floated past, some carrying passengers, egrets or herons. On the Chaco bank, eight black vultures drooped like damp folded umbrellas on the branches of a half-submerged tree. A tributary led away into a tangle of mangroves, cane thickets and low thorn scrub. An Indian fisherman balanced in a dugout canoe, waiting for the wash of our boat before plunging his spear.

The rain continued. There was nothing for it but lunch. In the restaurant, sitting in singular splendour, I ordered wine. The Mennonites frowned, murmuring to each other in Plattdeutsch, a variety of low German now extinct in the country of its origin. Palm hearts with mayonnaise and vegetable soup were followed by a tough steak, clearly from one of the stringy beasts of the Chaco, usually boiled down for Oxo cubes. The Mennonites still stared balefully, making me nervous. So I ordered more wine.

George Masterman, an Englishman who went to Paraguay as chief military apothecary, hired by the dictator Francisco Solano López and later incarcerated by him, had a perhaps understandably jaundiced view of the river trip: "One feature of the rivers of Paraguay, and a very depressing one to the traveller, is the absence of life from their banks. One steams up for league after league against the turbid stream, and no sign of man or his industry, or scarcely, indeed, of any living creature, is visible."

He mentioned the occasional alligator, but if they were still there, they kept a low profile. Even the British adventurer Cunninghame Graham, whose enthusiasm for Paraguay sent James Craig Kennedy to New Australia, had to admit: "As a steamer slips along the bank, nothing for miles and miles is seen but swamp, intersected by backwaters, in which lie alligators, electric eels and stinging rays. Far as the eye can reach are swamps, swamps and more swamps, a sea of waving pampas grass ... but here and there at intervals of many leagues, a clearing in the forest where some straggling settlement exists ..."

We shuddered to a stop. I went onto the wet deck to watch. On the Chaco shore was a place achingly desperate in its isolation — two thatched buildings that looked vaguely official, one of them a school with flagpole and playing field. A hundred metres along were sagging thatched huts; washing flapped on a line, fowls pecked. And beyond, endless swamp and scrub and nothingness. An Indian family were lined up in front of the huts, dolefully staring at us. They despatched a rowboat with two children, a boy of perhaps ten and a tiny fellow of about four. We lowered our gangway and a youth in military uniform, a baseball cap on his head, swaggered down, jumped into the rowboat and chucked a sodden newspaper into the ten-year-old's lap. Our engines started up again as the three rowed to shore — towards the little thatched huts, the Indian family, the flapping washing, the schoolhouse and the flagpole. I wondered about the life of the young man, about the future of the children in that desolate place. Were they descended from the once mighty Guaycurus or Payaguas?

If the river scenery was dull, its history was not. Theodore Roosevelt, with the American presidency behind him, journeyed up the Paraguay in 1913 and noted that it had been plied by craft, fortified and settled by soldiers, priests and merchants, "long before the Mississippi had become the white man's highway".

In 1536 Juan de Ayolas had led a fleet of Spanish ships bearing soldiers, horses and armaments up the Paraná and the Paraguay in search of El Dorado. Indian nations along the rivers fought the invaders, the Abipones alone massing 10,000 warriors. The conquistadores killed all who blocked their progress. A German adventurer with them recorded that the Abipones of the Paraná launched a war fleet of 500 canoes, but "we slew a goodly number of them with our guns, they having never in their lives before seen either a gun or a Christian".

Near the conical hill Cerro Lambaré, which announces the present day site of Asunción, the Spaniards encountered a settled agricultural people, the Guaraní, who amiably offered food. But the Spaniards, to ensure a supply line, attacked instead. A three-day battle ensued. Seeing hundreds of his people killed, the Guaraní *cacique* or chief negotiated a peace and sent some young women to clinch the deal. The Spaniards liked the Guaraní way of doing things. The settlement of Nuestra Señora de la Asunción was established and became the capital of the Vice-Royalty of La Plata.

The Spaniards saw that the Paraguay River bisected the country with almost mythological clarity. To the east the land was soft and undulating, with neat gardens tilled by the comely and industrious Guaraní. To the west it seemed to be, like the edges of their maps, where dragons lurked. The Chaco was hard and forbidding, resistant to agriculture, home only to nomads. Most feared were the Guaycurus, who controlled the land, and the Payaguas, warlike pirates with fleets of canoes, who held dominion over the river. These tribes were the traditional enemies of the Guaraní, who enlisted the Spanish as their allies and protectors.

For 200 years the warrior nations of the Chaco proved implacable foes. The Guaycurus fled from the Spanish cavalry at first, in terror of the thundering four-legged beasts. But soon captured horses were an essential part of their battle strategy and their nomadic life. Martín Dobrizhoffer, a Jesuit priest, observed: "Their only care is that of their horses and arms, in the management of which their skill is admirable. War, or more correctly pillage, is the only occupation they reckon most honourable."

Spanish conceptions of honour were different. In 1677 José de Avalos, commander of the Spanish garrison at Asunción, feigned peace negotations with the Guaycurus, to be concluded by his own marriage to a chief's daughter. All the most distinguished Guaycuru *caciques*, their families and retinues, arrived in Asunción for the celebration. They were feted with food and drink. At a prearranged signal Spanish soldiers turned on them and 300 Guaycurus were massacred.

The war of resistance escalated. Dobrizhoffer recorded the fearsome raids of the river pirates, the Payaguas: "These savages, though more like beasts than men in their outward appearance ... continued to pillage the Spanish colonies ... Heaps of dead bodies, crowds of boys and girls driven away, houses reduced to ashes, wares and all kinds of precious furniture carried off, and churches laid waste — these are all the monuments of the barbarous ferocity of these pirates."

But within one hundred years of Dobrizhoffer's account, the Payaguas had become a mendicant people, living in a squatter settlement across the river from Asunción, objects of pity for a British travel writer in 1852: "The Payaguas are very queer creatures: they are tame Indians ... allowed to drag on their miserable life unmolested, on the soil taken from them by the white men ... they wander about the town and pick up a living by selling birds and little things which they make, wherewith they buy in the market such food as they cannot catch for themselves."

A Payagua *cacique* had shown a flicker of the old spirit in 1869. After selling ostrich feathers and carved gourds to the English apothecary George Masterman, he refused to pose for a photograph, replying "that he was not going to have his ugly face copied for white men to laugh at, and stalked angrily away". But Masterman determined he was not to be beaten. He appealed to the garrison commander who had the whole tribe brought from the Chaco under armed guard.

> I took several portraits easily enough; for they stood as fixedly as if they had been carved out of wood, and were desperately frightened at the camera. Amongst them was an old woman, said to be more than a hundred years old, a dreadful old woman, with a scarcely human face, long white hair hanging down to her waist, and withered, fleshless limbs. I have never seen such an object as she looked, upside down, in the focusing-glass.

The warrior Guaycurus took longer to subdue, but by the 1870s they too had become hawkers of curios to passengers of passing river steamers, "holding up tiger skins to signify their readiness to trade".

But in the end Paraguay, alone in Latin America, became an officially bilingual *mestizo* nation. The Guaraní people east of the river saw their old rivals vanquished and eventually absorbed their Spanish conquerors, utterly. They were the true survivors.

*

The rain stopped. The Mennonites and backpackers returned to the deck. I tried to talk to a Mennonite woman but she moved hastily away. I had cast myself in a role with my incessant journal writing, the wine. A scarlet woman? Or a slightly dotty middle-aged lady like Greene's Aunt Augusta?

We passed a swampy island. Hundreds, maybe thousands, of black cormorants clung to spindly branches or bobbed in the water, their long black necks held high, like fussy swimmers protecting their hairdos. Through the trees swooped two huge white birds, their black-tipped wing spans over two metres across, effortless in flight.

On the eastern shore, scrub had become a dense wall of forest. As dusk settled we hove to off a town, Puerto Rosario. Streets in a grid pattern, almost heroic in their attempt to impose geometric order on wilderness. Neat pillbox houses with glowing windows. Our dinghy went ashore with cargo, returned with a passenger, and we were on our way again.

As the sun slipped down behind the Chaco wastes, a cold wind whipped off the river. I took a shower before dinner and changed into warmer clothing. Heading for the restaurant I passed a young Paraguayan couple hunched on the deck. The pretty girl, aged about eighteen, her head on her knees, was moaning softly. I asked if I could help. The man looked distraught but waved me on.

The main course was cold schnitzel and salad. The bearded Brazilian was in stale Lothario mode, determined to lock glances. I skirted around him to join the table of young English people. One of them, reading *New Scientist*, introduced herself as Virginia, a medical student. Her friend Patrick worked with computers, and her sister Claudia was still deciding what to be when she grew up, but might study archaeology. They'd been in Peru and were in love with Inca ruins.

We ordered more wine and soon were alone in the restaurant, swapping travellers' tales. The young Paraguayan man I had seen on the deck came to the door, wild eyed. His girlfriend was very sick, he said — was anyone a doctor? Virginia offered to help but said she was only a student, perhaps he should speak to the captain — an idea he rejected with alarm. We followed him outside.

The girl María was in pain and bleeding heavily. I offered my cabin and we settled her on the lower bunk. Virginia called for some items to be brought from her pack. After some time she emerged. She had supplied sedatives and sanitary napkins and the girl was resting more calmly. María had been to Asunción for an abortion. They were illegal in Paraguay, and since the Pope's visit in 1988 even harder to obtain. She had been to some backstreet place. But the bleeding was easing and Virginia hoped she would be all right until the morning.

I looked in on them. The young man, Ramón, cradled María in his arms on the lower bunk, but went to sit up with muttered apologies. I motioned him back and joined the English people on deck until they too retired.

*

The moon was riding high. I leaned against the rail, watching the phosphorescent spume of our bow wave. Our boat hugged the eastern shore, close enough to hear plopping sounds in the mangroves and the cry of a nightbird in the immense dark wall of trees. The *Carlos Antonio López* seemed puny in the vast expanses of sky, water and forbidding forest. We could have been travelling in any time, up any great river in the tropics, in the heart of a dark continent. I fantasised being Hepburn on the *African Queen* but it was unrewarding without a Bogart, even in grumpy mode.

I thought instead of Joseph Conrad. "Going up that river," he wrote, "was like traveling back to the earliest beginnings of the world, when vegetation rioted on the earth and the big trees were kings. An empty stream, a great silence, an impenetrable forest … The long stretches of the waterway ran on, deserted, into the gloom of overshadowed distances …"

We rounded a great bend and at last there were signs of human life, a few lights winking among the trees.

While his fellow passengers ate rotten hippo meat and plotted his murder, Conrad's narrator, Marlow, chugged inexorably upriver, in search of a tortured soul sequestered somewhere in its far reaches. Mr Kurtz, mad or bad, "desired to have kings meet him at railway stations on his return from some ghastly Nowhere, where he intended to accomplish great things". Marlow found Kurtz only to witness his death and was told later that he "would have been a splendid leader of an extreme party".

I guessed the lights signified that we were approaching the sequestered retreat of another tortured extremist, now long dead. The handful of low houses along the shore, a few with dimly lit windows, was all there was of the village of Antequera. We stopped, a dinghy came out, and we exchanged mail and cargo.

I stared into the enveloping darkness of forest beyond that small beach-head of civilisation. About 70 kilometres along a cart-track east from Antequera, I knew there was a ragged little settlement. Like Colonia Cosme, it was situated in the fork of two rivers. And it too was now virtually a ghost town, home for a few remnants, people with coppery skin and blue eyes, of mixed Paraguayan and European blood, descendants of utopia. Not New Australians but New Germans.

In 1886, seven years before Lane and his followers made landfall, Elisabeth Nietzsche, sister of the philosopher, arrived in Paraguay with her husband, Doktor Bernhard Förster, to implement their particular blueprint for paradise. They were accompanied by fourteen peasant families from Saxony, the breeding stock for an experiment in biological purity, the vanguard for an Aryan master race.

Förster was notorious in Germany for his anti-Semitic propaganda and had been dismissed from his teaching position in Berlin for racist agitation. He dreamed of a place where he could put his ideas on nationalism, anti-Semitism, Lutheranism and vegetarianism into practice. Because it was remote, unpopulated and, above all, uncontaminated by Jews, he chose Paraguay.

The Times of London mocked "the most representative Jew-baiter in all Germany" and his mission as "the comedy of the modern Pilgrim Fathers":

> He is a man, like too many of his countrymen, of one idea, and that idea is Germany for the Germans, and not for the Jews. Finding that idea unrealistic in his native country, he, with a few devoted men like himself, has sailed to a far country, there to found a new Deutschland, where synagogues shall be forbidden, and Bourses unknown.

Politically Förster and his wife Elisabeth were as far to the right as Lane was to the left, but their ambition was similarly boundless. In the Paraguayan wilderness they hoped to create "the nucleus for a glorious new Fatherland that would one day cover the entire continent".

As with Lane, it had taken two years of vigorous propaganda, fundraising and organising of supporters before they were ready for departure. Elisabeth hoped her brother Friedrich would join them, but notions of nationalism and anti-Semitism were repugnant to Nietzsche; he consistently expressed distaste for his sister's experiment in Paraguay.

Förster, Elisabeth and their followers travelled by steamer to Asunción. "This mission has a name," Förster wrote, "the purification and rebirth of the human race, and the preservation of human culture." It was not a good omen when the youngest daughter of the Fischer family died of fever during the trip.

Elisabeth stayed on in the Paraguayan capital while Förster and most of the colony men travelled north to Antequera and 70 kilometres through the forest to their chosen site. They cleared trees and set up a few rough dwellings.

Then they laboured to build an imposing residence, a virtual mansion with airy rooms and a deep thatched roof. It was called Försterhof and was to be home for the rulers of the colony. "Just think how grand it would sound," Elisabeth had written to her husband, "Förster of Försterhof."

The peasants from Saxony made do with grass huts.

In March 1888 Elisabeth arrived for the inauguration ceremony, clearly regarding herself as a royal taking possession of her principality. In a letter to her mother she described her welcome by humble local people who offered flowers, cigars and handed her their babies for benediction. "Suddenly, eight splendid horsemen appeared. They were our New Germans who had come to greet us ... We were not received with a cannon salute, but cheerful gunshots rang out as we approached and a charming small wagon appeared, decorated with palm leaves like a green arbour and carrying a small red throne." One of the loyal colonists made a speech of welcome and shouted "Long live the Mother of the Colony". Accompanied by the chant of *Deutschland, Deutschland über alles* Elisabeth drove on to her new house.

The Paraguay Government, encouraging immigration after the disastrous War of the Triple Alliance, assisted generously with the purchase of land but, as later with the Australians, it applied conditions: 140 families had to be settled within two years, otherwise the purchase money was to be returned or the land forfeited. Förster signed, certain that once they were established, hundreds would want to escape the blight of Jewry in Germany.

He published a booklet describing the opportunities for energetic Aryan settlers who could sweep all before them compared with the lazy Paraguayans: "The principal characteristics of the Guaraní are indolence, sluggishness and indifference. The Paraguayan is content with little, but this contentment is a vice rather than a virtue. A paradisiacal situation, of living without labour, which might seem ideal to the work-shy Jew, is achievable in these tropical and semi-tropical zones." The Paraguayans were passive and without initiative, he wrote, perhaps the most biddable people on earth, "but you can't trust the word of a Paraguayan".

"We have found the nearest thing to paradise on Earth," Elisabeth wrote to Friedrich, by then achieving fame for *Thus Spoke Zarathustra* and *Beyond Good and Evil*. But he declined her invitation to invest in the scheme and pointed out that "our wishes and our interests do not coincide insofar as your project is an anti-Semitic one. If Dr Förster's project succeeds, then I will be happy on your behalf and as far as I can, I will ignore the fact that it is the triumph of a movement that I reject. If it fails I shall rejoice in the death of an anti-Semitic project".

Elisabeth was discovering ambitions as a writer, which would later find expression, when her brother was incapacitated by a stroke and mental illness, in reworking his papers to bring his views more into accordance with her own. Meanwhile she described arcadian bliss in Paraguay for a German newspaper: "After supper we sit in the garden and look into the distance ... there are fields, gilded with red from the evening sun on both sides of the river, interspersed with fields of lowing cattle. What a peaceful, happy picture this affords, nothing is alien ... the singing of German men reaches us from a garden a little way off. How the jungle trees must wonder at these strange new sounds wafting through the tree-tops ... Up into the star-studded southern night sky, into the mysterious gloom of the jungle: *Deutschland, Deutschland über alles, über alles in der Welt.*"

She enthused that the produce of the land was so abundant it fell from the trees, the Paraguayan servants so simple and malleable they fell over themselves to serve their white masters, and a pan-continental railway would soon pass by their doors, connecting them with the Rio de la Plata and Peru. It was all as flimsy and fanciful as *nanduti* lace, spun from her fevered imagination.

In fact most of the colony crops were a failure and, without adequate transport, none were economically viable. The settlers scratched a wretched living, fought with the neighbouring Paraguayans, hated their grass and mudbrick shacks and resented the order to stand to attention when their self-appointed *caudillo* rode past on a white horse.

Bernhard Förster had developed a severe case of grandiosity and contemplated offering his services as President of Paraguay. (He was a little previous with the notion; later, the son of a German brewer achieved the same ambition.)

Though forty families arrived from Germany, over a quarter departed within the first two years. Förster was obliged to refund the price of their land and still had to find over 100 families to satisfy the Paraguay Government. He borrowed more money, with no hope of repayment. He sent desperate begging letters to Germany. He became increasingly deranged and spent long periods away from the colony, on the pretext of raising finance, indulging in drunken binges at the Hotel del Lago at San Bernardino, a German settlement near Asunción. In June 1890, aged forty-six, Förster took strychnine and morphine and was found dead in his hotel room. Elisabeth arrived by the first riverboat and persuaded a Paraguayan doctor to testify cause of death as a "nervous attack". She was then free to construct a noble obituary, characterising Förster as a man who had died like a Wagnerian hero, a martyr for his people.

Elisabeth had a new mission as a myth maker. She returned to Germany. Friedrich, released from a lunatic asylum to the care of his mother, sometimes undressed in public, or thought he was the Kaiser or the Duke of Cumberland. But in more lucid moments Elisabeth read him passages from *Thus Spoke Zarathustra*. She was finding quiescence an admirable quality in the men in her life. She began editing her brother's papers and also worked on a book, published five months later, *Bernhard Förster's Colony New Germany in Paraguay*. Bernhard was "a battling hero worthy of Valhalla, in the image of whose face the true Christ is united with the real German race, who has fallen on a foreign field for his belief in the German spirit".

Elisabeth came back to Paraguay in August 1892 to find the colony in disarray. Most settlers had left or were leaving for Germany, Brazil, Argentina or more accessible parts of Paraguay. Those who could not afford to go made clear their resentment of the lies she had published. One declared: "The first condition for any improvement in New Germany is the removal of Frau Förster."

Elisabeth sold her house and departed the colony forever. She had her new career to attend to in Germany, re-editing and often re-writing her brother's papers to suggest he shared her virulent anti-Semitism, and to reflect more lustre on herself and her threadbare political ideas.

Her lush and inaccurate biography of Friedrich Nietzsche, portraying herself as muse and confidante, brought her fame, control of his papers and a berth for life at the Nietzsche Archive established at Weimar. Her tampering with Friedrich's work contrived to make him an apostle of German imperialism, militarism and anti-Semitism and a prescient herald for Hitler's rise to power. Through her industrious manipulation, Nietzsche became forever associated with Nazism.

Elisabeth succeeded beyond even her own feverish dreams. She was nominated three times for the Nobel Prize for Literature, corresponded with Mussolini and was visited by Hitler, who deferred to the powerful old woman as if she were the mother of the Fatherland. In 1934 she was gratified by his instructions for a special ceremony at San Bernardino in Paraguay, where the first National Socialist party outside Germany had been formed. Children of party members sang as a bag of real German soil was solemnly sprinkled over Bernhard Förster's grave.

When Elisabeth died the following year at the age of eighty-nine, a Nazi guard of honour — the SA, the SS and the Hitler Youth — was provided for her funeral. The Führer was chief mourner.

Her colonial experiment in Paraguay had been a disaster but, from its ruins, Elisabeth had emerged triumphant: a famous writer, friend of the powerful, recipient of many honours and, by the end of her long life, unofficial matriarch of her nation.

In a curious way the same description could be applied to Mary Gilmore. She survived the failure of her very different colony in Paraguay, to achieve literary eminence, public honours and national icon status.

The two women of course never met. But it is poignant to speculate that Elisabeth Förster must have come within cannon-ball range of Mary's mentor, William Lane. Elisabeth did not leave Paraguay until late August 1893. Lane and the first Australian colonists arrived in early September.

Perhaps somewhere on the Río de la Plata the two fanatic visionaries, armed with almost diametrically opposed blueprints for reorganising mankind but similar in their certitude, were on ships passing in the night.

*

Ben Macintyre's book *Forgotten Fatherland* is brilliant in tracing Elisabeth Nietzsche's story.

The author visited the site of Nueva Germania in 1991 and found seven or eight families with names such as Fischer, Schubert, Stern, Schütte, Halke and Schweikhart — descendants of the Saxon farmers who came with the Försters. They lived in adobe thatched cottages and tilled neat fields, but he had a sense of the encroaching forest biding its time.

He concluded: "They remained what their ancestors had been, nineteenth-century German peasants, even poorer now than they had been then." The old people were clinging to their language and Lutheran religion "like a raft which was sinking under them". But they seemed to gain comfort in asserting a sense of superiority over the Paraguayans, and many boasted of Aryan purity in their own family line.

The young were drifting away. Among those who stayed, many did not speak the German language, preferring Guaraní.

All that remained of the Försterhof mansion, Macintyre wrote, were some timbers used for a chicken coop. But the older people relayed the verdict of their parents and grandparents: Förster had been an arrogant swindler, but Elisabeth was "a brave woman ... and beautiful".

Some of the men from Nueva Germania had gone to fight for the Fatherland in World War II. The little schoolhouse was closed in mourning when Germany was defeated. But although the Paraguay government had made a hasty declaration for the Allies three months before their final victory, its tolerance of fascist sentiments was well known. Nazi war criminals fled to the country for sanctuary, losing themselves in the large German community.

At Nueva Germania the descendants of an experiment in biological purity spoke of a stranger who stayed among them in the 1950s. When a body was exhumed in Brazil in a blaze of publicity over thirty years later, a few of them thought they recognised a former neighbour. The face in the photographs was that of Josef Mengele, the Auschwitz doctor who carried out sadistic experiments on thousands of twins and other helpless inmates, contriving to make Aryans of Jews and gypsies by torture; manipulating their genes, bleaching their skins, dyeing brown eyes to blue. All in the name of racial purity.

*

When I returned to the cabin the young couple were curled together, Ramón snoring. I climbed onto the top bunk and slept fitfully, alert to María's intermittent soft moans. During the night I heard the cry of a bird from the trees on the shore, a melancholy ulullation of descending notes. I wondered if it was the *urutaú*, in Guaraní myth the soul of a woman grieving for her lost lover and for her country laid waste by so much sadness.

*

There was a dip in the morning light as we passed under another of the great bridges spanning the river. To our starboard Concepción announced itself by the twin belltowers of its great cream-coloured cathedral, presiding feudally over the clutter of one-storey stucco buildings, brick smokestacks and rusting sheds which tumbled chaotically to a line of palm trees and the river. Its seedy tropical decadence seemed art directed for a Graham Greene film.

Hansom cabs with worn leather bonnets and pony traps were pulling up in front of the colonnaded Customs house, skinny horses harnessed into box carts, jostling for position in the mud.

As we eased in, sacks, boxes and baskets were thrown to eager hands on the wharf, while *campesinos*, market women, Indians in woven ponchos, a baby-faced soldier and the priest occupied the front stalls for the weekly theatrical event. But one figure towered above them all, ninety-year-old Norman Wood. He grinned, bobbing his black umbrella at me. He was wearing a tweed jacket and a jaunty deerstalker's cap. His son Enrique was with him, a head shorter, thickset and chunky, looking something of a brigand with a Zapata moustache and a leather hat crammed on his curly black hair.

*

Concepción was Don Norman's patch of Paraguay. The river port had been his home for over forty years and he was a figure of consequence. As we engaged an ancient taxi in the brick-paved main street, townsfolk greeted him — a *carreta* driver, a girl on a motor scooter, and the Bishop of Concepción who confessed, grinning, that he was still recovering from Don Norman's birthday fiesta. "*Mucho* whisky!"

"The architectural pretensions of Concepción are very moderate," a 1917 British travel book damned with faint praise. "The lesser cities of Paraguay have much to recommend them, but as a rule their merits incline rather towards the picturesque than towards any striking features of architecture or of urban design."

Since my visit seven years earlier only the decay had advanced. The few fine colonial buildings, the shopfronts and low stucco houses, whitewashed, ochre or pastel stained, were cracked and dilapidated, the side streets still muddy quagmires ploughed by oxen carts and pony traps which outnumbered the lorries and battered pick-up trucks.

Stroessner's dictatorship had been overthrown and the dreaded incarceration camp on Pena Hermosa Island, north of the town, was no longer congested with political prisoners. But the new government was still Colorado and had not been lashing out on civic improvements. Concepción was traditionally a stronghold for the opposition Liberals. Only the smuggling trade with Brazil, through the border town of Pedro Juan Caballero, kept the place going.

But the coup meant that Enrique Wood and his family had come back to live. When I'd met him in 1982 he had been home on a brief visit, but lived in Brazil, a veterinary surgeon working with cattle. He had confided then, in a low voice, that he was a socialist. He had thought it safer, like a few hundred thousand Paraguayans, to stay out of the country for his health. He left after being arrested and detained three times by the secret police. One arrest, on Independence Day, had been simply for wearing a shirt of the wrong colour — the blue of the Liberals.

In *Travels with My Aunt*, Graham Greene's retired bank clerk had been warned: "It's the National Day … If you go into town carry something red … It's the colour of the governing party. The Liberal party is blue, but it's unhealthy to carry blue. No one does."

"I was very young then," Enrique had told me, "I was only wearing the blue shirt because I liked it. The second time I was arrested I was a student in Asunción. Apparently there were some communists in the hostel where I was living. The police came at dawn and told me to come to police headquarters. They told me to hurry or they'd break my bones. I said 'Okay, no problem. I will go with you'. The third time I *was* political. I was shouting against Stroessner: 'Out military, out from power!' I was arrested and warned I'd go to gaol. After that I left the country."

Enrique was now involved in buying and selling cattle. As the taxi churned through the mud, he proudly pointed to the icecream parlour he had set up for his wife, Marita. But he was still a socialist, he told me in Spanish, though he couldn't see much connection between himself and Lane's people. "They all seemed a bit *locos*, and racist too. The first thing they did was throw the Indians off their land. That was the sort of thing Stroessner did. The Indians were cleared out of the forests to make way for people from Brazil with money."

"Better not to talk politics," said Don Norman, nodding meaningfully towards the driver. "You never know … Old Alfie's just over the border. He might be back one of these days."

Don Norman's rambling stucco house was on a corner block. A shopfront to the street had once been a saddlery. It was now the parlour and was never used. It was the museum for family history: five chairs in a row, a writing desk and a glass-fronted cabinet which displayed floral cups and saucers, replacements for those smashed by the bullock on Lillian

Wood's first night at Cosme. A portrait of the old lady herself was on the wall, next to a more elaborately framed one of Don Norman's Paraguayan mother-in-law, Doña Sarturnina Vergara. There was a print of *The Royal Family at Balmoral*, with Charles and Anne as young children, and a plate commemorating the Pope's 1988 visit to Paraguay.

The true heart of the house was a roofed courtyard with a long dining table. Most rooms gave onto it through curtained doorways and the courtyard was open to the garden. "Why would we ever need to lock up?" laughed Don Norman. "We have nothing worth stealing."

A foolishly amiable Labrador called Fury, clearly no watch dog, hurled himself at us in ecstasy. I said that his name didn't seem to suit. Don Norman agreed, "but he was the ninth dog we've had. All the others had names starting with F, so I had to come up with something".

He led me to the kitchen across a covered passage-way where a skinny black cat was suckling two kittens in a basket beside the fuel stove. Fury declared his love. It was unrequited, hissed the cat. Don Norman, clearly unfamiliar with domestic arrangements, fussed around looking for the makings for *yerba mate*. He was relieved when his wife and Melania the maid walked in carrying baskets of vegetables from the market.

Doña Leonarda, a strong handsome woman of seventy, embraced me, sent us out to the table with a pot of *mate* and set about making lunch. "He's been looking forward to talking English again," she told me in Spanish. "He never gets a chance these days."

*

After the revolution of 1921–23, Norman Wood left Cosme and took a job in the Chaco at the Pinasco tannin factory, near the Brazilian border. The axe-breaker *quebracho* logs were pulped, bagged and sent downriver to Asunción, where the extracted tannin was used for curing leather. "It was a hard life, even harder for the ordinary workers. I didn't like it." In Peter Upton's novel *Green Hill Far Away*, banned by the Stroessner regime, a tannin factory camp at the edge of the river, a scrofulous settlement around grey sheds and towering chimneys, was described as a living hell for the labourers press-ganged to work there.

After a few months Norman Wood wrote to Liebigs Extract of Meat Company. This British concern developed the concentrated essence of beef invented in 1847 by a pioneer of organic chemistry, Justus von Liebig, recognising its potential in the Chaco on land too poor for raising prime beef. By the 1880s the Liebigs company had become rich from its huge estancias and produced corned beef, bonemeal and the familiar Oxo cubes. It still does.

Norman Wood's most marketable talent was his fluency in English, Spanish and Guaraní. He was offered a job supervising the store at Estancia Arrecife in the Chaco. "I started as the bookkeeper, looking after the accounts, paying the men and distributing the rations and meat. But as often as possible I'd saddle up a horse and make myself useful at a *rodeo*. That's when they'd round up the half-wild cattle and identify those that needed curing, those that had maggots in their navels or tails. We'd ride hard and catch them and bring them to the men waiting to attend to them with carbolic. The wounds would be filled with horse dung and a bit of palm leaf tied to the beast's tail to show it'd been treated."

His skills with horses and cattle were recognised and he was given experience on other Liebig estancias. "One of my bosses was Rufino Vidal, a famous barbarous horseman, but he taught me a lot. In return I tried to teach him about keeping the books, but that was the most difficult job I ever had. He never got the hang of it. He was only happy in the saddle."

Norman himself was rarely out of the saddle, living the frontier life from which myths are manufactured. He could have been "The Man from Snowy River" but it wasn't Australia; a cowboy but it wasn't the American Wild West; a *gaucho* but it wasn't the Argentine. He simply called himself a cattleman. But, tall and straight, truly one of Lane's manly bushmen, he must have cut a dashing figure. "I had baggy pants called *bombachas*, a sash around the waist to hold them up, long jack-boots, a sombrero, a knife and a North American Colt 44 revolver."

He did not escape the attention of the girls in the nearest market town of Concepción, and he noticed them. With his meagre salary he couldn't think of getting married, although he courted a young Paraguayan school-teacher, Emiliana Martinez. But then Liebigs promoted him to assistant manager to an Englishman, Mitchell, on Maldonado, a large estancia in north-eastern Paraguay. With an increased salary and regular rations, he married Emiliana at last.

They were together for almost ten years. In 1931 their daughter Ruby Rose was born, followed two years later by another girl, Lily. "But Emiliana was never a healthy person, always very frail." In 1936 she died giving birth to a third daughter, Elsa.

Don Norman was promoted to *mayordomo* or manager of Maldonado, in charge of thousands of cattle. As he rode among them, the animals' fate sometimes gave him pause. "There's something sad about it. You looked at these marvellous looking steers and knew they were going to be reduced to a dark coloured paste. Oxo cubes. They say it's no damned good for your health but others think it's strengthening. I don't know."

He employed a young woman, Leonarda Mazacotte, as nurse and governess for his three daughters. Leonarda, of Paraguayan, Italian and dark Brazilian ancestry, was eighteen and beautiful. She confided that she had thought Norman Wood the most wonderful man she had ever met. And still did.

He told me, with a twinkle in his eyes: "She even learned to make sweet damper, just the way the Australians made it! I thought I'd better marry her. And she was very pleased about that. We've never had any trouble all our lives. She has never said a cross word to me."

Norman and Doña Leonarda had seven children. They were proud of their first child Rodrigo, who had become a successful bank manager; their only daughter, Marisa, had married well and lived in Asunción. Their other boys all lived in or around Concepción.

*

Most of those boys gathered in the courtyard for lunch.

The second son, Roberto, swarthy and solidly built, called in on his way out to his cattle property in the Chaco. His younger brother Ricardo had just come from there, where he worked on another estancia. Thin and moody, he washed off the dust before sitting down. "Ricardo lives with us," said Don Norman, "but he has a problem. He likes *caña* too much." The fifth son, Eduardo, a cotton farmer, lived too far downriver to visit often, but the youngest, Norman Federico, called Freddie, lived at the house. Plump and amiable, in his late twenties, he ran a produce store in Concepción selling grain and *yerba mate*. His wife Anna taught music. Their three-year-old son William was with his grandparents all day, clearly a joy in their lives.

It was a warm extended family and lunch was the time they met together. A chunky vegetable soup, thickened with cornmeal and cheese, was followed by roast chicken, baked potatoes and salad. With a flourish Don Norman produced a bottle of wine.

Before everyone in the household retired for the siesta, he showed me a present he had received for his ninetieth birthday. An old cattleman friend, Don Candido Benitez, had tooled a picture of a horseman on saddle leather. The intricately chiselled message to "*Al Gran Amigo* — Don Norman Wood — *90 años*" ran purple with affection as it recalled: "the times that have passed, when in the fresh early dawn in the north, mounted on fine horses of the Treble brand, going to the camp, sharing the happy songs of the birds, with the sun rising over hills in the distance, we would eat the delectable fruit of the north, the *guaviramí*. After that the hard work of the camp ..."

*

After the siesta Don Norman found a use for the parlour. We sat there to tape more of his memories. With his brothers gone he was conscious that the baton had passed to him as The Patriarch of Cosme and he wanted his story on record. His awareness of the fragility of life had become acute in that year, 1989: a grandson, Donald, had shot himself while playing with a gun; a son, Felice, had died from cancer.

With a shaky hand Don Norman drew a family tree. Felice had been born in 1944, some years after the three daughters of Emiliana Martinez, and before the birth of Rodrigo in 1947, the first of Doña Leonarda's seven children. "Who was the mother of Felice?" I asked, confused.

Don Norman smiled softly. "Let's just say she was a little girl who kept making a nuisance of herself and getting in my way. But a nice little girl."

Not for the first time I thought that the lovable old man was a lovable old rogue.

The year Rodrigo was born, 1917, was the time of the bloodiest revolution in Don Norman's memory. It began after an attempted coup against the military dictator, Higinio Morínigo, who had support from the Colorado party. The stronghold of the Liberals and the other opposition groups was in the north. They virtually declared war on the Colorado south.

At Nueva Germania, the Liberals made the Försterhof mansion their headquarters, firing through windows at the Colorados. As they retreated, the house was ransacked of the remaining heavy German furniture, including Elisabeth Förster's piano.

Norman and Leonarda were at Estancia Maldonado when Liberal rebels burst into the house during the night. Don Norman opened the storeroom at gunpoint and the rebels helped themselves to food, emptied the wardrobes of clothing and took all Doña Leonarda's jewellery. "They left us more or less standing in our night-shirts, cleaned us out. But we were lucky. In other places people were killed in such raids."

It was only a few days after Leonarda had given birth to Rodrigo and she was still weak. Surprisingly, the rebels had not taken all the horses.

Don Norman drove his wife and son in a horse cart, travelling all through the night to Concepción, to stay at her mother's house until the insurrection was over.

After that experience Don Norman decided he was a Colorado party supporter, so when General Alfredo Stroessner came to power in 1954 he was relieved. It seemed political stability had come at last.

He remained at Maldonado until his retirement from Liebigs. He had been able to run a few head of his own cattle on the property and from their sale bought the house in Concepción. He had his pension from Liebigs and had contributed to a state superannuation scheme, the *Provisión Sociál.* He was further gratified by the apparent solidity of the Stroessner regime when the fund paid up.

*

A clamorous morning penetrated my misty cocoon of mosquito netting: bells of the cathedral tolling, carts trundling, roosters crowing, birds twittering outside the window. I lay thinking how satisfying it was to wake to the sounds of an earlier century. Then a van with a loudspeaker held the town captive, blaring a promotion for a *kung-fu* movie at the local cinema, punctuated by blasts of rock music.

Enrique took us for a drive, calling first at the home of his brother Roberto and his shy blonde wife, Elsie. She was another descendant of Cosme, the granddaughter of Alfred Davey, a former Queensland farmer once described by Arthur Tozer as "the most practical and intelligent worker we have had".

The youngest of Elsie and Berto's four children, Norman Kitchener, crawled over his grandfather's knees. They had a cattle property of about 1,000 hectares in the Chaco. Berto said they supplemented their income by selling iguana skins and ostrich feathers purchased from the Indians. Elsie also made soft cheese, without refrigeration the only way to dispose of milk from their cattle.

Word travels fast in Concepción and we were soon joined by Elsie's sister Gladys, another blonde, but elegant and hypertense, her hair stylishly coiffeured. She had had a year's schooling in the United States on a Field Association scholarship and was married to a cattle rancher, Robert Smith-Pfannl, of mixed German-American descent. I was given to understand that they had a more substantial property than her sister Elsie. As afternoon tea was served, with a sweet damper sent over by Doña Leonarda, Gladys fretted about the absence of cake forks.

"What the hell," said Don Norman. "Let's just eat the damn thing!"

*

We crossed the river and entered the Chaco. Beyond here there be dragons, I'd decided. In the Chaco there were Indians who had escaped herding into reservations, still hunting wild. There was a living fossil, a species of pig discovered only in 1975, that had been believed extinct since the Pleistocene. There were Mennonites on tidy farms. And there were cattle runs. Descendants of Australian socialists hoped to become rich from them.

It was an unrewarding vista. The flat plain of soggy tussock grass and low bushes was studded with caranday palms, tall thin trunks, sometimes 9 metres in height, seeming disproportionate to the fanned leaves at their crowns. Lakes, pools and puddles, choked by the assertive spatulate leaves and mauve flowers of the water hyacinth, lurked hidden to swallow the unwary walker. Long-horned cattle foraged through the marshland, searching out grass, their hooves making plopping noises. These watery wastes seemed to bear no relation to the stories I'd heard of the war against Bolivia, fought out in a flinty pitiless desert. But it was the same land: sometimes desert, sometimes swamp, always inhospitable. This flooded plain was the Low Chaco.

Beyond was the Middle Chaco, a terrain of scrub, cactus and *quebracho* trees.

Then the thorn forests of the High Chaco began, a land of spikes and spines baked by the sun, extending to the foothills of the Andes. There wild creatures roamed at night — giant armadillos, long-nosed anteaters, boars, maned wolves, pumas and jaguars. Some of these creatures developed a taste for human flesh during the war against Bolivia.

The Chaco was as discouraging as the land to the east of the river was arcadian. A Paraguayan writer described it as "a plain with the soul of a mountain, motionless and hard as rock".

Mosquitoes clouded around us. We came across more bony cattle, cropping at low sage bushes. Don Norman cast a professional eye over them, and said he'd had enough.

We returned across the great concrete bridge, built at venally inflated cost during the Stroessner era, to what passed for civilisation. All around the town dense forest crowded in. By the waterfront was a monument to Marshal Francisco Solano López and his battle cry, "*Vencer o morir.*" Conquer or die.

About 100 kilometres to the north-east, near the frontier with Brazil, was Cerro Corá, the place on the Aquidabán River where López made his final stand.

"He fought bravely to the last," said Enrique. "He could have run away, but he didn't. Every Paraguayan knows his last words: *Muero con mi patria!* — I die with my country!"

I had read that the marshal's horse got bogged and that, attempting to run for it, he was stuck in the mud himself when the lance of a Brazilian cavalryman brought him down. There were also tales of his fabulous insurance policy, of how, as he and Madame Lynch fled north, they had lingered to stash a priceless treasure. It was said that fourteen servants were assigned to bury the contents of many carts — silver and gold, jewellery and paintings. Then the fourteen servants were shot in the back and their throats were cut.

Enrique was appalled. "López had to do some hard things, but he wouldn't have done that. This was British propaganda that you read?"

"A book by a British writer."

"*Claro!* For us López was a good man, a leader who made the rest of South America take notice of Paraguay. Why do English people want to call him a mad dictator? Racism, that's why. They try to do dirt on my country and I hate them for that!"

In his vehemence, he had broken into English. Don Norman looked across at his son, astonished. "I didn't think Enrique could speak it at all these days. He used to try a bit as a child. He used to follow English visitors around and learn words that way, but I thought he had forgotten all of it. There's some Aussie in him after all!"

*

I accompanied Doña Leonarda on her daily excursion to the market. The scene would not have been very different at the turn of the century: oxen *carretas*, donkey carts and hansom cabs lined up in the mud at the market's borders with a few cars and trucks. A man in a pony trap cracked his whip, his red-striped poncho swirling. Women in woollen bonnets huddled by mounds of fruit and vegetables, produced *empanadas* and omelettes from little stoves for the passing trade or heated *mate* kettles over fires. Flies buzzed around the open butchers' stalls where hunks of meat, hooves, pieces of stomach, spleen and coils of intestine were set out like gloves, lace and ribbon at an uptown haberdashery counter.

The market's picturesque qualities came from abject poverty. Cows foraged in rubbish bins. The second-hand clothing stalls exuded dank smells of sweat and hopelessness. Women turned over stained pieces of rag in futile search of a bargain.

"It's Stroessner who left the country this way," said Enrique on our return. "There was so much corruption. The money went to him and a few of his generals. And he's smuggled out a lot of the wealth that belonged to the people. There are still many Stroessner crooks in the government, though others have been brought to justice."

Don Norman said he had always been considered a Colorado supporter himself — Enrique was the only Liberal in the family — but he had had no idea of the extent of the thieving going on, although occasionally he had heard stories. There was the case, he remembered, of a Liebigs' manager who had been told he could take over an estancia in return for cooperation. "He said to them, 'But it belongs to the company' and they answered that didn't matter: 'We can fix it so it belongs to you'. The fellow was tempted but didn't go through with it."

Even their local mayor in Concepción forgot about looking after the streets and became rich taking over properties and cattle. "But after Stroessner was overthrown," said Don Norman, "they found a lot of money missing in the departments he controlled and he was sent to gaol. Some of them have got away out of the country, but others are in prison, and there's many more to be investigated. It seems they've been robbing the country for millions. Every day there's something new in the paper about someone else who's been stealing."

Don Norman said he was embarrassed to tell an Australian like me about such things.

"Why?"

"Because Australians aren't like that. My father always told us about how Australians are straight and honest. I've always admired them for that."

I started to tell him about the recent Fitzgerald inquiry in Queensland, about the number of politicians who had been found grossly corrupt and the police chief ending up in gaol.

Don Norman was deeply shocked. "I didn't think Australians would do such things!"

I omitted some of the more sordid details, for now I too felt embarrassed. I didn't want to destroy the illusions of ninety years.

*

On Sunday night we went to Mass in the cathedral. Don Norman said he wasn't so very devout himself, "but I go now and then to please the missus". While he waited for her, he sat at the courtyard table strumming a guitar. It was his mother's favourite song, "A Starry Night for A-Rambling". Doña Leonarda came out looking elegant in a blue dress and black lace mantilla.

In the beautiful cathedral they shared a hymn book and Don Norman sang in a confident baritone. As they queued before the altar to receive communion, he stumbled and held onto a pew, looking old and frail.

I was flying out in the morning. On that last night he wanted to stay up and talk by the old fuel stove. He would like to go back to Cosme, he said, but now that Roddy McLeod was dead there was no one there but his nephew Francisco. "He's not done too badly. He's got two trucks and works the timber. He goes out shooting partridges when he has a day off. He's the only man to have ever made a success of Cosme, my nephew Frisky." The only real attraction to lure him back now was the cemetery, he said, but he was not going to get sentimental about it.

I've had a good life and I'm not yet thinking of it being time to die. You can tell the people who listen to these tapes of yours that I've always wanted to go to Australia but now I'm satisfied to stay here and finish my life in Paraguay. I'm quite all right, I don't have any need for very much. I can live on what I've got and I can help people. I have my family and they all gather around whenever there's any trouble. I am well protected. I have a wife who is a Paraguayan, a good woman who has never been annoyed with me, not on any occasion. She has given me seven children and there are thirty grandchildren. And somehow or other they all seem to like and respect me.

From the time I had first met Don Norman in 1982 I had come to love the old man. As I kissed him goodnight, we both knew it was for the last time.

19
The Green Hell

On the Chaco shore of the river… the rank dense growth is altogether impassable. It is the utter desert as far as man is concerned, intolerable to him with mosquitoes and ague. If he penetrate it but a little way, awe seizes him to behold that gigantic network of plants that shuts him in as in a prison. In these dark depths one is oppressed by a feeling of suffocation, of restrained freedom, as in a nightmare …

E. F. Knight, *The Cruise of the Falcon*

… these must be the ashes of Eden, all that was left of it after the Fall, over which the sons of Cain now wander in their khaki and olive-green… But in this accursed Eden no miracle is possible.

Augusto Roa Bastos, *Son of Man*

The Dakota took off from Concepción. I settled back uneasily, alert to the bumps, rattles and asthmatic stutters of the twin engines. The horror stories about air travel in South America crowded in, the chance of being blown away as an afterthought with some cocaine baron or ex-president on the run, or finding oneself on the in-flight menu after a crash landing in the Andes. Paraguay's internal airline, Transporte Aéreo Militar or TAM, is run by the airforce. The decrepit fleet of Dakotas dates from World War II. Gloomily I considered the fact that Dustin Hoffman's precise autistic character in *Rain Man* did not pick TAM as his airline of choice. He preferred Qantas.

But my companion, Gladys Smith-Pfannl, grand-daughter of Australian socialists Alf and Mary Davey of Cosme, used TAM like a taxi. I remarked that I could see the point of a poor country selling seats on airforce flights when they were not needed for military purposes.

"*No* seats are for military purposes," she laughed. "The generals run the airline strictly for profit."

There didn't seem to be any drug barons or ex-presidents among the dozen passengers, but Gladys could have been taking their loot to Switzerland. Blonde, elegant, cherry-red suit and stiletto heels.

She and her rancher husband Robert and their dark-eyed daughter Carolina were going to Asunción to attend a wedding that evening, quite a society do. Gladys said she would be spending the afternoon at the hairdresser and beauty parlour. The wedding would be a chance for Carolina, a student at the University of Concepción, to meet some "nice" people. Another daughter was currently on an American Field Association scholarship in the Caribbean. "If you have daughters you do what you can for them. Especially if you live in Concepción, which isn't the centre of the universe."

They spent half of every week at their house in town and the rest of the time at one or other of their ranches in the Chaco. She produced photographs taken at a recent *asado*: the family relaxing at a table outdoors with wine, while some *rheas*, native ostriches, sprinted through the background of the shot, feather dusters on the move.

I stared down at the vast dun and olive wasteland threaded with dry watercourses and faint red dirt tracks which seemed to go nowhere. Extending between the Paraguay River and Bolivia's Andean foothills, the Chaco, at 260,000 square kilometres, is bigger than Arizona, and is about two-thirds of modern Paraguay's land area. But it is often said that more people are buried beneath its surface than have ever lived on it. I guessed the Chaco Indians were left out of that particular equation; they usually didn't count.

A parched desert of dust, cactus and thorn scrub for most of the year, between December and March downpours and melting snows from the Andes produce a vast, steamy, mosquito-infested swamp. In either season the heat is intolerable, but in summer temperatures soar to 49 degrees centigrade. From the time of the Conquistadores, people seemed to relish the region's awfulness, referring to it as *L'Inferno Verde* — the Green Hell.

But the Chaco is home to animals and a brilliant variety of birds, its name derived from the Quechua Indian word *chacu*, meaning "an abundance of animal life". Riotous menageries, animals that logic denies together outside the pages of *The Swiss Family Robinson* are found there — rattlesnakes and scorpions, jaguars, ocelots, monkeys and armadillos, deer, maned wolves, tapirs and a prehistoric hog — co-existing in a land which once discouraged all but the most intrepid hunters.

The indefatigable television naturalist David Attenborough went there in 1958 in quest of a *tatu carreta*, a giant armadillo nearly 2 metres long. He did not find his cart-sized creature but, in *Zoo Quest in Paraguay*, he recorded his amazement at another discovery. The wilderness guide who took him to the Chaco was Sandy Wood, a burly Paraguayan who spoke Spanish, Guaraní and a couple of other Indian languages. "In addition — and astonishingly, for he had never been outside South America in his life — he spoke English with a broad Australian accent."

> Paraguay is full of people of foreign stock. Poles, Swedes, Germans, Bulgarians and Japanese, all have flocked to this small republic in an effort to escape land shortage or religious oppression, political tyranny or the law. Sandy's parents had come with nearly two hundred and fifty other Australians just before the end of the last century ...

It was actually Sandy's grandparents, William and Lillian Wood, who came. Sandy was one of the swashbuckling sons of Alex Wood and Peggy McLeod. Attenborough learned from him the story of the Australian socialists.

Sandy had felled timber, worked cattle, been a hunter, "and his placid temperament made him an ideal guide". He knew how to cope with the Green Hell. Attenborough found him in Asunción, "in a bar in the centre of the town, where he was obviously preparing himself to withstand weeks of total drought in the Chaco. He bought us a beer".

No doubt, like the *palo borracho* tree, Sandy was conserving moisture. Attenborough discovered that the Chaco, one of the world's last unconquered frontiers, had an extensive arsenal to repel invaders and ensure the survival of its own. Even the vegetation was defensive:

> All the plants bore savage spines which protected them from the grazing cattle, desperate for fodder in the drought, and many had also developed devices to enable them to conserve water during the dry season. Some did so in their huge underground roots, others, like the hundred-armed candelabra-like cactus, in their swollen fleshy stems. The *palo borracho*, the drunken tree, conserved moisture in its distended bloated trunk, thickly studded with conical spines. These trees, perhaps, epitomized the character of the armoured vegetation of the Chaco ...

There had always been a few prepared to penetrate the region for the riches to be exploited: prospectors for oil and minerals, hunters of feathers, pelts and paws, cattle ranchers and loggers of the most marketable resource, the axe-breaking *quebracho* tree, prized both for a wood so hard it paved provincial roads and for its tannin-producing bark. But since the recent sealing of the Trans Chaco Highway, traversing 750 desolate kilometres to connect Asunción with Bolivia, the exploiters were advancing in force.

But the ones who came in their thousands and stayed, proving they too were made of stern stuff, were the Mennonites. Their main congregation was at Filadelfia, the town they created in the middle of the Chaco, 450 kilometres north-west of Asunción. They named it for The City of Brotherly Love, though a visitor described it, with its neat scattered houses, icecream parlours, supermarkets and used-car lots, as "an empty, one-lane, red-mud version of the Wild West. On all sides, you can see the town end and the nothingness begin".

Mennonites were a branch of the sixteenth-century Anabaptists, followers of a Dutch priest, Menno Simons, who rejected Catholicism to join the Anabaptist movement in 1636, seeking a society run on strictly Biblical lines. Another branch broke away to form the Amish.

For 300 years the Mennonites were on the move in search of a country that would allow them to live and practise their religion in isolated peace. They insisted on the preservation of their medieval language Plattdeutsch, their distinctive traditional dress, their right to educate their children in their own way and a tradition of pacificism. From Holland they moved to Prussia, then some to North America, others to southern Russia. The Bolshevik revolution of 1917 caused Russian Mennonites to join their brethren in Canada. But when the Canadian government introduced compulsory secular education, they fled in great numbers again. They settled in Mexico, but the introduction of a national security scheme offended their implicit faith in God's providence. In 1921 an advance group of Mennonites went to Paraguay. For three centuries they had been wandering, seeking a sanctuary where they could reject the customs and conveniences of modern life. At last they had found a place no one else seemed to want.

The Paraguay government offered them 120,000 hectares in the Chaco. This was just two-thirds of the grant received by the Australian pioneers in the fertile land to the east thirty years earlier, but no doubt the government had acquired a certain caution. But the Mennonites, hard-working rural people with no desire to interfere in local politics, seemed ideal immigrants to a country still suffering the chronic population deficit caused by the War of the Triple Alliance. And so they proved to be, although their aim, like the Australians, was to keep to themselves, avoiding intermarriage with Paraguayans. Their religious fervour and their distant location made them spectacularly more successful in achieving it.

Like Lane they wanted effectively to live in a country within a country. This was more feasible in the remote thorn scrub. They negotiated a charter in July 1921 which guaranteed them practical self-government, exemption from military service, generous tax advantages, suspension of tariff duties on basic imports for ten years, and complete freedom of immigration. In return they promised to be good citizens, to pay taxes and produce food not only for themselves but for local markets.

In 1926 the paddlewheel steamer *Apipé* brought the first batch of 309 Mennonites to their promised land. Within six months over 2,000 of them, mostly Canadians, were settled in the Chaco at Colonia Menno. However, they were unprepared for the harsh conditions. In the first year a number died from typhoid fever and there were many desertions.

But news of the settlement spread and others arrived from Russia, Poland, Germany, Manchuria, Canada and the United States. They settled in thirty-six villages in a new colony, Fernheim, Distant Home, and the town which became the Mennonite capital, Filadelfia.

The land was resistant. Floods, droughts and grasshopper plagues destroyed their crops and marauding animals killed their stock. Brigands attacked lonely farmhouses. The Mennonites, who called themselves *die Stillen in Lande*, the unobtrusive ones, did not fight back but put their trust in God.

Within a few years of their arrival, these pacifists found themselves living in a war zone. In 1932 hostilities broke out between Paraguay and Bolivia for possession of the Chaco, the land that no one but the religious exiles had seemed to covet. Paraguay mobilised, but the Mennonites were exempt from military service.

When the fighting came close to Colonia Menno, the Paraguayan commander ordered their evacuation. But the Bolivians fell back before a concerted Paraguayan attack, and the front moved further away. The order was withdrawn. The peaceful colonists, in gratitude, offered bountiful hospitality. Women in long dresses and prayer bonnets pressed cakes on their saviours, astonished Paraguayan soldiers existing on hard tack and a litre of water a week. Though the war in the Chaco continued for three years, most of the Mennonites stayed on.

After 1947 a third colony, Neuland, was settled, mainly by Ukrainian German refugees released from prisoner-of-war camps, some of whom had served willingly, and others who had been dragooned, in the German army during World War II.

Today about 15,000 Mennonites live in the three colonies of the Chaco, in neat villages of wooden farmhouses, with their own banks, schools and hospitals. Their farming cooperative grows cotton, sorghum and castor beans and an efficient dairy industry sends cheese and butter to market in Asunción.

The Mennonites have proved themselves the country's most successful colonists. They have large families and gather together to sing hymns in the evening. They continue to reject many amenities of modern living — indoor plumbing, radio and television — and often manage without electricity. Mostly they have accepted the need for motor vehicles, though a few still farm without tractors, despite the hardship for themselves, their horses and bullocks in the intense heat.

On the roads around Filadelfia women in dark dresses and small white prayer caps and men in dungarees and straw hats can be observed gravely travelling in horse-drawn buggies; but most find pick-up trucks more practical. Their children congregate at the video store which offers James Bond, *Mad Max* and the latest from Sly Stallone.

Many of the young men are reportedly disaffected with the traditional way of life; they favour wearing jeans and riding motorbikes, smoke openly and secretly enjoy *caña*. Some have sex with local Indian women, though few marry them. They hitch to Asunción or Santa Cruz in Bolivia along the Ruta Trans-Chaco. Military and oil trucks and an increasing number of tourist buses thunder along the highway, daily invading the enclave of the traditionalists.

But these exiles from persecution have been invaders too. The Chaco was the last refuge for Paraguay's Indians who subsisted by hunting, gathering and fishing. The Mennonites proved it could be settled for agriculture, presaging the end for the old nomadic way of life. Now only 50,000 pure-blood Indians remain. The Toba-Maskoy were moved by government order from their ancient lands in the central Chaco to make way for farming. Since 1980 some 10,000 Indians have settled in the Mennonite area and there are numerous stories of their exploitation as labourers.

In his book, *Land Without Evil*, journalist Richard Gott does not have a good word to say about the Mennonites, viewing them as "fearsome religious maniacs with limitless funds" who inexorably dominate the agricultural economy of the region, excluding the Indians from any chance at competition.

But the followers of Menno Simons insist they are simply preserving the sanctuary they have won after hard struggle, obeying the instructions in Genesis: "Be fruitful, multiply and replenish the Earth."

*

If war in the Chaco was a shock for the Mennonites, it was received as an outrage by the League of Nations, which pointed out indignantly that it had banned war.

There had long been resentment between Paraguay and Bolivia over the desolate lands of the Chaco. It had its origins in the peace settlement of 1878, negotiated after the War of the Triple Alliance. Rutherford B. Hayes, an otherwise undistinguished President of the United States, acted as arbitrator. He approved a significant loss of the defeated nation's territory to Argentina and Brazil, but ruled Paraguay should keep most of the Chaco. Humiliated and devastated, this concession of territory became crucially important to Paraguay's national pride.

But the arbitration ignored Bolivia's claims to the area from colonial days. These became more strident after the War of the Pacific of 1883, when a defeated Bolivia lost its Pacific coastline to Chile and became land-locked. The River Pilcomayo flowed across the Chaco to the Paraguay River; it was believed that control of its dubiously navigable waters could provide the Andean nation with the same access as Paraguay, via the Paraná and Plata rivers, to the Atlantic.

The discovery of oil in the Chaco foothills of the Andes fuelled Bolivia's claims. Wildly exaggerated stories swept La Paz and Asunción of immense lakes of petroleum lying just below the surface of the Chaco, fabulous riches for the nation that owned them. Each displaying a fine disregard for their earlier hostilities, Chile urged Bolivia on while Argentina supported Paraguay. Each side accused the other of more powerful, shadowy backers: Bolivia maintained that Great Britain and Royal Dutch Shell were behind Paraguay, which counter-charged that the Standard Oil Company of New Jersey was financing Bolivia's arms build-up.

In 1928 a Paraguayan skirmish against a Bolivian base almost precipitated the conflict. Friction between border patrols escalated, rumour and tension increased, while international attempts to arrange mediation came to nothing. In June 1932 Bolivian soldiers seized a Paraguayan post. The second bloodiest war in Latin America's history was on.

The League of Nations convoked emergency sessions in Geneva and issued statements against the two warring nations for failing to note that this method of resolving disagreements had been forbidden. It was the first serious test of the League's efficacy and it proved wanting, the first wrecker's hammer against its elaborate structure.

Bolivia had three times the population of Paraguay, three times the annual budget and a strong army led by an experienced though erratic German mercenary, General Hans von Kundt. It boasted an arsenal of 160,000 rifles, 1,400 machine-guns and 60 aeroplanes. Against Paraguay's 12,000 rifles, 150 machine-guns and 8 rather ancient aircraft, Bolivia looked invincible.

Those who had not studied Paraguay's fighting record in the War of the Triple Alliance confidently predicted that it would soon be overwhelmed by its stronger opponent and the conflict speedily resolved.

It lasted three years. It was fought in unimaginably harsh conditions with tenuous communication and supply links for both armies, though Paraguay had the advantage of a railroad penetrating 160 kilometres into the Chaco. The Bolivian government was unstable and corrupt, and its supply lines were vastly over-extended. Its soldiers suffered terribly away from their mountain altitudes. In the heat and humidity of the hated tropic lowlands, they died like flies.

The Paraguayans had the strength their turbulent history had instilled, a fierce, almost mystical, sense of nationalism. They were led by an able president, Eusebio Ayala, and had a brilliant military commander in Colonel, later Marshal, José Félix Estigarribia. The troops had a genuine conviction that they were fighting for their homeland. Inadequately equipped, many barefooted and without proper rifles or ammunition, often armed only with machetes, the Paraguayan soldiers made daring guerrilla raids to capture the equipment they needed.

The opposing armies had Spanish in common so, for security reasons, the Paraguayans communicated in the field only in Guaraní. The Indian tongue, familiar to all Paraguayans, intensified their sense of identity. After the war there was an outburst of literature in Guaraní.

The Chaco War offered the world the tragic spectacle of two poor and largely Indian-populated republics striving to liquidate one another. Conspiracy theories raged. To some, the battling nations seemed merely expendable frontline troops while the real commanders, Britain, the United States and their associated petroleum interests, simply bided their time for the division of the spoils.

For the Uruguayan writer, Eduardo Galeano, the spectacle was intolerable:

> Bolivia and Paraguay are at war. The two poorest countries in South America, the two with no ocean, the two most thoroughly conquered and looted, annihilate each other for a bit of a map. Concealed in the folds of both flags, Standard Oil and Royal Dutch Shell are disputing the oil of the Chaco.

In this war, Paraguayans and Bolivians are compelled to hate each other in the name of a land they do not love, that nobody loves. The Chaco is a gray desert inhabited by thorns and snakes; not a songbird or a person in sight. Everything is thirsty in this world of horror. Butterflies form desperate clots on the few drops of water. For Bolivians, it is going from freezer to oven: They are hauled down from the heights of the Andes and dumped into these roasting scrublands. Here some die of bullets, but more die of thirst.

Clouds of flies and mosquitos pursue the soldiers, who charge through thickets, heads lowered, on forced marches against enemy lines. On both sides barefoot people are the downpayment on the errors of their officers. The slaves of feudal landlord and rural priest die in different uniforms, at the service of imperial avarice.

One of the Bolivian soldiers marching to death speaks. He says nothing about glory, nothing about the Fatherland. He says, breathing heavily, "A curse on the hour that I was born a man."

It was the war in which descendants of New Australia and Cosme, including some who had already fought for the British Empire, made the commitment to Paraguay.

Some of the young men were of conscript age and had no say about going, but others who could have stayed at home decided to volunteer anyway. "We were Paraguayans," said Rod McLeod. "We were born in Paraguay. It was our war."

"The ladies of Cosme said it *wasn't* our war," Norman Wood reminded him. "They said it was between the Paraguayans and the Bolivians and nothing to do with us."

"But the ladies didn't understand the situation. They said, 'They're just bally natives!' "

Don Norman agreed that the Cosme women like his mother had never really accepted being in Paraguay. "They thought Cosme was a part of Australia or England. Over afternoon tea they'd argue about the war and say it wasn't our look-out. But of course they were wrong. Bolivia had the arms, and tanks and flame-throwers, and could have overrun us all."

"The Paraguayans always called me *gringo*," said Rod McLeod, "but they didn't say that I was a *gringo* when they wanted me to go to the war."

Four others from Cosme went with him: the brothers Mort and Sid Apthorpe, Donald Wood, and his elder brother Alex, a veteran of the Black Watch in Palestine. "Ack went up with them, but he soon came back sick. He couldn't stand it."

Rose Menmuir told me some of the men went into hiding. "They were called 'ghosts of the forest', because they hid in the *monte*. They only returned at night to their homes. My brother Wallace volunteered to join the army, but he had no intention of going. He just dissolved into the forest around Cosme and became a ghost too. But my other brothers Don and Ack went. Ack was only in the rearguard and twanged a guitar, but Don was in the big fight. He lost his hearing from the bombs."

Twice as many volunteered or were conscripted from New Australia: Ricardo Smith, Douglas Kennedy and his younger brother Nigel, two Adams boys, a young American called Shepperson, a Jones, a Drakeford, a King and a Bates.

In the Chaco wastes Paraguayans and Bolivians engaged each other; in three torrential rainy seasons struggling through deep mud and swamp, dying from disease more often than from inflicted wounds, in a desperate trench warfare that sometimes resembled the foulness of the Somme two decades earlier. At other times the combat resembled nothing that Europe had seen for a thousand years. A Paraguayan regiment which had run out of ammunition charged, swinging machetes. They left 200 headless Bolivians on the field.

The three long dry seasons were remembered with even greater horror, men on each side staggering across a blistering desert, maddened by thirst. "Someone should open a window somewhere to let in a little air," wrote a Bolivian. "The sky is a huge stone in which the sun is set." In the searing heat, millions of yellow and white butterlies fluttered over the corpses, sucking moisture from their eyelids.

"It was a hell of a place," said Rod McLeod. "They'd give you about a litre of water a week. Sometimes you didn't get any. When you ran out you had to poke your bayonet into certain trees and hold your little dish as moisture seeped out. Water was the most trouble. You could live a long time without eating, but not without drinking."

Donald Wood served in Regimento Itá Ybaté No. 9, named after a battlefield in the War of the Triple Alliance. His worst experience was an ambush by the Bolivians in a ravine called Cañada Strongest. If he had come across Douglas Kennedy there he would not have recognised him; they had never met and common links with a failed utopia would have meant little under bombardment. "They let us have everything they had, mortars, cannon and bombs from the air, but at last we found a break in their lines, and most of us got out... I think they took about 2,000 prisoners."

Among the Paraguayans captured at Cañada Strongest — the number is still debated — was Douglas Kennedy from New Australia.

Wood, later hospitalised for shell-shock, soldiered on: "Apart from the fighting, the living conditions were about zero. We were always hungry, always thirsty and always dirty… Sometimes we were whole days with only one cup of water, and the heat was terrible. There were times when we went without a drop of water the whole day. We used to dig up roots and chew them to suck the moisture. I often remembered Dad's tales of the Never Never Land in Australia, and reckoned that the Chaco must be something like it."

Water. I thought of lines by Kipling, the soldier's poet, writing of war in another parched land:

> But when it comes to slaughter
> You will do your work on water,
> An' you'll lick the bloomin' boots of 'im that's got it.

Donald Wood was with a companion near Villa Montes, inside the Bolivian frontier, when "a thin black soldier came up and asked us where the water hole was. I showed him the road and as he went off, my friend said, 'That man is from Cosme'. So I called him back and had a good look at him, and when he talked I saw a slight resemblance to Sid Apthorpe. I said, 'Are you Sid?' He nearly jumped out of his skin. He said 'Yes, but who the hell are you?' We were both so black that we didn't know one another."

Nigel Kennedy went to the war when he turned eighteen in 1933. "I had papers to say I was English if I'd wanted to use them, but I'm Paraguayan and I thought I should go and fight. My other brothers wanted to get us out of it, but I said, 'No, I want to go and have a bad time. I see these people coming back howling and I want to go and see if it's true, this desperate time they have out there.' "

"And it was true?"

"It was worse than true."

When Nigel arrived at the front, near the Bolivian border at Fortín El Carmen, he had not been assigned a regiment, but was an *agregado*, a freelance. "The Paraguayans were forming a pincer movement behind the Bolivian lines, two regiments on one side and three on the other."

Marshal Estigarribia had about 21,000 men to oppose an estimated 50,000 of the enemy along a 320-kilometre front. His First Corps struck in the north and after a seven-day battle took 7,000 prisoners. But the Bolivians commanded the road, preventing the Paraguayan water trucks from getting through. During the battle, Nigel was made a water carrier, struggling 30 kilometres through thorn scrub.

"We had the water in 50-litre bins. Two of us would take a bin with a pole on our shoulders. It took us at least a day and a night to walk 30 kilometres through the *monte*, carrying our guns and other equipment as well. We were about 500 metres behind the Bolivian lines. We could hear them and we were scared of their aeroplanes, circling overhead looking for us. The heat was terrible."

The journalist Peter Kihss covered the war for the *New York Times*: "The Paraguayan water supply was brought, a glass per soldier per day, from distances twenty-four hours of travelling away… And it was not brought when weather conditions were bad, as they frequently were, or when Bolivian airplanes pierced the forest veil with bullets."

Nigel Kennedy was assigned a regiment, but soon after became ill with dysentery and was sent to a field hospital. There he was treated by a man who had been the local doctor in the town of San José, near New Australia. After recovery, the doctor kept him on for a time as an orderly at the hospital.

Because of this brief medical experience, Nigel Kennedy was sent to a first-aid post at the new front, a place called Capiírendá. "All the badly wounded came to us from the front line. We'd look after them, tend their wounds, until the trucks could come and get them. Some were very seriously wounded and couldn't travel because of the bad roads. They'd either recover or die. Most died."

Peter Kihss sent a despatch to the *New York Times*, describing a visit to a first-aid post: "In such country, wounds or exhaustion meant death… It took so long to get wounded men back to first aid that their bodies were covered with white grubs before suffering could be alleviated. Then surgeons made swift incisions, spread ether and waited until the worms drew away before they could even begin to see the wounds drilled by bullets… There were men there who resembled rag dolls emptied of their contents."

"We had hardly anything to treat them, no penicillin in those days, no sulfur drugs," said Nigel Kennedy. "There were amputations without anaesthetic. I always had to help the doctor when he cut off legs and arms. Sometimes he had to amputate a second time because of gangrene. Sometimes the gangrene would go still further and they would die. A lot of people died. I buried a lot of people in Capiírendá."

He dreaded the wet season. "When it rained and rained, the trucks couldn't come anymore. But the Bolivians still came to attack us, right behind the lines. Their aeroplanes used to come and bomb us there at Capiírendá. One doctor got bombed. He was thrown up into the air and came down again."

Astonishingly, the bombing did not kill the doctor, but soon after, Kennedy witnessed his end. "He did a stupid thing. We used to hide in the trees to watch the Bolivian trucks pass. But instead of choosing a thick tree-trunk like we did, he stood behind one which grew like a slab, very thick on one side and thin on the other. A bomb came at him from that angle, cut his head in half and scattered his brains."

After the rain the land dried up again. The Chaco War was remembered above all as *La Guerra de la Sed*, the War of Thirst. Out of it came a body of powerful literature as writers on both sides of the conflict attempted to grapple with the meaningless horror and futility of war.

From the Paraguayan side came *Hijo de Hombre* — Son of Man — the great novel by Augusto Roa Bastos. It is a series of narratives, concluding with the Chaco War, in which the whole of Paraguay and its bloody history is seen as an immense prison from which man can be delivered only by his fellow man.

The transportation of water, with its baptismal allusion, in pitiful amounts across immense distances to the soldiers of the desert, is unable to keep pace with the stalking of death:

> Suffocating heat. Each particle of dust seems to be swelling by spontaneous combustion, so that we are crushed by a transparent, red-hot ingot. Thirst, the White Death, walks among us arm in arm with the other, the Red Death, both of them cloaked with dust. Neither the stretcher-bearers nor the water-carriers give themselves any respite. But they cannot keep pace. There are not more than about ten trucks to bring the precious liquid to the men of the two divisions. From the base of operations, the water-carriers transport the cans on their shoulders through the intricacies of the wood, where the greater part of their contents is spilt, evaporates or is stolen. In forty-eight hours we officers have received half a canteen, and the troops scarcely half a mug, of almost boiling water, per man... Whole platoons, mad with thirst, desert the firing-line and fall on the water trucks ...

An important character is one of the *chóferes del Chaco*, the drivers of the water-trucks which perilously negotiate the trackless wastes of the Chaco under the strafing of the Bolivian planes. He sacrifices his life to bring a day's respite to men who no longer have a drop of water for the shedding of tears, and who will die of thirst the following day. "I have a mission. I am going to carry it out. That is all I know."

The Bolivian writer Augusto Céspedes produced *Sangre de mestizos* — The Blood of the Mestizos — a collection of short stories about the war. One story, "The Well", is a day-by-day account of a group of Bolivian soldiers digging an immensely deep well in a desperate quest to slake their thirst.

> ... there is not a drop of water, which, however, does not prevent men at war from living here. We live, wasted, unhappy, aged before our time, the trees with more branches than leaves, the men with more thirst than hate.

The Bolivians reach 70 metres without finding a trace of water, but by then their excavation work has given life its only meaning.

> Will there ever be an end to this? We no longer dig to find water, but in obedience to some fatal plan, some inscrutable design. The days of my soldiers are sucked into the maelstrom of this tragic hollow which swallows them blindly in its strange, silent growth, screwing them into the earth ... Up here above, the well has taken on the outlines of something inevitable, eternal and powerful as war.

When Paraguayan soldiers, hounded by thirst, launch an attack, the Bolivians defend the well with ferocity, as if it is brimming with water. Many soldiers on both sides are killed and their corpses thrown into the well. A use has been found at last for the yawning dry hole in the desert.

In three years of fierce fighting some 95,000 men lost their lives, 25,000 of them Paraguayan. At least six men from New Australia were among them: Jones, Drakeford, King, Bates, Shepperson and Nigel's twenty-year-old brother, Douglas Kennedy.

After the ambush and his capture at Cañada Strongest, Douglas was put to work on road construction from the Andes for the Bolivian army. He died of pneumonia and malnutrition on 18 April 1935 at Oruro, the tin-mining town on the Andean high plain. He was buried at Cochabamba, the grim news relayed to his family by an English prisoner.

"Douglas the fair youth now rests from his sufferings and sadness in the distant cemetery of Cochabamba," reported an Asunción newspaper. "In the midst of his unhappiness he had the good fortune to find one of his father's countrymen who softened his last moments of life with loving attention, but was unable to save him... sincere homage from the thankful hearts of the Paraguayans."

Those who survived returned, drained and bewildered, just as the

ex-combatants of Gallipoli and the Western Front came back to Australia
and to Paraguay fifteen years before, struggling to make the transition
from the trenches to what passed for normal human society.

Roa Bastos portrays a soldier arriving back at his village, his face "scarred
by the thorns of the Chaco, and stained purple by gunpowder. One
cheekbone had been half shot away". Crushed and beaten by the terrible
war and his awareness of what human beings can do to each other, he is
unable to accept his new hero status:

> Quite a crowd had gathered. They all cheered with rather hollow enthusiasm.
> I joined in, not to do honour to the ex-soldier of the Chaco, but to put a little
> spirit into that sad shadow standing under the mid-day sun, the unadorned,
> indomitable shadow of a man.

Other returning soldiers react differently, wreaking vengeance on a local
strongman who had long oppressed them:

> When they returned from the Chaco, the Goiburú twins executed Melitón
> Isasí in a manner which horrified the whole village… they tore down the
> Christ from the cross and tied up in his place the castrated corpse of the *jefe
> político*… with a flabby face and bloodshot eyes over which the shadows of
> the vultures were already wheeling.

One of the young men who had gone from New Australia was the son
of Shepperson, a North American settler. Nigel Kennedy said the young
soldier came back from the war with typhoid fever. He walked from the
highway and was a short distance from the village of New Australia when
he fell down on the road. "He couldn't make it to his home. He was in
sight of it when he died. He was buried in our cemetery."

In 1938 a formal peace treaty confirmed Paraguay's military ascendancy
and awarded it the bulk of the disputed territory. "I've read different books
on the Chaco War," Nigel Kennedy told me, "and I sometimes get the
idea that we took more land off the Bolivians than really belonged to us."
But Paraguay's was a hollow victory. No oil in viable quantities was ever
found in the wastelands where almost 100,000 soldiers had died.

The carnage had been of use to the European powers, however. Like
the Spanish Civil War, it provided a chance to study strategies with
modern weaponry, a dress rehearsal for World War II.

Since the time of the great Guaraní nation, before the arrival of the
Conquistadores, the Chaco, "a plain with the soul of a mountain", had
always loomed in a threatening way for those who lived in the soft lands

to the east of the Paraguay River. Now it had carved a dark place forever in the national consciousness.

The soldiers who lost their lives in the war became martyrs who struggled not just against the Bolivians but against a more ancient, spectral enemy. The anniversary of the signing of the peace treaty, 12 June, became an important national holiday for Paraguayans, invested with the emotional potency that Anzac Day has for Australians.

Every year Chaco War veterans lead a march to the war memorial, usually the statue of a soldier on a plinth, in towns all over the country. Now the veterans who survive, in their eighties and nineties, come by car, wagon or wheelchair, though a few still insist on marching while they can.

Nigel Kennedy still goes to the ceremony at Nueva Londres. The last of the Cosme descendants to take part was Rod McLeod, wearing his dapper pinstripe suit to the service at Caazapá. But he was still arguing with the authorities, trying to obtain a document entitling him to a war pension, just before his death in 1989.

An army officer who had risen through the military hierarchy during the Chaco War always made his presence felt at these memorial ceremonies, all his medals flashing: General Alfredo Stroessner.

*

The Dakota flew low over a green swamp criss-crossed by meandering waterways and studded with palm trees like buttons on a quilt. Gladys explained that it was the region of the Chaco known as Departamento Presidente Hayes. Like most Paraguayans, she was aware that it was named in gratitude for the favourable arbitration of an American president generally forgotten in his own country.

"There used to be lots of flamingoes down there, but they seem to have gone."

I'd read something else about the region I thought better not to mention: Stroessner and his head of secret police, Pastor Coronel, had a way with political opponents, the same efficient disposal method now known to have been used by their friends in the Argentine military junta. The South Atlantic was available to the Argentines. In Paraguay dissidents were taken up in a light plane and pushed out high over Departamento Presidente Hayes. But the method was expensive. They couldn't do it for everybody. There were variations on the theme.

The Dakota landed at Asunción and I walked across the tarmac with the Smith-Pfannls to the vast bravura structure of the air terminal with its concrete flying buttresses. "Aeropuerto Silvio Pettirossi" announced the sign, with a glossy new tourist brochure indicating it was named after a famous Paraguayan aviator.

But until recently it had been "Aeropuerto Presidente Stroessner", erected to the greater glory of a dictator who seized power after a succession of shaky governments in the political vacuum left by the Chaco War.

20

Fields of God

The history of Paraguay does not go far back, and yet it is one of the most remarkable in the world, and full of instruction to communists and other theorisers on the perfect social state. Here, remote from the sea in an earthly paradise, dwelt a mild, kindly, but brave race, that of the Guaraní Indians. To them in the commencement of the seventeenth century came the Jesuit fathers ...

E. F. Knight, *The Cruise of the Falcon*

You bade the Red Man rise like the Red Clay
Of God's great Adam in his human right,
Till trailed the snake of trade, our own time's blight,
And man lost Paradise in Paraguay.

G. K. Chesterton, "To the Jesuits"

I woke from my siesta at the Hotel Vienna in Encarnación to hear singing coming to me in drifts across the town of low red-roofed houses at the edge of the wide Paraná River. One voice soared above the others, pure as a bird. It seemed like Fitzcarraldo's vision of opera in the wilderness. The choir was rehearsing at the cathedral.

Encarnación is not the wilderness, but a sleepy country town 370 kilometres south-east of Paraguay's capital. It evokes the nineteenth century, a wood-burning steam train with a black plume of smoke passing through to the terminus, and *carumbés*, little yellow-painted hooded horse carts clattering briskly through the streets. But it faces the twentieth century, the gleaming skyscrapers of the Argentine city of Posadas, 4 kilometres across the river. They are seen as twin towns, but Encarnación is Danny de Vito to the Argentine Schwarzenegger.

Before the War of the Triple Alliance, Posadas was a part of Paraguay. It was known as Candelaria, and was the administrative centre for the Jesuit empire. Encarnación, founded in 1615, was one of thirty missions, but all its original buildings have long since been destroyed. The beautiful Spanish cathedral was a much later construction, though many in the choir, their voices swelling, had ancestors, Guaraní converts, who had taken part in the dream.

William Lane and those with a historical bent among the Cosme colonists were aware of the saga of the great Jesuit missions. They could not fail to be impressed by the world's most long-lasting and extensive experiment in communal living, the ruins of its towns and villages within a few days walk of their own modest commune in Paraguay. The Russian Revolution of 1917 marked the beginning of a collectivisation scheme which exceeded the Jesuits' in scale, but the missions lasted far longer than the Soviet Union.

The Jesuit Fathers came to the New World with an idealistic vision of a communal society, acknowledging Thomas More's *Utopia* as an influence. In the late sixteenth century they began gathering the Guaraní of eastern Paraguay, a handsome, clever and resourceful people, into communities known as Reductions. For 180 years, hundreds of thousands of Indians lived and worked in harmony in thirty missions extending over an area the size of France. That they attained a level of high culture was indisputable, their physical attractiveness, skill and grace coveted by slave traders from Brazil, their economic proficiency envied by the Spanish settlers, their combined power bitterly resented. The Jesuit Fathers were too effective in establishing their state within a state. In 1767, in a decree of breathtaking political expediency, King Charles III of Spain banished the Jesuits from Latin America. The settlers and slave traders moved in, the mission buildings fell into ruins, the Indians fled.

Three years after the decree dismantling a great civilisation, Captain James Cook sailed into Botany Bay on the barque *Endeavour* and nominated it as a possible site for a colony. Another 123 years later a group of Australians sailed from those antipodean shores, intent on settling near the old mission lands of the Guaraní.

The Jesuit experiment was an inspiration for Lane, particularly as he reverted to a religious frame of mind, for its blend of pragmatic communalism and devotion to God. He was fond of saying that he designed the single men's barracks at Cosme — a long pavilion with rooms opening to an arcade — on the living accommodation of the Indian acolytes. He did not articulate another aspect of the missions he probably admired, the unchallenged supremacy, however benevolent, of the good Fathers.

In October 1896 two colonists, John Dias and Jack Amor, made an eighteen-day walking tour to the Jesuit ruins near Encarnación. They returned to give an address to Cosme's Literary and Social Union. Dias had been profoundly moved by the sight of great roofless cathedrals being reclaimed by the jungle, the artistry of toppled and broken sculptures, "one statue of Our Lord lying in the dust, His nose broken and one of His feet missing".

John Lane, an avid reader, provided historical background in a lecture which, on his eventual return to Queensland, he repeated for a Workers' Educational group: "Wonderful were the results obtained by the Jesuits. Their influence became almost supreme throughout Paraguay. Under the able teaching of the priests, the Paraguayans became skilled in farming and the mechanical arts. Those were Paraguay's halcyon days." He explained how the Jesuits taught their converts they could not love God unless they loved and helped each other; how in the villages the people were organised into communes. They lived in simple plenty, poverty being banished from the land. The sick and aged were supported. In 1896 John Lane was still optimistic about the success of Cosme's own small experiment, but found it poignant that the Jesuits could be "traced only in the names of the villages, in the ruins of their churches, and in the traditions of the country people".

One man in his lifetime made a direct linear connection between the Jesuit missions and the New Australia experiment. He was the parliamentarian, historian, writer and adventurer, Robert Bontine Cunninghame Graham who, with Keir Hardie, founded the Scottish Labour Party. A descendant of Robert the Bruce and the earls of Menteith, he had been praised for his dedication to socialism by William Lane in the Queensland *Worker*. He had shared platforms with Friedrich Engels, William Morris and the anarchist Prince Kropotkin, and been gaoled in 1887 for taking part in a demonstration in Trafalgar Square in support of Irish Nationalists. "I am a believer," he said, "in the theories of Karl Marx, to a great extent, but, both as regards Christianity and socialism, I care more for works than mere faith." Later he expressed distrust of socialism's move towards dogma and demagogy.

But he subscribed to *Cosme Monthly*, "the little journal published on yellow packing-paper", and it was through his urging that his friend James Craig Kennedy came to Paraguay in 1899, though Kennedy chose to settle at New Australia. At the time Cunninghame Graham was obsessed with Paraguay, for he was writing a book about the history of the Jesuit missions — *A Vanished Arcadia* — published in 1901.

In 1871, just after the War of the Triple Alliance, Cunninghame Graham had visited one of the old missions, where a few white-clad Indian women and children were clinging to vestiges of the past way of life. He was just nineteen years old and had been two years in South America, living a gaucho life, working with horses and cattle.

The terrible war was the final act of destruction for the missions, where a pitifully few Guaraní had lingered after the expulsion of the Jesuits a century earlier. A biographer noted that "Cunninghame Graham was the last historian of the Jesuit republic to have had first hand experience of it".

In 1873 the young horseman visited another semi-ruined mission on the day of the Feast of the Blessed Virgin. He was deeply moved to see women and children with armfuls of flowers, marching silently along forest tracks towards the great church to the tolling of bells. Few males were to be seen.

> On the neglected altar, for at that time priests were a rarity in the Reductions, the Indians had placed great bunches of red flowers, and now and then a humming-bird flitted in through the glassless windows and hung poised above them; then darted out again, with a soft, whirring sound. Over the whole *capilla*, in which at one time several thousand Indians had lived, but now reduced to seventy or eighty at the most, there hung an air of desolation. It seemed as if man, in his long protracted struggle with the forces of the woods, had been defeated, and had accepted his defeat, content to vegetate, forgotten by the world …
>
> As there was no one to sing Mass, and as the organ long had been neglected, the congregation listened to some prayers, read from a Book of Hours by an old Indian, who pronounced the Latin, of which most likely he did not understand a word, as if it had been Guaraní. They sang "Las Flores á Maria" all in unison, but keeping such good time that at a little distance from the church it sounded like waves breaking on a beach after a summer storm.

*

I had come to Encarnación to see the ruins and to visit Alcides Wood, a colony descendant. A forty-something lawyer, he had spent five years in Australia road-working, plumbing and welding. Now he was a Paraguayan senator. His blonde wife Mary was a public notary, still pleased to have caught her husband with the help of a splinter off the wooden cross of Father Luis Bolanos at Caazapá.

The Woods lived in a mansion, a newly-built pleasure dome they had decreed for themselves, surrounded by stone walls and wrought-iron gates, sprawling over three blocks at the highest point of the town. We arrived as the sun was setting and had drinks on the terrace to take in the scene: the twinkling skyscrapers of Posadas like a dream city on the far bank, their lights dancing and dappling in the luminous water; to the left, the miraculous swooping lines and high tension cables of a new bridge, Encarnación's Golden Gate.

"I liked Australia very much," Alcides said, "but I got sick of explaining where Paraguay was. People thought it was somewhere in Africa. To make things easier I'd say I came from Mexico. '*Now* I get you,' they'd say, 'why didn't you say so the first time?' This country is my home. I'm glad I came back. I had to hold down other jobs while I studied at the university, and Mary and I had a young family which made it hard. But it's all been worth it."

Alcides' father, Donald Wood, fought in the Chaco War and had died in 1978. Alcides took me to meet his mother, Deolidia, vivacious and kindly, one of the five Fernandez girls who had caused such a stir when their father bought into the village at Cosme. In a conversation exclusively in Spanish, I apologised for my lack of fluency. "Never mind about that," Doña Deolidia told me. "If you want to stay on in Paraguay, it's Guaraní that you need. Stay with me a few months and I'll have you talking like a native."

Alcides' awareness of the story of the Jesuits in Paraguay was drawn mainly from *The Mission*, David Puttnam's film with Jeremy Irons and Robert de Niro. Dubbed in Spanish, it was popular at the local video store. But it was filmed over the border in Brazil, because President Stroessner would have seen it as subversive. After all, it was about a flowering of the human spirit, ultimately crushed by an iron fist. Such themes were by definition anathema to Stroessner.

The following day Alcides dropped me at the bus station. I boarded a battered vehicle crowded with cheerful locals, pop music blaring, and negotiated with the hip young conductor to let me off at the *ruinas jesuíticas*.

*

Before the arrival of the Spanish, it has been estimated that there were 200,000 Guaraní Indians in eastern Paraguay, gentle people blessed with a well-watered land, rich soil for their gardens, abundant fish in the rivers and game in the forests. Hunger was rarely a problem. Their only concern was the defence of their lands against occasional raids across the river by the other original inhabitants of Paraguay, the warlike nomadic tribes of the Chaco.

Then came the Conquistadores. They were looking for fabled deposits of gold and silver, and most pushed north-west across the Chaco to the Andes and the strongholds of the Incas.

It seemed the Guaraní had nothing the Spanish wanted to steal — except their women who were comely, and their land which was fertile. The attractions were sufficient. The Spanish formed a garrison at Asunción and decided to stay. The new town became the headquarters of the Vice-Royalty of La Plata, administering all Spanish territory in southern South America until overtaken, forty years later, by Buenos Aires.

The Guaraní rapidly acquired certain craft skills of the Europeans and adapted to farming with introduced horses and cattle. For the Spanish they were servants and concubines. The harems of Asunción became legendary among envious compatriots in Buenos Aires. But women were accorded a relatively high status in Guaraní society, attested by the persistence of their mother tongue within the new order. There was a good deal of social mobility. Many unions were solemnised by marriage, and the *mestizo* offspring were not considered marginal citizens.

The Conquistadores' arrival in the New World had opened a vigorous theological debate in Europe concerning whether the Indian had a soul. In 1537, the year Asunción was founded, Pope Paul III made a crucial ruling: the Indian possessed a soul capable of salvation. This meant that, in the view of the Church, the Indian was a true human being, a recognition not accorded by the secular powers in Asunción until 420 years later, after the lobbying of a descendant of New Australia.

The Guaraní were a spiritual people, believing in Tupá, a single creator god, whose symbol and home was the golden sun. They accepted that "Tupá created trees and made the forest; he covered the naked banks of streams with grass and flowers; he made the giant anaconda and the deadly coral, the monkey and the fox, and every living thing. After long thought he created man."

It was a point of contact with Christianity. In 1588 three Jesuit missionaries arrived in Asunción seeking souls to be saved. They were members of the Roman Catholic Society of Jesus, founded by Ignatius Loyola in Rome fifty-five years earlier. They were hampered in their work by the Spanish colonists, who resented the Jesuits' attempts to gather the Indians into settlements or *encomiendas*, limiting their own access to them.

The Jesuits protested to Philip II of Spain, who in 1608 gave instructions to the Governor of Asunción: "It is the express wish of the King that the Indians of Paraguay shall not be subdued except by the sword of the spirit and that no other persons than the missionaries shall reside in the *encomiendas*. He has no desire to deprive the natives of their natural freedom, but wishes to liberate them from their savage and depraved mode of life, to bring them to know and adore the true God, and thus to assure their happiness."

In 1609 a new group of Jesuits selected one of the wildest and most impenetrable parts of South America for their missionary work, the province of Guairá on the upper reaches of the Paraná River, near the border with present day Brazil. It was a terrain of thick forest, of towering pines and cedars, of valleys and cliffs cut by rushing torrents and cataracts. Here the Guaraní were hunter-gatherers rather than cultivators. But it was far from the Spanish settlers.

Unfortunately it was more accessible for the *bandeirantes*, ruthless mixed-blood Portuguese slave-hunters, who made raids across the Paraná from their base in Sao Paulo. Slavery was legal in the Portugese colony, and a Brazilian historian has estimated that in the sixteenth and seventeenth centuries alone the *bandeirantes* captured as many as 350,000 Indians, mostly selling them to plantations north of Sao Paulo. They also sold their prisoners to the colonists of Paraguay. Although under Spanish law slavery was prohibited, Madrid was far away and infringements were almost never prosecuted.

In 1612 a remarkable priest, Father Antonio Ruiz de Montoya, came to Guairá to make contact with the Indians. He spent long periods in the forests alone, travelling through wild country with sandals or bare feet, subsisting on game and berries and a little mandioca flour. He related strange experiences, including witnessing an anaconda swallow an Indian whole, only to vomit him up again, all the unfortunate man's bones crushed. But he had a much more alarming snake story: an Indian woman, "carelessly washing some clothes on the banks of the Paraná, saw one of these beasts and it unexpectedly attacked for the purpose of violating her. The woman was speechless with fright on seeing the huge snake so licentious, and the latter, carrying her to the opposite bank of the river, carried out its lascivious purpose". Perhaps it was the berries. Or the effect of his stern celibacy among the near-naked and sensuous Guaraní.

But Antonio Ruiz de Montoya, who invited the nomadic Indians he encountered to join the missions and find protection from the slave-hunters, was perhaps the greatest of the Jesuit Fathers in Paraguay. According to Cunninghame Graham, he united "the qualities of a man of action to those of scholar and missionary. Without his presence most likely not a tenth part of the Indians would have escaped".

The tribes of Guairá were wooed to transform themselves into settled agriculturalists, but the Jesuits retained a traditional tribal structure as far as possible. The missions were organised as chiefdoms, with a chief responsible for up to thirty families. Their language was respected, and Father Montoya created the first Guaraní dictionary and grammar and went on to translate the catechism and hymns. In 1627, when Montoya was appointed head of the priests in the region, more than 40,000 Indians were living in eleven large communities.

The *bandeirantes*, "a nest of hawks", Cunninghame Graham called them, viewed the mission Indians as "pigeons ready fattening for their use". It was so much easier to attack these great settlements of disciplined and accultured people than to chase through the jungle after roaming bands of agile wild Indians.

The Portuguese brigands made a major assault in 1629 and carried off 1,500 Indian captives. Chained together they were sent on a forced march through the dense forest, 1,300 kilometres to Sao Paulo. The route was littered with the corpses of those unable to keep up. The Jesuit Fathers were unable to oppose this brigandage by force, but two of them went with their flock, caring for the wounded and giving absolution to the dying. In Sao Paulo they appealed to the authorities for justice but were laughed at.

Encouraged by this success, the *bandeirantes* renewed their expeditions. A priest wrote, "what is of the gravest concern is that the Indians imagine that we gathered them in, not to teach them the law of God, but to deliver them to the Portuguese".

*

A paprika-red road threaded through rolling green country, broken by corduroy patches where the red earth had been ploughed, passing beside a river where people were fishing near holiday cabins called Hawaii and Castel Gandolfo, through stands of waving sugarcane, groves of orange trees, apple orchards a mist of pale pink blossom. The curved tiled roofs of barns and outbuildings were dappled with lichen, silvery *criolla* cattle grazed in well-tended pasture and arum lilies grew in the shadowy borders of clear bubbling streams.

Latin rock music blasted from the bus speakers, and the young conductor hummed along as he swung at the door, taking fares with cowboy insouciance, smoothing the crumpled Paraguayan notes and fanning them like a poker hand. As I made jottings on a pad, fellow passengers peered over my shoulder with beaming, undisguised interest.

A man in a straw hat was waiting by the gate of a farmhouse. We stopped and he boarded. He had the copper Paraguayan complexion, greying blonde hair and pale blue eyes.

Now houses and barns, built with strong, wide boards, presented the bright-coloured simplicity of a child's picture book. We rumbled into the old German village of Colonia Hohenau. A square-towered Lutheran church made a postcard view on the hill and cabins with shuttered windows nestled under the pine trees. It was here that a Bavarian called Hugo Stroessner met a fifteen-year-old *mestizo* beauty, Heriberta Mattiauda. Hugo married her and set up a brewery in Encarnación. In 1912 their son Alfredo was born.

I had read stories too that Josef Mengele, the Auschwitz death-camp doctor, had lived in this area in the late 1950s. I begrudged the fact that life must have been very pleasant for him.

*

In 1631 an army of slave-hunters gathered for another massive raid. Father Antonio Ruiz de Montoya decided the Guairá settlements must be abandoned.

He organised an exodus of Biblical dimensions, assembling 12,000 Guaraní Indians and a flotilla of 300 longboats. They set off down the Paraná River with the *bandeirantes* in pursuit. When they reached the great waterfalls of Guairá, they disembarked to make the horrendous 114-metre descent down the cliff-face. Montoya hoped some longboats would survive the cataract. All splintered into fragments. "Not one escaped; and so the pilgrimage began, almost without provisions and without arms, in the middle of a country quite uncultivated, and where game was scarce."

The Jesuits and their charges made a journey of many months, hacking their way with machetes through the morass of tropical forest, enduring rains that never seemed to end, each man and woman carrying a child or necessary goods on their backs, the Portugese always behind them, waiting to catch the stragglers.

At last they reached the gentle rolling country near present-day Encarnación, where some missions had already been established at the time of those on the Upper Paraná. The refugees had walked 800 kilometres to reach this promised land. Thousands had died on the way.

The survivors barely possessed the will or energy to establish new settlements. In one community alone, 600 perished from famine. But within a few years there were thirty permanent communities around Candelaria, home for 100,000 Indians. One of the largest was the mission of Trinidad.

*

One walks through a wooden gate and quite suddenly the ruins of Trinidad are spread out, more massive than expected, more beautiful than imagined. The roofless colonnades and cloisters of perhaps twenty long red buildings made looming shadows across the grass. The sun beat down on pink honeycombed stone. Ageing date palms rustled in the afternoon stillness. Statues of angels with chipped noses and wings stared sightlessly across the empty plazas where once Indian acolytes had tended the gardens, raised voices in praise to their new god. A tethered nanny-goat with a kid foraged, bleating half-heartedly. In the brochures this was one of Paraguay's prime attractions but only three other tourists wandered the site, insubstantial figures in the distance. Undulating green hills extended to the horizon. On these pasture lands large herds of cattle had once grazed, sometimes over 50,000 head on a single mission, and thousands of sheep and horses.

The overwhelming sense was of peace, that it would have been a good place to live. It was easy to imagine bells tolling the faithful to prayer, workers coming from the fields, the voices of the choir in the cathedral, children chanting at school, artisans tapping at sculptures, fowls pecking at the kitchen door.

Most of the mission villages were designed along a similar pattern to Trinidad, around a central plaza where sheep cropped the grass. Dominating the square was always the church and, on another side, storehouses, library, school and priests' quarters.

On the remaining two sides were the long colonnaded dormitories where the Indians lived, each family to a room, with more dormitory blocks fronting other streets and plazas behind them. The rooms, on average some 7 metres square, were adequate, as they were generally used only for sleeping. In the balmy climate families did most of their cooking and living out of doors. There was a separate large house for widows and orphans, the aged and the disabled.

The great church at Trinidad, begun in 1706, was considered the most impressive of all those on the missions, capacious enough to hold 5,000 people at worship. It was believed to have been designed by the famous Milanese Jesuit architect, Brother Gianbattista Primoli. Built of the local red stone by Guaraní artisans, it was 58 metres long with a nave 11 metres wide, flanked by vaulted side aisles and crowned by a massive dome and lantern. Scaffolding now enclosed sections of wall. The church was in the process of careful restoration. One relic, a carved stone pulpit, had been shattered into 1,500 pieces, but was replaced in its original position.

I walked through the vast roofless space, trying to imagine the voices in harmony, in praise of the god who had replaced Tupá so resoundingly. Statues of apostles, mostly headless, in a procession of alcoves were mute witnesses to the glories of the past and the vengeance which had followed. In a half-restored wall frieze, supplicants knelt down among a tangle of birds and creatures of the forest, angels with wings like herons fluttering over them. The angels were playful, their faces discernibly Guaraní. In another frieze they frolicked with bassoons and flutes, a clavichord and a harp. One played an organ while a winged companion worked the bellows. The joyfulness of the Indian creators was palpable.

*

In this region, still called Misiones, the great Jesuit state of thirty Reductions came into being.

But first the raids by the Portuguese had to be stopped. Father Montoya journeyed to Spain and made a compelling case to the Council of the Indies that mission Indians should be allowed to bear arms. His request happened to coincide with Spain's reluctant acknowledgment of Portugal's claims to the vast land area of present-day Brazil. King Philip IV approved a controlled distribution of firearms among the Indians, recognising the value of a fortified bulwark at the border of Spanish territory.

When the *bandeirantes* mounted another slave-hunting expedition in 1641 they came into collision with an army of Guaranís, commanded by Jesuit priests. They retreated in confusion. Many were slain.

For over a century, the missions were free of the slave-traders. But the Jesuits' victory had created implacable enemies among the Spanish colonists, envious of their power, resentful that they could not enter the missions or even trade with them. They coveted the Indians as labour. They were finding it harder to obtain servants as the general population of Paraguayan Indians declined through disease, maltreatment and overwork. "They died like plants," a priest observed, "which, grown in the shade, will not bear the sun." Inside the missions the population increased.

The colonists charged that the Jesuits, with their armies to back them, aimed to set up a free state, independent of the Spanish crown. They spread rumours of a fabulous treasure of gold and silver, concealed within the missions. Cárdenas, Bishop of Asunción, accused the Jesuits of teaching heresy in their catechism. Once again the Black Robes were obliged to plead their case at the Court of Madrid. The Spanish king, Philip V, ordered that the Jesuits be left in peace.

So, over one hundred years before the bluff Yorkshire sea captain made his landing at Botany Bay, and during the worst excesses of the slave trade in Africa and the Americas, the great experiment of the Jesuit missions moved into its most flourishing period. In his lecture for the Cosme colonists, John Lane placed it in historical perspective:

> Wonderful were the results obtained by the Jesuits ... When all elsewhere in the great south land was racked and tortured by cruel conquerors; when in the sister continent to the north, British, French and Colonial struggled in bitter conflict, using the scalping knife of the savage to aid the fell work of the musket; when British seamen shipped their wretched human cargoes from the African slave coast to toil under the lash of American masters; when across the broad Atlantic the torch of Old World tyranny shed its baleful light over downtrodden peoples, and Europe shook with the tramp of marching armies; during all this worldwide strife, this savagery of civilisation, Paraguay, under the kindly sway of the good fathers, knew peace, contentment and prosperity ...

*

The daily routine at a mission was divided between work in the fields, study, prayer and music. The land and livestock were owned by the community and farmed in common to meet basic needs. But each family had its own garden plot to cultivate as it wished. In addition, everyone took a turn working the Fields of God which provided for the general maintenance of the mission and for the old, the sick and the needy. The crops were wheat and maize, cotton and tobacco, vegetables and sugarcane. Citrus seed imported from Spain thrived. Soon groves of orange trees, heavy in golden fruit, became a distinctive sight not just on the missions but throughout eastern Paraguay.

Within the settlements money was unknown and exchanges were by barter in kind. A flying bridge worked by a cable was erected across the 4-kilometre-wide Paraná to send goods from missions on one side to the other. In order to pay their required taxes to Spain and to purchase necessities, such as metal tools, from the outside world, export crops were developed. The Jesuits mastered the difficult technique of transplanting *yerba* striplings, a variety of holly, from the remote *yerba* forests and laid them out in plantations. The crushed and toasted leaves, popular as a tea throughout southern South America, became a highly profitable line, along with honey, hides, wool, cotton and linen cloth. They built roads and boats to take their produce to market.

Figures of saints were held aloft on the early morning procession to the fields. Indian men in trousers and coarse ponchos, women in loose white cotton shifts called *tupois*, chanted and played drums and flutes as they marched. At sundown they returned home singing and, after a rest, assembled in the church to chant the rosary before supper. The Jesuits recognised and encouraged the Guaranís' natural love of music. One priest was said to have challenged: "Give me an orchestra and I shall conquer at once all these Indians for Christ."

Mass was celebrated with an orchestra: oboe, fagot, lute and harp, cornet, clarinet, violin and viola. Theatrical performances were held nearly every Sunday, the Indian children transfixed by medieval miracle plays such as "The Fight Between Archangel Michael and the Dragon". There were frequent dances and every year a great feast, with much tolling of bells, for the patron saint of the settlement. Cunninghame Graham described the spectacular welcome for visiting dignitaries: "Great arches festooned with flowers extended across the streets; birds of brilliant plumage, chained pumas, and bowls of fish marked the route; masses of flowers and sweet-smelling plants lay on the ground ... Fireworks at night brought the festival to a brilliant end."

A mission was usually under the guidance of two priests, although a large settlement like Trinidad probably had more. Aided by Indian chiefs appointed *mayores*, they were responsible for the spiritual development and welfare of their charges and administered discipline when necessary. There was no capital punishment, but crimes such as drunkenness resulted in a flogging.

The black-robed Fathers were uneasy about the sensuality of the Guaraní and considered it best controlled by marriage. From a very young age the sexes were separated and forbidden to enter the church by the same door. Indian boys were encouraged to wed at seventeen, the girls at fifteen. A critic notes the restriction that, "Neither women nor girls were ever allowed to set foot in the houses of the Jesuits". The Fathers may have applied this rule to protect themselves from temptation for, unlike priests from other orders in Paraguay, they maintained a remarkable record of celibacy.

Singing and dancing were a popular evening recreation and some specialist craftsmen made exquisite musical instruments: flutes, harps, violins and harpsichords. At Trinidad organs were constructed and church bells cast in a bell foundry. "The Guaranís," one historian concluded, "seemed to possess the faculty of being able to reproduce anything, no matter how intricate, that was laid before them."

Artists produced sumptuous paintings, sculpture and bas relief, imitating the baroque art of Europe, but incorporating armadillos and passion flowers, monkeys and ferns, the flora and fauna of the forest they knew. Others, according to Cunninghame Graham, learned more practical skills:

> As well as agriculture and *estancia* life, the Jesuits had introduced amongst the Indians most of the arts and trades of Europe ... they wove cotton largely; sometimes they made as much as eight thousand five hundred yards of cloth in a single town in the space of two or three months. In addition to weaving, they had tanneries, carpenters' shops, tailors, hat-makers, coopers, cordage-makers, boat-builders, cartwrights, joiners, and almost every industry useful and necessary to life. They also made arms and powder, musical instruments, and had silversmiths, musicians, painters, turners, and printers to work their printing-presses: for many books were printed at the missions, and they produced manuscripts as finely executed as those made by the monks in European monasteries.

It was paradise of a kind. But there were critics. Voltaire was vitriolic in *Candide* about "his reverence, the Colonel" who dined on gold plate while the Indians ate maize in the field:

> "So you have already been to Paraguay?" said Candide.
> "Indeed I have," replied Cacambo. "It's a wonderful system they have. There are thirty provinces in their kingdom, and it is more than three hundred leagues across. The reverend fathers own the whole lot, and the people own nothing: that's what I call a masterpiece of reason and justice."

Mostly the missions inspired romantic admiration in Europe. Later even Voltaire revised his opinion, declaring that the Jesuit experiment in Paraguay "appears alone, in some way, the triumph of humanity", even "expiating the cruelties of the first conquistadors".

The idea of The Noble Savage was much in vogue in the eighteenth century, the belief that human beings were naturally good if only they could be freed of the impediments and perversions of civilisation. But, in embracing the sanctuary of the missions, the Guaraní were living support for another theory: they had escaped The State of Nature with its "continuall feare, and danger of violent death", according to the philosopher Thomas Hobbes, where the life of man was "solitary, poore, nasty, brutish, and short".

It is certain that they came willingly. With only two Jesuit priests, on average, in any settlement for some 4,000 Guaranís, they could not have been prevented from leaving. They did not do so, clearly preferring life in the missions to the dangers of the forest with its predatory bands of slave-hunters.

However, the Indians' lives were not all candle-lit processions and singing along a flower-strewn path. They laboured hard, were punished for misdemeanours, and were obliged to conform to a highly ordered regime with little hope of advancement in status. The father-priests have been criticised most for their authoritarianism and for their failure to offer a full education to the clever and eager Guaraní. With hindsight this can be recognised, but it must surely take a very punitive judgmentalism to be too harsh on the Jesuits, considering the life of bondage and slavery experienced by Indians elsewhere in the Americas.

It does seem though that the great libraries of the missions and the superbly executed manuscripts were the province of an elite few. There was a nominal attempt to send all children to school, but in a populous settlement two or three priests couldn't manage real teaching for all. Only the most promising choristers and children from families of chiefs and mission functionaries were chosen for a more intensive education. Those few, perhaps thirty in each mission, were, unsurprisingly for the period, all boys. They were taught to read and write in Guaraní, using dictionaries and grammars compiled by the priests, so ensuring the survival of the Guaraní language. They learned a little Spanish and a parroted Latin. More reprehensible, in the 180 years of the Jesuit missions, not one Guaraní was ordained into the priesthood, "not one attained to any higher dignity than that of sacrist. And yet these Jesuits were short of personnel and were obliged to get novices from a distance and with great difficulty".

The father-priests ran a most benevolent society but, for all that, it was a despotism. Like William Lane, they believed they knew best for the common good. The Indians were their special charges, to be guided, watched over and above all preserved from every temptation.

In the great church at Trinidad there was a baptismal font backed by a bas-relief carving of the Holy Trinity. There was said to be a hollowed space behind the bas-relief where a priest could conceal himself and strike awe in the congregation with "an echoing rendition of the Voice of God".

The Jesuits' attitude was characterised by extreme paternalism, wrote the historian Adalberto López; they treated the Indians like backward children, never expected to grow up. Resourcefulness was not encouraged in the neophytes, only blind obedience to their spiritual fathers. "When they became men, the Indians had no chance of putting childish things away."

It was the wealth of the missions which aroused most resentment among the Spanish colonists, especially the flourishing *yerba* trade. Cunninghame Graham claimed that the Jesuits anticipated socialism, "at least, so far as that they bought and sold for use, and not for gain ... neither the money nor the goods were used for self-aggrandisement, but were laid out for the benefit of the community at large".

Although this may have been the ideal, critics such as the Argentine historian Leopoldo Lugones argue that the Jesuits accrued handsome profits and returned only 10 per cent to the communal fund, the balance going to the Church. After the expulsion of the Jesuits in 1767, an inventory taken in the Misiones area measured the wealth the Society had amassed in dimensions almost justifying the rumours of fabled treasure: "Vast herds of animals including 724,903 cattle, 230,384 sheep, 99,078 horses and mares, 46,936 oxen, 13,905 mules and 7,505 asses." According to H. G. Warren in *Paraguay: An Informal History*: "If one attempts to value the Indian laborers at $200 each, and assigns a nominal value to livestock, buildings, land and church ornaments and plate, the thirty missions may be said to have been worth about $28,000,000 ... a figure that would arouse cupidity in any government." It seemed though that there was little evidence of personal venality on the part of the Fathers. Warren concludes: "The Black Robes as a society were wealthy; individually, they were honest and poor."

It was their economic success which brought about the Jesuits' downfall. It was an intolerable irritant to lay producers and traders, whose taxes were higher, labour force smaller and marketing machine more cumbersome. As the missions gained more converts and the population of Indians outside continued to decline, the hostility of the Spanish settlers was barely contained. It is likely that they would have attacked earlier if the Jesuits had been without military power. As it was, while the settlers continued to voice their complaints in Madrid, the Fathers continued to import guns and ammunition and to train their Guaranís in the art of war. And they continued to build great churches. The finest of all was planned a short distance from Trinidad at Jesús.

*

I took another local bus 10 kilometres north to the village of Jesús, a collection of unkempt wooden houses set back among pine trees. A massive stone church loomed on the hill above.

I walked up the red dirt road towards it, following a dark-skinned girl of about ten who was tugging a recalcitrant black and white cow by a rope. A group of men drinking *caña* and beer outside a cantina shouted ribald comments.

There was no entrance barrier at the top of the hill. One simply walked through a trefoil Moorish arch into the great roofless cathedral, described by a bishop in 1759 as "comparing with the largest in America". Built of ashlar masonry, one of its architects was Antonio Ribera, whose father was responsible for many important buildings in Madrid. Rows of half-finished columns supported only the sky. Vestries and priests' quarters led off through archways and cloisters. Deep-silled windows looked out on apple blossom country. Palm trees were silhouetted in the bright sunlight. The dormitories where the Indians had lived were rubble, overgrown by soft meadow grass. I almost stumbled over the low stone parapet of a well. Water gleamed, a yawning distance below.

The plump cow, a bell around its neck and dragging its rope behind it, was cropping the soft grass scattered with tiny yellow flowers like butter-cups. The young girl disappeared down the slope towards a tiled roof farmhouse in the distance. There was not another soul in sight in the vast and infinitely sad ruin.

Jesús was intended to be the most splendid achievement of the Jesuit builders. In 1767 it was still in the process of construction when the Society was expelled from Latin America. The new civil administrator promised the Indians living on the mission that the work would be completed. It never was.

*

The end for the Jesuits came with appalling suddenness.

For decades Spain and Portugal had argued over the definition of their possessions in South America. In 1750 they concluded a Boundary Treaty, agreeing to draw a line north from the Uruguay River, with Spain to control all the land to the west and Portugal to the east.

As a result of this division, seven of the best mission settlements fell into Portuguese territory, where slave-trading was legal. After nearly two centuries of occupation the Jesuits and Indians were summarily evicted.

When a commission arrived to take over the region, they refused to go.

A combined Spanish and Portuguese army of 3,000 men was sent to drive them out. The Indians took to arms. Although most of the Fathers abstained, at least one priest, an Irishman, Thadeus Ennis, joined the rebels. (A basis for the character portrayed in *The Mission* by Robert de Niro.) The war lasted almost five years. Of the estimated 2,200 in the Guaraní army, some 150 were taken prisoner and a few escaped. The overwhelming majority, 1,500 Indians, were slaughtered.

They had been expended for the sake of a line on a map. But soon it was acknowledged that the Boundary Treaty did not work. After numerous contraventions, Carlos III of Spain annulled it in 1761. The war had been for nothing. The Jesuits were permitted to re-occupy the seven missions, but they had overreached themselves in showing their strength of arms. The Spanish colonists and government officials in Paraguay, disappointed in their hopes of seeing the hated Black Robes vanquished, renewed their petitions to the king. The Fathers, they argued, were intent on setting up an empire of their own and had the military force to do it. Old stories of secret treasure were revived. The complaints coincided with a waning of Jesuit power in France and elsewhere in Europe. A variety of adversaries, both lay and clerical, were seeking to destroy the Society, whose members were viewed as too politically active and too attached to the papacy. In 1759 it was banished from Portugal and its territories and, three years later, made illegal in France.

Carlos III made an expedient decision to preserve his temporal realm and abandon an unpopular cause. In 1767 he decreed the expulsion of all Jesuits from Spain and its dominions in the Americas.

The task of expulsion was entrusted to Francisco Bucareli, the Viceroy of La Plata. At night soldiers entered the Jesuit houses in Buenos Aires and the great university at Córdoba which had the only significant library existing at that time in Latin America. The Fathers were turned out and the papers relating to their missions burnt. Bucareli then proceeded north with his army and, one by one, took possession of the thirty Jesuit missions. The overwhelming fear of the Spanish authorities was of an Indian uprising. The Fathers offered no resistance, but "peacefully gave up the keys of all their houses, and submitted quietly to be made prisoners and be carried off in chains from the territories which they and their order had civilized and ruled over almost two hundred years". On their way to exile in Italy, they counselled the Indians to acquiesce and avoid further bloodshed. "One word from the Provincial," wrote Cunninghame Graham, "would have set the missions in a blaze ... The dogged Paraguayan Indians, ancestors of the infantry which, under López, died so bravely under the fire of the Brazilian guns, would, in their red cloaks and scanty linen clothes, have marched ... against the enemies of the 'father-priests'."

In an exercise in damage control some mission Indians were brought to Buenos Aires for an official explanation. The French explorer Louis Antoine de Bougainville, by chance in port at the time, met some of them: "They ... seemed to have that stupid air so common in creatures caught in a trap. Some of them were pointed out to me as very intelligent but, as they spoke no other language but that of the Guaranís, I was not able to make any estimate of the degree of their knowledge. I only heard a *cacique* play upon the violin, who, I was told, was a great musician."

The Indians from the San Luis Gonzaga mission sent a touchingly respectful letter of protest to the Viceroy: "Withal we are the vassals of God and of the King ... so we pray to God that that best of birds, the Holy Ghost, may descend upon the King ... Furthermore, we desire to say that the Spanish custom is not to our liking— of everyone taking care of himself, instead of helping one another ..."

Priests from other orders were sent to Paraguay to replace the Jesuit Fathers, and "most of them at once took Indian women as their mistresses, a thing the Jesuits had never done", wrote a historian. The Spanish settlers promptly raided the missions for servants, effectively slaves, and took off large herds of cattle and horses. The best grazing land went to the highest bidder. Religious artefacts were stolen, statues decapitated, beautiful carvings, engravings and books in the Guaraní tongue destroyed. Castilian Spanish was imposed as the obligatory and only language. Schools and workshops were closed down, crops failed to be planted and hunger was commonplace. Those Indians who could, made their escape. Some became tradespeople, servants or prostitutes in the towns but thousands took up a nomadic life in the forests, a life unknown to most of them. They were inexperienced and vulnerable, easy prey for the slavers from Brazil. The *bandeirantes* became more brazen, and advanced on the missions. The Guaraní could not defend themselves as their arms had been confiscated. The new administrators and Spanish landowners declined to defend them.

Mission settlements were burned down. "Undergrowth invades pasture and wheat fields," recorded the Uruguayan writer Eduardo Galeano. "Pages are torn from books to make cartridges for gunpowder. The Indians flee into the forest or stay to become vagabonds, whores and drunks. To be born Indian is once again an insult or a crime."

By 1811, when Paraguay declared its independence from Spain, most of the majestic churches and mission buildings were in ruins, the creeping forest advancing, roots and lianas thrusting through the stonework. Sixty years later Cunninghame Graham visited one of the few still inhabited settlements and concluded: "For my own part, I am glad that ... I saw the Indians who still lingered about the ruined mission towns, mumbling their maiméd rites when the Angelus at eventide awoke the echoes of the encroaching woods, whilst screeching flocks of parrots and macaws hovered around the date-palms that in the plaza reared their slender heads, silent memorials of the departed Jesuits' rule."

By the time he wrote his book, his anger at the way the dream of the black-robed Fathers was destroyed had not abated:

> The semi-communism which the Jesuits had introduced was swept away, and the keen light of free and vivifying competition (which beats so fiercely upon the bagman's paradise of the economists) reigned in its stead ... Rightly or wrongly, but according to their lights, they strove to teach the Indian population all the best part of the European progress of the times in which they lived, shielding them sedulously from all contact with commercialism, and standing between them and the Spanish settlers, who would have treated them as slaves. These were their crimes. For their ambitions, who shall search the human heart, or say what their superiors in Europe may, or perhaps may not, have had in view? When all is said and done, and now their work is over, and all they worked for lost (as happens usually with the efforts of disinterested men), what crime so terrible can men commit as to stand up for near upon two centuries against that slavery which disgraced every American possession of the Spanish crown? ... Foredoomed to failure, it has disappeared, leaving nothing of a like nature now upon the earth. The Indians, too, have vanished, gone to that limbo which no doubt is fitted for them.

A short distance from the ruins, some of the mission descendants had returned. They were running a stall for tourists. "Guantanamera" came optimistically from a transistor, but no one was sitting under the Pepsi Cola beach umbrellas. Some mangy animal skins, hard to identify, were pegged up, flapping. I asked the Indian couple behind the counter about the great deserted church behind us. They grinned, indicated they only spoke Guaraní, but sold me a bamboo flute and a feathered head-dress. Something pecked at my ankes — a pet toucan with top-heavy orange beak, its tail feathers bedraggled. A little monkey with darting yellow eyes fretted psychotically at the end of a chain, baring its teeth.

Historians have pondered why the almost 200-year occupation of the Jesuits has left so little trace on modern Paraguay. Perhaps it is because, for all their idealism and good intentions, what the Fathers created was a static and artificial enclave. It was spectacularly more successful and lasted far longer than William Lane's, but was ultimately doomed for the same reasons. Unless a community is completely sealed off — like some science-fiction space station — it cannot function long without impact from the temptations, economic fluctuations and political pressures of the larger society surrounding it (the Mennonites notwithstanding either).

Within the enclave, the Guaraní learned to be docile students, clever imitators of a culture that was not theirs. But except in the most marginal way — such as the forest creatures at the borders of their wall friezes — they were not expressing themselves. By denying them a full education and limiting their response to new influences, the priests suppressed their growth.

The Guaraní hadn't asked for the Spanish to come, they hadn't asked for the Jesuits, they hadn't asked for a new god to replace Tupá, they certainly hadn't requested the slave-traders. But they had responded with a resilience and an intelligence which was their own. Like the colonised everywhere, after the invaders had arrived there was no going back. The way forward for the Guaraní was in the larger society, despite all its inequalities and perils. In mixing their blood with the Spanish but preserving their language, they survived to create the distinctive nation of Paraguay.

Evidence of the Jesuit occupation *has* remained: in the orange groves surrounding every farmhouse and penetrating the most remote *montes*, and in the lyrical national music for harp and guitar, so different from the music of all the surrounding countries.

Perhaps there is another unfortunate legacy, an inclination of the Paraguayan people to submit to authority which caused them, after the departure of the father-priests, to submit for another two hundred years to a series of ruthless dictators.

*

I returned by bus, marvelling again at the crazy, mixed-up beauty of the landscape, apple blossom and bananas, pine trees and palms, macaws and Jersey cows, a deranged tropical transposition of Thomas Hardy's Wessex. This former mission land, Cunninghame Graham had bleakly predicted in 1901, was only "waiting the time when factories shall pollute its sky, and render miserable the European emigrants, who, flying from their slavery at home, shall have found it waiting for them in their new paradise beyond the seas".

In 1927, when the Mennonites were settling in the Chaco, the Jesuit order was allowed back into Paraguay. But their old mission lands were taken. Many German immigrants had arrived and formed another enclave in the region. They were industrious law-abiding people, and made good citizens of Paraguay.

In the late 1940s and 1950s they were joined by compatriots fleeing Germany's defeat in the second world war. Some had dark pasts.

I got off the bus in the village of Colonia Hohenau, where Alfredo Stroessner's parents had made an encounter disastrous for Paraguay. In a prominent position in the main street was the statue of an heroic young man, his muscular torso naked, wielding an axe. He was the embodiment of Aryan youth and purity, like a figure from Leni Riefenstahl's *Olympia*.

Consulting a newspaper clipping I was carrying, I called in at the Hotel Tirol, an alpine chalet with a steep sloping roof and low eaves to protect it from snow that never fell. The proprietor, Madame Michline Reynaers, bespectacled and in her seventies, smiled wearily.

"Yes, it's true. Journalists come here to ask this question, but leave all that be! *Verdammt noch mal!* It's old history. There are so many good things to know about Hohenau. But yes, he lived here in 1959, before he moved to Brazil. He did not hide his name. We all knew him as Herr Mengele, but we didn't know what he'd done. He used to come here for his meals, always polite, and he played the piano very beautifully."

21

The Dragonfly

Now
I am going far away
in order to disappear
with my brothers, in the land of my brothers …
           Aché-Guayakí weeping song

"… the Indians … do not seek for meaning: they *are*. They are not
heavy the way we are, they are light as the air; their being is a mere
particle of the universe, like a leaf or wing of dragonfly or wisp of
cloud. Unlike ourselves, they are eternal."
        Peter Matthiessen, *At Play in the Fields of the Lord*

The faces of the dark Madonna and Child were Guaraní, although
they were wearing golden crowns and sumptuous robes. The
seventeenth-century painting, on fragile vegetable cloth, was protected by a glass case and, like other relics of the Jesuit missions, hidden
from view behind the nave of Asunción's cathedral.

The Guaraní, mingling their blood with the Spanish, had inherited the
modern nation of Paraguay. But some missed out after the will was written.
At the side of the cathedral, concealed from the casual observer, the
homeless were dossing, bundles and bedding scattered along a colonnade,
laundry pegged on strings.

Roger Cadogan thought it a suitable use for the cathedral. In his halting
English he said he wasn't a Catholic, although he admired certain priests
for their work with the poor. "Like my father, and his parents who came
here from Australia, I am a free-thinker." The earnest nineteenth-century
expression summoned up the world of his grandmother Rose Summerfield, of mechanics' institutes and workers' lending libraries, debates on
Darwinism and free will, The New Woman and the perfectability of man
through science. Roger, youngest son of León Cadogan, in his mid-forties
with a soft, sensitive face, intended it as straightforward self-assessment.

As we crossed the square towards the Legislative Palace, a Makká Indian approached a group of tourists. He was in his costume — loin cloth, feathered headdress, a quiver of arrows slung from his shoulder — and they were in theirs — floral shirts, sun hats, shopping and camera bags. A string of red beads was exchanged and after a brief negotiation the Indian agreed to pose for a photograph. He stood impassively while his seamed aquiline features were captured for the folks back home. "He's like the Sioux more than anything," a man in a nylon golf cap pronounced authoritatively, bobbing down for another angle. "Those fierce eyebrows."

"I think he's really sweet," said his wife.

As we walked on, I asked Roger if it made him mad. He shrugged, blue eyes blinking short-sightedly behind thick spectacles. "The world is the world. I will not be able to change the world."

The Makká, he said, came originally from the Chaco. They'd been renowned hunters. At the new moon, the women danced in clearings with girdles of fire-flies to bring rain.

In the 1950s a large group of them were moved from their traditional lands to make way for cattle grazing and given a reservation on the other side of the river from Asunción. Displaced from everything they knew, they led wretched lives. But a Russian emigré, General Juan Belaieff, had employed the Makká as scouts during the Chaco War. He undertook a personal crusade on their behalf and succeeded in negotiating 145 hectares of land, deeded in their name. Also a clinic, school and soccer field. The Makká sold handicrafts, lived from the tourist trade. For a fee the women would pose bare-breasted for photographs in order to look "more native". "The Makká have been very clever at adapting to these new ways of making a living," said Roger. "They've a natural ability for commerce. They're the Venetians of Paraguay."

General Belaieff became a mentor for Roger's father, who always credited the old Russian for introducing him to scientific anthropology. Cadogan went on to gain international recognition, rating this entry in the 1993 edition of the *Historical Dictionary of Paraguay*, published in the United States:

Leon Cadogan 1899–1973. One of the foremost ethnographic experts in Paraguay. He was noted for his research on the origins, languages and customs of the Forest Indians of Eastern Paraguay. The son of Australian immigrants belonging to the New Australia Cooperative Society, he grew up in Villarrica where he devoted his life and work to the study of the Mbyá-Guarani and Aché Indians. He translated into Spanish the classic mythical Mbyá-Guarani texts, *Ayvu-Rapyta (The Basis of Human Language)* and *Yvra-Ne'ery* (The Word

Flows from the Trees). He was one of the first people to denounce the mistreatment of the Aché at the hands of the mestizo population.

Roger was continuing his father's work. He had abandoned a successful career in electrical engineering to set up The León Cadogan Foundation, and was studying anthropology at the university. But, whenever he could, he drove to the remote wooded hills of the Caaguazú region, and walked many kilometres through the *monte* to clearings where a pitifully few Mbyá-Guaraní received him as a trusted visitor. Experience had taught them to melt into the trees when other strangers came with guns, Bibles, bulldozers and theodolites. The economic miracle of the Itaipú Dam, on which Roger had worked as an engineer, and the rush for land in the eastern border region, were pushing these nomadic people to the edge of extinction.

"That's why I can't get angry about how the Makká are making a living," said Roger. "They *are* making a living. There's so little I can change about the world. There's even so little I can change about myself, although I might want to. Recently I've come to realise I'm a dictator in my house, with my wife and children. Maybe I'd like to change that. But I'm largely Paraguayan and my father's son. He was a dictator too. But I hope I share his main belief, in the dignity of the human being."

*

Roger's grandparents, Rose and Jack Cadogan, arrived at New Australia in June 1899, with young Harry Summerfield, her son from a previous marriage. The long trip from Sydney had been especially arduous for Rose, for she was eight months pregnant when they landed at the Asunción docks.

She was known for her grit and fiery determination. "I will not preach calmness to you," she had exhorted the Australian Socialist League in 1892. "No! No! Agitate! Agitate! I hope I'll die with that word on my lips. You must work, you must do battle, you must be filled with stern resolve to do and die in that glorious work."

Of Polish and Irish stock, known either as Rose Summerfield or by her maiden name, Rose Stone, she had come to prominence through the socialist and women's suffrage movements in Sydney. Her son León later described her as "a revolutionary activist in the broadest sense of the term". A powerful speaker and a women's organiser for the Australian Workers' Union, she contributed regularly to journals such as the *Worker, Hummer* and *Democrat*. She hosted discussion meetings at her home at Waverley, attended by rebels such as Larry Petrie and Ernie Lane. Through her position at the AWU she'd worked on Petrie's defence case when he was charged with bombing the blackleg ship, the *Aramac*. He credited her as largely responsible for getting him off.

An attractive woman, Rose caused something of a stir when she travelled outback to speak to shearers and rouseabouts of the AWU. William Wood met her at Bourke in 1892: "She gave an address there and I remember that long Tom Hall was rather smitten by her charms".

Wood and Tom Hall ended up in Paraguay, but Rose was still working for the union in 1894 when Gilbert Casey came back, recruiting for New Australia after the split with Lane. He convinced her that the original colony would stay true to its socialist ideals without its zealous leader, and she agreed to take on the organising of single women, a thankless task as it turned out. But she itched to make the journey herself.

By 1897 she no longer believed socialism could be achieved in Australia; in her judgment most Labor politicians were corrupt and parliament "a tool designed and carried out solely in the interests of the propertied classes".

Jack Cadogan was a socialist without her public profile, but jack of a few if not all trades — teacher, journalist and shearer's cook. His son León gave an ironic account of the paternal family background in his *Memorias*, published posthumously in Spanish:

> The Cadogans belonged to a branch of the English aristocracy. The family lived in London, where Cadogan Square is named after them. There were three brothers and one of them, our ancestor, was required to pay a tax which he considered unjust. He burnt his house down instead, sold his wife (with whom he wasn't getting on at all well), and set off for Wales where he lived a life of pillage in the manner of all good aristocrats. It was one of his descendants who emigrated to found the Australian branch of the family.

It was the fulfilment of a dream for Rose when she and Jack arrived in Paraguay though, as committed socialists, they must have found the reality of life at the former colony of New Australia a disappointment. It had become an Industrial Co-Partnership, presided over by her old friend Gilbert Casey, who was placing emphasis on individualism and personal profit. The family barely had time to settle in before Rose gave birth to a boy on 29 July 1899. She named him León after her favourite author, Leo Tolstoy. From the beginning she had a feeling he was going to be someone special.

*

Rose had a talent for poetry, although she put most of her efforts away in a drawer, where they were discovered after her death. But she was determined that her sons would not be deprived of culture by growing up in a backwoods village. León soon had a brother called Bronte in honour of the passionate writers of the Yorkshire moors. In the next few years she had two more sons, but abandoned literary models, calling them Eric and Hugh. She read them most of the English classics, and insisted León take piano lessons, which he detested, from the New Australia postmaster.

Jack Cadogan and his stepson Harry Summerfield (who soon adopted the Spanish version of his name, Enrique) had gone into the *yerba mate* business. The *Ilex paraguayensis* or *yerba* tree flourished wild in wooded country along the Tropic of Capricorn. The secret of growing it in plantations had gone with the Jesuits, and it was necessary to travel to the *yerbales*, remote forests to the north-east.

Jack and Harry were away for long periods with a convoy of bullock carts and a team of Indian workers. This suited Jack, accustomed to the nomadic life from his days as a shearers' cook, and he liked to drink, another reason to escape.

While he was away he left a trusted workman, an Indian called Agüero, to look after the house, do odd jobs, and keep an eye on León and his friend Harry Gorman. Jack was gone so long on an expedition in 1904 that Rose became anxious. She went in search of him, leaving the younger children with the Gormans. Five-year-old León was woken at dawn by cries for help from Agüero, and dashed outside to see his house being consumed by fire. "This event made a profound impression on me. I was sorry to lose a wonderful hat, the only one like it on the whole colony. But the good news that came from the calamity (for most clouds have a silver lining) was that the hated piano was burned."

After the disaster the Cadogan family lived in various houses abandoned by former colonists. They became friendly with Alexander Macdonald and his wife Rebecca. Macdonald, an impressively tall Scotsman, was a wanderer who regaled them with stories of his travels. He had worked in the Panama Canal Zone, served with the Egyptian army in the Sudan, had trekked through much of East Africa, and even been an advisor to Emperor Ras Desta of Abyssinia. Before sailing on the *Royal Tar* he'd been a farmer in Australia. The place names were a blur to young León, but what came through was that Paraguay had held this restless adventurer for more than a dozen years.

James Craig Kennedy was a frequent visitor, and the boy listened in as
the adults discussed the woes of the government and the country's latest
political crisis. Sometimes Jack would speak nostalgically about Australia
and León pictured it as a huge, bare, brown country populated by
bushrangers and kangaroos.

From Rose he heard stories about his Irish grandmother, Mary Dargan.
At twenty she had migrated from Clonmel, Tipperary, and become a
servant girl in Australia. Rose would sing old Irish songs she had learned
from her, of ghostly sailing ships with celtic troubadours, of a noble knight
and his young bride, of Fair Killarney's lakes and vales.

At nine León was reading widely, "having cut my teeth on *Ivanhoe, The
Three Musketeers, The Count of Monte Cristo* and *Robinson Crusoe*". But
his spoken English was less than perfect and Spanish almost unknown to
him. His language was Guaraní.

The overwhelming influence on his life at this time was Agüero and
the forest world to which the Indian introduced him. León and his friend
Enrique Gorman chafed each day for school to end, so they could escape
its narrow, punitive regime. Once the final bell went they were free to
collect their knives, bows and arrows and join their Guaraní mentor to
learn more of the inexhaustible mysteries of the *monte*.

> Agüero was quite pleased to have two keen young ruffians to train and we
> were soon expert in his primitive lore such as trapping birds, making bows
> and other weapons to slaughter birds and small game. He used to tell us of all
> the guises in which they appeared to people. We learned to ride, swim, and
> find wild honey, and to be sure to take off our hats when we passed the roadside
> cross of someone who had died or been murdered on the spot. When we knelt
> to drink water from a pool, as the animals do, we had to blow first on the
> water in the form of a cross.

Agüero offered them a storehouse of knowledge "indispensable for
those who want to be respected by their friends in the Paraguayan
countryside". He taught them about the plants and trees of the forest, the
molle tree which gave up a balsam which could heal deep wounds, the
paraparay for stomach troubles, and the fruit of the *mamon* which relieved
burning fevers.

They learned to tread carefully, for the forest was treacherous, with giant
blind spiders which could kill with one sting, and many venomous snakes.
But in the *monte* there lived a warrior bird, the *macaguá*. It engaged in
combat with snakes, one wing folded in front like a shield, while attacking
with its beak. If bitten by its opponent, the *macaguá* bird would hurry to

a certain plant, eat its seeds, and rally to attack again. The Guaraní had studied this behaviour and discovered the plant was a mild antidote for snakebite, fever and headaches.

The boys knew how to stalk armadillo and agouti, to recognise the tracks of a jaguar, to respect the gentle three-toed tapir, after which the Milky Way had been named *Camino de Antas*, the Tapir Road.

Agüero described a fearsome carnivore which lived in the grasslands. Jack Cadogan concluded the maneater must be a wolf, an animal sometimes reputed to attack humans. "This information ... suggested to us a way in which we could revenge ourselves for the punishment which our schoolmaster, Mr Wheeler, used to mete out to us every day."

One morning, when León and Enrique were within half a kilometre of the school, they began to run as if the devil was at their heels, shouting at the top of their lungs, "Wolf! Wolf!" The schoolmaster and children rushed out to meet them.

> Sweating and panting, we told them of an enormous wolf which had come after us. Mr Wheeler spent all the rest of the day escorting all his pupils to their homes, taking the kids three or four together on his old horse. The missionaries in charge of the school published an article in their magazine about the incident and I think that the only person who didn't believe the story was Agüero. Some time later, when the incident had been almost forgotten, he asked us innocently if we hadn't met any more wolves! He seemed quite satisfied by the progress of his pupils.

Agüero told them about more fantastic animals from Guaraní mythology. One bore a *carbúnculo* or ruby in its head that glowed at night. And a disgusting hoggish creature which lay on its back, creating a water-trough of its belly, in order to seize deer and small animals careless enough to drink from it. "In a big lagoon to the north of our district he told us that he had seen an enormous marine horse which lived at the bottom of the lake and which surfaced occasionally to cavort on the bank; of a serpent which occupied a cave near the neighbouring town which drew its victims in with its breath; of a horse-faced dragon which was in the distant hills guarding treasure left there by the Jesuits and whose roars in stormy weather could be heard for leagues."

Most fearsome of all were the gremlins and spirits which could take semi-human form. The kindest was Caagüy Pora, female guardian of the forest and the birds and beasts, who flew with long hair streaming in the wind, and spread her perfume on the water lilies. One of the darkest was the *pombero*. León believed in them implicitly. "Thanks to Agüero, the *tejú yaguá*, the *pombero*, *moñái* and *yasy yateré* were almost as real for me as the thrushes that sang in the scrub, the partridges which we hunted, and the pigeons whose cries we could hear in the grassy knolls ..."

*

"Most Paraguayans grow up believing in those spirits," said Roger Cadogan. "They're not just Guaraní anymore. They belong to everyone. They influence our lives."

We were drinking tea at dusk in Florence's garden beside the swimming pool. Adelita, the pretty maid, was pouring milk into saucers for the eight cats which frisked around, their eyes gleaming.

"There's the *luisón*, a huge and frightening dog which lives off corpses. It takes away the seventh boy in every family. For us it was terrible to think about the *luisón* when we were kids. I believed in it. Believed absolutely! Fortunately in our family we didn't have seven boys in a row."

Adelita froze at the name, listened intently.

"Then there's the *curupí*. A tall, skinny person, maybe four metres in height. He appears like a ghost on stormy nights and sometimes frightens people to death. But he is the guardian of crops and fertility."

He asked Adelita if she knew of the creature. She nodded, her eyes huge.

"The *yasy yateré* calls children from their siesta, making noises like a bird ..."

The old men at Cosme had told me about him, the little blue-eyed white boy who lured children into the forest and made them lose their wits. I said he seemed to me like Puck, a Trickster figure.

"Yes," said Roger, "the *yasy yateré* is just mischievous, he likes making trouble, but the *pombero* is really bad ..."

Adelita called to the other maid through the gauze fly-door. Giselle, older and more worldly-wise, came out. Adelita whispered and giggled nervously. They both stared.

"The *pombero* means harm to you," said Roger. "He's a creature of the night, a goblin covered all over with thick brown fur. He can stand upright or run on all fours, faster than the wind. His friends are toads and snakes. He comes whistling under your window ..."

Giselle was very stirred up and spoke rapidly in Guaraní.

"She says he's real," Roger translated. "If a girl gets pregnant and no one seems obvious as the father, people say it was the *pombero*. When a person looks like no one in particular in the family, it's said, 'He is the son of the *pombero*'. You can try to keep him away by leaving tobacco in the hollow of a tree."

Adelita was looking anxious and edged away. It was bad luck to talk about him, she said. Or even to *think* of him. It might make him come. Sometimes she couldn't sleep for many nights in a row, because she could hear him outside, whistling through a crack in the wall, prowling around, right here in this garden.

*

Jack Cadogan abandoned the *yerba* trade in 1908 and sold his bullocks and carts. His eyesight was going and he was drinking heavily. The family moved to the village of Yataity, north of Villarrica, on the suggestion of William Saunders who had a store there. They took over the business from him and most of the responsibility for running it fell on Rose.

For León it was devastating to be parted from Enrique Gorman and especially from Agüero. He was obliged to attend school in Villarrica and of necessity his Spanish improved.

A sudden windfall opened more of the world of Europe to him, just as that of the Guaraní was receding. Dr Bottrell returned to live in Britain. The Cadogans lost an intelligent and cultured friend but purchased his library. León, lonely and dislocated, became seriously ill and was confined to bed for many weeks. He immersed himself in the novels of Verne, Dickens, Scott and Dumas.

His illness was diagnosed as parasitic anaemia, often fatal in Paraguay. His parents took him from one doctor to another, potions and iron tonics were prescribed, but nothing worked. A visitor from New Australia, the feisty Alexander MacDonald, remembered a recipe imparted to him years before by a missionary in Panama. Rose prepared the medicine and her son made a recovery so spectacular that word spread of her miracle cure. Despite her protests she was regarded as a "witch doctor".

Country people with various complaints came begging for help. Rather than turn them away, she treated their malaria or *chuchu* fever with Warburg's tincture of quinine, and developed her own cure for hookworm. "Quack would have been the proper term for her, but she really did a lot of good. She had thousands of patients."

A violent insurrection of Liberal Party factions erupted in 1911 and lasted two years. "These uprisings," noted the historian H. G. Warren, "are a part of Paraguayan national life, an inalienable right of the people. Revolution in Paraguay, as in all of Latin America, is a social malaria, a fever that strikes almost without warning, subsides, then strikes again. Revolution is also a cure for governmental longevity and self-perpetuation, since it is an axiom in Latin American politics that the government does not lose an election."

León Cadogan, collecting firewood, hid in the bushes when he saw a group of men come marching along the road. "I saw, going towards Villarrica, a line of fifty-three peasants, manacled and roped together. They were 'volunteers' from Ajos and they were going to the army to join the ranks of Albino Jara whose headquarters were in Villarrica."

That night the rebels stayed in Yataity, the "volunteers" being locked up in the school. The men looted the town, a local resident was shot dead in the street, and their commander, a notorious brigand called Cardozo, raped a girl from the wealthy Alvarez family.

Next day Cardozo came into the Cadogan store with fifteen rifle-men who made a line along the wall.

Enrique Summerfield was serving behind the counter. Cardozo demanded sixteen silk neckerchiefs in blue, the colour of the Liberal party. This seemed a remarkably modest request, with fifteen rifles backing it up, but Enrique informed the rebel leader how much he should pay.

Cardozo replied that a gringo wasn't going to insult him. His henchmen raised their rifles. Enrique took his hand from the cash register and in it he had a cocked Smith and Wesson 38, centimetres from the heart of the bandit.

"Order them to fire, Cardozo," he said. "We'll fall together like men."

Jack Cadogan appeared at the back of the store. He ordered Enrique to lower the revolver and invited Cardozo into his office for a chat. When they emerged, Cardozo obtained his sixteen neckerchiefs. Enrique was taken to the police station as a prisoner, accompanied by Jack and Rose, to "satisfy the injuries suffered by a Paraguayan soldier". They freed him immediately while the rebels, each with a blue neckerchief, celebrated by firing rifles at street corners.

The episode spurred Enrique to return to Australia. In 1911 he took over the lease of a large cattle property in the Northern Territory. The family planned to follow him, but were prevented by the outbreak of war in Europe.

In 1915 Rose published a nostalgic poem in the *Australian Worker*:

I have wandered from my own land
And deeply drunk from Pleasure's stream;
I've seen strange sights on foreign strand,

Where life passed like a summer dream.
Tho' noble streams and lovely sights
Enchained my senses for a while,
Not all the thousand fond delights
My love from thee could e'er beguile, Australia.
I am longing for my own land,
My dear land, my home land;
I'm sighing for its peaceful shore,
'Neath its blue gums again to stand,
And scent the wattle blooms once more.

At fourteen León left school and became a shop assistant. His brothers Eric and Bronte followed Enrique to Australia when shipping routes reopened at the end of the war. The rest of the family were to join them, but the Paraguay Mercantile Bank crashed. Jack lost all his savings, just as Clara Laurence and Leonard Apthorpe did at Cosme. They were marooned in Paraguay.

For the Cadogans, sorrows came with a vengeance. Enrique had returned to Australia because of the dangers of frontier life in Paraguay. In the Northern Territory he was savaged by a crocodile and paralysed for life, later also contracting leprosy. His half-brother Eric was stabbed to death, in circumstances which remain hazy, by an Aborigine in Darwin. Bronte survived to fight with the AIF in New Guinea during World War II, was wounded, and died shortly afterwards.

Hugh, León's remaining brother in Paraguay, was press-ganged by rebels during a revolution in 1921, transported 100 kilometres south in a closed rail-car and given the option of fighting or facing a firing squad. León, aged twenty-two, went in search of him. He almost drowned swimming a river, was robbed by bandits, then captured by a roaming band of rebels and forced to ride with them. He escaped during a skirmish with loyalist forces and made his way home.

His brother Hugh was already there. He too had fled the rebel army and struggled, starving, semi-naked and ill, through the wild jungle of the Alto Paraná, the same unforgiving terrain through which Father Montoya and his Indians had made their desperate trek. Soon after his return, Hugh developed tuberculosis and died the following year. He was buried in the little cemetery at New Australia.

While the revolution still raged, León moved to Buenos Aires and found casual work as a bilingual translator. A photograph from the time

shows a neat young man with long-boned features and a steady gaze. But
more bad news brought him home.

His mother had been fighting cancer, and died on 15 April 1922, while
on a visit to New Australia. Jack Cadogan, by then almost completely
blind, was bewildered and stricken. A poem found among Rose's papers
was possibly written during her final illness:

> Say what has life to offer?
> A little joy and pain.
> Take all that it doth proffer
> Nor count the loss or gain.
> Today a little sadness,
> Tomorrow who shall pay?
> An hour of love and gladness
> Or hope gone far astray.
> A moment of fierce longing,
> A quelling of love's flame,
> And passions surging, thronging,
> And thoughts scarce dare to name.
> It's all good in its season,
> The life of saint or page,
> There's time for love and reason,
> A compensating stage.

On his return, León realised how homesick he had been. He had a sense
that his destiny lay in Paraguay, that all the pain in his life was steeling
him for a purpose.

*

León bought a property in the village of Natalicio Talavera near Villarrica,
and supported himself by saw-milling and distilling *caña*, a practice which
had been legalised. He settled down to look after his father, assisted by the
elderly Lizzie Jones, who'd come from Bundaberg, Queensland, with the
first batch on the *Royal Tar*.

"Poor old Jack Cadogan, he is now well into the sere and yellow," wrote
William Wood to a friend in Australia. "I was told a few days ago that Jack
is now almost blind and in very bad health. Vastly different to when I met
him in 1894 at Marathon Station near Hughenden, Queensland, where
he was cooking for the station hands at that year's shearing. I remember
he gave myself and George Whelan a good feed there, and plenty for the
track. Jack was hit very hard when Mrs Cadogan died."

In 1926 León married a Paraguayan woman, Mercedes Colmán. She took over the care of his father and he was able to make trips away from home on Jack's old business, collecting *yerba* leaves in the Caaguazú region.

This was difficult, uncomfortable and labour-intensive work in the damp forests. As his father had before him, he employed a team of up to thirty local Indians to do the collecting. They picked the leaves from the trees growing wild in the *yerbales*, packed them into great bundles and brought them by donkey or on their backs to the *barbacuá*, a large oven constructed in the forest. The leaves were toasted, losing most of their bulk in the process, bagged and taken in a convoy of carts to the crushing-works and market in Villarrica.

León sometimes thought about the legend of the *yerba* tree which Agüero had told him when he was young. Long before the Spaniards arrived the Guaraní had recounted the story of Caá Yara, a young girl whose parents took her to live in the forest to escape the evils of the world. The great god Tupá came to visit, disguised as a traveller, and was favourably impressed by the girl's beauty and kindness. In gratitude he gave Caá Yara the gift of immortality, and her spirit entered the *yerba* tree.

The Indians employed in the forest were Mbyá-Guaraní. Although Cadogan spoke Guaraní perfectly, their language, Mbyá, was very different. He learned the basics of it in order to communicate and wondered idly what stories and myths they had preserved as their own.

*

Although Paraguay was a *mestizo* nation, some Guaraní — perhaps 20,000 in all — had remained outside the melting pot, against increasing odds attempting to continue their traditional way of life. In the eastern region of the country there were four distinct groups: the Chiripá, Pai Tawutená, Aché-Guayakí and the Mbyá-Guaraní. The two latter groups were the most difficult to penetrate, explained Roger Cadogan:

> The Mbyá-Guaraní had lived in the forest for hundreds of years without contact with Europeans. They fought when approaches were made, because they knew and feared what would happen to them. They would get the diseases of the white people. They would be brutalised. They would lose their homes, their culture, their religion, their language. They would become the slaves of the white people. And they were right. Most Paraguayans saw the Indians as heathens, because they weren't baptised. Many had contempt for them as if they were animals. It was not considered a crime to kill an Indian.

In his book, *Picturesque Paraguay*, the former New Australia colonist, Alexander Macdonald, described a commonplace event: "If a party of native hunters hear the tapping of the Indian's axe, they sneak up quietly and murder the poor wretch up the tree with no more compunction than if they were killing a monkey. I asked one of these fellows why they killed these people without provocation. He shrugged his shoulders and replied, '*Quién sabe*. Don't you know that the skin of an Indian is tougher than any other for making hammocks?'"

Into the *yerba* forests the Paraguayans came, offering work to the Mbyá-Guaraní. Sometimes it was accepted willingly, in order to obtain knives and machetes, tools that made hunting more efficient. More often the Indians were press-ganged, becoming slaves. Cadogan's workers spoke with fear of the compound, or *obraje*, of a *yerba* company close by in the forest. Once people were taken to work there, they said, they never came out. Armed riders, such as the bandit Crispín Rojas, were employed by the company to patrol the lines. Deserters were shot. The Paraguayan author, Augusto Roa Bastos, wrote of the horror of such places for the *mensús*, the Indian workers:

> No fugitive has ever managed to escape alive from the *mate* plantations of Takurú-Pukú. This fact became a legend among the *mensús* and, fermenting in their imagination, rose like the malarial miasma of a swamp before the eyes of those who dreamed of escaping, and blighted their hopes. So very few dreamed of escaping. If they did, and if they tried to realise their dream, they only got half way. And so the legend was fed by the tale of yet another fugitive brought down by the fangs of the dogs and the Winchesters of the guards. No one had managed to escape.

"My father's involvement with the Mbyá-Guaraní at this stage," said Roger, "was purely commercial. But he saw them as human beings. It made him angry to see how they were treated, although he didn't know what to do about it."

*

One day Cadogan and his second-in-command, Mariano Doldán, riding through the forest, heard galloping behind them. They were overtaken by two horseman. The elder, swarthy and fierce, reined in and asked where they'd be sleeping that night.

"Our horses shall rest wherever darkness overtakes us," replied Doldán. "As for ourselves, Crispín Rojas, we suffer from insomnia, you understand,

and our bullets make a hell of a hole when they hit anything, *comprende?*"
The bandit smiled unpleasantly and comprehended that he would not
forget them.

León Cadogan decided that he didn't care for such encounters, he hated
to see how the Indians suffered, and he lacked the qualities to be a *yerba*
businessman. He returned to store-keeping.

In 1934 his father died. Life in the village of Natalicio Talavera became
increasingly unpleasant because of factional politics. Cadogan had been
appointed a Justice of the Peace and in that role was required to identify
bodies brought to the morgue. He reported that many were victims of
political assassinations and so was targeted as a Colorado by the local
Liberal branch. His position became untenable in 1937, after he involved
himself in a dispute over the appointment of a head teacher. "There was
really no politics in it," he commented later, "but everything becomes
politics in Paraguay if you go against the wrong group. The trouble
coincided with a change of government, and the people who had supported another candidate for the teacher's job became rather dangerous."

The Liberal party was back in power. Cadogan was woken in the middle
of the night by his wife's cousin, a Liberal, who told him that a decision
had been taken to eliminate him if he did not leave town immediately.

The Cadogan family packed up and moved into Villarrica where they
opened a store. Much of the management of it fell on Doña Mercedes,
who already had their seven children to look after. The marriage was in
trouble. León was aimless and depressed and, like his father, took to drink.

His fortunes changed when another revolution swept in General
Morínigo as president of a Colorado government. The new mayor for
Villarrica appointed Cadogan to the local police force, making him head
of the criminal investigation office.

He held the position for three years. It brought him in contact with the
underlife — extortion, smuggling, beatings and murders — in the large
country town. Corruption, he soon discovered, began in the police station.
A lawyer extracted bribes from discharged prisoners, saying the money
was for the chief of criminal investigations. Cadogan was tipped off,
caught the lawyer red-handed, and warned him that if he ever showed his
face in the station again, he'd be locked up.

He was now painfully aware of the injustices and oppression suffered
by ordinary country-people at the hands of local thugs and strong-men.
His anguish at his inability to change a corrupt system contributed, he
believed, to his later heart attack.

Sometimes the prisoners in the Villarrica lock-up were Mbyá-Guaraní. Not officially recognised as human beings, they barely existed in terms of the law, so were bewildered when its full punitive majesty descended on them. Cadogan spoke their language and acted as interpreter, explaining why, for instance, the removal of a watermelon from a garden patch was theft. Inevitably he ended up as their unofficial advocate for there was no one else to defend them, even when the crimes were serious. An Indian named Emilio (employers rarely bothered with tribal names) killed his boss for insulting his wife. Arrested and brought to Villarrica, Emilio begged Cadogan to emphasise that he alone was responsible for the murder, for he feared vengeance would fall on his whole family group. Cadogan represented him and Emilio escaped capital punishment, sentenced instead to a few years in gaol.

But mostly the Indian prisoners in the lock-up remained silent and distrustful, viewing Cadogan, a uniformed gringo, as an authority figure to be avoided. When they were released, as often as not because of his intercession, they fled back to the forest.

In 1940 a branch of the British Council was opened in Villarrica and Cadogan left the police force to become an English teacher. But he fell ill with bronchial pneumonia, exacerbated by the emotional stress accompanying the breakdown of his marriage. The separation from Doña Mercedes was bitter. Years later, his memoirs omitted to mention they had produced seven children.

He saddled his horse and headed off towards the wild Caaguazú region. He had recovered physically, "but spiritually and intellectually I was empty, a useless piece of meat, a worthless object".

By chance he met up with one of the Indians he had helped in the police lock-up and they celebrated their reunion with *yerba mate*. The man told him the Mybá legend of the moon, "how a woman the moon pestered flung black resin at his face, staining it for ever afterwards".

Cadogan then understood a saying he had heard among country-people when the moon changed faces: "It's merely the new moon still trying to wash his face." He realised that much general Paraguayan folklore was embedded in the Guaraní mythology which had attracted him since childhood. He had an undeniable conviction that he had discovered his purpose in life. "But how to learn more of Guaraní mythology, without finding a way of being accepted by the Indians?"

On his ride home, he called at the cattle property of a friend who employed Emilio, the Indian whose murder charge Cadogan contested years before. He called in the favour, asking Emilio to spread word that he would welcome any Mbyá-Guaraní who would visit his house in Villarrica. He stressed that he wished only to gain an understanding of their stories and legends.

Rumours rippled around the countryside, recalled Cadogan, "that there was a man 'with a hairy mouth and yellow hair', who was interested in the Mbyá people … From all around they came to Villarrica to ventilate their problems, air their grievances, or simply to verify in person that it was true that there was a Paraguayan who considered them to be human beings".

Two of them took him to meet the Mbyá of their tribal band in the forests of the Caaguazú, an arduous trek. "The Indians survived in a primitive condition in the *monte*," said Roger, who began visiting with his father when he was only a toddler. "They used to hunt monkeys, agouti, armadillo and tapir, and grow a little mandioca, maize and beans. Because their way of life was so poor, Paraguayans thought them worth nothing."

Don León was introduced to the Mbyá chief Pablo Vera, a man of great dignity, and a lasting friendship began between the two men. It was the first of countless trips for Cadogan, accepted by the small brown stocky people of the forest, naked but for loin-cloths made of vegetable fibre, wary because of previous horrific encounters of all strangers. He observed them hunting with bows and arrows, ate what they ate, slept in their mud and thatch huts. They watched him too with their dark Mongolian eyes and laughed, deep-throated and guttural, as he made detailed notes on the stories and legends they told him: about the fearsome Ogre Charia, about the opossum who raped a human woman, and of the origin of fire, the flames seized by a charmed toad from the vulture-sorcerers who held the secret.

Cadogan, a turbulent, restless man, found a measure of happiness. He had married again, to a sixteen-year-old Paraguayan girl, María Pabla Gato Vedé, and had found his role in life, studying the culture of the Guaraní. "From that time, he was involved with the Indians until the day he died. But he was working intuitively, instinctively as an anthropologist, without an understanding of it as a science."

A mentor arrived to guide his path. General Juan Belaieff, a former Czarist officer, had fled from the Russian civil war in 1924. This military technician and cartographer turned anthropologist was in his seventies when Cadogan met him. He made his extensive ethnographic library available, encouraging the younger man to learn French, although the volumes in Russian defeated him.

"They had long discussions into the night," said Roger, "about many things that concerned my father. Belaieff didn't believe the Indians' culture could stay intact. There were so many forces outside trying to destroy their way of life. He thought they had to be westernised to survive. My father argued against this. He said if you destroyed the Indians' culture, you destroyed them as a people."

In 1946 Egon Schaden, Professor of Anthropology at the University of Sao Paulo, came to Paraguay. He was impressed by Cadogan's work with the Mbyá-Guaraní, but convinced him he shouldn't attempt to make deductions and interpretations. What he had to offer, he said, was his access to the Mbyá and his fluency in their language. He should simply listen, observe and record.

In November that year Cadogan went to the Guairá province near the Brazilian border, in order to bring charges before the local magistrate against a landowner, Emilio Flecha, for the rape of an Indian woman. "At that time, an Indian was just a biped living outside the law," wrote Cadogan, "so it was not surprising that the official didn't pay the slightest attention to my report ... It was probably the first time for the Guairá that the national authorities had intervened in favour of the Guaraní race."

Shortly afterwards Flecha was under suspicion of having murdered an Indian servant called Carlos, who had disappeared after a dispute. Cadogan knew that charges could not be laid without a corpse, but if they were, the cost of legal defence would be at least 30,000 pesos. He proposed to Flecha that if the Indian's family was compensated for that amount, he would not pursue the matter further. The truculent Flecha finally agreed and Cadogan ensured the local Mbyá chief witnessed the transaction. "But I had to bite my tongue," he recalled, "when an old harpie, Flecha's mother, exclaimed: 'How much an Indian's cadaver costs now!'"

"When my father stood up for the Mbyá," said Roger, "it was the first time an outsider had done so. They loved him for that and were prepared to trust him at last." Cadogan had considered himself an advanced scholar of the lore of the Mbyá, but came to realise he had been marking time in kindergarten.

A tribesman called Mario Higinio was brought before the court in Villarrica, accused of having killed a Paraguayan, raping his wife and ritually eating his victim's flesh. "Whatever the truth," Cadogan wrote later, "cannibalism did not form part of the case." He managed to secure Higinio's freedom, on the condition that he remain in the custody of Chief Pablo Vera.

When the chief arrived to collect his charge, the three of them drank *yerba mate* in the shade of a mango tree. Higinio asked if Don León had been admitted to discussions concerning *ayvu rapyta*, the foundations of their language, or told of their secret songs and funeral dirges.

Pablo Vera was reluctant to answer. Higinio challenged him: "It's not right that you continue leading this man up the river. Who else concerns himself with us, the inhabitants of the forest? Is he not already a true compatriot, a true member of the group that gathers around our camp-fires?"

Cadogan's excitement is palpable in his memoirs: "This is the way in which I began the study of the hidden mythology and religion of the Guaranís, kept in secret over centuries, and divulged only to the members of the tribe who mastered the special ritual language, unknown in scientific circles."

"That was the breakthrough," said Roger. "Until then they had told my father lies. At least they hadn't told him the *important* truths. But at last Chief Pablo Vera revealed their history, customs and secret religion, things never told to a white person before."

The chief invited Cadogan to spend an entire year in the jungle with him, saying: "You will eat honey, corn and fruit, and from time to time a chunk of peccary meat. You should leave off reading, for the wisdom of paper will prevent you from understanding the wisdom we receive, which comes from above." Cadogan regretted that was impossible, but promised to come as often as he could.

He listened eagerly, taking notes, as the old chief told him the creation legend of the Mbyá. Apart from his later scholarly discourse, he set it down as a short story, "The Blue Bird", for his young granddaughter María Mercedes. He warned her not to expect, because the person who told it to him was a wise man, that he wore smart clothes or lived in a nice brick house with electric light and running water. "Nothing like that! He lived in a tumble-down hut; he barely had one torn shirt and a pair of patched pants; he went about barefoot, and in winter he slept near the hearth on a mat." But that should not be a surprise, he said, because great teachers like Christ and the Buddha had also lived very humbly. "I tell you all this so that you will understand that wisdom does not depend on wealth, skin colour, nor even sometimes on being able to write … Nor did the wise man who told me 'The Story of the Blue Bird' know how to read and write. He was an Indian, Chief Pablo Vera, whom you saw one time when he came to visit me, although perhaps you don't remember."

From the chief he learned the Mbyá story of how the world was made:

I will begin by telling you that, in the middle of the great impenetrable darkness, with no beginning and no end, which we call *Ptyu Ymá*, appeared suddenly Our First Father. At the same time, out of the darkness burst an Owl and a Blue Hummingbird. And from the breast of Our First Father shot a beam of light so powerful that it converted the sea of darkness into radiant sunlit day. Our First Father was of the height of a little child, and was seated on a low stool, which we call *apyká*, in the shape of an animal. A wide ribbon was tied around his head and in between the flowers that adorned it the Blue Hummingbird fluttered, sucking the nectar with which he fed Our Father.

Our First Father reflected: "In the world that is about to be created, there will be humans living and they will need light to illuminate the darkness ..."

The chief told Cadogan how the First Father summoned powerful spirits and assigned each a task: to provide light, so the people of the earth could hunt, and darkness, so they could rest; fire to prepare their food and survive cold, water for refreshment, and thunder and lightning so the people would not forget themselves and become too vain.

But the Blue Hummingbird had been given a special role: "Its task is to inform Him about the children that live upon the earth; if they laugh or cry, if they are treated well or badly, if they are healthy or ill. The Blue Bird watches over all the children of the world."

Cadogan's granddaughter never tired of the story. He wrote to her that the Blue Bird would always be there, "to tell you that your mother will never be far away, that she will hug you and kiss you and bring you presents and tell you not to worry ... The only difference between this Blue Bird of Our Father which brings you this message, and the hummingbirds which suck the nectar of the flowers in our gardens, is that this one does not die; he is eternal because he accompanies Our First Father in paradise."

General Belaieff lent Cadogan an old Jesuit book about the Guaraní language, *Tesoro de la Lengua Guaraní* by Father Antonio Ruiz de Montoya. He found it helpful as he compiled a Spanish-Mbyá-Guaraní dictionary. His own studies on the Mbyá began to be published, received with increasing respect in anthropological circles, and his reading extended to the work of other ethnographers, Curt Nimuendajú and Claude Lévi-Strauss among them. The latter was to return the compliment by quoting Cadogan almost exclusively on the Mbyá in his definitive *Introduction to a Science of Mythology*.

In a secret ceremony, Cadogan was initiated into the Mbyá tribe and given a special name. Roger told me, "It was a great honour. He didn't tell anyone the name while he lived. We only learned of it after he died. It was *Tupa Kuchuví Vevé*, which means Dragonfly".

In 1949 the government conducted a census among the Mbyá-Guaraní of Guairá, causing panic among them. They feared its purpose was to determine their exact number in order to "lock them up in the State *chacra*".

Their suspicions were correct. A state chacra or farm of 500 hectares had already been set aside. Cadogan argued vehemently against the plan, pointing out how the Mbyá clung to their traditions, including wide ranging hunting, and their need to abandon a place after a death. "When a man dies, the soul of divine origin returns to Paradise, while its base twin remains on the earth, in the shape of a dangerous ghost, the *Mbogua*. Due to fear of *Mbogua*, a hut or even a settlement where someone has died is abandoned immediately."

In response to his concern, the President of Paraguay, Dr Molas López, visited Villarrica and had a special audience with Cadogan and Chief Pablo Vera in a private room of the local club. The newspaper *El Surco* ran an article, "Cadogan's Indians". It omitted to mention, Don León commented drily, that the club manager had prevented him and his Indian friend from using the main entrance, and had fumed and fretted "while the President of the Republic, instead of heeding requests for favours, listened entranced for a whole hour to the peerless oratory of my friend and teacher, Pablo Vera".

Cadogan's stocks were running high. The following year a government position was created expressly for him: Curator of Indians for the Department of Guairá. "I had a salaried job permitting me to fully devote myself to the study of the Indians. My first task was to convince as many people as possible that the Indian is a human being."

*

In 1949 the Indian survivors of a massacre were taken naked and in chains to the town of San Juan Nepomucento, just a few kilometres from Cosme, and there exposed for public sale. Landholders bid for them, prodding the limbs of the men and women, assessing the potential of the children for domestic and sexual use. These people were Aché Indians, the most reviled of the forest-dwellers of eastern Paraguay. The common name for them was "Guayakí" which, in Guaraní, means rabid rats.

The prevailing view was reflected by a British writer who described a wild tribe, more primitive than the Mbyá, degenerate through interbreeding, naked and of whom "it is said that the children who have been left behind and captured when the tribe was suddenly surprised have been found to be incapable of learning to talk".

The invariable way a tribe was "suddenly surprised" was by armed manhunters, operating like the *bandeirantes* 300 years before. It was customary to slaughter most of the adult men, though some of them were chained and sold as slaves to ranchers or to the timber and *yerba* camps, the women taken for whores. The children were the prime object of the raids, fetching a higher market price, for they could be trained to the explicit wishes, the particular and personal fetishes, of their new owners. Small wonder some of them found it difficult to talk.

The British travel writer maundered on: "The ape-like characteristics of these tribes have been much commented upon, and the other natives regard them as so low in the scale of creation that they have no compunction in shooting them down at sight, looking upon them as little better than thieving monkeys. These 'Guaqui' Indians are reputed to have no houses or huts of any description, no clothes or ornaments, no knowledge of the use of fire, and no articulate language, facts which, if correct, would seem to class them as the lowest and most primitive human beings at present existing upon the earth's surface."

These gentle people, Aché-Guayakí, had in fact abandoned cultivation when *mestizo* and hostile Guaraní pressure forced them into the harder country of the Caaguazú Hills, limited their hunting-gathering expeditions with manhunts and reduced their numbers through disease. From many thousands at the beginning of the century, perhaps more than 10,000, there were an estimated 500 in the 1950s.

In their subtle and complex language they preserved the tragic history of their tribe in a cycle of laments, weeping songs of bitter beauty. Their new songs were about murder and bloodshed, brutal dislocation, the sundering of family ties, the benevolent "First Father" usurped by the "Big Bosses" of the work camps:

> We, who were once men,
> never, never will we
> rove freely between the trees of the forest.
> We will never leave
> our Big Boss,
> who put on a big chieftain's head-dress.
> Now we will never again

find sustenance between our forefathers,
the trees of the forest ...

Now our daughters
live in big houses of the masters.
We can never weep together again.

For 300 years the Aché had lived in fear of the white men, creatures too dreadful even to appear in their legends: "At the beginning of all things when the Great Jaguar told all the people what they were supposed to do on earth, he left the whites out. He was afraid of them himself."

Cadogan's designated government position was Curator of the Mbyá-Guaraní Indians of Guairá. But he widened his brief to include these most oppressed people of Paraguay. He began learning their language and compiling an Aché-Guayakí dictionary.

He filed an official protest about raids on Aché camps, the kidnapping of their children, and demanded government action. But a learned judge pronounced: "As these beings have not been included by any law with the inhabitants of the national territory, they lack the rights which the laws of this country accord to its civilised inhabitants. In consequence there is no sanction envisaged for those who kidnap them."

Cadogan's advocacy became pressing. In 1957 his efforts, in collaboration with some Catholic priests, were rewarded by a ruling of the Supreme Court: Indians were to be legally recognised as human beings. "By the end of 1957," Cadogan wrote of this, his proudest achievement, "all the inhabitants of Paraguay received official communication that the Indians were as much human beings as the other inhabitants of the land. A number of criminals were imprisoned for crimes against Indians; and from Villarrica to the Paraná the cry went up: 'It is now prohibited to kill Guayakís.'"

At the same time, Cadogan completed his major work on Guaraní myths and legends, *Ayvu Rapyta* (The Basis of Human Language). An Argentine ethnologist, invited to write the preface, declined, saying it was absurd "to attribute such elevated conceptions to neolithic savages". The book, published by the University of Sao Paulo in 1959, was prefaced instead by Professor Egon Schaden, who described Cadogan as the foremost authority on Guaraní culture.

The Stroessner government created a Department of Indian Affairs in 1958. This was as a result of the efforts of the defence minister, General Marcial Samaniego, who was impressed by Cadogan's work and nominated him to head the department. The sum of 200,000 guaraníes was allocated for priorities such as Indian health. But instead a man with

influence with the president got the job. The department was soon
notorious for its laxity and corruption, and its budget "found another
destiny".

In 1959 the department relocated a group of Aché-Guayakí to a
reservation, arguing that this would protect them from manhunts. It soon
became apparent that the Aché were being sold directly from the reservation into servitude. The coralling of the Indians was as convenient as the
Jesuit missions had been for the *bandeirantes*, presenting "pigeons ready
fattening for their use".

The forest Aché continued to be hunted down. Their pursuers, who
were often observed to be accompanied by soldiers, were able to use army
compounds as their bases and transported the captured Indians on
military trucks.

On the reservation the Aché were discouraged from passing on their
religious beliefs to their children, were actively forbidden to practise their
funeral rites or even to sing of their grief in weeping songs:

In the forest of the dead we shot wild boar, wild boars in the rain.
In the forest of the dead I mounted the truck, in the forest of the dead I was
driven away on the truck full of dead.
The truck of the dead bore me to Asunción.
I, when I was dead, with my friends the whites,
In the city of the dead we shot
At the dead bodies of the Achés, at the many dead bodies.
Dead bodies in the rain ...

The reservation Aché began dying in alarming numbers from influenza,
tuberculosis and malnutrition. There were rumours that they were brutally overworked, and subject to humiliation and torture. In 1963 seventeen Aché-Guayakí died of a mysterious disease. All the babies that year
were still-born. "If a medical mission is not established very soon," wrote
Cadogan to the Department of Indian Affairs, "the Guayakí race is
condemned to disappear."

In a solemn ceremony in the same year, President Stroessner unveiled
a huge and costly Monument to the Indian at Concepción, describing it
grandiloquently as "the greatest monument in the country, which will
perpetuate the memory of our forebears". Cadogan was aware of the risk
when he published an article in a magazine, *Comunidad*: "The most
interesting and least-known nation on earth is rotting here. The Government builds an extravagant monument to the Guaraní Indian at Concep-

ción, yet elsewhere the Indians are rotting with tuberculosis and small-pox!"

It was later recognised, too late for most of the Aché, that the government-run reservation was effectively operating as an extermination camp, despite the lone voices, warning that actual genocide was taking place: "Perhaps more Aché have died during the last few years on the reservation than outside. Reliable sources, such as the anthropologists Chase Sardi and Leon Cadogan and the church dignitary and anthropologist Father Meliá, have called the reservation a 'concentration camp', a 'dirty pigsty', or simply an 'Aché graveyard'."

In 1964 Cadogan denounced a prominent army general of trafficking in Indian slaves. It was a brave but foolhardy act. Immediately everything went wrong for him. His post as Curator of the Guairá Indians was terminated. An unpublished manuscript, of which he had only one copy, disappeared from his desk. The loss of his salaried position meant financial strain and domestic worries at home. Cadogan was under enormous stress: a heart attack was the result.

He described it as saving his life. During his convalescence he had so much evidence of affection and support that he felt spiritually renewed. Little things, like the woman of eighty who walked six kilometres to bring him two fresh eggs and some oranges. He received donations to continue his work and an inheritance from Australia, left by his brother Bronte. Don León reappraised his "position as a martyr" and realised he was not indispensable.

In 1968 a road was cut through the forests of north-eastern Paraguay to the Guairá cataracts, where Father Montoya and his mission Indians had fled the slave-traders. The waterfalls were to power Paraguay's economic boom. More water flowed across them than over any other falls on the planet, estimated sufficient to fill St Paul's Cathedral in three-fifths of a second. They were to be destroyed by the construction of the world's biggest dam, the Itaipú, a massive hydro-electric scheme developed as a joint venture with Brazil.

The forest home of the Aché had become accessible to entrepreneurs and land prices soared in the region. Large areas of forest were cleared for ranching. The Aché were an inconvenience. Father Bartomeu Meliá reported to the Paraguayan Bishops' Conference: "The new invaders of the forest, wood cutters, palmetto collectors and land-owners, want to have the forest clean; they are bothered by the presence of the ancient owners."

Official government policy was to remove the Aché to the reservation of Cecilio Baez. The government appointed a former bandit and man-hunter, Manuel de Jesús Pereira, known for his sexual predilection for young Indian girls, to run it. The place was described as "a small Belsen for Indians".

Leon Cadogan was sixty-nine and declining. He obsessively sought someone to take up the cause of the Indians and recognised Father Meliá, "a Jesuit well versed in linguistics and with excellent understanding of general anthropology ... the Ruiz de Montoya of our century". He took the priest with him to the Caaguazú hills and introduced him to his Mbyá friends, so passing him the baton.

After another heart attack, Cadogan was admitted to hospital. As well as the 120 ethnographic papers he had published in international journals, he'd completed the writing of his second major study of Guaraní mythol-ogy, *Ywyra Ñe'ery* (The Word Flows from the Trees). But he was too ill to take it further. Father Meliá proofed the book and arranged publication.

Cadogan presented the priest with his anthropological library, "to continue the struggle to defend the Indians".

*

In 1970, when León Cadogan was old and frail, and the Stroessner regime was moving into its most authoritarian phase, a young German anthro-pologist, Mark Münzel, came to Paraguay intending to study the religious customs of the Aché. "Instead I discovered," he wrote, "the murder of a nation." He resolved to collect what evidence he could of a government Indian policy "that could only be characterised as genocide". He was assisted by reports of eyewitnesses, "some of whom cannot be identified by name". One was Cadogan whom elsewhere he acknowledged for his crusade: "The destruction of Aché identity has been recognised by Leon Cadogan, the Paraguayan anthropologist and linguist."

Münzel personally observed a manhunt in progress, the captured Indians transported on army trucks. His protests were ignored and Colonel Tristán Infanzón, Director of Indian Affairs, sought his goodwill "by offering me first a 15-year-old girl and then one 11 years old, apparently for sexual purposes". Münzel despaired of the Aché's future:

> Stripped of human dignity and freedom and deprived of hope, the Aché tribes of Paraguay now face virtual extinction. These gentle forest-dwellers are the victims of genocide, perpetrated to be sure with shotguns and machetes, but also with that more subtle form of extermination designed to destroy any

vestige of cultural identification and expression. Untold suffering and degradation have become the fate of a once proud and independent tribe.

In 1972 Colonel Infanzón was named in an affadavit presented to the United Nations as a trafficker in young female Indian slaves.

In the same year, an American anthropologist, Eric R. Wolf, attempted to alert the US government to the violation and murder of the Aché. He pointed out that Americans could no longer hear the moans of the dying at Wounded Knee, "but maybe there is still time to save a few Aché".

To its credit, the Roman Catholic Church of Paraguay has spoken out against the genocide of the Aché and informed the Holy See. To their great credit, Paraguayan anthropologists have voiced their alarm and their protests, often at considerable personal risk to themselves. But where are all the other voices that need to be heard when defenseless people are butchered and debauched? ... What about the government of these United States, always so quick to employ the rhetoric of human rights when its interests are threatened? It gives aid to the government of Paraguay under whose aegis the campaign of extermination is being waged.

Wolf concluded that Americans had "good cause to listen to the Aché weeping songs":

Now
I am going far away
in order to disappear
with my brothers, in the land of my brothers ...

The terrible bird of bitterness will carry me away
as he always does.
Over my grave he will sweep the dust meticulously
and I will finally be happy
when I hear his mocking songs.

One of the first to have heard the weeping, who urged others to continue the fight, was León Cadogan. In his humanism, he acted on the ideals articulated by William Lane of justice, equality and freedom from oppression. But those ideals had been only for whites. Cadogan, born in a colony which had espoused the Colour Line, went on to fight the Colour Line which existed in the wider society. When he took up a crusade for the forest Indians, at the very bottom of the social and race hierarchy in Paraguay, he risked his livelihood, his health and, at last, his life.

He died on 30 May 1973 and was buried in Asunción's Recoleta cemetery. On a simple slab his name was chiselled and, underneath, *Tupã Kuchuví Vevé*, Dragonfly.

*

In less than a year a formal protest to the UN Secretary General was lodged by the International League for the Rights of Man and the Inter-American Association for Democracy and Freedom. It charged "the government of Paraguay with complicity in the enslavement and genocide of the Guayakí Indians in violation of the United Nations Charter, the Genocide Convention, and the Universal Declaration of Human Rights". It gave documentary proof of the deaths, through murder and enslavement, of 343 Aché in the four years to June 1972. Circumstantial evidence suggested another 600 deaths. The Paraguayan Bishops' Conference published a statement, signed by Father Meliá, in *La Tribuna*: "Our secretariat has in its possession documentation of massacres which establish genocide as a reality in Paraguay."

The *New York Times* reported the going rate for the sale of Aché children at US$2 a head.

In Paraguay the manhunts continued …

Stroessner's government moved to silence its internal critics. In 1975 Professor Miguel Chase Sardi, the Paraguayan anthropologist who, along with Cadogan and Father Meliá, had spoken out against crimes against the Aché, was arrested. Sardi was reportedly drugged, beaten, and submerged in the *pileta*, a bath of foul water and human excrement. In 1976 Father Bartomeu Meliá was deported.

Genocide in Paraguay was published in the United States, with contributions by Münzel, Wolf and other distinguished anthropologists and writers. It paid tribute to the fearless efforts of Cadogan, Sardi and Meliá, but concluded "those who would work to help forest Indians in Paraguay will continue to do so at dire peril".

*

The Dragonfly had been dead for twenty years when I visited in 1993. Paraguay's first democratically elected government had adopted protection of the forest Indians as official policy.

But there were few Aché left to protect. "There are now just over one hundred of them," said Roger Cadogan. "They're living on a government reservation, the Church is involved with looking after them. But without their forest life and their culture they die as a people. They are dying out."

He drove through the straggling outskirts of Asunción as we talked, mysterious about our destination. We were going to see something, he said, that tourists didn't see.

The León Cadogan Foundation now concentrated its few resources on the Mbyá-Guaraní. Because they traditionally combined their hunting with subsistence agriculture, they had a chance of surviving a while longer in the forest. "Right now we're helping a group who have a land conflict with Mennonites who've settled in the Caaguazú Hills and want to push the Mbyá off the land. Mennonites work hard, develop industries, pay taxes and so have sympathy from the government. The Indians have nothing and no influence. But all the time the forests are being cleared and the places where they can live are disappearing."

Roger had bought 500 hectares of forest in the Alto Paraná region so a number of Mbyá families could live there without fear of eviction. It was not a reservation, but wild country with no road access, where they could till the soil and hunt with bows and arrows. "It's not enough," he said, "but we have few resources. We sell second-hand clothing to try to raise funds. Money is always a problem. Land has a very high price in that area and the government doesn't want to spend on the Indians. It prefers spending on progress, on clearing the forests."

We pulled up at our destination, but the stench had been with us for some time. It was a putrid place, the Carteura, a vast rubbish dump bordered on one side by the Paraguay River, a noxious lagoon on the other. Dominating the site was the conical wooded hill, Cerro Lambaré, Asunción's most commanding landmark.

I had not considered before what lay behind that hill. Hovels and shanties thrown together from scrap cluttered the fringes, surrounded by oozing drains and mounds of debris, the homes of the rag-pickers. Hundreds were bent, sweating, with feverish industry sorting the city's detritus into separate piles — bottles, aluminium cans, plastic containers, rags, newspapers and cardboard — each pathetic bundle frantically defended from the inexorable advance of the bulldozers, scooping and ploughing across the site as the thin scavengers scurried from their path.

"Anne, you see we are a very poor people," said Roger. "This is how many Paraguayans still live. And they have priority over the Indians, who are at the bottom of the scale. The budget for Indian health has been cut back; the government says it has so many other problems to deal with.

Look how these ordinary Paraguayans are living. Every time the river floods they lose their homes and start again. They're an embarrassment to the government. But the Indians are out of sight."

I looked up at the Cerro Lambaré and the triumphant sculpture at its peak. Its hubris, dominating the human misery below, was obscene.

We followed a winding road to the summit. It offered an expansive view of the city, the skyscrapers gleaming in the sun, the fanciful palaces at the edge of the wide river, the yacht club with expensive craft bobbing at the marina. The vainglorious monument favoured that noble view. It was easy to overlook the tiny figures dodging the bulldozers far below.

The base of the monument was an imposing bronze statue of a Guaraní Indian, Chief Lambaré, who negotiated with the Conquistadores. Above was a tower with niches occupied by statues of generals and bully-boys. "President Stroessner had it built," said Roger, "to honour the heroes of Paraguay. He gave himself the best spot."

But the niche facing the city and the palaces was empty. A few days after the coup of 2 February 1989, the mayor of Asunción made himself very popular. He came up to the Cerro Lambaré with a team of workmen and removed the statue of Alfredo Stroessner.

The coup had only been possible once the United States withdrew its support for Stroessner's regime. He had become too great an international embarrassment, his regime too notorious for repression and corruption. A particular embarrassment was the treatment of the forest Indians.

"My father was one of the first to speak out," said Roger, "and I'm very proud of that. Now we're publishing his papers that couldn't be published here before. Too critical of Stroessner."

He paused, looking out over the city. "My father used to say he was proud of coming from those Australian socialists. But he was really a true Paraguayan. And if you want my opinion, over a long period nobody will remember that man William Lane and the Australian colony here in Paraguay. I think León Cadogan's work with the Indians will be remembered far longer."

22
Gringos

Not in Utopia, subterranean fields,
Or some secreted island, Heaven knows where!
But in the very world, which is the world
Of all of us — the place where in the end,
We find our happiness, or not at all!
William Wordsworth, *The Prelude*

An acre of Middlesex is better than a principality in Utopia.
Lord Macaulay, *Essays*

"Old Señora Lillian Wood used to complain that Cosme was 'far from nowhere and further yet'."

"That's right," agreed Florence, "that was one of Grandmother's sayings. In her opinion it was *donde el diablo perdió su poncho* — out where the devil lost his blanket."

She refilled fine china cups with Indian tea and offered cake. Max, her husband, had beaten a hasty retreat. Tea parties with relatives who only spoke Spanish were as popular with him as a convention of Black Panthers.

Lily Apthorpe, a large stately woman, Paraguay manager for an American cosmetics company, pronounced the cake as good as Lillian Wood's sweet damper. Eighty-year-old Doña Florencia Szell hedged, deciding that Lillian's damper took some beating.

Señora Szell was the daughter of an English recruit to Cosme, William Dick, who had left after the Divide, opened a store in Caazapá and married a German woman. He had continued to visit Cosme regularly to sell provisions and his daughter often went with him for the ride. Her best friend had been Mabel Apthorpe who later married Bill Wood. Now her daughter was married to their son Willie.

"I'll never forget the dances out at Cosme," she said, "mostly at the Fernandez house. There was a blind musician who used to come from Caazapá. He would play the guitar and sing serenades."

"He probably had something to do with me being here then," laughed

Lily, one of eight children of Mabel's brother, Mort Apthorpe, and Paulina, one of the Fernandez girls. "The colony was such a lovely place to grow up, we didn't know how lucky we were." She nudged Florence. "Remember how we used to go to the clear spring in the *monte* to fetch water for tea?"

"And our picnics at The Stony Crossing?" said Florence.

"And Grandmother Apthorpe playing the piano for us? And now," Lily mourned in her emphatic, torrential Spanish, "*nada, nada, nada!* Where Grandma's house used to be, there's just an old crepe myrtle tree. Nearly everything gone. I wish I'd kept some relics of the old days before they all disappeared. It's all so sad. I've often thought that if I'd lived a little longer on the colony I'd be able to speak English today. But then probably none of my brothers and sisters nor me would have landed professional jobs. We would have spoken English but we would have just stayed third grade."

"We *had* to come into town to live," said Florence. "Our parents wanted the best for us. And I think we extended the magic from the colony into our house in town."

"It was there at that place of yours," said Lily. "I'll never forget it."

*

In 1940 Bill and Mabel Wood and their family settled in Asunción at 180 Avenida Chóferes del Chaco. It was a large rambling house with whitewashed walls and a red-tiled roof, set in a huge garden adjoining an overgrown cemetery. A long path overhung by mango and guava trees led to the front gate. The rear boundary, beyond an orchard, was a clear rippling stream called Mburicaó where the children splashed and swam.

A famous Paraguayan poet, Manuel Ortiz Guerrero, collaborated with the composer Jose Asunción Flores to write a Guaraní song about that stream, "Mburicaó":

This beautiful stream
that runs gently by,
reminds me, when I sit close to it,
of you.
How I quietly caressed you,
scattered stones in the stream
where we hid
and this song made me tremble
when I listened to you.
Mburicaó,

you continue running
so smoothly,
yesterday, my sadness,
Mburicaó,
when I submerged completely
in your waters,
you tickled my stomach.

Today the Mburicaó is polluted, choked with litter, and oozes through a park on the site of the old house. The park is named Guerrero for the poet and the street for the heroic truck drivers, *chóferes*, of the Chaco War.

Bill Wood established a successful lumber business close by and employed Nelly, an elder daughter, as cashier. Young Florence, freckled, red-haired and ready for adventure, often accompanied him on trips up-country to buy timber.

There were lots of visitors. By this time Bill Wood — Don Guillermo — was recognised as the patriarch of the surviving Cosme colonists, a spokesperson for the Australians and often also for the British in Paraguay. During school term there were at least a dozen and sometimes twenty young people staying at the house, Bill and Mabel's own eight children — June, Diana, Nelly, Willie, John, Florence, Charlie and Daisy — and other descendants of the colony tribe — Sylvia McLeod, Francisco and Dora Wood, Baby and Roger Cadogan, Dora Szell and Lily Apthorpe.

Mabel Wood coped by cooking a pot of food that she called San Francisco in honour of Saint Francis, the miracle worker, because somehow it managed to feed everybody. Florence looked back with wonder and some guilt on how her mother worked.

> I think she was a martyr to put up with all those people trooping in and out. We didn't have a maid and it never occurred to us girls to help our poor beloved mother. She was eternally washing up, making dampers and scones and cakes. I don't remember ever seeing her away from the kitchen much. She went in there at five in the morning, and at eleven at night she was still there.
>
> We had a long table, but I don't think we owned a tablecloth. We had very plain cups and saucers and plates. We didn't have much money, but we had lots of luck and family and friends. I guess it was my parents' ease and friendship, but that house had charm. Everybody who used to go there remembers it with happiness and longing. There was something very special about it.

The children had a large menagerie of pets: rabbits, cats and a red pig called Hiro which used to sleep on Florence's bed. At last Don

Guillermo announced, "I'm sorry, but it's time to kill Hiro." Florence and her young brother Charlie protested, carried the weighty pig to the home of a friend who lived some distance away and hid him there for a fortnight. Their father tracked the pig down, killed him and cured him for bacon. They didn't speak to him for two months.

They also had a "stupid lovable collie-cross mutt" called Silky, a constant embarrassment, digging up bones in the adjoining cemetery and bounding into the house with them, dropping them as presents in front of people, once the British ambassador.

When the heavy rains came, sometimes whole skeletons emerged through the mud at the cemetery. Florence and Charlie recognised a business opportunity. They collected the bones and set up a stall at their front gate. Medical students turned up and bought their entire collection.

Because their parents were mostly preoccupied, the children ran wild, scrambling up into the trees, chasing butterflies, catching eels. One day Florence and Charlie found their father's old shotgun and over-tamped the gunpowder. "We aimed at the old weasel that ate our chickens and eggs. When we pulled the trigger we were blown about half a block away. I don't know what happened to the weasel but we split a mango tree apart and the gun was smoking. Dad came running up and said, 'Look what you've done to my poor gun!' We were shaken and covered with black soot but he hardly glanced at us."

The younger children walked each day to the elementary school a few blocks from their home, the girls attending in the morning and the boys in the afternoon. When Florence began at high school, the Colegio Nacional de Niñas, she took one of the Belgian-built tramcars which still rattle through the city's avenues. During the 1947 revolution, when "people were running around the streets with guns", Don Guillermo always waited anxiously for the children's return. At other times he seemed placid to the point of perversity. "John and Willie were hoeing in the back vegetable garden with bullets zipping by all around them. They said 'Dad, we'd better leave off — the bullets are getting close!' And he replied, 'Oh well, they haven't hit you yet, you can keep on a while longer.' Finally Mum put her foot down and insisted they come in."

The new school was a shock for the red-headed rebel as the teachers tried to impress on her the virtue of docility. "I guess I was too full of energy. There were two or three of us who were always in strife, slipping down the stair bannisters, throwing paper aeroplanes in class, painting our faces, and I was always talking my head off. I seemed to spend most of my time in the punishment corner. When my young sister Daisy enrolled, the director said, 'I can't believe she's your sister. She's an angel compared to you.' "

Every weekend friends and relatives converged on Chóferes del Chaco, travelling in from Cosme, Caazapá, Villarrica and the railway town of Sapucai. "It was always the place to stay when the colonists came into Asunción," said Lily Apthorpe. "In that house there was always a welcome. And I remember Uncle Bill Wood saying to me, 'Don't ever look behind you, because there everything is cold and sad. Look ahead, look ahead! You are a little god. Always love and respect yourself and others will too.' "

Florence entertained visitors with theatrical evenings. Naturally she was director. Her mother helped with costumes, her father with sets and props. She brought plays and poems from school and rehearsed her brothers and sisters. The big veranda was the stage with up to fifty in the audience. They would set out all their chairs and benches, neighbours brought their own, the overflow crowd sprawled on the floor.

"We performed tragedies and comedies, sang and recited poems. It was all in Spanish of course. Most of my cousins and aunts and uncles didn't understand English. Sometimes we'd recite a very romantic poem by Garcia Lorca. But people especially liked a tragic tale we put on by the Chilean poet, Pablo Neruda. We'd act out how the hero came to the cemetery looking for his dead girlfriend. He was so passionately in love with her that he had found the ability to bring her back from the dead on the stroke of midnight. There we were, right next to the cemetery, and, as a clock chimed, a coffin that Dad built for us would creak open. Everybody would scream. I'd step out, very pale, acting like a complete zombie, and say my lines in a trance:"

I see, when alone at times,
coffins under sail
setting out with the pale dead, women in their dead braids,
bakers as white as angels,
thoughtful girls married to notaries,
coffins ascending the vertical river of the dead,
the wine-dark river to its source,
with their sails swollen with the sound of death,
filled with the silent noise of death …

When music was needed to accompany the performances, there were three elder Wood cousins willing to strum a guitar, Sandy, Pat and David, the grown-up sons of Alex Wood and his wife, the former Peggy McLeod.

They were rumoured to be handy with knives and pistols as well as guitars, and Florence was in awe of them:

> Those cousins of mine were quite a bunch of characters. There were always rumours about what they were involved in, wheeling and dealing and probably smuggling. They all had distinctive looks: Sandy was a big, cuddly bear, Pat was lean and suave, and David was such a giant of a man that he usually went by the nickname Big. He was a con artist but a real charmer. If he said, "Tomorrow I'm going to make the big bucks," you could already visualise three million dollars in his hands. My dad used to say he was a good person to know from a distance: "If you get too close you might get burnt," he would say. But I have very good memories of those cousins because they always treated us well.

When a convincing villain was required for their dramas, Sandy would usually oblige. "He was so broad and fearsome, but he had a wonderful sense of humour. He snored terribly so he was never allowed to sleep inside the house but on a mattress outside. One time, when he'd had a very heavy night, all of us kids got hold of his mattress, carted it across the grass and dumped it in the pond. Even though he was in the water, he just kept snoring. We were afraid he was going to drown, so we poked him with a hoe to wake him up. He was a bit angry but he laughed later, so he really did have a sense of humour."

When the children needed a beauty for one of their shows, their elder cousin Peggy could sometimes be prevailed upon. Sometimes, but not often. Peggy was curvaceous, tall like her three brothers and in her own way as romantic and inscrutable. Her long blonde hair swooped across one eye, just like a Hollywood film star. But Peggy could rarely be bothered to attend family get-togethers. She had her own mysterious life in Asunción, and was sometimes seen speeding along the avenues in a convertible beside a foreigner in dark glasses, or disappearing through the portico of an expensive restaurant with a uniformed officer.

*

For three months of every year the Wood children and some of their cousins spent their school holidays at Colonia Cosme. They crammed into beds in every corner of the old slab timber, iron-roofed farmhouse and were under the firm control of Grandmother Lillian Wood.

The old lady's eyesight was going and her tiny stature had shrunk even further with age, but she still stomped about exerting her powerful personality, a cigar or cigarette stuck behind her ear, often singeing her grey hair. She had named most of her charges. Peter, another grandson, recalled that she rarely bothered to ask her sons and daughters what they wanted to call their offspring. "It was taken for granted the choice was entirely hers. She controlled us all to the fine tune she wanted."

William Wood Senior had died on 1 August 1935 after a visit to Asunción to attend a celebration hosted by the British consul for the Jubilee of King George V. In a letter to her Australian cousin, his daughter Rose explained that it was the first time he had left home for eighteen years and the excitement proved too much for him. After his return he seemed dazed, took to his bed and died in his sleep.

"He enjoyed his life on Cosme," Rose concluded. "Preferred it to returning to Australia even though all his relations are there. Mum of course left her heart in Australia and has always longed to go back but I doubt whether she would be happy there after an absence of forty years. All her old friends gone or forgotten, all her own sisters dead or out of touch, a mother over ninety and in her second childhood."

Lillian had been nineteen years old when she married William Wood and twenty-two when she came to Paraguay. "She thought it was a lark; she never dreamed she wouldn't be going back," Rose had told me. "When she still talked of going my brother would say, 'Mum, there's nobody there anymore. The Australia that you knew doesn't exist anymore. If you went over there, where would you go?' "

But Lillian still talked about the old Australian days with her friend Allan McLeod, and her thoughts kept drifting back. She wrote about her memories of Bourke and the coach to Queensland always crowded with people. She spoke of being "beached on a foreign shore by William Lane's dream". But her sons had fought for Paraguay against Bolivia, some had embraced Catholicism and Paraguayan wives, and the old original colonists were dying off one by one and were buried in the little cemetery near the sugarcane field. Lillian knew that it would be her final resting place too, under the red Cosme earth beside her husband.

"I think my grandmother Lillian Wood never really thought she left Australia," said Florence. "She always wore these long, long dresses, that I think were worn in the 1890s, and her house, I think, was like somebody would have had in Australia. What used to impress me was the zinc roof, very unusual in Paraguay. She told me that in the summer it kept you cool and in the winter it kept you warm. And it had lots of other functions — it had no bugs, and when it rained it didn't have to go through straw, but came directly from this clean roof into a tank. The zinc roof covered the dining and living rooms which had wooden floors, which she always kept beautifully polished. Of course all the other rooms had thatch roofs and floors of mud."

When Florence came to Cosme on holidays in her early teens, a copper-skinned dark-eyed little boy was living with her grandmother. She knew he was the son of her lissome blonde cousin Peggy, who had abruptly disappeared to Buenos Aires. No one was saying who the father was. Possibly no one knew. When the adults talked about Peggy and her son, they did so in hushed voices. But Grandmother Wood was bringing him up, they said, and that was the best thing, though it was a funny name she had chosen for him: Robin Wood. Strange to link such a swarthy little ragamuffin, obviously a real touch of the tar there, with a character from an English folk tale. Still, they said, in Paraguay few would make the connection.

The old lady found Robin a handful, rebellious and given to sudden rages. She was relieved when the older children arrived to distract him for a while. The small boy was ten years younger than Florence, "but as a kid, just like later, he was game enough for anything and he would tag along with us".

Like their parents before them, the children headed off into the *monte*. "The best thing about the colony was that there were no restrictions. We'd just pretend to obey Grandmother and say 'Yes, yes' and go off and have a wonderful time. We'd pick wild oranges and watermelons, cut down green bananas to eat and get terribly sick. We used to walk to The Stony Crossing and fish and swim in the marvellous clear water of the Capiibary. And we'd go riding horses bareback. You know, it was like Tom Sawyer, but in a different time."

Life on the colony was so exhilarating that the children didn't mind the lack of home comforts of Asunción. "Grandma cooked over a fuel stove and my job was to start the fire in the morning with camphor bracken. We used to drink *yerba mate* out there, which we didn't have so much at home." The lavatory was a little outhouse and Florence shame-facedly remembered tearing leaves out of the family Bible to use instead of the dried corn husks provided for the purpose.

But her grandmother's lifestyle exhibited certain refinements that she had never encountered and she decided these must be part of an Australian way of life. "She used to tell me how she brought all her beautiful china from Australia and it didn't survive. And there was a silver dish that got lost. But she treasured her pretty things, curtains and bedspreads that nobody else on the colony had. She kept her few pieces of china — she always called it 'crockery' — and her linen in a cedar chest. She always had clean crisp bed linen and she made a special pillow for me out of chicken feathers. It had an embroidered cover and she used to put a sprig of lavender underneath it."

In the land of orange trees Florence's most evocative memory of Lillian Wood's house was of the scent of apples. "She always kept a bowl of them on the mantelpiece, and we used to say 'Please Grandma, can't we eat the apples?' She would say, 'Wait a few more days, they smell so lovely, then we'll eat them.' "

Sometimes Florence would join her cousins for meals at the home of her maternal grandmother, Laura Apthorpe, who lived a few houses away. "But my English Grandma Laura — and if she's listening somewhere I hope she's not mad at me for saying this — couldn't cook so very well. We'd get porridge for breakfast, lunch and dinner, and sometimes a little bit of pork and some damper."

At Cosme meat had become a luxury, with only the occasional killing of a steer or a pig, but Lillian Wood had ingenious ways with food. She maintained her own patch of vegetables with great difficulty, watering it from a well over 20 metres deep. "She had a very small bucket, so it took about fifty buckets to water just a small patch of vegetables." Oil and flour were hard to obtain and Florence later discovered that her grandmother always cooked with cod liver oil, "but so deliciously that nobody realised it. So we were all robust and healthy. She used to make wonderful Australian dishes, scones and bread and sweet damper. All of us kids would eat first and then she would sit down and have her cup of tea and what she used to call her smoko. She always had a cigar after her evening meal. Once I stole one and tried it and I choked. She didn't punish me but she said it would be a nice lesson."

In the evenings they would sit out under the honeysuckle vine which shrouded the veranda, and the old woman would sing songs she knew from Australia. Florence softly sang one she remembered, faltering for the words:

> The sun is sinking in the west,
> Yoo-lah, yoo-lay,
> The time the darkies like the best,
> Yoo-lah, yoo-lay,
> Come out, you yeller girls and see,
> The sun is sinking in the west,

Come now, you yeller girls to me,
Yoo-lah, yoo-lay!

"She told us that she learned the songs when she was very young. Grandma Wood only spoke English, never Spanish and certainly not Guaraní. My cousin Dora couldn't understand a word she said, but she still used to sit and listen to her sing and read stories to us in English. Grandma would talk about what she remembered of her home town back in Australia where she lived as a girl, and how she came to South America in a big ship. It had been very cramped and cold."

And there were still evenings when Lillian sat at the piano, her hair adorned with fireflies she had caught herself, in some fanciful memory of better days at Cosme, her hands straying over the keys and a lost faraway look in her eyes.

*

Lillian Wood still kept in touch with some of the former colony women, even if it was only a letter at Christmas time. They had reached the age where their news was the documenting of the deaths of loved ones.

From the British Channel island of Guernsey she occasionally heard from Clara Stevenson, living in genteel retirement with Dave, first at the Bel Air hotel on the Esplanade at St Peter Port, then at a guest house. Dave made an obsessive ritual of his daily swim.

Guernsey was under German occupation during World War II but, according to Dave's great-niece Mary Leeser, "the German commandant was a very fair man. Life went on more or less as before and for a while the islanders had quite a good time". In 1941 Dave was admitted to hospital for a gallstone operation. The Germans allowed him the dispensation of milk and eggs. But as the war continued and supplies became short, the German officers fared well, but the soldiers and the ordinary island people were desperately hungry. "There wasn't a cat, dog, rat or mouse alive on the island and every berry or edible leaf had been made into some sort of brew." Dave died, aged eighty-two, on 5 November 1942, probably not from malnutrition, according to a neighbour, but from lack of medical supplies. "I don't think he ever fully recovered from the operation."

David Russell Stevenson was buried in the graveyard of the Anglican church of St John the Evangelist on Guernsey, with a dressed headstone of granite, the "dearly beloved husband of Clara L Jones". It was to be another twenty-two years before Clara was laid to rest beside him.

Lillian heard even more rarely from Mary Gilmore, but Mary had become such a famous personage that she received clippings about her. In 1937 Mary was made a Dame of the British Empire, after a nomination which argued: "She is one of the grandest personalities in Australia today and is fittingly recognised as a national poet … She has memorialised the passing of the Aborigines more effectively than any living writer." Her elevation was widely acclaimed and publicised, but her husband failed to come from Queensland to accompany her to the official celebration. Although Mary wrote to Will regularly, she had seen him only twice in twenty-six years of living apart.

During World War II, Mary came to even greater public prominence through her verse rallying Australians to resist invasion. Her poem "No Foe Shall Gather Our Harvest" was a lead feature of the *Australian Women's Weekly* in June 1940; it was read over the radio, recited at concerts, set to music, displayed in shop windows and published as a popular Christmas card.

After the fall of Singapore in 1942 Mary wrote a powerful and bitter poem condemning Britain's failure to defend the crucial island base. She sent a copy to Prime Minister John Curtin, declaring she was prepared to go to gaol for it. The wartime censor still insisted on modifications before "Singapore" was published, especially to the last anti-British lines:

Ask of those who pandered for power,
Traitors whatever their rank,
Who flung to the dogs the nation's pride
Till the very name, Singapore, stank.

In 1945, as the war with Japan was coming to an end, Mary lost the two most important men in her life. At the age of seventy-nine, Will Gilmore died from blood poisoning after scratching his arm with barbed wire while working on his Queensland property. The news came to Mary as an appalling shock, for she had not known he had been ill.

Just five months later Mary's son Billy — William Dysart Cameron Gilmore — died, apparently after drinking benzine. He had been an alcoholic for some years. Mary wrote in her diary: "Dad in February and Billy last night. There will be no more pain, my son, no more suffering. It is all ended for you now. Now you are my little boy again. The cruelty is all over and you are free."

Mary suppressed her own grief and anguish; that had always been her philosophy:

> Never admit the pain,
> Bury it deep;
> Only the weak complain,
> Complaint is cheap.
> Cover thy wound, fold down
> Its curtained place;
> Silence is still a crown,
> Courage a grace.

A fortnight after Billy's death the *Daily Telegraph* ran a double-page spread on "Dame Mary Gilmore: Labor's First Lady" in celebration of her eightieth birthday. It described how the "Grand Old Lady of the Australian Labor Movement, crusader in a host of humanitarian causes ... became leader of the women" in Paraguay. At her Kings Cross apartment she was reported to rise before dawn, did all her own housework, and kept open house "for friends and those who seek her guidance in writing, or her support for old or new causes".

Jenny Lane in Brisbane wouldn't have cared for that description of Mary. In 1947 there is no record of Jenny writing to Mary at the same time that she wrote to Lillian Wood and Clara Stevenson with her own bleak news, that her husband John had died at the age of eighty-one.

*

The midday heat shimmered against the white walls of the villa, bounced back from magenta bougainvillea, as we returned from shopping, grateful to step into the coolness, close the shutters and sink, like the rest of Asunción, into the sweet torpor of the siesta.

Mail had arrived from Brisbane. Florence opened a letter, read a newspaper clipping and passed it to me. It was from the *Courier-Mail* and concerned a man I had interviewed and considered a friend:

DEATH ENDS ANOTHER PARAGUAY LINK: The death of Eric Lane, 84, in Mt Olivet Hospital last Tuesday, has revived memories of a communist colony established in Paraguay last century by a group of disgruntled Australians. Eric was the nephew of the founder William Lane ... Eric's parents John and Jane remained in Paraguay until 1905 ... Arguments ended the colony. Its assets were sold up — and most of the expatriates returned to Australia ... although some of their descendants are still to be found in Paraguay ...

*

Lillian Wood's daughter Rose returned on a visit to Cosme in 1938. Her life in South Africa with her husband Alan Menmuir was a privileged one, although she regretted their inability to produce a child. An operation in Buenos Aires "to have my womb put straight" had been a failure.

Rose envied her part-Indian sister-in-law, María, nursing a new baby daughter born in November. Wallace Wood had taken on the upbringing of María's Paraguayan son, Chilito, but this little girl, like her sister Dora, was a Wood. She had fair skin and blue-green eyes and was named Lillian after her grandmother. Doña María adored her and was gratified that Rose seemed to as well.

Bill Wood volunteered to register the baby in Asunción. María was bewildered to find her officially recorded as "Rosemary Lillian" but everyone seemed to like the new name so she became accustomed to it. And it seemed a gracious tribute to a loving aunt. Then her husband put a startling proposition to her. It was sad for his sister, Wallace said, lacking children of her own; it would be a kindness to let Rose take little Rosemary back to South Africa for twelve months.

María's protests were overruled. All the Woods thought it was a good idea. Old Lillian, a formidable mother-in-law, chided her not to be selfish. Bill Wood made the arrangements. "Uncle Bill was the head of the family, the patriarch," María's youngest son, Peter, told me. "He organised how it would be done. There was never any signing of papers. My mother was not consulted at any stage in terms of adoption, and she said she never agreed to her child staying away longer than twelve months. But the Woods didn't take a great interest in what she said or how she felt."

Rose Menmuir returned to Johannesburg in July 1939 with the little girl. She had been in Paraguay almost a year and encouraged the belief among her relatives and friends in South Africa that Rosemary was her daughter by Alan Menmuir.

Twelve months later at Cosme, María gave birth to a son, Patricio. But she was missing Rosemary. She resented the way she had been pressured into parting with her for a year, and now that year had passed. She wrote saying she wanted her daughter back. In reply she received photographs and a glowing account of Rosemary's progress. But no mention of when she would be returned. War in Europe and the threat to shipping routes provided a plausible excuse.

In October 1941 Wallace and María had a blue-eyed son. Lillian Wood, retaining the seigneurial right to name her grandchildren, called him Alan.

The name rang no warning bells for María, who was looking forward to the return of her daughter at the end of the war. By March 1943 there was another sister for her, tiny blonde Virginia. She cut off a snippet of the new baby's hair and carefully put it in a tin box beside the dark tress belonging to Rosemary.

María was pregnant again when Cosme was rocked by scandal the following year. The beautiful ice-maiden Peggy Wood, having been a virtual prisoner of her grandmother for months, gave birth in January to an illegitimate dark-haired boy. María assisted old Lillian with the delivery. A few months later, when her own son Francisco was born, and Peggy was sent away in disgrace, María suckled Robin Wood at her breast with her son. "Much later my cousin Robin became famous," said Peter Wood. "People were always talking about him. My mother used to wonder, 'Does he know that I breast-fed him for four or five months?' "

In 1945 María received the news she had been yearning for. Rose Menmuir was returning with her six-year-old daughter. She wondered how much Rosemary would resemble the pretty child of the photographs. She knew the little girl spoke only English and she only Spanish and Guaraní, but she felt certain their natural love for each other would win out.

Rose arrived alone. "Aunt Rose's excuse," said Peter, "was that Rosemary hadn't been well enough to make the trip."

María was never to see her daughter again.

Rose stayed at Cosme a few months. She made her wishes clear to her brother Wallace who went to his wife with a considered family verdict rather than a proposition. Alan, four, and two-year-old Virginia would accompany Rose back to South Africa. "I don't know how they could have done it to my mother," said Peter. "Uncle Bill had a lot to do with it. He was prepared and organised and insisted Alan and Virginia would be good company for Rosemary. The Woods were a very dominant family. Grandma Lillian was like a general, and my mother was isolated, out of contact with her own people." Later he had asked María why she hadn't stood up to them: "She said she couldn't. Wallace told her it was the best thing for the kids and that anyway they'd be coming back after a short time. The only person, she said, who wasn't in favour, was her brother-in-law Norman. He told my father that he was gutless for allowing it."

There was even a plan that Francisco should go as well; he was a very little baby and at the last minute it was agreed he was not old enough to travel.

Alan had a four-year-old's understanding of what was happening and clung to María. "He didn't want to go at all and put up a real show. He cried and cried. Uncle Norman said to my father, 'Don't make him go'. But it was all decided. The children were taken away while my mother stood weeping."

Peter Wood was born in 1947, so "escaped being on the list". But he was still angry:

The argument was that the children would be better off. But you know, those of us who stayed on at Cosme didn't end up destitute either. We went to school, we studied, we mightn't have had wonderful facilities and comforts, but that was Paraguay.

In many ways Uncle Bill was one of the greatest people I've ever known and I'm sure he thought what he did was just. But I'm afraid there was a racist aspect to it as well. Years later he said about me, "Peter hasn't turned out so badly, considering".

I felt like saying, "What bulldust!"

*

By her mid-teens, Florence Wood showed less enthusiasm to spend her holidays at remote and primitive Cosme. There were ten adolescent girls living at the house on Chóferes del Chaco, and the games of childhood had been replaced by new interests — boys and "dating". There was Florence herself, now experimenting with cosmetics to hide her freckles, her sisters Diana and Nelly, Norman Wood's daughters Ruby, Dolly and Lily (who was envied by the others for having been a runner-up in the Miss Paraguay beauty contest), Connie Cadogan, Dora Wood and two other girls who weren't relatives, Celia González and Dora Szell. They were all growing up, becoming aware of their womanhood and their sexuality. When visitors arrived there was always a frantic dash to be first in the bathroom to primp in front of the mirror.

The girls had to be strictly chaperoned if they ventured in public with a boy. "I think the idea of chaperoning came from Spain," said Florence, "and in those days it was the thing to do. Most of the time my chaperones were my cousins, my youngest brother Charlie or sister Daisy, who just hated the job. As a matter of fact, it was uncomfortable for the man too. If he paid for your movie entrance or for candy, he had to pay for the chaperone as well."

Bill and Mabel Wood were prepared to be more tolerant if the young people stayed in the grounds of the house. Florence recalled that at night she and the other girls would be cuddling with their boyfriends on the grass under the guava and mango trees. At about 10 o'clock her father would stride along the path to the gate, banging a tin pot and admonishing: "Time's up, gentlemen! Go home, please."

On clear moonlit nights a group of them would gather in the back garden beside the stream Mburicaó, tell stories, sing the new North American hits, "Hello, Young Lovers", "Getting to Know You", and dance barefooted on the grass, "In the Cool, Cool, Cool of the Evening". Sometimes the three buccaneer cousins would join them, Sandy Wood bringing his new bride, the beautiful Clara Cuquejo. One night Clara stood on a rock in the stream and sang a song in Guaraní, and Florence noticed how Sandy's younger brother David, known as Big, watched her with burning eyes. "It was clear to me that Big was in love with her too. I used to think, 'Doesn't he realise that she's married?' I used to introduce all my girlfriends to him, but he would leave them cold to gaze with adoration on Clara again."

Other couples would be absent during the singing and dancing, hidden in the darkness of the trees. "But it was all very innocent," insisted Florence. "We really didn't know very much about sex."

She learned a puzzling story by eavesdropping on an elderly woman who was a regular visitor to the house. "She was about seventy years old," said Florence, "but you could tell from the twinkle in her eye that she was very, very sexy. When she saw a handsome man she used to say, 'Look at all the hairs on my arm. They're all standing up!'" One day Florence overheard this woman confiding to a friend about her "secret vice". It was her occasional habit, apparently, to put on a long blonde wig, high heels and a diaphanous skirt over stockings and suspender belt. She would go to the local fleapit cinema that screened erotic films, slipping inside when the lights were dim, but would take a strategic position where her entrance would be noticed. Then she would wait. A man would ease into the seat beside her. A hand would slide up her skirt. She would leave just before the lights went up. Recalling an episode for her friend, she grinned wickedly and sighed, "Oh, I had such a lovely time!"

One of the great excitements in the Wood household was when professional musicians arrived to perform a serenade commissioned by a suitor, a traditional Spanish custom.

The ten resident young women would peer through the shutters, whispering and giggling, as the wandering minstrels came up the long path, usually a singer and two or three guitarists. When the suitor was wealthy, or particularly enraptured, there might be a harpist and someone on accordion as well. The girls would speculate on the identity of the sponsor and strain to listen as a bemused Bill or Mabel Wood met the musicians at the door and the name of the lucky recipient was announced.

The musicians would set up under a window or at the edge of the veranda and launch into a bracket of three songs. A serenade's lyrics, in Spanish or Guaraní, always pursued the theme of passionate love:

> Oh maiden with the starry eyes,
> I lay my heart at thy dear feet.
> My heart dissolves itself in sighs.
> What answer wilt thou give, my sweet?

There was a certain etiquette to the business of receiving a serenade, Florence informed me. The girl shouldn't make an appearance — on a balcony or at the window — until the third song or she would seem too eager. But of course, if she didn't appear at all, that would be a deliberate insult to her admirer.

"What if she just wasn't at home at the time they called?" I asked.

"She'd be home. The fellow paying for the serenade would first make sure she was at home."

*

The singer, in spangled jacket, was concluding a speech in such voluble Spanish that I had done my usual trick of tuning out, and was startled when in fulsome conclusion, he beamed directly at me, "*para la australiana!*"

"Take a bow," Florence hissed through the applause, "they're going to serenade you."

The singer crooned, eight guitars strummed and thrummed, and I found it difficult to sustain a look of damp and ecstatic appreciation. There really was an art, I could see, to this business of receiving a serenade. The sponsors were my kind hosts, Lily Apthorpe and her regular escort, Marcelo. They had brought us to a grillhouse and dance hall, *auténtico paraguayo*. There wasn't a harp in sight. The harps were somewhere else, rippling out traditional *guaranias* for American and Japanese tourists.

I nodded and smiled fervently during the applause, then the band launched into a cha-cha-cha. Marcelo led me onto the dance floor, sweating with the exertion of partnering us three females, one after another, all evening; *noblesse oblige* of the Paraguayan male, for over one hundred years accustomed to a surfeit of women.

The music changed to a polka. Immediately, to my bewilderment, people cheered and clapped. Marcelo growled that it was the polka of the Liberal party.

"*No le gustó?*" I asked — You don't approve?

"*No me gustó!*" he replied in disgust. He decided to make a big statement of it. "*Soy Colorado!*" he shouted, waving his fist. People dancing nearby looked towards us with hostility. Lily Apthorpe waved to him to sit down. "I'm Colorado!" he shouted again, the veins standing out on his forehead. "Colorado and proud of it! And I'm still for Stroessner!"

I was suddenly very tired. "*Estoy cansada,*" I told him, moving off the floor.

*

By her mid-nineties Mary Gilmore had reached national icon status, a Grand Old Lady, favourite of journalists, ready to expatiate on almost any issue. But the topic she regularly revisited was her time in South America. She had been mourning its loss for sixty years.

> The roses climb on the roof of the house where William Lane lived ... the moon-flower twines from eave to eave, and other people's children play there now, other faces pass in and out at the open door.
>
> In the little house that was mine, one who was kind to me sits and looks at the evening sun, and watches the wattle-blossom and the white cedars cast their leaves; the cricket sings in the grass, and the wild bird nests in the trees ... And in my heart there is a great longing just to go back once more, to see, unseen, what is — and what was.

Mary's clippings were sometimes posted to Cosme, although by 1960 Lillian Wood was completely blind. But Wallace lived next door and, according to Peter, read to her every afternoon, sometimes sleeping on a mattress in the spare room.

Lillian still managed to cook and find her way around the kitchen. Doña María and her remaining children all had their appointed tasks. Peter recalled: "Grandmother wanted her cup of tea at six in the morning. All of us kids would take turns serving her, bringing in the corn, collecting wood chips for her fire. Nobody would argue the point with her. The only animal allowed inside was her cat, unlike the typical Paraguayan who lets chooks and pigs run through the house. She knew all of us by the movements we made. We'd be up a tree picking loquats and she would know exactly who was up there."

When Florence visited from Asunción she would take over the reading aloud. "In the evenings Grandma would sit in her rocking chair on the veranda, under the honeysuckle vine, and I would read to her while there was still light from letters from former colonists, most of them long dead, and from the many old books in her library. Every time I smell honeysuckle these days, I remember her."

Lillian Wood died in 1961 aged eighty-nine and was buried beside her husband at Cosme.

"Now I realise," said Florence, "that Grandmother was something of a feminist. She gave me some of my best values: punctuality and belief in myself. She always said, 'Even if you live in the *monte* you must be a human being and differentiate yourself clearly from the beasts. Never degrade yourself. Never forget that individuality is the most desirable thing in the world'."

One year later, on 3 December 1962, the death of Mary Gilmore was mourned throughout Australia by people of every social class. She was given a State Funeral and her extraordinary life documented in most of the major newspapers. Her ninety-seven years reached back to Abraham Lincoln's assassination and ended just after the launching of the first man into space. Yuri Gagarin was the hero of her last days.

She had seen tumultuous changes and had faced most of them with resilience and enthusiasm. "I began, myself, with a slush lamp," she had said, "went on to the tallow candle ... then to the imported stearine candle, to kerosene lamps, from kerosene to gas, from gas to electric light, and now we have ahead of us the atomic power to cover every mortal thing we can think of."

For the previous ten years, the Dame of the British Empire had been writing a regular column for the Communist Party newspaper *Tribune*, something she had begun in indignant response to the Menzies Government's 1951 attempt to have the Party banned. "Do not be stampeded by that word 'Communism' as flung about and shouted by our opponents," she wrote. "It is an old game of theirs. We had it flung at us when the Labor Movement first began ..."

"For years the 'comrades' exploited the vagaries of her failing judgment," commented the obituary writer in the *Sydney Morning Herald*. "It was proof of the affection in which she was held in her old age that the public readily forgave her for allying herself with the Communists."

The day after Mary's funeral, *Tribune* published the poem she had submitted as her final contribution to the paper:

When I am gone I ask
No mighty ones to follow me;
No lions, tigers, elephants or tall giraffes
But just the little ants —
The little folk
Who, day and night,
Carry the burden of the small,
And save the world —
These were my friends in life;
In death they will remember me.

*

In August 1963, two young Australian journalists driving a jeep from Rio de Janeiro to New York, announced the discovery of a "Queenslander tribe" in the interior of the continent. "The Australian Peasants of Paraguay — Our Forgotten Exiles", they wrote, "follow Australian customs, wear Australian clothes. They speak English with an Australian accent. They also speak Spanish, and the local Indian dialect, Guaraní. They live in modest huts, like other natives of the country. But gum trees grow around their homes. Their lives are hard and simple ..."

The Murray family were lined up for a group shot at Nueva Londres. A young Nigel Kennedy was photographed in baggy *bombachas* on his cattle property. At the house on Chóferes del Chaco in Asunción, William Wood, "grey-haired and weatherbeaten", was interviewed with his attractive 21-year-old daughter Daisy and his youngest son Carlos. They were baffled by the excitement surrounding their "discovery". They didn't know they'd been lost. They had been writing to relatives in Australia for years.

But in 1965, with the arrival of the author Gavin Souter to document the history of Lane's utopian experiment in Paraguay, the first-generation colonists, like Bill Wood, who had never felt truly Paraguayan, had a genuine sense that the Australia of their forebears was taking an interest at last. Don Guillermo accompanied Souter on a five-day trip to Cosme. "That visit meant a lot to my father," said Florence. "It was one of the most important events in his later life. He and Gavin corresponded for years afterwards."

Peter Wood remembered them arriving at Cosme after having swum their horses across the flooded Pirapó. "Gavin Souter sat on the edge of the veranda, exhausted. He hadn't been on a horse for a long long time.

He seemed a nice polite man but I couldn't communicate with him in English. I never imagined the difference he was going to make to my life."

Bill Wood urged the writer to do what he could to help some of his nephews migrate to Australia. "Uncle Bill sold him the idea," said Peter. "He didn't think there was much future for us in Cosme. We'd always felt a bit different to the other Paraguayan kids. I'd always had a consciousness of being a *gringo*. My uncles had adventurous blood, but none of them had gone away too far, other than in the first world war. But deep down they had this feeling that it would be good for some of us to go back where the family came from. My mother never tried to talk us out of it either. She saw it as a big opportunity. But she said, 'You know where your home is if you find you're not happy'."

*

With her red hair and volatile temperament, Florence was considered a definite problem. "I was always quite annoyed that I was different when I was growing up," she said. "I'd get called *gringa*. At that time I think there were only two girls with red hair and freckles in the whole country. When you're young you want to be just like your friends. Now I accept what I am."

Most Paraguayan men found her independence of spirit and directness of manner rather threatening. "That's why I could never find a Paraguayan husband. I found boyfriends, but when they had to clash with my mind, it was a 'goodbye' and that was it!"

"The Wood girls," said her cousin Robin, "have always been strong, free and a little wild. Maybe because of their family background they didn't have the usual shyness, they felt more secure than Paraguayan women. We have a joke about the Wood girls: 'Never make a proposal to them. Let them do it'."

At the time of Souter's visit, Florence was thirty, still unmarried, which her parents considered vaguely scandalous, and working as a secretary at the United States embassy.

Most of Bill Wood's children had landed jobs which utilised their bilingual ability: June and Nelly were air hostesses and both married American professional men and moved to the States; Diana, Willie and John had positions with banks in Asunción, Charlie and Daisy were employed by a tannin export company.

Florence had also worked as an air hostess when she was in her twenties. Based in Lima with Panama Airways, her regular route took her to Miami, stopping at Guayaquil, Panama, Havana and Kingston, Jamaica. "But I was too naive to know how to have a good time. My first date without a chaperone was in Lima, but I kept looking around, expecting someone to be with us."

She continued with the job for almost four years but quit after a macabre episode. A fellow air hostess and good friend lived in the apartment next door in Lima. One night Florence was woken by a faint cry and sounds of movement; she waited, heard nothing further and went back to sleep. The following morning she and the other hostess were on the same flight. When she couldn't raise her, she became anxious and finally had the landlord open the apartment. The window to the fire escape was open and there were signs of a struggle. The young woman was never seen or heard of again. The newspapers speculated that she had been kidnapped to the Middle East.

Florence returned to Paraguay and the job in the American embassy. But the family were becoming increasingly concerned about her unmarried state:

> Some of my brothers and sisters were so embarrassed they'd hardly speak to me. But actually I did have proposals, quite a few, but never from anybody you'd want. There was a boy with clammy hands, who never had anything to say to me on the subject, but asked my father if I'd marry him. Dad said, "You'd better discuss the deal with Florence. She's very independent minded." Well, I didn't want him. Then there was an Italian count, at least he was supposed to be a count, from some very aristocratic family, but he looked just like Dracula, so he was no good. There was also a Peruvian, who wanted to take me to live on some little farm way out in the Boondocks, and I didn't want that either. My brothers and sisters despaired of me. One day they stuck a notice on my back as I walked down the main street in Asunción. I couldn't understand why everyone was laughing. The notice read: "This woman needs a husband."

She took up a new job, as an administrative assistant with the Inter-American Geodetic Survey, a para-military United States group progressively charting Latin America's cities, harbours, rivers, roads and major physical features. The Pentagon was its principal client. "It was a small office with eleven North American men on the staff including a colonel, a lieutenant and two sergeants. There were also 385 enlisted Paraguayan men. I had to make up the pay-roll and take it all around the country in helicopters. I was also the receptionist, so it was an endless office job."

Her next beau was an American who worked in the IAGS office. "We were going out together but it was nothing special, so I was surprised when he proposed. It turned out he thought he could escape being drafted to Vietnam if he was married. I didn't think that was very romantic, but he gave me a diamond ring and everyone was pleased. He took me to an elegant place to celebrate and, at the end of the meal, he belched so loudly that the whole restaurant turned to stare. 'They do that in Japan to show the food was good,' he told me. I decided we weren't in Japan and I wasn't going to live with someone who belched like that every day. He married a Paraguayan girl instead, but he still got drafted to Vietnam."

Florence was thirty-five years old and insisted she was quite reconciled, even if her family wasn't, to the fact that she wasn't going to get married. Then one hot October day, when the perspiration was streaming down her face, and all the fans were blowing her hair around, Max White, a new American cartographer, turned up in the IAGS office.

*

Max had been listening, with throaty chuckles, from his favourite position, commanding the carved mock-Spanish bar. He liked his role as a John Wayne cavalry hero to the rescue.

"I worked for the airforce in the United States," he said, "and we needed an accurate survey all over South America in order to establish tracking stations for the Space Program. That's why I'd been posted to Asunción. When I first met Florence her hair was in rats' tails and I wasn't too impressed. But the next time I met her at a party. She was all dolled up and I thought 'Wow!' "

Within a month they were dating regularly. In January they were dancing close together when Max asked her if she would like to come to the States with him. "I wasn't sure what he meant," Florence laughed. "I told him, 'I've been to the States. That's no big deal.' "

"I asked her if she would come and live with me there," said Max, "and she looked as if she'd sucked on a lemon. I said, 'Well, hell, what I'm trying to get at is ... Would you like to marry me?' "

"I thought this might be my last offer," Florence continued calmly. "I thought I'd better take him up. Next day I was telling my parents that I enjoyed the dance the previous night. They said, 'That's good, dear.' I said, 'Max asked me to marry him.' They smiled vaguely and said that was nice too. Then their jaws dropped in amazement. '*What* was that you said?' Well, they couldn't wait to get on the phone and ask Max to come by."

Max added with a wry smile that when he came calling, Bill Wood met him in the drive. He expected the full parental inquisition.

"You're thinking of marrying into this family?" asked Don Guillermo.

Max admitted to that hope.

"You'd better read this then. After that we'll talk." His prospective father-in-law thrust a book into his hands and walked away. It was Souter's *A Peculiar People.*

> He wanted me to read that book and I realised it seemed to be quite important to him that I read it, so I thought all right, I'll read the damn book. I brought it back a couple of days later and I understood him then. And I understood her too and where the family came from. But I think the vision was stupid. Communism doesn't work anywhere without force. But actually the first impression I got after reading that book was that those discontented Australians were just like Americans travelling to the Old West. They were going to a wilderness. They packed guns on their belts and they shot ducks, and Indians too if they had to, and they planted what they could and hoped it would grow, so they'd be able to eat for another six months. They came here to be free. This is a basic American attitude. We want to be independent. We don't want the government or anyone else telling us what to do. So I could sort of relate to that story.

Florence and Max married in 1970 and moved to St Louis, Missouri. He worked on the tracking orbit for the Skylab Program and she became a receptionist in the Spanish Department at the university.

*

Diana, Florence's elder sister, suffered a stroke in 1966 which left her a permanent invalid. "That house had been a magic time in our lives, but the magic came to an end." In 1968 Bill and Mabel moved from Chóferes del Chaco. Diana died in 1975, two days before her forty-sixth birthday; the flowers Florence sent for that occasion served for the funeral.

During this difficult time an Australian film crew arrived to make a documentary on what survived of Lane's socialist colonies. Four of the Wood brothers — Bill, Alex, Norman and Wallace — obliged by sitting in a *carreta* as it traversed the rutted road to Cosme and re-enacted subsistence farming, broadcasting grain in an old colony garden. Bill was overwhelmed by the charm of the film's producer and presenter, Caroline Jones. He was gratified that people in Australia still seemed to care.

But his wife Mabel had never recovered from the loss of Diana and died on 30 October 1976, the day of their fiftieth wedding anniversary.

Bill Wood lived on for another ten years. He had been teetotal all his life, but about this time began allowing himself a careful daily "tot" of whisky. He would potter among his beehives, watching the workers fly in and out. He said that they ran a better colony than William Lane.

*

In 1978 Peter Wood was happily settled in Australia at Griffith in the Riverina district. He was established as a real estate agent, had married Betty Calabria, a girl from the large Italian community and had fathered three daughters.

In that year Virginia, one of the South African sisters he had never met, came to visit him. "We'd had some previous correspondence," said Peter. "I'd written first about 1968 saying I was her brother. Aunt Rose was upset about that, but it turned out that Virginia and Alan had discovered the story already. Rosemary apparently had more difficulty accepting it."

Virginia had forged a brilliant career in the United States and at the time was personal secretary to the chairman of the World Bank.

The brother and sister's initial meeting at Griffith airport was tense. "I was really studying you," Peter told Virginia later. "I noticed," she said. They talked until 4 o'clock in the morning. Virginia told him about the journey she had made to Cosme three years earlier. She had met the people she'd come to realise were her biological parents and felt a warm rapport with María, although hampered by language. But after the affluent life she had been used to in South Africa and in her subsequent career, the living conditions at Cosme, a village still unconnected to electricity, were very confronting. "The pigs and chooks were wandering through," said Peter, "and it was only later that I managed to instal a shower and flush toilet for my parents." Virginia only stayed a few days in Paraguay. What was important to María was that she had come.

After meeting Virginia, Peter got in touch with his brother Alan, a surveyor. He called in to see him in South Africa on his own way through to Paraguay but failed to persuade Alan to accompany him. However, they spent a week together, some of it out on a survey trip, and became close.

Four years later Peter succeeded in arranging a visit of momentous importance to María. He telephoned his mother: "I'm not going to surprise you with shock treatment. I'm bringing you some very important visitors."

"Are they really coming?"

"Yes."

Peter, Virginia and Alan hired a vehicle in Asunción and made the long trip along red dusty roads, and at last rattled across the Pirapó bridge and arrived at Cosme.

A crowd of relatives and onlookers had gathered, but two old people waited at the slab-timber, iron-roofed farmhouse. Wallace was eighty-one, stooped and a semi-invalid from the angina condition he had developed just before I met him on my first visit a few months earlier. María was seventy-three, a tiny woman who bore the years of sadness and hard work in the tropical sun on her lined face.

"My father was looking forward to seeing them," said Peter. "He had got better a few days beforehand, as if in expectation. He was out of bed and sitting in a chair. But for my mother it was overwhelming. When she embraced them it was very emotional, especially meeting Alan."

It was thirty-seven years since the brother and sister had been taken away, little Alan screaming and trying to cling to his mother.

He had told his brother of his reluctance to come to terms with their father after what he had done. Peter had replied, "You're coming to see your mother. But talk to Wallace. He's not a bad man. Circumstances may have made him different. But you've got a thing or two to learn from him."

Before he left Cosme, Alan had a private meeting with Wallace Wood. "I don't know the words he used," Peter said, "but he conveyed that he wasn't impressed with his performance, the way he had gone about things, lying to María. My father died still denying any part in a deception. But they were his children and I don't see how it could have been managed without his being involved."

Peter met his other sister, Rosemary, in Canada. She told him she felt unable to make the trip to Paraguay, but she wrote to María several times, acknowledging their connection and expressing a wish to meet.

Doña María had the letters translated and kept them. By the time she died in August 1993, much of her pain had been assuaged.

Peter Wood returned to Paraguay to bury his mother at the Cosme cemetery. In a little tin box he found her most precious possessions: photographs and all the letters from her eight children, a lock of baby hair from each, a list of birthdays and a careful record of the dates when three of them were taken away.

23

The Adventures of Robin Wood

"Things have a life of their own," the gypsy proclaimed with a harsh accent. "It's simply a matter of waking up their souls."
Gabriel García Márquez, *One Hundred Years of Solitude*

We have built us a dome
On our beautiful plantation,
And we all have one home,
And one family relation.
Oneida community hymn

Peggy Wood at twenty was known for her beauty. Her remarkable pale skin and long blonde hair had a devastating effect on men. In 1943, staying with her grandmother Lillian Wood at Cosme, she sent a chatty letter to her Aunt Rose in South Africa. She'd had a dream the previous night, Peggy wrote, about old Allan McLeod, her maternal grandfather who lived a few houses away on the colony:

> Grandad Allan, with his billygoat beard streaming in the breeze, was about to plunge into the briny ocean. "Into the sea," says Grandad, to Daddy and me and a lot of other Cosme-ites who were waiting to do the same. We were all going to commit suicide and he was showing us the way. Grandma says look it up in your dream book and tell us what it means ...

Peggy's dream probably had something to do with the fact that her holiday at Cosme was an enforced one. She was a virtual prisoner of her grandmother Lillian, who told her she had wantonly thrown away her life.

Early the following year, on 24 January, Peggy gave birth to a bastard, a little copper-skinned boy with a shock of dark hair. She steadfastly refused to name the father.

Her grandmother said she had shamed the family and the good name of Australians in Paraguay. Her brother Pat arrived and pronounced she should leave the country immediately to spare further embarrassment. It was decided that Peggy was too irresponsible to take care of the child. He would stay at Cosme with his great-grandmother, who had already chosen a name for him.

"My birth was a big drama," Robin Wood told me, laughing with the confidence of one who expected to make a theatrical progression through life. He sprawled, thickset and darkly handsome, beside the swimming pool, while inside the house his blonde Danish wife instructed removalists packing their furniture. "Today the family are much more relaxed, but at that time they still felt themselves to be foreigners and were very insecure. My mother was the first of that group to have a child out of wedlock. She was very beautiful, strong-willed and quite indifferent to people's opinions. I think she was born far ahead of her time."

Peggy had been living in Buenos Aires, he said, studying to be a nurse, but had returned to Paraguay when she discovered she was pregnant. "She came out to Cosme because I think she planned to have an abortion there with the help of one of the Indian women. But — fortunately for me — my great-grandmother Lillian got wind of it. She was hopping mad and decided to keep my mother in the house until she had the baby. She locked her in the little room next to the woodhouse and I was born there. Grandma Wood helped with the birth. Afterwards my mother left the country and didn't return for years."

*

"I didn't hear much about the scandal," said Florence. "It happened out at the colony and we were just on the edge of things. Peggy was twelve years older than me so we didn't mix together. But I always thought she was stunning, just like the movie star Veronica Lake. When she walked down the street, *everyone* would stop to gaze at her with their mouths open. I was skinny like a pole, so I wasn't crazy about walking anywhere with her. I'd hear all the compliments she'd get and think to myself, 'It's not fair! Why wasn't *I* born a blonde with big blue eyes?' But I remember my parents saying it was a shame that such a lovely girl had this misfortune, an illegitimate baby. But it's wonderful that Robin was born because he's turned out to be so talented and rich and successful."

She opened her scrapbook to show me the many clippings about her famous cousin Robin Wood. It seemed he was interviewed every time he dropped into the country which he represented as a cultural attaché, appointed by the Stroessner government. A double page spread in *ABC Color* documented his international lifestyle, his homes in Spain and Denmark, his articles for Italian *Playboy*, his plans for a movie, and reproduced frames from some of his comic-books, noting that their circulation in Spain and Latin America ran into millions. There was no mention of any eccentric Australian heritage. He was a Paraguayan hero.

*

Peggy was twenty-one when the family banished her. She returned to Buenos Aires and I wondered how she had survived. "She had good legs," shrugged her son, still exasperated and obsessed by her. "She was ravishing, a charmer when she wanted to be and a natural platinum blonde. She was never an actual callgirl, but I think she had a chain of men and lived off them. She always used men."

His earliest memories were not of Peggy, but of his great-grandmother Lillian, matriarch of the dwindling ragtag group at Cosme. "She was tough, she was hard, everybody was afraid of her." When his grandmother, the former Peggy McLeod, came to visit, the old lady would screech at her, " 'Eee lass, come and make the tea *now* ! And hurry up about it!' And the lass, my granny, was nearly sixty years old." He remembered a story they told at the colony about a German, Otto Meyer, who used to take his great-grandfather off for a drink. Meyer was so afraid of Lillian that he would creep around outside the house until William Wood could slip away. "A bottle of *caña* would be in order and the two would get sloshed. When they came back she would rush out, tiny as she was, and the German would run off in terror."

From a crate of books, Robin extracted *One Hundred Years of Solitude* by Gabriel García Márquez. "This always reminds me of the story of the Wood family, all the humanity and tragedy, the good things and the bad. The heroine of the book is Ursula, the mother who becomes the matriarch of the large family, the strong character who keeps them all together." He located a passage and read aloud:

> Ursula's capacity for work was the same as that of her husband. Active, small, severe, that woman of unbreakable nerves who at no moment in her life had been heard to sing seemed to be everywhere, from dawn until quite late at night, always pursued by the soft whispering of her stiff, starched petticoats. Thanks to her the floors of tamped earth, the unwhitewashed mud walls, the rustic, wooden furniture they had built themselves were alway clean, and the old chests where they kept their clothes exhaled the warm smell of basil.

His great-grandmother Lillian was just like that, he declared. She ran the family and the house like a general. Her floors were so clean he always imagined he could see his face in them, even though, like Ursula's, they were made of earth.

In Robin's opinion, the colony had been a world of solid women, resilient and practical, and crazy men:

> The men were dreamers. That's why they landed there. They had visions, they were always in the place where they didn't want to be. Like José, the patriarch in Márquez, they wanted to create a different, special place, and ended up with a mirage. My great-grandfathers were dreamers, Billy Wood, and Allan McLeod who played the violin and was a great reader with his one crystal eye. Those fellows pined after things they couldn't get and never grasped reality. Firstly going along with that big dreamer Billy Lane. The idea of no booze? Madness! A bunch of Irish, Scots and Australians all together, and Billy Lane said "No booze"? Forget it! They were into making moonshine before they even took off their shoes. And Lane also said, "No hanky panky with the local girls". And such beautiful women in Paraguay? Forget that too! What were the men supposed to do? Hanky panky with the cows?

Sometimes Robin's elder cousins, including Florence, whom he called Carrot Top, would come to Cosme. He remembered good times with them, picnics, fishing and swimming at The Stony Crossing.

Lillian, old, frail and finding him a handful, needed an occasional respite too. She sent him to Asunción to stay with his grandparents, but then they separated and Alex Wood took up with a Paraguayan woman. So he was shared out among his uncles and aunts, staying with Wallace and María at Cosme, with Donald and Deolidia Wood in the southern town of Encarnación, or returning with Florence to the house on Chóferes del Chaco. His uncle Bill Wood told him later that they were passing him from family to family because nobody really knew what to do with him.

When he was five years old Peggy returned to claim him. He was overwhelmed to discover that the willowy pale woman was his mother and that they were going to live together. She rented a house in Asunción for two years. Once there was a coup d'etat and he remembered sleeping with his mother on the floor because bullets were coming through the windows. He had memories of a man who used to visit every day. "He was a politician, a minister in the government, Minister of Security, I think, or Chief of Police. He was very tall and dashing and I felt he was a good man, I liked him very much. He was always kind to me and used to give me money. He had brown-greenish eyes and actually he did look rather like me, so he could have been my father, he could have been …"

*

As abruptly as she had arrived, Peggy left her lover and Paraguay. This time she took Robin with her to Buenos Aires, where she obtained governess work teaching English. They were always on the move, living in different pensiónes, until they settled in a room in a building with a restaurant on the ground floor. Peggy opened an account for Robin to have his evening meals. Often she would not return until the small hours of the morning, sometimes with a man.

Robin had to fend for himself. He would take himself off to school and come back at midday, make soup with cubes or fry some eggs.

> Then I'd be alone in the room all afternoon. I did a lot of reading. My mother had mountains of books and she used to get through a book a day. I read Hemingway when I was eight and loved *For Whom the Bell Tolls* and *The Old Man and the Sea*. I also liked Faulkner's *Absalom, Absalom*. But one of the main things I'd do would be to sit for hours cutting drawings from comics. I'd put them together in different ways to make up my own stories. Once I counted and I had over three hundred of them in a big box. At night I'd go to the restaurant downstairs and order dinner. I was eight or nine years old, sitting there at the table with my book propped up. For me this had become usual. It was my life.

But sometimes he and Peggy would have a night out together, taking in a film and discussing it afterwards at a restaurant. "She would be very analytical about the film, as I am today because of her. She was an intelligent woman, charming and witty, and sometimes we'd talk for hours." One night Peggy became very heated over an article she had read about Marilyn Monroe. "My mother thought it was the pits of journalism. It suggested Marilyn gave herself easily to men. Nobody, she said, should accuse a woman of that. 'Under what judgment?' she asked me. 'Men's judgment? Firstly, they go to bed with you and then they accuse you of being easy. That's typical!' She was an incredibly emancipated woman for her time. It just wasn't usual then for a woman to think like that. Especially not in Latin America."

He loved her but he hated her too. "As a mother she was a catastrophe." Often their discussions ended in arguments, insults, screaming matches, with bystanders looking on aghast. "We had fights in restaurants, in cinemas, just walking along. Once we had a scuffle in the street; I was kicking and shouting and shook her arm. A police car stopped. Of course they saw this little dark street-kid roughing-up the elegant white woman.

They zoomed to the rescue, jumped out in front of us to say, 'Can I help you, madam?'

'Well, why?' she asked.

'Because the brat's bothering you.'

She gave them a cold look. 'He's my son.' "

The arguments often began with Robin raising the question of his father's identity. He passionately needed to know. "I was always asking her. But she would always change her story. One time it was this one, and another time it was that one." For many years he felt certain he was the kindly Paraguayan government minister with his own dark-green eyes.

Doubt was cast on this version by his grandmother, who moved to Buenos Aires after her separation from Alex Wood. "Her candidate was an Argentine doctor who had been involved with my mother and loved her enormously. Apparently he had gone to the United States to specialise further, and hadn't known my mother was pregnant. When he came back, he wanted to marry her but she refused him and never told him that I was his son. That was my grandmother's story and I don't know, it could be true. My grandmother was a very serious woman without any imagination."

I wondered why Robin hadn't been curious enough to seek out the Argentine doctor later in life. He said that years afterwards, a journalist girlfriend met the distinguished specialist, married with two daughters, and suggested to him that he had a son. "And she told me that he absolutely panicked. I told my friend to leave the man alone, he had his own world. By then I was too old to need to find out who my father was. It was too late. That curiosity belongs to a certain age."

Robin thought that his mother must have hurt the doctor in the way she rejected him. "It seemed that there was something that pushed her to destroy whatever was positive in life. She couldn't live with men and she couldn't live without them. She would take them to the extreme and then she backed off. She had many affairs and a lot of men who loved her dearly, good men, kind men. One of them committed suicide when she deserted him. I think she was as cold as a fish, completely without passion. Sex was simply a way to get things. She had a brilliant personality but it was pure facade. In my opinion, when she was made, they simply forgot to put a heart in her."

*

When Robin was twelve he received an invitation from his mother's brothers to come to Paraguay for a holiday. The lonely adolescent leapt at it. Overnight he acquired three flamboyant uncles who lived dangerously on the wilder frontiers of life.

Sandy, nicknamed Bear, was the eldest, strong, thickset and broad with light-brown hair. He always had a humorous glint in his eyes.

Pat was soon viewed by Robin with mixed feelings: "He was a hard man. I used to think of him as the Bengal Lancer, because he was elegant, tall and slim, with a blonde pencil-thin moustache and the coldest blue eyes you've seen in your life. All he needed was a red jacket and a white salakoff and he could have been a cavalry man in the Charge of the Light Brigade."

But the youngest uncle, David Laurence, always called Big Wood, became his hero:

> He was huge. I reckon he was 190 centimetres in height and he weighed about 100 kilos, solid rock! Later I created a comic book character, a detective based on him, with white hair and a scar across his cheek caused by a spider bite. Big Wood was an adventurer. He used to work for the Americans, the United States Operation Mission, one of those vague branches of American influence officially in occupation to help Latin America. But their function was vague. Very vague. I went with him to parties where all these American marines were getting drunk like hell. They looked as tough as nails, as if they'd shoot their own mothers if their coffee wasn't hot enough. I didn't see them as kind little characters come to help poor deprived Latin Americans. Possibly they had something to do with the CIA, I don't know, maybe I have my writer's fantasy. But they didn't look terribly interested in the business of protecting the population. They looked more capable of exterminating it. And Big Wood was with them.

Big and Sandy periodically went to the Chaco to fell the prized *quebracho* trees. They took their nephew with them to that wilderness west of the Paraguay River where Sandy had an *obraje*, a timber compound. Robin decided it was a mystic place for his uncles, "where they could go with rifles and pistols, ammunition and food and live wild for two or three months, playing Boy Scouts". He didn't view their plans as very practical. Sandy had thousands of the hardwood logs stored there. "So many," said Robin, grinning, "that sometimes you couldn't see the Wood for the trees. The only problem was, it had to rain so there'd be enough water for them to dump the logs in the river and float them downstream. Sandy waited something like twelve years for rain. And the rain never came. Another insane project of the Wood men, those dreamers! They never went in for little things, but always for incredible enterprises, immense projects that never worked."

Sandy, "a husky, brown-haired Paraguayan ... with a broad Australian accent", was hired soon afterwards by David Attenborough, the television naturalist, who had come to Paraguay in search of a giant armadillo. "His linguistic skills, his knowledge of the forest and his placid temperament made him an ideal guide for us."

But working with his uncles in the Chaco, Robin sometimes found Sandy's placid temperament wearing. "If I did something wrong, Sandy would give me a long, earnest lecture and I'd be bored stiff. I'd be dying to get away. Whereas Big Wood would just whack me with a belt. It was painful but quick. I preferred that. With Big you knew where you were. He always said, 'You can do whatever you want, but if you do something stupid, you'll get it in the neck.' Fine. That was better."

Back in Asunción, Robin had a fight with a boy his own age, decisively beating him up. The incident was reported and two policemen arrived to take him to the police station. "Big Wood towered in front of these little men and told them to get lost. And, you know, they went. Next day I caught the kid and beat him up again."

Big Wood had become Robin's father figure. "He was my *macho* man. From him I learned all those typical male things, like 'If someone punches you, kick him in the balls. Be brave, be tough.' I admired him enormously because he was everything I wasn't. He was tall, he was blonde with blue eyes. He was tough and humorous and he had a passion for life. He didn't just live life, he devoured it. He had this incredible laughter which roared up from his stomach and you had to laugh with him. He was extreme. He couldn't do anything in moderation."

Big Wood lived with Sandy and his Paraguayan wife, Clara Cuquejo. "I think it was more or less a question of habit. They always lived together because the Wood boys always went everywhere together." Pat rented a house nearby and every afternoon the three brothers met for an *aperitivo*, mostly with little to say to each other. "Clara never understood that," said Robin. "The three fellows would sit on the porch, each with a book and his drink, reading for two or three hours without a word. Then Pat would stomp out, saying in his booming voice, 'Well boys, see you tomorrow.' He would go home to his terrified wife, and the other two would come in for the meal Clara had prepared."

Every Christmas, Big Wood and Pat would have a tremendous fight, according to Robin just for the ritual of it. "Big Wood would turn up in one of his white suits and horrible ties (he had some ties that would make you collapse — I remember a handpainted silk one with a palm tree and a Hawaiian dancer), and of course Pat would say, 'You look like a poof!' and it would be on. We knew Christmas had arrived. I saw one fight that was splendid, they really bashed each other black and blue. They were wild boys. They didn't have much room in their lives for women. They liked drinking with the boys and a tough, rough life. I think they were rather Australian in that way. They saw themselves as Australians. They had a poor opinion of the English."

*

Robin's sojourn with his uncles ended when his grandmother arrived to accompany him to Buenos Aires. Peggy wanted him back. She had married an Italian restaurateur called Roberto who encouraged a family life.

But Roberto got off to a bad start with his stepson by embracing him when they met. "I was shocked," said Robin. "I thought, 'Oh shit, what's this? We Woods don't kiss each other!' When I'd left my uncles in Paraguay, I'd called, 'Well, I'm going', and they'd looked up from what they were reading and said, 'All right, goodbye' and nothing else. They weren't demonstrative. From time to time, if I'd done things he approved of, Big Wood might pat me on the shoulder and say 'Well done', but that was it."

The gentle Italian seemed deeply suspect: he kept fit with gymnastics, jogged on the beach, he could paint and sing, enjoyed cooking, and readily expressed his emotions. "I thought obviously he must be a poof because no real man would do those things. At that stage I hated him. I wasn't prepared for affection."

Roberto had two sons from a previous marriage, one the same age as Robin and the other two years older. "One month later I'd beaten them up so often they were horribly afraid of me. They stayed out of my way."

The uneasy menage continued for eighteen months, then Roberto went bankrupt and his chain of restaurants passed to the receivers. Peggy deserted him. Neither mother nor son showed enthusiasm for setting up house together. The fourteen-year-old made an abrupt decision and took a bus back to Paraguay.

*

If young Robin had found the Chaco tough going, Big Wood and Sandy had a real challenge waiting for him. Their new enterprise was felling timber in the Alto Paraná, the wild frontier area of cliffs and cataracts bordering Brazil.

They had bought a seven-tonne Scania truck, "a ruin of a vehicle, another of their disasters", and sent Robin to live in the forest as overseer of the *peones*, the timber workers, some of them Mbyá-Guaraní. He was based for two or three months at a time at a camp called Capitán Meza. "It was a hell of a life, because the jungle there is a wild place. It was hot, humid and hateful, it rained a lot and when it did the truck couldn't move."

His job was to go with the truck after the trees were felled, supervising the transport of logs to the roaring Paraná River where they were floated down in rafts. "I was supposed to be some kind of *comisario*, which was a joke because I knew nothing about the whole thing. The *peones* were very fed up with me because I was ambitious. We used to start work about 3 o'clock in the morning, but at 12 o'clock they were used to coming back, because after that the heat of the sun was impossible. But I wanted to keep going, so I was a real nuisance, an idiot from the city who thought he could change things. The *peones* would get edgy and they were wild people, with plenty of knives, machetes and guns. They weren't jokers. Eventually I learned, and then I got on well with them."

Reflecting today on his time there, Robin Wood still considered the Alto Paraná the toughest area he had ever seen:

> It was a kingdom of its own. A human life wasn't worth anything. It's the border, so you can kill someone, go across the border, wait a year there and nobody cares. Because it was the border, there were lots of smuggling rackets. Big Wood was involved with smuggling. I also did a bit myself when we needed extra money. There were heavy taxes on coffee in Paraguay, so we'd go across to Brazil, load bags with coffee, cross the border again at night and sell them on the other side. We were just small time. Of course the whole government was involved with smuggling. Everything was contraband. Cars were stolen in Brazil, brought into Paraguay, and given a new number plate. They were known in Asunción as "the Brazilian cars". Everybody knew. It was a corrupt society, *baksheesh* everywhere. All those things you're supposed to learn about what you should and shouldn't do! I was taught that if you could get away with it, that was all right: stealing, smuggling, bashing, even murder. The only point was not to get caught. If you were caught, you were stupid and hadn't bribed the right person. There was no morality in it.

In the forest Robin and his men worked beside others employed by the timber *obrajes*, work compounds run on the same brutal lines as the *yerba* camps known to León Cadogan. These places were owned by rich, influential men who controlled empires similar to the rubber and coffee plantations of Brazil, the mines of Bolivia and Peru. "They were overlords, people from the capital who bought land for peanuts from the government, including whole villages with all their people. The misery of the people in those little villages was colossal. They were used to being oppressed, they'd never known anything but oppression."

For the author Augusto Roa Bastos, the *obrajes*, with their contempt for the value of human life, represented Paraguay in microcosm:

> Takurú-Pukú, then, was the citadel of a country which was a law to itself. It was cut off from the rest of the world by the extensive woods of the Alto Paraná, by the belt of marshland which is flooded at high-tide and which is infested by snakes and wild animals, by the high, craggy cliffs, by the broad, turbulent river and by the sudden downpours which, in a matter of minutes, fill the woods and marshes with torrents red as blood. But most of all it was cut off by the autocratic rule of the managers, who were answerable to nobody …

The compound workers were known as *mensús*, monthlies, "because they were supposed to be paid every month, but of course they weren't". Once they signed up, often at gunpoint, they had to buy everything from the company store. The prices were inflated, so instead of actually making money, the workers were always more and more in debt, effectively slaves. The owners hired armed guardians, *capungas*, to maintain a harsh discipline. The *comisario*, the local police chief, was usually on the payroll as well. "He backed up the bosses of the *obrajes*. If you argued with him, you got shot. Even if the bullet went in the back of your head, the story later was always one of self defence."

In Robin's own observation, workers who attempted resistance were summarily disposed of:

> They weren't missed. These things were common. There were always terrible stories about how any rebellion was dealt with in the *obrajes*. If a *peón* made too much money, one night he would just disappear. On one *obraje* there was a trapdoor in the office. I saw it myself and know the story is true. They would bring in a fellow who, for some reason or other, was making a lot of money. Instead of paying him, he would get a bullet. They'd open this trapdoor and the body would go straight into the river. Sometimes you'd see a corpse floating downstream.

There were brothels in the camps, employing prostitutes who came from the ramshackle border town of Puerto Stroessner. "But if women went to the *obrajes* with their men, they had to become whores, they had no choice. First the *capungas* would go through them, then there'd be maybe one hundred and fifty men. There was no getting out of there."

For most of the time during 1958 Robin was alone in the forest with the *peones*, Big Wood calling in between smuggling and his other activities. On rare occasions Robin was able to get away for a few days to stay with his great-uncle Donald and aunt Deolidia in Encarnación. "I hardly ever washed in the forest and I stank! Aunty Dolly would take her nose in two fingers and point me to the bath. She would say, 'Go and stay there for a couple of hours. When you come out, go back there and stay a couple of hours more.' "

The moral stench of where he had been didn't reach him until much later. "I'd become very callous. To see dead people was a normal thing. I never thought in terms of, 'What a pity he died'. I never thought it was anything special until later on, when I realised that I'd been witness to a lot of horror when I was a kid."

*

I asked Robin if his uncles had been involved in any killings. He shrugged: "We're talking about a very different era, but people look back with today's eyes. Sure, Big Wood once shot a fellow in the street. Today it would be murder, but he just shot him and there was no trouble."

My question was hanging there. And Robin himself?

"Would I tell you?" Plagued by some memory, he gazed at the flowering shrubs in the ordered suburban garden. "When people think of South America, they think of the cities and the tourist sights. But the jungle is another world, like being on the moon."

*

One incident during his time in the Alto Paraná pierced Robin's emotional guard. A man from a leper colony in the forest severed his arm with a machete. "His wife pushed him through the jungle in a wheelbarrow. When she got him to the hospital, the fellow was already dying. They took him inside and she simply sat at the entrance, waiting. She was there until at last someone told her that he had died. She stood up, tied four knots in the cloth where she kept some food, and left without a word."

Robin stayed on with the timber workers until one day the old Scania wouldn't go anymore. "There was no point in trying to repair it and no money anyway. So that was the end of *that* Wood project."

He went back to Asunción, to the house Sandy and Clara shared with Big Wood, and to more horror close to home.

Within a few weeks of his return, Pat, the cold-eyed Bengal Lancer with the pencil-thin moustache, died from cancer. His death at thirty-eight was appallingly sudden. It was not how they had expected Pat would go. "We'd all been a bit afraid of Pat," said Robin, "of his streak of violence and his fearlessness. In Paraguay under Stroessner it was always a worry that he wouldn't keep his voice down. Once a Paraguayan woman, coming out of an office, was waylaid and brutally arrested. Pat attacked those fellows, who were secret police, the very toughest of the government. He knew who they were but he still went for them, while everybody else kept walking and tried not to look. Those thugs were so astonished that he got away with it."

A month after Pat's death, Sandy was negotiating some deals in that particularly rampageous town, Puerto Stroessner on the Brazilian border. In Asunción Clara made preparations for the festive season. On Christmas Day, Big Wood and Robin were waiting with her, all of them puzzled that Sandy hadn't shown up, when someone arrived with a message: "Sandy had been shot. Eight bullets had gone through him but he was still hanging on. Puerto Stroessner was a real frontier town then, some huts, cabins and cantinas. Sandy had been arguing with a *pistolero*, a small-time bandit or ruffian, and he had given him a beating. In return Sandy copped eight bullets."

Big Wood jumped into a taxi and ordered the driver to go like the devil to Puerto Stroessner. He found his brother clinging to life and took him back in the taxi to Asunción, a round trip of 750 kilometres on dirt roads.

In the English Hospital Sandy seemed to be recovering but, after a few days, died of a massive heart attack.

Big Wood had always lived with Sandy and his wife. He was effectively the man of the house, taking care of the children during the long periods when Sandy had been away in the Chaco, waiting for the rains to float his logs to fortune. Although some of the Wood cousins thought there had been a secret passion between Clara and Big for years, Robin denied this with vehemence. "There'd never been any indiscretion between them at all. But they were used to each other and after Sandy's death they both felt lost."

Big, always awkward with emotions, came to his nephew one day and announced that he had decided to marry Clara. "That night I went with him when he went to propose to her. She agreed. She was shattered and desperate and sad, but they put together what was left of the wreck. Some years later she had another baby with Big. But he was always Papá for all of her children."

*

Robin returned to Buenos Aires. A bleak and dull period in his life began. He found work in a factory making Sellotape. "I had no qualifications and it was the only job I could find." He had to get up at 4 in the morning to be at the factory, on the outer limits of the city, by 6 o'clock, then worked a twelve-hour day. The huge rolls of Sellotape turned on a machine and his job was to cut them into sections. "Liquid kerosene had to be poured at the same time to make the cutting easier and it would fly all over me. My face was always burnt, my eyes were red and my hands were stained different colours. I did it for five years and that was the worst time in my life."

He lived in the inner-city *barrio* of San Telmo, these days newly gentrified with restaurants and antique shops, but then a slum district of migrant workers and poor students. He shared a room in a pensión with four other men. One tiny cooking plate was fought over by all. The pittance he earned never quite lasted a week and Sunday was the hungry day — unless he got lucky.

He was a bag of bones, he told me, grinning, but for some reason he had luck with girls. "Of course the girls I had were not precisely what I wanted, but beggars can't be choosers. Every time I met a girl who had a place of her own and could cook, that was a definite plus. I'd get a meal. Food was the main thing that preoccupied me. My mother discovered I'd been laying several of her girlfriends because of their dinners. She didn't appreciate that."

He and Peggy would occasionally dine together or see a film, but mostly he avoided her. He was too proud to ask to borrow money and she never offered. "I was handling my life badly but she was handling her's like hell. By then her beauty was fading, all the men had gone and her drinking was out of control. She was irrational and hostile, hitting the bottle and living like a recluse. After work she would lock herself in her room and read and drink until the next day. That's the period when the real deterioration started."

Peggy no longer had contact with her ex-husband Roberto, and Robin was surprised and wary when the suave Italian sought him out. At first the only advantage he recognised was the undeniably splendid source of free meals. Roberto had recovered from his bankruptcy and was now a millionaire with a chain of restaurants, pizza parlours, and one of the plushest nightclubs in Buenos Aires.

Roberto still kept fit at the gym and encouraged Robin when he took up karate lessons. "I'd visit him at his restaurant, an elegant place full of society people, and he would ask me to demonstrate the new kicks I'd learned. Then Roberto would try them too, punching, kicking out and bellowing. The *maitre de* and all the diners would stare in horror, but Roberto didn't care what they thought."

It seemed an enigma to Robin that his former stepfather, a physically ugly man, was so successful with women. He realised it was something to do with his charm and his gentleness and that, unlike his Wood uncles, Roberto actually liked women and found their company fascinating. "When Big Wood wanted a woman, he *used* one. When he wanted to have fun, he called for the boys, the whisky, the guitars."

Roberto suggested to Robin that there was something lacking in his own amatory approaches. "He thought I was too brutal. He told me his basic philosophy with women, what he called his Christmas philosophy: 'When a woman goes to bed with you,' he said, 'she's doing something that you want. And when you receive a present, you have to be well educated and thank her. You're not *taking* her, she's going to bed with you as a gift.' "

The debonair Italian advised Robin how to dress, mildly but firmly corrected his table manners, told him about wines, and regaled him with stories of the life to be lived in Europe. Big Wood had been a father figure. Now Roberto had become one also.

Those men completely filled that gap. One was my hero, and the other one became my guide. From one I learned how to survive, and from the other I learned how to live. Big taught me how to fight, how to be crazy, he was proud of all my wild part. "My kid can beat you up," he would say. He was my *macho* man, Crocodile Wood. I was his son, his creation. He made that wild aggressive boy I was, a "wild colonial boy". If I was sinister and full of hatred, that part probably came from my mother.

But Roberto was suave and cultivated and he taught me all the other things: "Fight only if you've got a reason. Don't fight for fun — it's never fun." Roberto showed me how to enjoy life and he gave me Europe. People are sometimes sympathetic and say to me, "You didn't have a father." But I had two, and I chose them. They fulfilled completely different needs for me. Most people have fathers that they're born with and stuck with. These men were fathers that I chose. They chose me too and they loved me.

Robin was reluctant to accept too much generosity from Roberto. The grim Sellotape factory remained the dominant reality in his life and, without education or qualifications, it seemed there would never be any escape.

He heard with envy that two of his cousins in Paraguay had been given passages to Australia because of the help of a famous author who had been to visit. He tried the Australian and Canadian embassies himself. "But I had no luck. I'd only had six years of school and I didn't speak English." He decided to volunteer for Vietnam, but the Americans told him he would have to go to the United States to enlist. "I told the idiots that if I had the money for the fare, I wouldn't be joining the army." He offered to work for five years on a kibbutz in exchange for a ticket to Israel, "but I was refused, told they only helped Jews. Then I tried to get jobs on ships, but they didn't accept me because I was too skinny and frail".

Robin was stuck in Buenos Aires, desperate, determined to escape.

*

My life is cut into three parts. The first, in Paraguay and Buenos Aires, was just incredible confusion. Then the time in the factory, the killing of my youth, that was hell. And by sheer accident the lucky third part began when I started writing and used that as a way to freedom …

Apart from his sexual exploits, Robin found pleasure in reading and sketching. He didn't consider he had any great artistic talent, but enrolled for night classes at an art academy. He respected one of the teachers, Don Eduardo, an elderly artist "who was such a genius that I hated him. He could do it with such ease while I had to work like an animal". After the class they often had coffee together and discovered common interests in archaeology and history. Don Eduardo lent him a book on Sumerian mythology.

One evening the old man mentioned his freelance work as a comic-book illustrator. He was dismayed by the latest batch of scripts he had received, all of them weak and unimaginative. "He showed them to me and suggested I have a go at writing one myself, perhaps one on Sumerian myth. I started that very night and thought it was great fun. I tapped out three stories and gave them to him at the next class. Then I forgot about them."

A few months afterwards, Robin Wood arrived late one rainy morning at the Sellotape factory. The company had a rigid policy: all latecomers were to be turned away. "That meant you wouldn't have money that day and you wouldn't eat, it was as simple as that." He pleaded with the official at the gate: "Look, I've come two hours by bus and walked seventeen blocks. I'm only fifteen minutes late …" He was told a rule was a rule.

Without the money for the return fare, he began the long trudge back to the city. As the rain became heavier he took shelter under the awning of a newspaper kiosk, browsing through the magazines. He picked up a comic-book, recognising Don Eduardo's artwork. On the first page, his own name jumped out. Heart beating, he leafed through to the last page, which previewed the next issue. There he was again: "Story by Robin Wood".

"That's me!" he told the kiosk man, who seemed faintly impressed.

Robin barely remembered the long walk through the storm. He seemed to be flying. In downtown Buenos Aires he dripped across a gleaming foyer and took the lift to the publisher's offices. "The secretary (who later had an affair with me) said she thought I was a tramp come to beg for food or old clothes. But somehow I got to see her boss. He said they liked my work and would buy everything I offered. He paid me on the spot for the three scripts I had with them. For each one I got the equivalent of my monthly salary at the factory. I went out to a good restaurant and had a lovely dinner. Then I bought fifty books at one go, because that's what I felt most, the lack of books."

In the next week he wrote fifteen scripts. It seemed ludicrous to be paid for having such fun. "Suddenly I was Cinderella! I rented a smart flat, I acquired a beautiful girlfriend. The only problem, I discovered, was that now I had money, the girls started to talk about marriage and babies. Suddenly it wasn't about screwing anymore, but about, 'Now Robin, we must talk about our future'. Probably because of my mother, the very thought of a relationship, let alone marriage, gave me the shivers."

*

Peggy was indifferent to his success. But Roberto couldn't stop bragging. "Of all the people who were pleased, he was the proudest. He pestered everybody, showing people in the restaurant copies of the magazines, saying 'Look here, my son. This is the work of my son!' He'd always had to find jobs for his kids, but I'd made my own way. Like him."

The only thing that continued to disappoint the Italian was Robin's

Robin Wood's interest in myth spawned a range of popular comic books.

manner of dressing. "I never learned to dress well. And he was such a dandy. I'd go to visit him at the restaurant and he'd say, 'You're the son I always dreamed of having, but you dress like *shit*.' And I'd say, 'What do you want, perfection?' "

Roberto had instilled fantasies of travel in Europe, of driving through Burgundy, sipping coffee on the Via Veneto, sunning on the Lido, sailing the Mediterranean. Suddenly all these were possible. A year after what he called his "breakthrough", Robin made a deal with the publishers. He would go abroad for a time but would send them his storylines by post. As it turned out, the arrangement continued for twenty-five years.

He went first to Italy, then for ten years he wandered, always limiting his possessions to a portable typewriter, a record player and one suitcase. He lived in Switzerland: "I'd met a Swiss girl. I bought a car there which I crashed immediately because I didn't know how to drive. I had a forged licence which I'd bought in Buenos Aires." He moved on to Spain, Morocco and Germany, took the Orient Express to Turkey, then travelled on to Israel. Storylines were typed in hotel rooms and villas and posted to Buenos Aires. Money transfers arrived to continue the lifestyle.

He went to London when he was twenty-eight, and found the experience confronting. "My name created expectations. I couldn't afford not to speak English. People imagined someone called Robin Wood should wear Lincoln Green or look like Peter O'Toole, blonde with blue eyes. With a Paraguayan passport, I was always being stopped. They'd look at me, how dark I am, and say, 'Robin Wood? And you can't speak English? For sure you're Robin Wood! Now open your suitcases!' It was too weird. At least now I can defend myself in English."

A telegram was waiting for him in London. It had arrived some time before, while he was travelling in Israel. It was from the Paraguayan government minister who had been kind to him as a boy. He was dying of cancer and asked Robin to return to Paraguay: he urgently needed to see him. Robin called Asunción: the man had died. Then a letter came from the widow. "She said she had no idea what he wanted to see me about … Perhaps he was my father. But I'll never know now."

He was soon overwhelmed by a greater loss: Roberto, a father of his choice, had died. "I was completely shattered. I cried my eyes out. Even today, when I have a success, I think, 'What a pity. Roberto would have enjoyed that so much'. Today there's still a gap there, a hole I've never managed to fill."

Robin returned briefly to South America. He was shocked at Peggy's decline. "She was fifty-five but like an old woman, completely decrepit. She would sit looking at the wall for hours, like a zombie. The real Peggy had gone; it was a question of waiting. At the end I had to take care of her because quite simply she couldn't do anything for herself. One night she died in her sleep."

He set up a fund to maintain his grandparents for the rest of their lives and returned to Europe. He bought a house in the seaside resort of Marbella in Spain. He had met a Danish girl he liked, Mette Jensen. He felt perilously close to having a relationship.

He fled instead, taking the Trans-Siberian and Trans-China trains to Hong Kong, then on an impulse travelled on to Australia to visit his Paraguayan cousins. They had made new lives in Sydney and the Riverina district, and seemed pleased with their lot. But the land of his forebears made no great impact on him; his thoughts were elsewhere. "After four weeks I felt I just had to return to Europe to see Mette Jensen. And one day Mette told me that she thought it would be a great idea to have a child. I thought she was joking. When I realised she wasn't, it was too late ..."

*

Mette, whom Robin clearly adored, waved as she left the house to collect their two sons from school. They'd be late today, she said, because of a farewell party for them. Australians were such friendly people, in many ways she was sorry to leave ... The removal men had gone, most of the furniture in the house was encased in cardboard packing.

But the fax was still quietly at work. Images fell and unfurled on the floor from half a world away. Bestiaries of mythical creatures, dragons, demons and serpents. Medieval knights. Bandits with wicked moustachios, bristling with pistols and bandoliers of ammunition. Voluptuous, near-naked women in fetching distress. All had been penned with the meticulous craftsmanship of a Dürer engraving by an old man in Argentina. Robin Wood now owned the production company. He would check these pictures against his master text and make adjustments. Then in Buenos Aires, text and image would be married and a new comic book printed and distributed to his audience of many millions throughout Spain and Latin America.

I looked through some back numbers. One of the most striking characters was a detective called Munro, a *macho* man who knocked down villains in swathes, the bandits, brigands and smugglers who lurked in the

Munro, a Robin Wood creation. A flaxen-haired giant whose comic book adventures had an enormous following in Latin America.

luxuriant tropical jungle that seemed his natural habitat. He was a white-haired giant with a spider-bite scar across one cheek.

*

During the most excessive years of the Stroessner regime, the period of the construction of the huge Itaipú dam, Big Wood came to visit Mette and Robin, at the time in Spain. He seemed very pleased with himself. Some people in Paraguay, those with the right contacts, he crowed, were making fantastically easy money. And he was one of them.

"Big had another of his crazy projects. He came with a letter of credit for US$78 million dollars from the Stroessner family. They wanted to sell lumber, sugar, coffee and this and that. The whole thing seemed to me incredibly odd. But he stayed at Marbella with us and got in contact with people, made trips to London and Madrid. Of course everything he could negotiate could be bought cheaper elsewhere, so the whole thing never worked."

Robin remarked that the deal reeked of corruption. " 'Of course!' Big replied. But he said he didn't give a shit. He was having a great holiday, they paid all his expenses, he could visit everybody, he loved it all. Why should he worry? 'No money,' he said, 'can be conned quicker than from an ambitious greedy fellow. I didn't even have to con them. They came looking for me!' "

The handsome giant from the vagabond days on the Alto Paraná had become bloated. Big Wood drank six bottles of wine every day. "In the morning he would sit on the terrace with a book and a bottle of wine and start pouring, very nicely and steadily. He would have more wine with lunch and dinner and a couple of cognacs. I thought, 'I'm seeing the same story repeated. This is my mother all over again. This won't last long'."

Big died a few years later, in his early sixties. "He pushed his body too far and one day he just had a heart attack. We've got a saying in the Wood family, that there's one generation 'Yes', and one generation 'No'. My Grandfather Alex and Uncle Bill Wood were a Yes Generation. Those old boys all seemed to have ordered lives and died in their eighties of boredom. But the children, my mother and her brothers, they were a Drama Generation. They were incredibly handsome, intelligent, charming and wild — but they were tragic."

*

I was talking to Robin Wood in his rented house in a leafy northern suburb of Sydney. I was about to depart on my third visit to Paraguay. He and Mette and the boys were returning to Europe after a year in Australia. It had been a nostalgic attempt to settle permanently and reclaim his family's heritage. "I felt I had to do it. Those old boys in Paraguay had talked to me about Australia so often that I felt I must be Australian."

Some time earlier I'd been invited to an *asado* at the house. Robin had entertained his local and visiting Paraguayan relatives, flipping beef ribs and *chorizo* sausages on a grill beside the swimming pool. The guests of honour were his banker cousin Rodrigo and wife Carmen from Asunción, their first time in Australia. They had toured Sydney and admired the harbour.

Rodrigo had leaned back in his chair and raised his glass of chardonnay to his cousin. "Our grandparents left Australia looking for paradise on earth. I've always wondered what they hoped to find. And now I know. They were looking for this. *Salud!*"

Robin could not agree. He had experienced no strong sense of home-coming. He had found Sydney suburbia dull, and the attachment to British traditions an unpleasant surprise.

> I remember once someone gave my grandfather Alex a calendar of the coronation of Queen Elizabeth. He asked, "Why would I want that crap?"
>
> "Because you're English, Mr Wood."
>
> He told them, "I'm not English. I'm Paraguayan and Australian. We don't want that stuff in our house."
>
> If those old boys were here today, they'd be asking for a republic. The Wood family were part of this country's history, they had the rebellious spirit that's such an important part of the Australian character. I know they marched off and left the country, but their fight wasn't with Australia — it was with the oppressive regime of the time. And I think what they wanted is still a dream today — a free Australia.

Europe was Robin's true home. When he went to Buenos Aires, he said, he always felt a certain discomfort, "iciness in my stomach". But he would always keep going back to Paraguay. "Now I like the country because I go there on my own terms, where before I was trapped." He would always go back, he said, because of his relatives:

> I have a passion about the Wood family. For me, we're like the Chosen People. Okay, one might wish God had chosen a bit better, but they're my people. I love my life, I love being European, but that sense of family makes me feel warm, like a cat cuddling in on a cold night.

You never feel alone when you have the memory of your people. I have all the stories from my uncles and great-uncles and grandfather. When people talk about the labour struggle in Australia, we were there. When they talk about Gallipoli, we were there. When they talk about the Somme, we were in that too, and in the Chaco War. They ended up in Paraguay because they were a romantic bunch of lunatics. Their downfall was an excess of charm and a lack of reality. But from the failure and the waste they survived. We've always survived, because we have this sense inside us that we're a clan on our own.

24
Paradise Mislaid?

I had begun, not only to dimly understand, but to enthusiastically
fall in love with the brutal and tender land of Paraguay ...
                    Ariel Dorfman, Foreword to *Son of Man*

At the last, your paradise is lost,
at the last, your garrison accursed,
at the last, your phantoms tranfixed by air
kissing the tread of the seal in the sand.
        Pablo Neruda, "The Magellan Heart"

The Old Money mansions of Asunción — Italianate with deep
porticoes and lichened steps, hidden in foliage — now often served
as embassies, clubs and government offices. But the New Money
was boisterous and assertive. In the post-Stroessner era, The Houses that
Corruption Built had become a popular tour. The unleashing of fantasies,
egos and dubious bank balances had produced a jumble of styles: designer
Malibu, tiled Moorish, Santa Fe with cactuses, Tudor with mullioned
windows, Swiss chalet with fretted barge-boards. Visitors could gawp at
the white columns of a Disneyland Tara, the slate towers of a French
chateau, the layered roofs of a Taiwanese millionaire's pagoda. Many
homes sprouted satellite dishes and boasted sleek European cars in drive-
ways. Window grilles, shutters and ornamental gates sequestered the
wealth inside, but allowed glimpses of blue swimming pools, tennis courts
and gardens of tropical exuberance, palms and jacarandas, bougainvillea
and pointsettia drooping over high walls, shading the sentries patrolling
the gates. The mansion that Chile's General Pinochet built was still empty.
Change of retirement plans. Alfredo Stroessner's was hidden by trees in
its vast private parkland opposite the United States embassy. He was in
Brazil. The sprawling brick bungalow of his former mistress was occupied,
but not by her. She was in Switzerland, keeping an eye on the bank
accounts.

We took in part of the tour on the last day of October 1993. It was early in the morning and we had other business. Six of us were crammed into a Toyota Landcruiser for a journey to Colonia Cosme. Some of us had hangovers from the previous night's celebration of the arrival, 100 years earlier, of the Australian colonists, all pledged to teetotalism.

The driver, Randolf Wood, a handsome dark-haired architect, was a descendant but spoke no English. His relatives all called him Randy. Aged forty, he was the eldest child of Pat, one of the three dangerous sons of Alex Wood, the "No Generation". Randolf had only been twelve when his father died of cancer. His mother, Rosa Morínigo de Wood, had raised the three children, who all now had university degrees and professional careers. They were a "Yes Generation".

At the party the previous night Randy had offered to take us to Cosme. Otherwise, he said, there was no chance of getting there. The road was so poorly maintained, the wooden bridges so treacherous, that the last 20 kilometres were now impassable except by four-wheel-drive. The village was almost as remote now as it had been one hundred years ago.

Sitting in front with him were his cousin Patricio Wood and his wife Mercedes, who had come for the centenary on the same flight as me from Australia. Patrico had been born at Cosme, the first son of Wallace and María. He had not been selected by his Aunt Rose for adoption and a new identity in South Africa, and so had spent much of his life at Cosme. In his forties he had migrated to Australia and become a successful builder on Queensland's Sunshine Coast. Returning to Paraguay for his Uncle Norman's ninetieth birthday fiesta, he had met and married Mercedes, the glamorous daughter of a colonel. She had dressed for our expedition in stylish sportswear and gold sandals.

Patricio was excited to be returning to the place of his birth. He had plans to build a modern bungalow and retire there. Mercedes confided darkly: "Over my dead body."

But Sylvia McLeod de Wood, sitting beside me in the back seat, understood her brother-in-law's enthusiasm. Cosme had been her life. Her grandfather, Rod McLeod, a labourer from Bourke in far western New South Wales, had come with William Lane and the first batch on the *Royal Tar*. The family had remained there and Sylvia had known the Wood family all her days. When she went to high school in Asunción, she boarded with Bill Wood's family in the house on Chóferes del Chaco. So did Patricio's younger brother, Francisco, and the two became sweethearts. After Gavin Souter's visit in 1965, Francisco was invited to go to Australia with his brother Peter. He stayed in Paraguay instead to marry Sylvia, who had become the Cosme schoolteacher. It seemed inevitable and right. They had three daughters and two sons and, for many years, a successful marriage.

But recently Francisco had taken up with a twenty-year-old girl at Cosme, a beautiful part-Indian descendant of the Titilah family. Sylvia was heartbroken. A handsome woman in her late forties with a coppery complexion and clear blue eyes, she was subdued during the trip. She was preparing for the ordeal ahead, confronting her estranged husband, collecting her possessions, and staking her claim to the family home.

There was something sad and funereal about this journey to a ghost village. The other outsider travelling, like me, to document its demise, was Stuart Heather, a roving foreign correspondent based in Buenos Aires for the Australian Broadcasting Corporation. He was preparing a television story on the centenary of the Australians' arrival.

On the outskirts of Asunción, Randy pointed out a derelict mansion. It was an instant ruin, a crumbling bargain-basement version of Washington's White House, surrounded by a few acres of rank, overgrown grass. Broken windows gaped. A caretaker sat, like Whistler's mother, on a straight-backed chair on an upstairs veranda. It was the unfinished home of Freddie Stroessner, the deposed president's younger son, a cocaine addict who had died the previous year of a heart attack. Lawyers were still sorting out the estate. Meanwhile the house rotted and the caretaker seemed an immovable fixture.

The Stroessner legacy was taking a lot of sorting out. Years after the coup, it had left its shadow on most Paraguayans, including the Australian descendants.

*

Generalissimo Alfredo Stroessner — Legion d'Honneur, Knight of the Order of St Michael and St George, Collar of the Order of the Liberator, Order of the Condor of the Andes, Order of the Chaco, Grand Cross with Diamonds of the Order of the Sun and Medallist of the Inter-American Junta of Defence — was spending his enforced retirement brooding on the ingrates he had enriched.

Stroessner came to power in 1954, using his position as commander-in-chief of the armed forces and his influence within the Colorado Party. From that time he ruled the country by martial law. Colorado red became the only safe political colour. Opponents who knew what was good for them — and at least half a million in just a few years did — fled across the borders. Political prisoners swelled the country's gaols and were subject to the ferocious ministrations of the secret police: the cattle prod, electrodes on the genitals and immersion in a tub of liquid excrement.

Other critics of the regime were dropped from light planes, high over the Chaco. Wire-bound bodies were found floating in the Río Paraguay, food for alligators. According to testimony submitted by Amnesty International to the Paraguayan Supreme Court in 1979, Miguel Angel Soler, Secretary of the Paraguayan Communist Party, was methodically taken apart, dismembered alive by chainsaw. It was said that Pastor Coronel, head of the secret police, relayed the whole procedure over the telephone to President Stroessner. To accompany Soler's screams, the torturers played at full volume the beautiful Guaraní music of Jose Asunción Flores. The composer was another enemy, a communist who had fled to the USSR, his music banned in Paraguay, except when needed for a specific purpose.

By the time Stroessner was ousted in February 1989 he had held absolute power for over thirty-four years, making him the longest-surviving dictator in the Western Hemisphere. Yet his regime, supported by the United States until the final few years, engendered little international criticism.

Stroessner kept a low profile. Unlike other Latin American *caudillos*, he didn't go in for mass rallies, he didn't feel the need to confirm the devotion of his people by waving from a balcony over the city square. He didn't make many lavish trips abroad or adopt a flamboyant lifestyle at home, he didn't drive fast cars or consort publicly with glamorous women. His wife Doña Eligia, a bulky matron, accompanied him to official functions, and though it was well known that he had a mistress, that was such an entrenched Paraguayan tradition it was almost patriotic. His other sexual needs were darker and more secret.

He oppressed, exploited and terrorised his country-people just like Papa Doc Duvalier of Haiti, Rafael Trujillo of the Dominican Republic, or the man he harboured, Anastasio Somoza Debayle of Nicaragua. But, until near the end, Stroessner escaped their bad press.

With his thinning hair, bloated features and paunch, he was mostly described in terms of a harmless small-town burgher. John Gunther, without any irony, thought he looked "like a Bavarian butcher". Graham Greene, who knew Stroessner was not harmless, described him in civilian clothes as "like the amiable well-fed host of a Bavarian *bierstube*". The journalist Alex Shoumatoff repeated the "Bavarian butcher" analogy and concluded that, as dictators went, General Alfredo Stroessner was "about a seven": "He couldn't compare with Pinochet or Galtieri; he didn't eat his enemies, as Bokassa and Idi Amin did."

*

In February 1954 Australia was thrilling to the visit of the young Queen Elizabeth. She brought with her an assortment of floral dresses and open-toed shoes and drove in cavalcade through crowds of cheering schoolchildren and along city streets. Perhaps she glimpsed the huge Union Jack that Mary Gilmore, by then writing for the communist paper *Tribune*, had hung from the balcony of her Kings Cross apartment.

The Australian descendants in Paraguay heard about the royal visit and it seemed an impossibly serene world away. Like other Paraguayans, they had experienced one political upheaval after another since the end of the Chaco War. In 1947 they had suffered a bloody insurrection for five months, during which a third of the country's population fled. When General Stroessner came to power in May 1954 as if he meant to stay, some of them were relieved.

Oscar Birks, great-grandson of George Napier Birks of New Australia, admitted as much: "Stroessner arrived after many years of revolutions and civil wars and people were tired of the instability. In one year we'd had three presidents. There was a president who lasted only one day, thrown out in another *coup d'etat* the next morning. It was impossible to work, to study, to produce or to plan. When Stroessner came and put order in the country with a strong hand, many of us were happy."

The Stronato, the Stroessner era, had begun. The new president consolidated his control of the army and the Colorado Party. He proved a skilful politician in neutralising the factions intriguing against him and built up a network of supporters obligated through his patronage. They got the best government jobs, with opportunities for enrichment, and were anxious to show their gratitude. The cult of *personalismo* developed: the radio stations began each day, after blaring "The Don Alfredo Polka", with a message from El Gran Líder: "The constitutional president of the republic, General Alfredo Stroessner, salutes the Paraguayan people and wishes them a prosperous day." The president's portrait appeared in every government office, his name on streets, public squares, a new international airport and a raffish border town. Even his brewer father scored a place-name, the former village of New Australia, after an unctuous senator declared there was no need "to pay homage to kangaroos".

Two-bit entrepreneurs seized new opportunities. An official in the

Ministry of Culture told me: "A bunch of crooks set up in business selling Stroessner's portrait to shopkeepers. They'd offer one to the owner of a grocery store, for instance. He'd have to buy it, afraid to say no in case they reported him and he was closed down for some trumped-up reason. So it was blackmail, a captive market. Every shop ended up with a portrait."

Since the Conquistadores Paraguay had never known anything but authoritarian rule, so Stroessner had centuries of absolutism to back him up. The country had always been governed by *mbaraté*, the principle of those with the biggest clout. A state of siege, in force when Stroessner first came to power, was renewed every ninety days with barely a break until 1987. This allowed for arrests and confinement without charge and prohibited public meetings and demonstrations. "We are a geographically defenseless country," the president argued, the measure was needed "to protect our democratic institutions against invasion by communist-infil-trated expeditionaries". In his view most dissenters were communists.

Stroessner had the allegiance of the army and brought the Colorado Party behind him with a mandatory ruling that all public servants and military personnel should become Party members and pay annual dues. Munificent revenues made the Party a force in the land with branches in every village. Local branch bosses wielded great influence. Nigel Kennedy at New Australia later became one of them.

Norman Wood told me in 1982: "Nowadays if you want to work anywhere, you have to be a Red. All schoolteachers and public servants have to sign up as Colorados. Even the distillers of *caña*, because that's a government business. English people wouldn't think that was the proper thing to do, but here it's always been that way. The people in power get the work and the money and those who aren't in power look around for something else to do."

At that time Don Norman had been reluctant to talk because "Old Alfie has many ears". But he was glad of the calm after the horrors of the 1947 civil war when Liberal rebels had threatened him and ransacked his house.

After the 1989 coup which astonished him by deposing Old Alfie so effortlessly, he still expressed gratitude for the long years of stability: "Under the Stroessner regime it was very peaceful. I believe people were afraid of him and his police. But in the outback, in the countryside, we caused no problems. We didn't ask for any favours and we were left alone doing our work. Those who caused trouble — political people and others who complained about not getting their whack — were put in gaol or sent out of the country. Or killed. It didn't matter; there was nobody to claim their bodies. They just buried them in gaol, I think." He gave me a dry look. "Well, it wouldn't suit the Australians or English. But that's one way of keeping order in a country."

In Stroessner's modernised Paraguay, observed Isabel Hilton in her *Granta* article, "The General", "there was, above all, peace, but it was a peace punctuated with episodes of savage violence directed against peasant organizations, trade unions, the Church or anyone who showed a capacity for organization outside the Colorado Party ... The Party enjoyed the privileges of the one-party state. And holding it all together, at the centre of the web, the all-pervading image of Stroessner".

A network of paid informers passed information back through the Party machine. The secret police were known as *pyragüés*, a Guaraní word meaning the hairy-footed ones. They were everywhere, silently watching and listening for those who disrupted the orange-blossomed calm: students who spoke out, peasants with a grievance, radical priests, meddling anthropologists, all obviously communists. Hippies, punks and homosexuals also disrupted the *tranquilidad*.

When she first came to Asunción from Spain, wrote the poet Josefina Plá, "I realised that I'd arrived in paradise. The air was warm, the light was tropical, and the shuttered colonial houses suggested sensual, tranquil lives." But walking in the streets at night, surrounded by the smell of jasmine, she was aware of furtive presences: "like any paradise, this one had serpents."

Many others thought only of the abundant fruits. By the inauguration of his third term in 1963, Alfredo Stroessner was genuinely popular with a majority of Paraguayans. They were constantly reminded of the improvements he had brought them. Asunción had drainage and running water, where before residents had purchased water from mule-carts. New sealed roads extended out from the capital, replacing the old mud tracks. Primary education was free and compulsory, though teachers and equipment were in short supply. The president took a twenty-one gun salute, the medals blazing on his uniform, as red-shirted cavalry, blue-uniformed police and tail-coated officials filed past. "Were it not for an occasional headless body floating down the Paraná River," a correspondent remarked, "it might be possible to consider the gaudily uniformed and bemedaled dictator of Paraguay — the last of the breed in South America — a character out of Gilbert and Sullivan."

The world first became aware of Stroessner's dark side when Nazi war criminals on the run found haven with him.

*

On that final journey to Cosme in 1993, speeding along a sealed road that had become familiar, we passed a turn-off for San Bernardino, a watering-place to the north on Lake Ypacaraí. It was once called Nueva Bavaria.

Settled by German colonists in the late nineteenth century, it had become a popular weekend resort for the elite of Asunción. On my previous visit in 1989, I had gone there with Florence Wood de White and Connie Cadogan, daughter of the anthropologist. We had taken the toll road, passing country club estates, tennis courts and time-share villas, the old houses of San Bernardino hidden among flowers and dense greenery, the new condominiums, restaurants and cafes cluttering the lakeshore.

We lunched at the Hotel del Lago, a relic of the German era with its colonnaded verandas, twin towers and crenellated roofline. As we sat on the terrace overlooking the swimming pool and the lake, we were briefly joined by a neat American with a crew-cut. Florence, who had worked at the United States embassy, introduced him as the ambassador, Timothy Towell. We exchanged pleasantries and he remarked wryly that all year he had been kept pretty busy.

According to the journalist Alex Shoumatoff, writing about the last days of Stroessner, this "conservative Yalie ... hardly the human-rights zealot" had been very busy indeed. Towell had taken up the post in Asunción just five months before the coup, and "had lucked into one of the most exciting experiments in democracy in the hemisphere, and he was a major player". The new Paraguay government had been anxious to win back American goodwill and Towell had played a key role in pressing for the release of political prisoners.

He commented, as he moved on to work the terrace, that if I was interested in history I had come to the right place at San Bernardino.

It was to the Hotel del Lago that Bernhard Förster came as a regular guest to escape Elisabeth's criticism and the ruins of his Nueva Germania scheme. In one of its rooms he was found dead from an overdose. He was buried in the little cemetery overlooking the lake. When I found the grave, it looked a bit neglected.

In 1934 the German schoolchildren of San Bernardino had stood around it, singing, while a solemn ceremony was enacted. Members of the local branch of the Nazi Party, the first in South America, who convened regularly at the Hotel del Lago, scattered real German soil, sent with express instructions from Adolf Hitler.

*

Germans had long been comfortable in Paraguay, with an estimated 100,000 today of Teutonic descent, one in every forty Paraguayans. When Stroessner, half-Bavarian and proud of it, came to power they were even more at home.

A friendship with the president was cultivated by Hans Rudel, a wealthy German businessman who settled in Paraguay in the mid-1950s. Rudel, a former hero of the Luftwaffe, had been presented by Hitler with the Knight's Cross with Golden Oak Leaves. It was well known that he had worked for Odessa, the covert organisation which smuggled former officers of the Waffen SS out of Europe.

The number of Nazis who arrived, fitted with new identities, has never been confirmed for obvious reasons. Eduard Roschmann, the Butcher of Riga, Martin Bormann and Klaus Barbie were all rumoured to be in Paraguay at different times. But Josef Mengele, The Angel of Death, perpetrator of grotesque medical experiments at Auschwitz, was a certain guest. He was also, according to some stories, for a time a friend and private physician to Stroessner. In a *New York Times* magazine article, a witness who had sighted Mengele's Paraguayan passport — which was not actually revoked until 1979 — told how the president personally attempted to buy his silence with an honorary officer's commission. There were later other alleged sightings of the Angel of Death — in the Chaco and at the village of Nueva Germania — but he used his own name in the southern town of Colonia Hohenau, birthplace of Stroessner's mother, where he took his meals at the Hotel Tirol. Some time around 1961 Mengele left for Brazil. Eighteen years later he drowned in a swimming accident and was buried near Sao Paulo. Genetic testing confirmed that the remains, exhumed in a blaze of publicity in 1985, were those of Mengele.

A Paraguayan government official, a reliable source, believed that although most shady arrivals paid heavily for their protection, "with Mengele it was ideological as well as the money he brought. Stroessner admired Hitler. He got advice on torture techniques, interrogation, how to conduct ideological warfare against the communists".

*

At the crossroads of Coronel Oviedo, the former village of Ajos, we stopped at a *hamburguesería* before turning south for Villarrica and the rough road beyond it to Cosme. Cars from Brazil and *rápido* buses refuelled at this midway point on the route. A few tacky shops displayed electronic goods, duty-free whisky and cigarettes for the passing trade.

Smuggling became the mainstay of the Stronato economy. "It's the national industry of Paraguay," Graham Greene's retired bank clerk was told in *Travels with My Aunt*. "It brings in nearly as much as the *mate* and a lot more than hiding war criminals with Swiss bank accounts."

Paraguay's position, in the centre of the continent, wedged between Brazil, Argentina and Bolivia, had always been its fortune and its tragedy. In the case of smuggling it was fortune for a few, the practice acknowledged at the highest level: "Stroessner's frequent use of the phrase '*el contrabando es el precio de la paz*' (contraband is the price of peace) signaled official approval of the traffic, which became a normal part of economic life."

The upper levels of the military, police and Colorado Party had access to its vast profits. They were awarded concessions, like medieval fiefdoms, according to their rank and perceived loyalty: Brazilian cars and coffee, Scotch whisky, American cigarettes, fake Rolex watches, perfume, electronic goods. These robbed the government of import and export duties which could have been used for social services, an apparently irrelevant notion, but were sources of enormous undeclared wealth for those prepared to show their gratitude to the dictator.

Residents who could afford the luxury goods, especially expatriates, enjoyed the cheap prices which prevailed even after the 1989 coup, during the administration of President Andrés Rodríguez. Florence's American husband, Max White, told me: "Well now, I can buy a very good bottle of Scotch here for $6, US money. The same bottle in the States would be four times that. And I don't understand this, but these cigarettes that I'm smoking have tobacco imported from Virginia, but they're a fraction of the cost, 35 cents a packet. I'm retired and under these circumstances, this is the best place in the world to live."

But one of Florence's many cousins, Alcides Wood, a lawyer, did not agree: "Everything was smuggled but it was bad for industry and for people who worked honestly. They brought in American cigarettes and they didn't pay tax, so the cigarettes were cheaper than those we produced in our own country. We produced rice but Argentina could grow it cheaper and it was smuggled over the border. We couldn't sell our own products, people lost

Munro, Robin Wood's comic-book hero, fought against bandits and smugglers — but he had few real-life counterparts in Stroessner's Paraguay.

their jobs and factories closed down. Smuggling was only good for the people making a profit from it."

The United States looked the other way at most of Stroessner's excesses. He was a staunch anti-communist, a dependable ally. But around 1970, according to Paul Lewis, author of *Paraguay Under Stroessner*, the smuggling rackets extended to gun running — German, Israeli and Taiwanese arms for South Africa — and hard drugs, creating some frost in a previously warm relationship:

> Evidence that top officers in Paraguay were at the centre of a drug network covering the whole Western Hemisphere began to crop up between 1970 and 1972. As American narcotics agents became more successful at intercepting shipments from Europe, a new route was opened up. Heroin was sent from Marseilles to Asunción, where it was transshipped to Miami and New York. According to one calculation, as much as 582 kilograms of pure heroin with a value of around $145 million arrived in the United States every year by this route. The mastermind of the operation was an expatriate Frenchman named Auguste Ricord, who went under the name of André and used a night club he owned outside of Asunción as his cover.

An American blockbuster film, *The French Connection*, was made about Ricord. To operate on such an extensive scale, Paul Lewis argued, the drug baron needed the connivance and protection of powerful men inside Paraguay. Referring to the published testimony of American narcotics agents, he claimed his chief backer was General Andrés Rodríguez, whose daughter was married to Stroessner's son Freddie. Another backer was General Patricio Colmán, one of the president's oldest and closest friends. "Both Rodríguez and Colmán had made their fortunes from the whiskey and cigarette concessions in the early 1960s, but now they were making bigger profits by turning their extensive ranches near Asunción into airstrips where private planes came and went by night, hauling their cargoes of narcotics ... A third key official was Pastor Coronel, who headed the secret police."

When American narcotics agents requested Ricord's arrest and extradition in April 1971, they were stonewalled for eight months, then the Paraguayan court refused the request, arguing that Ricord had committed no crime in the United States.

President Richard Nixon sent Stroessner a personal note, warning that the United States might cut off $11 million in direct aid and review Paraguay's sugar quota. Stroessner maintained he could not overturn a court's decision. Then he took a trip to Japan, to investigate the possibility of financial aid from there in case the Americans cut him off. Oscar Birks, one of the Australian descendants and the director of a large travel company, accepted Stroessner's invitation to organise a party of 120 businessmen and they accompanied the president to Japan. Aid was not forthcoming but some commercial prospects opened up.

In August 1972 Stroessner was delivered from an awkward situation when his good friend General Colmán, one of Ricord's patrons, died of an old bullet wound. The following day an appeals court in Asunción suddenly decided there were grounds for Ricord's extradition. The heavy of *The French Connection* had lost his connections in Paraguay. He was sent to New York and twenty years in prison.

Paraguay then developed a lucrative trade in marijuana, which flourished in the wild Alto Paraná, transporting it over the border to supply the growing urban market in Brazil. At the same time cocaine was smuggled from Bolivia to a few hundred obscure landing strips in the Chaco, from where it was flown to Miami.

Human contraband, other fugitives, were smuggled in as well. The stunningly beautiful country became a repository for the world's undesirables and for old dictators past their use-by date. It was like Madame Tussaud's waxworks, one writer commented, "except all the figures are living".

Argentina's Juan Perón, overthrown in a 1955 coup, fled to Paraguay and claimed diplomatic asylum. The author Eduardo Galeano concluded that the event was "celebrated in drawing rooms and mourned in kitchens" in the Argentine and told a story of Perón confiding his bitterness to his Paraguayan host:

> He half-closes his eyes and whispers: "My smile used to drive them crazy. My smile ..."
> He raises his arms and smiles as if he were on the palace balcony, greeting a plaza filled with cheering people. "Would you like my smile?"
> His host looks at him, stupefied.
> "Take it, it's yours," says Perón. He takes it out of his mouth and puts it in his host's hand — his false teeth.

Over 3,000 university students attempted to march through downtown Asunción in October 1955, demanding Perón's expulsion. The new regime in Buenos Aires sent dark hints that his continued presence would be "incompatible with the maintenance of harmonious relations between the two countries" and instituted an informal boycott of Paraguayan trade. Stroessner did a half-buckle and sent Perón to house arrest in Villarrica.

The former Argentine superstar, accustomed to the high life, did not appreciate the sleepy rural town and left for Panama, a favourite last resort for obsolete dictators.

Stroessner still put out the welcome mat. Spanish and Argentine Falangists, Croation anti-communist terrorists, crooks and embezzlers from all over the world — all were welcome, as long as they brought their entrance fee. Even Australians.

In April 1973 company directors Alexander Barton and his son Thomas fled Australia. They were wanted by the New South Wales police on twenty-eight counts concerning irregular financial dealings in their sale of aircraft to Laos and Cambodia and the asset stripping of numerous companies. Just one of them, Murumba Minerals, had assets with a book value of over A\$4 million in early 1973. By September shareholders discovered that the true value was estimated by company inspectors at just \$90. The Bartons had connections with over sixty Australian companies and \$22 million was said to be missing.

Alexander Barton, born in Hungary, had a chequered past in Australia in the septic toilet business, leaving bankrupt partners behind before entering the infinitely more lucrative world of company finance. After he slipped the country he was described in the New South Wales parliament as "probably the greatest rogue we have ever known in this state".

The Bartons were tracked to Brazil, but no extradition treaty existed with Australia. But in December 1973 the father and son turned up in Paraguay which did have such a treaty.

It seemed the Bartons had blundered. But while negotiations with the Australian government continued, on 12 August 1974 the Paraguayan Supreme Court granted the Bartons citizenship. They could not be extradited. Their new lawyer announced, "Now they are Paraguayan citizens living in Paraguay the Australian government has no chance at all of ever getting them back".

But the Asunción newspaper *ABC Color*, in Stroessner's view always a troublemaker, quoted the law: To qualify for citizenship a person had to prove residence in the country for at least three years.

The Bartons claimed they had been in Paraguay since 1970. *ABC Color* found immigration records to prove their stay had been just a few months.

That the Bartons had official protection had become too blatant. On 21 November the Paraguayan Supreme Court revoked their citizenship, declaring it had "granted nationality to the two men in good faith".

The Australian government promptly issued warrants for the Bartons' arrest and sought extradition. The father and son were placed under comfortable house detention in Asunción. It did not seem to unduly restrict their new business ventures, a consulting company they had set up and various real estate investments. They had bought land in the Chaco for a rumoured $380,000 and the stock of a milk-processing company. The Bartons' wives flew to Europe, "apparently on business".

On 27 November the two men, insisting they were victims of Australian political persecution, were transferred to the national penitentiary in Asunción. Stroessner's government considered the extradition request.

His government took its time. One year later the appeals court rejected extradition. The Australian *National Times* speculated that "the strong man of Paraguay, President Stroessner, is said to have a strong direct influence on the operation of the Paraguayan courts". The Bartons were released from gaol and jubilantly announced that they would remain permanently in Paraguay.

They had become celebrities in Asunción and made Australia much more famous than a mob of nineteenth-century dreamers ever did. Florence remembered coming home on vacation from the United States to hear her father and uncles talking of little else. "They told lots of jokes about the Bartons, who had suddenly made Australia the talk of the town. It all caused quite a stir."

Osvaldo González Real, a senior official in the Ministry of Culture, had an early connection with Australia: as a child he learned his first English from the beautiful Peggy Wood, who had shared an apartment with his sister; later he took lessons from Bill Wood at the British Council. He found himself fascinated by the Bartons: "Everybody knew about the amount of money they'd stolen because it was in the international press. The Bartons would have had to pay a huge fee for the government to refuse their extradition. About two million dollars was the going rate. And there was always an agreement to invest part of the money you'd brought, buying land, building hotels, things like that. There also had to be gifts for people in Stroessner's entourage. I think in the end the Bartons were pressed so much for money that they preferred to go back to Australia and be judged by Australian law."

In October 1976 Alexander and Thomas Barton, finding their position in Asunción increasingly uncomfortable, began negotiations with the New South Wales government. In January 1977 they returned to Sydney, to one of the most protracted corporate law cases in Australian history and a short stint in gaol.

If Paraguay had become like Madame Tussaud's, then the most noto-rious of the living effigies was Anastasio Somoza Debayle. Stroessner opened his doors to Somoza after Nicaragua's Sandinista revolution in 1979. His chartered jet was flown by Stroessner's personal pilot and he made himself at home with an entourage of twenty friends and relatives, investing in real estate, including the usual ranch in the Chaco, and living in high style. Supermarkets and restaurants were cleared every time he shopped or dined. Then, in a quiet residential street, an anti-tank rocket slammed into his armour-plated car, blowing Somoza to a footnote of history. It was a superbly executed operation. The most favoured theory was that the assassins were Argentine left-wingers who had been living in Asunción, planning it for a year. Others said it was Carlos, the interna-tional hit-man. Still others thought Stroessner's own thugs fired the bazooka. Somoza had outstayed his welcome when he stole a beautiful young mistress from the president's son-in-law, Humberto Domínguez Dibb.

There was talk that Idi Amin had bought land in Asunción and might be arriving. Augusto Pinochet of Chile certainly built a house in a lush residential area. After the coup which removed his strong-arm friend, Pinochet reconsidered his options. I often passed the empty mansion, just around the corner from Florence and Max. Sentries patrolled its walls.

Georges Watin, the would-be killer of French president Charles de Gaulle, had more than just *The Day of the Jackal*. In Asunción he enjoyed over twenty years basking in his fame from Frederick Forsythe's best-selling novel. Shortly before his death in 1994, Watin told *ABC Color* that he never regretted the assassination attempt.

"For us it was awful," said Osvaldo González Real. "The image that our country had abroad was of a refuge for gangsters and murderers. We were embarrassed when we travelled because people would say, 'Oh yes, Paraguay … The drugs! Mengele, who killed so many Jews! Somoza! And did you know the Bartons?' "

A former close associate of Stroessner said there were few quibbles about who entered the country, in fact just one: "He only drew the line with blacks. As long as you had plenty of hard currency, he didn't care how you got it. Another pirate on the pirate ship was always welcome." By the 1970s it was Taiwanese, South Korean and Hong Kong businessmen, all paying heavily for the privilege of setting up in Paraguay. For many of them it was a waiting room while they lobbied for United States visas.

While these newcomers gained admission, Paraguayans such as the novelist Augusto Roa Bastos remained in exile. In 1974 he published *I the Supreme*, a fictional biography of Dr Francia, the cruel and ruthless nineteenth-century dictator. Parallels with Stroessner were perceived by many Paraguayan readers and guaranteed his continued banishment.

In 1975 construction began on a project that was to be crucial to the nation's economy. There had been a shift in the regional balance of power. As Argentina lurched from one financial crisis to the next, Paraguay looked to Brazil and its growing prosperity for development capital. Stroessner praised Brazil's President Kubitschek as a "brilliant proponent of the Good Neighbour Policy".

The international oil crisis of the 1970s hampered Brazil's plans for industrial expansion. It sought to harness the hydro-electric power of the great Paraná River and needed Paraguay's cooperation. Brazil and a few multilateral banks put up the finance, but Paraguay was able to insist on joint control, ownership of half the energy produced, and the right to sell back its massive power surplus.

The Itaipú Dam inundated 1,400 square kilometres of land and submerged forever the Guairá Falls, the greatest cataracts on earth in terms of average annual flow. During the seven years of the dam's construction it provided employment for thousands of Paraguayans, including a young engineer, Roger Cadogan. Completed in 1982 for US$18 billion — ten times the original estimate — it is the world's largest hydro-electric scheme. The statistics are staggering: the dam wall is over 220 metres high, half the height of New York's World Trade Towers. Its eighteen turbines generate 12,600 megawatts, six times the capacity of the Aswan Dam, or equal to the power consumption of all of New York State, including New York City. As half the electricity from one turbine can fulfill all Paraguay's present energy needs, the country has become a large exporter of power to Brazil. But many Paraguayans believe the result has been to become a client state, effectively a colony of its huge neighbour.

Nevertheless, Itaipú attracted foreign investment and resulted in an economic boom with an estimated US$2 billion pumped into the economy. Paraguay attained the highest growth rate in Latin America. The scrappy border settlement of Puerto Presidente Stroessner, where Sandy Wood was shot, grew into a major commercial centre. Land speculators moved into the area near the dam site and over 300,000 Brazilian settlers arrived during the construction years, drawn by cheap land and low taxes. The traditional landowners, the Aché Indians, had been removed to reservations long before, despite León Cadogan's impassioned crusade.

Stroessner claimed that the Brazilian influx assisted the country by developing the backward eastern provinces of Paraguay, but its most immediate effect was to bolster his power base with a new form of patronage for his elite supporters. Army officers and Colorado Party leaders bought large tracts of land at cheap prices. Many then entered partnerships with Brazilian companies, splitting the profits from real-estate sales to new Brazilian immigrants.

But the move lost the president the support of the *campesinos*, his traditional constituency. Peasants evicted on invented charges, their farms sold under them, combined in a land reform movement. They were accused of links with student guerrillas and in 1976 a concerted effort was made to smash their organisation. An authoritative study claimed: "Fifty peasant leaders were killed, hundreds more fled into exile and over 5,000 were arrested in raids throughout the countryside."

The Church protested against the gross violation of human rights and drew the attention of the Carter administration in the United States to the number of long-term political prisoners, some of whom had been held for twenty years without trial.

But fortunes continued to be made. Asunción was a boom-town. The new wealth was in few hands, much of it collected under the table. Corruption reached prodigious levels. Suddenly Asunción boasted more Mercedes than any other capital in Latin America. Gimcrack skyscrapers sprouted beside the wide river, many to remain unoccupied for years, their windows blank.

"As the years went by," said Oscar Birks, "Stroessner thought no one could replace him, and he was surrounded by a small group, no more than forty people, who isolated him from the rest of the people and the country. The last ten years of Stroessner were very bad, there was so much corruption. For example, my company imported two hydrofoils for our tourist business. We needed government permission to import, so of course the government minister would insist on a feasibility study first, and the job would go to his son's company. That sort of thing happened all the time, at every level. If they needed furniture for a government office costing $100, they'd obtain an invoice for $1000. Or they'd say the department needed a car, buy it and take it home."

Alcides Wood said, "The law was whatever they felt like. Nothing was sure. You could never rely on the proper procedures being respected." Another cousin, Rodrigo, a merchant banker, found business dealings constantly compromised, "but if you made any complaint the police came for you. People were very afraid."

> We arranged many loans from countries outside. The loans were corrupt, between officials of our government and officials of the other governments. The French, the Brazilians, the Spanish, the Italians and many Arab loans. We're talking hundreds of millions of dollars. For instance a loan was arranged with the French for a cement factory. The real finance needed might be $100 million. The loan would be for $240 million and the difference would be creamed off. The bridge at Concepción where my father lived cost between $45 and $60 million. The loan from Spain was for $100 million. The difference disappeared in people's pockets. But all this became part of our external debt which is now over $2 billion. We're tired of paying it, something that we didn't ask for. The country has been bled dry by these people.

After the completion of the Itaipú dam, the president needed new public sector projects as sources for the dispensation of patronage. Otherwise his carefully constructed feudal power structure could collapse. By the mid-1980s Stroessner had parcelled out *all* of the state lands, allowed an increase in the contraband trade, but was still impelled to shop for huge foreign loans. Lucrative deals were obtained for the state steel enterprise and for cement plants. According to a recent study: "Each of these Brazilian-backed projects cost nearly half a billion dollars and provided a handy source of rake-offs and graft."

It was during this period that Big Wood went to Europe with his letter of credit for US$78 million from the Stroessner family. When I had spoken to his nephew Robin, he had been a little impatient of all the righteous condemnation of profiteering under Stroessner, even when expressed by his own relatives:

> Virtue works better when there's no temptation. Let's be realistic. When they made me a cultural attache and offered me a diplomatic passport, I didn't say no. But if they had not offered it to me, today I'd be mocking and laughing at those who were cultural attaches under Stroessner. But as I was one of them, I keep my mouth shut. I'm as corruptible as anyone else. I'm romantic but I'm also a cynical man, a realist. Would I say no to $4 million because I want to keep my dignity and honour? I was not in that situation, so I'm not going to judge. Of course I disapprove of corruption, more than anything because there was no decent result, nothing positive for the people of Paraguay. But look, nobody offered me the money, so I didn't have to make the decision.
>
> We should always remember the ugly girl who says, "I don't understand why that woman goes screwing all those fellows". Well, she never had the chance to say no. It's very easy for her to be virtuous when nobody wants her virtue.

When you don't have merchandise to sell, it's no surprise that your shop has no customers.

Everybody was suffering under Stroessner but a lot of people did whatever they could to advance themselves.

ABC Color published details of some of the scams. In March 1984 fifty soldiers arrived with machine-guns to close the newspaper down. It had annoyed Stroessner for far too long. Isabel Hilton acknowledged that, "*ABC Color*'s record is one of courage. In the seventeen years the paper published, [its] journalists were jailed on thirty-two occasions. It became the practice for everyone to keep an overnight bag in the office, in case of arrest". Its editor, Aldo Zuccolillo, one of Asunción's elite, was gaoled twice. In 1986 the military arrived in trucks to pull the plug on Radio Nandutí. A weekly newspaper *El Pueblo* was closed the following year.

Oscar Birks was then a correspondent for Time-Life. He organised the visit to Paraguay of a senior *Time* writer who wanted to interview leaders of the opposition parties. Birks arranged these appointments for the last day but, as a survival strategy, advised that the president should be interviewed at the beginning. He obtained Stroessner's consent, on the proviso that written questions were submitted.

After the final interviews with the opposition leaders, Birks dined with the journalist and took him to the airport. At dawn next morning he was conducted to police headquarters and left to languish some hours. When he was led in to the chief of police he had his story ready:

"Good morning, I know why you brought me here."

"Oh, you do?"

"Yes, because I had dinner last night with so-and-so from *Time* who's been in Paraguay interviewing various people."

"You know he interviewed some of the opposition?"

"Of course, I arranged it! But let me tell you that the first person he interviewed was President Stroessner. Why don't we phone the president now? I'm sure he will explain that to you. May I borrow your phone?"

"No, no, please, that won't be necessary!"

Birks was hastily released.

"Without that bluff," he told me, "the usual thing would have been to keep me four or five days without an explanation. There were other cases of people who were taken to the police department and two days later they were dead. A tortured corpse would be given to a family in a closed box: 'Here he is, go to the cemetery and bury him and say nothing'. Other people just disappeared; their families still don't know what happened to them."

"I actually never saw anything happening," said Florence Wood de White. "I was never aware at the time. If these things happened, they must have happened at a level that a non-political everyday person like me didn't know about. It may sound terrible but I never was worried about such things. As long as there were no revolutions and prosperity, that was what was important to me."

*

In Villarrica the children streamed through the school gates. Fresh young girls, *muchachitas*, with glossy black hair and clear brown complexions, they held hands, talking, giggling, chanting, running down the street, the skirts of their blue uniforms flying up around their legs.

The old paunchy president regarded all the schools in the country as his exclusive playpen. Alfredo Stroessner loved the *muchachitas*. They were, wrote Alex Shoumatoff, an old man's elixir, the solution to the problem of his waning powers.

> After a long morning Stroessner would park near one of the schools and watch them come out. When he had made his pick, his aides would find out who the girl was and approach the parents with an offer of cash or real estate. If all else failed the girl was kidnapped and given an injection that made her more cooperative ...

One of his procurers was Colonel Leopoldo Perrier, who scoured the countryside for eight- to twelve-year-old peasant girls and brought them to various safe houses and suburban villas that had playgrounds to keep them amused.

It was often said in Asunción that Stroessner found his regular mistress, Stella Legal, nicknamed Nata, by picking her out from a school procession. She was then only fourteen. According to another story, her mother had been her predecessor. Everyone expected him to get rid of Nata once she passed out of her teens; the girls were usually handed on to favoured army officers. But Nata had two daughters by the president and somehow she stuck and was still with him in her forties.

But more and more, he wanted the diversion of little girls. Their relatives kept quiet if they knew what was good for them. One girl from a middle-class family was given a trip to Disneyland as a reward, her parents accompanying her. On such matters journalists in Paraguay kept silent: the result of not doing so would have been a one-way flight over the Chaco.

However the *Washington Post* published a story in 1977 using information obtained from Malena Ashwell, the daughter of a Paraguayan official based in Washington. She related how, in an Asunción garden, she had inadvertently come across the unconscious bodies of three young girls, aged eight and nine. They had been sexually abused and were bleeding heavily. Ashwell learned that the premises where they were found were regularly visited by senior military officers and by Stroessner himself. After reporting her discovery, "she was taken to Investigaciones and tortured for three days. Only her parents' connections saved her".

In the same year, President Carter cut aid to Paraguay because of human-rights abuses. President Stroessner was becoming an embarrassment.

*

"If I were asked what was the drop that made the glass shatter," said Oscar Birks, "I would say the corruption. The last ten years were years of corruption, they were robbing the country and most people knew it. But I thought nothing would change until Stroessner died of sickness or old age."

"The Tyrannosaur" had been there too long, his movements were slow and cumbersome, his prey needed to be brought to him. It was rumoured that by the late 1980s Stroessner had become so mentally feeble he could not sign documents anymore — not even to have people arrested — and flunkeys around him ran a lucrative trade in his signature.

Opposition grew, quietly backed by the Church and led by Archbishop Abimael Rolón. Protestors took to the streets with demonstrations about land, press freedom and human rights. As they were arrested, courageous lawyers came forward to defend them. In 1988 the March for Life was held: 20,000 people, including many priests, walked silently through Asunción.

Stroessner could not conceive of relinquishing power; it was a family business. He pushed for his elder son Gustavo to succeed him. This dynastic ambition was a strategic mistake, threatening a longtime ally, General Andrés Rodríguez, whose daughter was married to Freddie Stroessner. Rodríguez was commander of the cavalry, fabulously wealthy, allegedly from the contraband trade, and he viewed himself as presidential material. He heard plans were in train to retire him.

On 2 February 1989 rumours of an impending coup circulated in Asunción, even reaching Florence Wood de White, who admitted to little interest in politics: "I had gone to the hairdresser that afternoon. Coming back home, the taxi driver said General Rodríguez had been called to visit the president and he thought there was going to be trouble."

It was a Thursday, the day before Carnival, and all over the country people were putting finishing touches to their costumes or dining out. "Always before Carnival there are dinners and dances at various clubs," said Oscar Birks. "Everybody goes out except old people."

Florence dined with her brother and sister-in-law. Returning home, she was puzzled by the lack of traffic on the streets and found a power blackout in her own neighbourhood. "It was so dark it was scarey. The phone was ringing. When I answered it my sister Daisy told me there was a revolution going on."

Just before midnight cannon and mortar rounds exploded on the Avenida Mariscal López and tanks rolled through the streets. Shells were lobbed at the Departamento de Investigaciones from gunboats standing off port in the Río Paraguay. Fighting was heaviest outside the barracks of the Presidential Escort Battalion, the only unit to remain loyal to the dictator.

Florence and Max White lived just a few blocks from the action. "We lay in bed," said Max, "hearing artillery shells going over the house. But we weren't too worried. There's a joke in the American services: 'If you hear an artillery shell, forget it. It's the ones you don't hear that you have to worry about.' "

It was thought the Presidential Escort troops were hiding Stroessner, but in fact he was at the home of his mistress, Nata Legal, on the Avenida Aviadores del Chaco. Soldiers burst through the front door as Stroessner fled out the back. He was given twelve hours to leave the country.

"People were still out dining in private clubs and discotheques when it happened," said Oscar Birks. "Of course it was not possible to go back home, but we could communicate by phone. We all listened to Radio Caritas, the radio station of the Franciscan Fathers. The only part of the city in darkness was where Stroessner's men were resisting, so that was a good thing. In the old times when there was a revolution, the first thing they did was cut the phones and the power."

"Our neighbours had a transistor radio," said Florence, "and some hours after midnight, President Rodríguez came on and made his proclamation."

In the southern town of Encarnación, Alcides Wood, president of the local Carnival committee, had stayed up talking with friends, making plans for the next day's festivities. His brother-in-law rang and told him to turn on the radio. "It was the *comunicado* that Stroessner was out. We were so glad of it we didn't go to bed at all, but stayed up drinking beer. The sun came out and we were celebrating still. That was the best beer I ever had."

Next morning there was dancing in the streets of Asunción. "People were singing, parading and shouting," said Florence. "Mainly the younger ones, those brave enough to go out, curious to see what had happened. But many people feared a counter attack."

Meanwhile General Rodriguez's men worked overtime. "They took pains to erase all evidence of the fighting," said Osvaldo González Real. "They cleaned the city with water-hoses, removed the spent shells and bodies." Estimates vary of how many had died during the uprising — between the official figure of 50 and a rumoured 1,000.

Those dancing in the streets abruptly forgot the Don Alfredo Polka and learned the steps of the Rodríguez Polka. General Andrés Rodríguez announced that he had carried out the coup "to defend democracy, for the respect of human rights and the defence of our Christian religion".

Elections were held on 1 May 1989 and Rodríguez was resoundingly confirmed as president, the saviour of Paraguay. An American journalist was impertinent enough to ask how he had become the richest man in the country on a salary of $500 a month. He replied, "I gave up smoking some time ago."

*

Caazapá was still a sleepy cow-town with hitching rails along the dusty main street. The statue of Father Bolanos still stood sentinel at the gate of the simple white church. An Indian in a poncho sprawled on a bench at the bus shelter.

But one thing was very different: the wall of the shelter and some stucco facades were haphazardly adorned with political graffiti, leftovers from the election of May 1993. Just a few years before, the clumsy daubings promoting opposition parties would have cost the street artists their lives or their freedom. Now they were the exuberant expression of the first period of sustained democracy the country had ever known, the first respite from an unbroken line of dictators since Paraguay parted from Spain in 1811.

Despite a shadowy past, General Rodríguez had been almost as good as his word. Under his stewardship the country's perennial state of emergency was lifted, opposition parties (though not the Communist Party) were legalised, the banned radio stations and newspapers returned to business, and hundreds of exiles, including the author Roa Bastos, were allowed to return.

Paraguay's great composer, Jose Asunción Flores, had died in exile in 1972. But his music could be heard again. His symphonic work *María de la Paz*, first performed by the Bolshoi Symphony Orchestra in the 1960s, had its premiere in Paraguay. The Orquestra Sinfónica de Asunción performed it in the presence of President Rodríguez.

Political prisoners were freed from the gaols and gave grim accounts of the treatment of former inmates who survived only as files in the archives of state security. The brutal reality of the thirty-four years of the Stronato came out with a vengeance, stories of the torture of *desaparecidos* and photographs of bones disinterred from mass graves. It was estimated that at least 1,500 people had been "disappeared".

Rodríguez launched investigations into the corruption of the previous regime, although he drew the line at his own activities. But some of the officials assisting with the investigations were former cronies of the old president. "There are quite a few people still in the government," said Osvaldo González Real, "who were very close friends with Stroessner, but they participated in the coup so they have that protection. Like they changed their minds. They became revolutionaries. But people have good long memories."

Many prominent figures from the Stronato era went to gaol, including the hated Pastor Coronel, the former head of the secret police. But others managed to flee the country, most notably Alfredo Stroessner himself. In Brazil he had thoughtfully softened his landing by financing an airport at Guaratuba, a southern coastal resort where he had a beach-house. Journalists improved their tans while they staked out the opulent bolt-hole. Some stories seemed over-heated. The former president, one wrote, required a blue carpet to be rolled into the sea when he took a dip.

To escape the press Stroessner's matronly wife and his daughters-in-law fled to Miami, and he and Gustavo relocated to a comfortable residence in Brasília. A constant source of speculation in Paraguay was how much money he had got away with, how much he had stashed in Swiss banks. Most people believed, like Osvaldo González Real, that Stroessner was "one of the wealthiest men in the world, because he had almost thirty-five years to fill his pockets. Everybody had to pay him a percentage".

A counter-revolution remained a perennial fear. Although the old president's mental faculties were said to have weakened, his ambition had not, which was dangerous in combination with unlimited funds. "His son Gustavo is a military man and they have so much money they could hire mercenaries and arms. And they still have many supporters in Paraguay."

Rodríguez arranged a new general election for May 1993 and, as he had promised, did not stand himself. The Colorado candidate, Juan Carlos Wasmosy, a leading cotton exporter, was elected as the country's first civilian president.

At the time of my visit I found that most Paraguayans shared a spirit of optimism, including the Australian descendants. At the centenary celebrations the previous day they had been only too happy to talk about it. "Now we can say what we feel," said Oscar Birks, "we have freedom of the press, and the judiciary is more independent."

"Everybody seems to want to talk about politics now," said Florence. "A few years ago nobody would. I certainly didn't dare."

"Democracy isn't something that you get by creating a decree," said the senator Alcides Wood. "Everybody's got to work for it. And we are doing that now. There are still some people to be put out of the way and a lot of things to be changed. It's very hard to just turn around and change the whole system immediately. I reckon we're doing well now, changing bit by bit, and it's working. There's no way back. We have to look forward and walk forward, but I think we'll get there."

His cousin Rodrigo agreed: "Paraguayans have new hope. But I still believe the road is going to be long for democracy. The people need to be educated. And there's still quite a few in the government who belonged to the Stroessner system. We have to get rid of them slowly but surely — and hopefully we will. I don't know what's coming next, but I have confidence. You could say a shy optimism!"

"We all feel that," said Randolf Wood, as he negotiated the Landcruiser over the ragged timbers of the old bridge across the Pirapó, built by his great-grandfather, Allan McLeod. "Paraguay is a country we love and now we can feel hope for its future. One of my relatives said last night, 'We are recovering again the paradise!' "

*

Partridges exploded from the grass and scurried across the track in front of us.

In the five kilometres from the Pirapó to the village there were more little bridges to cross, some of them just two planks across a rushing creek. It was necessary for Patricio to jump out to guide the wheels of the vehicle.

Three *campesinos* in wide straw sombreros recognised him and emerged from the *monte*. One, with a bandolier of ammunition, waved a brace of dead birds in greeting.

As we neared Colonia Cosme, Sylvia became very quiet, her tension painfully evident.

Her estranged husband, Francisco, was waiting at the brick house where they had spent their married life together. He greeted us, subdued and awkward. His new love, the young Indian woman, stayed out of sight.

The old Wood homestead next door was a ruin, its timbers sagging under the weight of the rusting iron roof, vines forcing their way through holes in the walls. But Patricio smiled happily as he led us over to it. He had big plans for his retirement. The old place would have to be demolished, he said, but he'd put up a smart prefabricated bungalow on the site. All the components would come in a sea-container from Australia. But the fruit trees could be saved. They'd soon have the garden looking lovely.

His wife Mercedes picked her way through the dust in gold sandals. She screwed up her nose at the fowls scratching through the house and leaving droppings on the floor and grinned ruefully at me: "It's all very well for you to say '*Qué lindo!* How pretty!' You don't have to think of living here. No electricity and no-one to talk to."

Patricio might have eaten the fruit of the *guabirá* tree, but I had the distinct feeling he would not be retiring to Cosme.

Dark clouds rolled across the sky. While Sylvia packed up her possessions, the rest of us walked in a straggling group to the cemetery.

The wide streets — a legacy of the master-plan for a great communist city — were grassy, only at the centre scarred red by the furrows of *carreta* wheels. They gave a pleasant sense of strolling through parkland. Cows ambled ahead, a gaggle of geese flapped towards a pond. Villagers stood and watched at the doorways of little houses with thatched or tiled roofs. A dozen children trailed us, their fascination undisguised; even in this remote village they were all clean and well-dressed. We passed a tiny cement pillbox with a sign grandly announcing "Administracion Nacional de Telecomunicaciones". At the open window a pretty freckled girl, earphones clamped on her red hair, sat operating a small telephone switchboard. Although Cosme still had no electricity, it had this link with the outside world. She told me her name was Neida Titilah Fernandez and leaned against the window, grinning, to pose for a photograph with her brothers. Descendants of William Titilah, who came from Scotland in 1897, they spoke not a word of English.

The cemetery was unrecognisable from my previous visit. Newly constructed bungalows surrounded it. The brambles had been cleared away and beaten earth pathways separated the brick and concrete vaults of Paraguayan Catholicism. The low colony graves, many lacking head-stones, barely made an impression.

A weathered fence-post with morticed rail-hole, made from sturdy lapacho wood, had been erected as a monument. Francisco said he had put it there because it was the last one left from the colony days. Paraguayans would never go to such trouble making a fence-post. He explained it all again for Stuart Heather's video camera. Then his brother Patricio, in smart Australian Akubra hat, was taped pointing out the last resting places of William and Lillian Wood, apologising that they were overgrown.

Patricio lingered by the sharp-angled new concrete tomb where his mother was buried. It was the first time he had seen it. Doña María Albina Cáceres de Wood had died just three months before, while he was still in Queensland. Stuart Heather turned his camera off. María's death was not part of the story.

I thought sadly of Don Norman. He had always said he wanted to be buried at Cosme but predicted he wouldn't be, "because my missus won't let me". Then he used to smile, confident that his adored younger wife, Doña Leonarda, would be there to look after him at the end. She died with shocking suddenness of a ruptured appendix in December 1991. Don Norman lost the will to go on and survived her by just four months. He was buried at Concepción.

The threatened storm was about to break. We hurried back to the old Wood homestead. I operated the video camera while Stuart stood beside a derelict wall with massive chimney-piece. He explained to television viewers in Australia that this little village of Cosme was a place of dreams and disillusionment. But today, he said, one hundred years after the sailing of the *Royal Tar*, little evidence remained of the original settlers. It was now a Paraguayan village.

As he packed up his gear he commented wryly, "We're both mining a diminishing seam."

Abruptly the black clouds burst. A deluge fell on Colonia Cosme.

*

Night was closing in with no abatement in the storm. The rain roared down, relentless. We sat inside Sylvia and Francisco's house, dolefully drinking *yerba mate*. The strain between the couple was acute. Francisco obviously wanted to be anywhere else, but politeness demanded he remain while the visitors did. We were all hemmed into a tiny space, captive to the rushing sheets of water.

Even in my childhood in New Guinea I could not remember a tropical downpour of such ferocity. But it occurred to me that the original settlers described something similar on their very first night at Cosme. "Rain was falling, and the ground was wet and sloppy, on the day of our home-coming," wrote Harry Taylor. "But there was no time, nor any inclination, to grumble at anything. We were on our own land and were there to make the best of things."

In the intervening hundred years there had always been Australian descendants at Cosme and the attachment to that little place was strong among them. But one by one, all those with memories of the original colony had died, and their children, who knew the story and could pass it on like sacred tribal lore, were scattering. Sylvia, whose grandfather came on the *Royal Tar*, would be returning to Asunción; Patricio, grandson of William and Lillian Wood, would probably settle elsewhere in Paraguay if he did not go back to Australia. Only his brother Francisco would remain at Cosme. He spoke no English, and the new life he had chosen for himself would be among Paraguayans. Though some of them, too, were descendants of the colony, they no longer kept alive the flame. The story of the dream was lost to them.

As I looked around our little group huddled under the drumming roof, I remembered that someone had written that there was nothing quite so depressing as a defeated, written-off utopia. Abandoned by its former supporters, "it stinks like an empty railway-carriage shunted into a siding ..."

Later I found the quote, by the Czech social theorist, Milan Simecka. It continued:

> ... Such a utopia is an embarrassing reminder of defeat and the fallibility of man's intelligence, a monument to the wreckage of dreams, and such monuments make a sad sight. Rarely do people speak respectfully of failed utopias

— on the contrary, they tend to evoke embarrassment and irritation, those sentiments which are brought on by a guilty conscience.

As the rain showed no signs of easing, Randy said we'd make a dash for it; otherwise the Pirapó River could rise and maroon us for days.

The windscreen wipers had little effect. The village might not have existed in the watery blackness, but for the blur of a few lamplit windows.

When we reached the first of the rivulets, it had become a torrent. Huddled under an oilskin on the far side, Patricio shone a torch on the narrow planks the Landcruiser perilously had to negotiate.

"I won't be in a hurry to come here again," Randy muttered darkly.

"There's nothing to come here for anyway," answered Mercedes. "*Nada!* Absolutely *nothing*."

*

A few days later, back in Asunción, I prepared to go out for the evening. From a short distance away came the sound of lusty singing. Fireworks illuminated the night sky. It was in honour of Alfredo Stroessner's birthday. There were a lot of people, Florence said, who still loved him, but the celebrations were mainly in one *barrio* which he had heavily endowed. "He made a broadcast on television a few weeks ago and they hope he'll come back. But I don't think he will. He's so old and senile, and they say he can hardly walk."

I had been invited to the home of a prominent architect, a patron of the arts with many connections with business and government, to meet some Argentine film-makers. Paraguay was playing host to a festival of Latin American films for the first time.

Even the swimming pool cabana and guest lodge was larger than the average home on Sydney's plush North Shore or Melbourne's Toorak. In the dining room of the mansion, mirrored panels slid away at the touch of a button by the kitchen staff. In the vast drawing-room with its baronial fire-place, paintings and sculptures were spotlit and old folios with medieval engravings lay open on low shelves. As we talked the music of Paraguay's Agustín Barrios floated among us, interpreted by John Williams for the classical guitar.

They were interested to hear of a screenplay I was writing about Mary Gilmore and her time at Colonia Cosme. The discussion of socialism, of ideas and youthful idealism, the trade union background in Australia which propelled the movement and the stages in the dissolution of the utopian dream, left my paltry Spanish far behind. Paraguay's leading film-maker, Hugo Gamarra, translated for me.

"But you're saying" — the architect leaned forward, his brow furrowed — "that she left Paraguay an enemy of socialism?"

I said that for many years afterwards in Australia, Mary wrote for a trade union journal, took up the crusade for Aboriginal rights and, in her old age, wrote for the Communist Party newspaper.

"Thank God!" exclaimed our impeccable host. "I thought you were going to tell us she betrayed the cause."

*

I boarded a fast bus which announced its destination as Puerto Stroessner. There is a satisfying Biblical symmetry to the names of three important towns in Paraguay: Concepción, Asunción and Encarnación. But there is nothing sacred about the brash town on the border, the country's second largest, linked to Brazil by the Friendship International Bridge. It grew out of smuggling, the fast money which accompanied the building of the Itaipú Dam, and the locust descent of one-stop international tourists come to gaze at the nearby cataracts. Boasting to be "South America's biggest late-night shopping centre", huge air-conditioned malls and street after street of characterless shops displayed cameras, radios, binoculars, rubber shrunken heads with nylon hanks of hair, Johnny Walker whisky, imitation perfume, musical condoms, butterfly place mats and plastic-coated piraña fish with grinning teeth. In the rush of renaming, it had officially become Ciudad del Este — City of the East. But no one in the discos, bars and tacky shops seemed to have noticed. They still called it "Stroessner" and it seemed to suit.

I passed an old circus poster, half peeling on a cement-block wall. *El Circo del Canguro Boxeador*, it proclaimed, with a cartoon of a kangaroo in boxing gloves. Another compatriot, far from home, beached on a foreign shore.

At the Friendship International Bridge a customs official waved on my taxi with barely a glance. The secretive land of Paraguay — home of dictators and despots, destination of dreamers — was left behind. A sealed road cut through rainforest to the famous Iguazú Falls, described by the Guaraní Indians as "the great waters at the world's end".

A deafening clamour shook the earth. The morning mist was lifting from subtropical jungle, merging with spume rising hundreds of metres into the air. The Iguazú River churned and crashed over a vast horseshoe-shaped chasm. Rainbows, born of the sun and the foam, materialised, shimmered and faded away. Tiny birds like larks, called *vencejos*, darted and swooped through the hurtling spray. Butterflies, thousands of them in clusters, hovered over the abyss.

I tried to blot out the tourists in yellow raincoats, the cameras, the joyflight helicopters scuttling overhead, tried to imagine the scene a hundred years before, when a group of Australian colonists from Cosme came upon these awesome cataracts with their Guaraní guides. Innocents abroad, troubled by the vicissitudes of life, the bickering and tensions within their failing utopia, one or two of them went on from here to Sao Paulo and a slow boat home. But here they glimpsed a physical paradise, a miracle undiminished.

The social paradise they had tried to construct had eluded them, as it had eluded other visionaries seeking to build a heaven below. Perhaps such attempts, given human fallibility, will always fail. But it could be the seeking and dreaming, the striving and building, the urge to perfection, that have real importance. Utopia, said Oscar Wilde, is "the one country at which Humanity is always landing". Perhaps it is the voyaging beyond the frontier — the daring to transcend everyday existence, the hope of bettering ourselves, the dreaming — that makes us truly human.

Epilogue

Such is life in Patagonia when the man in possession rules ...
Mary Gilmore

I left South America by way of Patagonia. I visited Estancia Condor, a vast domain of 2,000 square kilometres, where Will Gilmore had supervised the introduction of machine shears, and Killik Aike, where he was first employed and Mary had joined him, working as governess to the Felton family, until the death of José, an obscure *peón*.

By the time she reached Patagonia, Mary had changed. Though her tribulations at Cosme were still a sore point, later she saw that period of communal living as the seminal time in her long life. "I used to think to myself, 'Thank God for Paraguay', in spite of the hardships we endured, and what it taught me of other countries and for giving me knowledge and vision." It had been the crucible which consumed many others but from which she emerged tempered and strong.

"In one sense our experiment failed," she concluded. "In another I think it succeeded beyond our expectations ... In a broad sense, I believe we influenced socialist thinking everywhere, and perhaps are still influencing it."

I fought the buffeting wind in the bleak streets of Río Gallegos where Mary had lived alone for six months, teaching English, struggling with Spanish, dysentery, depression and fear of war — and always fighting the same wind.

Río Gallegos looked as if the most exciting thing that had ever happened was in 1905, when Robert Leroy Parker and Harry Longabaugh — alias Butch Cassidy and the Sundance Kid — held up a bank. But I learned it had seen more horrific events than any little town ever should.

*

The Australians had left their own country because of the system that favoured the land-owning class over the worker. They denounced the oppression of the squatters and forces of state power which caused them to flee, although, despite Henry Lawson's bombast, little blood ever stained the wattle during the strike of 1891.

They came to a continent where older rules applied, backed by grim force beyond their imagining; where the old class structures and feudal traditions Lane had sought to escape were fully entrenched, and where a new form of *caudillo* rule was vigorously asserted. Any notion of rights for the workers was implacably resisted.

Even twenty years after the Gilmores departed, there had been no real progress for labour in Patagonia. The local workers' organisations around Río Gallegos organised a general strike, focusing on the demands of the *peones* and sheepworkers on the estancias. Their demands included the right to be paid in money, not in kind, and a free afternoon a week to wash their clothes, things won long before by Australian workers. But, just as the shearers had in Queensland, they also insisted on clean living quarters, free lighting, the right not to work outdoors in the rain and, above all, to be able to form trade unions and be represented by workplace delegates.

The provincial governor was called in to arbitrate. He ruled in favour of the workers. The land-owners refused to grant the agreed conditions. Another general strike was called in October 1921.

An anarchist trade union organiser, Juan Soto, urged the men to stand their ground:

> You are workers! Carry on with the strike, to triumph definitively, to shape a new society where there are neither poor nor rich, where there are no weapons, where there are no uniforms or uniformed, where there is happiness, respect for the human being, where no one needs to bend the knee to a priest's cassock or before any boss.

It was for all the world the rhetoric of William Lane of the old Queensland *Worker* days.

As in Queensland, the Argentine government sent in a heavy contingent of troops to "re-establish order". They were joined by young Patriotic League volunteers, like the "special constables" of Queensland, looking for a fight. This combined force, led by Lieutenant Colonel Héctor Benigno Varela, pursued the illiterate, isolated and mostly unarmed rural workers and *peones*.

What happened next was unlike anything white Australia has ever seen. (The Aboriginal people might tell a different story.)

"No one is executed without a trial," recorded the writer Eduardo Galeano. "Each trial lasts less time than it takes to smoke a cigarette.

Estancia owners and officers act as judges. The condemned are buried by the heap in common graves they dig themselves."

On one estancia alone, La Anita, not far from Killik Aike, 200 employees were shot and buried in a mass grave. By December over 1,500 strike leaders and ordinary workers had been sent to the firing squad. Most of them had first been required to dig their own death pits.

The region had been satisfactorily pacified and for years the story of the massacres was suppressed. But gradually details emerged. It became known that after the last of the "troublemakers" had been killed, the British and Scottish landowners organised a reception at the English Club in Río Gallegos in Colonel Varela's honour. They cheered him and sang "For He's a Jolly Good Fellow".

*

I boarded an international flight from the tin-shed airport of Río Gallegos; it is a refuelling stop for the trans-polar flight to Sydney.

We circled the mud flats of Río Gallegos, crossed the desolate brown steppe of southern Patagonia, passed over the vast fiefdom of Estancia Condor. Suddenly, beneath drifting cloud, there were the mountain peaks of Tierra del Fuego, that uttermost part of the earth, separated from the mainland by the Straits of Magellan. An arm of the waterway was in clear view below, a wide blue chasm edged with boiling surf, offering a way for mariners who dared, through from the chill, grey Atlantic.

It may have been an illusion, but as we veered to the west it seemed the sun came out. And at last there was *my* ocean, the vast blue rolling Pacific, flecked by racing waves.

I thought of the little sailing ship *Royal Tar* making its way across the blueness down there, men and women walking the deck, betting on porpoises, not minding the cold, certain of the heaven on earth they were about to inherit, warmed by their optimism.

Notes

Abbreviations

SL: University of Sydney Library
ML: Mitchell Library of NSW
NLA: National Library of Australia

Introduction: Quest

p.2 "The Australian Peasants of Paraguay ...": articles by Theodore James & Anthony Paul, *Australasian Post*, 29 August 1963 and 5 September 1963; **p.2** "Queenslander Tribe Found ...": *Brisbane Telegraph*, August 1963; **p.3** Gavin Souter, *A Peculiar People: The Australians in Paraguay*, Angus & Robertson, Sydney, 1968, reprinted Sydney University Press, 1981; **p.3** "In the history of the world ...": *Chambers Journal of Popular Literature, Science and Art*, Fifth Series, No. 529, Vol. XI, 17 February 1894; **p.4** "must gather themselves together ...": William Lane, *The Workingman's Paradise*, by "John Miller" (William Lane), 1892 facsimile edition with Introduction by Michael Wilding, Sydney University Press, Sydney, 1980, p. 154; **p.4** "soft-handed theorists ...": William Lane, Queensland *Worker*, 23 April 1892; **p.4** "Under good management ...": Mansfeldt de Cardonnel Findlay, Second Secretary at British Legation in Buenos Aires, his report to the British Minister Plenipotentiary, quoted in Souter, *A Peculiar People*, p. 96; **p.5** "There will be a few hundred ...": Sydney *Bulletin*, 1893.

PART ONE
1. A Feather-Headed Expedition

p.12 "the boss promoter and chief prophet ...": *Bulletin*, 1 April 1893; **p.12** "An appeal was made ...": report of *Royal Tar* departure by "Rose de Boheme" (Agnes Rose-Soley), *Worker*, 22 July 1893; **p.13** "When we were all on board ...": Mrs J. Sibbald, *Sydney Morning Herald*, 20 August 1964; **p.13** The unemployed in Australia estimated at 50,000 in *New Australia*, No. 5, 25 March 1893, p. 2; **p.14** "Sixty quid's a lump, Jo": *Bulletin*, 11 March 1893; **p.15** "They say there's injuns ...": "Over There in Paraguay" by A Bushman, *New Australia*, 18 November 1893; **p.15** "We think that an acre ...": Prospectors' report by William Saunders, *New Australia*, 8 April 1893; **p.15** " ...the men are naturally ...": Theodore Child, "The Republic of Paraguay", article in Harpers magazine, July 1891, reprinted in *New Australia*, 29 April 1893; **p.16** "The world will be changed ...": William Lane, writing as "John Miller" in *New Australia*, 8 April 1893; **p.17** " ... as our bachelors ...": William Lane's address to Tasmanian women, quoted in Souter, *A Peculiar People*, p. 25; **p.18** "The Men of New Australia" by Mary Jean Cameron, writing as "M.J.C." in *New Australia*, 18 November 1893; **p.19** "I never felt so much like ...": Stevenson on Sydney Burdekin, quoted in Souter, *A Peculiar People*, p. 56; **p.19** " ... a sunburnt shearer ...": Lane, *Workingman's Paradise*, p. 10; **p.21** "She was ... tall ...": ibid., p. 8; **p.21** Sequel advertised in the cloth-bound first edition of *The Workingman's Paradise*; **p.21** "Not till you've been ...": Mary Gilmore's account of Stevenson's formal approach to her mother, in Mary Gilmore Papers, ML, A3292, Vol. 41, "Personal History — Henry Lawson and I"; **p.22** "You are mine ...": "A Bit About Two", short story by Mary Cameron in *New Australia*, 21 April 1894.

2. Something Better

p.27 "Little Billy Woods ..." from Henry Lawson, "That Pretty Girl in the Army", *A Fantasy of Man: Henry Lawson Complete Works*, Vol. 2, 1901–1922 (compiled and edited by Leonard Cronin with an introduction by Brian Kiernan), Lansdowne, Sydney, 1984, p. 105; **p.28** "There's no point ...": Gavin Souter, *A Peculiar People*, p. 273; **p.28** Kolotex Holdings Ltd, through their charity foundation, offered air fares; Mr Al Grassby, Member of the Legislative Assembly for Murrumbidgee found employment and accommodation in the Murrumbidgee Irrigation Area for two New Australians from Cosme; **p.29** "The young writers I have helped ...": Mary Gilmore, letter to Arthur Fadden, MHR, Leader of the Country Party, dated 9 May 1947, written when she was 82, in SL, Cosme Collection; **p.30** "my last glorification": W.H. Wilde, *Courage a Grace: A Biography of Dame Mary Gilmore*, Melbourne University Press, 1988, p. 460; **p.30** "poisoned by arsenic": Mary Gilmore, Notes to *Selected Verse*, Angus and Robertson, Sydney, 1948, p. 288; **p.30** In what was essentially a 49-point brag, a list of Mary's perceived achievements which she sent in 1947 to Arthur Fadden, leader of the Country Party, she wrote: "Co-opted to the first executive of the AWU and so first woman member of the Union ... Vote recorded as unanimous", Cosme Collection, SL; **p.31** "Being a teacher ...": Mary Gilmore, ibid.; **p.31** "I was only a girl ...": ML, A3292, Mary Gilmore Papers, Vol. 41, "Personal History — Henry Lawson and I"; **p.31** "It was a strange meeting ...": ibid.; **p.31** "Sometimes he asked ...": " 'Henry Lawson and Me', dictated by Mary Gilmore to Gertrude Lawson at the Hotel Imperial, Goulburn NSW in March or April 1924 when she stayed with me," ibid.; **p.31** "being rather a sharp ...": ibid.; **p.31** "There was a curious immaturity ...": ibid.; **p.32** There is possible confirmation of Mary's story of Louisa Lawson's sabotage in a letter written to Mary many years later by Henry's younger sister Gertrude: ibid.; **p.32** From Dave Stevenson's notebook, possibly his own work, quoted in Souter, *A Peculiar People*, p. 162; **p.32** Mrs Gilmore's advice that they wait: ML, A3292, Mary Gilmore Papers, Vol. 41, "Personal History — Henry Lawson and I"; **p.32** "Concerned in the New Australia ...": ibid.; **p.33** Henry Lawson, "Rejected" (1893) in "A Camp-Fire Yarn": *Henry Lawson Complete Works 1885–1900* (ed. Leonard Cronin), Lansdowne, Sydney, 1984, p. 312.

3. The Crucible

p.34 Helen Palmer, "The Ballad of 1891", written for the play *Reedy River*. *Builders' Labourers' Song Book*, Widescope, 1975, p. 69; **p.39** Jack Howe's record is cited in Patsy Adam-Smith, *The Shearers*, Thomas Nelson Australia, Melbourne, 1982, pp. 163 and 382: "The record for hand-shearing is held by Jack Howe, who shore 321 ewes in 7 hours 40 minutes at Alice Downs (Qld) in October 1892"; **p.41** I am indebted to Stuart Svensen, *The Shearers' War: The Story of the 1891 Shearers' Strike*, University of Queensland Press, Brisbane, 1989, pp. 41–44 for an account of "Conditions of Employment in the Queensland Pastoral Industry, 1891"; **p.41** "It was a hugger-mugger ...": Flora Louisa Shaw (Lady Lugard), *Letters from Queensland*, Macmillan, London, 1893, quoted in Joe Harris, *The Bitter Fight: A Pictorial History of the Australian Labor Movement*, University of Queensland Press, Brisbane, 1970, p. 81; **p.41** "they were in the habit ...": D. Crombie, *The Crombies and Camerons in Queensland*, Brisbane 198?, quoted in Svensen, *The Shearers' War*, p. 147; **p.42** "Unionism came to ...": W.G. Spence, *Australia's Awakening: Thirty Years in the Life of an Australian Agitator*, Australia: The Worker Trustees, Sydney & Melbourne 1909, p. 78; **p.43** re 1877 strikes: see Michael Wilding, Introduction to Lane, *Workingman's Paradise*, p. 25, citing Jeremy Brecher, *Strike!*, Straight Arrow, San Francisco, 1972, p. 21; Robert V. Bruce, *1877: Year of Violence*, Bobbs-Merrill, New York, 1959, p. 315; **p.43** Lane's books cited in Lloyd Ross, *William Lane and the Australian Labor Movement*, Sydney, 1935, reissued Hale and Iremonger, Sydney, 1980, pp. 30–31; **p.43** "would like to sweep ...": William Lane, *Boomerang*, 24 November 1888; **p.43** "a piebald people ...": William Lane, *Boomerang*, 7 January 1888; **p.45** "they debauch our children ...": William

Lane, *Boomerang*, 14 April 1888; **p.45** racism as outgrowth of job chauvinism: Humphrey McQueen has argued that in Australia "the Labor Party was racist before it was socialist" (Humphrey McQueen, *A New Britannia: an Argument Concerning the Social Origins of Australian Radicalism and Nationalism*, Penguin, Ringwood, 1970, pp. 52–53 quoted in Michael Wilding, Introduction to Lane, *Workingman's Paradise*, p. 36, who also cites, on Lane and racism: Gollan, *Radical and Working Class Politics*, pp. 116–18; Ray Markey, 'Populist Politics' in Ann Curthoys and Andrew Markus (eds), *Who Are Our Enemies? Racism and the Australian Working Class*, Hale and Iremonger, Sydney, 1978, pp. 66–79; Andrew Markus, 'White Australia? Socialists and Anarchists', *Arena*, 32–3, 1973, pp. 80–9); **p.45** "coffee-coloured brat ...": Queensland *Worker*, 2 April 1892; **p.45** "We don't want another ...": William Lane, *Boomerang* 7 April 1888; **p.45** "the same as the lowliest ...": Joe Harris, *Bitter Fight*, p. 66; **p.45** "It is yours ...": William Lane ("John Miller"), *Worker*, 1 March 1890; **p.46** "While the men of the South ...": William Lane, ("John Miller"), *Worker*, quoted in Ross, *William Lane and the ALM*, pp. 99–100; **p.46** "It is to industrialism ...": William Lane, quoted in Ross, ibid. p. 117.; **p.47** "men who are ...": ML, A1562-1, Lane to Demaine, 28 November 1889; *Worker* 11 July 1891, cited in Svensen, *Shearers' War*, pp. 223–24; **p.47** "I lived in a fever ...": Mary Gilmore Papers, ML, A3292, Vol. 41, "Henry Lawson — Personal History — Henry Lawson and I", Goulburn, Oct–Nov 1922; **p.48** re 1891 shearing contract: see Ross, *William Lane and the ALM*, p. 130; **p.49** "If they want conference ...": *Worker*, 7 February 1891; **p.49** re number of police, constables, soldiers: see R.J. & R.A. Sullivan, p. 82; **p.50** "The strike in Queensland ...": *Worker*, February 1891; **p.52** "We have given moral suasion ...": Svensen, *Shearers' War*, p. 108, quoting *Morning Bulletin*, 4 May 1891 — Taylor to Blackwell, 20 March 1891; **p.53** Soldiers greeted at railway station, see: Svensen, *Shearers' War*, p.126; **p.53** estimated 800 rifles: see Souter, *A Peculiar People*, p. 5; **p.53** Police and troops estimate: see E. R. Drury, Special Service by Corps of the Queensland Defence Force, James C. Beal, Government Printer, Brisbane, 1891, pp. 1,7, quoted in Michael Wilding, Introduction to Lane, *Workingman's Paradise*, p. 14; **p.53** "The government troops ...": *Worker*, 1891; **p.53** "Shearblade" Martin cited in Svensen, *Shearers' War*, pp. 128–29; **p.53** arrest of strike leaders: *Brisbane Courier*, 26 March 1891, interview with Fothergill and Blackwell, cited by Svensen, *Shearers' War*, pp. 128–29; **p.54** "This is Queensland freedom ...": *Brisbane Courier*, 1891, 8 April, 9 April, 17 April, cited in Svensen, *Shearers' War*, pp.166–67; **p.54** "Naturally the capitalistic opposition ...": Queensland *Worker*, 18 April 1891; **p.56** "New Order which ...": Lane, *Workingman's Paradise*, p. 225; **p.56** Poem "The Coming Victory" by "Union Girl, Clermont", *Worker*, 2 May 1891. See Souter, *Peculiar People*, p. 9; **p.56** "and one sees how hollow ...": "John Miller" (William Lane), "At the Conspiracy Trial", *Worker*, 30 May 1891; **p.57** "rowdier than the ...": *Worker*, 30 May 1891; **p.57** Henry Lawson, "Freedom on the Wallaby", *Worker*, 16 May 1891; **p.58** "no rich land-grabber ...": *Worker*, 20 February 1892; **p.58** "From Gaol to Parliament ...": *Worker*, 19 March 1892; **p.58** "we cannot call a meeting ...": *Worker* editorial, 30 April 1892; **p.58** "could not possibly ...": *Worker*, 23 April 1892; **p.58** "Come out from this ...": *Worker*, 6 August 1892; **p.59** "The only thing ...": quoted in Ross, *William Lane and the ALM*, p. 178; **p.59** "Only enthusiasts will ...": quoted in Ross, ibid., p. 179; **p.59** John Lane's condition for marriage related by Eric Lane, John's youngest child, interview with Anne Whitehead, 12 January 1988; **p.59** "offers inducements to ...": Charles A. Washburn, *The History of Paraguay* (2 vols), Lee and Shepard, Boston, 1871, Vol. II, pp. 606–7; **p.60** "Aryan climate ...": Quoted in Grant Hannan, "William Lane — Mateship and Utopia" (based on his unpublished MA thesis on the New Australia Movement, 1966, University of Queensland), in D.J. Murphy, R. B. Joyce, Colin A. Hughes (eds), *Prelude to Power: The Rise of the Labour Party in Queensland 1885-1915*, Jacaranda Press, 1970, p. 185; **p.60** William Lane (as "Sketcher"), "White or Yellow? A Story of Race War in A.D. 1908", serialised in 12 issues of *Boomerang* between February and May 1888; **p.60** "We must be white ...": Lane, *Boomerang*, 4 February 1888; **p.60** "Mum didn't go ...": Lizzie Martyn (née Butterworth) in

Windsor and Richmond Gazette, undated clipping in Mary Gilmore papers, ML; **p.61** "My mother argued ...": Eric N. Birks, "As a Boy in Paraguay", *Australian Quarterly*, No. 26, June 1935; **p.64** "I think the sharks ...": Julian Stuart, *Part of the Glory: Reminiscences of the Shearers' Strike Queensland 1891*, Australasian Book Society, Sydney, 1967, p. 149; **p.64** "The dark cell ...": quoted in Jarvis Finger, *The St Helena Island Prison*, Boolarong Publications, Brisbane, 1988, p. 14; **p.65** "When he came back ...": Stuart, *Part of the Glory*, p. 162.

4. New Australia Bound

p.67 "Notwithstanding everything that ...": *Bulletin*, 22 July 1893; **p.68** *Royal Tar*'s specifications in *New Australia* journal, 27 May 1893; **p.68** "Leaving Sydney Harbour ...": John Sibbald, "The Pioneer Voyage", *New Australia*, 18 December 1893; **p.69** "who's to do the washing-up ...": *Bulletin*, 10 June 1893; **p.69** "'Tween decks ...": Sydney *Daily Telegraph*, quoted in Ross, *William Lane*, p. 207; **p.70** "We did not ...": John Sibbald, op.cit.; **p.70** "The first revolt ...": James Molesworth, *Windsor and Richmond Gazette*, 12 August 1927; **p.71** "By this time too ...": Mary Leeser, great-niece of David Russell Stevenson and, by marriage, Clara Jones, interview with Anne Whitehead in Sydney on 10 November 1982; **p.72** "How well I remember ...": quoted in Souter, *A Peculiar People*, p. 56; **p.72** "I don't know much ...": letter from Moira Pye to Mary Leeser; **p.73** "On the voyage over ...": ML, A3292, Mary Gilmore Papers, Vol. 41, "Henry Lawson — Personal History — Henry Lawson and I"; **p.73** "he had to have an armed guard ...": Eric Lane interviewed by Anne Whitehead, 12 January 1988; **p.73** "When Lane moved ...": John Rich, quoted in Souter, *A Peculiar People*, p. 71; **p.73** "like a sulky child ...": G.W.W. Pope, quoted in Souter, *A Peculiar People*, p. 71; **p.74** "We know also ...": Mary Cameron, "Our Mates are Gone", *New Australia*, 1 August 1893; **p.74** Infant buried at sea referred to in Souter, *A Peculiar People*, p. 72; **p.74** John Sibbald, "The Pioneer Voyage", *New Australia*, 18 December 1893; **p.74** "The sky was clouded ...": Harry S. Taylor, *The Voice*, 1 December 1893; **p.77** News of eight seceders: see Souter, *A Peculiar People*, p. 97; **p.77** Gilbert Casey's speech: see Souter, *A Peculiar People*, p. 98; **p.79** "Incidents of the Second Voyage", *New Australia*, 15 May 1894.

5. The Big Village

p.82 "Here are the best ...": Captain Richard F. Burton, *Letters from the Battlefields of Paraguay*, Tinsley Brothers, London, 1870, p. 183; **p.83** "All foreigners begin ...": Jacobo Timerman, quoted in Jimmy Burns, *Beyond the Silver River: South American Encounters*, Bloomsbury, London, 1989, p. 1; **p.83** "On the way to Paraguay ...": John Lane, "New Australia — Paraguay and Cosme. Interesting Recollections, Lecture by Mr. J. Lane", Part 2 of lectures for the Brisbane Workers' Educational Association, published in three parts in the *Daily Standard* (Brisbane), 9, 10 and 12 May 1924; **p.84** "In this extraordinary ...": E. F. Knight, *The Cruise of the "Falcon": A Voyage to South America in a 30 Ton Yacht*, Sampson Low, Marston & Co, London, approx 1882; fifth edition 1886, p. 70; **p.89** "Drainage is left ...": Burton, *Letters from Paraguay*, p. 161; **p.89** "Tell Grace I am sorry ...": This and all subsequent Tozer quotes are from: Arthur Tozer — Letters to Henry John Tozer 1889–1904 (lent for copying by Mr H.V. Tozer, Barcelona, Spain, 1971.) ML, FM4/5443; **p.91** "The pampas are ...": W. H. Hudson, *Far Away and Long Ago: A Childhood in Argentina*, Century Hutchinson Ltd, London, 1985; **p.92** "their appearance is ...": Charles Darwin, *The Voyage of the "Beagle"*, 1845, reprinted Heron Books, Geneva, 1968, p. 42; **p.94** "a rather cut-throat place ...": Knight, *Cruise of the "Falcon"*, p. 70; **p.96** H. J. Tozer, *British India and Its Trade*, Harper's International Commerce Series, Harper & Brothers, London, 1902; **p.97** Batemans long established: Though a British waterworks engineer, James Bevans, had designed the water supply system for the city in 1822 (Andrew Graham-Yooll, *The Forgotten Colony: A History of the English-*

Speaking Communities in Argentina, Hutchinson, London 1981, p. 103), Batemans had been involved for at least twenty years, as in 1871 John Frederic Bateman published *City of Buenos Aires improvements*, report of the drainage and sewerage and water supply of the city, 21/9/1871. This was a study commissioned after the yellow-fever epidemic; **p.101** "Insistence on the alienation ...": H. J. Tozer, Critical Introduction to his translation of *The Social Contract or Principles of Political Right* by Jean Jacques Rousseau, with a Preface by Bernard Bosanquet, Swan Sonnenschein & Co, London, 1895, p. 96; **p.102** Souter on Leck, *A Peculiar People*, p. 33; **p.105** "The whole line of country ...": Darwin, *Voyage of the Beagle*, p. 68; **p.105** "to kill all stragglers ...": ibid., p. 103; **p.105** "I think there will not ...": ibid., p. 104; **p.106** "There is unquestionably ...": William Saunders, "Prospectors' Report — Brought by William Saunders Who Has Returned", *New Australia*, Vol. 1, No. 6, Sydney, 8 April 1893; **p.107** Douglas Stewart, "Terra Australis", from *Douglas Stewart: Selected Poems*, Angus & Robertson, Sydney, 1973, pp. 105–8; **p.107** "What a rush ...": *New Australia*, Vol. 1, No.3, Wagga, 28 January 1893; **p.109** "At Buenos Aires ...": Burton, *Letters from Paraguay*, p. 154.

6. Across the Silver River

p.111 On Garibaldi: Burton, *Letters from Paraguay*, p. 259; **p.111** "well-cooked and ...": ibid., p. 145; **p.114** "We haven't had much time ...": Harry S. Taylor, *The Voice*, 24 November 1893; **p.114** "The Paraguayan Consul ...": ibid.; **p.115** "This immigration ...": *El Siglo* (Montevideo), 16 September 1893 (Translated extract from Souter), SL Cosme Collection; **p.115** Fight on board described in Souter, *A Peculiar People*, p. 74; **p.115** "It got to high words ...": John Rich account, SL, Cosme Collection; **p.116** "After acting with injudicious ...": Souter, *A Peculiar People*, pp. 74–75; **p.116** "I can't help feeling ...": Tom Westwood, quoted in Souter, *A Peculiar People*, p. 75; **p.117** "The first stage in the history ...", *New Australia*, 16 September 1893 (Mary Gilmore has signed her name, acknowledging authorship, on the copy of this article, ML); **p.117** "He was a gaucho by instinct ...": Washburn, *History of Paraguay*, Vol. 1, p. 238; **p.117** "Is it not then bitter ...": W.H. Hudson, *The Purple Land* in omnibus volume, *South American Romances*, Duckworth, London 1930, p. 13; **p.118** "In the evening ...": Knight, *Cruise of the Falcon*, p. 64; **p.120** Account of *Lady Shore* from Andrew Graham-Yooll, *The Forgotten Colony*, p. 33; **p.121** "It is worth coming ...": Mary Gilmore, ML, Papers of Mary Gilmore, MC MSS 123, Prose 1902–1904; **p.121** "This day my feet ...": Mary Gilmore, Verse Notebook, 18 October 1891, ML, quoted in W. H. Wilde, *Courage a Grace*, p. 98; **p.122** "One looked out upon lines ...": This and following quotes unless otherwise noted are from: Mary Gilmore, ML, MC MSS 123, Papers of Mary Gilmore, Prose 1902–1904.; **p.123** "fine zinc dome ...": Captain Richard F. Burton, *Letters from Paraguay*, p. 99; **p.126** "modern industry must not ...": José Batlle y Ordóñez, quoted in Hubert Herring, *A History of Latin America: From the Beginnings to the Present*, Jonathan Cape, London 1954, p. 666; **p.127** "A whole country living ...": V. S. Naipaul, *The Return of Eva Peron*, p. 137; **p.127** "In a country of less ...": Mario Benedetti, interviewed by Greg Price, *Latin America: The Writer's Journey*, Hamish Hamilton, London 1990.

7. The Good Ship Paraná

p.128 "About Paraguay (By One Who Has Been There)", *Age* (Melbourne), 15 July 1893; **p.130** "It was eight on a July ...": Graham Greene, *Travels with My Aunt* (The Bodley Head, London, 1969), Penguin Books, London, 1988, p. 185; **p.131** "Its officers and stewards ...": Harry A. Franck, *Vagabonding Down the Andes*, T. Fisher Unwin Ltd, London, 1919, p. 600; **p.131** "pocket Botany Bay ...": Burton, *Letters from Paraguay*, p. 191; **p.131** Fate of Indians on Martín García: see Hubert Herring, *A History of Latin America*, p. 622; **p.131** corpses washed ashore: *Report of an Amnesty International Mission to Argentina: 6–15 November 1976*,

Amnesty International Publications 1977, p. 41; **p.132** "Disregarding the children's ...": Stewart Grahame, *Where Socialism Failed: An Actual Experiment*, John Murray, London, 1912, p. 69; **p.133** "The sides of the ...": *The Voice* (Adelaide), 8 December 1893; **p.134** "Their vessels are handsome ...": Knight, *Cruise of the Falcon*, p. 79; **p.135** "It is imperative ...": quoted in Souter, *A Peculiar People*, p. 76; **p.136** "Ugly church ...": Burton, *Letters from Paraguay*, p. 239; **p.136** "There is but little ...": Knight, *Cruise of the Falcon*, pp. 80–81; **p.136** "I have crossed ...": W. J. Holland, quoted in Deirdre Ball (ed.), *Argentina*, An Insight Guide, APA Publications (HK) Ltd, 1988, p. 78; **p.137** "From the very bowels ...": Eric N. Birks (grandson of George Napier Birks), article 'As a Boy in Paraguay', *Australian Quarterly*, No. 26, June 1935; **p.138** "when the gaucho ...": W. H. Hudson, *Far Away and Long Ago: A Childhood in Argentina* (J.M. Dent & Sons, London, 1918), Century Hutchinson Ltd, London, 1985, p. 251; **p.139** "all the cant about the gaucho ...": Bruce Chatwin, *In Patagonia* (Jonathan Cape, London, 1977) Pan Picador, London, 1979, p. 8; **p.139** "The river being flooded ...": Knight, *Cruise of the Falcon*, p. 211; **p.142** "I don't know which ...": Westwood quoted in Souter, *A Peculiar People*, p. 77; **p.142** Taylor's return to Australia: See Souter, *A Peculiar People*, p. 77; **p.142** "It seems to have ...": Harry Taylor, *The Voice* (Adelaide), 8 December 1893; **p.142** "In Paraguay, the river's ...": John Lane, "New Australia — Paraguay and Cosme. Interesting Recollections, Lecture by Mr J. Lane", Part 2 of lectures for the Brisbane Workers' Educational Association published in three parts in the *Daily Standard* (Brisbane), 9, 10 and 12 May 1924; **p.143** For details of arsenal: George Frederick Masterman, *Seven Eventful Years in Paraguay*, S. Low, Son & Marston, London, 1870, p. 142; **p.143** Paraguayans board iron-clads: Burton, *Letters from Paraguay*, p. 312; **p.144** "I will never forget ...": Mary Gilmore, "South America", NLA, Papers of Dame Mary Gilmore, MS 8766, Series 5, Prose; **p.144** "a brand new floating ...": Burton, *Letters from Paraguay*, p. 292; **p.144** "the party of pleasure ...": ibid., p. 135; **p.145** "by far the favourite ...": ibid., p. 294; **p.145** "the tripsters ...": ibid., p. 223; **p.145** "He has been the life ...": ibid., p. 308; **p.145** Story of Madame Lynch's shoes told in Gordon Meyer, *The River and the People* (Methuen, 1965), Readers' Union edition, London, 1967, pp. 71–72; **p.146** "the ambitious names of ...": Burton, *Letters from Paraguay*, p. 351; **p.146** "To be killed by such ...": ibid., p. 322; **p.146** "I felt something of the ...": ibid., p. 339; **p.146** "Mr Whytehead, the chief engineer ...": George Masterman, *Seven Eventful Years in Paraguay*, p.127 (Masterman always spelled his name "Whytehead"); **p.147** "leave anything with an exposed ...": Dr E. de Bourgade La Dardye, *Paraguay: The Land and the People*, George Philip & Son, London, 1892, pp. 70–71; also on fish, Gordon Meyer, *The River and the People*, p. 34; **p.148** "The whole ship's ...": ML, Mary Gilmore Prose 1902–04; **p.148** "the forest lies on each side ...": Mary Gilmore, ibid.; **p.148** "England wanted Paraguay ...": Mary Gilmore, "South America", NLA, Papers of Dame Mary Gilmore, MS 8766, Series 5, Prose; **p.149** "several white-clad damsels ...": Knight, *Cruise of the Falcon*, p. 236; **p.149** "Numerous women passed ...": Knight, *Cruise of the Falcon*.

8. Landfall

p.152 "... They all would sail ...": Christina Stead, *Letty Fox: Her Luck*, Peter Davies, London 1947, p. 501; **p.152** "I came to Paraguay ...": Graham Greene, *Ways of Escape*, Penguin Books, Harmondsworth 1981, p. 221; **p.154** "the only one that can run ...": Arthur Tozer, letter to H. Tozer, 21 October 1893; **p.154** "They are a superior class ...": Dr William Stewart report to Buenos Aires, quoted in Gavin Souter, *A Peculiar People*, p. 79; **p.154** "On landing and exploring ...": Knight, *Cruise of the Falcon*, p. 250; **p.155** Dr Francia addressing the Congress in Asunción on 18 June 1811, quoted in H.G. Warren, *Paraguay: An Informal History*, Greenwood Press, Westport Connecticut 1982 (originally pub. Norman, University of Oklahoma Press, 1949) p. 147; **p.155** "make him an altar boy": Quoted in Warren, *Paraguay*,

p. 174; **p.157** "hideous, burly and thick-set ...": Burton, *Letters from Paraguay*, quoted in Alyn Brodsky, *Madame Lynch and Friend*, Cassell, London 1976, p. 45; **p.157** re British equipment on railway: M. G. Mulhall, "The English in South America", *The Standard*, Buenos Aires 1878, p. 365, quoted in George Pendle, *Paraguay*, Oxford University Press, London, 1967, p. 19; **p.158** "he bit the nipple ...": Mary Gilmore, "Lopez", NLA, Papers of Dame Mary Gilmore, MS 8766, Series 5 Prose; **p.162** "The high society of Asunción ...": Hector Varela, *Elisa Lynch, por Orion* [pseud.], Buenos Aires 1870, quoted in Alyn Brodsky, *Madame Lynch and Friend*, Cassell, London, 1976, p. 102; **p.162** "The Spaniards used ...": Souter, *A Peculiar People*, p. 80; **p.162** "We slept in the open ...": James Molesworth, *Windsor and Richmond Gazette*, 12 August 1927; **p.163** "that would-be Napoleon ...": "Paraguay and Elsewhere in South America", ML, Mary Gilmore Prose 1902–04; **p.163** "They are in a disgraceful state ...": John Rich, quoted in Souter, *A Peculiar People*, p. 80; **p.163** "An old woman, seated ...": article by "One Who Has Been There", *Age*, 15 July 1893; **p.165** "the man from Paraguay": quoted in William E. Barrett, *Woman on Horseback: The Biography of Francisco Lopez and Eliza Lynch*, Peter Davies, London, 1938, p. 49; **p.165** "quite too busy ...": quoted in Alyn Brodsky, *Madame Lynch and Friend*, p. 60; **p.165** "would as soon break bread ...": ibid., p. 182; **p.165** "Sadism, an inverted patriotism ...": R.B. Cunninghame Graham, *Portrait of a Dictator*, Heinemann, London, 1933; **p.165** "He is, when he likes ...": George Thompson, *The War in Paraguay*, Longmans, London, 1869, p. 327; **p.166** "a monster without ...": ibid., p.v; **p.166** "Many of Madame Lynch's brasses ...": unidentified Buenos Aires newspaper quoted in Barrett, *Woman on Horseback*, p. 84; **p.166** Account of Mesdames Dupart and Balet in Brodsky, *Madame Lynch and Friend*, pp. 96–97; **p.167** "By ignoring Madame Lynch ...": Brodsky, *Madame Lynch and Friend*, pp. 105–107; the story is also told in Barrett, *Woman on Horseback*, pp. 93–95, both taken from the original source by Hector Varela (under the pseudonym "Orion"), *Elisa Lynch*, Buenos Aires, 1870, p. 330; **p.167** "At this fancy ball ...": Washburn, *History of Paraguay*, Vol. 1, p. 536; see also Brodsky, *Madame Lynch and Friend*, pp. 132–33, Barrett, *Woman on Horseback*, p. 140; **p.167** "The furniture, destined ...": Burton, *Letters from Paraguay*, p. 75; **p.169** "Interested motives ...": ibid., p. 328; **p.169** "a whole Race was incarnate ...": Natalicio González, *Solano Lopez y Otros Ensayos*, Editorial las Indias, Paris, 1926, quoted in George Pendle, *Paraguay*, p. 22; **p.169** Dom Pedro's empire: Barrett, *Woman on Horseback*, p. 129; **p.170** Brazilian national guard outumbered Paraguay's population: John Hoyt Williams, *The Rise and Fall of the Paraguayan Republic, 1800–1870*, Institute of Latin American Studies, University of Texas at Austin, 1979, p. 203; **p.170** Size of Paraguay's army: Hoyt Williams, p. 203; also Warren, *Paraguay*, pp. 213 & 218; **p.170** Size of Argentina's army, quoted in David Rock, *Argentina 1516–1982*, I.B. Tauris & Co, London, 1986, p. 127; **p.171** "It is a fatal war ...": Burton, *Letters from Paraguay*, p. xii; **p.171** "That battle ...": George Masterman, *Seven Eventful Years in Paraguay*, quoted in Warren, *Paraguay*, p. 234; **p.171** "They complained that ...": George Thompson, *The War in Paraguay*, quoted in Warren, p. 234; **p.172** "atrocities of López ...": Burton, *Letters from Paraguay*, p. xi; **p.172** "There certainly exists ...": General Martin T. McMahon to US House Foreign Affairs Committee, House Report No. 65, p. 223, quoted in Barrett, *Woman on Horseback*, pp. 278 & 345; **p.172** Eliza leading cavalry charge described in Barrett, *Woman on Horseback*, p. 264; **p.172** "López's determination was ...": Brodsky, *Madame Lynch and Friend*, p. 231; **p.174** "hobbling ... their bandages caked" described in John A. Crow, *The Epic of Latin America*, University of California Press, Berkeley (1946) 1980, p. 606; **p.174** "Marshal-President López, safely sheltered ...": Burton, *Letters from Paraguay*, p. 79; **p.174** Paraguay's population: figures quoted from Warren, *Paraguay*, p. 243; also Pendle, *Paraguay*, p. 22; and Herring, *A History of Latin America*, p. 675; **p.174** "seldom has aught ...": Burton, *Letters from Paraguay*, p. viii; **p.174** "a time of misery ...": from "Paraguay and Elsewhere in South America", ML, Mary Gilmore Prose 1902–04; **p.174** "The peace that came to Paraguay

..."': Herring, *History of Latin America*, p. 675; **p.175** "Weep, weep *urutaú* bird ...": "Nenia" by Carlos Guido y Spano, quoted in Crow, *Epic of Latin America*, p. 607; note that Souter credits the author as the Paraguayan poet Marcelino Pérez Martinez, *A Peculiar People*, p. 36; **p.175** "The Paraguayans exist no longer ...": Masterman, *Seven Eventful Years in Paraguay*, p. 342; **p.176** For arguments that Eliza made off with much loot, see Brodsky, *Madame Lynch and Friend*, pp. 241–251 and Warren, *Paraguay*, pp. 204–205; **p.176** "The defender undertook ...": Brodsky, *Madame Lynch and Friend*, p. 249; **p.177** "Colour Line" pledge: New Australia Co-operative Settlement "Articles of Association", quoted in Souter, *A Peculiar People*, p. 24.

9. Into the Wilds

p.180 "four kilos of pure Lebanese ...": Brodsky, *Madame Lynch and Friend*, p. 285; **p.181** "Elisa Alicia Lynch, who ...": ibid, p. 290; **p.182** "If not met ...": *Cosme Monthly Notes*, this warning in most issues in 1896; **p.183** "a handsomer one than Adelaide's ...": quoted in Souter, *A Peculiar People*, p. 80; **p.184** "This is quick for Paraguay ...": Arthur Tozer to H. J. Tozer, 21 October 1893; **p.185** "Women in long white sleeveless ...": R. B. Cunninghame Graham, "The Stationmaster's Horse" in *Tales of Horsemen*, Canongate, Edinburgh, 1981, pp. 49–51; **p.187** "We aristocrats were ...": Knight, *Cruise of the Falcon*, pp. 258–62; **p.188** "Assume at all times ...": Rev William Barbrooke Grubb, *An Unknown People in an Unknown Land. An account of the life and customs of the Lengua Indians of the Paraguayan Chaco, with adventures and experiences met with during twenty years pioneering and exploration amongst them*, Seeley, London, 1911, p. 27; **p.188** *El Centinela*, Asunción 1893, quoted in Souter, *A Peculiar People*, p. 81, also a free translation in SL Cosme Collection; **p.189** "We pegged out in the open ...": John Rich, quoted in Souter, *A Peculiar People*, p. 82; **p.189** "At nights, beyond the fires ...": Eric Birks, "As a Boy in Paraguay", p. 58; **p.189** "Puesto De Las Ovejas — The Sheep Station ...": quoted in Souter, *A Peculiar People*, p. 83; **p.191** "It was an inauspicious ...": James Molesworth, *Windsor and Richmond Gazette*, 12 August 1927; **p.191** "For the rest of that night ...": Stewart Grahame, *Where Socialism Failed: An Actual Experiment*, John Murray, London, 1912, p. 78.

10. The Promised Land

p.193 "Sing the song o' pizen snaix ...": Mary Gilmore, *New Australia*, 18 December 1893; **p.194** "All the rising ground is forest ...": Arthur Tozer, letter to H. J. Tozer, 21 October 1893; **p.195** "A picturesque revolver-girded ...": James Molesworth, "The Lame Tyrant of Paraguay", *Windsor and Richmond Gazette*, 12 August 1927. Molesworth must have been mistaken in describing Tozer, who always referred to himself as an Englishman, as a Scot; **p.196** "The Government have made ...": Arthur Tozer to H. J. Tozer, 21 October 1893; **p.196** "riding round in various ...": Arthur Tozer to H. J. Tozer, 28 January 1894; **p.197** "with a round, red face ...": Stewart Grahame, *Where Socialism Failed*, p. 81; **p.197** "the establishment of the New Australia Colony ...": Vol Molesworth, "New Australia — Reminiscences of a Pioneer — The Vanishing Tongues — By a First Batcher", Auburn NSW, 1918, SL, Cosme Collection; **p.197** "Two large logs ...": Vol Molesworth, ibid.; **p.198** "I find the people ...": Arthur Tozer, letter to H. J. Tozer, 21 October 1893; **p.199** re Fred White: see Souter, *A Peculiar People*, p. 86; Michael Wilding, *The Paraguayan Experiment: a documentary novel*, Penguin Books Australia, 1984, p. 126; **p.199** re planted saboteurs: Svensen, *Shearers' War*, pp. 231–32 quoting QSA COL/413 Allan to Horace Tozer, 1 May 1891; **p.199** "a colony of 50,000": The estimate of unemployed quoted in *New Australia*, No. 5, 25 March 1893, p. 2; **p.199** "There is one black sheep ...": Arthur Tozer, letter to H. J. Tozer, 21 October 1893; **p.199** "Attended Mass at 6 o'clock ...": Tom Westwood's diary, quoted in Souter, *A Peculiar People*, p. 86; **p.200**

"three fellows breaking ...": Arthur Tozer, letter to H.J. Tozer, 17 December 1893; **p.200**
"Thus was capitalism crushed ...": Vol Molesworth, "New Australia — Reminiscences";
p.200 "We have isolation ...": William Lane, *The Voice*, 1893; **p.200** "Fancy, in the town of
Ajos ...": Edward Channing, "News from the Settlement", *New Australia*, 20 January 1894;
p.201 "At a feast day in Ajos ...": Alf Walker, letter to Walter Head, quoted in Souter, *A
Peculiar People*, p. 87; **p.201** "Have you anyone in view ...": Arthur Tozer, letter to H. J. Tozer,
21 October 1893; **p.201** Registering the Sociedad as a company described in Souter, *A Peculiar
People*, p. 88; **p.202** "If Lane felt as he looked ...": John Rich, quoted in ibid., p. 89; **p.202**
"The malcontents are so buried ...": William Lane, letter to Walter Head, quoted in Wilding,
Paraguayan Experiment, p. 122; **p.202** "There is nothing for it but for me ...": William Lane,
letter to Walter Head, quoted in Souter, *A Peculiar People*, p. 90; **p.203** "a nondescript body
of payless ...": James Molesworth, "The Lame Tyrant of Paraguay", *Windsor and Richmond
Gazette*, 12 August 1927; **p.203** "I rode into Ajos ...": Arthur Tozer, letter to H. J. Tozer, 17
December 1893; **p.203** "It was the most brutal exhibition ...": Charles Manning, *Bulletin*,
31 March 1894; **p.203** "Hard words have been said ...": petition quoted in Souter, *A Peculiar
People*, p. 91; **p.204** New Australia loses one-third of its population: ibid., pp. 91–92; **p.204**
"Take them to hell!" quoted in ibid., p. 92; **p.205** "As the movement had caused ...":
Confidential Memorandum by M. de C. Findlay, quoted in Wilding, *Paraguayan Experiment*,
p. 159; **p.206** "very respectable people ...": ibid, p. 165; **p.208** "Mr Lane has very strong,
and very narrow ideas ...": ibid., p. 171; **p.208** "it is not improbable ...": Findlay report,
quoted in Souter, *A Peculiar People*, p. 96; **p.208** "He was surprised at the progress ...": Arthur
Tozer, letter to H. J. Tozer, 28 January 1894; **p.208** "They also were surprised at our progress
...": Arthur Tozer, letter to H. J. Tozer, 28 January 1894; **p.209** "The triple wedding was
engineered ...": *New Australia*, No. 18, 15 May 1894; **p.209** "For God has given a task ...":
William Lane, *New Australia*, quoted in Souter, *A Peculiar People*, pp. 100–101; **p.210** "awful
vein of snuffle ...": *Bulletin*, quoted in ibid., p. 100; **p.212** "I never felt so easy ...": Denis
Hoare letter, 16 May 1894, SL Rare Book Collection, Add MS 322; **p.213** Three men walk
off, then twelve: Souter, *A Peculiar People*, p. 105; **p.213** "we had songs and boxes ...": Frank
Birks, quoted in Souter, *A Peculiar People*, p. 105; **p.214** "We are tired of talking Socialism
...": Gilbert Casey quoted in Ross, *William Lane*, p. 178; **p.214** "At one time during our
conversation ...": Gilbert Casey, quoted in Souter, *A Peculiar People*, pp. 106–107; **p.215** "As
a matter of fact, the best thing ...": William Lane to Walter Head, quoted in ibid., p. 108;
p.215 "but then began murmurings & growls ...": Arthur Tozer, letter to H. J. Tozer, 29
April 1894; **p.217** "We had a split ...": Denis Hoare, letter 16 May 1894, SL RB, Add MS
322; **p.218** re McCreen boring holes in ships' hulls, see Souter, *A Peculiar People*, p. 215;
p.219 Story of McCreen child's grave told in Souter, *A Peculiar People*, pp. 215–16; **p.220**
"an abundant faith in our leader ...": Harry Taylor in Don Gobbett and Malcolm Saunders,
With Lane in Paraguay: Harry Taylor of The Murray Pioneer 1873–1932, Central Queensland
University Press in association with *The Murray Pioneer*, South Australia, 1995, p. 64; **p.220**
"Of his fitness for generalship ...": Harry Taylor, ibid, p. 62; **p.220** "one of the most
inaccessible ...": John Sibbald, quoted by Vol Molesworth, "New Australia — Reminiscences"; **p.221** "He has done his best ...": Arthur Tozer, letter to H. J. Tozer, 29 April 1894;
p.221 "The great scheme ...": Sydney *Bulletin*, 2 June 1894.

11. The Workingman's Paradise

p.223 "Kidd the new chairman ...": Arthur Tozer, letter to H. J. Tozer, 27 May 1894; **p.223**
"López and Walker walked ...": Arthur Tozer, letter to H. J. Tozer, 7 April 1895; **p.224** "Casey
will no doubt ...": Arthur Tozer, letter to H. J. Tozer, 22 June 1894; **p.224** "To save needless
enquiries ...": *Cosme Monthly Notes*, May 1895; **p.225** "absolutely destitute of household ...":
letter from George Napier Birks to his brother William, dated 10 August 1894 (possession of

descendant Jenni Woolard); **p.226** "Through other channels we hear …": Arthur Tozer, letter to H. J. Tozer, 12 August 1894; **p.227** "You may think that our life …": Denis Hoare, letter of 9 December, 1894. SL Rare Book collection, RB, Add Ms 321; **p.228** "It is not possible …": Souter, *A Peculiar People*, p. 117; **p.228** "There was Louis Simon …": Mary Gilmore in Julian Ashton, *Now Came Still Evening On*, Angus & Robertson, Sydney, 1941, p.133; **p.228** 'that this boat being allowed …": untitled essay, ML, Mary Gilmore Prose 1902–04; **p.228** "suspected of engineering …": Mary Gilmore in Ashton, *Now Came Still Evening On*, p.133; **p.228** "where Foley, despite his blindness …": Souter, *A Peculiar People*, p.117; **p.229** "When our people were approaching …": Denis Hoare, letter of 9 December 1894, SL Rare Book Collection, RB, Add Ms 321; **p.229** "Nice blanky position …": Walter Head, quoted in Souter, *A Peculiar People*, p. 119; **p.230** "for he has always been true …": Anne Lane, quoted in ibid., p. 124; **p.230** "The worse of it is …": William Saunders, quoted in ibid., p. 124; **p.230** re Walter Head's career as Walter Alan Woods, see ibid., p. 126; **p.230** "and until the end of his life …": ibid., p. 129; **p.231** Dear Will, you have heard …": Denis Hoare, letter of 9 December 1894, SL Rare Book Collection, RB, Add Ms 321; **p.232** "Dad used to tell them …": Lizzie Martyn (nee Butterworth), *Windsor and Richmond Gazette* (undated article in Mary Gilmore papers, ML); **p.232** "Plainly we were sick and tired …": Eric Birks, "As a Boy in Paraguay", p. 60; **p.232** "Get out of this …": Grace Birks, quoted in Souter, *A Peculiar People*, p. 138; **p.234** "One little tree snake …": Eric Birks, "As a Boy in Paraguay", p. 62; **p.234** "This flea-like pest …": ibid., p. 62; **p.235** "Near by the barn …": ibid., p. 59; **p.235** re Blackwell a dangerous firebrand, see Svensen, *Shearers' War*, p. 165, referring QSA COL/411, Ranking to Tozer, 29 March 1891; **p.235** "Things are quiet in Clermont …": Svensen, *Shearers' War*, p. 171; **p.236** "who came because they …": letter from George Napier Birks to his brother William, 18 February 1895 (possession of Jenni Woolard); **p.236** "In Adelaide one can choose …": John Sibbald, quoted in Souter, *A Peculiar People*, p.137; **p.236** "The fact is …": Henry Connelly, quoted in Souter, *A Peculiar People*, p.138; **p.236** re Pogson family: Howard C. Jones in a series of articles, "New Australia and Albury", *The Border Mail* (Albury), beginning 7 July 1993, lists the Pogson children as: Percy, Lucy, Olive, Maude (age 5 during voyage, later Maude Altona), Violet, Ivy, Gladys (born 7 July 1894, later Mrs Hooff), Flora (born 19 March 1896, later Mrs Cliff Martin); **p.237** "had to turn out early …": Lizzie Martyn (nee Butterworth), *Windsor and Richmond Gazette* (undated article in Mary Gilmore papers, ML); **p.237** re George Napier Birks' illness, see Souter, *A Peculiar People*, p. 140; **p.237** "Lying on his death-bed …": Eric Birks, "As a Boy in Paraguay", p. 63; **p.237** "as brilliant as any tree …": ibid., p. 61; **p.238** "going to the dogs …": letter from Arthur Tozer to H. J. Tozer, 26 January 1896; **p.239** "delightfully friendly and refreshing …": Rev. Charles Newbould, quoted in Souter, *A Peculiar People*, p. 216; **p.239** "One of the historic sights …": *Cosme Evening Notes*, quoted in Souter, *A Peculiar People*, pp.141–42; **p.239** re sale of herd and timber rights, see ibid., p.142; **p.240** "it was the other fellow's job …": Eric Birks, "As a Boy in Paraguay", pp. 62–63; **p.240** re Casey cohabiting with a Paraguayan woman: Arthur Tozer, letter to H. J. Tozer, 24 May 1896; **p.241** In January 1897 colony assets valued and divided: see Souter, *A Peculiar People*, p. 143; **p.244** "In spite of the epitaph mongers …": Gilbert Casey, quoted in Souter, *A Peculiar People*, p. 214; **p.244** "New Australia colony is coming …": Arthur Tozer, letter to H. J. Tozer, 5 July 1899; **p.245** re reasons for J.C. Kennedy settling at NA: Juan Y. Kennedy, letter to Mr D. B. Cody, (Melbourne) 8 June 1952, ML, MSS 654; **p.245** re Lane on Cunninghame Graham: *Worker*, 1 November 1891; **p.245** "The towns buried in vegetation …": Robert Bontine Cunninghame Graham, "Cruz Alta", *Thirteen Stories*, Penguin Books, Harmondsworth UK (1900), 1942, p. 51; **p.246** "You only need reading and writing …": J. C. Kennedy quoted in Souter, *A Peculiar People*, p.273; **p.248** "I am longing for my own land …": Rose Cadogan, *Australian Worker*, 1915; **p.249** "a big strong determined man …": *Western Champion*, quoted in Isabel Hoch, *Barcaldine 1846–1986*, Barcaldine Shire Council, 1986.

12. New London

p.255 "One makes friends quickly in Spanish …": Peter Matthiessen, *The Cloud Forest*, Harvill, Harper Collins, London, 1961, pp. 56–57.

13. Virgin Ground

p.258 "We still have a certain kind …": Margaret Thatcher, quoted in *Age*, 3 May 1982; **p.260** "was flaming the great communal fire …": Taylor, *With Lane in Paraguay*, p. 73; **p.260** "We are getting along far better …": Arthur Tozer, letter to H. J. Tozer, 12 August 1894; **p.261** "He would eat the beans …": James Molesworth memoir in SL, Cosme Collection; **p.261** "Monkey, whether it be …": *Cosme Evening Notes*, 5 October 1894; **p.261** "We were never reduced to rags …": Taylor, *With Lane in Paraguay*, p. 76; **p.261** "It must not be forgotten …": *Cosme Evening Notes*, 10 November 1894; **p.262** "The bushman is generally a big reader …": Arthur Tozer, letter to H. J. Tozer, 10 September 1894; **p.262** "I happened to score …": Arthur Tozer, letter to H. J. Tozer, 27 December 1894; **p.264** "Melbourne could never hold me …": William Wood Sr, 1922 letter to his niece Torry Johnston in Ballarat, SL, Cosme Collection; **p.264** "a poetic temperament and more …": Henry Lawson, "That Pretty Girl in the Army", *A Fantasy of Man: Henry Lawson Complete Works*, Vol. 2, 1901–1922 (compiled and edited by Leonard Cronin with an Introduction by Brian Kiernan), Lansdowne, Sydney, 1984, p. 105; **p.264** "After the meal, Henry …": William Wood to George Reeves, April 1926, "Bourke: A Letter from Paraguay", *Henry Lawson: By His Mates*, edited Bertha Lawson and John Le Gay Brereton, Angus & Robertson, Sydney, 1931, pp. 35–36; **p.266** "Before I left Sydney …": Wood to Reeves, ibid., p. 36; **p.267** "no bruise to indicate …": Arthur Tozer, letter to H. J. Tozer, 20–21 May 1895; **p.268** "The agent and mate had now …": D. R. Stevenson, "Three Men in a Boat", attachment to Arthur Tozer's letter to H. J. Tozer, 26 July 1895; **p.270** "It was not till I went to South America …": Mary Gilmore, "Dynamite. Larry Petrie", Papers of Dame Mary Gilmore, NLA, MS 8766, Series 5, Prose; **p.270** "Mrs Lane used to ask me …": Mary Gilmore, ML, A3292 Gilmore Papers, Vol. 41 — Henry Lawson: Personal History — Henry Lawson and I (Goulburn, Oct–Nov 1922), p. 20; **p.271** "a woman has lived vainly …": Mary Cameron, *New Australia*, 27 January 1894; **p.271** "You were a tall, straight, lissome …": Walter Alan Woods, letter to Mary Gilmore, 9 October 1924, quoted in Wilde, *Courage a Grace*, p. 96; **p.271** "a formidable woman …": Wilde, *Courage a Grace*, pp. 99–100; **p.272** "I think it likely that Lane …": Arthur Tozer, letter to H. J. Tozer, 7 September 1895; **p.272** "The camp very gloomy …": John Dias quoted in Souter, *A Peculiar People*, p. 160; **p.272** "took on the same intensely religious …": ibid., pp.160–61; **p.273** "I couldn't have been nursed better …": William Lane, letter to Will Saunders, quoted in Souter, *A Peculiar People*, p. 161; **p.273** "tried the patience of our nurses …": Billy Mabbott, quoted in ibid., p. 161; **p.273** "We nearly stowed away …": Mary calls him "R. Jones" but he is almost certainly Lawson's friend from childhood, Jack Jones, who wrote in his memories of Lawson: "Down in Sydney we roamed about a good deal together, and had many adventures. We nearly stowed away on the boat that left for Paraguay", *Henry Lawson — By His Mates*, p. 33; **p.273** "I sent my own people away …": Mary Gilmore, ML, A3292 Gilmore Papers, Vol. 41 — Henry Lawson: Personal History — Henry Lawson and I (Goulburn Oct–Nov 1922), p. 20; **p.274** "Most men in the street …": Graham Greene, *Travels with My Aunt*, (The Bodley Head, London, 1969), Penguin Books, Harmondsworth, 1988, p. 226; **p.275** "Imagine how the hearts of white women …": Eric N. Birks, "As a Boy in Paraguay", p. 63; **p.276** "a good looking active man …": Arthur Tozer, letter to H. J. Tozer, 29 January 1904; **p.277** "were taken naked and in chains …": Norman Lewis, "The Camp at Cecilio Baez" in Richard Arens (ed.), *Genocide in Paraguay*, Temple University Press, Philadelphia, 1976, p. 58; **p.278** "scarce the fifth part …": Nicolás del Techo, a Jesuit historian who put together a synthesis of the early chroniclers in *The History of the Provinces of Paraguay*, written and first published in the 17th century in Latin; an edited and truncated version was published in English in A.& J. Churchill's *Collection of Voyages and Travels*, Vol. 4, 1746, pp. 29–30; quoted in Richard Gott, *Land Without Evil: Utopian Journeys Across the South American Watershed*, Verso, London, 1993, p. 28; **p.279** "Once in Asunción …": Mary Gilmore, "Recollection", *Marri'd and Other Verses*, George Robertson & Co., Melbourne, Sydney, 1910, p. 6; **p.279** "The sun was blazing …": Mary Gilmore, "Paraguay and Elsewhere in South America", ML, Mary Gilmore Prose 1902–04; **p.279** "The colonists were Paraguayan …": Mary Gilmore, "Recollections of Colonia Cosme", ML, Mary Gilmore Prose 1902–04; **p.280** "The train had come in …": Eric Lane interviewed by Anne Whitehead at his home in Brisbane, 29 April 1986; Although Eric Lane never was in Paraguay, he was clear about his father's recounting of this episode; **p.280** "John Lane told me of the illness …": Mary Gilmore, "Life in Cosme", *The New Idea*, June 1904; **p.280** "was a bit of a Casanova …": Hilda Lane, letter to Gavin Souter, 23 May 1965, SL, Cosme Collection; **p.280** "She was a joke in Cosme …": ibid.; **p.280** "the hysterical man-woman": George Napier Birks, quoted in Souter, *A Peculiar People*, p.139; **p.281** "She is *not* married …": Tom Hall, quoted in ibid., p. 163; **p.281** "She is a great girl …": William Wood, quoted in ibid., p.163; **p.281** "David, cousin to Robert Louis Stevenson …": Mary Gilmore, letter to Hugh McCrae, 26 December 1928, quoted in Wilde, *Courage a Grace*, p. 105; **p.281** "At the time of my arrival …": Mary Gilmore, Article "Life in Cosme" in ML, Mary Gilmore Prose 1902–04, later revised and published in *The New Idea*, June 1904; **p.282** "My first house was of grass …": Mary Gilmore, ibid.; **p.284** "Soon after my arrival …": Mary Gilmore, "Life in Cosme", *The New Idea*, 6 July 1904, p. 25; **p.284** "The subjects taught include Reading …": Mary Cameron, school report, *Cosme Monthly Notes*, June 1896, quoted in Souter, *A Peculiar People*, p. 163; **p.285** "observation of birds": Mary Gilmore, "Life in Cosme", *The New Idea*, 6 July 1904, p. 25; **p.285** "It was not all over …": Mary Gilmore, "Life in Cosme", *The New Idea*, June 1904; **p.285** "he will aways be in considerable …": Arthur Tozer, letter to H. J. Tozer, 19 March 1896; **p.285** "My part of the work …": Arthur Tozer, letter to H. J. Tozer, 19 March 1896; **p.286** "my besetting sin is, I believe …": Arthur Tozer, letter to H. J. Tozer, 12 July 1896; **p.286** "Any information given by Bottrell …": Arthur Tozer, letter to H. J. Tozer, 19 March 1896; **p.286** Arthur Tozer, renewed request in letter to H. J. Tozer, 6 April 1896; **p.286** "The plainest thing written …": Mary Cameron, letter to W. G. Spence, approx. March–April 1896, W.G. Spence papers, ML, A1562/2, CY Reel 931; **p.287** "he had kissed her in England …": Mary Gilmore, "San Rosa — A Tale of the Pampa", ML, Mary Gilmore Prose 1902–04; **p.287** "like some vast Botanical Garden …": Mary Cameron, letter to W. G. Spence, approx. March–April 1896, W. G. Spence papers, ML, A1562/2, CY Reel 931; **p.287** "The sun was growing perceptibly …": Mary Gilmore, story "Jose the Paraguayan", Mary Gilmore collection, NLA, MS 309; **p.289** "And the Paraguay skies and nights …": Redgum, *Virgin Ground*, Cassette EPC 4137, CBS RecordsAustralia Limited, 1980; **p.290** "It appears to me that you …": Arthur Tozer, letter to H. J. Tozer, 12 July 1896; **p.290** "It is a very healthy but …": Arthur Tozer, letter to H. J. Tozer, 3 May 1896; **p.291** "But we may safely say …": "The Second Yearly Report of Cosme Colony, Paraguay, 12 May, 1896", *Cosme Monthly Notes*, May 1896; **p.291** "The comedy itself was played …": *Cosme Monthly Notes*, May 1896; **p.291** Mary Gilmore, "I Shall Not Sleep", *Marri'd and Other Verses*, p. 38; **p.292** "The furniture consists …": Arthur Tozer, letter to H. J. Tozer, 24 May 1896; **p.293** "He took me in his arms yesternight …": Mary Gilmore, "The Lover", *Marri'd and Other Verses*, p. 10; **p.293** "on account of sickness …": *Cosme Monthly Notes*, August 1896; **p.293** "Dear Harry …": Mary Cameron, letter to Henry Lawson, 5 August 1896. ML, Henry Lawson correspondence, AL 29/23.

14. Falling from Eden

p.296 "The plaza and the streets …": Taylor, *With Lane in Paraguay*, p. 82; **p.297** "Hurrah for the Social Revolution ...": Laurence De Petrie, *Hummer*, 18 June 1892 & 6 August 1892; **p.297** "the struggle for existence ...": Taylor on Petrie, *With Lane in Paraguay*, p. 92; **p.297** "vowed he would travel ...": "Jack Cade" (Ernest Lane), *Dawn to Dusk: Reminiscences of a Rebel*, William Brooks, Brisbane, 1939, p. 51; **p.297** "make an example of some plutocrats ...": alleged police evidence from railway worker Robert Fitzpatrick, SL, Cosme Collection; **p.297** "I had seen the paragraphs ...": Mary Gilmore, "Dynamite. Larry Petrie", Papers of Dame Mary Gilmore, NLA, MS 8766, Series 5, Prose; **p.297** "The Crows Kep' Flyin' Up", *Worker*, 9 September 1893; **p.298** "Not daring to face the public ...": Ernest Lane, *Dawn to Dusk*; **p.298** "with his face set for Cosme ...": Taylor, *With Lane in Paraguay*, p. 92; **p.298** "without a doubt one of the most ...": quoted in Souter, *A Peculiar People*, p. 171; **p.298** "Communism is all right ...": Petrie to W. G. Spence, 13 September 1896, ML, A1562 (2); **p.299** "Mary Gilmore wasn't very popular ...": Hilda Lane, letter to Gavin Souter, 23 May 1965, SL, Cosme Collection; **p.299** "the sort of head that ...": Harry Taylor, quoted in Souter, *A Peculiar People*, p. 175; **p.299** "and by the time he was up and about ...": Hilda Lane, letter to Souter, 23 May 1965, SL, Cosme Collection; **p.300** "much in love with him ...": John Le Gay Brereton letter to Mary Cameron, quoted in Wilde, *Courage a Grace*, p. 73; **p.300** 6 September decision to marry: see Mary Gilmore letters to Will Gilmore in Patagonia in ML, "Cosme Colony 1899–1902", loaned by George Mackaness, FM4/2280, letter dated 6–9–1901, "Five years ago today we became engaged, today is also Lane's birthday"; **p.300** "an accidental *rencontre* ...": Tom Hall, quoted in Souter, *A Peculiar People*, p. 175; **p.301** "But at last the nerve shaking thing ...": Mary Gilmore, letter (undated) to W. G. Spence, ML, A1564/1 Cosme Settlement, Paraguay Minute Books 1894–1900; **p.302** "Being poor we had what props ...": ML, Mary Gilmore Prose 1902–04; **p.302** "The guests were impressed ...": *Cosme Monthly Notes*, September 1896; **p.302** "an extraordinary sequence of tragedies ...": Souter, *A Peculiar People*, p. 174; **p.302** "was loaded with presents for the children ...": *Cosme Monthly Notes*, December 1896; **p.303** "Miss Cameron's resignation ...": *Cosme Evening Notes*, 6 February 1897; **p.304** re Edward Thompson's recruitment, see Souter, *A Peculiar People*, pp.176–77; **p.304** "In the first place the pioneers ...": Mary Gilmore, *The New Idea*, June 1904; **p.305** "kept everyone awake singing ...": quoted in Souter, *A Peculiar People*, pp.175–76; **p.305** Cosme Marriage Service, *Cosme Monthly Notes*; **p.305** "married Billy Gilmore — who my father said ...": Hilda Lane, letter to Souter, 12 September 1965, SL, Cosme Collection; **p.305** "At Homestead on May 29th ...": *Cosme Monthly Notes*, June 1897; **p.305** "All the usual friendly messages ...": William Lane, letter to Will Gilmore, 23 September 1897, quoted in Wilde, *Courage a Grace*, p.112; **p.306** "The record deer ...": *Cosme Monthly Notes*, July 1897; **p.308** "Amy has been very unwell ...": Arthur Tozer, letter to H. J. Tozer, 19 October 1897; **p.308** "a very acceptable wedding present ...": *Cosme Monthly Notes*, December 1897; **p.309** Mary Gilmore, "The Housewife", *Cosme Monthly Notes*, December 1897; **p.309** "the people from England & Scotland ...": Arthur Tozer, letter to H. J. Tozer, 19 November 1897; **p.309** "in social matters things have gone back ...": Arthur Tozer, letter to H. J. Tozer, 22 December 1897; **p.310** "camping out in some instances ...": *Cosme Monthly Notes*, January 1898; **p.310** Mary Gilmore, "Wedded", *Cosme Monthly Notes*, January 1898; **p.310** "This matter has been thoroughly thought out ...": Saunders, quoted in Souter, *A Peculiar People*, p. 179; **p.311** "on a conversation that took place ...": *Cosme Evening Notes*, March 1898, quoted in Souter, *A Peculiar People*, p. 179; **p.311** "It is not clear from the surviving records ...": Souter, *A Peculiar People*, p. 179; **p.311** "This getting 'nearer Nature' ...": Arthur Tozer, letter to H. J. Tozer, 23 January 1898; **p.313** "We shall work together on purely ...": Arthur Tozer, letter to H. J. Tozer, 4 March 1898; **p.313** "Monkey Stew", *Cosme Monthly Notes*, March 1898; **p.313** "That we had done more to disturb ...": Arthur Tozer, letter to H. J. Tozer, 6 April 1898; **p.314** Tozer's widow, Amy Tozer, in a footnote to the collection of Arthur's letters to Harry, wrote that in fact he had never had tuberculosis; that in 1912 he had been examined by a Harley Street specialist in London, "who could find no scar on lungs or any trace of lung trouble in his opinion". She said this opinion had been supported by a second specialist. But her son, H.V. Tozer, who had married Dr Bottrell's daughter, disputed this in another footnote: "when my father was x-rayed in Buenos Aires after his retirement there from England, the tubercular scars were apparent"; **p.314** "I understand that he never charges ...": Arthur Tozer, letter to H. J. Tozer, 7 March 1899; **p.315** "but I think all or nearly all will want ...": Arthur Tozer, letter to H. J. Tozer, 6 April 1898; **p.316** "Whips of dogma, stacks of selfishness ...": Petrie, letter to W. G. Spence, 4 August 1899, SL, Cosme Collection; **p.316** "I am looking forward to the next *Cosme Monthly* ...": Arthur Tozer, letter to H. J. Tozer, 15 May 1898; **p.316** "*Maintenance of Principles*. On May 9 ...": *Cosme Monthly Notes*, June 1898; **p.316** Cosme's population of 96: figures quoted in Souter, *A Peculiar People*, pp. 181–82; **p.317** "So I went to Lane and had a regular row ...": Arthur Tozer, letter to H. J. Tozer, 27 June 1898; **p.318** "A month before my child was born ...": Mary Gilmore, letter to W. A. Woods, 11 June 1903, quoted in *Letters of Mary Gilmore*, ed. W. H. Wilde and T. Inglis Moore, Melbourne University Press, 1980, p. 18; **p.318** "Will split the timber — lapacho ...": ibid. pp. 18–19; **p.319** "The slaughtered were quickly divided ...": *Cosme Monthly Notes*, November 1898; **p.319** "Freedom from petty worries ...": Arthur Tozer, letter to H. J. Tozer, 29 August 1898; **p.319** "There will be a few hundred people ...": Sydney *Bulletin*, 1893; **p.319** "is supposed to be at times a bit strange ...": Arthur Tozer, letter to H. J. Tozer, 5 February 1899; **p.320** "Once, just as I stepped into the bath ...": Mary Gilmore, "In Paraguay", ML, Mary Gilmore Prose 1902–04; **p.320** "A girl heard a rattle ...": Mary Gilmore, *The New Idea*, 6 July 1904; **p.321** "The devil of the Labour movement ...": Lane to Spence, quoted in Souter, *A Peculiar People*, p.186; **p.321** "He is still incorruptible, disinterested ...": Taylor, *With Lane in Paraguay*, p.105; **p.321** "To me this Labour movement endeavouring ...": Lane to Spence, quoted in Souter, *A Peculiar People*, p.186; **p.321** Of course he gave us a lot ...": Arthur Tozer, letter to H. J. Tozer, 5 July 1899; **p.322** "Those who are personally acquainted ...": John Lane, Brisbane *Worker*, quoted in Souter, *A Peculiar People*, pp.186–87; **p.322** "it strikes me that it is the thin edge ...": Arthur Tozer, letter to H. J. Tozer, 5 July 1899; **p.322** "Stevenson, since his return ...": Arthur Tozer, letter to H. J. Tozer, 5 July 1899; **p.322** "We were not communists, we were Laneites ...": Mary Gilmore, article "New Australia and Colonia Cosme, Paraguay", ML, Mary Gilmore Prose 1902–04; **p.323** "I often dread your feeling sorry ...": Mary Gilmore to Will Gilmore, 20 October 1899, quoted in Wilde and Inglis Moore, *Letters of Mary Gilmore*, p. 4.

15. A Wild Colonial Childhood

p.325 "They are dirty, ill mannered little savages ...": Arthur Tozer, letter to H. J. Tozer, 23 January 1898; **p.326** "There is a lot of anger ...": Mary Gilmore letter to Will in Patagonia, December 1899; **p.326** "She bathed among the men ...": ibid.; **p.326** "thoroughly suited to English people ...": Mary Gilmore letter to Will, 12 December 1899, quoted in Wilde and Inglis Moore, *Letters of Mary Gilmore*, p. 8; **p.327** "You don't understand how I am ...": Mary Gilmore, 8 December 1899, Wilde and Inglis Moore, *Letters of Mary Gilmore*, p. 7; **p.327** "I often wonder if the thought of me ...": ibid, 15 December 1899, p. 9; **p.327** "not attainable, real Communism that is ...": ibid., 25 February 1900, p. 12; **p.327** "to balance its snakes ...": ibid., 17 December, 1899, p. 10; **p.327** "He is worth all the rest ...": Dame Mary Gilmore, letters to Will Gilmore in Patagonia 23–9–1899 to 26–12–1901 (lent by George Mackaness), ML, Microfilm FM4/2280, 21 April 1900; **p.329** "You will understand what that means ...": Mary Gilmore to Will in Patagonia, April 1900; **p.330** "The poor woman had had a hard life ...": Arthur Tozer, letter to H. J. Tozer, 26 September 1900; **p.331** "I left the place ...": Mary Gilmore, letters to Will Gilmore in Patagonia, 23 May 1900; **p.331** Mary Gilmore, "Somehow We Missed Each Other", *Marri'd And Other Verses*, p. 93; **p.331** "I feel more homely ..." Mary Gilmore, letters to Will Gilmore in Patagonia, 23 May 1900; **p.332** "After a week of this my landlord …": Mary Gilmore, letter to W. A. Woods, 11 June 1903, Wilde and Inglis Moore, *Letters of Mary Gilmore*, p. 19; **p.332** "The funny thing …": Mary Gilmore, "Dynamite. Larry Petrie", NLA, Papers of Dame Mary Gilmore, MS 8766, Series 5, Prose; **p.332** "as he hasn't much chance …": Mary Gilmore, SL, Cosme Collection; **p.332** "I think Tozer has to recommend …": ML, Mary Gilmore, letters to Will Gilmore in Patagonia, 23 July 1900; **p.332** "because I don't want her to be Paraguayan …": Arthur Tozer, letter to H. J. Tozer, 24 January 1900; **p.334** "staring down soldiers' rifles …": Billy Bennett, quoted in Souter, *A Peculiar People*, p. 7; **p.334** Souter on John Lane as chairman, ibid., p. 194; **p.337** "One evening as I sat reading …": Mary Gilmore — *More Recollections*; Angus & Robertson, Sydney, 1935, pp. 128–30; **p.341** "Paraguay is the land of orange trees …": *New Australia*, 8 April 1893; **p.342** Gilmores' voyage from Buenos Aires: Mary Gilmore, autobiographical letter to W. A. Woods, 11 June 1903, in Wilde & Inglis Moore, *Letters of Mary Gilmore*, p. 20; **p.342** "named the land on one side …": Mary Gilmore, "Magellan", NLA, Papers of Dame Mary Gilmore MS 8766, Series 5, Prose; **p.342** "She was new to Gallegos and its ways …": Mary Gilmore, "Patagonia in the South", NLA, Papers of Dame Mary Gilmore MS 309; **p.343** "Everybody whom I have seen …": Mary to Will Gilmore, 5 January 1901, ML Letters from Mary to Will Gilmore in Patagonia, 23 September 1899 to 26 December 1901, lent by George Mackaness; **p.343** Barrel of water a block of ice: Mary Gilmore, ML Gilmore papers A3254, vol. 3, Diary, 7 March 1942; **p.344** "There was quite a gape of wonder …": Tom Hicks-Hall, quoted in Souter, *Peculiar People*, p. 185; **p.344** "said to be the best shearer in Patagonia": Mary to Will Gilmore, 25 August 1901, ML, letters from Mary to Will Gilmore in Patagonia, 23 September 1899 to 26 December 1901, lent by George Mackaness; **p.344** "I think the most awful girl that ever lived …": Mary Gilmore, letter to W. A. Woods, 11 June 1903, in Wilde & Inglis Moore, *Letters of Mary Gilmore*, p. 20; **p.345** "in a land where there were but few …": Mary Gilmore, "We Called Him José", (1903), ML, Mary Gilmore Prose 1900–1904; **p.345** "Look here, little girl …": Mary Gilmore, "Patagonia in the South", NLA Mary Gilmore Collection, NLA MS309; **p.346** "Even then I felt the frozen earth …": Mary Gilmore, *Old Days: Old Ways: A Book of Recollections*, Angus & Robertson, Sydney 1934, p. 62; **p.346** "like mutton hams from chaps and chillblains …": Mary Gilmore, "We Called Him José"; **p.347** "My heart stopped …": Mary Gilmore, "We Called Him José"; **p.348** "Oh, but you are such a good English scholar …": Mary Gilmore, letter to W. A. Woods, 11 June 1903, p. 20; **p.348** "the teaching I am doing …": Mary to Will Gilmore from Río Gallegos, 20 September 1901, ML Mackaness collection; **p.348** Mary to Will Gilmore from Río Gallegos, 16 October 1901, ML Mackaness collection: "I lent Mrs Lane *The Workingman's Paradise*. She is full of it, and is reading it now to her husband."; **p.348** "If you were to come in now …" Mary to Will Gilmore from Río Gallegos, 16 September 1901, ML Mackaness collection; **p.348** "Can you shear with a machine?": Mary to Will Gilmore from Río Gallegos, 12 September 1901, ML Mackaness collection; **p.349** "of the awful roughness …": Mary to Will Gilmore from Río Gallegos, 16 October 1901, ML Mackaness collection; **p.349** "Indeed, I have often thought …": Mary to Will Gilmore from Río Gallegos, 6 October 1901, ML Mackaness collection; **p.349** "It will be a serious matter …": Mary to Will Gilmore from Río Gallegos, 25 November 1901, ML Mackaness collection; **p.349** English bank officials offered defence of British women: quoted in Wilde, *Courage a Grace*, p. 120; **p.349** "It is terrible to be always alone …": Mary to Will Gilmore from Río Gallegos, 14 December 1901, ML Mackaness collection; **p.350** Mary refers to amoebic dysentery diagnosis: Mary to Will Gilmore from Río Gallegos, 25 November 1901, ML Mackaness collection; **p.350** "either to swear or cry": Mary to Will Gilmore from Río Gallegos, 5 December 1901, ML Mackaness collection; **p.350** "Half the lessons I gave at my own house …": Mary Gilmore, letter to W. A. Woods, 11 June 1903, p. 21; **p.350** "I wish we were away …": Mary to Will Gilmore from Río Gallegos, 16 December 1901, ML Mackaness collection; **p.350** "I was so glad to have missed him.": Mary to Will Gilmore from Río Gallegos, 21 December 1901, ML Mackaness collection; **p.350** "They say 'a bird in the air will carry a thing' …": Mary Gilmore, "We Called Him José"; **p.350** "Bed's made and cot's ready …": Mary Gilmore, letter to W. A. Woods, 11 June 1903, Wilde & Inglis Moore, *Letters of Mary Gilmore*; **p.351** "The village to us is better than the city …": John Lane in *British Socialist News*, quoted in Souter, *A Peculiar People*, p. 199; **p.351** "the tide of practical politics …": Souter, *A Peculiar People*, p. 199; **p.352** "Dad had a lovely set of letters …": Eric Lane to Anne Whitehead, 12 January 1988; **p.352** Jim Fitzpatrick, *The Bicycle and the Bush*: A Study of the Bicycle in Rural Australia, Oxford University Press, Melbourne, 1980; **p.353** "The Socialistic idea has become …": John Lane, quoted in Souter, *A Peculiar People*, p. 201; **p.353** "Cosmeism tended to kill …": Arthur Tozer, letter to H. J. Tozer, 7 March 1899; **p.353** "In Cosme there is no social evil …": *Cosme Monthly Notes*, January 1903; **p.354** "Many of those in the colony …": Arthur Tozer, letters to H. J. Tozer, 26 September 1900 and 29 July 1901; **p.354** "The women are old before …": Arthur Tozer, letter to H. J. Tozer, 26 September 1900; **p.354** "Tozer looked up at me …": quoted in Souter, *A Peculiar People*, p. 206; **p.354** "So far have had no reason …": Arthur Tozer, letter to H. J. Tozer, 15 February 1903; **p.355** "See you back soon": quoted in Souter, *A Peculiar People*, p. 204; **p.355** "opposing party — cooperators …": Ernie Lane, in ibid., p. 208; **p.355** "had to use the whip on him": Harold Wallis, quoted in ibid., p. 202; **p.355** "had the audacity to state that Cosme …": Ernest Lane, quoted in Ibid., p.208; **p.355** "I myself considered that Cosme's only chance …": John Lane, Lecture No. 3 on "New Australia and Cosme", SL, Cosme Collection; **p.362** "The political history of Australia …": Ricardo Caballero, "Las Raices Paraguayas de Australia", *ABC Color*, Asunción, 30 May 1982, translated from the Spanish by the late Don Guillermo Wood.

PART TWO

16. Coming of Age

p.367 "We thought to find the Happy Land …": H. S. T. (Harry Taylor), "To a Disappointed Communist", Brisbane *Daily Standard*, 1917; **p.373** "bust up the 'brotherhood' ": Arthur Tozer, letter to H. J. Tozer, 5 July 1899; **p.374** "exploiting the native …": Arthur Tozer, letter to H. J. Tozer, 26 September 1900; **p.375** "each of the nine members received …": Souter, *A Peculiar People*, p. 213; **p.375** "So here is the question …": Mary Gilmore — *Colonia Cosme*, first published in three parts in Sydney *Daily Telegraph*, November 1902, reprinted in *Australians Abroad*, ed. Charles Higham and Michael Wilding, F. W. Cheshire, Melbourne, 1967, p. 73; **p.376** "Here you have the puzzle …": William Wood, quoted in Souter, *A Peculiar People*, p. 214; **p.376** Donald Macdonell, described by Henry Lawson as one of the best of the "Bourke-Side Shearers" (he shore 214 sheep in a day with hand shears), helped form the Australian Workers' Union and the fledgling Australian Labor Party. By 1910 he was Colonial Secretary and Minister for Agriculture and in that position could have aided the Woods' return, but in October 1911 he died of cancer; **p.382** "go as far as the women of Finland …": Mary Gilmore, "Women's Page", NSW *Worker*, 30 January 1908; **p.382** "It is to women, the waiting mother …": Mary Gilmore, "Women's Page", NSW *Worker*, 7 January 1909; **p.383** "as horse and rider disappear …": Minnie Jacks letter to Mary Gilmore, SL, Cosme Collection; **p.384** "Ties of blood and kindred …": *Buenos Aires Herald*, quoted in Andrew Graham-Yooll, *The Forgotten Colony*, p. 231; **p.384** "D.R. Stevenson is in Egypt …": Minnie Jacks letter to Mary Gilmore, SL, Cosme Collection; **p.385** For the assault at Lone Pine I have referred to Patsy Adam-Smith, *The Anzacs*, Thomas Nelson, Melbourne, 1978, pp. 92–93; **p.385** "making the devil of a noise …": H. M. Denham, *Dardanelles*: A Midshipman's Diary 1915–16, John Murray, London, 1981, pp. 139–42; **p.386** "all the while the Tommy troops …": Adam-Smith, *The Anzacs*, p. 93; **p.386** "largely to the lack of energy of the commander, Sir Frederick Stopford …": Anthony Bruce, *An Illustrated Companion to the First World War*, Michael Joseph, London, 1989, p. 148; **p.386** "In the history of war there is no more signal …": C.E.W. Bean,

Official History of Australia in the War of 1914–18, Vol. II, *The Story of Anzac*, Angus & Robertson, Sydney, 1924; also *Frontline Gallipoli*: C. E. W. Bean diaries from the trenches, selected and annotated by Kevin Fewster, Allen & Unwin, Sydney, 1983, p. 206; also Peter Burness, *The Nek: The Tragic Charge of the Light Horse at Gallipoli*, Kangaroo Press, 1996; **p.388** "I couldn't tell who were the officers ...": Bill Wood quoted in Souter, *A Peculiar People*, p. 235; **p.388** "The truth is that after 100 years ...": *Frontline Gallipoli*: C. E. W. Bean diaries from the trenches, selected and annotated by Kevin Fewster, Allen & Unwin, Sydney, 1983, pp. 153–56; **p.389** "He still kept his section together ...": Private A. Hanson, "How Corporal Lane Died", undated article from *New Zealand Herald*, SL, Cosme Collection; **p.389** "The message from Anzac ...": William Lane, *New Zealand Herald*, quoted in Souter, *A Peculiar People*, pp. 221–22; **p.390** "The sea was hell and the shore ...": Henry Lawson, "Song of the Dardanelles", *A Fantasy of Man*, p. 615; as recited on tape by Norman Wood, Asunción 1982; **p.391** "Almost the whole of the 500,000 British troops ...": C. E. W. Bean, *The Australian Imperial Force in France 1916*, University of Queensland Press, St Lucia (1929), 1982, pp. 942–43; **p.392** "As *you* always knew, Dave was the one ...": Clara Stevenson to Jenny Lane, quoted in Souter, *A Peculiar People*, p. 235; **p.392** "my boy Norman the senior boy ...": William Wood to Mary Gilmore, SL, Cosme Collection; **p.395** Alex Wood's ambition re *The Thousand Nights and a Night*, quoted in Souter, *A Peculiar People*, p. 235; *The Thousand Nights and a Night*, translated from Arabic by Sir Richard Burton, 1885–88; **p.395** "Since I left my home far far to roam ...": poem "Paraguay" by Alf L'Hotelier, Balranald, *Australian Worker*, 3 August 1916.

17. The Guabirá Tree

p.396 "I thought of going to Australia ...": Bill Wood, SL, Cosme Collection; **p.396** "We advise them all not to come back ...": Minnie Jacks letter to Mary Gilmore, SL, Cosme Collection; **p.396** "Among the great trees of Paraguay ...": Harris Gaylord Warren, *Paraguay: An Informal History*, Greenwood Press, Publishers, Westport Connecticut (1949), 1982, pp. 16–17; **p.397** "This journal has lost ...": quoted in Souter, *A Peculiar People*, p. 222; **p.398** "and it will live as long ...": Queensland *Worker*, 30 August 1917; **p.398** "I have to face life without Will ...": Anne Lane, letter to John Lane, 5 November 1917, SL, Cosme Collection; **p.398** "'Billy' Lane is dead — dear old 'Billy' Lane ...": R. S. Ross, "Late Billy Lane — A Reminiscence and a Tribute", *Ross's Monthly*, September 1917, reprinted in *The Worker* (NSW), 4 October 1917; **p.398** "Just picture a wooden house ...": William Wood Sr, letter to Torry Hyatt (née Johnston) in Ballarat, 23 September 1921, Torry Hyatt Papers, NLA, MS 5741; **p.399** "developing a keen interest ...": William Wood Sr, letter to Torry Hyatt (née Johnston) 22 December 1922, Torry Hyatt Papers, NLA, MS 5741; **p.401** "The bloodthirsty Paraguayans have been ...": William Wood Sr, letter to Torry Johnston in 1922, SL, Cosme Collection; **p.401** "So Nellie is sweet 21 is she ...": Kathleen Wood to Torry Johnston, 1922, SL, Cosme Collection; **p.402** "Kathy, I think, would easily become an accomplished ...": William Wood Sr, letter to Torry Hyatt (née Johnston) 22 December 1922, Torry Hyatt Papers, NLA, MS 5741; **p.402** "nearly all the second generation has gone native ...": William Wood, *Windsor and Richmond Gazette*, 25 September 1925; **p.402** "But we can still see the sun ...": William Wood Sr, letter to George Reeve, November 1926, SL, Cosme Collection; **p.403** "I am sure we would joyfully ...": Reeve and Wood, *Windsor and Richmond Gazette*, 25 September 1925; **p.403** "Consequently I'm Grandad now ...": William Wood Sr, letter to Torry Hyatt (née Johnston), 23 September 1921, Torry Hyatt Papers, NLA, MS 5741; **p.404** "We hold not merely life-marriage ...": pledge quoted by Taylor, *With Lane in Paraguay*, p.107; **p.404** "The merging with the Paraguayan ...": Mary Gilmore — *Colonia Cosme*, first published in three parts in Sydney *Daily Telegraph*, November 1902, reprinted in Higham and Wilding, *Austra-*

lians Abroad, p. 73; **p.406** "When we have made some money we hope ...": Rose Menmuir to Torry Hyatt (née Johnston), 18 January 1936, Torry Hyatt Papers, NLA, MS 5741.

18. Heart of Darkness

p.410 "One feature of the rivers of Paraguay ...": Masterman, *Seven Eventful Years in Paraguay*, pp. 5–6; **p.410** "As a steamer slips along ...": R. B. Cunninghame Graham, *A Vanished Arcadia: Being Some Account of the Jesuits in Paraguay 1607–1767* (first published 1901), Century Classics, London 1988, p. 39; **p.411** "long before the Mississippi ...": Theodore Roosevelt, *Through the Brazilian Wilderness*, London, 1914; **p.411** "we slew a goodly number of them ...": "Voyage of Ulrich Schmidt to the rivers La Plata and Paraguai", in Dominguez, 1567, quoted in Richard Gott, *Land Without Evil: Utopian Journeys Across the South American Watershed*, Verso, London, 1993, p. 56; **p.411** "Their only care is that of their horses ...": Martín Dobrizhoffer, *An Account of the Abipones: an Equestrian People of Paraguay*, London (1784), 1822, Vol. 1, p. 97; **p.412** The story of 1677 Guaycuru massacre is told in Gott, *Land Without Evil*, pp. 52–53; **p.412** "These savages, though more like beasts ...": Dobrizhoffer, *An Account of the Abipones*, Vol. 1, p. 118; **p.412** "The Payaguas are very queer ...": C. B. Mansfield, *Paraguay, Brazil and the Plate: Letters Written in 1852–53*, London, 1856, quoted in Gott, ibid., pp. 58–59; **p.412** "that he was not going to have his ugly face ...": George Masterman, *Seven Eventful Years in Paraguay*, p.121; **p.413** "holding up tiger skins to signify ...": Marion Mulhall, *From Europe to Paraguay*, London, 1877, p. 38, quoted in Gott, *Land Without Evil*, p. 55; **p.414** "Going up that river ...": Joseph Conrad, *Heart of Darkness*, in *Great Modern Short Stories*, Random House, NY, 1942, pp. 46–47; **p.414** "desired to have kings meet ...": ibid., p. 97; **p.414** "would have been a splendid leader ...": ibid., p.103; **p.415** "the most representative Jew-baiter ...": *The Times*, 1 February 1883; **p.415** "the nucleus for a glorious new Fatherland ...": Ben Macintyre, *Forgotten Fatherland: The Search for Elisabeth Nietzsche*, Farrar Straus Giroux, NY, 1992, p. 3; **p.416** "This mission has a name ...": Bernhard Förster, *Deutsche Colonien in dem oberen Laplata Gebiete mit besonderer Berücksichtigung von Paraguay*, Naumberg, 1886 [*German Colonisation in the Upper La Plata District with Particular Reference to Paraguay*], quoted in Macintyre, *Forgotten Fatherland*, p. 5; **p.416** "Just think how grand ...": Elisabeth Nietzsche, quoted in Macintyre, *Forgotten Fatherland*, p.121; **p.416** "Suddenly, eight splendid horsemen ...": Elisabeth Nietzsche, quoted in ibid., p. 122; **p.416** "The principal characteristics of the Guaraní ...": Bernhard Förster, *Deutsche Colonien in dem oberen Laplata Gebiete mit besonderer Berücksichtigung von Paraguay*, pp. 73–74, quoted in Macintyre, *Forgotten Fatherland*, p. 63; **p.417** "We have found the nearest thing to paradise ...": Elisabeth to Friedrich Nietzsche, quoted in Richard Gott, "Pure Folly in Paraguay", *Sydney Morning Herald*, 3 June 1989; **p.417** "our wishes and our interests ...": Friedrich Nietzsche, draft letter to Elisabeth Nietzsche, before 5 June 1887, *Nietzsche Briefwechsel Kritische Gesamtausgabe* no. 854, ed. G. Colli and M. Montinari, Berlin & NY, 1975, quoted by Macintyre, *Forgotten Fatherland*, p.124; **p.417** "After supper we sit in the garden ...": Elisabeth Nietzsche, "A Sunday in Nueva Germania", *Bayreuther Blätter*, January 1889, quoted by Macintyre, ibid., pp. 125–26; **p.418** Förster's cause of death stated as "nervous attack": see Macintyre, *Forgotten Fatherland*, p.138; **p.418** "The first condition for any improvement ...": Max Schubert, "Colonial Society Newsletter", quoted in ibid., pp. 146–47; **p.419** 1934 ceremony at San Bernardino described in ibid., p.193; **p.419** "They remained what their ancestors ...": Macintyre, *Forgotten Fatherland*, p. 211; **p.420** "a brave woman ... and beautiful": ibid., p. 211; **p.421** "The architectural pretensions ...": W.H. Koebel, *Paraguay*, T. Fisher Unwin Ltd, London, 1917, pp. 261–62; **p.422** "It's the National Day ...": Graham Greene, *Travels with My Aunt*, p. 226; **p.423** re Liebig's offer of formula, I have referred to Andrew Graham-Yooll, *The Forgotten Colony*, p. 227; **p.427** "the most practical and intelligent worker ...": Arthur Tozer, letter to H. J. Tozer, 4 March 1898; **p.428** "a plain with the soul of a mountain ...": J. Natalicio González, *Proceso y formación de la cultura paraguaya*, Asunción 1938, quoted in Adalberto López, *The Revolt of the Comuñeros 1721–1735: A Study in the Colonial History of Paraguay*, Schenkman Publishing Co., Cambridge, 1976, p. 5; **p.429** Account of López murder of fourteen servants in Gordon Meyer, *The River and the People*, p. 88, which also cites Alexander Baillie F.R.G.S., *A Paraguayan Treasure: the Search and Discovery*, Simpkin, Marshall, London, 1887.

19. The Green Hell

p.434 "In addition — and astonishingly ...": David Attenborough, *Zoo Quest in Paraguay* (originally published Lutterworth Press, UK, 1959) anthologised in *The Zoo Quest Expeditions*, Penguin Books, Harmondsworth, 1980, pp. 246–48; **p.434** "in a bar in the centre of the town ...": Attenborough, *Zoo Quest Expeditions*, p. 303; **p.434** "All the plants bore savage spines ...": Attenborough, *Zoo Quest Expeditions*, p. 313; **p.435** "an empty, one-lane, red-mud ...": Pico Iyer, "Paraguay: 1992 — Up For Sale, Or Adoption" in *Falling Off the Map*: Some Lonely Places of the World, (Jonathan Cape, London, 1993), Black Swan edition 1994, p.181; **p.436** For the account of the Mennonites' settlement charter, I referred to Warren, *Paraguay*, p. 274; **p.437** 10,000 Indians settled since 1980 referred to in Riordan Roett and Richard Scott Sacks, *Paraguay: The Personalist Legacy*, Westview Press, Boulder 1991, p.101; also quotes David Maybury-Lewis and James Howe, *The Indian Peoples of Paraguay and Their Prospects*, Cultural Survival, Peterborough NH, 1980; **p.437** "fearsome religious maniacs ...": Gott, *Land Without Evil*, pp. 211–12; **p.439** Bolivian and Paraguayan military strengths quoted in Souter, *A Peculiar People*, p. 239; **p.439** "Bolivia and Paraguay are at war ...": Eduardo Galeano, *Memory of Fire, Vol 3: Century of the Wind*, translated by Cedric Belfrage (Quartet Books, 1989), Minerva Octopus paperback, 1990, p. 94; **p.441** Account of 200 headless Bolivians left on the field quoted in Souter, *A Peculiar People*, p. 240; **p.441** "Someone should open a window ...": Augusto Céspedes, "The Well" from *Sangre de Mestizos*, translated by Harriet de Onis, in *The Green Continent*, ed. Germán Arciniegas, Alfred A. Knopf, NY, 1945, p. 484; **p.441** Paraguayans captured at Cañada Strongest: General Estigarribia claimed "we lost no more than 600 prisoners" in (ed.) Pablo Max Ynsfran, *The Epic of the Chaco*: Marshal Estigarribia's Memoirs of the Chaco War 1932–1935, Greenwood Press, NY (1950), 1969, p. 149; **p.442** "Apart from the fighting, the living conditions ...": Donald Wood, letter to Gavin Souter, 29 November 1967, SL, Cosme Collection; **p.442** Rudyard Kipling, "Gunga Din"; **p.442** "a thin black soldier came up ...": Donald Wood, letter to Souter, 29 November 1967, SL, Cosme Collection; **p.442** Re Marshal Estigarribia's pincer movement: see Warren, *Paraguay*, pp. 311–12; **p.443** "The Paraguayan water supply was ...": Peter Kihss, dispatch for *The New York Times*, quoted in Jonathan Kandell, *Passage Through El Dorado*: *Traveling the World's Last Great Wilderness*, William Morrow & Co., NY, 1984, pp. 263–64; **p.443** "In such country, wounds ...": Peter Kihss, dispatch for *The New York Times*, quoted in ibid., pp. 263–64; **p.444** "Suffocating heat. Each particle ...": Augusto Roa Bastos, *Son of Man* (first published in Spanish, *Hijo de Hombre*, Editorial Losado S.A., Buenos Aires 1961), English edition translated by Rachel Caffyn, Victor Gollancz Ltd, 1965, this edition Monthly Review Press, NY, 1988, pp.179–80; **p.445** "I have a mission. I am ...": Roa Bastos, *Son of Man*, p. 229; **p.445** " ... there is not a drop of water ...": Céspedes, "The Well" from *Sangre de Mestizos*, pp. 482–95; **p.445** Chaco War losses: Souter, *A Peculiar People*, p. 241 gives figures quoted; Kandell, *Passage Through El Dorado*, p. 264 writes "Almost a hundred thousand soldiers died"; Charles J. Kolinski, *Historical Dictionary of Paraguay*, p. 52 states "about 80,000 killed, of which an estimated two-thirds were Bolivian"; **p.445** "Douglas the fair youth now ...": obituary for Douglas Kennedy quoted in Souter, *A Peculiar People*, pp. 241–42; **p.446** "Quite a crowd had gathered ...": Roa Bastos, *Son of Man*, pp. 236–40; **p.446** "When they returned from the Chaco ...": Roa Bastos, *Son of Man*, pp. 246–47.

20. Fields of God

p.450 Thomas More's influence noted in Crow, *Epic of Latin America*, p.192; **p.451** "one statue of Our Lord lying …": John Dias quoted in Souter, *A Peculiar People*, p. 175; **p.451** "Wonderful were the results obtained …": John Lane, lectures for the Brisbane Workers' Educational Association, published in Brisbane *Daily Standard*, 9, 10 and 12 May 1924; **p.451** "I am a believer …": quoted in Philip Healy, Introduction to R.B. Cunninghame Graham, *A Vanished Arcadia: Being Some Account of the Jesuits in Paraguay 1607–1767* (first published 1901), Century Classics, London, 1988, p. vii; **p.452** "Cunninghame Graham was the last historian …": Philip Healy, Introduction, *Vanished Arcadia*, pp. v–vi; **p.452** "On the neglected altar …": R.B. Cunninghame Graham, *Tales of Horsemen*, Canongate, Edinburgh, 1981, pp. 57–60; **p.454** "Tupá created trees and made …": For an account of pre-Conquest Guaraní society and their beliefs, I am indebted to Warren, *Paraguay*, pp. 11–12; **p.455** "It is the express wish of the King …": quoted in Charles Gide, *Communist and Co-operative Colonies*, translated by Ernest F. Row, George G. Harrap & Co, London, 1930, p. 62; **p.455** Capture of 350,000 Indians referred to in Kandell, *Passage Through El Dorado*, p. 291, quoting Brazilian historian Alfredo Ellis Junior; **p.455** "carelessly washing some clothes …": Father Antonio Ruiz de Montoya, *Conquista Espiritual del Paraguay*, quoted in Warren, *Paraguay*, p.10; **p.456** "the qualities of a man of action …": Cunninghame Graham, *Vanished Arcadia*, p. 53; **p.456** "a nest of hawks …": Cunninghame Graham, *Vanished Arcadia*, p. 55; **p.456** "what is of the gravest concern …": quoted in John Hemming, *Red Gold: The Conquest of the Brazilian Indians*, Macmillan, London, 1978, p. 257; **p.457** "Not one escaped; and so …": Cunninghame Graham, *Vanished Arcadia*, p. 82; **p.458** In one community 600 perished from famine: quoted in Crow, *Epic of Latin America*, p. 195; **p.460** "They died like plants …": Padre Nicolás del Techo, *The History of the Provinces of Paraguay*, quoted in Cunninghame Graham, *Vanished Arcadia*, p. 234; **p.460** "Wonderful were the results obtained …": John Lane, lectures, Brisbane *Daily Standard*, 9, 10 and 12 May 1924; **p.460** cable flying bridge referred to by Cunninghame Graham, *Vanished Arcadia*, p. 198; **p.461** "Give me an orchestra …": quoted by Philip Healy, Introduction to *Vanished Arcadia*, p. xi; **p.461** "Great arches festooned …": R.B. Cunninghame Graham, *A Vanished Arcadia*; **p.461** "Neither women nor girls …": Crow, *Epic of Latin America*, p. 197; **p.462** "The Guaranís seemed to possess …": Crow, *Epic of Latin America*, p. 198; **p.462** "As well as agriculture …": Cunninghame Graham, *Vanished Arcadia*, pp. 180–81; **p.462** "appears alone, in some way, the triumph …": Voltaire, *Essai sur l'histoire générale*, Ch. 154; **p.463** "solitary, poore, nasty, brutish …": Thomas Hobbes, *Leviathan* (1651), J. M. Dent & Sons, London, 1953, p. 65; **p.463** "not one attained to any higher dignity …": Gide, *Communist and Co-operative Colonies*, p. 75; **p.464** "an echoing rendition of the Voice of God …": Tony Perrotet (ed.), *Insight Guide — South America* (chapter on Paraguay by Kathleen Wheaton), APA Publications (HK) Ltd, 1990, p. 229; **p.464** "The Jesuit attitude towards the Indians …": López, *The Revolt of the Comuñeros*, p. 37; **p.464** "at least, so far as that they bought …": Cunninghame Graham, *Vanished Arcadia*, pp. 193–201; **p.464** Jesuits returned only 10 per cent to communal fund: quoted in Leopoldo Lugones, *El imperio jesúitico*, Buenos Aires 1904, cited in Crow, *Epic of Latin America*, p. 202; **p.464** "Vast herds of animals including …": Warren, *Paraguay*, p. 99; **p.465** Jesús "comparing with the largest in America": Bishop de la Torre, 1759, quoted in Introduction by Clement J. McNaspy to exhibition brochure, *Paradise Lost: The Jesuits and the Guaraní South American Missions 1609–1767*, Inter-American Development Bank, Washington, 1989; **p.466** Guaraní losses in five-year war quoted in Gide, *Communist and Co-operative Colonies*, p. 83; **p.467** "One word from the Provincial …": Cunninghame Graham, *Vanished Arcadia*, pp. 266–68; **p.467** "They … seemed to have that stupid air …": Louis Antoine de Bougainville, Ch. VII, *Description d'un voyage autour du monde* (1772), reprinted in *Colonial Travelers in Latin America*, ed. Irving A. Leonard, Alfred A. Knopf, NY, 1972, p. 190; **p.467** "Withal we are the vassals ...": quoted in Cunninghame Graham, *Vanished Arcadia*, p. 43; **p.467** "most of them at once took Indian women ...": Crow, *Epic of Latin America*, p. 204; **p.468** "Undergrowth invades pasture ...": Eduardo Galeano, *Faces and Masks*, Vol. II of *Memory of Fire*, p. 35; **p.468** "For my own part, I am glad ...": Cunninghame Graham, *Vanished Arcadia*, pp. 287–88; **p.468** "The semi-communism which the Jesuits ..." Cunninghame Graham, preface to *Vanished Arcadia*, pp. xxii–xxiii; **p.470** "waiting the time when factories shall ...": Cunninghame Graham, *Vanished Arcadia*, p. 286.

21. The Dragonfly

p.471 "Now I am going far away ...": Aché-Guayakí weeping song, recorded and rendered in free translation by Mark Münzel, "Manhunt" in *Genocide in Paraguay*, ed. Richard Arens, Temple University Press, Philadelphia, 1976, p. 30; **p.471** " ... the Indians ... do not seek for meaning ...": Peter Matthiessen, *At Play in the Fields of the Lord*, (Heinemann, London, 1966), Flamingo, imprint of Harpers Collins, London 1991, p. 309; **p.472** General Belaieff's negotiations for the Makká: described in Roett and Sacks, *Paraguay: The Personalist Legacy*, p. 102; **p.472** León Cadogan entry in Andrew L. Nickson, *Historical Dictionary of Paraguay*, 2nd edition, Scarecrow Press, Metuchen NJ & London, 1993; **p.473** "I will not preach calmness to you ...": Rose Summerfield, quoted in Souter, *A Peculiar People*, pp. 229–30; **p.473** "a revolutionary activist in the broadest ...": Leon Cadogan, *Extranjero, Campesino y Científico: Memorias*, edited Roger Cadogan, Fundación "Leon Cadogan", Centro de Estudios Antropológicos Universidad Católica, Asunción Paraguay, 1990, p. 50. (Unless indicated otherwise, all subsequent quotations are from Cadogan's *Memorias*. All extracts from this biographical memoir, written in Spanish, have been translated into English by Mary-Jane Field and Greg Price.); **p.474** Petrie's crediting Rose Summerfield referred to in notes in SL, Cosme Collection; **p.474** "She gave an address there ...": Letter from William Wood to George Reeve, *Windsor and Richmond Gazette*, 9 September 1927; **p.474** "a tool designed and carried out ...": Rose Summerfield, NSW *Worker* 15 January 1898, quoted in Verity Burgmann, *In Our Time: Socialism and the Rise of Labor, 1885–1905*, Allen & Unwin, Sydney, 1985, p. 32; **p.474** "The Cadogans belonged to a branch ...": Leon Cadogan, *Memorias*, p. 48; **p.476** For Guaraní mythology, see Leon Cadogan, "Some plants and animals in Guaraní and Guayakí mythology" in *Paraguay: Ecological Essays*, ed. J. Richard Gorham, Academy of the Arts and Sciences of the Americas, Miami Florida 1973, pp. 97–104; also León Cadogan, "*Las leyendás guaranies*", *Boletín Indigenista*, *VII*, No 4, Mexico 1947, pp. 378–82; **p.476** For additional material on *macaguá* bird and other creatures of the *monte*, I am indebted to the chapter "Nature, Miracles, and Myths" in Warren, *Paraguay*; **p.477** "Sweating and panting ...": Leon Cadogan, letter to Gavin Souter, SL, Cosme Collection; **p.479** "Quack would have been the proper term ...": quoted in Souter, *A Peculiar People*, p. 231; **p.479** "These uprisings are a part ...": Warren, *Paraguay*, p. 266; **p.480** "I have wandered from my own land ...": Rose Cadogan, *Australian Worker*, 1915; **p.482** "Say what has life to offer?": poem copied by Anne Whitehead from Rose Cadogan's papers in Paraguay; **p.482** "Poor old Jack Cadogan, he is now ...": William Wood, letter to George Reeve, *Windsor and Richmond Gazette*, 9 September 1927; **p.483** Caá Yara myth in Warren, *Paraguay*, p.14; also León Cadogan "Animal and Plant Cults in Guaraní Lore", *Revista de Antropologia*, XIV, Sao Paulo 1966, pp. 105–24; **p.484** "If a party of native hunters ...": Alexander K. Macdonald, *Picturesque Paraguay*, Kelley, London 1911, p. 393; **p.484** "No fugitive has ever managed ...": Roa Bastos, *Son of Man*, p. 80; **p.484** "Our horses shall rest wherever darkness ...": story quoted in Souter, *A Peculiar People*, pp. 232–33; **p.485** "There was really no politics in it ...": Leon Cadogan, quoted in Souter, *A Peculiar People*, p. 233; **p.487** Myths of Ogre Charia, rapist opossum and origin of fire: Claude Lévi-Strauss, *Introduction to a Science of Mythology*, Vol. I, *The Raw and the Cooked* (first published Librairie Plon, Paris, 1964), Jonathan Cape, London, 1970, pp. 74, 140, citing Leon Cadogan, "Ayvu

Rapita: Textos miticos de los Mbyá-Guaraní del Guaira", *Antropologia*, No.5, Boletim No.227, Univeridade de Sao Paulo, 1959, pp. 57–66, 80–81, 86–87, 197, 202; Creation myths of Mbyá: León Cadogan, *La literatura de los Guaraníes*, Editorial Joaquin Martiz, Mexico 1965; also "Les Guaranís", *Le Monde Diplomatique*, Paris, 16 January 1966; **p.490** "I will begin by telling you that …": León Cadogan, "Historia del pájaro azul" ("Story of the Blue Bird"), *Memorias*, pp.185–92; the 1949 census of the Mbyá-Guaraní listed 803 men, 786 women and 1,170 children; **p.491** "When a man dies, the soul …": Leon Cadogan, "The Problem of the Mbyá-Guaraní Population of the Department of Guayrá", report to the Paraguay government, pp. 77–81; **p.491** 1949 sale of massacre survivors: referred to by Norman Lewis, "The Camp at Cecilio Baez" in *Genocide in Paraguay*, p. 58; **p.492** "it is said that the children who have been left behind …": A. S. Forrest, *A Tour Through South America*, Stanley Paul & Co., London, 1913, pp. 237–38; **p.492** The figure of "ten thousand at the beginning of the century" is quoted by Norman Lewis, "The Camp at Cecilio Baez" in *Genocide in Paraguay*, p. 58; **p.492** Estimated 500 Aché-Guayakí in the 1950s: J.H. Steward & L.C. Faron, *Native Peoples of South America*, McGraw Hill, NY, 1959, p. 429; **p.492** "We, who were once men …": Aché "weeping song", recorded and rendered in free translation by Mark Münzel, "Manhunt" in *Genocide in Paraguay*, pp. 27–28; **p.493** "At the beginning of all things …": quoted by Mark Münzel, ibid., p. 26; **p.493** "As these beings have not been included …": Cadogan, *Memorias*, p.132; **p.494** Assistance of army in Aché hunts noted in Mark Münzel, "Manhunt" in *Genocide in Paraguay*, p. 21; **p.494** "In the forest of the dead we shot wild boar …": Aché "weeping song", recorded and rendered in free translation by Mark Münzel, ibid., pp. 25–26; **p.494** "The most interesting and least-known nation …": León Cadogan in *Comunidad*, quoted in Souter, *A Peculiar People*, p. 265; **p.495** "Perhaps more Aché have died …": Münzel, *Genocide in Paraguay*, p. 29; **p.495** Flow of Guairá cataracts: See Norris and Ross McWhirter (eds), *Guinness Book of Records*, Guinness Superlatives Ltd, Middlesex, 1974, p. 64; **p.495** "The new invaders of the forest …": *La Tribuna*, 13 August 1972; **p.496** "a small Belsen for Indians": Norman Lewis, *Genocide in Paraguay*, p. 59; **p.496** "Instead I discovered …": Mark Münzel, *Genocide in Paraguay*, p. 19; **p.496** "The destruction of Aché identity …": Mark Münzel, ibid., p. 34; **p.496** Münzel's observation of manhunt: ibid., pp. 27–28; **p.496** "by offering me first a 15-year-old girl …": ibid., p. 26; **p.496** "Stripped of human dignity and freedom …": ibid., pp. 19–21; **p.497** "but maybe there is still time to save …": Eric R. Wolf, "Killing the Achés", in *Genocide in Paraguay*, pp. 56–57; **p.497** "Now I am going far away …": Aché "weeping song", recorded and rendered in free translation by Mark Münzel, *Genocide in Paraguay*, p. 30; **p.498** Protest to the UN quoted in Norman Lewis, "The Camp at Cecilio Baez" in *Genocide in Paraguay*, p. 62; **p.498** Circumstantial evidence of another 600 deaths: see Münzel, *"Genocide in Paraguay*, p. 37; **p.498** "Our secretariat has in its possession …": *La Tribuna*, Asunción, 28 April 1974; **p.498** Aché children at US$2 a head: *The New York Times*, 29 August 1976, p. 37; **p.498** "those who would work to help forest Indians …": Richard Arens, ed. & Prefatory Note, *Genocide in Paraguay*, pp. xii–xiv.

22. Gringos

p.502 Manuel Ortiz Guerrero, verses from "Mburicaó", translated from the Guaraní by Florence Wood de White; **p.505** "I see, when alone at times …": Pablo Neruda — "Sólo la muerte" from "Residencia en la tierra", II (1935) p. 58 of Pablo Neruda — *Selected Poems* (A bilingual edition, edited by Nathaniel Tarn, translation of "Solo la muerte" by Nathaniel Tarn), Penguin Books Ltd, Harmondsworth, Middlesex, England, 1975; **p.507** "He enjoyed his life on Cosme …": Rose Menmuir, letter to Torry (Johnston) Hyatt, 1 August 1935, SL, Cosme Collection; **p.510** "There wasn't a cat, dog, rat …": Mary Leeser, great-niece of David Russell Stevenson and, by marriage, Clara Jones, interviewed by Anne Whitehead in Sydney on 10 November 1982; **p.510** "I don't think he ever fully recovered …": Letter from Mrs Lucy

Allisett, St Peter Port, Guernsey, 31 October 1967, SL, Cosme Collection; **p.511** "She is one of the grandest personalities …": quoted in "Biographical Notes" by Barrie Ovenden in (eds Dymphna Cusack, T. Inglis Moore, Barrie Ovenden) *Mary Gilmore: a Tribute*, Australasian Book Society, Sydney, 1965, p. 43; **p.511** Popularity of "No Foe Shall Gather Our Harvest": See Wilde, *Courage a Grace*, pp. 343–45; **p.511** "Ask of those who pandered for power …": Mary Gilmore, from original version of "Singapore", quoted in ibid., pp. 359–60; **p.511** "Dad in February and Billy last night …": Mary Gilmore diary, quoted in ibid., p. 380; **p.512** Mary Gilmore, "Never Admit the Pain" from *The Wild Swan* (1930), in *Selected Verse*, Angus and Robertson, Sydney, 1948, p. 103; **p.512** "Dame Mary Gilmore: Labor's First Lady": *Daily Telegraph*, 9 August 1945; **p.513** "to have my womb put straight": Rose Menmuir to Torry Hyatt, 18 January 1936, NLA, MS5741 Torry D. Hyatt Papers; **p.517** "Oh maiden with the starry eyes …": extract from a poem found among Rose Cadogan's papers after her death, either her own attempt at the serenade genre or her translation; **p.518** "The roses climb on the roof of the house …": Mary Gilmore, "Life in Cosme", *The New Idea*, 6 July 1904; **p.519** "I began, myself, with a slush lamp …": Dame Mary Gilmore in a recording for the Australasian Book Society, quoted in *Mary Gilmore: a Tribute*, p. 25; **p.519** "Do not be stampeded …": Quoted in *Mary Gilmore: a Tribute*, pp. 46–47; **p.519** "For years the 'comrades' exploited …": "Obituary — Teacher, Reformer, Poet" by a Special Correspondent, *Sydney Morning Herald*, 4 December 1962; **p.520** Mary Gilmore, "When I Am Gone", *Tribune*, 6 December 1962; **p.520** "The Australian Peasants of Paraguay: Our Forgotten Exiles": Theodore James (travelling with Anthony Paul), *Australasian Post*, 29 August & 5 September 1963; **p.524** 50 min documentary, *And Their Ghosts May Be Heard*, produced and presented by Caroline Jones, directed by Keith Gow, Film Australia 1975.

23. The Adventures of Robin Wood

p.527 "We have built us a dome …": Oneida song, quoted in Mark Holloway, *Heavens on Earth*, Turnstile Press, London, 1951, p. 178; **p.527** "Grandad Allan, with his billygoat …": Peggy "Bud" Wood, letter to Rose Menmuir in South Africa, 1943, SL, Cosme Collection; **p.529** "Ursula's capacity for work was the same …": Gabriel García Márquez, *One Hundred Years of Solitude*, trans. from Spanish by Gregory Rabassa, Pan Picador, London, 1978, 1983, p. 15; **p.534** "a husky, brown-haired Paraguayan …": David Attenborough, *Zoo Quest Expeditions*, pp. 246–48; **p.537** "Takurú-Pukú, then, was the citadel …": Roa Bastos, *Son of Man*, pp. 80–81.

24. Paradise Mislaid?

p.551 "I had begun, not only …": Ariel Dorfman, Foreword to *Son of Man*, p. 7; **p.551** Pablo Neruda, "The Magellan Heart", from *Canto general* (1950), translated by Anthony Kerrigan, in *Pablo Neruda — Selected Poems*: A bilingual edition, edited by Nathaniel Tarn, Penguin Books, 1975; **p.553** For an account of Stroessner's orders and decorations I am indebted to Isabel Hilton, "The General", *The Best of Granta Travel*, Granta Books, London, 1991; **p.554** "like a Bavarian butcher": John Gunther, "A Semi-Affectionate Look at Paraguay", *Inside South America* (Harper & Row 1967), Pocket Books, New York, 1968, p. 282; **p.554** "like the amiable well-fed host …": Graham Greene, *Travels with My Aunt*, p. 221; **p.554** "about a seven. He couldn't compare …": Alex Shoumatoff, "The End of the Tyrannosaur", *Vanity Fair*, September 1989, p. 232; **p.554** "We are a geographically defenseless country …": Stroessner, quoted in Herring, *A History of Latin America*, p. 820; **p.557** "there was, above all, peace …": Isabel Hilton, "The General", *The Best of Granta Travel*, p. 347; **p.557** "When I first came to Asunción …": Josefina Plá, quoted in Iyer, *Falling Off the Map*, p. 165; **p.557** "Were it not for an occasional headless body …": Herring, *History of Latin America*, p. 820; **p.558**

"conservative Yalie ... hardly the human-rights zealot ...": Shoumatoff, "End of the Tyrannosaur", p. 298; **p.559** Rudel's connection with Odessa: see Shoumatoff, p. 235; **p.559** Witness to Mengele's passport: John Vinocur, "A Republic of Fear", *New York Times* magazine, 23 September 1984; **p.559** "It's the national industry ...": Greene, *Travels with My Aunt*, p. 207; **p.560** "Stroessner's frequent use of the phrase ...": Richard Roett & Richard Scott Sacks, *Paraguay: The Personalist Legacy*, pp. 75–78; **p.562** "Evidence that top officers in Paraguay ...": Paul H. Lewis, *Paraguay Under Stroessner*, University of North Carolina Press, Chapel Hill, 1980, pp. 135–36; **p.562** "Both Rodríguez and Colmán had made ...": Lewis, ibid., p. 136; **p.563** For account of marijuana trade to Brazil: see *Paraguay Power Game*, Latin American Bureau 1980, p. 54; **p.563** Like Madame Tussaud's waxworks, "except all the figures are living": Iyer, "Paraguay: Up for Sale, or Adoption", *Falling Off the Map*, p. 163; **p.563** "celebrated in drawing rooms ...": Eduardo Galeano, *Memory of Fire*, Vol. 3: *Century of the Wind*, trans. Cedric Belfrage (Quartet Books 1989), Minerva Octopus Paperback 1990, p.156, citing as source Joseph A. Page, *Perón*, Vergara, Buenos Aires, 1984; **p.563** "incompatible with the maintenance of harmonious ...": quoted in Lewis, *Paraguay Under Stroessner*, pp. 77–78; **p.564** Re Bartons' asset stripping: Trevor Sykes, "The $1m Rape of Murumba — How a Company was Stripped", *Australian Financial Review*, 3 September 1973; **p.564** "probably the greatest rogue we have ...": Evan Whitton, "The Little Known Years of Alexander Barton", *National Times*, 24–29 September 1973; **p.564** "Now they are Paraguayan citizens ...": *Sydney Morning Herald*, 20 November 1974; **p.564** "granted nationality to the two men ...": *Sydney Morning Herald*, 21 November 1974; **p.565** Bartons' dealings while under house detention: *Sydney Morning Herald*, 20 November 1974; **p.565** "the strong man of Paraguay ...": Andrew Clark, "Bartons Before First Instance Court", *National Times*, 16–21 June 1975; **p.565** Bartons announce they're remaining in Paraguay: *Sydney Morning Herald*, 10 November 1975; **p.566** "He only drew the line with blacks ...": Shoumatoff, "End of the Tyrannosaur", p. 236; **p.567** "brilliant proponent of the Good Neighbour Policy": Lewis, *Paraguay Under Stroessner*, p.161, quoting Alfredo Stroessner, *Mensaje presidencial a la honorable Cámara de Representantes*, April 1957; **p.567** "as much electricity as all of New York State ...": Kandell, *Passage Through El Dorado*, p. 265; **p.568** "Fifty peasant leaders were killed ...": R. Andrew Nickson, *Paraguay*, World Bibliographical Series, 1987, pp. xviii–xix; **p.568** Re long-term political prisoners: Nickson, *Paraguay*, pp. xviii–xix; **p.568** Re more Mercedes than any other Latin American capital: See Isabel Hilton, "The General", p. 354; **p.569** "Each of these Brazilian-backed projects ...": Roett and Sacks, *Paraguay: The Personalist Legacy*, p. 129; **p.570** "*ABC Color's* record is one of courage ...": Isabel Hilton, "The General", p. 355; **p.571** "After a long morning Stroessner would park ...": Shoumatoff, "Tyrannosaur", p. 300; **p.572** "she was taken to Investigaciones ...": Shoumatoff, ibid., p. 301; **p.574** "I gave up smoking some time ago": Shoumatoff, "Tyrannosaur", p. 234; **p.575** Estimate of 1,500 *desaparecidos*: Shoumatoff, ibid., p. 235; **p.579** "Rain was falling ...": Taylor, *With Lane in Paraguay*, p. 73; **p.579** "it stinks like an empty railwaycarriage ...": Milan Simecka, translated by George Theiner, "A World With Utopias or Without Them?", in Peter Alexander & Roger Gill (eds), *Utopias*, Duckworth Press, London, 1984, p. 169.

Epilogue

p.583 "Such is life in Patagonia ...": Mary Gilmore, "We Called Him José", (1903) ML Mary Gilmore Prose 1900–1904; **p.583** "I used to think to myself, 'Thank God for Paraguay' ...": Mary Gilmore, "South America", NLA Papers of Dame Mary Gilmore, MS 8766; **p.583** "In one sense our experiment ...": Mary Gilmore, interviewed for article "They Tried to Find Utopia", *Sunday Herald*, 8 April 1949; **p.584** "You are workers! Carry on with the strike ...": Juan Soto, addressing the strikers in Patagonia in 1921, quoted in Ronaldo Munck with Ricardo Falcón & Bernardo Galitelli, *Argentina: From Anarchism to Peronism: Workers, Unions* *and Politics*, 1855–1985, Zed Books, London 1987, p. x; **p.584** "No one is executed without a trial …": Eduardo Galeano, *Memory of Fire*, vol. 3: *Century of the Wind*, translated by Cedric Belfrage (Quartet Books 1989), Minerva Octopus paperback, 1990, p. 53; **p.585** For suppression of Patagonian rebellion: see Ronaldo Munck with Ricardo Falcón & Bernardo Galitelli, *Argentina: From Anarchism to Peronism*, pp. 88–89; Andrew Graham Yooll, *The Forgotten Colony*, p. 236; see also Osvaldo Bayer, *La Patagonia Rebelde*, Nueva Imágen, Mexico 1980; Osvaldo Bayer, *Los Vengadores de la Patagonia trágica*, Galerna, Buenos Aires 1972; Jorge Abelardo Ramos, *Revolución y contrarevolución en la Argentina*, Plus Ultra, Buenos Aires 1976.

Index